Comparative Economic Systems

Comparative Economic Systems

Sixth Edition

Paul R. Gregory
University of Houston

Robert C. Stuart
Rutgers University

HOUGHTON MIFFLIN COMPANY   Boston   New York

We dedicate this book to our wives, Annemarie and Beverly.

Editor-in-Chief: Bonnie Binkert
Assistant Editors: Adrienne Vincent and Bernadette Walsh
Project Editor: Elizabeth Gale Napolitano
Production/Design Coordinator: Jennifer Meyer Dare
Manufacturing Manager: Florence Cadran
Marketing Manager: Juli Bliss

Cover Image: Herbert Bayer, "Chromatic Interlocking," 1969/70
Cover Design: Cathy Hawkes/Cat and Mouse Design

Printed in the U.S.A.

Library of Congress Catalog Card Number: 98-72033

ISBN: 0-395-90815-9

3 4 5 6 7 8 9-QF-02 01 00

Contents

Preface

We are gratified that our book, *Comparative Economic Systems,* has been a leading text for comparative economics since 1975. Our new sixth edition is the most significant revision ever. As times and events change, so must a book that looks at the way we organize economic systems. With the collapse of communism and the ongoing transition from planning to markets, we no longer have the major dichotomy of capitalism and socialism that was the prime focus of earlier editions. The economic world is full of innovative experiments on how to organize economies, such as the market socialist approach of China, the difficult transitions of the former Soviet states, the Asian Model of Southeast Asia, and even the creation of a single currency in Europe. The world economy has become irreversibly internationalized.

This edition presents the teaching of comparative systems in a new way. It shows how comparative economic systems will be taught in the twenty-first century. However, we should not forget how we got here. We should not forget the twentieth century's greatest experiment: the attempt to create a planned economy in Russia in the years following the Bolshevik Revolution of 1917 and the experience of dismantling these economic arrangements at the end of this century.

The sixth edition will explore the following topics:

- Emerging market economies of Asia and Eastern Europe
- Distinct "European Models" versus "Asian Models," the latter including Japan and the Tiger Economies
- How the economic system affects economic growth and performance in a wide variety of settings
- The transition process in Eastern Europe, Russia, the Baltic states, and Central Asia
- Modern economic topics such as growth convergence, monopoly rent seeking, corruption models and corruption indexes, and growth models

This edition will help instructors present comparative economic systems in the post-Soviet transition period. As our world becomes more internationalized, we expect growing rather than declining interest in comparative economics. We hope that this new edition will provide a road map for instructors to use in teaching this vital subject.

To assist the instructor in organizing the subject matter of a one semester course in comparative economic systems, we have sustained the general framework used in earlier editions, but with the substantial modifications noted above.

In Part I, we begin with a familiar discussion of basic issues—the nature of the field of comparative economic systems and how it has changed in the past decade, how economic systems are classified and analyzed, and how we might assess the impact of differing economic systems upon resource allocation. Finally, we discuss systemic change, a subject dramatically more important in the contemporary era than in the past. The material in this section is changed from past editions in several ways. First, for students with little or no life experience from the "plan era," we believe an overview of events is essential. Second, with the disappearance of the simple extremes of plan and market, emphasis on the tools of organization theory is of much greater importance than in the past. Third, the subject of systemic change was of limited interest during the plan era, focusing mainly on a never-ending series of failed reforms. Obviously, events of the 1990s have changed that posture, necessitating attention both to overall systemic change, the transition from plan to market, and to the subtle but critical changes taking place within existing systems, for example contemporary restructuring.

In Part II, we turn to a discussion of economic systems in theory. While the basic themes discussed here bear a close similarity to similar discussions in the past, there are important changes. First, it is difficult for a student to understand the complexities of the transition era if they have no knowledge of the theory underlying past system arrangements. Second, although the simple dichotomy of plan and market may have disappeared, contemporary systems are very much mixed systems with significant variations from one case to another. To understand these systems, it is essential to understand the nature of their components. Third, the task of understanding contemporary mixed systems is difficult. Fundamentally, our theoretical understanding of mixed systems is much less well developed than our understanding of simple polar extremes. Finally, our ability to understand change is limited, a major reason why there is so much interest in real-world cases of change in contemporary transition economies.

In Part III, we discuss economic systems in practice. Although we sustain discussion of the traditionally important cases, there are important changes in this section. First, while the discussion of the U.S. and Soviet experiences is traditional, we discuss China as an example of market socialism. China is treated as a country and as an economic system of great importance, especially its continuing efforts to grow in a global setting with elements of both market and plan. Second, we develop the discussion of the European model and the Asian model in comparable dimensions given the immense interest in both major cases and the potential for influence of one on another. Finally, we analyze the major reason for the emergence of the transition era, namely the economic collapse of the major planned socialist economic systems.

In Part IV, we turn to a discussion of transition era. This part is organized along familiar lines. We begin with a discussion of basic transition issues noting that the more general issue of change has already been discussed in Part I. Following the discussion of the framework of transition theory, we discuss major real world cases. The Russian case is one of great complexity and yet it is also one of major political importance in the global economy. The East European cases that we discuss are, on balance, success cases when compared to the Russian experience. Finally, we conclude with observations on the first decade of the transition era, noting the importance of transition issues for the global economy of the twenty-first century.

Our goal since the inception of *Comparative Economic Systems* has been to provide a tour through the contemporary literature on comparing differing economic systems. While we now organize the tour differently from the past, the content is very much the work of a large number of scholars to whom we are indebted.

Finally, we greatly appreciate the help and guidance received from the staff at Houghton Mifflin. Special thanks go to assistant editors Adrienne Vincent and Bernadette Walsh, project editor Liz Napolitano, and sponsoring editor Bonnie Binkert.

P.R.G.
R.C.S.

Comparative Economic Systems

PART I

Economic Systems: Issues, Definitions, Comparisons

1

Economic Systems After the Collapse of Communism

Comparative economic systems studies economic systems and their impact on the allocation of resources. Comparative economic systems focuses on how the **economic system,** or organizational arrangements, combine with economic policies in distinct natural and historical settings to influence economic outcomes. If the type of economic system and/or system components influences resource allocation in identifiable ways, we can select an optimal set of organizational arrangements to achieve our economic objectives (for example, rapid economic growth) from our endowment of scarce resources.

The *economic system is the set of institutional arrangements used to allocate scarce resources.* The limits of productive resources (labor, land, and capital) dictate the scarcity of resources. As a result of scarcity, societies must decide in an orderly way what is produced, how to produce it, and for whom it is produced. If such ordering arrangements are absent, anarchy and chaos will prevail.

Economic systems exist within countries both large and small, developed and less developed. Some countries are rich in human capital; others are rich in natural resources. These differences make it difficult to determine how the economic system will affect economic outcomes. Differences among countries and their endowments cloud the system's impact.

Economic systems are identified or classified according to their basic characteristics, such as **ownership** (private or nonprivate), **information mechanisms** (market or plan), **levels of decision-making authority** and responsibility (centralized or decentralized), and finally **incentive arrangements** (moral or material). Economic systems fall within a spectrum ranging from decentralized, market-driven, incentive-based "capitalist" systems to centralized, plan-directed "socialist" systems.

Prior to the 1990s, the study of comparative economic systems focused on two distinct models: capitalism and socialism. Now, at the end of this century, we must examine different issues.

The New World

If Rip Van Winkle woke up in 1999 after a twenty-five-year sleep, he would be hard pressed to recognize the world he had last seen. In 1975, at the beginning of his sleep, life was more simple. About one-third of the world's population lived under Soviet-style or Chinese-style socialism dictated by the Communist party leadership.

3

Although these economies were not prospering, they were muddling along without imminent threat of demise. The countries of Eastern Europe were held in the political and economic embrace of the Soviet Union. Although some reform of their Soviet-type economies had occurred, change was modest and often unsuccessful.

The Western world, in 1975, was recovering from energy shocks, recessions, and stagflation. How well they would deal with these issues remained open. The rest of the world, with the exception of Japan, appeared stuck at a low level of economic development. Latin America, South America, and Africa, were not progressing satisfactorily toward long-term economic growth and development.

Imagine Rip Van Winkle's shock on waking in 1999. The Soviet empire has disintegrated; Germany has reunited; the Communist party no longer exists as a centralized, controlling organization; China has been experiencing phenomenal growth; the "developing markets" of Southeast Asia, Latin America, and even Eastern Europe are attracting large sums of capital. Even small investors are betting on emerging market funds. Not much has changed with the industrialized countries of Western Europe. They are again recovering from recessions and are troubled by high unemployment.

The Collapse of Communism[1]

The year 1985 marked the starting point for serious change in the communist bloc. In this year, the newly selected general secretary of the Soviet Communist party, Mikhail Gorbachev, announced his intention to initiate "radical" reform of the Soviet political structure, society, and economy. Up until this point, the Soviet Union had been the most important example of a centrally planned socialist economic system. It had experienced serious problems in economic performance for decades but had limited interest in economic reform. Gorbachev's call for radical reform was initially greeted with considerable skepticism. After all, Gorbachev rose through the party ranks and therefore could be expected to cling to past goals and methods. Few observers in 1985 could anticipate that five years later, Mikhail Gorbachev would receive a Nobel Peace Prize for his bold reforms, especially those related to Eastern Europe and foreign policy.

As the Soviet leadership introduced one reform after another, even the most skeptical of observers came to see that real changes were intended. Thus, in spite of some discrepancies between the rhetoric of reform and the reforms actually instituted, the terms *glasnost, democratization,* and *perestroika* entered the Western vocabulary. Indeed, the pace of political and social change was rapid. Open criticism of the regime was tolerated; curbs on freedom of speech and of the press were significantly reduced; national and republican parliaments, city councils, and even factory managers were elected. Mass emigration of disaffected Soviet minorities was allowed, foreign travel became easier, religious activities were encouraged, and Marxist–Leninist ideology was disavowed. Most significant from a political and potentially economic perspective, the constitutionally guaranteed "leading role" of the Communist party became the subject of open discussion and debate. Indeed, political dominance of the Soviet Union by the Communist party would end in the summer of 1991.

The international consequences of liberalization in the Soviet Union were far-reaching. The lack of Soviet sympathy for conservative communist regimes in

Eastern Europe became apparent. Soviet tanks would no longer be used to prop up unpopular dictatorships. Caught in the pincers of liberal reform in the Soviet Union and the attraction of consumer affluence in Western Europe, former communist dictatorships tumbled one after the other. As neighboring communist regimes granted access through their territories, East German citizens fled to West Germany, threatening to depopulate the former German Democratic Republic. The Berlin Wall was opened in November of 1989 and subsequently dismantled. The émigrés' "voting with their feet" became so pronounced that the unpopular regime of Erich Honecker fell in November of 1989, to be replaced by that of Lothar De Maiziere, the last leader of East Germany before full reunification in 1990.

The overthrow of the East German communist regime was followed by a series of mostly bloodless revolutions in Eastern and central Europe. By the end of 1989, the Communist political structure in Czechoslovakia (the Czech and Slovak Federal Republic) was toppled, as Václav Havel was elected president and Alexander Dubček speaker of the parliament. Free popular elections held in 1990 sustained the mandate of Havel and his Civic Reform party. In Bulgaria, the Communist leader Todor Zhivkov was replaced in November of 1989. Finally, in the spring and summer of 1990, elections left a majority of communists in the Bulgarian parliament but resulted in the naming of a new president, Zhelyu Zhelev, a non-communist. In Hungary similar events unfolded. In the fall of 1989, agreement was reached on the creation of a multiparty system and on free elections to be held in 1990. In the spring of 1990, after elections were held, the United Democratic Front (a party in opposition to the reconstituted former Communist party) won, and Jozef Antall became prime minister. Events in Poland had generally anticipated those elsewhere. With the rise of Solidarity to political power in the summer of 1989, Tadeusz Mazowiecki became prime minister and General Wojciech Jaruzelski president. These arrangements, however, were short-lived. In September of 1989, General Jaruzelski announced that he would step down, a move that led to the election of Lech Walesa, who replaced Tadeusz Mazowiecki as the Polish leader. Finally, the despotic dictator of Romania, Nicolae Ceausescu, was executed in a bloody uprising. By the summer of 1990, elections placed Ion Ilies in the position of president, though unrest continued.

The process of political change in Eastern Europe typically followed a two-step pattern. First, the unpopular totalitarian communist regime was replaced by reform-minded communists, who formed coalition governments with non-communists. In this phase, the Communist party's monopoly on political power was broken. In the second stage, a non-communist coalition government was elected on a platform of closer alliance with the West and the establishment of a market economy. *Economic disarray resulting in popular discontent and the withdrawal of Soviet backing were two major forces that led to these developments.*

Events in China were equally dramatic, but they had quite different results. In the early 1980s, the aging Chinese communist leadership seemed determined to open the country to the West and to reform the Chinese planned economic system. The reintroduction of private incentives in agriculture and the initial influx of foreign investment boosted economic growth and brought about substantial improvements in living standards. However, liberalization quickly spilled over into political and social life. When, in the spring of 1989, opposition groups began to demand fundamental changes—an end to the Communist party monopoly, free speech, and democratic elections—the Communist regime decided to crack down on the reform movement. This decision culminated in the May 1989 Tiananmen Square massacre, the arrest of leading dissidents, and the introduction of sanctions by Western governments against the Chinese regime.

The Chinese retreat to political conservatism was in stark contrast to developments in the Soviet Union and Eastern Europe. Although the process of effecting economic reform in the Soviet Union has proved difficult, in Eastern Europe there was general acceptance of the long-term goals of reform: establishment of a market economy, multiparty elections, and free speech.

China continued economic reform, especially the freeing of private initiative and openness to the West, despite its rejection of political democracy. As China assumed domestic rule of Hong Kong in 1998, the future of Hong Kong's democracy remains unclear.

By the start of the 1990s, conservative communist regimes were found only in China, Cuba, and North Korea. Even Vietnam took preliminary steps toward reform and reconciliation with its archenemies in the West, a course that resulted in the restoration of diplomatic relations with the United States in 1994.

In the 1990s, sober reality replaced the euphoria of the late 1980s. The leaders of once administratively planned economies realized that the transition to a market economy was not painless and, moreover, that blueprints were not established. Severe production declines replaced the stagnating growth of the 1980s; inflation at times accelerated to hyperinflation rates as prices were freed and budget deficits soared. The freeing of prices redistributed incomes from state employees and pensioners to entrepreneurs and black marketeers.

Lagging political support for reform compounded these difficulties. The people had seen only the negative side of transition; they had yet to see the positive consequences. Therefore, in some cases, former communist officials, promising order, returned to power. Elsewhere, political stalemates between conservatives and reformers continued. In Russia, a reform-minded executive branch was pitted against an anti-reform legislature.

By the second half of the 1990s, some successes were evident. Poland, Hungary, the Czech Republic, Slovenia, and the three Baltic states were recording positive growth and low inflation. Some former Soviet republics (Kyrgystan, Armenia, and Moldavia) were making significant progress. In the meantime, China continued to boom under communist rule but with continued economic modernization. In a sense, by the mid-1990s, our attention was already shifting away from the troubled initial transition steps toward understanding the long-run patterns of change under markets.

The Industrialized West

Although change was less dramatic in the industrialized West, change did occur in the 1990s. With few exceptions, the 1990s witnessed voter repudiation of the more extreme forms of social democracy. The 1980s had been dominated by Reaganism in the United States and by Thatcherism in England—both movements designed to replace the ills of "big government" with the benefits of the market. In Germany, the conservative Christian Democratic party strengthened its hold over German politics at the expense of the Social Democratic Party until the late 1990s. Western conservatism set in motion policies designed to reduce the role of government in the economy and to shift existing government functions from federal to state and local levels. Tax reductions were used to improve incentives, welfare programs were cut, and privatization was encouraged in Great Britain, Germany, and France. Even Sweden, long a symbol of welfare statism, experienced a voter backlash against excessive social expenditures and high tax rates.

The conservative economic policies that characterized the industrialized West spread into Latin America, Africa, and Asia in the 1980s. In Latin America, programs were initiated to reestablish private enterprise, and experiments with planned socialism were largely aborted. In Southeast Asia, the remarkable rise of the "Four Tigers" (Singapore, South Korea, Taiwan, and Hong Kong) demonstrated that formerly poor Asian countries could industrialize rapidly and compete in world manufacturing markets using export-oriented economic policies. The strong economic performance of the Four Tigers contrasted sharply with the continued stagnation of Bangladesh and Pakistan, countries that continued to pursue economic policies of state interventionism and protection.

The 1980s and 1990s revealed the limits to conservative economic policies. United States political experience clearly showed public unwillingness to alter fundamentally the social security system put in place in the 1930s. Moreover, U.S. voters refused to accept pro-growth tax reforms that appeared to benefit the wealthy. And the British experience under Thatcher and John Majors revealed a general unwillingness to abandon the national health service or to support growth-oriented tax reform that appeared to favor upper-income groups. The elections of Bill Clinton and Tony Blair in England underscored the conclusion that certain provisions of the welfare state enjoyed considerable voter support.

The 1980s and 1990s saw a strong expansion of economic internationalism and an expanding role for multinational corporations. The West European governments agreed to a united European Union. The United States, Canada, and Mexico established a barrier-free North American market (NAFTA) in 1994. This decisive move toward economic integration has raised the issue of multinationalism versus national sovereignty—a divisive issue that must be resolved in the next century. Multinationalism threatens national identity and weakens sovereign control over economic destiny. How much autonomy should supranational European economic organizations enjoy? Should a European central bank administer a common monetary policy and a common European currency?

The highly publicized political movement toward economic multinationalism has been accompanied by a deeper and more gradual trend: the increased integration of the world economies. The major industrial firms of the West are no longer constrained by national boundaries. In fact, they are no longer national companies; rather, they have become multinational corporations. The IBMs, Siemens, and Sonys of the world are now equally at home in New York, Mexico City, Montreal, London, and

Singapore. An oil venture in Indonesia may be carried out by a consortium of British Petroleum, Royal Dutch Shell, and Exxon and may be financed by funds from the Bank of Tokyo and the Deutsche Bank. A slight change in U.S. interest rates can cause billions of dollars to flow from Hong Kong, Zurich, and Toronto to New York. Transactions between Venezuela and Austria are conducted in U.S. dollars.

The 1990s have held fewer surprises for the industrialized West. The major change has been the shattering of the myth of Japanese invincibility. Japan's growth rates have tapered off, and Japan has been bogged down by recessions in the 1990s. Although Japan's trade performance has remained strong, doubt has begun to grow about the wisdom of Japan's touted industrial policy and its policy of lifetime employment.

The recessions of the 1990s, which hit Western Europe, raised Europe's already high unemployment rates. Europe's hard times forced it to consider restructuring its social welfare policies and instituting policies to reestablish its competitive position in world markets.

The Third World

The most striking feature of the world economy of the 1990s is that prosperity remains limited to a small proportion of the world's population. More than three-quarters of the world's population continues to live in poverty. The average citizen of Asia, Africa, and Latin America remains largely untouched by the industrial–technological revolutions that have created enormous affluence in North America, Western Europe, and Australia. The twentieth century had offered only one example of a country that had made the transition from relative poverty to relative affluence: Japan in the 1950s.

In the last two decades of the twentieth century, a remarkable shift took place. Previously poor countries in Southeast Asia, Hong Kong, South Korea, Taiwan, and Singapore began to grow rapidly. Rapid growth culminated in the achievement of living standards that approached those of the industrialized West. These examples have begun to spread to other Asian countries, such as Indonesia, Thailand, and Malaysia, that are trying to duplicate this feat. Moreover, Latin American countries, such as Chile and Peru, have recorded rapid growth. The Asian miracle experienced setbacks in the second half of 1997 and the first half of 1998 as currency crises and bank failures caused economic slowdowns and even recessions in the region.

Economic Systems in the New Era

The dramatic events of the 1980s and 1990s—the end of the cold war, German reunification, the fall of communist political systems in Eastern Europe, and the dissolution of the Soviet Union—surprised most observers. These changes, unimaginable a few years earlier, raised new and challenging issues.

First, we had thought that the planned socialist economic systems would undergo slow reform designed to make the system work more effectively rather than to replace it. Any change would involve using elements of the market system to improve the existing system.

The unexpected willingness of the former communist economies to abandon their economic system means that we must now study the issue of **transition** rather than **reform** of an existing system. Moreover, for the success stories, we will increasingly view the transition economies within a framework of traditional perceptions—rather routine cases of growth and performance.

Second, the context of change has become ever more important, opening up new and complicated avenues of exploration. For example, although both the Ukraine and Poland are pursuing a transition from plan to market, their circumstances differ dramatically, a fact that will affect transition. Many forces beyond the economic system (such as historical development patterns, foreign trade exposure, and cultural identities) influence the transition—economic systems and system components are not neutral to the setting in which they arise.

Economists prefer to study general principles rather than becoming historical, sociological, or political experts on each country. If a country's **initial conditions** affect the pattern and pace of transition, we must learn to study the "special circumstances" of each transition. We must study the **path dependence** of each transition on its initial conditions.

Third, comparative economic systems, as traditionally studied, had become too narrow. Combining economic history, growth models, and comparative economics is necessary to understand system change. China is a large, relatively poor socialist economy attempting to introduce market forces. Does understanding the Chinese experience thus require a look at comparative economic systems or the study of theories of economic development and growth? The messages may not differ dramatically, and yet being explicit about the approaches is useful if we are to have confidence in our projections.

Despite the importance of understanding initial conditions that may have a strong noneconomic content, remember that comparative economic systems is a branch of economics. It must therefore combine all those branches of economics that speak to the issues of economic systems: how they perform, where they come from, and which system performs the best.

Modern Methodology of Economic Systems

Economists, for more than a century, analyzed how economies work in a setting of stable institutional arrangements. What happens, for example, if the money supply increases or if relative prices change? Only recently have economists become interested in the origins and evolution of the institutions themselves and begun asking how property rights and constitutional law affect economic outcomes.

The number of economic disciplines that are now relevant to comparative economic systems has expanded, and this expansion has enriched but complicated the field. Instead of labels to describe different economic systems, we look at the system and its components directly. In most societies, people pursue objectives through the use of organizations. Economic systems, then, are organizations that can be analyzed and understood through organization theory, institutional economics, information economics, and contemporary microeconomic theory. Organizations have structure and guidance systems, both of which can differ in varying degrees. Figure 1.1 provides a schematic picture of traditional and modern approaches to differing economic systems.

The modern approach emphasizes the multidimensionality and the infinite gradations of economic systems rather than trying to sort them into several categories. It is the characteristics of an economic system that are important, not the labels used. One economy may have more private ownership than another, but the other may have more government intervention in economic decision making. One economy may allow worker participation in corporate decision making, whereas another may allow government bodies to regulate prices. One economy may try to guide its long-term development by government industrial policy, and another may rely exclusively on private-enterprise decision making.

The Choice of Economic Systems

Recent history shows that we do have a choice of economic systems. The former Soviet Union and the countries of Eastern Europe are actively searching for their economic systems. It is still unknown what answers they will find. The industrialized West has operated with fairly stable economic systems for decades if not centuries, but even these societies must make continuous and often subtle choices concerning the shape of their economic systems. The emerging worlds of Asia and Latin America must make crucial choices concerning the economic systems that will bring them to an appropriate level of affluence.

FIGURE 1.1   The Spectrum of Economic Systems

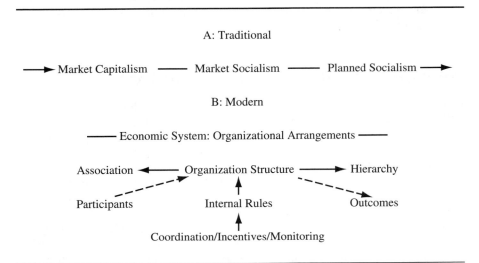

A: Traditional

Market Capitalism —— Market Socialism —— Planned Socialism

B: Modern

—— Economic System: Organizational Arrangements ——

Association ← Organization Structure → Hierarchy

Participants   Internal Rules   Outcomes

Coordination/Incentives/Monitoring

If choosing the economic system were not possible, the study of comparative economic systems would be less compelling. Insofar as people, through the ballot box and through their private and public lives, make choices that affect the economic system, it is important to stay informed about the strengths and weaknesses of alternative economic systems.

The first full-fledged experiment with economic systems began in the Soviet Union in the late 1920s, a decade after the October revolution of 1917. After World War II, the Soviet experiment expanded into Eastern Europe, China, North Korea, Cuba, and North Vietnam. At its peak, about one-third of the world's population lived in countries generally described as socialist economic systems dominated by Marxist–Leninist orthodoxy and communist political systems.

The spread of Soviet-style communism stimulated a debate about which economic system is "better." Viewed with hindsight, the answer to this question appears obvious. But the question of relative superiority has not always been easy to answer.

In the 1930s, the contrast between the depression-ridden West and the industrializing Soviet Union cast real doubt on the superiority of capitalism. At this time, the weaknesses of the capitalist system were all too evident, whereas the flaws of the Soviet system were hidden behind a veil of official secrecy and claims of extraordinary successes. The immediate postwar period of the 1950s saw the remarkable economic successes of West Germany and Japan, but the slow growth of the United States and Great Britain caused some to question the vitality of the capitalist system. In contrast, a confident Soviet Union launched the first piloted space vehicle and declared its intention to "bury" the West. Few will forget the flamboyant performances of then Soviet leader Nikita Khrushchev as he boasted about Soviet economic performance. Yet even Khrushchev warned the Soviet people that in the face of the Soviet ability to build basic industrial capacity, the system might well have "steel blinders" and might lack the ability to adjust and diversify. The era of Leonid Brezhnev revealed to what degree the Soviet economy was, in fact, unable to adjust to change.

The gap between the economic performance of East and that of the West became more pronounced in the 1980s. The West experienced a sustained recovery from the oil shocks of the 1970s and began its longest uninterrupted business expansion in 1981. The East, on the other hand, continued its secular decline. In the Soviet Union, this decline came to be called the "period of stagnation." Promises that things would be better in the future lost their meaning to people who had made considerable sacrifices from the 1930s through World War II, and even thereafter, in spite of the "thaw" of the Khrushchev years. Even more troubling was the lack of growth in productivity. In the face of limits to the growth of inputs, the call for greater reliance on "hidden reserves" proved fruitless. The search for greater efficiency became paramount.

The contrast between the economic growth and consumer affluence of the West and the secular stagnation and consumer poverty of the East set into motion the "radical" reform process that installed non-communist regimes in much of Eastern Europe. News publications in both East and West declared the final victory of capitalism over socialism and proclaimed Marxist–Leninist thought an historical dead end. The Soviet experiment may be dead, but its appeal could be resurrected. If an appropriate path to transition cannot be found and the end result is chaos, enthusiasm for the old system could be revived. Some could claim that although it did not work well, at least it worked.

In our personal and business lives, we copy success. The same is true for economic systems. In the years after World War II, many thought that the Soviet experiment was a success and sought to copy it. In the 1990s, the success of the "Four Tigers" prompted other Asian countries, such as Indonesia, Thailand, and the Philippines, to emulate them. Chile's rapid economic growth has served as an example for other countries in Latin America.

Just as individuals learn from the examples of others, countries learn from the successes and failures of other countries. The ultimate goal of the study of comparative economic systems is to gain a sense of what works and in what settings.

Summary

The field of study known as comparative economic systems examines how differences in economic systems influence resource allocation. The **economic system** is the set of organizational arrangements that, along with differences in national economic policies and natural settings, influence the outcomes of economic activity. Economists interested in different economic systems attempt to define the nature of the system and system differences and to isolate their impact on resource allocation. The traditional "isms" of **capitalism**, **socialism**, and **communism** were the defining characteristics in comparative economic systems for many years. Recent events have, however, shifted concern away from capitalism and communism toward an understanding of a broader spectrum of organizational variants. These variants are defined in terms of the key features of the structure and functioning of organizations—specifically, the **ownership** arrangements (private, public, or mixed), the **information mechanisms** used within organizations (market, plan, or mixed), the levels of decision making (**centralized**, **decentralized**, or mixed), and the incentive arrangements designed to motivate system participants (**monetary**, **moral**, or mixed).

Economic systems arise in real-world (country) settings and can be changed and modified over time. The most important difference among various economic systems today (as opposed to, say, 20 years ago) is precisely the issue of change. The world is no longer divided into neat competing blocs of capitalist and socialist or communist countries. What we see instead are economies undergoing change. The major direction of the former communist economies is **transition**—the movement from the administrative-command system of socialism to market capitalism. The major direction of change in the industrialized West has been the search for improved policies and better organizational arrangements.

Significant events have occurred in Asia, where the Four Tigers have achieved such high rates of growth that they now number among the world's affluent economies. China, though retaining communist political control, has been able to open up its economy to the outside world and to unleash private initiative. Clearly, those interested in comparative economic systems must study these phenomena.

The tools of comparative economic systems have changed. No longer are we dealing with fixed systems. Rather, we are examining economic systems that are in the process of change. Traditional economic analysis is not able to analyze the changes in institutions, so we must look to organizational theory, institutional economics, information economics, and other developing branches of economics to find answers. Because change depends on **initial conditions,** the course of change is **path-dependent.**

Successful economic systems are copied by others. They therefore exert influence well beyond their own borders.

Key Terms

economic system	information mechanisms	economic policies
capitalism	centralized	reform
socialism	decentralized	transition
communism	monetary incentives	initial conditions
ownership	moral incentives	path dependence

Notes

1. The concept of communism as used here refers to the former political systems of the Soviet Union and Eastern Europe, whereas the economies of these former communist states were generally characterized as planned socialist economic systems.

Recommended Readings

David Remnick, *Lenin's Tomb: The Last Days of the Soviet Empire* (New York: Random House, 1993).

Joseph E. Stiglitz, *Whither Socialism?* (Cambridge, Mass.: The M.I.T. Press, 1994).

Gale Stokes, *The Walls Came Tumbling Down: The Collapse of Communism in Eastern Europe* (New York: Oxford University Press, 1993).

Robert C. Stuart and Paul R. Gregory, *The Russian Economy: Past, Present, and Future* (New York: HarperCollins, 1995).

World Bank, *From Market to Plan: World Development Report 1996* (Washington, D.C.; World Bank, 1996).

2

Definition and Classification

Comparative economic systems has been described as "a field in search of a definition."[1] The search for definition has become more complex now that we can no longer divide the world into capitalist and socialist economies. Today, those who study comparative economic systems must confront a dynamic world of change.

Comparative economic systems studies economic outcomes in different institutional, geographic, and political settings. The **economic system**, along with the conventional inputs of land, labor, and capital, matters in observable and understandable ways. Beyond the economic system and traditional inputs, economic outcomes are also influenced by social, economic, cultural, geographic, and random forces. We must develop methods to understand and to control (hold constant) all of the relevant variables in order to isolate and understand the influence of the economic system.[2]

Relating the economic system and other inputs to the observed economic outcomes is a formidable yet feasible task. We know that the level of economic development affects economic outcomes. The level of economic development can be measured, albeit imperfectly, by per capita gross domestic product and other such aggregates. We can estimate relationships between, for example, shares of industry and agriculture in national product and the level of economic development. In this way, we control for differences in the level of economic development. But what about the **nontraditional inputs**? Social, cultural, and historical forces maybe of even greater importance, and yet they are difficult to quantify and to relate to the development experience in a systematic fashion.[3]

Economic Systems: Definition and Classification

We seem to know intuitively what an economic system is, yet there is little agreement on a definition. Traditionally, systems have been classified along an ideological spectrum of the "isms"—feudalism, capitalism, socialism, and communism. This classification identified a system by one or two important characteristics, such as ownership of the means of production.

The modern approach is to classify economic systems in terms of the organizational features that they exhibit. **Organizations** exist in a large number of forms: corporations, proprietorships, legislatures, unions, and churches. They vary in complexity. The organization of a giant multinational corporation is more complex than that of a small family business. No matter how simple or complex, they can all be described in common terms, such as the nature of information mechanisms, behavior rules, decision-making arrangements, and property rights. Organizational arrangement vary broadly, so in the language of the "isms," it is therefore less likely to find pure capitalism or pure socialism than mixed systems with a variety of component characteristics.

In this book, we use the theory of organizations to define and classify economic systems. Organization theory provides a more finely calibrated approach and allows for more diversity than the older capitalism/socialism dichotomy. We continue, however, to use these concepts, because

> Capitalism, communism, socialism, and kindred terms, whatever system traits they may in actuality represent, have a life of their own. They live as symbols or clusters of symbols in the minds of participants in all modern systems . . . , and they may have a profound influence on the way actual systems change or on the reasons why they fail to change.[4]

Definition

We use the definition proposed by Assar Lindbeck, one that emphasizes the multidimensional aspect of an economic system.[5]

An **economic system** is a set of mechanisms and institutions for decision making and for the implementation of decisions concerning production, income, and consumption within a given geographic area.

According to this definition, the economic system consists of mechanisms, organizational arrangements, and decision-making rules. An economic system can vary in any of its dimensions, particularly in its structure, its operation, and its adaptability to change through time. It "includes all those institutions, organizations, laws and rules, traditions, beliefs, attitudes, values, taboos, and the resulting behavior patterns that directly or indirectly affect economic behavior and outcomes."[6]

Economic systems are **multidimensional**, a feature that can be formalized in the following manner:

$$ES = f(A_1, A_2, \ldots, A_n) \tag{2.1}$$

As equation 2.1 indicates, an economic system (ES) is defined by its attributes (A_i) or characteristics, where there are n such attributes. An economic system cannot be defined fully in terms of a single characteristic such as property ownership; rather, the full set of characteristics must be known before ES is specified. We shall focus on four general attributes ($n = 4$) that are critical in differentiating economic systems:

1. Organization of decision-making arrangements: structure
2. Mechanisms (rules) for the provision of information and for coordination: market and plan
3. Property rights: control and income
4. Mechanisms for setting goals and for inducing people to act: incentives

These four characteristics have been chosen because economic systems differ along these dimensions. They have also been chosen because they affect economic outcomes. We do not list features that are relatively uniform across systems—for example, the organization of production in factory units.

Characteristics of Economic Systems

We shall now examine each of the four characteristics and explain why economic outcomes differ with respect to them. Initially, the characteristics appear to have little in common with characterizations of economic systems as capitalist or socialist. However, this chapter later brings them together to formulate working definitions of capitalism and socialism based on the nature of organizational arrangements. This combines the contemporary and traditional approaches to understanding different economic systems.

The Organization of Decision-Making Arrangements

Nobel laureate Herbert Simon writes that "organization refers to the complex pattern of communications and other relations in a group of human beings."[7] According to J. M. Montias, "an organization consists of a set of participants (members) regularly interacting in the process of carrying on one or more activities. . . ."[8] The organization must be allowed to have some turnover in its membership and must be able to change the activities it pursues. Organized behavior has certain advantages over unorganized behavior. In an organization, goals exist, information is created, and assumptions and attitudes are formed, all of which play a part in the making of decisions.

According to organization theory, individuals participate in organized behavior, pursuing **self-interest** constrained by **bounded rationality**.[9] Self-interest may be construed as the maximization of some utility function constrained by a broad range of human limitations, such as the ability to generate, process, and utilize information. These characteristics lead to two major classes of organizational problems. The first, **technical–administrative problems**, derive from individuals who are limited in their ability to make decisions because of, for example, incomplete information. The second, **agency–managerial problems**, derive from individuals who, while pursuing self-interest, may pursue objectives differing from those established for the organization.

To handle these problems, an organization must establish rules concerned with setting up subgroups within the organization, assigning tasks, coordinating activities, monitoring activities, and describing the nature of incentive arrangements. These rules, along with such external factors as cultural and historical influences, largely determine the nature of the organization and lead to basic and important distinctions among economic systems.

The rules within an organization determine how the activities of the organization are carried out. The two extremes of organizational structure are **hierarchy** and **association**. In an organization based on hierarchy, superiors (**principals**) establish objectives and issue orders to subordinates (**agents**) who are supposed to carry out assigned tasks to achieve organizational objectives. In an association-based organization, by contrast, decision making occurs among individuals where there is no superior–subordinate relationship, but rather equality among the individuals.

Except in the case of very simple organizations (such as an owner-operated company with no employees), a hierarchy is present. There can be substantial differences in, for example, the number of levels in the hierarchy, the allocation of tasks among these levels, and the span of control or the number of subordinates directed by a superior.

Armen Alchian and Harold Demsetz[10] suggest one reason why hierarchy exists. Technology requires members of the organization (say, a firm) to work together in "team production." Because the team effort produces output, it is difficult to assess each individual's contribution. Such a setting may cause some to slacken work effort unless a superior monitors work and relates rewards to this effort.

There are other reasons for hierarchy in organizations.[11] Some individuals are risk takers, whereas others avoid risk. Employees agree to work for an owner and to obey the owner's instructions. The owner reaps the rewards of profits if the business succeeds but also risks sustaining losses if the business fails. Production is often carried out in a hierarchical setting because management problems are at times too complicated to organize production through markets.

Principal–Agent Problems An organization is characterized by the levels at which resource-allocation decisions are made and executed. In a **decentralized** organization, decisions are made primarily at low levels of the organization, whereas a **centralized** organization, most decisions are made at high levels.

Such characterizations are in fact simplistic, though as a practical matter, levels of decision making are important for assessing how organizations achieve objectives. Decision-making levels are assessed in terms of the organization's structure, the manner in which the organization generates and utilizes information, and finally, the way it allocates authority and responsibility for decision making among the levels of the organization.[12]

In most organizations, a superior–subordinate (or principal–agent) relationship implies that agents are organized as groups, subunits, or smaller organizations. For example, an enterprise may be a branch of a larger company that is itself owned by a conglomerate. A government enterprise may be subordinated to a government department that in turn is subordinated to a ministry.[13]

Organizations enter into contractual relationships in which they can act either as a principal or as an agent. A **principal** is a party that has controlling authority and that engages an agent to act subject to the principal's control and instruction. An **agent** is a party that acts for, on behalf of, or as a representative of a principal.

Firm X is a principal when it enters into a contract with Firm Y. The contract requires that Firm Y (the agent) supply Firm X with specified amounts of a product at specified prices over a specified period of time. Firm X is also a principal when it signs a contract with an employee (the agent) that calls for the employee to perform specific services at a specified wage for a specified period of time. Once an agency relationship is established, the principal is responsible for monitoring performance to ensure that the agent is providing the services specified in the agreement. When both the principal and the agent are motivated toward the same goal, or when the performance of the agent can be easily monitored, conflicts between the principal and the agent are unlikely to arise. However, when the parties have different goals and when monitoring is difficult, conflicts between principal and agent are expected.

The physical allocation of resources takes place in the enterprise, yet the decisions that determine resource allocation may be made either at the enterprise level or above. The resource-allocation decision could be made at the lowest level (at the enterprise), at an intermediate level (the company or the branch department), or at a high level (the conglomerate corporation or the ministry).

Two factors determine the level of the resource-allocation decisions: the way **authority** is distributed within the hierarchy and how the hierarchy utilizes **information**.

Information Problems   In a perfectly centralized economy, the authority to make decisions rests in a single central command that issues orders to lower units in the organization. The perfectly decentralized case would be a structure where all decision-making authority rests with the lowest subunits (households and individual firms), independent of superior authorities. In the real world, authority is typically spread through various levels in the hierarchy.

The level of decision making depends on the handling of information. Perfect centralization of information means that a single decision maker possesses all information about all participants, their actions, and their environment. Decentralization means that decision makers possess less than complete information. An "informationally decentralized" system generates, processes, and utilizes information at the lowest level in the organization without exchanging information with higher levels in the organization. In a decentralized system, information on prices is exchanged only among the lowest units. Conversely, an "informationally centralized" system involves the generation, processing, and utilization of information by superior agencies and the subsequent transmission of only limited pieces of information to lower subunits.

Perfect centralization of information is not possible because of the mass of information on prices, locations, outputs, and technologies. Economic systems and their constituent organizations must have some degree of information decentralization. In fact, lower-level units have an information advantage over their local circumstances compared with higher-level organizations. Information advantages offer agents the opportunity to engage in **opportunistic behavior** relative to their principals. Opportunistic behavior means that the lower-level unit can use its information advantage against the interests of its superiors.

Opportunistic behavior of this type can take two forms: moral hazard and adverse selection.[14] **Moral hazard** occurs when the lower-level unit exploits an information advantage to alter its behavior after entering into a contract with the upper-level unit. For example, a buyer may promise a supplier steady purchases at fixed prices if that supplier acquires specialized equipment suited only to that buyer's product. After the equipment has been installed, the buyer, as the sole buyer of that product, reduces its purchases or price. **Adverse selection** occurs when agents conceal information from the principals, making it impossible for their superiors to distinguish among them. For example, all enterprises may claim that they cannot adopt a new technology proposed by the ministry. Some can and others cannot, but those that can conceal this fact from the ministry. The ministry therefore may be forced into inefficient decision making, such as requiring all firms to adopt the technology.

Information disadvantages require careful consideration of incentive systems to limit the effects of moral hazard and adverse selection.

Identifying levels of decision making from organization charts can be misleading. Figure 2.1 shows why. In column A, there are three levels in the hierarchy. In column B, there are two—resulting, say, from eliminating the intermediate level or from combining the lower and intermediate levels. At first glance, the change from A to B appears to be a move toward the centralization of decision making. The removal of the intermediate organization seems to concentrate decision-making authority at the center. But elimination of the intermediate organization *might* cause authority to devolve to the subunits. In fact, a critical distinction between the stylized system variants of the past (market or plan) and the mixed systems of the present is the myriad of complex organizational variants being developed in contemporary economies.

Market and Plan

The **market** and the **plan** are the two major mechanisms for providing information and for coordinating decisions in organizations. It is common to identify centralization with plan and decentralization with market, but there is no simple relationship

FIGURE 2.1 Levels of Decision Making in an Economic System

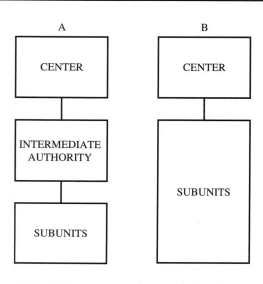

between the level of decision making and the use of market or plan as a coordinating mechanism. In market economies, it is possible to combine a considerable concentration of decision-making authority and information in a few large corporations with substantial state involvement and yet to have no system of planning as such. On the other hand, economies that are characterized as planned can vary substantially: Witness the centralized planning of the former Soviet Union, the "indicative" planning system of France, and the combinations of plan and market that exist in other countries. To identify an economy as planned does not necessarily reveal the prevalent coordinating mechanism or, for that matter, the degree of centralization in decision making. Both depend on the *type* of planning mechanism.

Markets or Plan? Coase   Nobel laureate Ronald Coase posed the question of why some activities are carried out through markets, whereas others are carried out by directives (plan) within enterprises.[15] Coase concluded that activities will be carried out by directives whenever the **transaction costs** of using markets are too high.

The coordination of decision-making activities in markets has costs. The participants in market-coordinated activities must develop appropriate contracts based on market-generated information and must bear the legal and financial consequences of unfulfilled contracts. Business firms can limit the costs of market coordination. Consider, for example, the task of building a jet aircraft. Managerial coordination can reduce transaction costs and negotiations and can enforce a myriad of contracts through directing employees to fulfill required tasks, thus limiting the need for subcontractors. As long as the cost of organizing an activity inside the firm remains below the cost of organizing that activity using markets, the task is carried out within the firm.

Coase applied his theory of transaction costs to explaining why economies organize themselves into business organizations. His ideas could be applied on a grander level to explain why some organizations, such as economic systems, may wish to carry out all their transactions by directive or command and not use markets at all. If the system's directors conclude that the transaction costs of using markets are everywhere too high, they might decide that a planned economy is better than a market economy.

Planned versus Market Economies   A **planned economy** is one wherein agents are coordinated by specific instructions or directives formulated by a superior agency (a planning board) and disseminated through a plan document (sometimes termed directive planning). The participants are induced to carry out the directives via appropriate incentives or threats, which are designed by the planning authorities. The specifics differ from one case to another, but in a planned economy, economic activity is guided by instructions or directives devised by higher units and subsequently transmitted to lower units. Rewards depend on the achievement of plan directives. A planned economy and a **market economy** are mutually exclusive: In the former, resources are allocated in accordance with the instructions of planners, who thereby usurp the role of the market as allocator of resources.

In the case of a market economy, the market—through the forces of supply and demand—provides signals that trigger organizations to make decisions on resource utilization. The market thereby coordinates the activities of decision-making units. Households earn income by providing land, labor, and capital, and with this income they buy the goods that firms supply. Firms and households respond to the market. Other mechanisms for information or coordination are not necessary, and decision-making authority is vested at the lowest level of the economic system.

In **indicative planning**, the market serves as the principal instrument for resource allocation, but a plan is prepared to guide decision making. An indicative plan is one in which planners seek to project aggregate or sectoral trends and to provide information beyond that normally supplied by the market. An indicative plan is *not* broken down into directives or instructions for individual production units; enterprises are free to apply the information in the indicative plan as they see fit, though indirect means are often used to influence economic activity.

The ultimate decision makers are different in planned and market economies. In a market economy, the consumer can "vote" in the marketplace and exercise **consumer sovereignty**. If consumer sovereignty prevails, then the basic decision of what to produce is dominated by consumers in the marketplace. In a planned economy, on the other hand, decisions are made by the planners, and hence **planners' preferences** prevail. Where planners' preferences dominate, the basic decision of what to produce is made by planners.

In a planned economy, planners must base their instructions to production units on some social preference function (that is, some known ordering of society's desires). For political reasons or to promote incentives, however, planners may well have to take into account consumers' preferences. It is difficult to envision a pure planners' preference system, where the wishes of the consumer are totally disregarded.

Neither would one expect pure consumer sovereignty to prevail in a market economy. In market economies, governments can exercise considerable influence over what goods and services are produced. Furthermore, factors such as public goods, externalities, and the market power of large concentrated firms abridge the consumer's ability to dictate resource allocation.

Property Rights: Control and Income

"*Ownership* refers to an amalgam of rights that individuals may have over objects or claims on objects or services" and "these rights may affect an object's disposition or its utilization."[16] Ownership rights may be divided into three broad types. First is the *disposition* of the object in question—the transfer of ownership rights to others, as in the selling of a privately owned automobile. Second, ownership may include the right to *utilization*, whereby the owner can use the object in question in a manner deemed appropriate. Third, ownership implies the **right to use the products and/or services** generated by the object in question.

Ownership rights may be temporary or permanent, and they may well rest with different individuals at any time. The individual who rents an automobile has the right to the *utilization* of that automobile but not to its *disposition*. The owners of a private firm have a claim over the profits of the firm, even though the operation may be significantly circumscribed by government rules and regulations. De jure ownership rights may differ significantly from de facto rights. For example, although members of Soviet collective farms (*kolkhoz*) "owned" the assets of the farm, departing members could not sell their share of these assets.

There are three broad forms of property ownership—**private**, **public**, and **collective** (cooperative). Under private ownership, each of the three ownership rights ultimately belongs to individuals, whereas under public ownership, these rights belong to the state.

Differences in ownership rights affect economic outcomes. Consider an economic system in which all three ownership rights belong to individuals. As the owners seek to maximize their lifetime incomes, capital will be disbursed so as to yield the highest rate of return commensurate with the risk involved. If capital is owned by the state, the rules of capital allocation may be different. Greater attention may be paid to long-term social rates of return. Moreover, time preferences may differ according to whether individuals or the state owns the capital. The distribution of income will differ according to private or state ownership: Property income will accrue to private owners in the one case, to the state in the other. Finally, because the allocation of capital ultimately determines the direction of economic activity, the ownership of capital determines whether allocation is done by private individuals or by the state.

Clearly, ownership arrangements are important in the classification of economic systems. As previously noted, in the traditional classification in terms of the "isms," ownership arrangements are a distinguishing characteristic among the different arrangements. Moreover, in the Marxian schema, changes in ownership of the means of production signalled changes in the economic system. Additionally, unlike differing levels of decision making in an organization, it is possible to identify and measure differences in property ownership arrangements among different groups in a society.

In the contemporary era, it is widely argued that if markets replace plans as decision-making frameworks, then private ownership must be the basis of market allocation mechanisms. The nature of ownership and of its influence on resource allocation is a complex subject. Indeed, in terms of the broad ownership arrangements we have identified, most economic systems are, in fact, mixed systems. Even in economic systems that may be classified as market or capitalist systems, not only are there major differences in the nature of private ownership, but also major segments of the economy are dominated by what has been broadly termed public ownership, where traditional ownership rights are much less well established. We know much more about decision making in the private sector.[17] The nature of decision making and its impact on resource allocation in a state enterprise or a state bureaucracy is much less well understood in both theory and practice. An economic system must organize both private and public decisions. Identifying the nature of differing mixes of decision-making arrangements, especially the effect these differences have on resource allocation, is a major challenge for the field of comparative economic systems.

Incentives

An organization (economic system) can also be characterized in terms of the incentives that motivate people. "Goals and incentives are . . . vital links in understanding the transformation of property rights and informational inputs into effective actions."[18]

An incentive mechanism should induce participants at lower levels (agents) to fulfill the directives of participants at higher levels (principals). An effective mechanism must fulfill three conditions.[19] First, the agent who is to receive the reward must be able to influence the outcomes for which the reward will be given. Second, the agent's principal must be able to check on the subordinate to see whether tasks have been executed properly. Third, the potential rewards must matter to the agent.

In a hierarchy in which superiors issue binding directives to their subordinates, incentives would not be necessary if the principal had perfect information. Armed with perfect information, the principal would automatically know whether the agent was carrying out designated tasks properly. In complex organizations, however, principals typically lack such perfect information. The subordinate knows much more about local circumstances than the superior, and the superior cannot issue perfectly detailed instructions to the subordinate. Because of the imperfect information of the principal, the agent gains local decision-making authority in a number of realms. The principal needs to devise an incentive system that will induce the agent to act in the interests of the superior when the subordinate makes such local decisions. If the principal's incentive system is flawed, then the agent will not act in the interest of the superior.

The information disadvantage of superior organizations relative to their agents affects the way the system is organized. If it is not possible to devise incentive systems that cause agents spontaneously to work in the interests of superior organizations, a more centralized solution may be required. If incentive systems do not elicit information, the superior organization may impose decisions on the subordinate organization without consultation. If private insurance companies cannot elicit information on disabilities or on driving habits, in a cost-effective way, then government agencies, rather than private markets, may have to provide disability or automobile insurance. Information disadvantages explain why governments instead of private markets handle unemployment and poverty insurance.

The superior can devise and use either material or moral incentives to motivate the subordinate. Material incentives have typically been dominant in modern economic systems, yet some systems have attempted to emphasize moral rewards. **Material incentives** promote desirable behavior by giving the recipient a greater claim over material goods. **Moral incentives** reward desirable behavior by appealing to the recipient's responsibility to society (or the company) and accordingly raising the recipient's social stature within the community. Moral incentives do not give recipients greater command over material goods. In simpler terms, the difference between material and moral incentives is the difference between giving an outstanding performer a cash bonus and bestowing a medal.

Different justifications for material rewards have been advanced. According to the neoclassical theory of distribution, those who provide inputs to the system (private owners in a market system) are rewarded according to their productivity. Material incentives are a reward for higher productivity. A case for material incentives can be made even when capital is not privately owned. Marx argued that material rewards are necessary for socialist societies to progress. When ownership of the means of production becomes public and socialism is attained, differential material rewards should persist, but moral incentives (to build socialism for future generations) becomes more important. Eventually, when a stage of material abundance is reached, distribution can be based on the notion "from each according to his ability, to each according to his needs." In the Marxian framework, one would expect material rewards to be gradually replaced by moral incentives.

The issue of incentives in the contemporary analysis of different economic systems remains complex.[20] First, from the perspective of the "isms," much of the early literature dealt with the equity aspects of differing reward systems and made assumptions about individual behavior and how that behavior changes as systems evolve— for example, in the Marxian schema. Indeed, one of the most critical features of socialism was achieving a distribution of income more equitable than that under capitalism. Second, much of the contemporary literature on incentives focuses on **incentive compatibility** or on designing incentive systems for complex organizations such that participant behavior achieves system objectives in the most efficient manner. Much of this research has been cast within the framework of organization theory focusing on firm (enterprise) behavior. In this latter case, the variety of special circumstances arising in real-world organizations is immense, and the difficulties of relating the features of organizations to those of economic systems is great.

Comparing Economic Systems: A Mode of Classification

This chapter has examined the attributes that characterize economic systems. Figure 2.2 summarizes the alternative options available for each attribute. Four criteria for distinguishing among economic systems have been selected. Although additional criteria could have been introduced, these four are especially useful. They result in a threefold classification of economic systems: *capitalism, market socialism*, and *planned socialism*. As Figure 2.3 shows, each system is characterized multidimensionally in terms of the four criteria we have established.

Capitalism is characterized by private ownership of the factors of production. Decision making is decentralized and rests with the owners of the factors of production. Their decision making is coordinated by the market mechanism, which provides the necessary information. Material incentives are used to motivate participants.

Market socialism is characterized by public ownership of the factors of production. Decision making is decentralized and is coordinated by the market mechanism. Both material and moral incentives are used to motivate participants.

Planned socialism is characterized by public ownership of the factors of production. Decision making is centralized and is coordinated by a central plan, which issues binding directives to the system's participants. Both material and moral incentives are used to motivate participants.

These definitions raise as many questions as they answer. They merely state the most important characteristics of economic systems; they do not tell us how and how well each system solves the economic problem of resource allocation. Under capitalism, how do the owners of the factors of production actually allocate their resources, according to what rules, and with what results? Under market socialism, how can

FIGURE 2.2   Attributes of Economic Systems

Attribute:	Options:
Organization of Decision Making	Centralization, Decentralization } MIXED
Provision of Information and Coordination	Market, Plan } MIXED
Property Rights	Private, Cooperative, Public } MIXED
Incentive System	Moral, Material } MIXED

public ownership of the factors of production be made compatible with market co-ordination? In fact, is public ownership *ever* compatible with market coordination? Under planned socialism, how is information gathered and processed to allocate resources effectively? How is it possible to ensure that the system's participants will follow the center's directives?

The "Isms" and Organizations

This chapter has introduced some basic ideas about different economic systems, using both the traditional models of capitalism and socialism and the contemporary framework of organization theory. As succeeding chapters pursue these themes in greater depth, it will be useful to focus on the simple system variants in familiar schematic form.

Figure 2.4 presents the traditional circular flow diagram (panel A) to represent the market capitalist economy. In panel B, a typical hierarchy represents the socialist economy of the planned or market type.

These system types are similar in the process of resource allocation. Both have major system variants that arise in a geographic (country) setting with political governance arrangements. Both face scarcity and opportunity costs and need to allocate

FIGURE 2.3   The Classification of Economic Systems

	CAPITALISM	MARKET SOCIALISM	PLANNED SOCIALISM
Decision-making Structure	Primarily Decentralized	Primarily Decentralized	Primarily Centralized
Mechanisms for Information and Coordination	Primarily Market	Primarily Market	Primarily Plan
Property Rights	Primarily Private Ownership	State and/or Collective Ownership	Primarily State Ownership
Incentives	Primarily Market	Material and Moral	Material and Moral

resources rationally to achieve societal objectives. Both use organized behavior as a fundamental framework for coordinating the activities of system participants as they pursue the allocation of resources. But the settings, objectives, and the systems used to achieve the objectives differ, as do many of the economic outcomes.

The market capitalist economy (Figure 2.4, panel A) typically has a relatively decentralized economy in which association, driven by economic gain, results in organized behavior to achieve system objectives determined largely in the marketplace. Markets for factors and for products are based on private property and the "invisible hand," which provide information necessary for making and coordinating decisions about resource allocation as participants respond to material incentives. Market forces drive the basic decisions about production, distribution, and accumulation. When examining the contemporary transition systems of Eastern Europe, we will see that there is a faith that markets are efficient, though government intervention "regulates" most market capitalist systems to offset perceptions of market failure.

The socialist economy (Figure 2.4, panel B) is typically some variant of the hierarchical form of organization. In the planned variant, decision making is relatively centralized, and a planning mechanism generates information that it uses to coordinate decision making. In this system, the state directs the basic decisions about production, distribution, and accumulation. These decisions are then formulated and executed through the planning system using state-owned resources. Superiors issue

FIGURE 2.4   System Variants: Capitalism and Socialism

Panel A
The Circular Flow: Markets

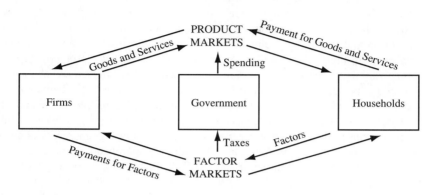

Panel B
The Hierarchical Command Economy

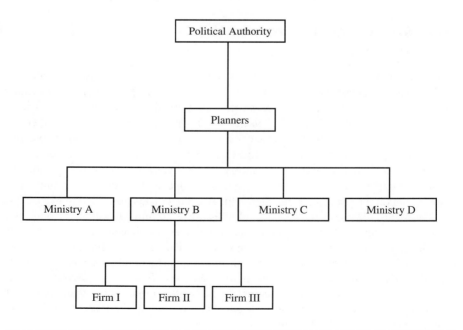

plan directives to subordinates generally through intermediate ministries, and participants respond to the directives, influenced by both material and moral incentives.

In the market socialist variant, market mechanisms can be substituted for various components of the allocation process, but in such models the state generally
retains a central role in many facets of resource allocation.

After considering these simple schematic representations, the reader might well
ask why, if the market is a generally efficient mechanism for resource allocation
requiring minimal intervention, anyone would wish to construct the hierarchical system presented in Figure 2.4, panel B. After all, many of the basic problems of relating organizations to resource allocation introduced in this chapter are abundantly
evident in the hierarchical model. If one finds the classical Marxian schema a useful
approach to explaining historical evolution, then socialism seems inevitable and perhaps should be viewed as a superior system, especially from the perspective of equity.
But even in terms of the contemporary theory of organizations, the hierarchical model
cannot be dismissed, for its structure and its features are embedded in the capitalist
economic system as firms both large and small. In fact, many corporate entities in
market economies have larger and more complex structures than individual small
countries. In essence, as this chapter has emphasized, both costs and benefits can be
discovered in a variety of different organizational arrangements. Thus it is not surprising that an optimal economic system in any given setting comprises a variety of
differing organizational arrangements and guidance mechanisms for the purpose of
resource allocation.

Transition and Change in the
Twenty-First Century

Throughout the twentieth century, we focused on the differences between capitalism
and socialism. These were viewed as the two competing philosophies concerning
how we should organize resource allocation. With the collapse of the socialist
administrative-command economy in the late 1980s and early 1990s, our attention
has been redirected. Now we must consider the transition of the former planned
socialist economies, whose hierarchical organization and lack of market allocation are depicted in Figure 2.4. Transition requires that a hierarchical organization be
converted into a decentralized market system. Product and factor markets (including
capital markets) must replace the hierarchical arrangements described in Figure 2.4.

With the collapse of the socialist administrative-command system, we must also
redirect our attention to the variations and differences among economic systems that,
by and large, allocate resources through markets. The primary advantage of our definition of economic systems in terms of multidimensional attributes is that we can
use differences in attributes to distinguish different types of economic systems
among those economies that use market resource allocation. Rather than comparing
capitalism and socialism, we are now interested in finding the type of market economic system that yields the "best" performance.

Summary

The field of comparative economic systems focuses on identifying the differences in economic systems and assessing the impact of these differences, along with analyzing the effect of traditional inputs (land, labor, and capital) and nontraditional inputs (culture, history, and geography) on the allocation of resources in a given geographic (country) setting.

An economic system consists of the organizational arrangements used to make decisions about resource allocation and can be identified in terms of a variety of important system characteristics, such as system organization (structure), use of market or plan for generating information, and coordination of ownership arrangements and incentives.

Traditionally, pure systems have been classified as market capitalist, market socialist, or planned socialist, depending on the prevailing configuration of the key defining factors. Although this classification helps us understand real-world systems, today we focus on understanding the defining organizational arrangements that occur in the real world in differing mixes and thus influence resource allocation in a variety of ways.

Organizations involve individuals pursuing objectives. In an organization, individuals may function in groups or singly, and objectives can be formulated in a variety of ways. However, the organizational rules that guide system participants in the pursuit of these objectives define the structure of the organization. The structural extremes are hierarchy (where superiors issue orders to subordinates) and association (where individuals have roughly equal rights). An economic system must generate and use information for decision making and coordinate the use of resources to achieve the economic goals it sets.

Organizational decision making is often characterized in terms of levels—that is, whether decision making is centralized (made at upper levels in the hierarchy) or decentralized (made at lower levels in the hierarchy). Levels of decision making are often characterized in terms of information (sources and uses) and/or the authority and responsibility to make decisions. Planned economies may be viewed as hierarchical in structure and centralized in that superiors or principals give instructions to subordinates or agents. Market systems are often defined by association in structure, where impersonal markets rather than instructions are the dominant source of information and the mechanism used for the coordination of economic activities. In fact, both mechanisms have costs and benefits and can both be found in varying degrees in most modern real-world economic systems.

Control over resource use is important, so differences in ownership arrangements or property rights (private property versus state or social ownership) are critical to understanding allocation arrangements and differing economic outcomes in different economic systems. Private property is associated with the functioning of markets and has always been a major characteristic of capitalist economic systems. Some form of state or social ownership of property is associated with socialism, a fact that alters both the way property is used and the distribution of rewards from that use.

Finally, for participants in economic systems to achieve objectives, they must be appropriately motivated. Incentive arrangements can differ broadly (moral or material) and technically, but they must induce system participants to achieve system objectives efficiently with available scarce resources.

Key Terms

economic system
nontraditional inputs
organization
self-interest
bounded rationality
technical–administrative problems
agency–managerial problems
hierarchy
association
principal
agent
market
directive plan
indicative plan

decentralized
centralized
authority
information
opportunistic behavior
moral hazard
adverse selection
market economy
property rights
material incentives
moral incentives
incentive compatibility
transaction costs

Notes

1. Alexander Eckstein, "Introduction" in Alexander Eckstein, ed., *Comparison of Economic Systems: Theoretical and Methodological Approaches* (Berkeley: University of California Press, 1971) p. 1; John Michael Montias, *The Structure of Economic Systems* (New Haven: Yale University Press, 1976).
2. This issue is discussed in Appendix 3A.
3. Relatively little attention has been paid to the relationship among the nontraditional inputs (social, cultural, and historical forces), the traditional inputs (land, labor, and capital), the economic system, and the resulting outcomes. See, for example, Douglass C. North, *Institutions, Institutional Change and Economic Performance* (Cambridge: Cambridge University Press, 1990). For the way other social sciences approach the study of organizations, see, for example, Terry M. Moe, "Politics and the Theory of Organization" *The Journal of Law, Economics and Organization*, 7 (1991), Special Issue, 106–129; Christopher Winship and Sherwin Rosen, eds., "Organizations and Institutions: Sociological and Economic Approaches to the Analysis of Social Structure," *American Journal of Sociology*, 94 (1988), Supplement.
4. Montias, *The Structure of Economic Systems*, p. 8.
5. Assar Lindbeck, *The Political Economy of the New Left: An Outsider's View,* 2nd ed. (New York: Harper & Row, 1977), p. 214.
6. Frederic Pryor, *Property and Industrial Organization in Communist and Capitalist Nations* (Bloomington: Indiana University Press, 1973), p. 337. Adapted from T. C. Koopmans and J. M. Montias, "On the Description and Comparison of Economic Systems" in Eckstein, *Comparison of Economic Systems*, pp. 27–28.

7. Herbert A. Simon, *Administrative Behavior*, 2nd ed. (New York: Free Press, 1966), p. xvi.

8. Montias, *The Structure of Economic Systems*, p. 8.

9. This discussion is based on the excellent survey by Avner Ben-Ner, John Michael Montias, and Egon Neuberger, "Basic Issues in Organizations: A Comparative Perspective," *Journal of Comparative Economics* 17 (1993), 207–242. For an early discussion, see Benjamin Ward, "Organization and Comparative Economics: Some Approaches," in Eckstein, *Comparison of Economic Systems*, pp. 103–133.

10. A. A. Alchian and H. Demsetz, "Production, Information, Costs and Economic Organizations," *American Economic Review* 62 (December 1972), 777–795. A classic in the study of organizations is Simon, *Administrative Behavior*; for a contemporary survey, see Paul Milgrom and John Roberts, *Economics, Organization and Management* (Englewood Cliffs, N.J.: Prentice-Hall, 1992); see also the classic work of Oliver E. Williamson, *The Economic Institutions of Capitalism: Firms, Markets, Relational Contracting* (New York: The Free Press, 1985) and Armen A. Alchian and Susan Woodward, "The Firm is Dead; Long Live the Firm: A Review of Oliver E. Williamson's 'The Economic Institutions of Capitalism,'" *Journal of Economic Literature* 26 (March 1988), 65–79; Alfred D. Chandler, "Organizational Capabilities and the Economic History of the Industrial Enterprise," *Journal of Economic Perspectives* 6 (Summer 1992), 79–100.

11. For a different approach, see Raaj Kumar Sah and Joseph E. Stiglitz, "The Architecture of Economic Systems: Hierarchies and Polyarchies," *American Economic Review* 76, 4 (September 1986), 716–727; see also Roy Radner, "Hierarchy: The Economics of Managing," *Journal of Economic Literature* 30 (September 1992), 1382–1415.

12. There is a large body of literature concerned with issues of centralization and decentralization. For early contributions, see Leonid Hurwicz, "Centralization and Decentralization in Economic Processes," in Eckstein, *Comparison of Economic Systems* pp. 79–102; Leonid Hurwicz, "Conditions for Economic Efficiency of Centralized and Decentralized Structures," in Gregory Grossman, ed., *Value and Plan* (Berkeley: University of California Press, 1960), pp. 162–183. Thomas Marschak, "Centralization and Decentralization in Economic Organizations," *Econometrica* 27 (1959), 399–430. A summary of different meanings can be found in Pryor, *Property and Industrial Organization*, Ch. 8; for a recent discussion of the issues, see Robert G. Lynch, "Centralization and Decentralization Redefined," *Journal of Comparative Economics* 13 (March 1989), 1–14; Donald Chisholm, *Coordination Without Hierarchy* (Berkeley: University of California Press, 1989).

13. Much attention has been paid to the principal–agent relationship. See, for example, Stephen A. Ross, "The Economic Theory of Agency: The Principal's Problem," *American Economic Review Papers and Proceedings* (May 1973); Glen MacDonald, "New Directions in the Economic Theory of Agency," *Canadian Journal of Economics* 17 (1984), 415–440; George Baker, Michael Jensen, and Kevin Murphy, "Compensation and Incentives: Practice vs. Theory," *Journal of Finance* 43 (1988), 593–616; Bengt Holmstrom and Paul Milgrom, "Multitask Principal–Agent Analyses: Incentive Contracts, Asset Ownership, and Job Design," *The Journal of Law, Economics, & Organization* 7 (1991), Special Issue, 34–52; John Pratt and Richard Zeckhauser, eds., *Principals and Agents: The Structure of Business* (Cambridge: Harvard Business School, 1985).

14. It is argued that with the presence of adverse selection and moral hazard, incentive arrangements must be altered. For an early discussion of incentive arrangements in a systems context, see David Conn, ed., "The Theory of Incentives," *Journal of Comparative Economics* 3 (September 1979); for a discussion of incentives in simple cases, see Bernard Caillaud, Roger Guesnerie, Patrick Rey, and Jean Tirole, "Government Intervention in Production and Incentives Theory: A Review of Recent Contributions," *Rand Journal of Economics* 19 (1988), 1–26; Nahum D. Melumad and Stefan Reichelstein,

"Value of Communication in Agencies," *Journal of Economic Theory* 47 (1989), 334–368; David E. M. Sappington, "Incentives in Principal–Agent Relationships," *Journal of Economic Perspectives* 5 (Spring 1991); for a discussion of incentive arrangements under adverse selection and moral hazard, see Liang Zou, "Threat-Based Incentive Mechanisms Under Moral Hazard and Adverse Selection," *Journal of Comparative Economics* 16 (March 1992), 47–74.

15. Ronald H. Coase, "The Nature of the Firm," *Economica* 4 (1937), 386–405. Reprinted in George Stigler and Kenneth Boulding, eds., *Readings in Price Theory* (Homewood, Ill: Richard D. Irwin, 1952).

16. Montias, *The Structure of Economic Systems*, p. 116; for an early survey of the literature, see Erik Furubotn and Svetozar Pejovich, "Property Rights and Economic Theory: A Survey of Recent Literature," *Journal of Economic Literature* 10 (December 1972), 1137–1162; for a discussion in the comparative context, see Pryor, *Property and Industrial Organization*; for a recent discussion, see Alan Ryan, "Property" in John Eatwell. Murray Milgate, and Peter Newman, eds., *The New Palgrave: Dictionary of Economics* (New York: Stockton Press, 1987), pp. 1029–1031; Louis Putterman, "Ownership and the Nature of the Firm," *Journal of Comparative Economics* 17 (1993), 243–263; John P. Bonin, Derek C. Jones, and Louis Putterman, "Theoretical and Empirical Research on Producers' Cooperatives: Will Ever the Twain Meet?" *Journal of Economic Literature* 31 (September 1993), 1290–1320.

17. For a discussion of decision making in the public sector, see V. V. Ramanadham, *Public Enterprise: Studies in Organizational Structure* (London: Frank Cass, 1986); for a discussion of nonprofit organizations, see Avner Ben-Ner and Theresa Van Hoomissen, "Nonprofit Organizations in the Mixed Economy: A Demand and Supply Analysis," *Annals of the Public and Cooperative Economy* 62, 4 (October–December, 1991), 519–550; Susan Rose-Ackerman, ed., *The Economics of Nonprofit Institutions: Studies in Structure and Policy* (New York: Oxford University Press, 1986); Burton A. Weisbrod, *The Nonprofit Economy* (Cambridge: Harvard University Press, 1988); Jean-Jacques Laffont and Jean Tirole, "Privatization and Incentives," *Journal of Law, Economics & Public Organization* 7 (1991) Special Issue, 84–105.

18. Pryor, *Property and Industrial Organization*, p. 338.

19. Montias, *The Structure of Economic Systems*, Ch. 13.

20. For a broader approach to the relationship between participants in an organization and those who make decisions, see Paul Milgrom and John Roberts, "An Economic Approach to Influence Activities in Organizations," *American Journal of Sociology* 94 (1988) Supplement, s154–s179.

Recommended Readings

Traditional Sources

A. A. Alchian and H. Demsetz, "Production, Information, Costs and Economic Organizations," *American Economic Review* 62 (December 1972), 777–795.

David Conn, ed., "The Theory of Incentives," *Journal of Comparative Economics* 3 (September 1979).

H. Demsetz, "Toward a Theory of Property Rights," *American Economic Review* 57 (May 1967), 347–359.

Alexander Eckstein, ed., *Comparison of Economic Systems: Theoretical and Methodological Approaches* (Berkeley: University of California Press, 1971).

Erik Furobotn and Svetozar Pejovich, "Property Rights and Economic Theory: A Survey of Recent Literature," *Journal of Economic Literature* 10 (December 1972), 1137–1162.

John Michael Montias, *The Structure of Economic Systems* (New Haven: Yale University Press, 1976).

Egon Neuberger, "Classifying Economic Systems," in Morris Bornstein, ed., *Comparative Economic Systems: Models and Cases*, 4th ed. (Homewood, Illinois: Richard D. Irwin, 1978).

Frederic Pryor, *Property and Industrial Organization in Communist and Capitalist Nations* (Bloomington: Indiana University Press, 1973).

———, *A Guidebook to the Study of Economic Systems* (Englewood Cliffs, N.J.: Prentice-Hall, 1985).

Herbert A. Simon, *Administrative Behavior*, 2nd ed. (New York: Free Press, 1966).

P. J. D. Wiles, *Economic Institutions Compared*, (New York: Halsted, 1977).

———, "What Is Comparative Economics?" *Comparative Economic Studies*, 31 (Fall 1989), 1–32.

Oliver E. Williamson, *Markets and Hierarchies* (New York: Free Press, 1975).

Basic, General, Contemporary Sources

Armen Alchian and Susan Woodward, "The Firm Is Dead; Long Live the Firm: A Review of Oliver E. Williamson's 'The Economic Institutions of Capitalism,'" *Journal of Economic Literature* 26 (March 1988), 65–79.

Avner Ben-Ner, John Michael Montias, and Egon Neuberger, "Basic Issues in Organizations: A Comparative Perspective," *Journal of Comparative Economics* 17 (1993), 207–242.

Paul Milgrom and John Roberts, *Economics, Organization and Management* (Englewood Cliffs, N.J.: Prentice-Hall, 1992).

Frederic L. Pryor, "Corporatism as an Economic System: A Review Essay," *Journal of Comparative Economics* 12 (September 1988), 317–344.

Oliver E. Williamson, *The Economic Institutions of Capitalism: Firms, Markets, Relational Contracting* (New York: The Free Press, 1985).

———, ed., *Organization Theory: From Chester Barnard to the Present and Beyond.* (Oxford: Oxford University Press, 1990).

Organizations: Historical Aspects

Alfred D. Chandler, "Organizational Capabilities and the Economic History of the Industrial Enterprise," *Journal of Economic Perspectives* 6 (Summer 1992), 79–100.

James S. Coleman, "Constructed Organization: First Principles," *The Journal of Law, Economics, & Organization* 7 (1991), Special Issue, 7–23.

R. R. Nelson and S. G. Winter, *An Evolutionary Theory of Economic Change* (Cambridge: Harvard University Press, 1982).

Douglass C. North, *Institutions, Institutional Change and Economic Performance* (Cambridge: Cambridge University Press, 1990).

The Structure of Organizations

Sanford Grossman and Oliver Hart, "The Costs and Benefits of Ownership: A Theory of Vertical and Lateral Integration," *Journal of Political Economy* 94 (August 1986), 691–719.

Raaj Kumar Sah and Joseph E. Stiglitz, "The Architecture of Economic Systems: Hierarchies and Polyarchies," *American Economic Review* 76 (September 1986), 716–727.

Paul Milgrom, "Employment Contracts, Influence Activities and Efficient Organizational Design," *Journal of Political Economy* 96 (February 1988), 42–60.

Herbert A. Simon, "Organizations and Markets," *Journal of Economic Perspectives* 5 (Spring 1991), 25–44.

Joseph E. Stiglitz, "Symposium on Organizations and Economics," *Journal of Economic, Perspectives* 5 (Spring 1991), 15–24.

Principal–Agent Relationships

Joseph Farrell, "Information and the Coase Theorem," *Journal of Economic Perspectives* 1 (Fall 1987), 113–129.

Bengt Holmstrom and Paul Milgrom, "Multitask Principal–Agent Analyses: Incentive Contracts, Asset Ownership and Job Design," *The Journal of Law, Economics, & Organization* 7 (1991), Special Issue, 34–52.

Glen MacDonald, "New Directions in the Economic Theory of Agency," *Canadian Journal of Economics* 17 (1984), 415–440.

John Pratt and Richard Zeckhauser, eds., *Principals and Agents: The Structure of Business* (Cambridge: Harvard Business School, 1985).

Incentive Arrangements

David Conn, "Effort, Efficiency, and Incentives in Economic Organizations," *Journal of Comparative Economics* 6 (September 1982), 223–234.

Jean-Jacques Laffont and Eric Maskin, "The Theory of Incentives: An Overview," in Werner Hildenbrand, ed., *Advances in Economic Theory* (Cambridge: Cambridge University Press, 1982).

Louis Putterman and Gil Skillman, "The Incentive Effects of Monitoring Under Alternate Compensation Schemes," *International Journal of Industrial Organization* 6 (March 1988), 109–120.

Yingyi Qian, "Equity, Efficiency, and Incentives in a Large Economy," *Journal of Comparative Economics* 16 (March 1992), 27–46.

David E. M. Sappington, "Incentives in Principal–Agent Relationships," *Journal of Economic Perspectives* 5 (Spring 1991), 45–66.

Liang Zou, "Threat-Based Incentive Mechanisms Under Moral Hazard and Adverse Selection," *Journal of Comparative Economics* 16 (March 1992), 47–74.

Property Rights

H. Demsetz and K. Lehn, "The Structure of Corporate Ownership: Causes and Consequences," *Journal of Political Economy* 93 (December 1985), 1155–1177.

Louis Putterman, "Ownership and the Nature of the Firm," *Journal of Comparative Economics* 17 (1993), 243–263.

Alan Ryan, "Property," in John Eatwell, Murray Milgate, and Peter Newman, eds., *The New Palgrave: Dictionary of Economics* (New York: Stockton Press, 1987), pp. 1029–1031.

Xiaoki Yang and Ian Wills, "A Model Formalizing the Theory of Property Rights," *Journal of Comparative Economics* 14 (June 1990), 177–198.

The Theory of Cooperatives

John P. Bonin, Derek C. Jones, and Louis Putterman, "Theoretical and Empirical Research on Producers' Cooperatives: Will the Twain Ever Meet?" *Journal of Economic Literature* 31 (September 1993), 1290–1320.

Nonprofit Organizations

Susan Rose-Ackerman, ed., *The Economics of Nonprofit Institutions: Studies in Structure and Policy* (New York: Oxford University Press, 1986).

Walter Powell, ed., *The Nonprofit Sector: A Research Handbook* (New Haven: Yale University Press, 1987).

Burton A. Weisbrod, *The Nonprofit Economy* (Cambridge: Harvard University Press, 1988).

The Public Sector

Abram Bergson, "Managerial Risks and Rewards in Public Enterprises," *Journal of Comparative Economics* 2 (September 1978), 211–225.

A. Boardman and A. Vining, "Ownership and Performance in Competitive Environments: A Comparison of the Performance of Private, Mixed, and State-Owned Enterprises," *Journal of Law and Economics* 32 (1989), 1–33.

Estelle James, Egon Neuberger, and Robert Willis, "On Managerial Rewards and Self-Selection: Risk Taking in Public Enterprises," *Journal of Comparative Economics* 3 (December 1979), 395–406.

Jean-Jacques Laffont and Jean Tirole, "Privatization and Incentives," *The Journal of Law, Economics, & Organization* 7 (1991), Special Issue, 84–105.

3

Evaluation of Economic Outcomes

This chapter explains how observed economic outcomes can be systematically related to the economic system. This, after all, is the central focus of comparative economic systems. We wish to judge which economic systems perform best and how to alter economic systems or system components to improve performance. The task of relating outcomes to systems raises a number of key methodological issues.

Models versus Reality

The previous chapter examined in abstract terms three general types of economic systems: capitalism, planned socialism, and market socialism. Each exhibits different organizational arrangements and decision-making rules. In the real world, however, actual systems tend to be mixed systems, a fact that complicates an assessment of outcomes. Moreover, given the collapse of the administrative-command system in the former Soviet Union and Eastern Europe, we are now more interested in assessing performance within the capitalist system.

Comparative economic systems can be structured on two levels: models and reality.[1] The justification for examining and comparing **system models** is the same as that made for economic theory. Theories or models enable us to abstract from reality to understand basic issues; they provide a means to make comparisons in simple ways; they provide a means for predicting outcomes to establish a "norm" for assessing ultimate real-world outcomes.

Having justified the use of abstract system models, it is now important to understand that the economic outcomes observed are those of real-world systems working in actual geographic settings influenced by a variety of system and nonsystem forces.[2] Most important, however, is that these real-world systems are typically mixed. Thus there are a number of basic issues that we should bear in mind while attempting to relate outcomes to systems.

First, to the extent that theoretical system models are used, it is important to compare model with model, or the reality of a given model (say market capitalism) with the model of market capitalism. Comparing the outcomes of, say, a planned socialist economic system with the model of market capitalism is not generally useful, though models of planned socialist systems are generally much less developed than those of market capitalist systems, which makes cross-comparisons appealing in some cases.

Second, in comparing real-world outcomes with system models, it is difficult, if not impossible, to quantify measures of economic systems and system differences. Outcomes are generally measurable, but system characteristics are much less so. We can use broad measures to capture system characteristics, such as the size of government or shares of private ownership. Because economic systems are multidimensional, however, such broad measures capture only a portion of reality.

Third, many forces beyond the economic system influence outcomes. Although this issue is discussed in greater depth in Appendix 3A, it is important to emphasize that although some nonsystem forces are measurable, others are not, which makes it difficult to generalize about system and nonsystem forces and their relationships to outcomes.

Fourth, most real-world systems are mixed systems, which is of great importance in the contemporary analysis of economic systems in an era when market-type systems dominate. Is the United States more "capitalistic" than Germany or Singapore and, if so, by how much?

Such questions cannot be answered satisfactorily. More subtle and difficult to assess, moreover, is the variability of system components. For example, it has generally been noted that different economic systems all use the firm as a basic unit of industrial production. But firms can differ significantly—in terms of ownership, for example. Public- or government-owned corporations are very different from private corporations, and both differ from cooperative arrangements. These differences are difficult to isolate and to measure such that their impact on outcomes can be assessed.

The Forces Influencing Economic Outcomes

To capture some of the ideas outlined above, we propose some simple notation. If we could measure the **economic system (ES)** in a manner that provided ordinal or cardinal rankings, we would still have to measure economic **outcomes (O)** in a meaningful manner.

Economic outcomes depend on factors other than the economic system—natural resource endowments, the level of economic development, the size of the economy, labor and capital inputs, random events, and so on. These are termed **environmental factors (ENV)**. Finally, economic outcomes depend on the **policies (POL)** that the policy makers in economic systems choose to follow.

$$O = f(\text{ES, ENV, POL}) \qquad (3.1)$$

where

> O   denotes economic outcomes
> ES   denotes the economic system
> ENV   denotes environmental factors
> POL   denotes policies pursued by the economic system

Equation 3.1 and Figure 3.1 highlight the methodological problems of determining the impact of the economic system (ES) on the observed outcomes (O)—the

FIGURE 3.1   Forces Influencing Economic Outcomes

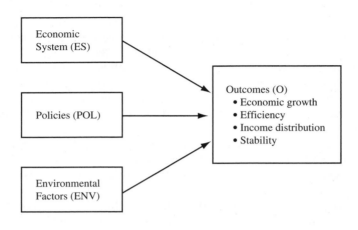

ceteris paribus ("other things being equal") problem. Insofar as the outcomes observed depend on factors in addition to the economic system, one cannot isolate the
impact of the system without first controlling for, or holding constant, the influence
of the environmental (ENV) factors and the policy variables (POL). But how is this
problem handled, and to what extent can ENV and POL factors be identified? To
illustrate the problem, some basic examples from the real world can be used.

Labor productivity (an "outcome") in the former Soviet Union was relatively low
compared with that in Western Europe and the United States.[3] Assuming accurate
measurement, is the observed outcome the result of the economic system (planned socialism), environmental factors, policy factors, or some combination of these forces?
This question is not easily answered. For example, the level of economic development
in the former Soviet Union (as measured, say, by per capita domestic product) was
well below levels in the United States and Western Europe, and historical evidence
shows that the level of productivity is positively associated with the level of economic
development. In this case, is the productivity gap observed in the former Soviet Union
a function of the economic system, or are other factors involved?

Appendix 3A contains simple statistical techniques to handle these sorts of measurement problems, and yet basic difficulties remain because many of the variables of
interest (notably the economic system) are in fact difficult to measure in any meaningful manner.

This discussion of measurement problems has focused on the nature of the economic system and environmental factors. But how is it possible to identify the policy
(POL) differences across economic systems? Again, examples are useful.

Three countries that have grown rapidly over the past decade are China, Chile,
and Singapore. In an effort to determine what factors led to this rapid growth, we
would look for changes that would have accelerated growth. In the case of China, we

might look at its decision to open up the economy to foreign investment. In Chile, we might look at the privatization of its pension system, which promoted increased capital formation. In the case of Singapore, we might look at its market-oriented programs carried through by a nondemocratic government.

Should we classify these changes as *changes in the economic system* or as *changes in policy?*

A factor is classified as **policy** if it can be significantly changed without changing the underlying economic system. It is, by contrast, a direct attribute of the economic system if it cannot conceivably be altered without an alteration of the economic system. Such an approach provides us with some conception of how policy influences and system influences might differ.

Policies tend to be closely intertwined with the economic system. They are nonetheless important to the evaluation of economic systems. In most instances, trade aversion leads to a lower standard of living than would have prevailed had there been international specialization. The standard of living is often used as a performance indicator. Should this weakness be attributed to the economic system or to policies pursued by the economic system?

To understand the impact of the economic system on economic outcomes, one must understand the effects of all other significant environmental and policy factors. In other fields of economics, the economic system is taken as "given," and one can more easily isolate the effect of changes in a particular variable on economic outcomes.

The Evaluation of Outcomes: The Success Criteria Problem

When the outcomes of differing economic systems are compared, we wish to determine which economic system performs "best" in achieving its goals. How are we to evaluate the differing outcomes in order to decide which is "best"? Two crucial problems arise.

First, to evaluate the outcomes of differing economic systems, we must select a set of performance criteria. Because people typically do not agree on the appropriate criteria, the selection tends to be subjective.

Second, even if agreement can be reached on a list of criteria for evaluating outcomes, how will the criteria be added together if economic systems yield different results? In such instances, the disparate results must be somehow added together by assigning *weights* for aggregation. This produces a single index of achievement, which can then be used to compare systems. Clearly, the weights selected will determine the value of the index of achievement, but they are themselves subjective and depend on the values held by the particular observer.[4]

It is logical to think that the economic system should have as its objective the achievement of a maximal value of the economic outcome (O), subject to the constraints imposed by the economic system (ES), policies (POL), and environmental factors (ENV), which include technology and resource constraints. The objective is to

Maximize: O

Subject to (ES, ENV, POL)   (3.2)

From this, it would seem that evaluating the performance of economic systems would be (theoretically at least) a rather simple matter. After adjusting for differences in environment and policy, one would have only to determine which system achieved the highest economic outcome. If there were agreement on the measurement of outcomes, it would work this way. Instead, the economic outcome (O) is a function of a series of performance indicators:

$$O = \sum_{j=1}^{k} a_j o_j \qquad\qquad (3.3)$$

where

o_j = desirable (or undesirable if negative) economic outcomes
a_j = the relative importance of the various outcomes

Consider the following example, in which two economic systems designated A and B are judged according to two criteria. System A receives a score of 1 and 2 on the two criteria. B receives a score of 2 and 1 on the two criteria. Which system has outperformed the other depends on the relative weights applied to the two criteria.

Just as individuals assign different weights (a_j) to different economic goals, so one would expect economic systems to assign different weights to those goals.[5] Furthermore, the evaluation of these goals changes over time. One need only consider the changing priority of economic goals in the United States or note that capitalist societies attach different weights to the items on a rather similar list of economic goals or objectives.

Equation 3.3 summarizes the crux of the problem. Because different societies assign different subjective weights (a_j) to economic outcomes (o_j), the measurement of economic performance depends not only on o_j but also on a_j, which must remain subjective. For example, one economic system may assign priority to economic growth and allocate resources accordingly. In so doing, it attaches relatively low weights to the other goals. Another economic system may attach a dominant weight to price stability and allocate its resources accordingly. It is likely, in this scenario, that the first system will perform better in terms of the growth objective and that the second system will perform better in terms of price stability. Which system has outperformed the other? The answer depends on one's personal judgment of which goal is more important.

The Determination of System Priorities

How are **national priorities** determined in practice? The involvement of substantial subjective elements does not mean that priorities are not in fact established, although they do change over time partly as a function of change in the economic system itself.

The determination of national priorities differs from system to system. In societies where political power is largely centralized, the prevailing political authority exercises decisive control over the formation of national goals. In the former Soviet Union, for example, the Communist party historically played a dominant role in goal formation.[6] This does not mean that other forces had no influence, but their roles were relatively limited. (In socialist societies, where political power was substantially concentrated, the process of modernization itself led to some pluralization of the society and to the formation of influential interest groups.)[7]

In democratic societies, establishing priorities is more complicated. This complexity is reflected in the various arrangements through which individuals can express preferences by voting. The vote may indicate a preference among political candidates with differing positions on national issues, or it may be a "vote" cast in the marketplace indicating what goods and services are desired. However, pressure groups such as trade unions, manufacturers' associations, and professional associations can and do exert substantial influence. Even though majority voting prevails, legislation that advances minority interests may be passed.[8] Also, even in a pluralistic democratic society, as power becomes concentrated (whether in the hands of individuals in the form of wealth or in the hands of lobby groups or corporations), there is a tendency for the goal formation process to change.[9] In a democratic society, the change may take place slowly. In a society where power is centralized, change may be more sudden, though not necessarily revolutionary.

If various goals are laudable, why not pursue all of them? Specific goals can often be achieved only by sacrificing other, less important goals. The necessity of choosing to pursue some goals at the expense of others is a consequence of the fundamental scarcity of resources, which prevents every economic system from producing unlimited quantities of goods and services. Instead, choices must be made among goals.

The nature of the tradeoffs is not always clearly defined. Can unemployment in the United States be lowered without increasing inflation? Is sustained economic growth compatible with a cleaner environment? Can the affluent economies of Europe maintain generous welfare and benefits programs without sacrificing economic growth? Can China maintain an open economy *and* the political dictatorship its leaders desire? The existence of tradeoffs matters in at least two ways. First, we cannot assess the performance of economic systems without understanding the tradeoff among alternatives. Second, when one goal must be sacrificed to achieve another, we should not criticize a system for not achieving a goal that it has, in effect, decided not to pursue.

Performance Criteria

We have selected those performance criteria that are generally applied to assess economic outcomes. We realize that any such list will omit some criteria (military power, for instance, or environmental quality) that are important. We shall use the following criteria to evaluate economic outcomes:

1. Economic growth
2. Efficiency
3. Income distribution (fairness)
4. Stability (cyclical stability, avoidance of inflation and unemployment)
5. Viability of the economic system

Economic Growth

The most widely used indicator of economic performance is economic growth. **Economic growth** refers to increases in the volume of output that an economy generates over time or to increases in output per capita.[10] We are interested in economic output and its growth because, for a particular economic system at a particular time, the material well-being or welfare of its population can be approximated by the volume of goods and services per capita at its disposal.[11] Changes in the volume of output per capita over time normally bring about changes in the welfare of the population in the same direction. Using this interpretation, we can compare levels of well-being in different systems at any time, or over time, to evaluate the rate at which economic progress is being made.

Because economic growth is so widely employed as a performance indicator, it is useful to spell out some complications. First, measurement problems arise in assessing economic growth, especially when different economic systems are compared.[12] Second, it is difficult to untangle the causes of differences in economic growth. They may be a consequence of the economic system, but they may also result from environmental and policy factors. The process of economic growth is so complex that it defies easy description; therefore, we can never be sure of the system's impact on growth. For example, the most rapidly-growing countries of recent years are located in Asia: China, Singapore, and Taiwan. They began their rapid growth from low levels of income. To what extent was this rapid growth the consequence of changes in the economic system rather than a result of the low "baseline" level of development? If one compares the growth of two economic systems over time, when each system begins with a different base, one may expect, *ceteris paribus*, differences in growth performance.

Third, the uncertain link between the growth of output and increases in quality of life should be emphasized. Economic growth is enhanced by capital formation, but to expand the capital stock, saving (refraining from current consumption) is required. It may well be that the savings of the present generation will bear fruit in the form of improvements in the living standard of later generations. The decision to postpone present consumption in favor of future consumption must be confronted in any economic system, whether the choice is made primarily by consumer or by planner. The outcome of this decision has an impact on growth performance and on current living standards. For example, the Four Tigers of Southeast Asia recorded very high saving rates, and these high rates of capital formation clearly contributed to their rapid growth. In effect, they sacrificed the present for the future.

It was argued that capitalist systems consistently underrate the merits of future consumption and hence save too little to make adequate provision for the future.[13]

Thus we anticipate higher savings ratios in socialist systems and, accordingly, a more rapid rate of growth of the capital stock and, *ceteris paribus*, a higher rate of growth of output. The failure of the Socialist economies to generate more rapid growth *despite* high rates of saving was one reason for their collapse.

Efficiency

A second measure of system performance is economic efficiency. **Efficiency** is the effectiveness with which a system utilizes its available resources (including knowledge) at a particular time (**static efficiency**) or through time (**dynamic efficiency**).[14] Static and dynamic efficiency are interrelated in a complex manner, but both are multidimensional in the sense that they depend on a wide variety of factors.

The concept of efficiency can be conveniently illustrated by the production possibilities schedule shown in Figure 3.2. The initial production possibilities schedule (*AB*) illustrates all feasible combinations of producer and consumer goods that a particular economic system is capable of producing at a particular time by using all available resources at maximal efficiency. The production possibilities schedule shows that, given its existing resources, the system has a menu of production choices open to it. Economic systems must choose where to locate on the schedule.

FIGURE 3.2   The Production Possibilities Schedule

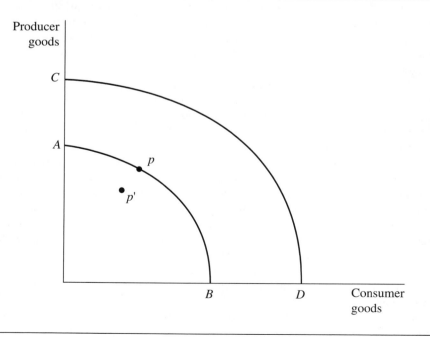

In capitalist societies, the consumer–voter dominates this choice. In planned social-ist societies, planners make the decision.

The labels we have attached to the axes in Figure 3.2 are arbitrary. We could have chosen other goals and could have examined a number of possible tradeoffs. However, the *shape* of the production possibilities frontier is not accidental. The fact that it is a curve convex from the origin illustrates a basic fact of economic life: As one attempts to produce increasing amounts of, say, consumer goods, one has to give up ever larger amounts of producer goods to obtain identical increases in consumer goods. In more technical terms, there is a diminishing marginal rate of technical substitution between the production of consumer goods and the production of producer goods.

The production possibilities schedule is a useful device for illustrating the con-cept of efficiency. We have already indicated that *AB* represents the capacity of a par-ticular economic system at a particular time. Static efficiency requires an economic system to be operating on its production possibilities frontier—for example, at point *p*. Output combinations beyond *AB* are impossible at that time; combinations inside *AB* are feasible but inefficient. An economic system that has the capacity *AB* but is producing at point *p′* is statically inefficient, because it could move to point *p* and produce *more of both* goods with no increase in available resources.

Dynamic efficiency is the ability of an economic system to enhance its capacity to produce goods and services over time without an increase in capital and labor inputs. Dynamic efficiency is indicated by movement of the frontier outward from *AB* to *CD* (without an underlying increase in resources); the distance of this move-ment indicates the change in efficiency.

Like other indicators of system performance, static and dynamic efficiency are subject to complex measurement problems. The basic approach to measuring static efficiency is to make productivity calculations, as measured by the ratio of the out-put to inputs. Dynamic efficiency is measured by the ratio of the growth of output to the growth of inputs.

Economic growth and dynamic efficiency are not the same. The output of a system may grow by increasing efficiency (finding better ways of doing things with the same resources) or by expanding the amount of, say, labor but using that labor at a constant rate of effectiveness. The former is often termed **intensive growth**, the latter **extensive growth**.

The concepts of intensive and extensive growth are important in understanding the growth experiences of different economic systems. Later chapters show that the former planned socialist systems of the Soviet Union and Eastern Europe tended toward high-growth systems in their early years and then exhibited substantial and continuing slowdowns in their later years. Although the growth slowdown is an outcome for later discussion, the early rapid-growth experience has been widely attributed to a strategy of extensive growth—a growth-oriented policy supported by an economic system designed to harness inputs and to allocate those inputs to growth-generating sectors such as heavy industry. As economies reach higher levels of economic development, growth in output is increasingly derived from intensive economic growth. Mature economies no longer experience the increases in popula-tion and saving rates necessary to sustain extensive economic growth.

Income Distribution (Fairness)

How "fairly" an economic system distributes income among households is the third criterion for assessing economic performance. Technically, **income distribution** is measured by the **Lorenz curve** or **Gini coefficient**, as shown in Figure 3.3. Our ability to measure income distributions does not, however, answer the question of what constitutes a "good" distribution. There may be substantial agreement on the definition of bad income distributions (for example, where 1 percent of the population receives 95 percent of all income); judgments about intermediate cases are more difficult to make.

What constitutes an equitable distribution of income?[15] Equity involves fairness, though what is considered fair differs from case to case and over time. One criterion of fairness might involve reward according to contribution to the production process. In a capitalist society, personal income is determined by the human and

FIGURE 3.3   Measuring Income Inequality: The Lorenz Curve

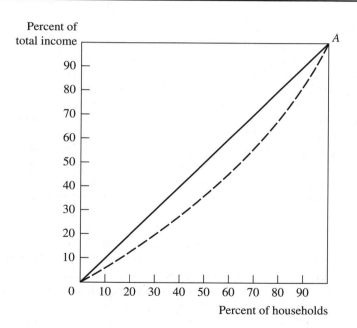

Explanation: Percent of households is measured on the horizontal axis, percent of income on the vertical axis. Perfect equality would be, for example, where 10 percent of households received 10 percent of all income. This would be illustrated by a 45-degree line between the origin (0) and point *A*. Inequality can be illustrated by the dashed line. The further the dashed line bows away from the 45-degree line, the further from equal the distribution of income. In the diagram, for example, the bottom 20 percent of households receive 10 percent of the income. A comprehensive measure, known as the *Gini coefficient,* is typically used to measure income inequality. The Gini coefficient is the area between the 45-degree line and the dashed line divided by the entire area under the 45-degree line.

physical capital one owns and by their prices as determined by factor markets. Income differences reflect differences in effort (provision of labor services), differences in frugality (provision of capital), inheritance of physical and human capital, luck, and so on. The market distribution of income may be modified by the tax system and by the provision of social services. The extent to which government redistributive action is justified on equity grounds is a matter of continuing controversy in capitalist societies. Under socialism, the factors of production are, with the exception of labor, publicly owned. Capital and land are both socially owned in a socialist society; hence their remuneration belongs to the state, not directly to individuals.

Stability

The fourth criterion is economic stability. By **stability** we mean the absence of significant fluctuations in growth rates, the maintenance of acceptable rates of unemployment, and the avoidance of excessive inflation. Economic stability is a desirable objective for two reasons. The first is that various segments of the population are damaged by instability. Individuals on fixed incomes are hurt by unanticipated inflation; the poorly trained are hurt by unemployment. Second, cyclical instability can lead to losses of potential output, making the economic system operate inside its production possibilities schedule.

Capitalist economies have historically been subject to fluctuations in the level of economic activity—in other words, to business cycles.[16] In planned socialist economies, aggregate economic activity (including investment) had been subject to the control of planners. Although cyclical activity could have occurred in planned socialist economics—through planning errors or transmission through the foreign sector—the economic growth of a socialist society was less likely to suffer cyclical fluctuations.

Stability of economic growth is of practical importance. Potential lost at any particular time is lost forever. A system that, because of cyclical instability, does not reach its potential cannot be expected to achieve its potential rate of growth through time. Thus the matter of cyclical instability, the length and the severity of cycles, and the forms in which they find expression are important indicators of the relative success of economic systems.

Inflation, a second manifestation of instability, may appear in open form as a general rise in the price level, or it may occur in repressed form as lengthening lines for goods and services, regional and sectoral shortages, and the like. In capitalist economies, inflation typically occurs in the first form; in the planned socialist economies (where planners set prices), it historically manifested itself in repressed form. In any event, excessive inflation is viewed as an undesirable phenomenon; it can distort economic calculation (where relative prices are used as sources of information), cause increased use of barter, and alter the income distribution.

Excessive **unemployment** is also undesirable. It implies, along with the personal hardships of those unemployed, less than full utilization of resources. It is difficult, however, to measure causal factors and to compare unemployment rates across economic systems, because the planned socialist economies for many years did not maintain records on unemployment (which was said to have been "liquidated").

Moreover, the standard definition of unemployment (the unemployed are those seeking employment but unable to find jobs) leaves room for differences in interpretation. There are different types of unemployment, ranging from unemployment associated with the normal changing of jobs to chronic, hard-core unemployment.

These definitions, however, fail to account for the more subtle but important concept of **underemployment**, or the employment of individuals on a full-time basis at work in which they utilize their skills at less than their full potential. Underemployment (which was common in the planned socialist economies) is less visible than unemployment, but it can have a similarly adverse effect on capacity utilization. It typically takes the form of overstaffing, a situation in which ten people are employed for a job that could be accomplished just as well by five.

Viability of the Economic System

The ultimate test of an economic system is its long-term viability. The basic premise of Marxian economics is that over the course of history, "superior" economic systems replace "inferior" ones. In the Marxian scheme, capitalism replaces feudalism and then socialism replaces capitalism. Inferior systems are beset by internal contradictions that make it impossible for them to survive over the long term. Marx depicted capitalism as an unstable system suffering from a number of insurmountable internal contradictions. These internal contradictions, he believed, ensured the eventual demise of capitalism and its replacement by the "superior" system of socialism.

Since the beginning of the Soviet experiment with planned socialism (and its eventual expansion to one-third of the world's population), there had been little discussion of the long-term viability of the planned socialist variant. Rather, discussion had focused on the *relative* economic performance of planned socialism. Most experts felt that planned socialism, though inefficient, would be able to muddle along—to survive at relatively low levels of efficiency and consumer welfare.

Events of the late 1980s highlighted the issue of the long-term viability of planned socialism. Significantly, the goal of the reform movements in the former Soviet Union and in Eastern Europe is transforming the planned economic system into a market economic system. The rejection of the planned socialist system by the political leadership casts serious doubt on this economic system's ability to deliver an economic performance strong enough to ensure its continued existence.

Among the other basic performance criteria—economic growth, efficiency, income distribution, and stability—the long-term viability of the economic system stands out as the dominant test of performance. If an economic system cannot survive, it has clearly proved itself inferior to those systems that can.

It may be premature to declare the planned socialist system dead. The move away from socialism in the former Soviet Union and in Eastern Europe could be reversed. Socialism continues to have appeal in China, which is combining communist dictatorship with market reform and the opening up of the economy to international trade and investment.

Tradeoffs

The four performance criteria we have discussed are not all-inclusive. Other criteria could be added, such as military power, environmental quality, and democratic political institutions. The four criteria we have selected are those typically used to measure economic performance.

If all performance criteria were compatible, measuring economic performance would be less complicated. If the achievement of higher growth meant the automatic achievement of the other goals, countries would need only to aim for one goal and expect to achieve the others spontaneously. This is not the way the world works. Frequently, the achievement of one goal requires the sacrifice of another.

Consider a society that sets a "fair" distribution of income as its overriding economic goal, where "fairness" requires an equal distribution of income. Dividing output equally among families means that those who have worked harder, who have worked more effectively, or who have taken risks receive the same as those who have not. If unequal effort receives equal reward, this society offers no incentives to encourage hard and effective work, risk taking, and innovation, and in the long run these activities would cease to occur. An equal distribution of income would therefore harm both efficiency and economic growth.

Consider a society that establishes rapid growth as its overriding goal and seeks to achieve this growth by requiring all teenagers and retired persons to work and by forcing households to save unreasonably large sums for capital formation. Such policies would create economic growth through extensive means (growth through expansion of inputs), but they would probably reduce static efficiency and dynamic efficiency. The capital and labor employed at the margin would not be effective; the loss of household production might make people work less effectively.

Consider a society that wishes to guarantee employment to all those able and willing to work. This guarantee is made in the form of an implicit *job rights* contract, which declares that the state will, as a last resort, provide a job and an income to all.[17] Such a job rights contract would mean that workers have a job no matter how ineffectively and unconscientiously they work. Under such an arrangement, effort would slacken, absenteeism would rise, and employee discipline would fall. These events would depress economic efficiency and cause the society to produce below its production possibilities.

Economic Systems and Performance

Societies do have a choice of economic systems. The countries of the former Soviet Union and Eastern Europe are currently searching for a new economic system. China is experimenting with the combination of political dictatorship, planning, public ownership, and market reform. The nations of the industrialized West are faced with ever-changing choices related to tax systems, industrial policies, and privatization. They must face hard choices between improved growth and efficiency, on the one hand, and, on the other, more equity and stability as provided by their massive social welfare systems. The relatively backward countries of Asia, Africa, and Latin America must decide whether to adopt the free-market policies deployed by the Four Tigers.

Comparative economic systems addresses the effect of the system on economic performance. The big issue is the effect radically different economic systems— market economies or planned socialist economies—have on economic performance. Although the countries of the former Soviet Union and Eastern Europe appear to have rejected this socialist model, it is still important to evaluate its performance, both to complete the historical record and to assess accurately the performance of those countries that continue to use it in modified form, such as China.

It is more difficult to judge the effect of differences in institutional arrangements on performance in countries that use basically the same economic system. What is the effect, for example, of worker participation in management on German economic performance? What has been the effect of exceptionally high marginal tax rates in Sweden? With interest in the planned socialist economy declining, comparative economics will focus much more on such issues. In fact, a number of studies have been done that relate differences in institutional arrangements and policies—such as the independence of the central bank and the generosity of the social safety net—to economic performance.

Social experiments, both broad and small, can be costly if erroneously performed. Consider the failed U.S. effort to reform health care in the mid-1990s. America's eventual choice will be enriched by the availability of social experiments that have been conducted in Canada, the U.K., and Germany, which reveal consequences of the choice of various policies. Japan, in its reexamination of its industrial policies in the late 1990s, can glean guidance from the experiments with industrial policies in other countries. The poor countries of Asia and Africa can learn from the privatization and free-trade experiments of Hong Kong and South Korea.

Performance Comparisons: The Twenty-First Century

A number of issues will complicate performance comparisons in the new century. Much of the assessment of the performance of different systems in the last half-century was based on the assumption that systemic change was not great in either capitalist or socialist economic systems. Change or reform in the planned socialist economic systems was predicted to be modest. The era of transition presents the need to examine economic systems that are really not in place. In this new setting, the tendency is to look more at transition indicators (for example, the implementation of privatization) as an outcome of the transition process rather than as basic performance indicators per se. Moreover, as performance across economic systems is assessed, classification, as previously emphasized, will be more subtle and thus more difficult. What model should be used to assess the progress of economic development in Uzbekistan? Against which other countries should the progress in Uzbekistan be judged? In such a setting, the framework of economic development may be more useful than that of comparative economic systems.

Finally, the issue of data availability has taken on new importance. Those formerly planned socialist economies that are now in transition have steadily shifted away from the old definitions and concepts toward standard international concepts in, for example, national income accounting. But as subsequent chapters will show, data availability and reliability remains a serious problem and complicates attempts to understand contemporary performance, let alone to make accurate comparisons with the past. These complications are especially important in an era of evolving efforts to improve the nature of basic international economic comparisons.

Summary

The central focus of comparative economic systems is the characterization of differences in economic systems and assessment of the influence of those differences on outcomes. The field of comparative economic systems sustains comparative analysis using both theoretical or abstract system models and real-world variants. In the former, it is important to compare theoretical variants, whereas in the latter, complicated measurement problems limit our ability to relate observed outcomes to theoretical ideals.

In addition to the influence of the economic system (ES), outcomes are influenced by a variety of forces conveniently aggregated as environmental factors (ENV) and policy factors (POL). As outcomes are related to differences in these three major forces, it is difficult—though important—to isolate the impact of each while holding constant the influence of the others. Although Appendix 3A discusses statistical means to achieve such results, problems of method and measurement limit such efforts in the real world.

As outcomes of economic activity in different economic systems are evaluated, it is important to identify clear performance criteria and develop some (generally subjective) weighting criteria to aggregate these criteria. Although the result of such an exercise is necessarily subjective, there is nevertheless a considerable measure of agreement on the criteria that might be used to assess economic performance.

Although most observers of different economic systems would recognize the importance of a variety of both economic and noneconomic criteria, four basic economic performance criteria stand out: economic growth, efficiency, income distribution, and stability. All are critical to economic growth and economic development, though in real-world economic systems, the formation of societal objectives is a complex social process the nature of which changes through time.

Economic growth refers to increases in the output of goods and services produced in a system (country) and/or to increases in output per capita. Economic development is a broader concept that includes societal changes and improvements in the well-being of the population.

The second criterion, efficiency, refers to the effectiveness with which a system uses its resources at a given time (static efficiency) or through time (dynamic efficiency). Though difficult to measure with precision, the concept of efficiency is frequently related to the concepts of extensive economic growth (growth achieved through the expanded use of inputs) and intensive growth (growth achieved through the better use of available inputs). Experience suggests that as economic systems grow and develop, they typically rely increasingly on intensive growth as a source of expanded output and as a means to raise the well-being of the population.

The third criterion of economic performance is the nature of the resulting income distribution. Apart from extremes, the matter of a "good" distribution of income is inherently subjective, though economists argue that the nature of the income distribution is related to the effectiveness with which participants pursue system objectives.

The fourth criterion of economic performance is stability, which refers to the ability of an economic system to grow without such significant cyclical fluctuations and to avoid inflation and unemployment.

Possibly the ultimate test of an economic system is its viability. In the contemporary setting, relating the system characteristics outlined in the preceding chapter to the performance criteria is an important but difficult task. As previously emphasized, most systems are in fact mixed systems where system characteristics are difficult to identify and measure, and the tradeoffs among differing outcomes are subtle and not always understood.

Key Terms

system models	economic growth	Gini coefficient
economic system (ES)	efficiency	stability
outcomes (O)	static efficiency	inflation
environmental factors (ENV)	dynamic efficiency	unemployment
policies (POL)	intensive growth	underemployment
success criteria	extensive growth	fairness
aggregation	income distribution	
national priorities	Lorenz curve	

Notes

1. For a survey of issues related to system models, see Morris Bornstein, ed., *Comparative Economic Systems: Models and Cases*, 7th ed. (Homewood, Illinois: Irwin, 1994), Chs. 1 and 2. The use of deductive models has been criticized in a work by Trevor Buck. Buck argues that the predictions derived from utopian models (in particular, those of perfect capitalism, central planning, and self-management) are identical and that "empirical evidence cannot test utopian models." For an elaboration of these views, see Trevor Buck, *Comparative Industrial Systems* (New York: St. Martin's, 1982), Ch. 1.

2. The approach used here is suggested in Tjalling C. Koopmans and John Michael Montias, "On the Description and Comparison of Economic Systems," in Alexander Eckstein, ed., *Comparison of Economic Systems: Theoretical and Methodological Approaches* (Berkeley: University of California Press, 1971), Ch. 2; see also John Michael Montias, *The Structure of Economic Systems* (New Haven: Yale University Press, 1976).

3. For a discussion of the productivity issue in this case, see the work of Abram Bergson, especially "Comparative Productivity," *American Economic Review* 77 (June 1987), 342–357.

4. See Koopman and Montias, "On the Description and Comparison of Economic Systems," pp. 27–78.

5. For the matter of goals or objectives as viewed within the field of comparative economic systems, see Montias, *The Structure of Economic Systems*, Ch. 3; G. M. Heal, *The Theory of Economic Planning* (New York: North Holland, 1973), Ch. 2.

6. For a brief treatment of the role of the Communist party in the formation of national economic objectives in the former Soviet Union, see Paul R. Gregory and Robert C. Stuart *Soviet and Post-Soviet Economic Structure and Performance*, 5th ed. (New York: Harper-Collins, 1994).

7. For a discussion of the various paradigms of political economy, see Barry W. Poulson, *Economic Development: Private and Public Choice* (New York: West Publishing Company, 1994), Part II.

8. The literature on modern public choice has reached some disturbing conclusions about the rationality of majority-rule voting procedures in single and multi-issue settings. See James Buchanan and Gordon Tullock, *The Calculus of Consent* (Ann Arbor: University of Michigan Press, 1962); James M. Buchanan and Robert Tollison, eds., *The Theory of Public Choice II* (Ann Arbor: University of Michigan Press, 1984); for a summary of issues, see Barry W. Poulson, *Economic Development* (New York: West Publishing Company, 1994), Ch. 4.

9. This is a standard element in the socialist critique of capitalism: that under capitalism the impact of the consumer is in fact quite limited, constrained by powerful lobby groups, large corporations, and the like. For a classic treatment, see John Kenneth Galbraith, *The New Industrial State* (Boston: Houghton Mifflin, 1967); Assar Lindbeck, *The New Left: An Outsider's View*, 2nd ed. (New York: Harper & Row, 1977); Samuel Bowles, David M. Gordon, and Thomas E. Weisskopf, *Beyond the Waste Land: A Democratic Alternative to Economic Decline* (New York: Anchor Press/Doubleday, 1983); for a brief summary of these issues, see Poulson, *Economic Development*, Ch. 1.

10. There is much literature on the subject of economic growth. For an introduction, see Malcolm Gillis, Dwight H. Perkins, Michael Roemer, and Donald R. Snodgrass, *Economics of Development*, 3rd ed. (New York: W. W. Norton, 1992; Bruce Herrick and Charles P. Kindleberger, *Economic Development* (New York: McGraw-Hill, 1983), Ch. 2.

11. The contemporary literature on economic development in fact looks well beyond simple indicators such as per capita output. See, for example, Poulson, *Economic Development*, Ch. 1.

12. The methodological problems of cross-country comparisons have received a great deal of attention in the literature. For early discussions in the U.S.–Soviet context, see Robert W. Campbell, N. Mark Earle Jr., Herbert S. Levine, and Francis W. Dresch, "Methodological Problems Comparing the U.S. and U.S.S.R. Economies," in United States Congress, Joint Economic Committee, *Soviet Economic Prospects for the Seventies* (Washington, D.C.: U.S. Government Printing Office, 1973), 122–146; for an analysis of growth patterns, see

Hollis Chenery and Moshe Syrquin, *Patterns of Development 1950–1970* (London: Oxford University Press, 1975); Moshe Syrquin and Hollis Chenery, "Patterns of Development, 1950–1983," World Bank, Working Papers Series No. 41, 1989; Ross Levine and David Renelt, "A Sensitivity Analysis of Cross-Country Growth Regressions," *American Economic Review* 82, 4 (September 1992), 942–963.

13. This is a rather standard socialist criticism of capitalism. See, for example, the classic work by A. C. Pigou, *Socialism versus Capitalism* (London: Macmillan, 1960), Chapter 8, or the extended discussion in Maurice Dobb, *Welfare Economics and the Economics of Socialism* (Cambridge: Cambridge University Press, 1969); see also Janos Kornai, *The Socialist System* (Princeton: Princeton University Press, 1992).

14. A great deal of attention has been paid to the issue of efficiency in connection with the growth analysis of the former planned socialist systems. For a summary of this literature and its application to the Soviet case, see Paul R. Gregory and Robert C. Stuart, *Soviet and Post-Soviet Economic Structure and Performance*, 5th ed. (New York: HarperCollins, 1994), Ch. 10.

15. For an introductory discussion of income distribution, see, for example, Roy Ruffin and Paul Gregory, *Economics* (New York: HarperCollins, 1993); for a development perspective on the distribution of income and wealth, see Poulson, *Economic Development*, Ch. 7.

16. The basic theory of business cycles can be found in any basic work on macroeconomics. See, for example, Andrew W. Abel and Ben S. Berkake, *Macroeconomics* (Reading, Mass.: Addison-Wesley Publishing Company, 1992), Ch. 11. There has been a great deal of interest in the issue of cycles in the formerly planned socialist economic systems. For a summary, see Paul R. Gregory and Robert C. Stuart *Soviet and Post-Soviet Economic Structure and Performance*, 5th ed., Ch. 11.

17. David Granick, *Job Rights in the Soviet Union: Their Consequences* (Cambridge: Cambridge University Press, 1987).

Recommended Readings

Traditional Sources

Kenneth Arrow, *Social Choice and Individual Values*, 2nd ed. (New York: Wiley, 1963).
Trevor Buck, *Comparative Industrial Systems* (New York: St. Martins, 1982).
Edward F. Denison, *Why Growth Rates Differ* (Washington, D.C.: The Brookings Institution, 1967).
———, *Accounting for Slower Economic Growth* (Washington, D.C.: The Brookings Institution, 1979).
John W. Kendrick, *Understanding Productivity* (Baltimore: Johns Hopkins University Press, 1977).
Etienne, S. Kirschen and Lucien Morrisens, "The Objectives and Instruments of Economic Policy," in Morris Bornstein, ed., *Comparative Economic Systems: Models and Cases*, 7th ed. (Homewood, Ill. Irwin, 1994), 49–66.
Simon Kuznets, *Modern Economic Growth: Rate, Structure and Spread* (New Haven: Yale University Press, 1966).
John Michael Montias, *The Structure of Economic Systems* (New Haven: Yale University Press, 1977).
P. J. D. Wiles, *Distribution of Income East and West* (Amsterdam: North Holland, 1974).

Economic Growth and Productivity

Robert J. Barro, "Economic Growth in a Cross Section of Countries," *Quarterly Journal of Economics* 106 (May 1991), 407–444.

"Empirical Evidence in Economic Growth Theory," *American Economic Review: Papers and Proceedings* 83, 2 (May 1993), 415–430.

Malcolm Gillis, Dwight H. Perkins, Michael Roemer, and Donald R. Snodgrass, *Economics of Development*, 3rd ed. (New York: W. W. Norton, 1992), Chs. 2–3.

Bruce Herrick and Charles P. Kindleberger, *Economic Development*, 4th ed. (New York: McGraw-Hill, 1985).

Ross Levine and David Renelt, "A Sensitivity Analysis of Cross-Country Growth Regression," *American Economic Review* 82, 4 (September 1992), 942–963.

Angus Maddison, "Growth and Slowdown in Advanced Capitalist Economics," *Journal of Economic Literature* 25, 2 (June 1987), 649–698.

E. Wayne Nafziger, *The Economics of Developing Countries*, 2nd ed. (Englewood Cliffs, N.J.: Prentice-Hall, 1990), Ch. 3.

Robert Summers and Alan Heston, "A New Set of International Comparisons of Real Product and Price Levels: Estimates for 130 Countries, 1950–1985," *Review of Income and Wealth* 34 (March 1988), 1–25.

Income Distribution

Anthony B. Atkinson and John Micklewright, *Economic Transformation in Eastern Europe and the Distribution of Income* (Cambridge: Cambridge University Press, 1992).

Malcolm Gillis, Dwight H. Perkins, Michael Roemer, and Donald R. Snodgrass, *Economics of Development*, 3rd ed. (New York: W. W. Norton, 1992), Ch. 5.

Margaret E. Grosh and E. Wayne Nafziger, "The Computation of World Income Distribution," *Economic Development and Cultural Change* 34 (January 1986).

Jacques Lecaillon, Felix Paukert, Christian Morrison, and Dimitri Germidis, *Income Distribution and Economic Development: An Analytical Survey* (Geneva: International Labor Office, 1984).

E. Wayne Nafziger, *The Economics of Developing Countries*, 2nd ed. (Englewood Cliffs, N.J.: Prentice-Hall, 1990), Ch. 6.

Barry W. Poulson, *Economic Development* (New York: West Publishing Company, 1994) Ch. 7.

Cyclical Stability

Morris Bornstein, "Unemployment in Capitalist Regulated Market Economies and Socialist Centrally Planned Economies," in Morris Bornstein, ed., *Comparative Economic Systems: Models and Cases*, 7th ed. (Homewood, Illinois: Irwin, 1994), 597–605.

Carlo Frateschi, ed., *Fluctuations and Cycles in Socialist Economies* (Brookfield, Vermont: Avebury Publishers, 1989).

David Granick, *Job Rights in the Soviet Union: Their Consequences* (Cambridge: Cambridge University Press, 1987).

Paul R. Gregory and Robert C. Stuart, *Soviet and Post-Soviet Economic Structure and Performance*, 6th ed. (New York: Addison Wesley Longman, 1997), Ch. 11.

Barry W. Ickes, "Cyclical Fluctuations in Centrally Planned Economies: A Critique of the Literature," *Soviet Studies* 38, 1 (January 1986), 36–52.

Appendix 3A: Measuring the Impact of the Economic System

We are interested in isolating and measuring the impact of the economic system on economic outcomes for two major reasons. First, if differing system arrangements matter in the process of resource allocation, then it is critical to understand the relationship between system or system characteristics and outcomes such that the former can be altered to influence the latter. Historically, much of the interest in differing system arrangements has focused on this issue: how resource allocation differs in knowable ways among system variants, especially the capitalist–socialist comparison. Second, in this era of transition, the nature and success of transition from plan to market is in part determined by the starting point from which the transition process begins. To put it another way, many have argued that indeed the planned socialist system did matter and that its procedures of resource allocation resulted in a set of structural distortions compared with the outcomes that might have resulted under different allocation procedures. Thus it has been widely argued that the formerly planned socialist systems emphasized economic growth through forced saving and investment, the latter directed toward industry, and especially heavy industry, to a degree not generally observed in market economic systems. Can these sorts of differences be measured such that economic structures at the beginning of transition can be better understood? In effect, the success of the contemporary transition experience is often directly related to the point of departure and the transition policies developed and implemented. Moreover, one could argue that transition will end when prior structural distortions are substantially reversed—in effect, long-term convergence has been achieved.

To measure the system effect, we have chosen differences in patterns of urbanization as an example for two reasons. First, there is a large body of evidence relating levels of urbanization to levels of economic development for a large number of countries that differ in known and measurable ways. Second, it has been widely argued that the planned socialist systems exercised a great deal of control over the urbanization process. Thus the case of urbanization seems important for understanding system differences, and it is also an approach that can be generalized to understand other differences, such as differences in industrial structure, consumption, international trade patterns, and the like.

Comparative Urbanization Patterns: System Influences

The relationship between economic development, as measured by per capita gross domestic product (GDP) and the proportion of a country's population living in urban areas (URB) is depicted in Figure 3.4, which shows that urbanization is positively related to GDP per capita.

Suppose we wish to determine whether urbanization patterns differ systematically between socialist and capitalist systems. Data for the late 1980s revealed that about 65 percent of the Soviet population lived in urban centers, whereas the equivalent figure

FIGURE 3.4   Urbanization and Economic Development

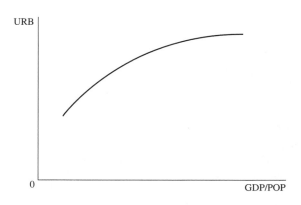

for the United States was about 75%. Can we conclude that the Soviet Union was less urbanized than the United States? According to Figure 3.4, lower Soviet urbanization should be expected because the Soviet Union was at a lower level of economic development than the United States. There are two possible explanations for these patterns; each is developed in Figure 3.5.

Panel A of Figure 3.5 provides one possible explanation of the observed urbanization pattern: Urbanization patterns have been similar in socialist and capitalist economic systems, and apparent differences have emerged simply because urbanization *levels* have been related to levels of economic development. Because the Soviet Union was at a lower level of economic development than the United States, the Soviet level of urbanization was also lower. Had the Soviet Union suddenly achieved the same level of development, the two countries would have had the same urbanization rate.

Panel B suggests a different interpretation: Socialist and capitalist urbanization patterns are systematically different. Even when we control for the level of economic development, socialist systems are less urbanized, which suggests that there are characteristic features of socialism—possibly aspects of the economic system or policies—that systematically influence urbanization.

Chapter 3 outlined an approach to isolating the impact of the economic system and assessing that impact (both its direction and its magnitude) on observed outcomes. In notational form, the following approach was suggested:

$$O = f(\text{ES, ENV, POL}) \tag{3A.1}$$

Outcomes (O) are a function of the economic system (ES), the environment in which the economic system functions (ENV), and, finally, policy (POL). Can we, in practice, empirically estimate the foregoing relationship for real-world economic systems? In this particular case, the outcome (O) is the level of urbanization, the environmental or controlling factor (ENV) is the level of economic development,

FIGURE 3.5   Urbanization in Different Economic Systems

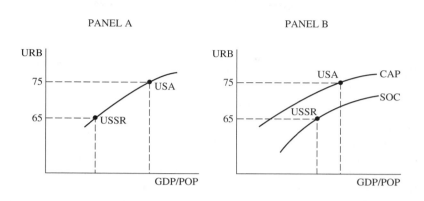

measured by per capita gross domestic product; the economic system (ES) is considered explicitly—it is either capitalist or socialist:

$$\text{URB}_i = a + b(\text{GNP/POP})_i + u_i \tag{3A.2}$$

This relationship, which is assumed to have the usual characteristics (a positive relationship between per capita income and urbanization), makes it possible to examine statistical regularities across a number of systems. In practice, there are several ways to estimate equation 3A.2 to capture the economic system. Statistically, the task is to observe a particular relationship (in this case, urbanization) in samples drawn from two populations (capitalist and socialist) and to determine whether the results obtained can be assumed to have come from two different populations.

The Forecasting Approach

Equation 3A.2 can be estimated from data drawn from a sample of capitalist or market systems. Deriving estimates for the parameters of the equation (the constant a and the coefficient b), results in a simple model from which predictions can be made. Specifically, using sample data on per capita gross domestic product from capitalist systems, we would use the predictive equation to forecast values for URB_i in socialist systems. The forecast value provides the expected level of urbanization of each socialist country, assuming that they exhibit the "normal" capitalist relationship between income and urbanization. The actual socialist values of URB_i can then be compared with those predicted by our equation. Assuming that our predictive equation captures the "normal" capitalist relationship, differences between predicted and actual values of URB_i would indicate whether socialist countries are, relative to capitalist countries, underurbanized, overurbanized, or about the same.

This approach has the distinct advantage of indicating how particular socialist countries behave relative to "normal" patterns. As it stands, however, we have no test of the statistical significance of our results. Finally, should we observe that the deviations are not uniformly positive or negative, some additional criterion of evaluation would be necessary.

The Dummy Variable Approach

An alternative method is to use dummy variables.[1] In this approach, equation 3A.2 is respecified as follows:

$$\text{URB}_i = a + b(\text{GDP/POP})_i + c\text{DUM} + u_i \qquad (3\text{A.3})$$

We assign the dummy variable the value 1 for socialist systems and the value 0 for capitalist systems, and then we estimate it by using an aggregated sample of socialist and capitalist countries. The statistical importance of the economic system in influencing urbanization levels is assessed by determining the significance and magnitude of the coefficient attached to the dummy variable.

A variant of the dummy variable approach is used to isolate differences in *both* the intercept and the slope, thus providing a better explanation of why the socialist and capitalist patterns differ. Were we to use this variant in our present example, the dummy variable would be defined as before: 1 for socialist systems and 0 for capitalist systems. A second dummy variable would be defined as follows:

$$\text{DUMG} = (\text{DUM})(\text{GNP/POP})$$

In this variant, the equation to be tested would be

$$\text{URB}_i = a + b(\text{GNP/POP})_i + c\text{DUM} + d\text{DUMG} + u_i \qquad (3\text{A.4})$$

As before, we would make this estimate by using data from capitalist and socialist systems, and the results would be assessed by examining the magnitude and significance of the coefficients. The c coefficient captures differences between intercepts, and the d coefficient captures differences between slopes, in the urbanization–income relationship.

The Chow Test

A third method for examining system differences in a relationship such as equation 3A.2 is the Chow test.[2] In this approach, equation 3A.2 is estimated separately, once using capitalist and once socialist, sample data. Two sets of parameter estimates exist: one for the socialist, the other for the capitalist sample. The Chow test is used to determine whether the coefficients (for example, the coefficient b in equation 3A.2) are in fact statistically different in the sense that they can be said to come from different populations. If the Chow test shows the parameters to be statistically different, then the conclusion is that the economic system acts to render the relationship between per capita income and urbanization different.[3] The empirical evidence on urbanization patterns seems to support the outcome postulated in panel B of Figure 3.5.[4] However, although considerable emphasis is placed on this sort of analysis in our characterization of different outcomes across economic systems, the analysis presents a number of problems. The modeling of the relationship between systems and outcomes remains simplistic. Moreover, econometric issues such as appropriate specification, along with the usual problems of data availability in the international context, complicate our attempts to analyze these relationships.[5]

Notes

1. The problem posed in this appendix is of a basic and general nature. For the techniques of analysis, see William H. Greene, *Econometric Analysis*, 2nd. ed. (New York: Macmillan 1993), pp. 3–32.
2. For a discussion of the Chow test, see *Econometric Analysis*, pp. 211–212.
3. For a useful comparison of various approaches, see Edward A. Hewett, "Alternative Econometric Approaches for Studying the Link Between Economic Systems and Economic Outcomes," *Journal of Comparative Economics* 4 (September 1980), 274–294. Also see John Michael Montias, *The Structure of Economic Systems* (New Haven: Yale University Press, 1976), Ch. 5.
4. See Gur Ofer, "Economizing on Urbanization in Socialist Countries: Historical Necessity or Socialist Strategy?" in Alan A. Brown and Egon Neuberger, eds., *Internal Migration: A Comparative Perspective* (New York: Academic, 1977), Ch. 16. For a broader discussion, see Henry W. Morton and Robert C. Stuart, *The Contemporary Soviet City* (Armonk, N.Y.: M. E. Sharpe, 1984).
5. For a recent alternative to traditional approaches, see Peter Murrell and Randi Ryterman, "A Methodology for Testing Comparative Economic Theories: Theory and Application to East-West Environmental Policies," *Journal of Comparative Economies* 15, 4 (December 1991), 582–601.

4

Reform and Transition: Evolution or Revolution?

The economic system, the environment in which the system functions, and the economic policies all influence economic outcomes. Many of these influencing forces can, however, be changed. Although the terminology lacks precision, it is useful to think of **economic reform** as attempts to modify an existing system, whereas **transition** refers to the shift from one system to another—for example, the contemporary replacement of plan by market in the countries of the former Soviet Union and Eastern Europe.

Reform of Economic Systems

Although economic reform applies to both capitalist and socialist economic systems, change occurs differently in different systems. Economic reform in capitalist systems is generally evolutionary in nature, gradual in pace, and, to a significant degree, introduced on a decentralized basis through market-type institutions. In socialist systems, however, change tends to be revolutionary in nature and abrupt and is usually introduced by a central authority—for example, the former Communist parties of Eastern Europe and the Soviet Union. China's move toward modernization also was decided on and introduced by its communist leaders.

No matter how systemic change is classified, modifications that economic systems undergo do change their character. The introduction of command planning and collectivized agriculture in the Soviet Union at the end of the 1920s and the subsequent introduction of such arrangements into Eastern Europe and China after World War II are examples of fundamental and rapid changes in economic systems. In these cases, decision-making arrangements were centralized, the market was replaced by the plan, state ownership supplanted private ownership, and moral incentives became increasingly important. The replacement of command planning by worker-managed socialism in Yugoslavia in the 1950s is another case of fundamental change. Finally, in recent times, Eastern Europe and the Soviet Union are attempting to shift from plan to market allocation.

If economic reforms in socialist economic systems can generally be identified as "packages" introduced by a central authority, the reforms of capitalist systems are more difficult to characterize. Today's industrialized countries operate differently from those of 100 years ago. Changes have occurred gradually, without clear milestones.

When resources are allocated through markets, changes in allocation procedures are less visible than when a central authority makes sweeping changes by fiat. Some milestones can be identified. Britain's passage of the Corn Laws in the 19th century turned the English economy into the world's first open economy. Bismarck's introduction of social security legislation changed Germany's economic system, as did the passage of social security laws in the United States during the Great Depression. Further examples include privatization during the Thatcher years in Great Britain, in the United States the Great Society of Lyndon Johnson in the 1960s, New Zealand's liberalization reforms conducted between 1985 and 1995, Chile's macroeconomic and privatization reforms under Pinochet, Singapore's creation of a forced saving program starting in 1955, and Germany's privatizations of the 1990s.

Economic reform attempts to change system characteristics, but the ultimate intent is to change economic outcomes. Should the implementation of economic reform be judged by outcomes, or should we look directly at the changes made in the characteristics of the economic system? If neither outcomes nor characteristics change, has the reform been a failure or has it been less than a full-blown economic reform?

Economic Development and Systemic Change

The characterization of systemic change is influenced by the models or frameworks used for interpreting change. The work of the classical economists in the 19th century made our view of economic development appear pessimistic despite the perceived merits of the invisible hand for the allocation of resources. Economic development, they argued, required capital accumulation, which would be insufficient to offset the impact of diminishing returns. At best, a continuing reproduction of an existing state was possible, and it was more likely that stagnation would result. In the 20th century, economists spawned a variety of explanations, some focusing on the technical underpinnings of economic growth and structural change, others focusing more broadly on social change in historical perspective. In the different approaches to change, a point of contrast has been between those who have argued within a neoclassical static general equilibrium theory and those who attempt a more general dynamic framework to understand why, in fact, an equilibrium at a particular point in time may not be sustained.

Karl Marx, who sought to demonstrate the inevitability of change through the natural evolution of one system into another, formulated the most famous theory of system change. Whether Marx's approach is used as a framework in which to interpret change or as a set of tools to understand the foundations of socialist objectives, his analysis deserves attention.

Within the broader framework of theories of dynamic change, the contributions of Joseph Schumpeter, Janos Kornai, and of New Institutionalists such as Douglas North and Mancur Olson move beyond the static framework of neoclassical economic theory by seeking to explain organizational change.

Marx's Theory of Change

Karl Marx (1818–1883) concluded in *Das Kapital* that capitalism is an unstable economic system whose lifespan is inevitably limited.[1]

Marx's theory of capitalism is based on his materialist conception of history,[2] which teaches that economic forces (called **productive forces**) determine how production relations, markets, and society itself (the **superstructure**) are organized. Weak productive forces (underdeveloped human and capital resources) result in one arrangement for producing goods and services (**production relations**), and strong productive forces lead to different, more advanced production arrangements. A society with underdeveloped economic resources has underdeveloped production relations and superstructure (manifested in barter exchange, serf labor, a rigid social hierarchy, and religious biases against commerce). As the productive forces improve, new economic and social relationships emerge (such as hired rather than serf labor and monetary rather than natural exchange). These new arrangements are not compatible with the old economic, cultural, and social relationships. When they come into contact, tensions and conflicts mount.

Eventually, incompatibilities become so great that a qualitative change (usually the result of violent revolution or war) occurs. New production relations and a new superstructure, compatible with the new productive forces, replace the old order. These **qualitative changes** are inevitable because societies are destined to evolve from a lower to a higher order.

The engine of change is the conflict between old and new, primarily in the form of class antagonisms (the emerging capitalist class versus the landed gentry in feudal societies, the worker versus the capitalist in capitalist societies). The process of evolutionary and inevitable qualitative change through the competition of opposing forces (**thesis versus antithesis**) is the foundation of Marx's theory of **dialectical materialism**, which was based on the teachings of the German philosophers George Wilhelm Hegel and Ludwig Feuerbach.

The upshot of Marx's materialist conception of history was his contention that societies evolve according to an inevitable pattern of social and economic change in which lower systems are replaced by more advanced systems. In this manner, feudalism is bound to replace slavery, capitalism inevitably displaces feudalism, and socialism eventually replaces capitalism.

The victory of capitalism over feudalism represented a qualitative step forward for society. A highly efficient productive machine (capitalism) replaced an inefficient one (feudalism) based on semiservile labor and governed by traditional landed interests. Two landmarks signaled the emergence of capitalism. The first was the initial accumulation of capital by the emerging capitalist class—a process Marx called **primitive capitalist accumulation**. The second indicator was the formation of a "free" labor force at the disposal of capitalist employers. Laborers were separated from control over land, tools, and livestock and were left with only their own labor to sell. At this point the capitalist, who now controlled the means of production, hired this free labor, and capitalist factories were established. In this manner, the basic class conflict of capitalism was created—the conflict between the working class and the capitalist, who "owns" the labor services of the worker.

The feature that distinguishes labor from the other factors of production is that the employer can compel workers to produce a value that exceeds the value that workers require to maintain themselves. However, the employer is not required to pay workers the full value of their production—only enough to allow them to subsist. One worker may have to work 8 hours to produce a value sufficient to meet subsistence needs, yet the employer can force the worker to create a surplus, which will accrue to capitalists, by working 12 hours—4 hours more than are required for subsistence. The exploitation of labor is the source of capitalist profits, which Marx called **surplus value**.

Marx pictured capitalism, in its early stages, as a world of cut-throat competition. The capitalist was driven to maximize profits (surplus value) and to accumulate more capital out of profits. Capitalists, operating in intensely competitive markets, are forced to introduce cost-saving innovations lest their competitors do so first and drive them out of business. One capitalist introduces a new labor-saving technology, attracts competitors' customers through lower prices, and experiences a temporary increase in profits above "normal" levels. The profits are short-lived, however, because competitors respond by introducing the same cost-saving techniques, and new competitors enter the market in response to windfall profits. Excess industry profits are eliminated, and no capitalist ends up better off. But when fixed capital is substituted for labor, the profit rate declines. There is an inherent tendency to substitute capital for labor, even though labor is the sole source of surplus value. Marx predicted that the profit rate would fall, with disastrous consequences for capitalism.

As the profit rate falls, capitalism's internal contradictions and weaknesses become apparent. In an effort to halt the decline in profits, capitalists increase the exploitation of their workers, and alienation and exploitation intensify. The declining profit rate leads to the failure of marginal businesses, and bankrupt capitalists now swell the ranks of the unemployed. Those fortunate enough to be employed are exploited and alienated; the unemployed fare even worse.

A more ominous phenomenon is overproduction. Workers are kept at subsistence wages by high unemployment; capitalists, driven by the desire to accumulate capital, are not willing to increase their spending on luxury goods. Moreover, the ranks of the capitalists are thinning, as monopolies drive out smaller capitalists. Yet all the while, the productive capacity of the economy is growing because of the growing capital-intensity of industry. Aggregate demand falls chronically short of aggregate supply; recessions and then depressions occur, and worldwide crises become commonplace. The declining profit rate leads to declines in investment spending and to further shortfalls in aggregate demand.

Marx described only generally the final stages of the **capitalist breakdown**. Overproduction, underconsumption, disproportions, and the exploitation and alienation of workers combine to create the conditions necessary for the violent overthrow of capitalism.[3] Workers unite against the weakened capitalist class and, through a violent *world* revolution, establish a new socialist order. Marx had little to say about this new order. Implicit in Marx's writings on the final stage of capitalism is that contradictions will be more intense in the most advanced capitalist countries; the socialist revolution would be initiated there.

Joseph A. Schumpeter: The Evolution of Capitalism

Joseph Schumpeter described the dynamics of capitalist economies.[4] Although Schumpeter was pessimistic about the survival of capitalism and predicted its eventual replacement by socialism, he nevertheless viewed this demise rather differently than Marx.

Schumpeter argued that the capitalist economy could not be understood within the framework of static economic analysis—that is, the pursuit of objectives by existing institutions. Capitalism, he argued, is fundamentally dynamic and can be understood only if change is explained. The important issues, therefore, are not how an organization functions at a point in time, but rather how that organization comes into being and how it evolves over time as a mechanism generating economic growth.

The driving force of evolution in the capitalist system, according to Schumpeter, is innovation, or the development and implementation of new products, new ideas, and new ways of doing things. This drive, he argued, is carried out by an entrepreneurial class, driven by and rewarded through a profit motive. Indeed, the development of new ideas broadly defined was for Schumpeter a process termed **creative destruction**, as the new replaced the old.

According to Schumpeter, the life of a capitalist enterprise was one of struggle. By having a better idea, a superior innovation, or a new product, the enterprise would be able to drive more mature rivals from the field. However, any competitive advantage would be short-lived. Eventually, every business must face creative destruction, even monopolists and giant concerns. Business rivals are constantly in search of better production techniques and better products. Today's dominant firm (the railroad) will become tomorrow's dinosaur as better products (trucking and air freight) are introduced. Today's secure monopoly (AT&T) becomes tomorrow's competitive battlefield.

Schumpeter viewed the capitalist economy not in terms of the competitive ideal but rather as characterized by concentration. Concentration would lead to the routinization of the entrepreneurial spirit and a lack of social willingness to reward risk takers. The decline in entrepreneurial activity would be a fundamental reason for the eventual decline of capitalism.

Although there are similarities between the Schumpeterian and Marxian interpretations of capitalism (the importance of classes, the cyclical nature of economic activity, the role of profit, and a tendency for profit rates to decline), the Schumpeterian focus is on the innovative power of capitalism and on how to preserve innovation.

The New Institutional Economics

Both Marx and Schumpeter were interested in how institutions change and in how these changes affect economic life. The new institutional economics focuses directly on how institutions evolve and on the effect of this evolution on economic performance.[5] The new institutional economics has a number of precursors. The early writings of Nobel laureat Friederick Hayek considered the process by which economic institutions change and evolve over time. Hayek argued that economic institutions arise according to a *spontaneous order* in which new organizations, laws, regulations, and customs are tested by daily economic life. Those arrangements that "work" are retained by society; those that do not work fall by the wayside in a Darwinian manner. The corporation arose as a way of raising capital and sharing risk in medieval times. It survived because it served a useful economic function. Worker guilds also arose during the medieval period, to evolve later into craft unions. They served their purpose for a long time, but they will disappear when they outlive their usefulness.

According to Hayek, the institutions of economic life exist in the form of written and unwritten information that is passed from one generation to the next. They are the result of "human action" but not of "human design." They do not have to be codified into law or written into corporate charters or contracts. They evolve in bits and pieces, so no single person or entity knows them in their entirety. Rather, these bits and pieces are known and understood by those who require each bit of specialized knowledge in order to conduct their economic lives. An example is money. All economies use money, but no one designed money. Because money is something that fills a void, it resulted from spontaneous human actions.[6]

Ronald Coase is also a precursor of the new institutional economics. Coase, whose ideas we discussed in Chapter 2, explained the rational economic logic according to which organizations are created. Business enterprises are created when the transaction costs of organizing production through markets are too high. Political and social institutions arise in the same fashion. Communities form school districts when the transaction costs of organizing the education of children through individual market contracts are too great. Governments finance the procurement of certain goods when the transaction costs of arranging voluntary contributions are too great.

The basic proposition of the new institutional economics, as practiced by Douglass North, Gordon Tullock, Mancur Olson, and many others, is that we can study the evolution of institutions and their effect on economic life by using the logic of economic rationality as reflected in the pursuit of self-interest. Specifically, we can explain many major changes in the course of economic history by examining changes in property rights transactions costs and rent-seeking opportunities.[7] For example, the increase in agricultural output and the urbanization of Britain during the Industrial Revolution were enhanced by changes in property rights in the English countryside, as changes in laws and customs reduced the transaction costs of enclosing agricultural land into separate estates. England's making more rapid economic progress than France during the 19th century is explained by the creation of stable financial markets as a consequence of parliamentary restraints on arbitrary royal actions. England's long-term decline in the 20th century is explained by its social and political stability, which allowed rent-seeking *distributional coalitions* to form. The persistence of sharecropping in the American South is explained by imperfect capital markets and excessive information costs. The resistance of French peasants to producing cash crops in the 19th century is explained in terms of risk avoidance and the natural insurance provided by the growing of subsistence crops.

As Nobel laureat Douglass North explains, standard microeconomic theory cannot account for the effects of time and institutions on economic performance. Instead, standard theory holds time and institutions constant.[8] The new institutional economics argues that changes in institutions can be explained in terms of standard economic logic. They can be explained by changes in property rights, innovations that change transaction costs, information asymmetries, and opportunities for voluntary behavior.

According to the new institutional economics, market institutions—corporations, futures markets, contract law, cartels, commercial banks—were created because they happened to be economically rational given the circumstances of time and place. If economic conditions change—if something happens to lower transaction costs, raise information costs, or change property rights—then our economic institutions will change accordingly.

Whereas Marx viewed institutional change as inevitable and as following a predetermined path, the new institutional economics views institutional change as being dictated by economic variables, whose course of change cannot be predicted in advance; nor does this course of change follow an inevitable path. This path depends on the starting point, as measured by an economy's history, culture, resource endowments, and the like—that is, on its *initial conditions*. The path then depends on the course of transaction costs, property rights, and other factors. The course of change is *path-dependent* in that it depends on the initial conditions from which progress begins.

Change in Socialism

Whereas Marx and others believed in the inherent instability of capitalism, a number of critics argued the exact opposite: that socialism is an inherently unstable economic system. Socialism's critics warned against socialist experiments on the grounds that once started, they might be difficult to stop.[9] If a socialist economy was indeed established, it would prove unworkable and would be destined either to collapse or to operate at very low levels of efficiency.

Hayek and Mises

As we have noted, the Austrian economist and Nobel laureate Friederick Hayek argued that capitalism develops its institutions in an efficient manner.[10] If an attempted institutional change does not improve the efficiency of the system, it will disappear. Hayek, together with his colleague Ludwig von Mises, founded a school of economic thought now called the Austrian school. Both economists praised the efficiency with which market economies process and utilize information on relative prices. Hayek wrote that the principal problem of economics is "how to secure the best use of resources known to any member of society, for ends whose relative importance only these individuals know."

How is the economy to utilize knowledge about product prices, qualities, and location that is not available to any one person or institution in its entirety? These economists believed that the specialization in information about the price system enables each individual to participate effectively in the economy, acquiring knowledge only about those things that he or she needs to know. Hayek writes of the "marvel" of the price system:

> The marvel is that in a case like that of a scarcity of one raw material, without an order being issued, without more than perhaps a handful of people knowing the cause, tens of thousands of people whose identity could not be ascertained by months of investigation, are made to us the material or its products more sparingly; i.e., they move in the right direction.*

Mises was an early critic of socialism. In his classic article "Economic Calculation in the Socialist Commonwealth," published in 1922, Mises anticipated most of the modern-day problems of the socialist economies, arguing that socialist economies would lack market exchange and would hence lack the vital information provided by the price system. Without relative prices, socialist managers would lack the information to make rational economic decisions. Moreover, lacking property rights, socialist managers would not behave in an economically rational manner but rather would overdemand and waste scarce resources.

According to Hayek and Mises, socialism lacked the informational basis for rational economic calculation, and its institutions were created by "human design" rather than by a spontaneous order.

Experiments with socialism, such as took place in Russia after the Bolshevik revolution of 1917, created an economic system of planned socialism that contained a number of internal contradictions. Mises and Hayek felt that a socialist economy would be too complex to plan from the center and would require more information on technology, prices, quantities, and assortments than a central planning board could digest. Moreover, they felt that the task of planning and management could not be effectively decentralized, because in the absence of private property, even the best-intentioned managers of state enterprises could not make economically correct decisions.

For these reasons, Mises and Hayek felt that such socialist experiments as those in the Soviet Union would fail and that the experiment would eventually be abandoned. In this sense, the theories of Mises and Hayek are models of the change of socialism back to capitalism on the grounds of socialism's inferiority as an economic system.

Source: Friederick A. Hayek, "The Price System as a Mechanism for Using Knowledge," *American Economic Review* 35, no. 4 (September 1945): pp. 519–528.

Kornai: The Economics of Shortage

The Hungarian economist Janos Kornai, also argued that socialism was inherently unstable because of its natural tendency to generate shortage.[11]

Kornai argued that the planned socialist economy is a **system of shortage**, where shortage is a systemic, perpetual, and self-reproducing condition. Others had argued earlier that persistent shortages or excess demand in the socialist systems are functions of identifiable, though not necessarily easily corrected, forces. Consumer goods are simply not a high priority but rather are supplanted by producer goods and military production. Errors in planning, inadequate incentives, and other system characteristics lead to continuing shortages.

From a very different perspective, Kornai argued that the economy of shortages arises from the nature of the enterprise in the planned socialist system. The socialist enterprise operates under fundamentally different rules from the capitalist enterprise. The capitalist enterprise is motivated to maximize profits. It makes its input and output decisions on the basis of prices established in markets. As a profit maximizer, the capitalist enterprise has little incentive to overdemand resources. If it employs more resources than technology requires, its profits suffer. The capitalist enterprise operates under a **hard budget constraint**. Faced with input prices and output prices, the capitalist enterprise must cover its costs while earning an acceptable rate of return on invested capital. If it fails to meet its budget constraint, the capitalist firm will fail in the long run. The capitalist firm must live within its means. The hard budget constraint "polices" capitalist enterprise activities and effectively eliminates shortage (in the sense of excess demand for inputs).

The socialist firm operates in a supply-constrained economy. Socialist planners have as their objective the rapid expansion of outputs, and they judge the performance of socialist enterprises on the basis of output expansion. The manner in which socialist enterprises select inputs to meet their output objectives is of less importance than the output targets themselves. Although socialist enterprises face prices for inputs and outputs, their resource-allocation decisions are aimed at meeting output targets. Relative prices play only a minor role.

The capitalist enterprise that fails to live within its means is punished by bankruptcy. The socialist enterprise that fails to cover costs plus a rate of return on the state's invested capital does not suffer the same consequences. Socialist planners value enterprises for their outputs; socialist enterprises that make losses remain in business by virtue of state subsidies. Accordingly, socialist enterprises face a **soft budget constraint**. Socialist enterprises can live beyond their means, if necessary, over the long run.

The hard budget constraint forces capitalist enterprises to limit their demands for inputs. The soft budget constraint on socialist enterprises fails to reward them for restricting their input demands. Hence the socialist system generates continuous excess demands for inputs. The supply of inputs falls chronically short of the demand for inputs, and persistent shortages or imbalances result.

Economic systems must allocate resources in an orderly fashion. Persistent imbalances and chronic shortages detract from the orderly allocation of resources. With imbalances, those who obtain resources may be those who will not put them to their best and highest use. Kornai's analysis of socialism is related to the complexity and motivation issues raised by Mises and Hayek. Kornai's conclusion is that the socialist motivation system and inattention to relative prices disrupt the orderly allocation of resources under socialism. Accordingly, socialism will not be an efficient economic system.

The New Institutional Economics Critique of Socialism

Public choice economists, in particular the late Mancur Olson and Peter Murrell, argue that the process of change in socialist economies will be dictated by the extent to which the system's directors (say, a monolithic Communist party directed by a small elite) can prevent rent-seeking distributional coalitions from emerging.[12] As long as the socialist system is rigidly controlled by the system's dictator, that dictator will strive to allocate resources to maximize growth. It will be in the dictator's interest, as the beneficiary of economic growth, to create high savings rates, new technologies, and managerial behavior that elicits maximal enterprise capacity. By imposing terror or other coercive policies, the dictator can force agents throughout the economy to work toward the goal of economic growth.

As time passes, however, the power of the dictator may weaken. Dedication to the goal of "overtaking the West" may diminish. Various interest groups (such as a military lobby or a heavy-industry pressure group) emerge, and the primary interests of every such group is promoting its particular branch or enterprise at the expense of others. These coalitions find ways to insulate themselves from the pressure of the dictator, such as concealing information from the center or appropriating resources that could have been used more productively by others. They develop ways to promote their own interests at the expense of the interests of the economy as a whole.

As the power of separate interest groups increases, the center finds it more difficult to impose discipline on the periphery. Power is devolved from the center to lower levels. Interest groups form into *distributional coalitions* to promote their own interests. Instead of resources being devoted to generating the highest possible growth rates, resources are dissipated among distributional coalitions, who evade central controls and use resources for their own benefit.

The net result of the rising power of interest groups is that growth rates decline and efficiency of resource use drops. The dictator cannot maintain a strong hand forever, but the system works well *only* under a strong hand. As growth rates decline, distributional coalitions become bolder. They begin to engage in outright corruption and theft. No one considers the interest of society as a whole; attention is paid only to the narrow interests of vested interest groups.[13] Moreover, given that each distributional coalition has vested interests to protect (such as special access to scarce goods and the opportunity to buy at below-equilibrium prices), there is no support for reform, which means that the system will not be able to take corrective action.

The new institutional economics invokes these reasons to explain the inevitable deterioration of the planned socialist economy. Schumpeter felt that creative destruction could spell the end of capitalism. In this case, the inevitable creation of distributional coalitions will spell the decline of socialism.

Changes in Capitalist Economies

Change in capitalist economies is more gradual and less visible than change in socialist economies, which tends to come from above. Careful analysis of long-run changes can, however, reveal the process of change in capitalist economies. Some aspects of change can be captured by quantitative statistics, which enables us to see the type and magnitude of change in capitalist economies.

Property Rights: Private versus Public

The ownership of property is a fundamental distinguishing characteristic of economic systems that can be measured, albeit imperfectly. Significant changes in the shares of public and private ownership of property can alter the nature of a capitalist economic system. Indeed, if the state owned a major share of existing property, we would no longer classify the system as capitalist.

Real-world capitalist systems are mixed, some having higher shares of public ownership than others. **Privatization** occurs when property that had been state owned is sold to private owners. State ownership increases when privately owned property becomes publicly owned, or **nationalized**. The shares of public ownership can be increased either by government spending that creates new government-owned capital (such as the U.S. government's Tennessee Valley Authority initiated during the Great Depression) or by direct government buying of existing facilities. By selling its shares of British Air, for example, the British government increased the share of private ownership in the United Kingdom. And by buying a failing steel company, the British government increases the share of public ownership.

Public sentiment in favor of public ownership was highest in the United States during the Great Depression. In the United Kingdom, the elections of labor governments in the 1940s and 1950s provided political support for nationalization, whereas the lengthy tenure of a conservative government from the mid-late 1970s through the mid-1990s showed support for privatization. Alternating socialist and conservative governments in France also reflect rising and falling sentiment for privatization or nationalization. In Germany, both socialist and conservative governments have consistently favored privatization since the end of World War II. The German government has sold its shares of major corporations to private owners throughout the postwar era. It is currently undertaking its largest privatization, the sale of Deutsche Telekom.

In the United States, government shares of structures and land have not changed noticeably since the early 1930s, nor has the share of output produced by government enterprises. After a rise in public ownership in the early 1930s, the share of government ownership has remained fairly stable, despite a substantial increase in output shares consumed by government.

Table 4.1 shows the government shares of fixed capital in 1955, 1980, and 1987 in seven industrialized capitalist countries including Greece. The differences in ownership shares partially result from different accounting procedures, but even so, substantial changes in government ownership shares within each country cannot be observed from these figures. In some countries, government ownership shares have fallen (Canada and Greece). In others, they have risen (United Kingdom and Sweden). In the majority of countries, government shares of capital have been stable over the 25-year period. In France, West Germany, and Finland, government ownership shares either were unchanged or changed only slightly.

Figure 4.1 shows that the production of government enterprises as a percent of GDP varied considerably among industrialized countries but that there was no strong trend prior to the 1980s. Overall there has been little change in private and public ownership shares in capitalist countries, which suggests that these countries have reached a basic consensus on the distribution of public and private ownership. Changes in governments over the years have not notably altered this consensus.

The conservative governments elected in the United States and Western Europe in the 1980s brought a rising tide of privatization. It is difficult to tell whether this trend will continue long enough to change fundamentally their shares of private and public ownership, but in view of the long-term stability of ownership shares, this outcome seems unlikely.

Although government production and shares of capital appear steady, the government's claim on production has increased in most countries. The government does not produce more or own more capital (as a percent of GDP), but its expenditures on goods and services and transfers have been steadily rising (see Table 4.2). The contemporary debate, therefore, is about the government's share of production, not about its ownership of resources.

TABLE 4.1 Share of Government Ownership of Fixed Capital, Capitalist Countries (percentages of total)

	1955	1980	1987
Canada	22	24	23
Finland	—	16	16
France	16	17	—
Greece	3	1	—
Sweden	4	7	—
United Kingdom	11	14	—
West Germany	7	8	8
Unweighted average	11.2	9.9	—

Source: OECD, *Flows and Stocks of Fixed Capital, 1955–1980* (Paris: OECD, 1983); OECD, *Flows and Stocks of Fixed Capital, 1962–1987* (Paris, OECD, 1989).

FIGURE 4.1   Public Enterprise Share of GDP (selected industrialized countries)

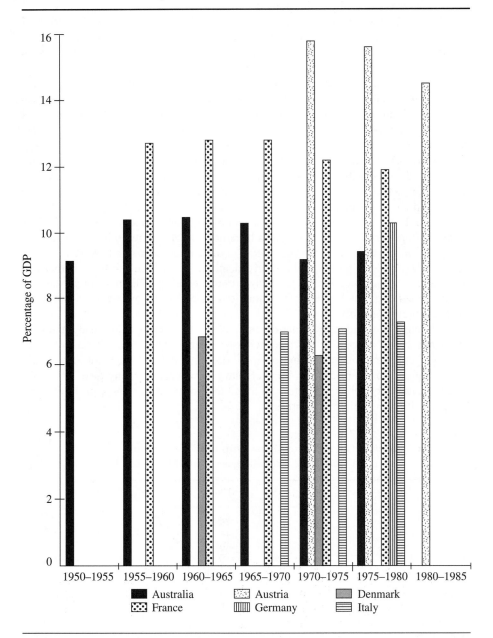

Source: From "The Role of Public Enterprises: An International Statistical Comparison," in Robert Floyd, Clive Gray, and Robert Short (eds.), PUBLIC ENTERPRISE IN MIXED ECONOMIES (Washington, D.C.: IMF, 1984), pp. 110–196. Reprinted by permission of the International Monetary Fund.

TABLE 4.2   Central Government Expenditure as
a Percentage of GNP

	1972	1990
Canada	20.2	23.4
Finland	24.3	31.1
France	32.3	43.0
Greece	27.5	50.9[a]
Sweden	27.7	42.3
United Kingdom	32.0	34.8
Germany	24.2	29.4
United States		

[a]1986

Source: The World Bank, *World Development Report 1992*
(New York: Oxford University Press, 1992), Table II.

Trends in Competition

Changes in **competition** alter the nature and operation of a capitalist economy, but they do not result in the system's ceasing to be capitalist. A capitalist economy in which monopoly is the prevalent form may operate inefficiently and may cause consumers to pay high prices, but it is still a capitalist economy.

The degree of competitiveness is affected by antitrust laws, regulations, and trade policies. It is difficult to generalize about trends in state policy toward competition. The best-documented trend is the postwar relaxation of international trade barriers. The industrialized capitalist countries created international arrangements for dismantling the restrictive trade barriers that were erected during the Great Depression, and there is little doubt that the degree of international competition expanded at a rapid rate throughout the postwar period. Trade barriers were lowered in both product markets and factor markets (see Figure 4.2). In the late 1990s, one can speak of a world capital market in which financial capital flows freely and quickly among Europe, North America, and the industrialized Asian countries.

Deregulation is another visible indicator of state policy toward competition. When a potentially competitive industry is regulated by the state, the degree of competition is reduced. The trend toward deregulation started in the United States in the late 1970s, and it spread from North America to Western Europe and Japan in the 1980s. Deregulation has been most prominent in transportation, communications, and banking, but it remains to be seen whether other capitalist countries will deregulate to the extent of the United States and whether the deregulation experiment will continue into the twenty-first century. The example of U.S. deregulation has clearly been spreading. The European Union has scheduled the deregulation of passenger airline traffic, telecommunications, and financial services as part of Europe's move to a single market.

FIGURE 4.2   Average U.S. Import Duties, 1900–Present

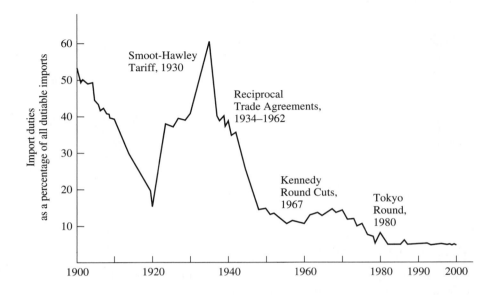

Sources: Historical Statistics of the United States; Statistical Abstract of the United States.

The least visible aspect of state competition policy—and the most difficult to characterize—is antitrust policy. Most industrialized capitalist countries allow more exemptions from antitrust laws than the United States, which exempts primarily farming operations and labor unions; however, antitrust laws that prevent abuse of monopoly power exist in nearly every capitalist country. Unlike the U.S. laws, which declare all formal price-fixing agreements illegal, other industrialized capitalist countries judge price-fixing arrangements on the basis of whether they result in reasonable prices.

In the United States, there have been few major changes in antitrust legislation since the 1930s. The changes that have occurred have taken place in the courts. Initially, the courts interpreted the antitrust laws as outlawing anticompetitive behavior, but in the early 1950s, antitrust laws were interpreted as outlawing monopoly power per se, whether this power was abused or not. The 1980s and 1990s have seen a move toward a more liberal interpretation of antitrust laws, stemming from the recognition that businesses must compete in international markets against close substitutes and that antitrust laws should not be used to penalize competitive successes.

Growing international competition and deregulation should increase the degree of competition in capitalist countries. Moreover, rapid technological progress produces a wider variety of competitive products and promotes competition. William Shepherd has attempted to measure the changing degree of competition in the U.S.

economy. He concludes that the American economy became more competitive after 1960 as a consequence of growing international competition and deregulation.[14] According to Shepherd, the share of the U.S. economy that was effectively competitive remained fairly stable at 52 to 54 percent between 1939 and 1958 but rose to 77 percent by 1980. Similar studies have not been conducted for the other industrialized capitalist countries, so we do not know whether the American experience is representative. However, because virtually all industrialized capitalist countries have been subject to growing international competition, the impact of this development may be equally strong in other capitalist countries.

An important perspective on deregulation in the American economy is provided by the major changes in airlines, telecommunications, trucking, and other important sectors of the economy during the 1980s.[15] According to a recent survey of the outcomes of this deregulation, in 1977 fully regulated industries produced 17 percent of gross national product, whereas by 1988 this share had decreased to 6.6 percent.[16] Although the results of this deregulation experience have often been controversial, economic analysis suggests that the benefits have outweighed the costs, resulting in significant net gains for the American public.

Income Redistribution

Capitalism uses material incentives to motivate economic behavior, and a move away from material incentives would signal a fundamental change in the capitalist economic system. If a capitalist state altered the distribution of income earned in factor markets, earnings in factor markets would become less decisive in determining command over resources. For example, if the tax system equalized the distribution of income after taxes, material rewards would cease to guide economic decision making. Changes in tax policy can indeed change the nature of the capitalist economic system.

For a tax system to have a large impact on the reward system, taxes must make up a large share of factor income, and the tax system must redistribute income. Income is redistributed via either a **progressive tax** (which redistributes proportionally away from high-income earners) or a **regressive tax** (which redistributes proportionally away from low-income earners). In a progressive tax system, the tax's share of income rises with income; in a regressive system, that share falls. In order substantially to redistribute income away from high-income earners, the tax system must take up a large share of factor income and must be highly progressive.

Table 4.3 gives information on changes in the tax system's shares of income and in the shares of income taken by several different taxes. The table shows that in all the capitalist countries surveyed, taxes rose as a percentage of GDP. The most modest rise was in the United States—from 27 to 29 percent; the largest rise was in Sweden—from 28 to 50 percent.

The shares of income taxes and taxes on goods provide indirect information on the redistributive role of the tax system. Taxes on income tend to be progressive, whereas taxes on goods are regressive. Assuming no significant changes in income tax rates by income bracket, the tax system would become more progressive as a whole when the share of income taxes rose. The tax system would become more

TABLE **4.3** Changes in the Capitalist Tax System

	Taxes as a Percentage of GDP			Share of Total Taxes						Social Security Transfers as Percentage of GDP		
				Income Taxes[a]			Taxes on Goods					
	1960	1980	1992	1970	1985	1992	1970	1985	1992	1960	1981	1988
United States	27	29	29	48	42	42	19	18	17	5.0	11.1	10.6
Canada	24	32	37	45	43	45	32	33	26	7.9	9.9	12.0
France	32	42	44	18	18	17	38	29	27	13.5	20.3	21.7
Italy	27	30	42	17	36	39	38	26	27	9.8	5.7	17.3
Japan	20	25	29	41	46	42	22	15	14	3.8	10.6	11.8
Sweden	28	49	50	54	42	39	29	25	27	8.0	18.2	15.1[b]
United Kingdom	28	35	35	40	38	36	29	31	34	6.8	12.9	16.0
Germany	30	38	40	32	33	32	32	27	27	12.0	17.2	—

[a]Individual and corporate
[b]1987

Sources: Statistical Abstract of the United States (international comparisons); OECD, *Historical Statistics* (Paris: OECD, 1990).

regressive as a whole when the share of taxes on goods rose. Table 4.3 reveals a mixed picture. In six of the countries, the income tax share of total taxes remained stable or fell. In the other two countries, the income tax share rose. In only two countries (Italy's rising share and Sweden's falling share) were the changes substantial. The table also shows a generally declining reliance on taxes on goods. The share of taxes on goods fell substantially in France, Italy, and Japan. Only Canada recorded a small increase in the share of taxes on goods.

Not having readily available information on income tax rates, we can draw only cautious conclusions about Table 4.3. There has been a substantial increase in the share of taxes of factor income in the industrialized capitalist countries, but there has not been a substantial shift in the form of taxation. Although there has been a slight drift away from taxes on goods and toward taxes on income (which should increase progressivity), these changes have been relatively minor, except in Italy. The overall conclusion is that the redistributive role of the tax system has not changed much in capitalist economies, even though the share of taxes has been rising.

What have capitalist governments done with the increasing tax share of GDP? The last columns show the dramatic rises in the shares of social security transfers as a percentage of GDP. The effect of social security transfers on economic rewards depends on how these transfers are distributed. If they are distributed according to contributions, they do not alter the factor distribution of income. If they are distributed in a manner unrelated to contributions (such as in poverty programs), they do alter the distribution of income.

The evidence that has been collected for the United States shows that although the tax system does not materially alter the distribution of income, the distribution of transfers does.[17] The major instrument of state income redistribution in the United States is the distribution of transfer payments to low-income recipients. The growing GDP share of social security transfers suggests that a significant alteration in material rewards may have occurred in capitalist economic systems through the distribution of social security transfers to the less advantaged.

Worker Participation

A basic characteristic of capitalism is that the owners of capital (individual proprietors, partners, and corporate shareholders) are rewarded out of profits.[18] Workers are paid wages that do not vary directly with profits. Capitalism can change its character by sharing profits and management control with workers. Such a change would require new incentive arrangements.

Because profits fluctuate more than wage income, the owners of capital are, in effect, making a deal with workers that as long as the business remains solvent, workers will receive their contracted wages. Owners of capital, who bear risk in the form of fluctuating returns on capital, earn a return to reward them for taking that risk. The worker accepts a contractual wage and, in return, is prepared to follow the directions of management.

The fundamental nature of the relationship between worker and owner of capital can be altered by profit sharing. If rewards to workers depend in part on the profits of the business, the worker becomes a partial capitalist and bears a part of the risk of fluctuating profits. If workers' incomes depend entirely on the profits of the enterprise, then they basically become capitalists.

The advantages of a profit-sharing economy are that workers are more materially interested in the profitability of the enterprise. They are more inclined to work in the interests of the enterprise than before, and they are less inclined to shirk work. A profit-sharing economy has another advantage: If workers' pay rises and falls with profits, the economy becomes more flexible. Recessions cause wages to drop, and falling wages stimulate employment.

The notion of profit sharing is not new, but it has gained increasing attention in capitalist economies because of the large-scale use of profit sharing in postwar Japan.[19] In Japan, worker bonuses average about one-quarter of annual earnings, and they are paid out of profits. Although the relationship between profits and worker bonuses is not clear-cut, Japanese workers certainly benefit from higher profits in the form of higher year-end bonuses.

Government Intervention

Capitalist economic systems rely on the market mechanism to provide information for decision makers. At the same time, there is much debate over the extent to which various failures of the market mechanism might be reduced or eliminated by state intervention.

A significant change in policy has been widespread acceptance of the notion that government is responsible for macroeconomic stability. This change—called the **Keynesian revolution**—took place in the period since World War II, especially in the 1960s and thereafter. Capitalist governments use fiscal and monetary policies to pursue stabilization. Most capitalist systems have put in place a variety of monetary and fiscal mechanisms designed to implement stabilization policies. Although the role of the state in macroeconomic stabilization remains a subject of discussion and controversy, capitalist countries have generally experienced greater macroeconomic stability in the second half of the 20th century, despite major energy shocks in the 1970s, than in the first half of the 20th century or in the 19th century. Business cycles have become less severe.

A different sort of change in capitalist systems is represented by the introduction of some sort of planning mechanism—and thus a reduction in reliance on the market mechanism. Great Britain, a country known for the important role government plays in its market economy, has had very limited experience with national economic planning. France, on the other hand, is well known for its application of **indicative planning**, an approach to planning designed to achieve better decision making based on more and better information without being vulnerable to the possibility of authoritarian control in an otherwise democratic system.

There are cases where market capitalist systems have developed some form of planning to supplement and/or modify market outcomes. The Scandinavian countries are cases in point. In the United States, there is no planning in the sense of utilizing a national economic planning mechanism, though one could argue that a great deal of planning does occur through large government branches, powerful corporate entities, and the like. Recent discussion has focused on the perceived need for an **industrial policy** to develop and implement policies designed to promote the health of the capitalist economy—for example, through technological change.[20] Interest in industrial policy peaked with the apparent success of Japan's industrial policy in the period 1950–1970. In Japan, a powerful alliance of government officials, commercial banks, and industrial conglomerates (Sony, Mitsubishi, and so on) decided what products and industries were to be promoted. The prolonged slump of the Japanese economy in the 1990s has reduced interest in industrial policy.

Change in Socialist Economies

Although change in the capitalist West may appear to be significant, it has been mild compared to change in the socialist economies located in the former Soviet Union, Eastern Europe, and Asia. With the minor exceptions of Cuba and North Korea, planned socialist economies either have been dramatically changed through the process of **reform** or are being abandoned through the process of **transition.**

As we have said, reform is the process of changing (improving) an existing system. Transition is the movement from one economic system (planned socialism) to another (capitalism).

In all cases, reform and transition have been motivated by economic performance. In the cases of the former Soviet Union and Eastern Europe, the decision to begin transition was motivated by declining growth rates, the failure to find ways to grow through **intensive growth** (rather than **extensive growth**), rising consumer dissatisfaction, and the general sense of being left behind by the other world economies.

Many reasons have been advanced to explain the general slackening of their economic performance, but the fact remains that the planned socialist economies found the transformation from extensive to intensive growth very difficult. The basic Stalinist model, though draconian and costly, nevertheless served to bring idle and underused resources into the production process. However, the luxury of idle resources was, for many socialist systems, over by the late 1960s. Economic growth and the expansion of consumer well-being had to come from improved productivity, or what socialist systems described as **intensification**.

We do not know exactly why intensification in socialist systems proved so difficult. Clearly there were consumer pressures in these systems, and clearly they grew more complex over time. Advances in planning methods did not keep pace with the demands on the planning system. The diffusion of technology was inadequate. These systems were not demand-driven, and enterprise rules generally did not stimulate growth in productivity and cost reduction. Efficiency was simply not a hallmark of the Stalinist command economy. Moreover, in contrast to the cyclical nature of productivity problems in market systems, socialist systems seemed to experience long, steady declines in productivity growth through the 1980s.

Interest in socialist reform began in the 1960s and grew in the 1980s and 1990s. By the mid-1980s, performance in most socialist systems had slipped alarmingly.

With inadequate incentives, there appeared to be little hope for improved productivity. Moreover, most socialist countries had not been able to compete well enough in export markets to afford significant imports of consumer products. Seen in this perspective, the imperative of reform was evident, although the sudden spread of radical change in the late 1980s caught most observers by surprise.

Backdrop of Reform

The Soviet experiment with planned socialism began in earnest in the late 1920s with the introduction of command planning to industry and of forced collectivization to agriculture. The economic system that Stalin created in the late 1920s and early 1930s proved durable. It was introduced into Eastern Europe by Soviet troops at the end of World War II, and it found its way into China with the victory of communist forces there.

Prior to the early 1960s, reform of the Stalinist economic system was not possible. According to Stalinist dogma, the system was perfect. Any failures encountered were the result of human error or sabotage. Such thinking did not provide fertile ground for reform. The death of Stalin and the ensuing mild liberation allowed discussion of reform to begin. The problems of the planned socialist economy were apparent, and it was natural to consider improving the system.

The Soviet Communist party officially approved such discussion when *Pravda* published the reform proposals of Evsei Liberman in 1962. In this fashion, reform discussion was initiated in the Soviet Union and Eastern Europe. Although official reforms in the Soviet Union were modest, reforms in Eastern Europe were more substantial. Hungary, for example, initiated a long and careful reform process designed to orient its economy more toward the consumer. None of these reforms, either in thought or in content, was designed to replace the planned socialist economy with a market capitalist economy.

China, after experiencing cataclysmic political upheavals in the 1950s and 1960s, embarked on its own reform program in the late 1970s. The Chinese path to reform focused on unleashing private initiative in agriculture and small business and on opening the Chinese economy to world capital and product markets. China's suppression of student revolts in June of 1989 signaled that China was not prepared to combine economic reform with democracy. China's example stands out as a reform that has generated rapid economic growth.

Socialist Reform Models

Reform of planned socialist economic systems focused on changes in some or all of the system components.[21] However, prior to the dramatic changes of the late 1980s and 1990s, most reform in socialist systems was very modest and was characterized as an attempt, by means of very limited changes, to make the existing system work better.

Socialist economic reform has focused on reform models that differ in intensity. We characterize socialist reform in terms of three basic variants: **making planning**

work better, **changes in organizational arrangements**, and **decentralization** of decision making.

Improving the Planning Mechanism   Improving planning is a weak alternative—one that signals unwillingness to make serious changes in the economic system. The arguments in support of this alternative are that problems of economic performance arise largely because planning has not been perfected and that planning can be improved through the application of more sophisticated computer technology. To the extent that enterprise managers make bad decisions because they lack information, ready access to accurate information through an advanced computer network would alleviate the problem. It is assumed that better planning methods, better information channels, and more attention to incentive compatibility can perfect the planning system and improve economic performance. The 1970s were devoted to a number of attempts to improve planning both in the Soviet Union and in Eastern Europe.

Organizational Reform   Changing the organizational arrangements of the existing plan structure represents a second reform alternative. A typical organizational reform is the introduction of intermediate organizations into the organizational hierarchy. Ministries, it was argued, are too distant from the enterprises they supervise. Moreover, each ministry supervises enterprises that produce too diverse an array of products. Ministries cannot keep in touch with enterprise behavior and do not truly understand the problems peculiar to the enterprises they oversee. Thus an intermediate agency or association should be placed between the ministries and groups of enterprises that produce similar products. The intermediate association, it is argued, could understand and manage a particular group of firms more successfully.

Another way to implement organizational reform would be to shift the emphasis from sectoral to regional planning. An economy planned on a sectoral basis may place the interests of the branch over national interests. A shift to regional planning might loosen the grip of an entrenched bureaucracy and encourage a better flow of information among units in the economy. It was this type of reform that Nikita Khrushchev tried, without success, in the Soviet Union in the late 1950s and early 1960s. Most—though not all—past reform attempts in socialist systems have been organizational in nature.

Decentralization   Decentralization, the third broad category of socialist economic reform, is a shifting of decision-making authority and responsibility from upper to lower levels. Decentralization is often viewed as "real" reform that can fundamentally change the nature of economic systems and, especially, reduce the role of central planning.

Decentralization implies that decisions about resource allocation will be shifted downward in the economic hierarchy. Most important, in a decentralized economy, decisions are not made by planners but are reached at lower levels by means of what are frequently termed **economic levers**—prices, costs, profits, rates of return, and the like. Decentralization of decision making entails both the devolution of decision-making authority and responsibility *and* the use of different decision-making tools in the process. To put it another way, although planning still exists, decentralization implies that local decision makers pay less attention to planners and more attention to market signals.

This type of economic reform has been characterized as real reform or significant reform to distinguish it from organizational change. In contemporary terms, it is likely to be called radical reform. Its existence raises new and difficult questions about the development of markets—and thus market signals—in systems previously dominated by planners, by state ownership of property, and by an absence of market signals.

Record of Socialist Reform

With the exception of China, which has recorded rapid economic growth since the introduction of its reforms in the late 1970s, the other attempts to reform the planned socialist economies through organizational change, improvements in planning, and decentralization failed. In the case of China, it is unclear whether China is actually on a path of transition from a planned socialist to a market economy or whether it is engaged in the reform of its current system. Much of Chinese heavy industry remains owned and controlled by the state, China's capital stock is still largely in state hands, and a system of central planning persists.

The failure of reform in the Soviet Union and Eastern Europe had far-reaching consequences culminating in the decision to abandon the planned socialist system and to move to a market capitalist system. As the dominant force in the former Soviet bloc, in the Soviet Union is where the actions that made this move possible originated.

Declining economic performance in the Soviet Union and Eastern Europe, despite repeated reform efforts in the 1970s and early 1980s, convinced the leaders of the Soviet Communist party that radical change was necessary. They appointed a relatively young and vigorous general secretary, Mikhail Gorbachev, to lead this reform effort, which Gorbachev immediately described as radical to distinguish it from the modest reforms of the past. Internationally, Gorbachev relaxed Soviet control over Eastern Europe. As a result, these countries gained their political independence and their freedom to experiment with reform and transition. The collapse of the Soviet Union in December 1991 allowed an additional 15 former republics of the Soviet Union to select their economic systems freely.

Transition

We shall devote a great deal of attention to transition models in later chapters. Once a society has decided in favor of transition, it must decide the speed and sequencing of transition. It may determine that transition should occur on all fronts as quickly as possible. This approach to transition is called *shock therapy.* It may, on the other hand, decide that transition should occur gradually and not on all fronts simultaneously. This approach is called *gradualism.*

The economies of Eastern Europe and the Soviet Union began their transitions in the late 1980s (Eastern Europe) and in late 1991 or early 1992 (the former Soviet

Union). Hence we have a growing body of information on transition successes and failures. We appear to have a number of transition successes (Poland, Hungary, the Czech Republic, Slovenia, and the Baltic states). We appear to have even more transition failures. We shall study the characteristics of transition in later chapters.

We can draw a number of general conclusions about the course of transition so far: First, we can say that transition has indeed brought about remarkable changes in every country undergoing transition, be it a transition success or failure. Figure 4.3 shows the degree to which property rights changed from state to nonstate ownership just a few years after transition began in Russia. Transition is for real, and it appears to be including steps that would be very difficult to reverse.

Second, transition is not easy. Although Poland, Hungary, the Czech Republic, and the Baltic states have shown signs of success, no country has yet to complete the process of transition. Transition has been costly both politically and economically. Each country undergoing transition has experienced substantial declines in output, dramatic changes in the distribution of income, and rampant inflation. These costs have created political backlashes that have often returned to power those who favor the old system.

Third, there is no single path to transition. Some countries have tried a gradual approach; others have tried "shock therapy." Although the results are inconclusive, it appears that gradualism does not reduce the costs of transition.

Fourth, the combination of transition and a young democracy has proved to be difficult. Politicians in newly democratic countries must somehow enact transition policies that are costly in terms of lost political support. This difficult combination has created considerable interest in the Chinese reform model, which has combined market-oriented reforms with Communist party dictatorship.

Although the final outcome is still not known, the former Soviet Union and Eastern Europe have taken the first steps of dismantling the power structure on which their planned economic systems were based. The planned socialist economy no longer exists. What has yet to happen is replacement of the old system with a new, stable economic system.

Summary

The central focus of this chapter is change. Economic reform usually consists of attempts to improve the functioning of an economic system that basically remains unchanged. Transition, on the other hand, is the replacement of one economic system with another, for example replacing plan with market in contemporary Eastern European. If it is difficult to classify systemic change precisely, it is equally difficult to assess results. In cases of major changes, such as privatization in Eastern Europe, there is a tendency to examine the degree of privatization at a stage when the impact on resource allocation (the outcome) is tenuous.

Systemic change is part of the more general process of economic development. In the mid-1800s, Karl Marx proposed the most famous theory of system change. Marx argued from a materialist/determinist/revolutionary perspective that revolutionary

FIGURE 4.3 (a)   Nongovernmental Shares of Capital (Russia)

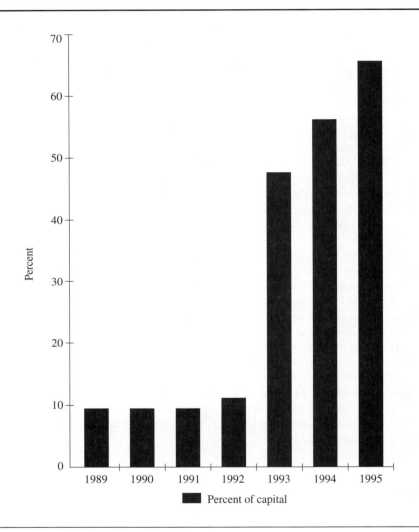

system change was an inevitable product of class struggle in an efficient but inequitable system (capitalism) that would result in socialism and ultimately communism. Although the conflict between the economy (productive forces) and the organization of the society (production relations) would inevitably lead to change, capital accumulation and the exploitation of labor under capitalism would nevertheless build an economic base from which the more equitable socialist system could emerge.

Other models of capitalist change include Joseph Schumpeter's dynamic model of capitalism. Schumpeter depicts capitalism as a constant struggle by firms for long-term survival in the face of creative destruction.

FIGURE 4.3 (b)   Distribution of Russian Labor Force (type of enterprise)

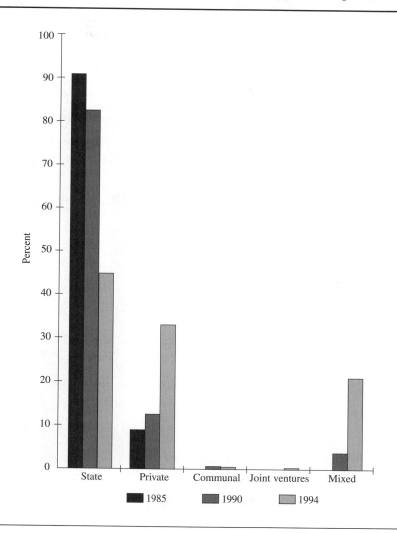

The new institutional economics seeks to explain institutional change by examining property rights, transaction costs, and rent seeking. In so doing, these theorists use Ronald Coase's notion of transaction costs and Friederick Hayek's notion of spontaneous order.

Contemporary theories of socioeconomic change have focused on the role of institutions—how they emerge, why they differ in different systems, and how they change through time. The **Austrian school**, represented most notably by Ludwig von Mises and Friederick Hayek, argued that the task of planning in the planned socialist economy is too complex to be reasonable and that, in the absence of private

FIGURE 4.3 (c)   Privatization of Russian Housing (cumulative totals; percent privatized)

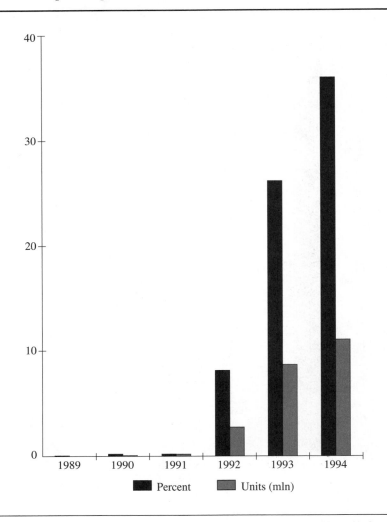

Sources: Natsional'nye scheta Rossii v 1989–1994 gg. (Moscow: Goskomstat, 1995), p. 71; *Sotsial'naia sfera Rossii* (Moscow: Goskomstat, 1995), p. 26.

property, decentralization of decision making would not be effective as a means to allocate resources.

New institutional economists argue that socialist performance will decline when dictatorship disappears and distributional coalitions form. Distributional coalitions will retard economic reform.

Janos Kornai argues that the socialist system is fundamentally a shortage economy, largely because enterprise rules in such a system differ from those in market capitalist economies and do not present the firm with a hard budget constraint—that is, the need to use scarce resources effectively.

Change in capitalist systems is viewed as evolutionary and can be analyzed by examining changes in property rights, trends in competition, income distribution, the role of government, and the organization of the workplace, notably worker participation.

In the past, socialist economic reform was an attempt to make the planning system function effectively. Such reforms in socialist economic systems were of minimal value. Transition in the contemporary era, or the shift from one system to another, remains difficult, and important cases of modified reform (China) are important to our understanding of systemic change.

Key Terms

economic reform
transition
Marx's theory of capitalism
superstructure
productive forces
production relations
qualitative changes
thesis versus antithesis
dialectical materialism
primitive capitalist accumulation
surplus value
capitalist breakdown
creative destruction
spontaneous order
economics of shortage
hard budget constraint
soft budget constraint
privatization
nationalization

property rights
competition
income redistribution
progressive tax
regressive tax
worker participation
role of government
Keynesian revolution
indicative planning
industrial policy
socialist economic reform
intensification
changes in organizational arrangements
decentralization
economic levers
reform
transition
distributional coalitions

Notes

1. Karl Marx, *Capital* (Chicago: Charles Kerr and Company), Vol. I, 1906; Vols. II and III, 1909. Two works that seek to describe the basics of Marx's economics in the language of conventional economic theory are Oskar Lange, "Marxian Economics and Modern Economic Theory," *Review of Economic Studies*, Vol. II (June 1935); and Murray Wolfson, *A Reappraisal of Marxian Economics* (New York: Columbia University Press, 1966).

2. Our discussion of the economic theories of Marx and Engels is based primarily on the following sources: Paul Sweezy, *The Theory of Capitalist Development* (New York: Monthly Review Press, 1968); Wolfson, *A Reappraisal of Marxian Economics* (New York: Columbia University Press, 1966); Alexander Balinky, *Marx's Economics: Origin*

and Development (Lexington, Mass.: Heath, 1970); John Gurley, *Challengers to Capitalism: Marx, Lenin, Mao* (San Francisco: San Francisco Book Company, 1976); William Baumol, Paul Samuelson, and Michio Morishima, "On Marx, the Transformation Problem, and Opacity—A Colloquium," *Journal of Economic Literature* 12 (March 1974), 51–77; *Grundlagen des Marxismus–Leninismus: Lehrbuch*, German translation of the 4th Russian edition (Berlin: Dietz Verlag, 1964); Karl Marx and Friedrich Engels, *The Communist Manifesto*, in Arthur Mendel, ed., *Essential Works of Marxism* (New York: Bantam Books, 1965), pp. 13–44; Paul Samuelson, "Understanding the Marxian Notion of Exploitation: A Summary of the So-called Transformation Problem Between Marxian Values and Competitive Prices," *Journal of Economic Literature* 9 (June 1971), 399–431; and Leon Smolinsky, "Karl Marx and Mathematical Economics," *Journal of Political Economy* 81 (September–October 1973), 1189–1204.

3. According to Sweezy, *The Theory of Capitalist Development*, Ch. 11, the Marx–Engels description of the end of capitalism and the coming of socialism was scattered and sketchy. Their failure to deal more thoroughly with the breakdown of capitalism led to the breakdown controversy among socialist writers—Eduard Bernstein, M. Tugan-Baranovsky, Karl Kautsky, Rosa Luxemburg, and others. The central issue of this controversy was whether a violent overthrow of capitalism was obviated by reform of the capitalist system and the capitalist government. For Lenin's view of Kautsky and "revisionism," see V. I. Lenin, *State and Revolution*, in Mendel, *Essential Works of Marxism*, pp. 103–198; and V. I. Lenin, *Izbrannye proizvedeniia, Tom I* (Moscow: Gospolitizdat, 1960), pp. 56–63 ("Marxism and Revisionism").

4. The basic works are Joseph Schumpeter, *Capitalism, Socialism, and Democracy*, 3rd ed. (New York: Harper, 1950) and Joseph Schumpeter, *The Theory of Economic Development* (Cambridge: Harvard University Press, 1934).

5. We use the term *new institutional economics* to apply to a broad range of schools of economic thought. Our usage includes fields such as the new economic history, public choice economics, and the new political economy.

6. On this, see Friederick von Hayek, *Studies in Philosophy, Politics, and Economics* (New York: Norton, 1969).

7. See, for example, Jon Cohen, in Thomas Rwaski, ed., *Economics and the Historian* (Berkeley: University of California Press, 1996), pp. 60–84; Douglass North and Barry Weingast, "Constitutions and Commitment: The Evolution of Institutions Governing Public Choice in 17th Century England," *Journal of Economic History* 49, 4 (December 1989), pp. 803–832; Mancur Olson, *The Rise and Decline of Nations* (New Haven: Yale University Press, 1982).

8. Douglass North, "Economic Performance Through Time," *American Economic Review* 84, 3 (June 1994), pp. 359–368.

9. F. A. Hayek, *The Road to Serfdom*.

10. F. A. Hayek, ed., *Collectivist Economic Planning*, 6th ed. (London: Routledge and Kegan Paul, 1963), Ludwig von Mises, "Economic Calculation in Socialism," in Morris Bornstein, ed., *Comparative Economic Systems*, rev. ed. (Homewood, Ill.: Irwin, 1969), pp. 61–68.

11. See Janos Kornai, *Economics of Shortage*, Vols. A and B (New York: North-Holland, 1980); "Resource Constrained versus Demand Constrained Systems," *Econometrica* 47 (July 1979), 801–819; *Anti-Equilibrium: On Economic Systems Theory and the Tasks of Research* (Amsterdam: North-Holland, 1971); and Janos Kornai, *Rush versus Harmonic Growth* (Amsterdam North-Holland, 1972); *Overcentralization in Economic Administration* (London: Oxford University Press, 1959); and *Growth, Shortage, and Efficiency: A Macrodynamic Model of the Socialist Economy* (Berkeley: University of California Press, 1983).

12. See Peter Murrell and Mancur Olson, "The Devolution of Centrally Planned Economies," *Journal of Comparative Economics* 15, 2 (June 1991), pp. 239–266. Also see Richard R. Nelson and Sidney G. Winter, *An Evolutionary Theory of Economic Change* (Cambridge: Harvard University Press, 1982) for a discussion of the contemporary transition experience from an evolutionary perspective. See, for example, Peter Murrell, "Can Neoclassical Economics Underpin the Reform of Centrally Planned Economies?" *Journal of Economic Perspectives* 5, 4 (Fall 1991), 59–76; Peter Murrell, "Evolution in Economics and in the Economic Reform of the Centrally Planned Economies," in Christopher C. Clague and Gordon Rausser, eds., *Emerging Market Economies in Eastern Europe* (Cambridge: Blackwell, 1992).

13. For descriptions of how these interest groups engage in rent-seeking behavior, see Josef Brada, "The Political Economy of Communist Foreign Trade Institutions and Policies," Michael Mandler and Randi Ryterman, "A Detour on the Road to the Market Coordination, Queues, and the Distribution of Income; and Michael Alexeev, "If Market Clearings Are So Good Then Why Doesn't (Almost) Anybody Want Them?" all in *Journal of Comparative Economics* 15, 2 (June 1991).

14. William G. Shepherd, "Causes of Increased Competition in the U.S. Economy, 1939–1980," *Review of Economics and Statistics* (November 1982), 613–626.

15. Clifford Winston, "Economic Deregulation: Days of Reckoning for Microeconomists," *Journal of Economic Literature* 31, 3 (September 1993), 1263–1289.

16. Robert Crandall and Jerry Elig, *Economic Deregulation and Customer Choice: Lessons for the Electric Industry* (Center for Market Processes, George Mason University, 1996).

17. Edgar K. Browning, "The Trend Toward Equality in the Distribution of Net Income," *Southern Economic Journal* 43 (July 1976), 914.

18. The theoretical foundation of a profit-sharing capitalist economy is provided by Martin L. Weitzman, *The Share Economy* (Cambridge: Harvard University Press, 1984) and Martin L. Weitzman, "The Simple Macroeconomics of Profit Sharing," *American Economic Review* 75 (December 1985), 937–953. For an excellent survey of recent developments in the theory of producer cooperatives, see John P. Bonin, Derek C. Jones, and Louis Putterman, "Theoretical and Empirical Studies of Producer Cooperatives: Will the Twain Ever Meet?" *Journal of Economic Literature* 31, 3 (September 1993), 1290–1320.

19. For an analysis of Japanese profit sharing, see Merton J. Peck, "Is Japan Really a Share Economy?" *Journal of Comparative Economics* 10 (December 1986), 427–432.

20. For a discussion of industrial policy in the American contemporary American context, see R. D. Norton, "Industrial Policy and American Renewal," *Journal of Economic Literature* 24, 1 (March 1986), 1–40.

21. There is a large body of literature on reform in the former planned socialist economies. For a summary with emphasis on the Soviet case, see Paul R. Gregory and Robert C. Stuart, *Russian and Soviet Economic Structure and Performance*, 6th ed. (Reading: Mass.: Addison Wesley Longman, 1997).

Recommended Readings

Marixst Thought

Paul A. Baran, *The Political Economy of Growth* (New York: Monthly Review Press, 1957).
William Baumol, Paul Samuelson, and Michio Morishima, On Marx. The Transformation Problem and Opacity—A Colloquium," *Journal of Economic Literature* 12 (March 1974), 51–77.

John Gurley, *Challengers to Capitalism: Marx, Lenin, Mao* (San Francisco: San Francisco Book Company, 1976).

Oskar Lange, "Marxian Economics and Modern Economic Theory," *Review of Economic Studies* 2 (June 1935).

Karl Marx, *Capital* (Chicago: Charles Kerr and Company), Vol. I, 1906; Vols. II and III, 1909.

Ernest Mandel, *Marxist Economic Theory* (New York: Monthly Review Press, 1970).

Arthur Mendel, ed., *Essential Works of Marxism* (New York: Bantam Books, 1965).

Joan Robinson, *An Essay on Marxian Economics* (New York: Macmillan, 1966).

Paul Samuelson, "Understanding the Marxian Notion of Exploitation: A Summary of the So-called Transformation Problem Between Marxian Values and Competitive Prices," *Journal of Economic Literature* 9 (June 1971), 399–431.

Joseph Schumpeter, *Capitalism, Socialism and Democracy*, 3rd ed. (New York: Harper, 1950).

————, *The Theory of Economic Development* (Cambridge: Harvard University Press, 1934).

Leon Smolinsky, "Karl Marx and Mathematical Economics," *Journal of Political Economy* 81 (September–October 1973), 1189–1204.

Paul Sweezy, *The Theory of Capitalist Development* (New York: Monthly Review Press, 1968).

Murray Wolfson, *A Reappraisal of Marxian Economics* (New York: Columbia University Press, 1966).

Socialist Changes

Janos Kornai, *Anti-Equilibrium: On Economic Systems Theory and the Tasks of Research* (Amsterdam: North-Holland, 1971).

————, *Economics of Shortage*, Vols. A and B (New York: North-Holland, 1980).

————, *Growth, Shortage, and Efficiency: A Macrodynamic Model of the Socialist Economy* (Berkeley: University of California Press, 1983).

————, "Resource Constrained versus Demand Constrained Systems," *Econometrica* 47 (July 1979), 801–819.

————, *Rush versus Harmonic Growth* (Amsterdam: North-Holland, 1972).

————, *The Road to a Free Economy* (New York: W. W. Norton, 1990).

————. *The Socialist System: The Political Economy of Communism* (Princeton, N.J.: Princeton University Press, 1992).

Richard R. Nelson and Sidney G. Winter, *An Evolutionary Theory of Economic Change* (Cambridge: Harvard University Press, 1982).

The Capitalist Economy: Selected Aspects of Change

Richard R. Nelson and Sidney G. Winter, *An Evolutionary Theory of Economic Change* (Cambridge: Harvard University Press, 1982).

R. D. Norton, "Industrial Policy and American Renewal," *Journal of Economic Literature* 24, 1 (March 1986), 1–40.

Nitin Nohria and Robert G. Eccles, eds., *Networks and Organizations: Structure, Form, and Action* (Boston: Harvard Business School Press, 1993).

Richard B. Freeman, "Unionism Comes to the Public Sector," *Journal of Economic Literature* 24, 1 (March 1986), pp. 41–86.

William G. Shepherd, "Causes of Increased Competition in the U.S. Economy, 1939–1980," *Review of Economics and Statistics* (November 1982), 613–626.

Grahame Thompson, Jennifer Frances, Rosalind Levacic, and Jeremy Mitchell, eds., *Markets Hierarchies and Networks: The Coordination of Social Life* (London: Sage Publications, 1991).

Michael L. Vasu, Debra W. Stewart, and S. David Garson, *Organizational Behavior and Public Management*, 2nd ed., revised and expanded (New York: Marcel Dekker, 1990).

Leonard W. Weiss and Michael W. Klass, eds., *Regulatory Reform: What Actually Happened* (Boston: Little, Brown, 1986).

Oliver E. Williamson and Sidney G. Winter, eds., *The Nature of the Firm: Origins, Evolution and Development* (Oxford: Oxford University Press, 1991).

Clifford Winston, "Economic Deregulation: Days of Reckoning for Microeconomists," *Journal of Economic Literature* 31, 3 (September 1993), 1263–1289.

The Socialist Economy: Reform and Transition

Robert W. Campbell, *The Socialist Economies in Transition: A Primer on Semi-Reformed Systems* (Bloomington: Indiana University Press, 1991).

Christopher Clague and Gorden Rausser, *The Emergence of Market Economies in Eastern Europe* (Cambridge, England, Blackwell, 1992).

Sabastian Edwards, "The Sequencing of Economic Reform: Analytical Issues and Lessons from the Latin American Experience," *World Economy* 1 (1990).

Paul R. Gregory and Robert C. Stuart, *Russian and Soviet Economic Structure and Change*, 6th ed. (Reading, Mass: Addison Wesley Longman, 1997), Ch. 12.

Edward P. Lazear, *Economic Transition in Eastern Europe and Russia* (Stanford: Hoover Institution, 1995).

Peter Murrell, "Public Choice and the Transformation of Socialism," *Journal of Comparative Economics* 14 (June 1991), 203–210.

PART II

Economic Systems in Theory

5

Theory of Capitalism

This chapter is about the *theory* of capitalism. Subsequent chapters discuss capitalism in practice. This chapter asks: How well should capitalist market economies *in theory* resolve the problem of allocating scarce resources among competing ends? This issue is important for two reasons. The first is that the theories of capitalism and socialism yield hypotheses concerning expected differences in performance, and those hypotheses can be tested against real-world experience. The second is that one may be most interested in what the theoretical models themselves suggest about the performance of economic systems under *ideal conditions*. Because actual economies diverge from the ideal, it could be argued that they cannot be used as a test of the system's "true" performance and that the performance issue must be resolved at the theoretical level.[1]

How Markets Work

The theory of capitalism focuses on *markets* in which the interaction of demand and supply determine prices for factors such as labor (factor markets) and products such as consumer goods (product markets). These markets (see panel A of Figure 2.4) provide a mechanism for harmonizing consumer desires with producers' ability to satisfy these desires.

Equilibrium and the "Invisible Hand"

The pioneering analysis of market capitalism is Adam Smith's *The Wealth of Nations*, published in 1776.[2] Speaking against the mercantilist position that free trade could lead to a country's ruin, Adam Smith argued that a highly efficient and harmonious economic system would emerge if competitive markets were left to function freely without government intervention.

Smith's underlying notion was that if individuals were given free rein to pursue their own selfish interests, then the **invisible hand** of competitive markets would cause them to behave in a socially responsible manner. Products desired by consumers would be produced in the appropriate assortments and quantities, and the most efficient means of production would be used. No government or social action would be required, for individuals acting in their own interests could be counted on to do the right thing. In fact, government action would probably interfere with this natural process, so government should be limited to providing essential public services—national defense, a legal system to protect private property, and highways—that private enterprise could not produce on its own. An equilibrium of consumers and producers would be created spontaneously in the competitive marketplace, for if the actions of consumers and producers were not in harmony, the market price would adjust to bring the two groups into equilibrium.

Smith's notion of a natural tendency toward an efficient economic equilibrium was the foundation for the liberal economic thought of the 19th century. In the words of one authority, Smith's most important triumph was that "he put into the center of economics the systematic analysis of the behavior of individuals pursuing their self-interest under conditions of competition," and this remains "the foundation of the theory of resource allocation."[3] Most of the later theorizing aimed at a further elaboration of Smith's vision of market capitalism.

Market Equilibrium

Adam Smith's description of markets was incomplete. Partial equilibrium assumes that two motivating forces drive market capitalism: the desire of producers to maximize profits and the desire of consumers to maximize their own welfare (utility) subject to the constraint of limited income.[4] Under competitive conditions, producers will be prepared to supply larger quantities at higher prices, combining inputs to minimize costs. Consumers, seeking to maximize their welfare, will purchase less at higher prices. The producer and consumer meet in the marketplace, where their conflicting objectives are brought into equilibrium. If the quantity demanded exceeds the quantity supplied at the prevailing price, the price automatically rises, squeezing out some demand and evoking a larger supply until all those willing to buy and all those willing to sell at the prevailing price can do so. At this point, an equilibrium price is established, the market clears, and there is no tendency to depart from the equilibrium unless it is disrupted by some exogenous change (see Figure 5.1).

This description underscores how market resource allocation works under competitive conditions. All other things being equal, an increase in consumer demand for a particular product disrupts the established equilibrium, and the price starts to rise. As the price rises, producers find it in their interest to supply larger quantities. If larger profits can be obtained at the new price, additional producers enter the market. On the demand side, the rise in the price causes substitution of now less-expensive commodities and income effects, thereby reducing the quantity demanded (see Figure 5.2). The increase in demand causes resources to be shifted automatically to the product in greater demand, and the wants of the consuming public are met without intervention from outside forces. Consumers are said to be sovereign because the economy responds to changes in their demand.

Efficiency of Market Allocation

There are two arguments for the **efficiency of market allocation**. One depends on the market being competitive—that is, consisting of a large number of buyers and sellers, none of whom has the power to influence the market price. The other efficiency argument rests on the ability of markets to use information effectively.

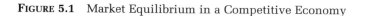

FIGURE 5.1   Market Equilibrium in a Competitive Economy

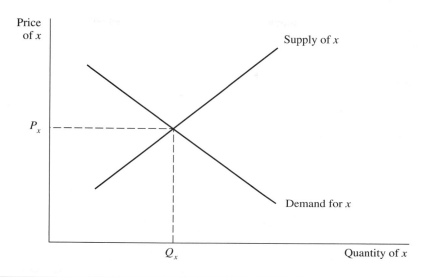

Explanation: In a competitive market economy, the price at which x sells will be P_x. If the price were *below* this level, the quantity demanded would exceed the quantity supplied. The *shortage* of x would cause the price of x to rise. If the price were *above* P_x, the quantity supplied would exceed the quantity demanded. The surplus of x would then cause the price of x to fall. Only at P_x is the quantity supplied equal to the quantity demanded (Q_x).

The first argues that in perfectly competitive markets, production will take place to the point where the marginal cost of society's resources equals the marginal benefit or utility to consumers. Firms that operate in competitive markets produce the level of output that equates price and marginal cost, and that price is set in the marketplace. When costs and benefits are not equal at the margin, society can gain by producing more or less of the product. For example, if price exceeds marginal cost, the product yields more benefits than costs and society can gain by producing more. If marginal costs exceed price, too much of the product has been produced and production should be reduced.

The Austrian economists Friederick Hayek and Ludwig von Mises wrote about the *relative* superiority of market economies over planned socialist economies.[5] Their arguments rest on the efficient manner in which market economies mobilize and utilize information, in contrast to the inefficient use of information in socialist economies. Hayek wrote that the principal economic problem is not how to allocate given resources but "how to secure the best use of resources known to any member of society, for ends whose relative importance only these individuals know. Or, to put it briefly, it is a problem of the utilization of knowledge not given to anyone in its totality." Economic agents (consumers and producers) specialize in information about prices, products, and location that is relevant to them in their daily lives. Economic

FIGURE 5.2   Consumer Sovereignty in a Competitive Economy

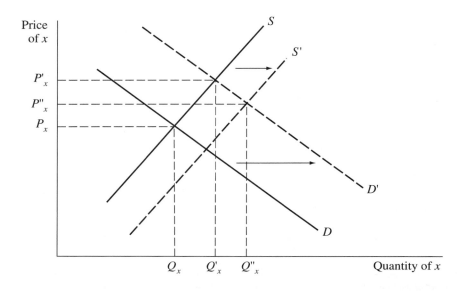

Explanation: We begin with the market for *x* in equilibrium at price P_x and quantity Q_x. *There is an increase in consumer demand from D to D'.* As a consequence, the price of *x* rises to P'_x and the equilibrium quantity *rises* to Q'_x. If economic profits are being made at this new price, new firms will enter the market and the supply curve will eventually shift to S'. Now a new long-run equilibrium is established at price P''_x and quantity Q''_x. An increase in consumer demand *automatically* leads to an increase in the quantity produced. The long-run effect on market prices depends on the entry of new firms at the higher price.

agents need not know all prices, products, and locations to behave efficiently in the marketplace. According to Hayek and Mises, the fact that market economies efficiently generate information in the form of market prices, which enable producers and consumers to plan their actions in a rational manner, is the principal advantage of capitalism and will ensure its relative superiority over planned socialism. This is their argument for the theoretical and practical superiority of capitalism. The planned socialist economies would prove too difficult to manage because of the complexity of information and incentive problems.

State Intervention

The picture of capitalism that we have developed is one of a harmonious and efficient resource allocation system strongly inclined toward equilibrium in production, especially under competitive conditions. This harmony occurs without the benefit of government intervention and control. Critics of the harmonious model point to the need for **state intervention** to deal with monopoly power, externalities, public goods, and income distribution problems. They also stress the inherent cyclical instability of capitalism and the problems of making rational public choices.

The appropriate level of state intervention into the affairs of private enterprise is one of the most disputed issues in economics. The neoclassical position, descended directly from Adam Smith, is that in the absence of monopoly power, and in the absence of external effects, the economic role of the state should be strictly limited. The state should supply only those public goods—such as national defense, public roads, a legal system, and foreign policy—that private enterprise on its own would not be able to provide in optimal proportions. The theory of public goods explains why laissez-faire capitalism will underproduce such goods.[6] The question we consider here is in what instances state intervention is necessary to correct deficiencies in market allocation.

Monopoly Power

The nonoptimality of monopoly has been emphasized since, and even before, publication of *The Wealth of Nations*.[7] The crux of the monopoly problem is the monopolist's inclination to restrict output below the level that would prevail in a competitive situation. Monopolists underproduce and overcharge relative to competitive producers. Monopoly causes a deadweight loss, in that the gains of the monopolist are less than the losses to consumers. Figure 5.3 demonstrates that monopolies produce less and charge higher prices than competitive markets.

Monopoly behavior is not explained by extraordinary greed on the part of the monopolist, who is simply attempting to maximize profits. By definition, the monopolist is the sole producer in a particular market. Therefore, to sell a large volume of output, the monopolist must lower the price. Perfectly competitive producers, as price takers, can sell all they desire at the market price. Monopolists fail to expand their output to the point where the marginal cost (which measures the marginal cost of output in terms of society's resources) equals price (which measures the marginal benefit of output to society). Rather, monopolists who wish to maximize profits must restrict their output.

Economic theory suggests four approaches to the control of monopoly, three of which require state intervention. The first is to use the state's authority to *tax and subsidize* to correct the underutilization of resources by monopolistic producers. The basic idea is to combine subsidization with consumer and producer **taxation** to induce the monopolist to expand output to the competitive level, while at the same time producing a social tax dividend for society. The obvious difficulty is that tax authorities must make quite sophisticated calculations. The use of **subsidies** and taxes to obtain an optimal allocation of resources from a monopolist does not seem too practical, although the theory of how to do so is clear.

The second form of state intervention is **direct regulation** of monopoly. Theoretically, state regulatory authorities could dictate that the regulated monopoly produce the efficient quantity of output at which *P* equals *MC* and force the monopolist to charge a regulated price equal to marginal costs. In this manner, the regulators

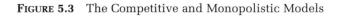

FIGURE 5.3   The Competitive and Monopolistic Models

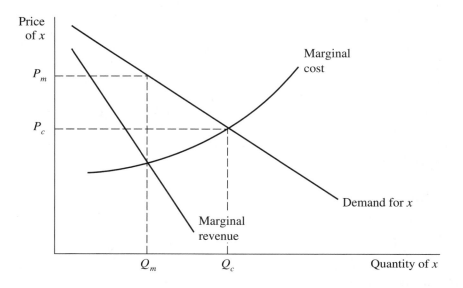

Explanation: This diagram presents the models of price and output determination under conditions of perfect competition and monopoly.

Let us suppose that industry X could be organized either as a monopoly (with a single producer) or as a competitive industry (with a large number of producers). The marginal costs are the same whether the industry is a monopoly or is perfectly competitive. The industry demand schedule and the industry marginal-cost schedule are given in the diagram. The latter is the marginal-cost schedule of the monopolist (in the case of the monopolistic industry) or the sum of the individual marginal-cost schedules of producers (in the case of the competitive industry).

Because the demand schedule is negatively sloped, the monopolist's marginal revenue is less than the product price. To maximize profits, the monopolist produces that output (Q_m) at which marginal cost and marginal revenue are equated and sells this output at the price dictated by the market (P_m). Competitive producers produce output levels at which the product price and marginal costs are equal; therefore, the supply schedule of the competitive industry is the industry marginal-cost schedule. The competitively organized industry produces Q_c, and the product sells for P_c.

The monopoly produces less than the competitive industry and charges a higher price. The monopolist charges a price greater than the marginal costs of production, whereas the competitive industry equates price and marginal cost. Because price and marginal revenue are not equal, an economy made up of monopolies is not efficient.

could dictate directly an efficient allocation of resources. There are two practical difficulties with this approach, however. How are regulators to know market demand and monopoly marginal costs? The monopoly might be tempted to inflate its costs by lax management or other means in order to obtain a higher regulated price. The second difficulty is that marginal-cost pricing would probably force the monopolist to operate at a loss if marginal costs were still declining at the output where *P* equaled *MC*. The existence of regulated losses would require a system of subsidization, which would tend to disrupt the optimal allocation of resources.

The third approach is that recommended by Milton Friedman—to *leave* **natural monopolies** *alone* because regulation is poorly managed and encourages monopolists to be inefficient.[8] The unregulated monopoly, prompted by the desire to maximize profits and keep potential competitors out of the market, would supply a larger quantity at a lower price than that charged by a regulated monopoly. Moreover, even monopolists must face some form of competition in the long run and cannot get by indefinitely with an inefficient use of resources.

The final collective approach applies to cases where competitive production is also possible. The state, through enforcement of antitrust and anticartel legislation and through the removal of legal obstacles to competition, could *transform the industry from monopolistic to competitive.*

Modern theory has pondered whether there are natural limitations on monopoly power. Unless freedom of entry were highly restricted, monopolists would avoid charging monopoly prices for fear of attracting competitors in the long run.

External Effects and Collective Action

External effects are brought to bear in situations where the actions of one producer or consumer directly affect the costs or utility of a second producer or consumer.[9] External effects are effects that take place outside of the price system. These external effects may be harmful, in which case they are called an **external diseconomy**, or they may be salutary, in which case they are known as an **external economy**. An example of an external diseconomy of production is the dumping of wastes into a river by one producer, requiring a producer downstream to increase costs by installing water purification equipment.

When external effects are present, the allocation of resources is not optimal, even if the economy is perfectly competitive. Producers of the external effect are not required to take the external impact of their actions into account when making decisions. Rather, they seek to maximize their private profit on the basis of the **private costs** of production, not on the basis of **social costs**. The producer of an external harmful effect therefore produces an output level in excess of the optimum, for the private producer tends to underestimate the true social costs of production (Figure 5.4).

Economic theory suggests remedies to correct for misallocations caused by external effects. One is the internalization of such effects—for example, by merging both the enterprises producing and those being affected by external effects. Consider the example of the waste-dumping factory. If it merged with the downstream factory, the water purification costs would become private costs for the combined enterprise, and waste dumping would be limited as a natural consequence of profit maximization.

In the absence of opportunities for internalization, remedies may require state action, such as taxation and subsidies, to equate private and social costs. If an excise tax equal to the external diseconomy could be levied on the producer, private costs would equal social costs. To maximize private profits, the producer would be forced to limit output to the level at which price and marginal *social* costs are equal—the condition required for an efficient allocation of resources.

FIGURE 5.4   The Inefficiency of External Costs

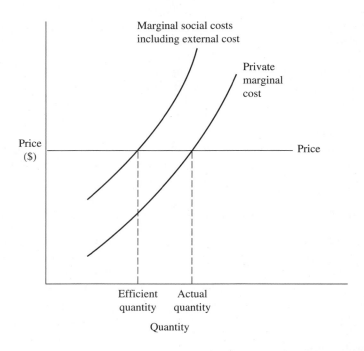

Explanation: When externalities are present, enterprises base their decisions on private marginal costs. This perfectly competitive firm produces where *P* = private marginal costs, not where *P* = full marginal cost. Thus externalities cause competitive firms to produce more than the optimal quantity.

When appropriate taxes and subsidies cannot be levied, one alternative is state regulation. Government regulators determine the optimal allocation of resources and administratively decree that producers supply the optimal output. The major drawback is that enforcement and policing costs may be quite high, for it is not clear how one would obtain compliance with regulations. Moreover, there is the enormous problem of calculating private and social marginal costs—the data required for effective regulation.

A third approach to the externality problem is voluntary agreements among the parties involved. This notion was first suggested by Ronald Coase.[10] He contends that under certain conditions, the creator and recipient of the external effect can come to a mutually satisfactory agreement that restores an optimal allocation of resources. Whenever harmful externalities exist, the affected parties have opportunities for gains from trade by striking deals. In the absence of legal obstacles, the amount of shared gains from an agreement must exceed the costs of transacting the agreement. Coase's novel conclusion, therefore, is that if the transaction costs of reaching an agreement are small, private agreements can correct the misallocation of resources caused by external effects. If mutually acceptable bargains are not reached in the presence of small transaction costs, then the divergence between private and social costs is probably inconsequential.

The most important drawback to voluntary agreements is exactly the problem of transaction costs and other impediments to agreement, especially when the number of parties involved is large. When a small number of parties are involved, voluntary agreements are feasible. When the agreement must be ratified by a large number of parties, some of whom have relatively small stakes in the matter, the probability of reaching a mutually acceptable agreement is small.

Problems of Public Choice

Public goods—national defense, police protection and a legal system, dams, flood control projects, and the like—will not be supplied in efficient quantities by the private economy for two principal reasons: Nonpayers (called free riders) cannot be prevented from enjoying the benefits of the public good, and one person's use of the good does not generally prevent others from using it. Both of these features make it difficult for the private sector to produce public goods.

How efficiently will government supply such public goods? How rational is public choice? Public-choice theorists, such as Nobel laureate James Buchanan, have concluded that certain factors prevent public choices in a democratic (majority-rule) society from being made in an efficient manner.[11]

Efficiency in the case of a public good requires, at a minimum, that the marginal benefits enjoyed by users of the good equal or exceed its marginal costs. Will this necessarily be the case in a society in which public-choice decisions are made by majority-rule voting? Public-choice theory outlines a number of potential problems. First, **majority voting** fails to take into consideration the intensity of preferences among voters. A number of voters may have intense feelings about a specific public-expenditure decision, whereas others may be virtually indifferent. Yet each person's vote counts equally, and changes in preferences typically do not change the voting outcome. This is called the **median voter rule**. Second, there may be a tendency toward vote trading when voters must decide on a number of public-choice issues. A group that favors one public-expenditure program may offer its support for the public-expenditure program of a second group if that group will form a majority coalition. Through such logrolling techniques, public-expenditure programs may be enacted where marginal costs exceed marginal benefits. Moreover, politicians are in the business of getting reelected and are likely to serve special-interest groups that are instrumental in financing election campaigns. The voter, on the other hand, does not have a great incentive to be well informed about public-choice issues. Individual voters are aware that their votes are unlikely to change any outcome, and the costs of gathering information on the large number of technically detailed government programs are high. It is therefore in the rational voter's economic interest to remain "rationally ignorant." Logrolling, vote trading, and rational ignorance cause governments to authorize public programs that are not economically efficient.

Income Distribution

In a capitalist economy, people who own resources that command a high price have higher incomes than those who own resources that command low prices. How equally or unequally should income be distributed? To what extent should the state redistribute income?

The marginal productivity theory of **income distribution** follows from the fact that the private owners of labor, land, and capital are paid the marginal revenue product of their factor. If the factor market is perfectly competitive, the owner receives the actual value of the marginal product of the factor. Thus, argue some economists, the resulting distribution of income is "just," because factor owners receive a reward that is equal to the factor's marginal contribution to society's output. Bestowing rewards according to marginal productivity encourages the owners of the factors of production to raise the productivity of their factors. If the state were to alter this distribution, there would be less incentive to raise the marginal productivity of one's own factors. There would be less investment in human capital and less risk taking, and society's output would accordingly be less.

Critics of this "natural justice" view point out that the marginal productivity of any factor depends on the presence of cooperating factors. An American coal miner may work with millions of dollars of capital equipment, whereas the Indian coal miner works just as hard with only a pick and shovel. The marginal productivity of the American coal miner is therefore many times that of the Indian coal miner. Moreover, marginal productivity is affected by human capital investment, and not everyone has equal access to education.

There are a number of arguments in favor of a redistributive role for the state. First, people are not indifferent to the welfare of others, and their own welfare is diminished by poverty around them. Yet despite altruistic motives, there are strong incentives against charitable contributions. Any one person's contribution can have only a negligible effect on poverty. The insignificance of any one donor creates a substantial free-rider problem, which means that voluntary contributions are unlikely to have a significant impact on the distribution of income. Government income redistribution programs eliminate the free-rider problem. Only the state is in a position to alter the distribution of income.

The philosopher John Rawls has advanced another argument in favor of state intervention.[12] Rawls argues that an unequal distribution of income persists because those who benefit from income inequality are unwilling to accept changes that favor the poor. People are unwilling to agree to redistribution because those who will be rich know fairly early in life their chances of being rich. For this reason, a social consensus can never be formed whereby the rich agree to redistribute income to the poor.

Rawls asks how people would behave if they did not know in advance their lifetime endowment of resources. How would they react if they operated behind a "veil of ignorance"? Rawls maintains that under this condition, people would naturally act to minimize the risks of being poor and would therefore reach a social consensus in favor of a fairly equal distribution of income. If people, operating behind a veil of ignorance, would naturally favor an equal distribution of income, then society should have an equal distribution of income. Insofar as voluntary charitable giving will not effect this result, the state is justified in redistributing income from the rich to the poor.

Macroeconomic Instability

A major challenge to the neoclassical vision of self-regulating capitalism was mounted by John Maynard Keynes in *The General Theory of Employment, Interest, and Money*, published in 1936 against the backdrop of the world depression.[13] The depression seemed to deny neoclassical notions of an automatic tendency toward equilibrium over time. Keynes's assertion that activist government action was required to stabilize capitalist economics has come to be called the **Keynesian revolution**.

Keynes   Keynes disputed the mainstay of classical equilibrium theory, Say's Law.[14] According to **Say's Law**, there can be no lasting deficiency of aggregate demand because the act of producing a given value of output creates an equivalent amount of income. If that income were not spent directly on consumer goods, it would be saved. The savings would end up being spent as well, for interest rates would adjust to equate *ex ante* savings and *ex ante* investment. Accordingly, depressions could not be caused by deficiencies in aggregate demand. If we were only patient, eventually prices and wages would adjust to bring about an equilibrium at full employment. If unemployment did exist, it would be because workers were unwilling to accept the lower real wages required for labor market equilibrium. As long as prices and wages are flexible, there will be an automatic adjustment mechanism to restore full employment.

Keynes argued that there is no assurance that equilibrium will occur at full employment or that the automatic adjustment mechanism will work with reasonable speed. Thus—and this is the foundation of the Keynesian revolution—it is the responsibility of government to ensure full employment.

Keynes disputed the conclusions of the neoclassical school in the following manner. First, he argued that wages and prices are not nearly so flexible (especially downward) as the neoclassical economists believed. He pointed out that despite considerable unemployment, money wages were not falling in England in the 1920s and 1930s. Second, he argued that aggregate saving is not significantly affected by the interest rate; rather, it is principally dependent on the level of income. According to Keynes, the investment–savings relationship would be especially troublesome because of the cyclical instability of investment expenditures; only by chance would enough investment be forthcoming to guarantee full employment.

Keynes saw no reason why macroequilibrium should occur at a rate of output sufficient to ensure full employment. Therefore, it is the responsibility of government, by appropriately raising or lowering its spending and taxes (**fiscal policy**) or by controlling investment spending (through **monetary policy**), to ensure that equilibrium occurs near full employment. Because investment spending is quite unstable, government must be prepared to counteract investment fluctuations with compensatory actions.

After World War II, Keynes's advocacy of discretionary monetary and fiscal policy became widely accepted by economists and public officials, who felt justified in abandoning the traditional hands-off policies favored by the neoclassical school. Federal budgets could be openly in deficit in order to stimulate the economy. In the United States, for example, tax cuts and tax increases were imposed for the express purpose of manipulating aggregate demand. The practice of demand management became standard procedure in Western Europe, Japan, and Canada. Monetary policy also became an instrument of macroeconomic regulation. In the height of optimism in the mid-1960s, there was talk of being able to "fine-tune" the economy, and the business cycle was declared dead.

Self-Correcting Capitalism: Monetarism and Rational Expectations
Keynes and his contemporary followers questioned the cyclical stability of capitalism. Without government intervention to moderate business cycles, there will be a significant loss of output and employment. Keynesian economics advocates **policy activism**—the discretionary use of monetary and fiscal policy to try to prevent or ameliorate the business cycle. Activist monetary and fiscal policy is required to keep the economy on an even keel.

The **monetarists**, under the intellectual leadership of Milton Friedman, and rational expectations economists, led by Robert Lucas, argue against the use of activist macroeconomic policy to combat capitalism's cyclical instability.[15] They argue that capitalism is considerably more stable than Keynes thought. In fact, the Great Depression was an aberration caused in large part by blunders in economic policy. The capitalist economy has a built-in self-correcting mechanism that will restore it to full employment or to the natural rate of unemployment. If the economy is operating at an unemployment rate above the natural rate, a slowing down of the inflation rate (or even deflation in extreme cases) will restore the economy to full employment. Lower prices raise aggregate supply, and aggregate employment rises until the natural rate is reached.

The monetarists argue against the use of activist policy. Because fiscal policy is decided primarily by politics rather than economics, monetary policy has been the most flexible tool of activist policy. Monetarists maintain that activist monetary policy is as likely to do harm as good. Lengthy and indeterminate lags separate recognition of a macroeconomic problem, the taking of necessary monetary action, and realization of the effect of that action on the economy. An anti-inflationary policy adopted during a period of rising prices may begin to affect the economy at the very time an expansionary monetary policy is required. Rather than running the risk of policy mistakes, the monetarists favor a fixed-monetary-growth rule, which would bind monetary authorities to expand the money supply by a fixed rate each year (roughly equal to the real growth of the economy) regardless of the state of the economy.

Advocates of the **rational-expectations theory** also argue against activist policy. They maintain that activist policy will have the desired effect on the economy only if the policy catches people off guard. If taxes are lowered for the purpose of stimulating employment, and people know from experience that lower taxes raise inflation, then people will take actions to defeat the policy. If monetary authorities expand the money supply to raise employment, and workers and employees know that more monetary growth means more inflation, then the higher wages and prices will not raise employment or real output.

Real business cycle theorists argue that the business cycle is caused by random shocks and cannot be controlled by factors other than the self-correcting mechanism. The basic message of the monetarists, the rational expectations economists and the real business cycle theorists is that capitalism is much more stable than Keynes thought and that activist policies are likely to harm the economy. It is better to rely on the self-correcting forces of the capitalist economy to restore it to equilibrium than to count on government policy makers to do so.

Growth and State Policy

An economy must grow for living standards to rise. Will a market economy grow appropriately on its own or is state action required to promote and direct growth?

The Austrian economist Joseph Schumpeter argued that market economies are well suited to create growth.[16] Schumpeter saw growth as a process of **creative destruction**. A particular company or industry will find new ways to produce products or find new products to develop. Such adaptability can become the engine of growth for the entire economy, pulling along laggard branches. The company's success, however, will result in its eventual decline as competitors create substitutes and invent improved technologies.

To prove that economic growth follows the path of creative destruction, Schumpeter pointed out that no company or industry has been able to maintain a dominant position over the long run. The railroads were dominant in the 19th century; now they face tough competition from superior technologies, such as truck and air transport. IBM dominated computer production until new technologies allowed smaller, more efficient companies to grab pieces of IBM's market share.

Although economists such as Schumpeter argue that market economies can grow on their own and can be trusted to select those industries that will grow more rapidly than others, a significant number of economists believe that **industrial policy** can manage growth. Industrial policy uses the state to promote, subsidize, and generally manage the economic growth of a country. The proponents of industrial policy argue that private markets cannot effectively produce growth. Returns from research and development are insufficient to encourage private sector financing. The state must therefore fund R&D, perhaps in partnership with private industry. The proponents of industrial policy also argue that private industries are not farsighted; they are unable to identify growth industries of the future. Thus government must find, support, and subsidize the growth industries of the future. The real-world model for industrial policy is Japan, which apparently used industrial policy to develop its automobile and electronics industries.

The Performance of Capitalist Economic Systems: Hypotheses

Chapter 3 discussed criteria by which to judge the performance of economic systems: efficiency, stability, income distribution, economic growth, and viability. What hypotheses, if any, follow from the theory of capitalism in each of these areas? First, let us say that it is difficult to formulate hypotheses at this point, because our principal concern is the efficiency of capitalism vis-à-vis other economic systems; these hypotheses would best be stated in relative terms. (See Table 5.1.)

Efficiency

Capitalism should provide a high level of efficiency, especially in the static case. The more competitive the economy, the more efficient the economy. The producer's desire to maximize profits and the consumer's desire to maximize utility lead to a maximal output from available resources under conditions of perfect competition. Imperfect competition and external effects reduce this efficiency. Another point promoting static efficiency is capitalism's apparent ability to process and utilize information more effectively than an economic system in which the market is lacking. Probably the most important point is that profit maximization, under all market arrangements, strongly encourages the efficient (least-cost) combination of resources to produce output.

Stability

Stability is the ability of an economic system to grow without undue fluctuations in the rate of growth and without excessive inflation and unemployment. Of course, it is a subjective judgment what "undue" and "excessive" mean in such a context. Keynes argued that capitalist economies are not stable, at least in terms of short-run automatic equilibrating forces. Monetarists and rational-expectations theorists believe that capitalist economies are (or could be) inherently more stable if left to their own devices,

TABLE 5.1   Hypothesis on the Performance of Capitalist
Economic Systems

Criterion	Performance
Efficiency	Good
Stability	Potentially poor; debate over government role
Income distribution	Unequal in the absence of state action
Economic growth	No clear *a priori* hypothesis; greater efficiency versus potentially lower capital formation

so there is considerable disagreement on this point. However, capitalism continues to suffer periodic bouts of inflation, unemployment, and growth fluctuations, which the general public regards as troubling.

Income Distribution

The theory of capitalism cannot make definitive judgments about equity and how resources should be divided among the members of capitalist societies. Only value judgments can provide answers. We lack a consensus about "fairness," and without an agreed-upon definition it is difficult to arrive at hypotheses. Instead, we can only consider empirical measures of income distribution and make statements like the following: Income is distributed more nearly equally in society X than in society Y. It is difficult to proceed further and say that income is distributed "better" ("more fairly") in X or in Y.

The theory of capitalism, however, does suggest the likelihood of significant inequalities in the distribution of income. The factors of production are owned predominantly by private individuals, and the relative value of these factors is determined by the market. Insofar as human and physical capital and natural ability are not likely to be evenly distributed, especially when such things can be passed from one generation to another, private ownership of the factors of production raises the likelihood of an uneven distribution of income and wealth among the members of capitalist societies. Exactly how unevenly income and wealth are distributed will depend on the distribution of human and physical capital and also on the redistributive role of the state.

Economic Growth

One of the supposed advantages of planned socialist economies is their ability to direct resources to specific goals, such as economic growth and military power. To a greater extent than capitalist economies, they can marshal resources for economic growth, if they so desire, by controlling the investment rate and the growth rate of the labor force. Although capitalist governments can and do affect the investment rate, the amount saved is largely a matter of individual choice, and it is likely that individual choice will result in lower savings rates than will a planned socialist economy. Thus if the growth of factor inputs is left to individuals, one would hypothesize a slower rate of growth of factor inputs and hence of economic growth, *ceteris paribus*, under capitalism.

A counterbalancing factor must be considered: the hypothesized efficiency of capitalist economies. Static efficiency means that a maximal output is produced from available resources and (with a given saving rate) a greater volume of savings is available relative to less efficient production methods. Moreover, there is the unresolved matter of the dynamic efficiency of capitalist economic systems. Up to this point, capitalist theory has had relatively little to say about dynamic efficiency. It is conceivable that the greater static and dynamic efficiency of capitalism can compensate for the lesser control over the growth of productive resources.

Viability of the Capitalist System

The viability of capitalism has been demonstrated by both theory and historical experience. Capitalist theory points to its inherent tendencies toward equilibrium. And historical experience shows that capitalism has survived several centuries and that there are no signs of impending collapse.

Summary

This chapter focuses on the theory of resource allocation in the market capitalist economic system—in particular, on the way resources are allocated and the role the state should play in the allocation process. The traditional neoclassical model maintains that capitalist economies have a strong tendency toward equilibrium and that they generate and process information efficiently. Under competitive conditions, they use resources efficiently. Market capitalism promotes consumer sovereignty, which allows consumers to determine what will be produced. From a policy perspective, in the perfectly competitive market capitalist economy, government would play a very limited role, avoiding interference in the operation of business.

Critics of this model of self-regulating market capitalism have focused on several perceived weaknesses. In his classic work dating from the late 1930s, John Maynard Keynes attempted to demonstrate that such an economy could establish a stable macroeconomic equilibrium at less than (or greater than) full employment. Thus, given the possibility of persistent and unacceptable unemployment, Keynes argued that it is the responsibility of government through fiscal and monetary policies to bring about an appropriate (full-employment) equilibrium.

A major line of criticism focuses on the argument that in the real world, perfectly competitive markets are likely to be replaced, in part, by imperfectly competitive markets, where resources are misallocated and that regulation and taxation are required to offset potential abuses arising from monopoly power.

The outcomes of the market economy have also been criticized from the perspective of externalities. As we saw in this chapter, the basic neoclassical model assumes that all costs and benefits, both private and social, can be measured and accounted for in the resource-allocation process. Economists have demonstrated that in a variety of circumstances, there are likely to be externalities—that is, costs or benefits external to, and thus not accounted for by, the decision maker as resource allocation takes place. In this setting, it is argued that government intervention may be necessary to achieve an optimal allocation of resources.

Despite the above criticism, the notion of self-regulating market capitalism remains controversial. For example, the monetarist view of the market economy has mounted a major counterattack against the Keynesian revolution, arguing that, on balance, government intervention in the economy is not necessarily stabilizing and thus should be minimized. Indeed, some have argued that capitalism is capable of handling problems of market imperfections and externalities without significant, if any, government intervention.

What hypotheses can be put forward concerning the economic performance of the market capitalist economy? The traditional view holds that the markets tend to result in an efficient allocation of resources but that economic activity remains unstable or cyclical. It is usually argued that the distribution of income will be less even than in those systems where greater degrees of social ownership or government redistributive effort are present; however, the matter of an appropriate distribution of income is controversial on both equity and efficiency grounds. No firm hypotheses are suggested regarding economic growth in the market capitalist economy.

Key Terms

invisible hand	public goods
consumer sovereignty	majority voting
efficiency of market allocation	the median voter rule
state intervention	income distribution
monopoly	Keynesian revolution
taxation	Say's law
subsidies	fiscal policy
direct regulation	monetary policy
natural monopoly	policy activism
external effects	monetarists
external diseconomies	rational-expectations theory
external economies	creative destruction
private costs	industrial policy
social costs	

Notes

1. Examples of how the latter approach has been applied are found in Abram Bergson, *The Economics of Soviet Planning* (New Haven: Yale University Press, 1964); Jaroslav Vanek, *The Participatory Economy* (Ithaca, N.Y.: Cornell University Press, 1971), Chs. 2 and 3; and Benjamin Ward, *The Socialist Economy* (New York: Random House, 1967), Chs. 8 and 9. We also refer the reader to our discussion of the socialist controversy in Chapter 7.
2. Adam Smith, *The Wealth of Nations*, ed. Edwin Cannan (New York: Modern Library, 1937).
3. George Stigler, "The Successes and Failures of Professor Smith," *Journal of Political Economy* 84 (December 1976), 1199–1214.
4. It is difficult to single out a few individuals and claim that they are the major contributors to partial-equilibrium analysis, but these three would appear on most lists: Alfred Marshall, *Principles of Economics*, 8th ed. (New York: Macmillan, 1948); J. R. Hicks, *Value and Capital*, 2nd ed. (Oxford, England: Oxford University Press, 1946); and Paul Samuelson, *Foundations of Economic Analysis* (Cambridge, Mass.: Harvard University Press, 1948).
5. Friederick Hayek, "The Price System as a Mechanism for Using Knowledge," *American Economic Review* 35 (September 1945), 519–530; and Ludwig von Mises, *Socialism: An Economic and Sociological Analysis* (New Haven: Yale University Press, 1951).

6. Paul Samuelson, "The Pure Theory of Public Expenditure," *Review of Economics and Statistics* 36 (November 1954), 26–30.
7. For a brief but lucid discussion of monopoly theory, see George Stigler, *The Theory of Price*, rev. ed. (New York: Macmillan, 1952), pp. 204–222.
8. Milton Friedman, "Monopoly and Social Responsibility of Business and Labor," in Edwin Mansfield, ed., *Monopoly Power and Economic Performance*, 3rd ed. (New York: Norton, 1974), pp. 57–68; and George J. Stigler, "The Government of the Economy," in Paul Samuelson, ed., *Readings in Economics*, 7th ed. (New York: McGraw-Hill, 1973), pp. 73–77.
9. The discussion of externalities is based on the following sources: E. J. Mishan, "The Postwar Literature on Externalities: An Interpretive Essay," *Journal of Economic Literature* 9 (March 1971), 1–28; George Daly, "The Coase Theorem: Assumptions, Applications, and Ambiguities," *Economic Inquiry* 12 (June 1974), 203–213; and Eirik Furobotin and Svetozar Pejovich, "Property Rights and Economic Theory: A Survey of Recent Literature," *Journal of Economic Literature* 12 (December 1972), 1137–1162.
10. R. H. Coase, "The Problem of Social Costs," *Journal of Law and Economics* 3 (October 1960), 1–44.
11. James Buchanan and Gordon Tullock, *The Calculus of Consent* (Ann Arbor: University of Michigan Press, 1974); Kenneth Arrow, *Social Choice and Individual Values* (New Haven: Yale University Press, 1976); for a discussion of differing views of the state, see Barry W. Poulson, *Economic Development: Private and Public Choice* (New York: West Publishing, 1994).
12. John Rawls, *Theory of Justice* (Oxford, England: Clarendon Press, 1976).
13. John Maynard Keynes, *The General Theory of Employment, Interest, and Money* (New York: Harcourt, 1936). The most important early work to interpret Keynes's general theory for nonspecialists was Alvin Hansen, *A Guide to Keynes* (New York: McGraw-Hill, 1953).
14. There is considerable controversy over what Keynes actually meant to say in *General Theory*, and some authorities argue that the more popular interpretations of Keynes are incorrect. For discussion of this controversy, see Don Patinkin, *Money, Interest, and Prices*, 2nd ed. (New York: Harper & Row, 1965); Axel Leijonhufvud, *On Keynesian Economics and the Economics of Keynes* (New York: Oxford University Press, 1968); Herschel Grossman, "Was Keynes a 'Keynesian'? A Review Article," *Journal of Economic Literature* 10 (March 1972), 26–30; and Alan Coddington, "Keynesian Economics: The Search for First Principles," *Journal of Economic Literature* 14 (December 1976), 1258–1338. For an historical perspective on the Keynesian revolution, see Alan Sweezy *et al.*, "The Keynesian Revolution and Its Pioneers," *American Economic Review, Papers and Proceedings* 62 (May 1972), 116–141.
15. The discussion of the monetarist school is based on the following sources: Milton Friedman, ed., *Studies in the Quantity Theory of Money* (Chicago: University of Chicago Press, 1956); Milton Friedman and A. J. Schwartz, *A Monetary History of the United States* (Princeton, N.J.: Princeton University Press, 1963); Milton Friedman, *Dollars and Deficits* (Englewood Cliffs, N.J.: Prentice-Hall, 1968); Franco Modigliani, "The Monetarist Controversy, or, Should We Forsake Stabilization Policies?" *American Economic Review* 67 (March 1977), 13; Edmund Phelps, *Microeconomic Foundations of Employment and Inflation Theory* (London: Macmillan, 1974); and Milton Friedman, "Inflation and Unemployment," *Journal of Political Economy* 85 (June 1977), 451–472.
16. For a contemporary view of the Schumpeterian contribution, see F. M. Scherer, "Schumpeter and Plausible Capitalism," *Journal of Economic Literature* 30 (September 1992), 1416–1433. For a discussion of contemporary issues in economic growth, see

Paul M. Romer *et al.*, "New Growth Theory," *Journal of Economic Perspectives* 8 (Winter 1994), 3–72.

Recommended Readings

Traditional Sources

F. M. Bator, "The Simple Analytics of Welfare Maximization," *American Economic Review* 47 (March 1957), 22–59.

Abram Bergson, "A Reformulation of Certain Aspects of Welfare Economics," *Quarterly Journal of Economics* 52 (February 1938), 310–334; reprinted in R. V. Clemence, ed., *Readings in Economic Analysis* (Reading, Mass.: Addison Wesley, 1950), Vol. I, pp. 61–85.

James Buchanan and Robert Tollison, eds., *Theory of Public Choice: Political Applications of Economics* (Ann Arbor: University of Michigan Press, 1972).

James Buchanan and Gordon Tullock, *The Calculus of Consent* (Ann Arbor: University of Michigan Press, 1974).

Edward Chamberlin, *The Theory of Monopolistic Competition*, 6th ed. (Cambridge, Mass.: Harvard University Press, 1948).

R. H. Coase, "The Problem of Social Costs," *Journal of Law and Economics* 3 (October 1960), 1–44.

Alan Coddington, "Keynesian Economics: The Search for First Principles," *Journal of Economic Literature* 14 (December 1976), 1258–1338.

A. S. Eicher and J. A. Kregel, "An Essay on Post-Keynesian Theory: A New Paradigm in Economics," *Journal of Economic Literature* 13 (December 1975), 1293–1314.

Milton Friedman, *Dollars and Deficits* (Englewood Cliffs, N.J.: Prentice-Hall, 1968).

———, ed., *Studies in the Quantity Theory of Money* (Chicago: University of Chicago Press, 1956).

Robert J. Gordon, "What Is New Keynesian Economics?" *Journal of Economic Literature* 28 (September 1990), 15–71.

J. de V. Graaff, *Theoretical Welfare Economics* (London: Cambridge University Press, 1957).

Herschel Grossman, "Was Keynes a 'Keynesian'? A Review Article," *Journal of Economic Literature* 10 (March 1972), 26–30.

J. R. Hicks, *Value and Capital*, 2nd ed. (Oxford, England: Oxford University Press, 1946).

Axel Leijonhufvud, *On Keynesian Economics and the Economics of Keynes* (New York: Oxford University Press, 1968).

John Maynard Keynes, *The General Theory of Employment, Interest, and Money* (New York: Harcourt, 1936).

E. J. Mishan, "The Postwar Literature on Externalities: An Interpretive Essay," *Journal of Economic Literature* 9 (March 1971), 1–28.

Franco Modigliani, "The Monetarist Controversy, or, Should We Forsake Stabilization Policies?" *American Economic Review* 67 (March 1977), 1–19.

A. C. Pigou, *The Economics of Welfare*, 4th ed. (London: Macmillan, 1946).

John Rawls, *Theory of Justice* (Oxford, England: Clarendon Press, 1976).

Joan Robinson, *The Economics of Imperfect Competition* (London: Macmillan, 1959).

Paul Samuelson, "The Pure Theory of Public Expenditure," *Review of Economics and Statistics* 36 (November 1954), 26–30.

———, *Foundations of Economic Analysis* (Cambridge, Mass.: Harvard University Press, 1948).

Tibor Scitovsky, *Welfare and Competition*, rev. ed. (Homewood, Ill.: Irwin, 1971), Chs. 20 and 21.

Adam Smith, *The Wealth of Nations*, ed. Edwin Cannan (New York: Modern Library, 1937).

The Neoclassical Model

David M. Krebs, *A Course in Microeconomic Theory* (Princeton N.J.: Princeton University Press, 1990).

Eugene Silberberg, *The Structure of Economics: A Mathematical Analysis*, 2nd ed. (New York: McGraw-Hill, 1990).

Hal R. Varian, *Intermediate Microeconomics: A Modern Approach*, 2nd ed. (New York: Norton, 1990).

Macroeconomic Theory

Andrew B. Abel and Ben S. Bernake, *Macroeconomics* (New York: Addison-Wesley, 1992).

William H. Branson, *Macroeconomics: Theory and Policy*, 3rd. ed. (New York: Harper-Collins, 1989).

Richard T. Froyen, *Macroeconomics: Theories and Policies*, 4th ed. (New York: Macmillan Publishing Company, 1993).

Robert J. Gordon, "What Is the New Keynesian Economics?" *Journal of Economic Literature* 28 (September 1990), 15–71.

———, *Macroeconomics*, 5th ed. (Glenview, Illinois: Scott, Foresman, 1990).

Robert E. Hall and John B. Taylor, *Macroeconomics*, 3rd ed. (New York: Norton, 1991).

N. Gregory Markiw, "A Quick Refresher Course in Macroeconomics," *Journal of Economic Literature* 28 (December 1990), 1645–1660.

N. Gregory Mankiw *et al.*, "Keynesian Economics Today" *Journal of Economic Perspectives* 7 (Winter 1993), 3–82.

Paul M. Romer *et al.*, "New Growth Theory," *Journal of Economic Perspectives* 8 (Winter 1994), 3–72.

Market Failure: Imperfect Competition, Income Distribution, and Public Choice

Nicholas Barr, "Economic Theory and the Welfare State: A Survey and Interpretation," *Journal of Economic Literature* 30 (June 1992), 741–803.

Dennis W. Carlton and Jeffrey M. Perloff, *Modern Industrial Organization* (New York: HarperCollins, 1990).

Douglas F. Greer, *Business, Government, and Society*, 2nd ed. (New York: Macmillan, 1987).

F. M. Sherer and David Ross, *Industrial Market Structure and Economic Performance*, 3rd ed. (Boston: Houghton Mifflin, 1990).

R. D. Norton, "Industrial Policy and American Renewal," *Journal of Economic Literature* 24 (March 1986), 1–40.

Barry W. Poulson, *Economic Development: Private and Public Choice* (New York: West Publishing, 1994).

Leonard W. Weiss and Michael W. Klass, eds., *Regulatory Reform: What Actually Happened* (Boston: Little, Brown, 1986).

Clifford Winston, "Economic Deregulation: Days of Reckoning for Microeconomists," *Journal of Economic Literature* 31 (September 1993), 1263–1289.

6

Theory of Planned Socialism

Chapter 2 introduced two variants of the socialist economy: centrally planned socialism and market socialism. This chapter discusses the former, and then Chapter 7 looks at market socialism. Before the two major organizational variants of the socialist economy are discussed, it is important to introduce the basic ideas that define the nature of **socialism**.

The Socialist Economy

The characterization of the socialist economy in Chapter 2 focused on the nature of decision-making arrangements, property rights, and incentive arrangements. These arrangements, along with different policies and a different political system, lead to outcomes different from those observed under capitalism. Unlike the neoclassical paradigm of the market capitalist economy, no widely accepted theoretical paradigm of the socialist economy exists.[1] Much of the literature on socialism focuses on its noneconomic aspects and especially on the nature of socialist society. Indeed, many socialists characterize their economic system as one not only based on fundamental social changes with special emphasis on equity but also designed to improve the capitalist system.

Let us consider how socialism resolves the four fundamental tasks of any economic system—what to produce, how to produce, who gets the product, and how to provide for the future.

First, although the output mix could in theory be the same in capitalist and socialist systems, such an outcome is unlikely. Typically, the socialist economic system is accompanied by a strong central state, which along with state ownership of resources allows considerable state influence over what will be produced. In most socialist economies, the output mix favors public goods, defense goods, and the socialization of consumption as opposed to the expansion of private consumer goods.

Second, the structure of the socialist economy, through state controls and ownership arrangements, can be dictated by forces that may or may not resemble those of the market. Thus the state dictates sectoral expansion and, within sectors, the arrangements for production. Moreover, socialists have viewed the technology of production as much simpler than that thought to prevail in the market economy. As a result, the appropriate mix of factor inputs (capital and labor) appears limited and constrained by technology, making an assumption of constant-factor proportions

115

over extended periods of time quite reasonable. In such a setting, information problems are not serious, and engineers rather than economists can resolve the factor proportions issue. Not surprisingly, factor prices are of limited importance in deciding the appropriate input mix.

Third, state ownership of the means of production has fundamental implications for income distribution. For the household, the primary source of income is labor. Private income from capital is absent. Moreover, in a system where the socialization of consumption is an objective, one would expect a more equitable distribution of income than in a market capitalist economy. This expectation—one of the strongest basic tenets of socialism—relies on assumptions about basic human needs, human participation in the economy, and how these basic needs ought to be fulfilled. It is therefore argued that under socialism, human needs change, that their fulfillment can, in fact, be socialized, and that no major differences exist in the ability to benefit from increases in income, all of which assumptions support an egalitarian distribution of income.[2]

Finally, the economy's provision for the future differs in the socialist case. The capitalist market economy tends to overstate the worth of present consumption at the expense of future consumption. Thus the socialist economy follows policies that expand present savings to offset individual shortsightedness and expand well-being in the future.

Its advocates view socialism as an economic system that can offset the perceived faults of the market capitalist economy. The socialist economy places greater emphasis on economic equality and socialization and, in doing so, uses a variety of state controls and policies to offset the problems of unemployment, inflation, and slow economic growth, which are perceived as inevitable under capitalism.

Although a look at historical experience helps us judge the relative merits of different economic and associated political systems, it is difficult to compare the paradigm of the market with that of the socialist economy because there is no single dominant socialist paradigm. This is why little attention is given to socialist economic thought in the general history of economic thought. Views of the socialist economy have varied through history. Beyond the economic aspects of socialism, a great deal of attention has focused on the nature of a socialist society and its evolution. Not surprisingly, therefore, as we focus on how systems evolve through time, we find that a great deal of attention is paid to Marx and subsequent Marxian thinkers. As we will see, Marx analyzed capitalism, but in doing so, he envisioned socialism (and ultimately communism) as an inevitable outcome of the process of social change.

The Marxist–Leninist View of Socialism

Although Marx did not analyze socialist working arrangements, he did develop a framework for predicting the triumph of socialism over capitalism. For Marx, the historical evolution from primitive societies to communism was inevitable.[3] Capitalism, because of its exploitation of workers and internal contradictions, would be replaced by socialism. Capitalism would be an engine of economic progress, the results of which would be more evenly shared under socialism.

Socialism itself would be an intermediate step, a system ultimately to be replaced by communism. **Communism**, the highest stage of social and economic development, would be characterized by the absence of markets and money, abundance, distribution according to need, and the withering away of the state. In the meantime, under socialism, vestiges of capitalism would continue and some familiar institutions would remain. The state would be transformed into a **dictatorship of the proletariat**. Marx emphasized a strong role for the state, a role that was subsequently strengthened by V. I. Lenin.[4] Under socialism, though, the state would be representative of the masses and therefore noncoercive. The state would own the means of production as well as rights to surplus value. Under socialism, each individual would be expected to contribute according to capability, and rewards would be distributed in proportion to that contribution. Subsequently, under communism, the basis of reward would be need. However, need would presumably have a meaning rather different from the one assigned to it under capitalism, where wants are continually expanding.

Many changes and additions have been made to the Marxian model originally developed in the 19th century. Lenin wrote extensively on the role of the state under socialism, especially on the tactics of revolution.

Lenin emphasized that inequalities and capitalist vestiges would still exist under socialism and that, accordingly, coercive actions by the state would be necessary.[5] Indeed, during the war communisim period in the former Soviet Union, Lenin promoted a peculiar view of the state in which the task of administering the economy's affairs was viewed as simple, capable of being handled by anyone.[6] There was no need, Lenin argued, for specialists, because the tasks of management were quite routine. These views were subsequently modified, although they form the basis of later Soviet thinking on management.

Marx, Engels, and Lenin wrote about the role of the state and income distribution under socialism. They did not deal with the more fundamental issue of how scarce resources were to be allocated during the socialist phase.

The Socialist Controversy: The Feasibility of Socialism

Resource allocation under socialism has been widely discussed over the past century, and the discussion has been loosely termed the **socialist controversy**. Socialist economic theory must explain how resources are to be allocated under socialism. If the socialist economy is planned, how will planners make rational decisions about the use of scarce resources? Is private ownership necessary for the proper functioning of markets?

Barone: A Theoretical Framework

The first consistent theoretical framework of resource allocation under socialism was developed by the Italian economist Enrico Barone. In 1907, Barone published "The Ministry of Production in the Collectivist State."[7] Here he argued, though in a limited and purely theoretical way, that prices, understood as **relative valuations**, are not bound to the market. A **central planning board** (hereafter designated CPB) could establish prices, or "ratios of equivalence" among commodities.

Barone's model consisted of simultaneous equations relating inputs and outputs to the ratios of equivalence. When solved (Barone admitted that a real-world solution would be impractical), the equations could provide the appropriate relative valuations of resources required to balance demand and supply. A CPB armed with perfect computation techniques would require perfect knowledge of all relevant variables, specifically (1) individual demand schedules, (2) enterprise production functions, and (3) existing stocks of both producer and consumer goods. Barone's principal conclusion was that the CPB's computed resource allocation would be similar to that of competitive capitalism. In fact, he saw no reason for substantial differences.

One could question the practicality of this approach, both at the time Barone was writing and even in the present state of improved computer technology. Nevertheless, it demonstrated that the relative valuations of resources essential for rational resource allocation could be discovered by imputation (solving equations) rather than through the particular institutional arrangements of the market.

The Challenge of Mises and Hayek

The discussion of this matter went little further until the 1920s and 1930s, when three important developments took place. First, Ludwig von Mises and Friederick Hayek mounted a formidable and now famous attack against the case for rational resource allocation under socialism.[8] Second, a number of Soviet authors made significant contributions to the theory of planning, then in its formative stages. Third, the noted Polish economist Oskar Lange set forth his famous model of market socialism, to be discussed in the next chapter.[9]

Hayek and Mises's challenge was directed toward the problem of allocating producer goods in a socialist economic system, a task presumably in the hands of the state (with the allocation of consumer goods left to the market). Mises argued that for a state to direct available resources rationally toward the achievement of given ends, even if resource availabilities and ends were known, a knowledge of relative valuations (prices) would be essential. He maintained that the only way to establish these valuations would be through the market mechanism, which is absent in a socialist state where producer goods are owned and allocated by the state. If prices are the vehicle by which relative scarcities are reflected, why not artificially simulate prices via a system of equations as proposed by Barone? Mises and Hayek argued that it would be difficult if not impossible to separate the allocation function from the workings of the market. Both, he suggested, are tied together through the profit motive and the existence of private property.

Much has been written about the profit motive and private property.[10] Mises argued that individuals are motivated by the urge for material self-betterment, which translates into utility and profit maximization. Second, individuals and enterprises are motivated to produce goods and services as efficiently as possible so as to increase profits. Third, the drive for achievement cannot be socialized; that is, the urge for betterment cannot be translated from the individual to the group. Furthermore, if resources are owned by the state, profits accrue to the state, not to individuals. Thus, Mises argued, the motivation for utilizing available resources in the most efficient way is lost.

The responses to Hayek and Mises's critique have varied. There have been two main interpretations. The first is that they were saying that socialism could not "work" in the sense that resource allocation would be impossible in the absence of a market mechanism. The second and more common interpretation is that socialism cannot work *efficiently*. In fact, the debate over the relative merits of socialism and capitalism has focused on the question of relative efficiency.[11]

The Planned Economy: Organizational Arrangements

Figure 2.4 (panel B) depicts the hierarchical nature of a planned socialist economic system. Unlike the market economy, where resource allocation takes place on a relatively decentralized basis through supply and demand, allocation here is guided by the planning mechanism. What is planning, and how does it differ from other forms of resource allocation?

The socialist political authority exercises considerable control over broad economic objectives. Having characterized objectives, the planning authority is responsible for developing a plan or document outlining how resources will be used to achieve the objectives. The task of developing a plan is dealt with at length in this chapter.

Once a plan is developed, it is disseminated to the participants (enterprises) in the economy, whose responsibility it is to execute the plan. Plan instructions tell the enterprises what to produce, how to organize production (technology), and to whom to distribute the products through the state distribution system. In this setting, the flow of information and commands is from enterprise to planner and vice versa; only limited interaction occurs among enterprises. Agencies (ministries) between the planners and the enterprises coordinate the information flows by product type—for example, steel, agricultural products, and machinery. Ideally, the directives of the plan, based on adequate and appropriate information, are complete and clear to the enterprises, and incentive structures are harmonized with central directives. Real-world planning systems differ from the ideals of a perfectly administered economy. In both theory and practice, the market mechanisms are very different, though in both cases the basic task of efficiently utilizing resources to achieve desired objectives is fundamentally the same.

Resource Allocation Under Planned Socialism

The socialist controversy raised the key issues of resource allocation under conditions of socialism. On the one hand, it raised the complexity issue for planned socialism. Barone showed that the CPB would, in theory, have to gather data and solve simultaneous equations for millions of products. Such a task would be beyond the capabilities of any real-world CPB. On the other hand, the socialist controversy raised the motivation issue for both planned and market socialism. If the means of production are owned by society at large, how are managers to be motivated to combine resources efficiently and to take innovative risks?

The discussion that follows pursues these questions for planned socialism. It begins with the origins of the theory of planned socialism in its first real-world experiment, the Soviet Union in the 1930s, and then proceeds to the theory of planning.

Origins: The Soviet Union in the 1920s

The 1920s have been described as "the golden age of Soviet mathematical economics."[12] There was relatively open discussion in the Soviet Union, including discussion about the appropriate path and mechanisms for economic growth under socialism.[13] The emphasis was on formulating a socialist path of development, guided by Marxist–Leninist ideological principles. Pioneers in mathematical economics, a key area for the subsequent development of the theory of economic planning, were very active. Under these conditions, it is not surprising that prior to the Stalinist crackdown of the late 1920s, Soviet planners and theoreticians pursued the theory of planning under conditions of social ownership. Possibly the most important practical work of this period was the development of **balances of the national economy**, forerunners of the input–output analysis of Wassily Leontief, and of **material balances**, the planning system later used in planned socialist economies. The development of the material balance approach remains a major (though simple) contribution of considerable practical importance.[14]

The material balances formulated by Soviet economists focused on the need to determine aggregate demands and supplies for basic industrial commodities and to bring them in balance without relying on market forces. More specifically, the theoretical underpinning of the material balance approach (input–output analysis) demonstrated that the productive relations of an economic system could be approximated by a system of simultaneous equations along the lines suggested by Barone.

A significant omission in the Soviet discussion of the 1920s was the matter of how enterprises might be guided at the micro level. Some Soviet economists even argued that the whole discussion of relative values (prices) under socialism was irrelevant because the **law of value** would not exist under socialism.

Although there is no necessary inconsistency between Marxian economics and mathematical economics, Stalin thought otherwise. This view ended open discussion in the Soviet Union, a situation that did not change until after Stalin's death in the early 1950s.

Economic Planning: A Paradigm for Planned Socialism

It is not surprising that the Soviet discussions of the 1920s focused on **national economic planning**. If market resource allocation is to be eliminated, some alternative arrangement must be used in its place.

There has been a tendency to associate national economic planning with socialism in both a political and an economic context. Actually, planning is consistent with a wide variety of organizational and ideological arrangements. Nevertheless, the idea that an economic system could be centrally planned stems in large part from the experience of the former Soviet Union. Even in the countries where most national planning was done—for example, the Soviet Union—the theory of planning was only a set of pragmatic principles; there was no "theory" comparable to the paradigm of the market economy. In this sense, most real-world national planning is a pragmatic exercise.

Planning is a term with differing connotations. Various authors have used different definitions, but there are basic elements in common. Gerald Sirkin writes, "Planning is an attempt, by centralizing the management of the allocation of resources sufficiently, to take into account social costs and social benefits which would be irrelevant to the calculus of the decentralized decision maker."[15] The emphasis here is the appropriate *level* of decision making and the social versus the private element in the decisions taken.

Abdul Qayum defines planning as "a systematic and integrated program covering a definite period of time, approved or sponsored by the state to bring about a rationalization of resources to achieve certain national targets using direct and indirect means with or without state ownership of resources."[16] Here we have a broader and more inclusive definition, which nonetheless includes elements of the previous definition—notably, the implication of centralization in the decision-making process.

Michael Todaro, writing in the context of development planning, defines planning as follows: "Economic planning may be described as the conscious effort of a central organization to influence, direct, and, in some cases even control changes in the principal economic variables (GDP, consumption, investment, savings, and the like) of a certain country or region over the course of time in accordance with a predetermined set of objectives."[17] Todaro further emphasizes that the key concepts are influence, direction, and control, and he defines an economic plan "as a specific set of quantitative targets to be reached in a given period of time."

The concept of plan formulation has been described succinctly by G. M. Heal, who writes that it can be viewed as "solving a constrained maximization problem."[18] Plan formulation involves doing the best one can to achieve objectives, albeit with limitations on available resources.

In contrast to the increasing specificity of these definitions, it is interesting to consider the definition from the Soviet period:

> Socialist planning is based upon strict scientific foundations; it demands the continuous generalization of the practical experience of the construction of Communism as well as the utilization of the accomplishments of science and

technology. To operate the economy according to plan means to foresee. Scientific foresight rests on the reconciliation of the objective economic laws of socialism. Plans carry in socialism the character of objectives. The planned direction of the economy requires that priorities be established and the main priorities of the economic plan are the branches of heavy industry, for they determine the development of all industrial branches as well as the economy as a whole.[19]

Although some of the elements of this Soviet definition (for example, the "objective economic laws of socialism") may be difficult to interpret, the definition contains some familiar concepts, such as the ability to foresee and the existence of objectives.

These definitions, though differing in specifics, differ relatively little in substance. They agree that a **national economic plan** is a mechanism to guide the activity of an economy through time toward the achievement of specified goals. The notion of *control* is fundamental to the concept of planning. Planning is more than forecasting. Although forecasting involves projections of future economic activity, planning is substantively different: The planner attempts to *alter* the economy's direction of movement and hence to change economic outcomes. It is convenient to categorize planning as either indicative or directive. In the case of **indicative planning**, targets are set in the hope of affecting economic outcomes by providing information external to the market; typically, individual firms receive no directives from planners. In the case of **directive planning**, however, targets are set by planners with the expectation of directly altering outcomes, because plan targets are legally binding on enterprises. A popular expression in the Soviet Union was that "the plan is law." Indicative planning will be discussed in more detail in a later chapter.

If the economic activity of a country is to be planned, three basic steps are required. First, a plan has to be constructed that specifies the goals or objectives to be achieved and the means for achieving those goals within a specified time frame. Second, there must be an organizational mechanism for executing the plan and, in particular, a means to guarantee that agents will in fact attempt to achieve plan goals. In short, there must be an incentive system to harmonize the behavior of agents with goal achievement. Finally, there must be a means to evaluate outcomes and, where they differ from targets, to ensure appropriate feedback to adjust the direction of economic activity.

The literature on national economic planning can be conveniently divided into two categories. First, there is the literature devoted to the planning methods actually utilized in the planned socialist economic systems. This literature describes material balance planning, the Soviet origins of which we have already discussed. Second, there is the literature on national economic planning models, which usually employ some optimizing procedure. Although the basic principles of planning are common to both, the planned socialist economies have utilized the material balance approach.

Material Balance Planning

The material balance approach to national economic planning has been widely used in the planned socialist economic systems. The central planning board (CPB) specifies a list of goods and services that are to be produced in the plan period. Once the

CPB determines the inputs (land, labor, capital, and intermediate products) needed to produce one unit of output (generally on the basis of historical input–output relationships), it can draw up a list of inputs necessary for meeting the specified output objectives. Obviously, the CPB would like to produce as much output as possible, but the availability of inputs limits how much can be produced given available technology.

The CPB must ensure a **balance** between outputs and inputs. For each factor input and intermediate good, the amount needed to produce output (the demand) must be equated with the amount available (the supply). If a balance between the two sides does not exist, administrative steps must be taken to reduce demand and/or expand supply. A balance must exist for each item, and there must also be an aggregate balance of demand and supply.

On the supply side, there are three main sources of inputs: production, stocks on hand, and imports. On the demand side, there are two main elements: **interindustry demand**, where the output of one industry (for example, coal) is used as the input for another industry (for example, steel), and **final demand**, which consists of output that will be invested, consumed by households, or exported. Thus adjustment is possible on both the demand and supply sides, and it is through administrative adjustment that demand and supply are balanced. This adjustment procedure is in basic contrast to market economies, where prices adjust to eliminate imbalances.

For any economy, maintaining an appropriate balance between the supplies and demands for all products would be an enormous task, a point emphasized by Hayek and Mises. In fact, the planned economies that use the material balance approach plan only the most important inputs and outputs, handling others on a more decentralized basis. Although this means that only a portion of total output is under the control of central planners, it is nevertheless sufficient to exert a major degree of influence over the economic outcomes.

Even in this more limited context, Barone's question—how to solve the equations—remains a problem. The problem of balancing supply and demand can be conveniently formalized in the following manner:

$$\text{Sources} \qquad\qquad \text{Uses}$$
$$X_1 + V_1 + M_1 = X_{11} + X_{12} + \cdots + X_{1n} + Y_1$$
$$X_2 + V_2 + M_2 = X_{21} + X_{22} + \cdots + X_{2n} + Y_2$$
$$\vdots$$
$$X_n + V_n + M_n = X_{n1} + X_{n2} + \cdots + X_{nn} + Y_n$$

where n items are included in the balance, and

X_i = planned output of commodity i
V_i = existing stocks of commodity i
M_i = planned imports of commodity i
X_{ij} = interindustry demand; that is, the amount of commodity i required to produce the planned amount of commodity j
Y_i = the final demand for commodity i; that is, for investment, household consumption, or export

Table 6.1 depicts a simplified material balance. Note that for each commodity a balance exists. In the case of steel, there are three sources on the supply side: production of 2,000 tons, no stocks on hand, and imports of 20 tons, for a total supply of 2,020 tons. On the demand side, there are six users of steel: the coal industry using 200 tons, the steel industry using 400 tons, the machinery industry using 1,000 tons, the consumer goods industry using 300 tons, exports of 100 tons, and domestic use of 20 tons, for a total demand of 2,020 tons. In this example, supply and demand are balanced at 2,020 tons.

Computational, administrative, and data-gathering limitations set an upper limit on the number of items that can be handled by material balance planning. Typically, the items that are of major significance to the achievement of state objectives are included in the plan. Items not included in the plan are planned at a lower level in the hierarchy. Plan authorities have discovered that the economy can be effectively controlled by manipulating a relatively small number of important inputs.

How does the CPB know how much of each input ($X_{ij}s$) will be necessary to produce a unit of output? The coefficient relating input to output is typically derived from the previous year's planning experience and adjusted somewhat (usually upward) to allow for investment and productivity improvements. Moreover, these coefficients are normally assumed to be constant over varying ranges of output—an assumption that causes problems when an industry is expanding and experiencing increasing (or decreasing) returns to scale. Gathering the information necessary to keep the coefficients up to date is a real problem. Most planned socialist systems rely on communications with enterprises, a process that is time-consuming and not necessarily reliable.

Material balance planning must deal with the interrelatedness of economic sectors. Suppose, for example, that a need arises to expand the output of a particular commodity or a previously unknown input shortage is discovered. If more steel is needed, more coal will also be needed for the production of the steel. But to produce more coal, more electricity is needed, and on, and on, and on. These so-called second-round effects reverberate throughout the economic system, making it very difficult to obtain a balance. To what degree can planners take second-round effects into account? In theory, a number of reformulations of the plan would be necessary. In practice, most planners allow for the initial or most serious repercussions, leaving the remainder to be absorbed as shocks by the system.

A plan that achieves a balance of supplies and demands is a **consistent** plan. The balancing of demands with supplies is the essence of material balance planning. But what about optimality? **Optimality** implies selecting the *best* plan of all those consistent plans with which it would be possible to achieve a balance. The best plan is the one that maximizes the planners' objectives. Although it is mathematically possible to elaborate the criteria for selecting an optimal plan from among a number of consistent plans, most planned socialist economies are able to prepare two or three variants at best, and there is no reason for the selected variants to be optimal.

When we examine Soviet planning in practice, we shall have a chance to consider further aspects of material balance planning. At this juncture, let us simply observe that material balance planning was a mechanism that worked, though at a

TABLE 6.1 Sample Material Balance

	Sources			Intermediate Inputs Required by				Final Uses	
	Output	Stocks	Imports	Coal Industry	Steel Industry	Machinery Industry	Consumer Goods Industry	Exports	Domestic Uses
Coal (tons)	1,000	10	0	100	500	50	50	100	210
Steel (tons)	2,000	0	20	200	400	1,000	300	100	20
Machinery (units)	100	5	5	20	40	10	20	10	10
Consumer goods (units)	400	10	20	0	0	0	100	100	230

Demonstration that a balance exists:

Sources of coal: 1,010 tons = uses of coal: 1,010 tons
Sources of steel: 2,020 tons = uses of steel: 2,020 tons
Sources of machinery: 110 units = uses of machinery: 110 units
Sources of consumer goods: 430 units = uses of consumer goods: 430 units

Source: Paul R. Gregory and Robert C. Stuart, *Soviet Economic Structure and Performance* (New York: Harper & Row, 1986), p. 169. Reprinted by permission of HarperCollins Publishers, Inc. Copyright © 1986 by Paul R. Gregory and Robert C. Stuart.

low level of efficiency. Furthermore, it enabled the planners to select key areas on which pressure could be applied to seek rapid expansion, regional economic growth, or whatever. On the other hand, it was cumbersome, and achieving a balance frequently required buffer or low-priority sectors (typically consumer goods) that could absorb planning mistakes.

Raymond Powell examined how economies that operate through material balance planning were able to survive and generate growth.[20] Powell pointed out that material balance planning does not prevent agents and principals in the economy (managers, ministers, and planners) from responding to nonprice scarcity indicators. Because there will inevitably be planning errors (imbalances between output targets and the inputs allocated to produce these targets), managers and planners will be confronted with various indicators of scarcity. Managers will recognize that some materials are harder to acquire than others or that some materials held by the enterprise are scarcer than others. Ministries will receive warnings from their enterprises concerning production shortfalls and material shortages and will have to assess the reliability of this information. On the basis of this **nonprice information**, resources will be reallocated within the firm according to perceived indicators of relative scarcity. Managers may allocate internal resources (personnel and trucks) to seek out and transport scarce materials. Ministries and central planners will reallocate materials to enterprises that, according to the scarcity indicators they receive, have relatively high marginal products. According to Powell, these natural responses to scarcity indicators introduce into material balance planning the rationality that allows it to function and survive.

The Input–Output Model

The **input–output model**[21] offers an alternative approach to administrative material balance planning. In theory, it gives planners an opportunity to determine balances quickly (through high-speed computers) and hence to explore alternative resource allocations.

An input–output table is a graphical presentation of the national accounts of an economy and illustrates the flows among the various sectors. The economy is divided into **sectors** of which there are two broad types—those that produce output (final output for consumption or intermediate output) and those that use final output (either as an intermediate input to further production or as a final consumption item). Sectors may correspond to industries, the number of which depends on the degree of disaggregation. Naturally, the greater the number of sectors, the more accurately the table reflects real economic interrelationships. At the same time, data and computational problems normally place severe limits on size. A simple input–output table is presented in Figure 6.1.

The sum total of goods and services produced (gross domestic product) is equal to the sum total of factor incomes (gross domestic income) used to produce this output. This concept is illustrated in the input–output table. The sum of all inputs used in, say, agriculture (sum of entries in the second column) is numerically equal to the total output of the agricultural sector (sum of entries in the second row). Each column

FIGURE 6.1   Schematic Input–Output Table

USING SECTOR	INTERMEDIATE USE			FINAL USE			TOTAL OUTPUTS
PRODUCING SECTOR	Steel	Agriculture	Other branches	Consumption	Exports	Other branches	
Steel							
Agriculture	INTERINDUSTRY, QUADRANT I			FINAL USE, QUADRANT II			
Other branches							
Land							
Labor	VALUE ADDED, QUADRANT III			DIRECT FACTOR PURCHASE, QUADRANT IV			
Capital							
TOTAL INPUTS							

in the input–output table illustrates both the source and the amount of input that will be used from each source in producing output. The inputs are of two types: **primary inputs** (labor, capital, and land) and **intermediate inputs** (steel, agricultural products). At the same time, each row shows how the output of the particular sector (agriculture in this case) is distributed among the various users (of agricultural products). In this table, there are two types of users: industries that use agricultural products as intermediate inputs for manufacturing, and final consumers who use agriculture products directly without further processing.

The input–output table is a simple yet highly useful picture of resource flows in an economic system. We should emphasize, however, that input–output economics relies on several crucial and limiting assumptions.

1. *Aggregation:* Obviously, the fewer the sectors, the easier it is to manipulate the table. The larger the number of branches, the more realistic the table, but the more difficult it is to compile and manipulate. On the other hand, generalized branches such as "agriculture" and "manufacturing" tell us little about the real working arrangements of an economy.

2. *Time frame:* The simple model presented here is *static* and does not, therefore, allow for change through time. The amount of labor required to produce a unit of steel is assumed not to change over time.
3. *Returns to scale:* We are assuming constant returns to scale. That is, the input–output ratios are the same, regardless of the *volume* of output being produced.

Our interest focuses largely on Quadrant I, for here are the **technical coefficients** that relate inputs to outputs. Specifically, this quadrant tells us how much of a particular input is required to produce a unit of a particular output. Clearly this technical relationship is crucial for specifying what will be produced and what inputs will be available for this production activity. How are these coefficients determined?

If there are i rows and j columns in the input–output matrix, then any cell can be described as a_{ij}, which represents the amount of i that is used to produce a unit of j as a proportion of the total output of j. These technical coefficients are defined in the following manner:

$$a_{ij} = \frac{x_{ij}}{X_j}$$

where

x_{ij} = the amount of input i used in industry j
X_j = the total output of industry j

What is the relationship between the input–output framework and material balance planning? First, knowledge of the matrix of technical coefficients is crucial to the development of a plan, whether that plan is constructed by a simple material balance technique or by more sophisticated methods. For example, if a plan is to be feasible, input availabilities must be sufficient to produce desired outputs. Clearly, knowledge of the technical coefficients can assist in making such a determination.

Second, if one knows the relationship between inputs and outputs, then with a given feasible objective, one in effect knows the relative worth (value) of different inputs in the production process. Thus a set of **relative prices** can be determined from the input–output model.

Third, the basic input–output model, even with a fair degree of aggregation, provides the planner with important information about the relationship between inputs and outputs.

Suppose the technical coefficients (a_{ij}) are known. How can the planner determine whether a particular objective is possible with available inputs? The input–output model says that for n sectors, the total production of each sector is the sum of intermediate demand and final demand. In notational form, this relationship can be expressed as follows:

$$\sum_{j=1}^{n} x_{ij} + Y_i = X_i \tag{6.1}$$

But we know something about the amount of i needed to produce a unit of j. Specifically, this relationship is

$$x_{ij} = a_{ij}X_j \tag{6.2}$$

Substituting equation 6.2 into equation 6.1, we derive the relationship

$$\sum_{j=1}^{n} a_{ij}X_j + Y_i = X_i \tag{6.3}$$

Rearranging terms yields

$$Y_i = X_i - \sum_{j=1}^{n} a_{ij}X_j \tag{6.4}$$

Equation 6.4 expresses the basic relationship among final demand, interindustry demand, and total production. This basic relationship can be more conveniently expressed in matrix notation as follows:

$$X = AX + Y \tag{6.5}$$

or by rearranging terms:

$$Y = (I - A)X \tag{6.6}$$

where

I = identity matrix
X = a vector of planned outputs
A = the matrix of technical coefficients
Y = a vector of final outputs

If the matrix of technical coefficients (A) is known to the planner, then the feasibility of a given vector of plan targets (X) can be readily determined by matrix multiplication. Clearly, even if the focus of the planner should change, knowing any two of the three components of this relationship makes it easier to determine the third component.

How useful is this model in practice? Although aggregation reduces the realism and the practical applicability of the model, it nevertheless remains useful as a method of checking the feasibility of alternative scenarios. The input–output model performs a number of functions: It provides a mathematical formulation of material balances, and it shows how supply–demand balances can be achieved mathematically via computers. Although problems that arise in the real-world collection and manipulation of data limit its applicability, the input–output model supplies the theoretical underpinnings of material balance planning.

Optimization and Economic Planning

Soviet material balance planning was the actual planning method used by the Soviets to allocate resources. As we have noted, Soviet material balance planning was a pragmatic method for planning an economy by administrative means. Its objective was to provide a rough balance between supplies and demands of a relatively limited number of key industrial commodities. Because of its administrative complexity, Soviet material balance planning aimed at achieving a balance; it did not aim at achieving the optimal balance.

The theory of economic planning focuses on the problem of achieving an *optimal* balance. It shows how, in theory, planners can plan for the economy to produce the optimal combinations of outputs, subject to the constraint of limited land, labor, and capital resources. No present-day economy actually allocates resources by using administrative planning techniques that select detailed optimal combinations of outputs. Although the solution to such a planning problem is evident in theory, in practice it is elusive.

The planning problem can be expressed in the following manner:

$$\text{Maximize } U = U(X_1, X_2, \ldots, X_n) \qquad i = 1, \ldots, n \qquad (6.7)$$

Here X_i are products that are produced subject to existing technology:

$$X_i = f(u_1, u_2, \ldots, u_m) \qquad (6.8)$$

where u_j are resources (land, labor, materials, and others) and are subject to

$$u_j \le b_j \qquad j = 1, \ldots, m \qquad (6.9)$$

where b_j represents resource availabilities, and u_j represents the total amount of resource j used by all producers. Moreover, resources are employed at zero or positive levels:

$$u_j \ge 0 \qquad (6.10)$$

The goal of planning is to achieve the maximal value of equation 6.7, which is termed the **objective function**. The objective function summarizes the planners' economic objectives and provides a precise relationship between the utility derived by society (U) and the output of goods and services (X_i) from which that social utility, or satisfaction, is derived. In turn, the magnitude of goods and services available is a function of resource availabilities (u_j) with given technology. Resources cannot be used beyond their available supplies (b_j), either in the aggregate or for any individual resource.

The critics of the Barone model explained why such optimal planning is virtually impossible in practice. First, an economy produces millions of distinct products and factor inputs. Even with powerful computers, it is not possible to solve the millions of simultaneous equations for the optimal combinations of inputs and outputs. To reduce the computational problem to manageable proportions, planners would have to work with aggregations of distinct commodities (such as tons of steel or square meters of textiles). Real-world economies do not operate with aggregated commodities. Factories require steel goods of specific grades and qualities. To go from a planning solution based on aggregate inputs or outputs to real production and distribution processes is an extremely complicated problem. Second, even if planners could gather the necessary information and make the complicated calculations, it is still not clear how to get enterprises actually to produce the planned commodities by using optimal combinations of inputs. This is the problem of creating an incentive scheme that encourages firms to implement the optimal production and distribution computed by planners. A related problem is the generation and processing of data. The information burden on planners is already excessive even if there is accurate and unbiased reporting by the enterprises. However, planners might find it difficult to elicit accurate information from enterprises, because their success or failure might hinge on these statistical reports.

A final problem with optimal planning is obtaining agreement on the objective function of society. How are planners to know what goods and services are more important than others? Presumably, planners would have some insights on this issue, but the more complex the economy became, the more difficult it might be to determine the relative social valuations of different goods and services. In a complex economy, planners must know whether industrial plastics are more important than stainless steel or ceramics, all of which might serve similar functions as substitutes.

Coordination: How Much Market? How Much Plan?

In our discussion of planning, two themes emerge. First, there is the matter of how much control the central planning board is to exercise over economic outcomes. Should all decisions be made from above by planners, or should there be some decentralization to lower levels? Second, there is the matter of actually solving the plan to achieve both consistency and optimality. In most planned socialist systems, the practical approaches to these problems involve simplification through limitation of the formal planning procedures to important outputs and inputs, and a downgrading of the optimality criterion. Furthermore, mistakes are typically absorbed by low-priority (buffer) sectors. Also, most real-world systems utilize intermediate arrangements that combine plan and market. For sectors viewed by the planners as crucial to the achievement of state objectives (for example, steel), the CPB plays an important role; for sectors viewed as substantially less important (for example, light industrial goods), the CPB may play a minor role. Most approach planning as only a partial means for the allocation of resources. The "priority principle" (that is, focusing on important sectors such as steel and chemicals) serves to limit the range of inputs and outputs planned at the center. Plan techniques are of the material balance type; they are substantially distant from the more sophisticated and theoretically elegant optimization models that we have described.

Critics of the planned socialist system argue that the complexities of the real world make it impossible for the CPB to handle its tasks, let alone to expect the individual firm to follow its directives. The supporters of planned socialism, on the other hand, have argued that choices in production and consumption are generally much simpler than neoclassical economic theory implies. These sorts of issues remain at the center of the debate over the relative merits of the plan versus the market.

The theory of planning stresses the **formulation of a plan**, consisting of a set of objectives and the means for achieving the objectives. However, plans are of little value unless they are implemented. Implementation calls for incentives that induce economic agents to achieve the goals planners have set. The record of the Soviet Union and other planned socialist economic systems shows that ensuring appropriate motivation is a serious problem. Managers frequently work with plan objectives that are poorly specified, if not contradictory. When managers are asked to **execute plans** with limited information under such conditions, a large element of informal (and often dysfunctional) decision making takes over where plan directives were intended to be dominant.

The Performance of Planned Socialism: Hypotheses

Chapter 5 put forth several hypotheses concerning the expected performance of capitalist economic systems in terms of the performance criteria of economic growth, efficiency, and income distribution. We shall now attempt to do the same for socialist economic systems.

Because we have no paradigm of socialist economic systems, the formulation of hypotheses is especially difficult. Moreover, it is difficult to formulate hypotheses independently of the performance of real-world socialism. We now know a great deal about the efficiency problems of planned socialism in practice. Although it does not constitute a scientific approach to hypotheses formulation, real-world experience is hard to ignore.

Income Distribution

The first hypothesis is obvious. Income should be more equally distributed under planned socialism than under capitalism. The state (society) owns capital and land, and the returns on these assets go to the state. It is conceivable, but not likely, that the state will distribute this nonlabor income *less* equitably than capitalist societies. Presumably, authorities in planned socialist economies attach considerable importance to the "fair" distribution of income. We therefore expect income to be distributed relatively equally in a planned socialist economy.

Efficiency

The critics of planned socialism believe that planned socialist economies have difficulty in efficiently allocating resources. Planners, they feel, would have great difficulty in processing information, constructing a plan, and motivating participants. Moreover, the planned socialist economy would not automatically generate relative prices that would enable participants to make good use of resources. These theoretical difficulties suggest the hypothesis that planned socialist economies operate at relatively low levels of efficiency. Planning techniques that aim at optimality still have limited real-world applicability, and planned socialist economies have had to use material balance planning procedures that are unlikely to place them on their production possibilities frontiers (see Figure 3.2). In fact, the aim of material balance planning is consistency, not optimality. Thus the hypothesis that the planned socialist economies do not perform well in terms of both dynamic and static efficiency appears to be a fairly safe one.

Economic Growth

In planned socialism, the state is able to exercise greater control over investment and savings rates than under capitalism. This is true because virtually all nonlabor income accrues to the state. One would therefore expect a higher savings rate under both forms of socialism, because the socialist state is likely to adopt rapid growth as a priority objective (the building of socialism).

In the planned socialist economies, rapid growth is promoted both by the high savings rate and by the planners' direction of resources into growth-maximizing pursuits. At first glance, therefore, it would appear that one should hypothesize a higher growth rate for the planned socialist economies. The complicating factor, however, is the hypothesized lower efficiency of the planned socialist economies. Thus we must again refrain from stating a strong hypothesis about the relative growth of planned socialism, an issue that must be investigated empirically.

Stability

We hypothesize that the planned socialist economies will be more stable than their capitalist counterparts. In making this statement, we do not deny that significant concealed instabilities (repressed inflation, underemployment) will be present in the planned socialist economies. We base our hypothesis of greater stability on the following considerations. First, investment spending will be subject to the control of planners and will probably be maintained at a fairly stable rate. Thus fluctuations in investment spending (a major source of instability in capitalist economies) will probably be small. Second, material balance planning will lead to an approximate balance of labor supplies and demands. Third, supplies and demands for consumer goods will be subject to a great deal of state control (planners set industrial wages and determine the output of consumer goods). Moreover, the state will be less subject to popular pressures to pursue inflationary monetary policies. Fourth, firms operating under pressure to meet output targets will provide workers with guaranteed jobs.

Summary

This chapter examines socialism with special emphasis on central planning as a mechanism to organize resource allocation. Although there is no single dominant paradigm of the socialist economy, socialism typically combines a strong state with public ownership and a set of policies designed to change economic outcomes that are typically associated with market capitalism. The socialist system focuses on an output mix distributed largely through labor incomes and socialized consumption to pursue an egalitarian distribution of benefits. The socialist system also maintains substantial state control over the nature and expansion of industry, especially economic growth.

In the absence of a theoretical paradigm of the socialist economy, emphasis is placed on the evolution of systems and especially on the view of Marx and Lenin that socialism is an inevitable outcome of social and economic progress. Much of the 20th century has witnessed a continuing debate about the feasibility of socialism as an economic system. Indeed, at the beginning of the century, Barone demonstrated the theoretical feasibility of socialist resource allocation, but he failed to provide a workable real-world scheme for such a system. Although a fundamental objective of socialism is equity based on an egalitarian distribution of income, much of the criticism rests on the inefficiency of resource allocation in an economy where markets do not exist.

Mises and Hayek argued that socialism would be inefficient if not unworkable, largely because of computational problems, evaluation difficulties, and fundamental incentive problems.

In the socialist economy where central planning is used, resources are allocated through a national economic plan. Typically the economy is organized in a hierarchical fashion using a central planning board (CPB). The CPB is responsible for preparing a plan document—basically a sources and uses statement—that directs producing enterprises as they allocate inputs to produce goods and services. Whereas input–output analysis is a theoretical basis of planning, most real-world planned socialist systems use a system of balances, or material balance planning. The former Soviet Union pioneered the development and implementation of the balance approach to planning.

In a sense, the theory of planning could serve as a theoretical paradigm for the socialist economy. Planning, however, is a general approach to the basic problem of rational resource allocation, emphasizing the development of an optimal plan that maximizes an objective function subject to a variety of constraints, especially resources. Although the theory of planning is a general paradigm, real-world applications have typically suffered from both information and incentive problems.

These latter difficulties have led to modifications of planning arrangements and to the use of mixed systems in real-world socialist applications. Thus an attempt is often made to combine the perceived equity of socialist arrangements with the efficiency of the market, the latter serving as a way to limit the burdens placed on planning agencies.

Key Terms

socialism

communism

dictatorship of the proletariat

socialist controversy

relative valuations

central planning board

balances of the national economy

material balances

law of value

national economic plan

indicative planning

directive planning

consistent plan

balance

optimality

input–output model

sectors

primary inputs

intermediate inputs

aggregation

technical coefficients   plan formulation
relative prices   plan execution
objective function

Notes

1. See A. C. Pigou, *Socialism Versus Capitalism* (New York: St. Martin's, 1960), Ch. 1. For a brief definition, see Benjamin N. Ward, *The Socialist Economy* (New York: Random House, 1967), Ch. 1; for a broader definition, see J. Wilczynski, *The Economics of Socialism* (London: Unwin Hyman, 1970), Ch. 1; for a contemporary summary, see Tom Bottomore, *The Socialist Economy: Theory and Practice* (New York: Harvester Wheatsheaf, 1990).

2. If the marginal utility of income is identical and declining for all individuals, then an equal distribution of income would maximize social benefit.

3. In the Marxian schema, capitalism is the engine that was to create the developed and industrialized economy; socialism would be concerned with providing an "equitable" distribution of the productive capacity developed under capitalism. Although socialism was not intended to be the mechanism for economic development, this is precisely the role in which it has been cast.

4. For a survey, see R. N. Carew Hunt, *The Theory and Practice of Communism* (Harmondsworth, England: Penguin Books, 1963), Chs. 6 and 15.

5. Lenin's views on this matter are elaborated in his *State and Revolution*, published in 1917.

6. This view, though largely discredited during the period of war communism in the Soviet Union, has remained influential in present-day Soviet attitudes toward industrial and agricultural management. This attitude is used to support the argument for technical rather than managerial training in large enterprises.

7. The important articles on this debate can be found in F. A. Hayek, ed., *Collectivist Economic Planning*, 6th ed. (London: Routledge and Kegan Paul, 1963).

8. See Ludwig von Mises, "Economic Calculation in Socialism," in Morris Bornstein, ed., *Comparative Economic Systems*, rev. ed. (Homewood, Ill.: Irwin, 1969), pp. 61–68.

9. The best source for the original article by Oskar Lange and related discussion is Benjamin Lippincott, ed., *On the Economic Theory of Socialism* (Minneapolis: University of Minnesota Press, 1938), reprinted by McGraw-Hill in 1964.

10. Pigou, *Socialism versus Capitalism*, Ch. 1.

11. Abram Bergson, *Essays in Normative Economics* (Cambridge, Mass.: Harvard University Press, 1966), Ch. 9; also see Abram Bergson, Market Socialism Revisited," *Journal of Political Economy* 75 (October 1967), 663–675; for contemporary views, see Don Lavoie, *Rivalry and Central Planning: The Socialist Calculation Debate Reconsidered* (New York: Cambridge University Press, 1985); Peter Murrell, "Did the Theory of Market Socialism Answer the Challenge of Ludwig von Mises? A Reinterpretation of the Socialist Controversy," *History of Political Economy* 15 (September 1981), 261–276.

12. See Leon Smolinski, "The Origins of Soviet Mathematical Economics," in Franz-Lothar Altmann, ed., *Jahrbuch der Wirtschaft Osteuropas* [Yearbook of East European Economics], Band 2 (Munich: Gunter Olzog Verlag, 1971), pp. 137–154.

13. The most famous Soviet growth model is by P. A. Feldman and is discussed in Evsey Domar, *Essays in the Theory of Economic Growth* (New York: Oxford University Press, 1957), pp. 233–261. The classic work on the Soviet industrialization debate is Alexander Erlich, *The Soviet Industrialization Debate, 1924–1928* (Cambridge, Mass.: Harvard University Press, 1962).

14. R. W. Davies and S. G. Wheatcroft, eds., *Materials for a Balance of the National Economy 1928/29* (Cambridge, England: Cambridge University Press, 1985).

15. Gerald Sirkin, *The Visible Hand: The Fundamentals of Economic Planning* (New York: McGraw-Hill, 1968), p. 45.

16. Abdul Qayum, *Techniques of National Economic Planning* (Bloomington: Indiana University Press, 1975), p. 4.

17. Michael P. Todaro, *Development Planning: Models and Methods* (Nairobi: Oxford University Press, 1971), p. 1.

18. G. M. Heal, *The Theory of Economic Planning* (New York: American Elsevier, 1973), p. 5.

19. *Political Economy: A Textbook*, 4th ed. (Berlin: Deitz, 1964), pp. 496 and 499.

20. Raymond Powell, "Plan Execution and the Workability of Soviet Planning," *Journal of Comparative Economics* 1 (March 1977), 51–76.

21. H. B. Chenery and P. G. Clark, *Interindustry Economics* (New York: Wiley, 1959); R. Dorfman, P. Samuelson, and R. Solow, *Linear Programming and Economic Analysis* (New York: McGraw-Hill, 1958); W. W. Leontief, *Input–Output Economics* (New York: Oxford University Press, 1966); Michael P. Todaro, *Development Planning: Models and Methods* (Nairobi: Oxford University Press, 1971); and Vladimir Treml, "Input–Output Analysis and Soviet Planning," in John Hardt *et al.*, eds., *Mathematics and Computers in Soviet Planning* (New Haven: Yale University Press, 1967); for a discussion in the development context, see E. Wayne Nafziger, *The Economics of Developing Countries*, 2nd ed. (Englewood Cliffs, N.J.: Prentice-Hall, 1990), Ch. 19.

Recommended Readings

Traditional Sources

Abram Bergson, "Socialist Economics" in Howard Ellis, ed., *A Survey of Contemporary Economics* (Philadelphia: Blakiston, 1948).

———, "Market Socialism Revisited," *Journal of Political Economy* 75, (October 1967), 655–673.

R. N. Carew-Hunt, *The Theory and Practice of Communism* (Harmondsworth, England: Penguin, 1963).

G. D. H. Cole, *Socialist Economics* (London: Gollancz, 1950).

Maurice Dobb, *Welfare Economics and the Economics of Socialism* (Cambridge, England: Cambridge University Press, 1969).

F. A. Hayek, ed., *Collectivist Economic Planning*, 6th ed. (London: Routledge and Kegan Paul, 1963).

Michael P. Todaro, *Development Planning: Models and Methods* (Nairobi: Oxford University Press, 1971).

Benjamin N. Ward, *The Socialist Economy* (New York: Random House, 1967).

The Socialist Economy

Pranab K. Bardhan and John E. Roemer, eds., *Market Socialism: The Current Debate* (New York: Oxford University Press, 1993).

Tom Bottomore, *The Socialist Economy: Theory and Practice* (New York: Harvester Wheatsheaf, 1990).

Bernard Crick, *Socialism* (Minneapolis: University of Minnesota Press, 1987).

Don Lavoie, *Rivalry and Central Planning: The Socialist Calculation Debate Reconsidered* (New York: Cambridge University Press, 1985).

Andrew Levine, *Arguing for Socialism: Theoretical Considerations* (London: Routledge and Kegan Paul, 1984).

Peter Murrell, "Did The Theory of Market Socialism Answer the Challenge of Ludwig von Mises? A Reinterpretation of the Socialist Controversy," *History of Political Economy* 15 (September 1984), 261–276.

———, "Incentives and Income Under Market Socialism," *Journal of Comparative Economics* 8 (September 1984), 261–276.

Alec Nove, *The Economics of Feasible Socialism* (Winchester, Mass.: Unwin Hyman, 1983).

S. Pejovich, *Socialism: Institutional, Philosophical, and Economic Issues* (Norwell, Mass.: Kluwer Academic Publishers, 1987).

James A. Yunker, *Socialism Revised and Modernized: The Case for Pragmatic Market Socialism* (New York: Praeger, 1992).

Economic Planning

John Bennett, *The Economic Theory of Central Planning* (Cambridge, Mass.: Blackwell, 1989).

Morris Bornstein, ed., *Economic Planning, East and West* (Cambridge, Mass.: Ballinger, 1975).

Roger A. Bowles and David K. Whynes, *Macroeconomic Planning* (London: Unwin Hyman, 1979).

Phillip J. Bryson, *Scarcity and Control in Socialism* (Lexington, Mass.: Heath, 1976).

Parkash Chander and Ashok Pavikh, "Theory and Practice of Decentralized Planning Procedures," *Journal of Economic Surveys* 4 (1990), 19–58.

Pawel H. Dembinski, *The Logic of The Planned Economy* (Oxford, England: Clarendon Press, 1991).

G. M. Heal, *The Theory of Economic Planning* (New York: American Elsevier, 1973).

Zoltan Kenessey, *The Process of Economic Planning* (New York: Columbia University Press, 1978).

Don Lavoie, *National Economic Planning: What Is Left?* (Cambridge, Mass.: Ballinger, 1985).

Abdul Qayum, *Techniques of National Economic Planning* (Bloomington: Indiana University Press, 1975).

Gerald Sirkin, *The Visible Hand: The Fundamentals of Economic Planning* (New York: McGraw-Hill, 1968).

Nicolas Spulber and Ira Horowitz, *Quantitative Economic Policy and Planning* (New York: Norton, 1976).

7

Theory of Market Socialism

Market socialism is, as the term suggests, a hybrid of market and state ownership. It is an economic system that combines social ownership of capital with market allocation. As such, it offers the potential of combining the "fairness" of socialism with the efficiency associated with market allocation. The state owns the means of production, and returns to capital accrue to society at large. Because resources are allocated primarily by markets, many of the problems of planned socialism—the administrative and computational burdens and the problem of valuing resources—appear to be avoided.

This chapter presents the theory of market socialism. Unlike the perfectly competitive model of capitalism, there is no single paradigm of market socialism. Instead, there are alternative visions of market socialism, one characterized by state ownership of the means of production, the other by worker ownership. Both visions rely on markets (or at least artificial markets) to do the job of resource allocation.

Whereas it is possible to study the actual workings of both market capitalism and planned socialism, the world has little experience with market socialism. This lack of real-world practice makes the theory of market socialism even more important. We must rely heavily on theory to understand the properties of this type of economic system. As this chapter shows, market socialism has both advantages and drawbacks. The major problems appear to be how to motivate participants to use resources efficiently and how to make markets work when private individuals do not own capital.

The appeal of market socialism is obvious. The widespread rejection of planned socialism in the late 1980s and 1990s has elevated market socialism to the status of the major alternative to capitalism. The reform leadership of the Soviet Union and Eastern Europe may ultimately find market socialism a more palatable solution than market capitalism insofar as it promises to avoid the more negative features of market capitalism. Put another way, the demise of communism in Eastern Europe does not mean the demise of socialist thought and especially democratic variants of socialism. The latter will continue to have appeal, especially in poor countries striving to achieve improved standards of living.

Market Socialism: Theoretical Foundations

The problems of optimal planning—computational difficulty and motivation—make market socialism appealing. Permitting the market to direct a number of resource-allocation decisions reduces the burden on the **central planning board** (CPB). Also, by allowing individual participants to respond to market incentives, market social-ism may offer greater inducements to combine resources efficiently at the local level.

Advocates of market socialism have had to answer two questions raised by Hayek and Mises (see Chapter 6). If the means of production are owned by society, what assurances are there that capital will be used efficiently? And will the social ownership of capital distort incentives or lead to perverse economic behavior?

The Lange Model

The most famous theoretical model of market socialism is the **trial-and-error model** proposed by the Polish economist Oskar Lange.[1] This model focuses on the use of a general equilibrium framework (emphasized in the writings of Barone, Pareto, and Walras), approaching a "solution" through a number of sequential stages (emphasized by Walras).

A number of economists (most notably H. D. Dickinson and Abba Lerner) con-tributed to the Lange model, and a number of variants of the model exist.[2] Further-more, the **Lange model** of market socialism differs from our definition of market socialism in that Lange envisioned only indirect usage of the market.

What are the essential features of the Lange-type market socialist model? The model posits three levels of decision making (see Figure 7.1). At the lowest level are firms and households; at the intermediate level, industrial authorities; and at the highest level, a CPB. The means of production, with the exception of labor, are state-owned. Consumer goods are allocated by the market.

The CPB would set the prices of producer goods. Producing firms would be informed of these prices and would be instructed to produce in accordance with two rules: Produce the level of output at which price is equal to marginal cost, and mini-mize the cost of production at that output. Households could make their own deci-sions about how much labor to supply.

Because the initial prices of producer goods would be arbitrarily set by the CPB, there is no reason to believe that as firms followed the rules (assuming that they did in fact follow the rules), the "right" amount of goods and services would be pro-duced and supplies and demands would be in balance. What would the planners do if there were an imbalance?

If there were an excess supply of a particular good, its price would be lowered by the CPB. If there were excess demand, its price would be raised by the CPB. Thus, in a sequential process, the CPB would adjust prices until they were at the "right" levels—that is, where supply and demand were balanced.

In addition to setting prices, the central planning board would also allocate the social dividend (rents and profits) earned from the use of productive resources owned by the state. This dividend could be distributed in the form of public services or investment, the latter decision made in conjunction with the intermediate indus-trial authorities. The state would have a substantial degree of power because it could determine both the magnitude and the direction of investment, though Lange argued that investment funds should be generally allocated to equalize marginal rates of re-turn in different applications. Considerable central control over the economic system

FIGURE 7.1   The Organization of Market Socialism in the Lange Framework

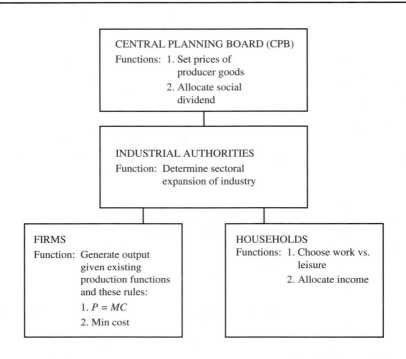

would be maintained by the CPB. At the same time, prices would be used for decision making to relieve the CPB of a substantial administrative task.

Let us examine some of the proposed advantages of the Lange model. Lange envisioned that with the means of production owned by the state, both the *rate* and the *direction* of economic activity would be determined in large part by the state. Thus the returns from and the influence of private ownership would be removed. Accordingly, the distribution of income would be substantially more even than under capitalism. Furthermore, the mix of output would be different, and insofar as the investment ratio would be a major determinant of the rate of economic growth, this rate too would be largely state-determined. Both these features of the Lange model (a more even distribution of income and state control over investment) are presumed advantages.

Lange argued that externalities could be better accounted for because the state could manipulate resource prices. Other economists—for example, Jan Tinbergen and Maurice Dobb—have argued that, in general, decisions made at higher levels rather than lower levels are likely to be "better" in terms of preventing undesirable environmental effects.[3] Lange further presumed that state control over savings and investment would reduce cyclical instability, a mainstay in the socialist critique of capitalism.

Real-world market systems depart from the perfectly competitive model. Simulation of the market, argued Lange, would utilize the positive aspects of the market while eliminating its negative characteristics. In this context, it is ironic that Lange said little about the problems that would arise when difficulties of entry, economies of scale, and changes in technology were present. These forces are crucial in determining the degree of competition in a capitalist economic system. Might not some of these problems arise in the real-world operation of a Lange-type model?

Critics of the Lange Model

The Lange model captured the fancy of many observers over the years, but it has not been without critics. Lange himself recognized that the many tasks assigned to the CPB could lead to a large bureaucracy, long considered a negative feature of socialism. The most outspoken critic on this score has been the Nobel laureate Friederick Hayek. Hayek has suggested that although the task set for the CPB might be manageable in theory, it would probably be unmanageable in practice.[4]

Abram Bergson and others have pointed to a key problem in the Lange model: that of ensuring appropriate managerial motivation.[5] How would he intermediate authorities, and especially enterprise managers, be motivated to follow Lange's rules of conduct even if they knew marginal costs? The problem of establishing a workable incentive structure has been a major theme in modern socialist economic systems.

Bergson also emphasized the possibility of monopolistic behavior in the Lange framework—if not at the enterprise level, then at the intermediate level. This problem and the matter of relating one level to another are substantially neglected in the original formulation of the Lange model.

Although the Lange model uses features of capitalism, it is also characterized by many elements normally associated with socialism. The scholarly literature, therefore, has tended to focus on whether the Lange model can operate in reality and, if so, how effectively. The Lange model has also sparked great interest because most existing socialist systems use a crude form of trial and error for the setting of prices, at least for consumer goods. Real-world reliance on the trial-and-error methods is important, for mathematical models of planning (and price formulation) have been of limited practical use in spite of their theoretical elegance.[6]

Market Socialism: The Cooperative Variant

A second variant of market socialism is the **cooperative economy** or **labor-managed economy** or, more specifically, the **producer cooperative**.[7] The interest in worker participation stems from both the theory of cooperative economic behavior elaborated in this section and the systems of worker management used in Yugoslavia, Western Europe, and now Eastern Europe.

The cooperative model of market socialism stems from the notion that people should participate in making the decisions that affect their well-being. Jaroslav Vanek, a major early advocate of the **participatory economy**, emphasizes this theme:

The quest of men to participate in the determination and decision-making of the activities in which they are personally and directly involved is one of the most important sociopolitical phenomena of our times. It is very likely to be the dominant force of social evolution in the last third of the twentieth century.[8]

Vanek uses five characteristics to identify the participatory economy:

1. Firms will be managed in participatory fashion by the people working in them.
2. Income sharing will prevail and is to be equitable—that is, "equal for labor of equal intensity and quality, and governed by a democratically agreed-upon income-distribution schedule assigning to each job its relative claim on total net income."[9]
3. Although the workers may enjoy the fruits of the operation, they do not own, and must therefore pay for, the use of productive resources.
4. The economy must always be a market economy. Economic planning may be used through indirect mechanisms, but "never through a direct order to a firm or group of firms."[10]
5. There is freedom of choice in employment.

In essence, resources are state-owned but are managed by the workers in the enterprises, whose objective is to create a maximal dividend per worker. Cooperative socialism belongs to the more general category of market socialism, because there is state ownership of the means of production but also an exchange of goods and services in the market without intervention by central planners. Producer goods would use market prices, as opposed to prices manipulated by the CPB in the Lange framework. The cooperative form of socialism has been viewed as an important and path-breaking addition to socialist thinking, especially by those who would identify with democratic socialism as a political system.

Theoretical analysis of the cooperative model dates from an article by Benjamin Ward published in 1958 and the subsequent early elaboration of the participatory economy by Vanek and thereafter by many authors.[11] Resources (with the exception of labor) are owned by the state and will be used by each firm, for which a fee will be paid to the state. Prices for both producer goods and consumer goods will be determined by supply and demand in the market. Enterprises will be managed by the workers (who may hire a professional manager responsible to them), who will attempt to maximize the dividend per worker (**net income per worker**) in the enterprise. With this objective, management must decide on input and output combinations.

In addition to levying a charge for the use of capital assets and for land, the state will administer the public sector of the economy and may levy taxes to finance cultural and industrial development. In this environment, how will the cooperative firm behave? Let us examine two cases: first, the short run, where there is a variable supply of labor but capital is fixed; second, the long run, where both labor and capital are variable.

The cooperative model assumes that the enterprise manager wishes to maximize net earnings per worker (Y/L) and that output (Q) is solely a function of the labor input (L) in the short run. The output can be sold on the market at a price (P) dictated by *market* forces. The firm must pay a fixed tax (T) on its capital. In the short-run variant, capital is fixed; so is the tax. Under these conditions, the firm will seek to maximize the following expression:

Maximize $$Y/L = \frac{PQ - T}{L} \tag{7.1}$$

where

Y/L = net income per worker
P = price of the product
Q = quantity produced
T = fixed tax levied on capital
L = labor input

Maximum net income per worker in equation 7.1 will be achieved when the amount of labor hired (L) is such that the value of the marginal product of the last worker hired is the same as the average net earnings per worker, or, in terms of the notation of equation 7.1, when the following balance is achieved:

$$P \cdot MP_L = \frac{(PQ - T)}{L} \tag{7.2}$$

where

MP_L = marginal product of labor

The logic of this solution is quite simple. If the enterprise can increase average net revenue by hiring another worker—that is, if the marginal product of the last worker hired is greater than average net revenue—then the worker should be hired, and average net revenue can be increased. The addition of workers should continue until the value of the marginal product of the last person hired and the average net revenue are the same. If the manager were to hire, at the margin, a worker the value of whose marginal product were less than the average net revenue per worker, then the net income of the remaining workers would fall.

In the *long run*, the cooperative must select its optimal capital stock (K), on which it will pay a rental charge (r) per unit of capital used. The firm now seeks to maximize its average net revenue as given by the following expression:

Maximize $$Y/L = \frac{PQ - rK}{L} \tag{7.3}$$

where

K = amount of capital
r = the charge per unit of capital

The maximal value of this expression (average net revenue per worker) will be achieved in a manner similar to that of the short-run case. As long as the value of the marginal product of capital ($P \cdot MP_K$) is greater than the rental rate (r) paid on capital, more capital should be hired and utilized until the return and the cost are equalized ($P \cdot MP_K = r$). This rule applies to the perfectly competitive capitalist firm and the Lange-type firm as well. The same rule as for equation 7.2 would apply for the hiring of labor, except that the charge for variable capital would have to be deducted as follows:

$$P \cdot MP_L = \frac{PQ - rK}{L} \tag{7.4}$$

These two cases, the short run and the long run, are both simple variants of the cooperative model. The short-run case is elaborated diagrammatically in Figure 7.2. Note that the model assumes that both product and factor markets are perfectly competitive and that there is no interference by the state.

The cooperative model works through product and factor markets. Households supply labor services as a consequence of maximizing household utility in the choice of work versus leisure. Labor supply schedules are determined in this way, as are demand schedules for consumer goods. Firms maximize net revenue per worker and in so doing are prepared to supply goods and services at various prices and at the same time purchase inputs at various prices.

FIGURE 7.2   The Cooperative Model

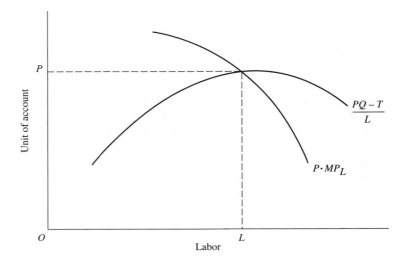

Explanation:

$$\frac{PQ - T}{L} = net \text{ receipts per worker}$$

$$P \cdot MP_L = \text{marginal value product of labor}$$

If the cooperative wishes to maximize the value of net receipts per worker, it should hire labor until the value of the marginal product of the last worker hired is the same as the net receipts per worker. In the diagram, the cooperative would hire *OL* labor, and each worker would receive *OP*.

There is a close relationship between the cooperative model and the competitive capitalist and Lange models. In essence, the cooperative model captures the efficiency features of both. In the Lange model, the firm follows two rules, equating price and marginal cost and minimizing average cost of production. In the cooperative model, these two rules are replaced by a single rule (in the short run represented by equation 7.2). In the case of the capitalist market economy, the firm follows the rule of equating marginal cost and marginal revenue, which in the case of perfect competition reduces to the Lange rule; so here too, the cooperative variant simply replaces this rule with equation 7.2.

There is now a considerable body of literature on the cooperative model and its variants. Many pertinent issues have been raised by the model's critics as well as by its admirers.

Criticism of the Cooperative Model

The cooperative model has been analyzed in detail by Benjamin Ward. Ward notes that the two key features of the model are "individual material self-interest as the dominant human motivation" and "the resort to markets as the means of allocating resources."[12] Ward devoted considerable attention to analyzing the response of the cooperative to various changes in capital charges, taxes, input prices, and product prices.[13] For the capitalist and the Lange-type firm, an increase in price induces an increase in output (that is, a positively sloped supply curve). Ward demonstrated that the cooperative supply curve may well be negatively sloped (that is, an increase in price generates a *decrease* in output), especially in the short run.[14] If true, this would certainly be a perverse and undesirable result, especially in an economy where resources are allocated by the market. Such a result might (though it would not necessarily) threaten both the existence and the stability of equilibrium in product markets.

Ward also argued that if two cooperatives producing an identical product use different technologies, there will be a misallocation of labor and capital that would not occur if the two were capitalist firms.[15] In the case of the capitalist firms, both would hire labor until the wage was equal to the value of the marginal product ($W = P \cdot MP_L$), for both would face the same market-determined wage (W) and hence would generate the same value of marginal product. In the case of the cooperative, however, unless the production functions are identical, the average net revenue per worker will differ between the two cooperatives. Although each cooperative equates average net revenue per worker with the marginal product of the last worker hired, overall output could be increased by moving workers to the cooperatives where the value of the marginal product is higher.

Ward also argued that the cooperative might be undesirable if it existed in a noncompetitive environment.[16] Specifically, he contends that the monopolistic cooperative would be less efficient than either its competitive cooperative twin or its monopolistic capitalist twin. The monopolistic cooperative would hire less labor, produce less output, and charge a higher price than either the competitive cooperative or the monopolistic capitalist firm.

Critics of the Lange model raised the issue of how to ensure appropriate managerial motivation. To the extent that the cooperative utilizes hired professional management, the problem of how to motivate and regulate managers will exist. Ward noted that in some cases the cooperative would have the incentive to expand, although in the absence of private property holding, it is not clear who the entrepreneur would be.[17] It is possible that the state would play an important role here because it would control some of the investment funds.

Advantages of the Cooperative Model

Strong support for the cooperative model comes from Jaroslav Vanek, who argues that the participatory economy is an element of social evolution that will be especially important in future years.[18] In addition to prescribing the participatory economy for present-day economies, Vanek argues that it is also the best alternative for developing economies.

Vanek does not agree with Ward's criticisms. He argues that if two cooperative firms have access to identical technology, and if there is free entry and exit, the input–output decisions of the cooperatives will be identical to those of two capitalist firms operating under the same conditions.[19] Moreover, Vanek argues, the result will be much more desirable socially, because in the capitalist case the workers are rewarded according to the value of the marginal products, whereas under the cooperative case, workers are rewarded according to the decision of the collective, which they themselves control.

Vanek also maintains that under certain likely cases, the supply curve of the cooperative firm will not be negatively sloped as Ward suggests. Vanek shows that if the cooperative is a multiproduct firm, or if it faces an external constraint (for example, a limited supply of labor), the firm's supply curve will be positively sloped.

Vanek argues that the imperfectly competitive cooperative firm will be superior to the imperfectly competitive capitalist firm because it will have no incentive to grow extremely large and hence to dominate a particular market. Further, the cooperative will have no incentive to act in a socially wasteful manner—to create artificial demand for a product through advertising. Finally, Vanek maintains that both the demand for investment and the supply of savings will tend to be greater in the cooperative than in the competitive capitalist environment.

Many of the issues surrounding the comparative performance of cooperative and capitalist firms seem highly abstract and theoretical. They are, however, of basic importance to the efficiency of each system. The response of the cooperative firm to market signals determines the extent to which it can meet consumer goals and, in the long run, the extent to which an appropriate industrial structure is established in line with long-term development goals and aspirations.

Many of the supporters of the cooperative model, especially Vanek, argue that beyond these specific performance characteristics, the crucial features of the cooperative would be its "special dimensions." Among the most important is elimination of the capitalist dichotomy between management and labor. It is also argued that there would be greater social justice in the distribution of rewards.[20]

The Participatory Economy in the Twenty-First Century

The pioneering work of Benjamin Ward in the late 1950s and the subsequent elaboration by Jaroslav Vanek in the late 1960s spawned a large and ever-growing body of literature devoted to the broad concepts of labor management and, more specifically, producer cooperatives as a means to organize production in an economy. A recent discussion of this literature by John Bonin, Derek Jones, and Louis Putterman provides an excellent basis for understanding the state of the cooperative idea in the 1990s.[21]

The body of literature on cooperatives is large but diverse and mainly theoretical; there has been little empirical verification. This is partly because the practical use of cooperatives in real-world economies has been limited, though it has grown in recent years. The lack of empirical work on cooperatives reflects the absence of appropriate data for evaluation purposes; it also reflects the nature of the theoretical models, which tend to be highly abstract, and the great deal of diversity among cooperatives in real-world economies.

In addition, many of the outcomes of the earlier simple models are evidently not robust under more realistic circumstances. For example, contemporary research demonstrates that the existence of a negatively sloped supply curve depends heavily on the original assumptions of early models and is not generally found in contemporary specifications where "the focus shifts to the membership as the constituent decision-making body or when reasonable labor supply considerations are added."[22] Moreover, limited empirical evidence seems to support the contemporary view.

Contemporary empirical evidence on issues related to worker effort and productivity in producer cooperatives does not provide clear-cut answers. Bonin *et al.*, in their survey of this empirical literature, found that participation variables are important when explaining differences in outcomes. There seems to be a positive relationship between profit sharing and productivity; however, isolating the impact of other types of participation has proved difficult.

Finally, the literature places considerable emphasis on the potential problems of self-financing of producer cooperatives, on the assumption that members will distribute internal funds to themselves rather than expand the capital stock in the absence of appropriate property rights. On the basis of existing empirical evidence, Bonin *et al.* conclude that no econometric evidence supports this proposition.[23]

Despite the relatively few producer cooperatives in contemporary market economies, their existence provides growing evidence that presents them much more favorably than the early and simple models of cooperative behavior. Furthermore, future empirical research will undoubtedly reveal at least partial answers to yet-unanswered questions and will shed more light on the evolutionary aspects of cooperatives in market economies.

We must consider that aspects of the participatory economy are encountered in most market economies. Many major U.S. corporations have employee stock options (ESOP) plans whereby, over time, employees come to own considerable shares of the company. The second-largest airline in the United States (United Airlines) is employee-owned. In Germany, worker representatives occupy positions on boards of directors. These "experiments" may provide insight into how a participatory economy will work.

Feasible Socialism in the Twenty-First Century

Some might argue that the demise of the major planned socialist economic systems of the former Soviet Union and Eastern Europe significantly reduces the potential appeal of socialism as an economic system. There is, however, interest in the reasons for the demise of these systems and in the possibility of defining a socialist system that not only eliminates these reasons but sustains the basic tenets of socialism—most notably an egalitarian distribution of benefits. As a result, the discussion of **feasible socialism** and the socialist economy will continue into the twenty-first century.

In a detailed argument, James Yunker presents what he terms a case for "pragmatic socialism" based on public ownership and a bureau of public ownership "to enforce upon the executives who manage the publicly owned business corporations a strong profit motivation."[24] This board will also oversee disbursement of the social dividend in an egalitarian manner. In addition to dealing with issues such as transition, Yunker devotes substantial attention to such critical areas as investment, growth, and entepreneurship in the socialist economy.

In another contribution to feasible market socialism, Pranab Bardhan and John Roemer argue that the socialist economies that failed were characterized by public or state ownership, noncompetitive and nondemocratic politics, and command/administrative allocation of resources and commodities.[25] They maintain that "competitive socialism" could be envisioned through the negation of the latter two characteristics of the failed economies. Bardhan and Roemer focus on competitive markets but include an important role for the state, a system using banks for insider monitoring to solve the traditional problems of enterprise decision making, and the development of political accountability for a state that supervises the banking structure.

In a further discussion of market socialism, Andrei Schleifer and Robert W. Vishny argue that the Bardhan–Roemer approach would not work primarily because of the characterization of the state.[26] Specifically, Schleifer and Vishny argue that under market socialism, the state's objectives will dominate those of firms, that the state will not necessarily pursue economic efficiency, and that government's pursuit of its objectives will be less destructive under capitalism than under socialism.

These ongoing discussions are meant neither to characterize market socialism in any detail nor to assess its positive and negative features. Rather, these discussions send several important signals. First, as previously emphasized, the demise of socialist economic systems in the former Soviet Union and the countries of Eastern Europe does not end discussions about socialism in general and market socialism in particular. Second, much of the discussion here focuses on the nature of the state in a socialist system and on how agency and incentive problems can be resolved.

Contemporary organization theory provides useful insights into these problems. Finally, the appeal of a more egalitarian distribution of income remains, yet limited attention is given to the noneconomic aspects of socialism that many argue are critical to understanding the nature of socialism.

The Performance of Market Socialism: Hypotheses

With the exception of Yugoslavia, a small country beset by insurmountable political and ethnic problems, we lack real-world experience with market socialism of either the Lange or the worker-managed type. Consequently, we do not have the advantage of long historical experience to test hypotheses concerning the economic performance of market socialism. The following paragraphs represent our best analytical—though somewhat speculative—efforts.

Income Distribution

The easiest hypothesis to formulate concerns the distribution of income under market socialism. Inasmuch as capital continues to belong to society, we would expect income to be distributed more nearly equally under market socialism than under capitalism. Even in the case of worker-managed enterprises, the state must be paid a fee for the use of capital, and the state would presumably divide such income among the population on a fairly equal basis. Some reservations must be expressed, however. As critics have pointed out, prosperous worker-managed firms might protect extraordinarily high earnings by excluding outsiders. This type of behavior could lead to significant inequality in wage income.

Economic Growth

Proponents of market socialism claim that market socialism would yield relatively high rates of growth, primarily because society would plow earnings from capital back into the economy. This conclusion, however, assumes that the socialist state would not be pressured into putting the "social dividend" into current consumption in the form of subsidies and social services. Such pressure would be particularly strong in the case of democratically elected socialist governments. For these reasons, we believe it risky to presume that market socialism will yield higher investment rates—and hence higher rates of growth—than the capitalist model. The outcome is far from certain.

Efficiency

The theory of market socialism does not yield strong propositions concerning economic efficiency. Arguing that market socialism can indeed be more efficient than capitalism, its advocates cite the lack of monopoly, the greater attention to externalities, and individual participation in decision making. Its critics, however, mount equally convincing arguments about the inefficiency of market socialism: motivation problems, perverse supply curves, and the difficulty of finding equilibrium prices. Accordingly, we cannot venture any hypotheses about the relative efficiency of market socialism.

Stability

Advocates of market socialism make the following case for greater economic stability: The state will have greater control over the investment rate, so sharp fluctuations in investment can be avoided. Counterarguments exist, however. If market socialist economies (we are using the Lange model) have trouble adjusting prices to equilibrium, macroeconomic instabilities associated with nonequilibrium prices might be experienced. Moreover, democratically elected officials will be under strong pressure to pursue "popular" economic policies (the political business cycle), while feeling less pressure from market forces to tighten the reins on economic policy. Again, we cannot propose any strong hypotheses concerning the relative stability of market socialism.

Market socialism has sufficient appeal to make it a serious model for discussion—Western Europe has experimented with programs of partial worker management, and major corporations in the United States now have employees as their majority shareholders. Market socialism has appeal for Eastern Europe because it combines the elements of market and socialist economies.

Summary

Market socialism has significant appeal because it promises to combine attractive features of capitalism (especially the efficiency of the market mechanism) with similarly attractive features of socialism (a more equitable distribution of income). Although there is no generally accepted paradigm of the market socialist economy, the positive and negative features of market socialism (the socialist controversy in Chapter 6), along with specific variants suggested by various authors, present a picture of the market socialist idea that culminates in the contemporary discussion of the "economics of feasible socialism."

Probably the most famous model of market socialism is that suggested many years ago by the Polish economist Oskar Lange. The Lange model combines public ownership with a "trial-and-error" approach to establishing equilibrium and determining output, because individual enterprises are expected to follow market-type rules, specifically by producing where price and marginal cost are equal and by minimizing cost. Households supply labor services, and the state distributes the social dividend. Sectoral expansion is also dictated by the state.

Although the original model developed by Lange was simple, its considerable appeal focuses on a number of key issues, especially those raised in the socialist controversy. Critics, however, have generally viewed the model as computationally inefficient, lacking appropriate and necessary managerial motivation, and possibly subject to monopoly problems.

The general idea of a participatory economy is very appealing, especially in less-developed countries. Unlike other suggested models of the socialist economy, the contemporary theory of the cooperative has much theoretical rigor, and yet its real-world application is quite limited.

Although the specifics of different variants of the cooperative idea vary greatly, the basic construct typically involves worker management in enterprise decision making. Workers share profits and pay a rental charge for the use of productive assets that society at large owns. The cooperative differs fundamentally from the typical capitalist firm, which maximizes profits (or some variant of profits). The cooperative, however, maximizes profit per worker, which is usually termed a dividend.

Advocates of the cooperative model argue that such a system would be fair, efficient, and stable and would offer the population a number of less-quantifiable yet potentially attractive features, such as the possibility of substantial participation in economic decision making.

Critics of the cooperative model maintain that such an economic system would be unstable, offer no potential efficiency advantages, and suffer from problems of **managerial motivation**.

Although there are relatively small numbers of producer cooperatives in contemporary market economies, the significant body of theory combined with recent, if limited, empirical research suggests that some of the negative features of the early cooperative models (the negatively sloped supply curve, difficulties of generating capital internally, and the like) are not evident in models with differing and reasonable specifications; such negative features have not been confirmed by empirical evidence.

Key Terms

market socialism	labor-managed economy	short-term equilibrium
central planning board	producer cooperative	long-term equilibrium
Lange model	participatory economy	feasible socialism
trial-and-error model	net income per worker	managerial motivation
cooperative economy		

Notes

1. Benjamin Lippincott, ed., *On the Economic Theory of Socialism* (Minneapolis: University of Minnesota Press, 1938).
2. See, for example, F. M. Taylor, "The Guidance of Production in a Socialist State," *American Economic Review* 19 (March 1929); reprinted in Lippincott, *On the Economic Theory of Socialism*, pp. 39–54; H. D. Dickinson, *Economics of Socialism* (London: Oxford University Press, 1939); and Abba P. Lerner, *The Economics of Control* (New York: Macmillan, 1944).

3. See the discussion in Maurice Dobb, *The Welfare Economics and the Economics of Social-ism* (Cambridge, England: Cambridge University Press, 1969), p. 133 and footnotes thereto.

4. F. A. Hayek, "Socialist Calculation: The Competitive Solution," *Economica* 7 (May 1940), 125–149; reprinted in Bornstein, *Comparative Economic Systems*, pp. 77–97.

5. Abram Bergson, *Essays in Normative Economics* (Cambridge, Mass.: Harvard University Press, 1966), Ch. 9.

6. The sophisticated works of Soviet mathematical economists have been brought to Western readers by Zauberman, Ellman, and others. See Alfred Zauberman, *The Mathematical Revolution in Soviet Economics* (London: Oxford University Press, 1975); Michael Ellman, *Soviet Planning Today* (Cambridge, England: Cambridge University Press, 1971); Martin Cave, Alastair McAuley, and Judith Thornton, eds., *New Terms in Soviet Economics* (Armonk, N.Y.: M. E. Sharpe, 1982).

7. For a recent discussion of the state of the literature on producer cooperatives, see John P. Bonin, Derek C. Jones, and Louis Putterman, "Theoretical and Empirical Studies of Producer Cooperatives: Will the Twain Ever Meet?" *Journal of Economic Literature* 31 (September 1993), 1290–1320.

8. Jaroslav Vanek, *The Participatory Economy* (Ithaca, N.Y.: Cornell University Press, 1971), p. 1.

9. *Ibid.*, p. 9.

10. *Ibid.*, p. 11.

11. For Ward's original contribution, see Benjamin Ward, "The Firm in Illyria: Market Syndicalism," *American Economic Review* 48 (September 1958), 566–589. See also E. Domar, "The Soviet Collective Farm as a Producer Cooperative," *American Economic Review* 56 (September 1966), 734–757; and Walter Y. Oi and Elizabeth M. Clayton, "A Peasant's View of a Soviet Collective Farm," *American Economic Review* 58 (March 1968), 37–59. For a general treatment of Vanek's argument, see Vanek, *The Participatory Economy*; and for a detailed analysis, see Jaroslav Vanek, *The General Theory of Labor-Managed Market Economies* (Ithaca, N.Y.: Cornell University Press, 1970). Since these early contributions, the literature has expanded rapidly. For a survey, see John P. Bonin and Louis Putterman, *Economics of Cooperation and the Labor-Managed Economy* (New York: Harwood Academic Publishers, 1987); see also John P. Bonin, Derek C. Jones, and Louis Putterman, "Theoretical and Empirical Studies."

12. Ward, *The Socialist Economy*, p. 183.

13. *Ibid.*, Chs. 8–10.

14. *Ibid.*, pp. 191–192.

15. *Ibid.*, pp. 184 ff.

16. *Ibid.*, pp. 201 ff.

17. *Ibid.*, Ch. 9.

18. For the general treatment, see Vanek, *The Participatory Economy*.

19. See Vanek, *The General Theory*.

20. For background on participatory socialism, see Ellen Turkish Comisso, *Worker's Control Under Plan and Market* (New Haven: Yale University Press, 1979), Chs. 1 and 2; Hans Dieter Seibel and Ukandi G. Damachi, *Self-Management in Yugoslavia and the Third World* (New York: St. Martin's, 1982); Howard M. Wachtel, *Workers' Management and Workers' Wages in Yugoslavia* (Ithaca, N.Y.: Cornell University Press, 1973), Ch. 2.

21. John P. Bonin, Derek C. Jones, and Louis Putterman, "Theoretical and Empirical Studies."

22. *Ibid.*, 1299.

23. *Ibid.*, 1316.

24. James A. Yunker, *Socialism Revised and Modernized: The Case for Pragmatic Market Socialism* (New York: Praeger, 1992), p. 38.

25. Pranab Bardhan and John E. Roemer, "Market Socialism: A Case for Rejuvenation," *Journal of Economic Perspectives* 6 (Summer 1992), 101–116.

26. Andrei Schleifer and Robert U. Vishny, "The Politics of Market Socialism," *Journal of Economic Perspectives* 8 (Spring 1994), 165–176; for the Bardhan/Roemer reply, see Pranab Bardhan and John Roemer, "On the Workability of Market Socialism," *Journal of Economic Perspectives* 8 (Spring 1994), 177–181.

Recommended Readings

Traditional Sources

H. D. Dickinson, *The Economics of Socialism* (London: Oxford University Press, 1938).

Abba P. Lerner, *The Economics of Control* (New York: Macmillan, 1944).

Benjamin Lippincott, ed., *On The Economic Theory of Socialism* (New York: McGraw-Hill, 1964).

Jaroslav Vanek, *The General Theory of Labor-Managed Economies* (Ithaca, N.Y.: Cornell University Press, 1970).

———, *The Labor-Managed Economy* (Ithaca, N.Y.: Cornell University Press, 1971).

———, *The Participatory Economy* (Ithaca, N.Y.: Cornell University Press, 1971).

Benjamin N. Ward, "The Firm in Illyria: Market Syndicalism," *American Economic Review* 48 (September 1958), 566–589.

———, *The Socialist Economy* (New York: Random House, 1967).

The Lange Model

Abram Bergson, "Market Socialism Revisited," *Journal of Political Economy* 75 (October 1967), 663–675.

Benjamin Lippincott, ed., *On The Economic Theory of Socialism* (New York: McGraw-Hill, 1964).

Market Socialism: The Labor-Managed Variant

Katrina V. Berman, "An Empirical Test of the Theory of the Labor-Managed Firm," *Journal of Comparative Economics* 13 (June 1989), 281–300.

John P. Bonin, Derek C. Jones, and Louis Putterman, "Theoretical and Empirical Studies of Producer Cooperatives: Will the Twain Ever Meet?" *Journal of Economic Literature* 31 (September 1993), 1290–1320.

John P. Bonin and Louis Putterman, *Economics of Cooperation and the Labor-Managed Economy* (New York: Harwood Academic Publishers, 1987).

Saul Estrin, "Some Reflections on Self-Management, Social Choice and Reform in Eastern Europe," *Journal of Comparative Economics* 15 (June 1991), 349–361.

Derek C. Jones and Jan Svenjar, eds., *Advances in the Economic Analysis of Participatory and Labor Managed Firms*, Vols. 1–4 (Greenwich: JAI Press, various years).

Kathryn Nantz, "The Labor-Managed Firm Under Imperfect Monitoring: Employment and Work Effort Responses," *Journal of Comparative Economics* 14 (March 1990), 33–50.

Hugh Neary, "The Comparative Statics of the Ward–Domar Labor-Managed Firm: A Profit–Function Approach," *Journal of Comparative Economics* 12 (June 1988), 159–181.

V. Rus and R. Russell, eds., *International Handbook of Participation in Organization* (New York: Oxford University Press, 1989).

Fernando B. Saldanha, "Fixprice Analysis of Labor-Managed Economies," *Journal of Comparative Economics* 13 (June 1989), 227–253.

Feasible Socialism: Contemporary Views

Pranab Bardhan and John E. Roemer, "Market Socialism: A Case for Rejuvenation," *Journal of Economic Perspectives* 6 (Summer 1992), 101–116.

———, eds., *Market Socialism: The Current Debate* (New York: Oxford University Press, 1993).

———, "On the Workability of Market Socialism," *Journal of Economic Perspectives* 8 (Spring 1994), 177–181.

Alec Nove, *The Economics of Feasible Socialism* (Winchester, Mass.: Unwin Hyman, 1983).

S. Pejovich, *Socialism: Institutional, Philosophical and Economic Issues* (Norwell, Mass.: Kluwer Academic Publishers, 1987).

Andrei Schleifer and Robert W. Vishny, "The Politics of Market Socialism," *Journal of Economic Perspectives* 8 (Spring 1994), 165–176.

James A. Yunker, *Socialism Revised and Modernized: The Case for Pragmatic Market Socialism* (New York: Praeger, 1992).

PART III

Economic Systems in Practice

8

The American Economy: Market Capitalism

Now that we have outlined the basic models of market capitalism, planned socialism, and market socialism, it is time to examine the real-world variants of these different economic systems. We look at several variants of market capitalism and begin with the United States.

As the world's most advanced industrial nation, the United States serves as the most important representative of market capitalism. It generates the world's highest per capita income and the largest total output. Our study of the American economy begins with the structure and operation of product and factor markets and changes that occur over time.

Next, we turn to the economic role of government and why the public sector generates considerable controversy. We examine public goods, regulation, and antitrust policy. Finally, we examine stabilization and policies with regard to the distribution of income.

Why study the American economy in a book on comparative economic systems? For many readers, the American economy is immediately familiar because it is the system within which we work. The American economy is a large and wealthy economy that has enjoyed considerable success. Although it is a mixed system, it relies predominantly on markets with less government intervention than in many other capitalist economies. It is also the most technologically advanced economy, and many experiments, such as deregulation, originated in the United States.

Resource Allocation in the Private Sector

The American economy can be divided into two major sections: the **private sector** and the **public sector**. How important is the role of government (the public sector) in the American economy? The role of government in the United States is more limited than in most other advanced industrialized economies. Even in the case of natural monopolies, the U.S. government plays a limited role and has no apparatus for economic planning. Most resource-allocation decisions are made in the private sector, though in areas such as public utilities, government regulation is active.

The term *private sector* refers to the business sector in which private ownership prevails and government regulation or intervention is limited. According to estimates developed by Milton Friedman, roughly 25% of economic activity in the United States in 1939 was government-operated or government-supervised, leaving roughly

75% conducted in the private sector.[1] Frederic Scherer estimates that in 1965, the government-regulated sector accounted for 11% of GNP, and the government-operated sector accounted for another 12%. The resulting total of 23% is close to that for 1939.[2] Clifford Winston estimates that in 1977, 17% of the U.S. GNP "was produced by fully regulated industries," whereas in 1988, this share had fallen to 6.6%.[3] The U.S. private sector today amounts to for well over 80% of the American economy.

Figure 2.4 uses a circular-flow diagram to represent the organization of a typical market capitalist economy consisting of three main actors—firms, households, and the government—that interact through product and factor markets. In the factor market, households provide factor inputs and earn income, and firms respond to household demand, producing goods and services that are paid for with household incomes in the product markets. Government intervenes in these markets for a variety of reasons. Markets provide through prices the information used to guide decision making. Organizational arrangements are critical to understanding outcomes. It is therefore important to examine closely the major actors in the U.S. market economy.

Business Organization

Business enterprises in the United States are divided into three categories on the basis of legal organization: sole proprietorships, partnerships, and corporations.

The **sole proprietorship** is owned by one individual, who makes all the business decisions and absorbs the profits (or losses) that the business earns. A **partnership** is owned by two or more partners, who make all the business decisions and share in the profits and losses. The major advantages of these forms of business organization are their relative simplicity (the proprietorship is simpler than the partnership) and that, under existing tax law, their profits are taxed only once. They have two major disadvantages: (1) the owners are personally liable for the debts of the business, and (2) the ability to raise capital is limited, dependent as it is on the owners' ability to borrow against personal assets.

The third form of business organization, the **corporation**, is owned by its stockholders and has authorization to act as a legal person. A board of directors, elected by the stockholders, appoints management to run the corporation. The advantages of the corporation are (1) that its owners (the stockholders) are not personally liable for the debts of the corporation (limited liability), (2) that its management can be changed if necessary, and (3) that it has more options for raising capital (through the sale of bonds and additional stock). A major disadvantage of the U.S. corporation is that its income is taxed a second time when corporate earnings are distributed to stockholders as dividends. Double taxation gives American corporations an incentive to reinvest earnings rather than pay out dividends.

These three forms of business organization are supplemented in the United States by innovative legal arrangements (such as limited liability partnerships) designed to circumvent a variety of problems, yet the threefold classification remains valid. Figure 8.1 and Table 8.1 show the distribution of U.S. enterprises according to the legal form of business organization. Although sole proprietorships account for most American businesses, they account for only a small percentage of business

FIGURE 8.1   Proprietorships, Partnerships, and Corporations, 1994

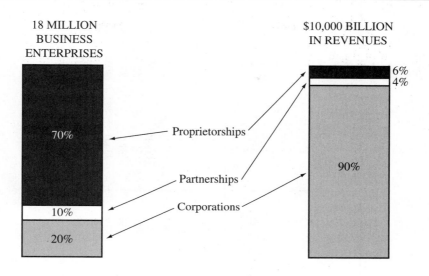

18 MILLION
BUSINESS
ENTERPRISES

$10,000 BILLION
IN REVENUES

6%
4%

70%

Proprietorships

90%

Partnerships

10%

Corporations

20%

Source: Statistical Abstract of the United States.

revenues. Corporations, though few in number (about 20 percent of the total), account for 90 percent of business revenues. The larger size of the corporation is explained by limited liability and the greater ability of the corporation to raise capital. The sole proprietorship is important in agriculture, retail trade, and services; the partnership is important in finance, insurance, real estate, and services; the corporation is the dominant form in other sectors.

The Product Market

Resource-allocation arrangements depend on the degree of **market power** in different product markets. There is no accurate measure of market power, but the most frequently used measure is the **concentration ratio**. The concentration ratio gives the percentage of industry sales accounted for by the largest 4, 8, or 20 firms. For example, a 4-firm concentration ratio of 80% means that the 4 largest firms account for 80% of industry sales. An industry with a very low concentration ratio is generally a "competitive" industry; one with a very high concentration ratio is an "oligopoly" or near-monopoly. The comparison is flawed for various reasons: the difficulties of defining industry boundaries; the availability of competitive substitutes; the fact that some firms operate in regional and local markets, others in national and international markets; and so on.

The degree of **competition** in the U.S. economy is hard to measure. Most concentration studies focus on manufacturing, which, although it is the most visible

TABLE 8.1   Proprietorships, Partnerships, and Corporations, by Industry, 1990

Industry	Number (thousands)			Business Revenues (billions of dollars)		
	Proprietorships	Active Partnerships	Active Corporations	Proprietorships	Active Partnerships	Active Corporations
Total	14,298	1,635	3,628	693.0	405.0	10,440
Agriculture, forestry, and fishing	342	131	123	15.0	8.0	81.0
Mining	155	46	42	7.0	20.0	88.0
Construction	1,757	62	393	101.0	30.0	505.0
Manufacturing	431	26	301	25.0	55.0	3,276.0
Transportation, public utilities	623	22	156	31.0	27.0	844.0
Wholesale and retail trade	2,438	173	1,012	234.0	90.0	3,095.0
Finance, insurance, and real estate	1270	853	592	50.0	71.0	1,868.0
Services	7,039	299	109	226.0	162.0	680.0

Source: Statistical Abstract of the United States.

branch of U.S. industry, accounts for less than one-fourth of national income. Many industries that produce raw materials, such as agriculture, forest products, and coal, are organized competitively. Yet government price-support programs in agriculture have affected the behavior of agricultural producers, and the owners of coal mines often band together in associations. Retail stores and most services operate in local markets and in a competitive environment.

Estimates of the overall level of competitiveness (including agriculture, manufacturing, trade, and services) are few and far between. Milton Friedman's estimates for the year 1939 indicate that the private sector was then between 15% and 25% "monopolistic" and between 75% and 85% "competitive."[4] A contemporary study (Table 8.2) finds that the degree of competition has increased for the U.S. economy as a whole since the 1960s.[5]

Competitive Industries   Competitive producers are **price takers**. They cannot influence prices, so they maximize profits by expanding their output to the point where marginal cost is equal to the product price. If for some reason (say, an unexpected shift in demand) above-normal profits are earned, excess profits disappear as new firms enter the market.

Prices are formed in competitive industries by supply and demand. Take the case of basic agricultural products (wheat, pork bellies, soy beans, frozen orange juice), which are traded on commodity markets. These markets are called **perfect markets**, because at any time, all buyers pay the same price. All potential buyers and sellers are participants in the market, and information concerning prices is available almost instantaneously. All participants know, for example, the price of a bushel of wheat at any time.

Producers and users of commodities, however, are not the only participants in the market. Commodity speculators buy and sell in the hope of buying at a low price and then selling high. Commodity markets establish not only prices of commodities for immediate delivery but also prices (called **futures prices**) for deliveries at some specified date in the future. An American wheat farmer can contract, even before the crop has been planted, to sell next year's harvest at a specified price in the commodity market.

Most competitive industries are not perfectly competitive because they sell slightly differentiated products. Even though a product is differentiated, producers have little control over price. In each market, prices are established by supply and demand, and **arbitrage** (buying in the cheap market and reselling in the expensive market) prevents large price disparities between markets. Although these markets are not perfectly competitive, they closely approximate perfect competition.

Imperfectly Competitive Industries   Competitive markets work in a fairly invisible and low-key manner. Highly concentrated, noncompetitive industries follow a wide variety of behavior patterns.

The surprising feature of U.S. manufacturing is that the degree of concentration appears to have scarcely changed since the turn of the century (see Table 8.3). According to G. Warren Nutter's famous study, in 1900 roughly one-third of manufacturing net output came from industries wherein the four largest firms accounted for

TABLE 8.2   Trends in Competition in the U.S. Economy, 1939–1980

Sectors of the Economy	Share of Each Sector That Was Effectively Competitive (percent)		
	1939	1958	1980
Agriculture, forestry, and fisheries	91.6	85.0	86.4
Mining	87.1	92.2	95.8
Construction	27.9	55.9	80.2
Manufacturing	51.5	55.9	69.0
Transportation and public utilities	8.7	26.1	39.1
Wholesale and retail trade	57.8	60.5	93.4
Finance, insurance, and real estate	61.5	63.8	94.1
Services	53.9	54.3	77.9
Total	52.4	56.4	76.7

Note: In this table, an effectively competitive industry is one in which the 4-firm concentration ratio was below 40 percent, entry barriers were low, market shares were unstable, and prices were flexible. The extent of oligopoly in the economy is the measure of the combined shares of dominant-firm and tight-oligopoly industries.

Source: William G. Shepherd, "Causes of Increased Competition in the U.S. Economy, 1939–1980," *Review of Economics and Statistics*, November 1982, 613–626. Used by permission of Elsevier Science Publishers, Amsterdam.

half or more of industry output. In 1963 and 1982, the figure was still one-third. Morris Adelman reports similar findings for the period 1947–1958, when the average concentration ratio of the four largest firms in each industry rose only from 35% to 37%. Between 1931 and 1960, the share of the 117 largest manufacturing firms in total manufacturing assets remained stable at 45%.[6]

Economic theory suggests that concentrated industries with a great deal of market power will enjoy larger profit rates. Joe S. Bain and H. Michael Mann have shown that profit rates in the 1930s and 1950s tended to rise with concentration and with barriers to entry, although this effect was more pronounced in the 1950s.[7] More recent studies find that at concentration ratios above 70%, concentration is strongly related to profit rates. Barriers to entry appear to have an even stronger positive effect on profit rates. At lower rates of concentration, the relationship among profits, concentration, and entry barriers appears weak or even nonexistent.[8]

Another gauge of the degree of competition in the U.S. economy is how much output would increase if monopoly were eliminated. Researchers—notably Arnold Harberger and David Schwartzman—have calculated such "monopoly welfare losses."[9] They conclude that if monopoly were to disappear, national income would increase by less than 1%. These calculations do not deny that the distribution of income between the monopolist and the consumer is distorted by monopoly. Rather, what is calculated is the "dead-weight loss" of monopoly—that is, the net loss of output due to monopoly.

TABLE 8.3   Trends in Concentration in American Manufacturing: Two Measures

Year	Percentage of Output by Firms with 4-Firm Concentration Ratio of 50 percent or Above (1)	Percentage of Output of 100 Largest Firms (2)
1895–1904	33	n.a.
1947	24	23
1954	30	30
1958	30	32
1972	29	33
1977	28	33
1982	24	33

Sources: G. Warren Nutter, *The Extent of Enterprise Monopoly in the United States,* 1899–1939 (Chicago: University of Chicago Press, 1951); pp. 35–48, 112–140; F. M. Scherer, *Industrial Market Structure and Economic Performance* (Boston: Houghton Mifflin, 1980), pp. 68–69; *Concentration Ratios in Manufacturing, 1977 Census of Manufacturing,* MC77-SR-9; *1982 Census of Manufacturers,* MC82-S-7.

Critics of monopoly such as Gordon Tullock and Anne Krueger have pointed out that monopoly rent seeking raises society's losses above dead-weight losses.[10] Examples of monopoly rent seeking include bribing public officials to gain monopoly franchises and lobbying to gain protection from foreign imports. Because substantial profit gains accrue to the monopolist, people are prepared to expend substantial resources to turn a competitive industry into a monopoly. Harvey Leibenstein emphasized the "organizational slack" or "X-inefficiency" of monopoly. Because monopolists are faced with less competition, they are under less pressure to minimize costs of production. The competitive firm that fails to minimize costs may be forced out of business, but the monopoly can relax. If one takes monopoly rent seeking and X-inefficiency into account, society's losses from monopoly may be considerable.

Harold Demsetz argues in a different vein that the higher profits of large enterprises result from their superior cost performance.[11] If prices are set competitively so that each firm acts like a price taker, then economic profits accrue to those firms that have lower costs of production. The higher profit rates found in highly concentrated industries are the result of the superior efficiency of large firms.

The Labor Market

Labor is allocated largely through labor markets[12] in the United States. In competitive labor markets, employers demand larger quantities of labor at low wages. The supply of labor is a positive function of the wage rate offered, and a wage rate equating the supply and the demand for labor is established automatically in the marketplace.

There are no measures of how competitive the U.S. labor market is. Obvious examples of highly competitive labor markets include markets for domestic help, farm labor, most white-collar occupations, and banking employees. Labor market analysis focuses on the causes of deviations from the competitive model: union power, government intervention, and discrimination.

Unions   Less then 15 percent of the U.S. labor force belongs to labor unions. In the 1930s, union members accounted for 6 to 7 percent of the labor force. Union membership rose in the 1940s and peaked at 25 percent in the mid-1950s. Since then the percentage has declined—despite the notable increase in union membership among public employees—largely because of the rapid growth of white-collar employment. Government employees now count for the majority of unionized workers. The American trade union movement is more decentralized than its counterparts in Europe. More authority rests with local unions, and the movement has failed to produce its own political party. The American union movement consists of loose federations of local unions banded into national unions. With notable exceptions, bargaining over wages proceeds on a company-by-company basis. In recent years, however, the trend has been toward collective bargaining at the national level and bargaining over local issues at the local level.

Most American unions are associated with the AFL-CIO (American Federation of Labor–Congress of Industrial Organizations). The AFL-CIO accounts for almost 80 percent of all union members.

American workers were slower to organize than their European counterparts, because unfavorable legislation existed until the early 1930s: The Sherman Antitrust Act of 1890 was initially applied against "monopolistic" labor unions, court orders prohibited union activity, and "yellow dog" contracts required employees to agree not to join a union. The Norris–LaGuardia Act of 1932 and the Wagner Act of 1935 laid the legislative foundation for the growth of unionism.

How much have unions altered the process of labor allocation? There are wide differences of opinion. Some (Milton Friedman, for example) argue that unions have had only a minimal impact on employment and wages. Unions act as highly visible **intermediaries** between the forces of supply and demand, and the pattern of wages and employment is virtually identical to that which would have prevailed without unions. Collective bargaining cannot negate the forces of demand over the long term, because too-high wages would result in a substitution of other factors for labor.

Most studies show that unions raise wages in unionized industries. Unions control wages through their power to strike and to control the supply of (and in some cases, through work rules, the demand for) labor. Unions raised wages in the unionized sector some 25 percent during the mid-1930s, 5 percent during the late 1940s, and some 10 to 15 percent during the 1950s. The most recent studies show that union wages are 15 to 18 percent higher than they would have been in the absence of unions. For the entire economy, the impact of unionization is probably small. Union wages are emulated in the nonunionized sector, and higher union wages reduce employment in the unionized branches and hence place downward pressure on wages in nonunionized branches.

What has been the effect of unions on productivity? Economists have traditionally believed that unions have a negative effect on productivity through disruptive strikes, featherbedding practices, and distortion of union–nonunion wages. Some economists have questioned this view. Albert Hirschman, Richard Freeman, and James Medoff maintain that unions actually raise productivity by giving union members a collective voice. Without union representation, the only way workers can raise their voice against bad employers is to exit—that is, to leave the enterprise. With unions, workers can gain effective representation and can work from within to improve conditions. Unions can have a positive effect on productivity in three ways: Unions reduce worker turnover and thus limit hiring and training costs. In the union setting, senior workers are more likely to provide informal training and assistance. And the union provides for an improved information flow between workers and managers.

Government Intervention in the Labor Market   A second extramarket force in the labor market is government. Government affects wages through licensing and other procedures that regulate the supply of labor in particular occupations. It also affects the supply of labor in the long run through its policies toward public education and job training. Moreover, antidiscrimination legislation, hiring quotas, and the like affect employment practices. Probably the most disputed role of government is minimum wage legislation. Its opponents argue that minimum wages disrupt the market process and create unemployment among the poor workers the legislation seeks to assist. Supporters argue that minimum wages are unlikely to have a significant effect on employment and are necessary to protect weak workers, who are at a disadvantage in the bargaining process. Minimum wages remain controversial, as evidenced by the substantial political battle over raising the minimum wage in 1997.

Discrimination   The third extramarket force in the labor market is **discrimination** by race and gender, which excludes particular races and sexes from particular occupations (such as specific craft unions) and channels them into overpopulated occupations. An example is the channeling of women into public school teaching. A great deal of research has attempted to estimate the effect of discrimination on earnings of African Americans, Mexican Americans, and women. The general consensus is that discrimination does exist, once other factors such as background and education are held constant, but that its overall effect on wages in the United States has been limited. Within specific occupations, the discrimination effect on the observed minority wage differential is small. The most significant impact of race and sex discrimination results from the exclusion of minorities from specific occupations.

How U.S. policy deals with discrimination is another area of controversy. Some favor affirmative action to make up for past discrimination. Others favor a race- and gender-neutral approach. Several states have in fact introduced legislative initiatives to do away with state affirmative action programs.

The Capital Market

The **capital market** brings together suppliers and users of credit. Businesses undertake investment projects as long as the anticipated risk-adjusted rate of return exceeds the cost of acquiring capital funds. At the margin, projects are undertaken wherein the rate of return just equals the cost of borrowing. Accordingly, the lower the cost of acquiring investment funds, the higher the demand for investment will be.

The supply of investment funds to the capital market depends on the savings of individuals, government surpluses or deficits, retained profits, and depreciation. In the U.S. capital market, the supply of investment funds is seldom channeled directly from the saver to the investor. Such transactions are normally handled by **financial intermediaries**, such as commercial banks, savings banks, and insurance companies. In the corporate sector (which accounts for some three-fourths of business borrowing), the corporation can raise capital by issuing debt, by issuing additional stock, or by using retained earnings.

A striking feature of American capital markets (and capital markets in general in industrialized capitalist countries) is the prevalence of financial intermediation. Financial intermediaries borrow funds from one set of economic agents (people or companies with savings) and lend to other economic agents. Financial intermediaries serve a useful purpose by making it unnecessary for borrowers and lenders to seek each other out. A commercial bank, for example, borrows from its depositors (by accepting checking and savings account deposits) and then lends to a corporation building a new plant. If borrowers and lenders had sought each other out, the lender would have received a higher rate of interest and the borrower would have paid a lower rate of interest. The fact that lenders and borrowers pay for financial intermediation suggests that the service performed is a valuable one. Of the private domestic capital advanced for private investment in the early 1980s, about 90 percent was supplied through financial intermediaries.

The U.S. capital market is a well-organized market in the sense that national securities markets (the New York and American Stock Exchanges, markets for federal funds, and others) bring together all potential borrowers and suppliers of investment funds, and information concerning investment alternatives is readily and almost instantaneously available to all participants. It is misleading to speak of a U.S. capital market, for there is an *international* capital market. The huge amount of international data in the financial section of the daily newspaper demonstrates this fact. The net result is an approximate equalization of rates of return on all investments *at the margin* once they are adjusted for risk.

This equalization of rates of return at the margin is an important positive feature of capital markets, because it leads to an efficient allocation of capital resources. If rates of return were not equal at the margin, then capital funds could be redistributed from projects with a lower rate of return to those with higher rates, and output could be increased without an increase in capital resources.

Government in the American Economy

When examining socialist economic systems, it is customary to study how market forces arise in the socialist economy. Similarly, it is important to discover how and why government becomes involved in a predominantly market economy and to examine the results of such intervention.

Government intervention in the American economy is usually justified as a response to various types of market failure. As Chapter 5 emphasized, markets can fail in a variety of ways. Similarly, government response can take a variety of forms, which usually involve some mix of direct production (**public goods**), redistribution of income, and/or regulation.

Though all agree that some degree of government activity is necessary, beyond this limited consensus there is much disagreement.[13] Public-choice theory does not provide significant guidance in determining how much government involvement is appropriate, and yet an examination of most market capitalist economies indicates that government activity has been growing over time.[14]

The Scope of the Public Sector

The data presented in Figure 8.2 shed light on the role of government in the American economy. The government's claim on labor and capital resources indicates how productive resources are divided between government and business uses. Government (federal, state, and local) employs approximately 16 percent of the American labor force and owns approximately 18 percent of the stock of structures, one-eighth of all land, and one-twentieth of all inventories. Government owned approximately 15 percent of the national wealth and accounted for some 7 percent of total labor, capital, and land inputs in the late 1950s.

Government's share of productive resources has increased steadily over the last hundred years. At the turn of the century, government accounted for some 4 percent of employment and owned 6 percent of the stock of structures and 13 percent of the stock of land. By 1939, the government's share had increased substantially (to 18 percent of structures and 19 percent of land), whereas its share of the labor force had risen to about 10 percent. Since the late 1930s, government's share of employment has increased by 80 percent, but its share of national wealth has risen only slightly. We have reached a national consensus on the distribution of wealth, which has remained fairly stable for about 50 years. There is now little serious talk of large-scale nationalizations, and most of the major decisions in this area (broadcasting, communication satellites, atomic energy) have come down on the side of private ownership.

Government produces about 13 percent of national income, of which the overwhelming portion is produced by "general government." The business sector accounts for more than 80 percent of national income; the remainder is accounted for by government and not-for-profit institutions. The encroachment of government enterprises on private business has been minimal. Government enterprises account for less than 2 percent of the national income. Rather than government enterprises

FIGURE 8.2   Indicators of Government Participation in Economic Activity and
Wealth in the United States, 1900–1995

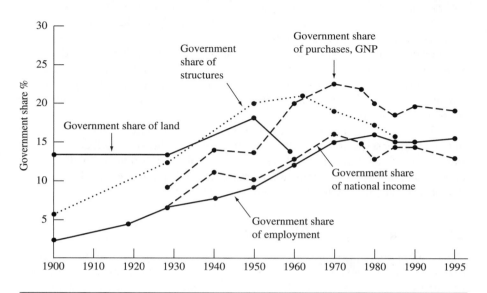

The dots (•) indicate the years of observations.

Source: Handbook of Economic Statistics 1992, CPAS 92–10005, September 1992, *Economic Report of
the President* (selected years); *Statistical Abstract of the United States* (selected years).

supplanting private enterprises, it has been the expansion of general government
activities that has accounted for rising government output.

The government's share of national income has been rising steadily over the last
hundred years (4 percent in 1869 to 8.5 percent in 1919 to 13 percent in 1994). Since
the 1930s, the increase in the federal government's share has been more substantial
than that of state and local government. Since 1929, business's share of national income has fallen from 91 to 81 percent at the expense of the rise in general government and not-for-profit institutions.

Government purchases account for about one-fifth of the total. Interestingly,
most of the historical increase in the share of government purchases has been due to
rising state and local government spending and federal defense spending.

It is important to put these U.S. developments in perspective. An examination of
other industrialized capitalist countries (Figure 8.3) shows that the scope of the public sector in the United States is average or even below average if one considers that
most countries do not bear a substantial defense burden. If one looks only at non-
defense spending, the U.S. government's share of total spending is relatively small
by international standards. The rising share of government output and expenditures
is also unexceptional; it has characterized the economic growth of capitalism for
more than a century. The U.S. tax burden is also relatively modest.

FIGURE 8.3   The Size of Government in the United States and Other Countries, 1960, 1970, and 1992

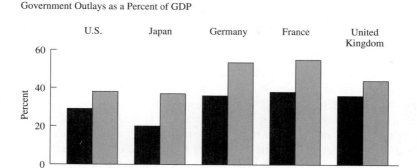

Government Outlays as a Percent of GDP

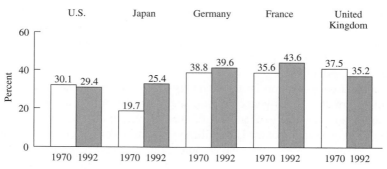

Taxes as a Percent of GDP

Sources: Handbook of Economic Statistics 1992, CPAS 92–10005, September 1992, *Statistical Abstract of the United States,* 1995, p. 860.

Some people view the rising share of government with alarm; others consider it too small. All one can say for sure is that in the United States, the allocation of resources between the public and private sectors is basically a matter of public choice.

Public Goods: The Case of National Defense

Government bears the principal responsibility for providing public goods, although in the real world there are few "pure" public goods. The activity that dominates the public-goods market in the United States is national defense, which is the best theoretical example of a public good; we shall therefore use it to illustrate how the U.S. government deals with public goods.

Two issues must be considered. The first is how decisions are reached concerning national defense's share of total public resources. The second issue is the market structure under which defense goods are produced.

Resource Allocation by the Defense Industry   The share and product mix of national defense are decided by the political process. The nexus between the government and the large manufacturers of military hardware has been called the **military–industrial complex**. Three explanations of weapons procurement have been offered: the strategic, the bureaucratic, and the economic.[15]

The strategic explanation is that defense planners determine weapons procurement on the basis of rational calculations about the foreign military threat. The bureaucratic explanation is that defense spending is the product of a tug of war among the various interests that make up the military–industrial complex, not of any rationally calculated plan of national security. One branch of the military exerts pressure for its weapons system, while a rival branch applies similar pressure in favor of its project. Or one manufacturer exerts, through strategic members of Congress or lobbyists, pressure in favor of its design for a weapons system. According to the bureaucratic explanation, the overall distribution of resources depends on the outcome of this struggle of vested interests.

New Left economists offer a third explanation. Defense spending is based on its impact on the overall economy. An expanding defense budget is necessary to preserve full employment. Contracts for major weapons systems are granted, not to produce the most effective system, but to preserve established contractors located in politically important states.[16]

A related consideration is the extent to which the private defense contractors themselves are able to influence defense spending. According to some, major defense contractors are able to exert control over the allocation of defense resources.[17]

The market structure of the U.S. military–industrial complex consists of the U.S. government, as a monopsonistic buyer, purchasing from a small number of defense contractors. The government purchases a weapons system from a single supplier, who is granted a monopoly to develop the system. Often there is no serious negotiation with potential competitors. Defense contracts are typically let on a cost-plus basis, whereby the manufacturer agrees to supply a particular weapons system at a negotiated cost plus an agreed-upon profit margin. Because there is little competition among producers, and because the manufacture of a new weapons system is characterized by technological uncertainty, the government cannot judge whether the manufacturer is operating efficiently.

Suggestions for reform of military procurement center on either the nationalization of the defense industry or the introduction of more competition.[18] The major disadvantage of nationalization is that government production would not be cost-effective. Therefore, the most effective approach appears to be more competition.

Personnel and National Defense   Until 1973, the personnel needs of the armed forces were met by a national draft operated by the Selective Service System. Conscription was employed to fill the gap between the number of volunteers joining the military at established wage rates (the supply) and the quotas established by the armed services (the demand). The costs of maintaining the armed forces therefore consisted of payments to armed service personnel *plus* the loss of income incurred by those draftees who had to forgo higher incomes outside the military. To some extent, however, individuals with higher earning capacities were excluded from the draft by educational and occupational exemptions.

Military personnel prior to 1973 were handled largely outside of the labor market. With the winding down of the Vietnam War, the U.S. government turned to a voluntary army in 1973. Military personnel needs were to be met by raising military pay and benefits to the level required to bring the supply of and demand for military personnel into approximate balance. This use of the market represents a return to the practice of using hired troops. It has the advantage of relying on freedom of choice of occupation and avoiding the economic inefficiency of conscripting individuals with high earning capacities. Its disadvantages are that the armed forces are made up primarily of the disadvantaged, for whom military pay scales are attractive, and that the whole notion of national service is circumvented. The effectiveness of the volunteer army was tested in the Persian Gulf War with apparently favorable results.

Trends in Military Spending   In 1959, the federal government spent $308 billion (1992 prices) on national defense. Defense spending rose during the Vietnam War to a peak of $400 billion (1992 prices) in 1968. Defense spending then fell to $265 billion (1992 prices) in 1976. When Ronald Reagan was elected President in 1980, defense spending was $280 billion. Under Reagan, they rose to $409 billion in 1987. During Bill Clinton's presidency, defense spending fell from $375 billion in 1992 to $320 billion in 1996.

Unlike other categories of government spending, all of which have shown a steady tendency to increase, U.S. defense spending depends on military campaigns and on which major party controls the White House and the Congress. The sharp reductions in military spending in the 1990s indicate that defense spending is not dictated by the military–industrial complex and that the U.S. economy can prosper with declining defense spending.

Health, Education, and Welfare

U.S. government public assistance has been limited to public education, some low-cost health care for the poor, and social security insurance for retirement, disability, and unemployment. Such services are typically supplied on a mixed private-enterprise–public-service basis with the user paying a portion of the cost.

The mix of private and public support has shifted toward public provision, reflecting a changing public attitude toward government responsibility. Over the last half-century, this change has been most dramatic in the areas of health expenditures, social welfare expenditures, and social insurance (Table 8.4), which earlier had been regarded as private or charitable obligations. Prior to the 1930s, almost all retirement, health, and unemployment insurance was purchased on a voluntary private basis; in 1929 only 10% of personal health expenditures were funded by

TABLE 8.4   Expenditures on Public Assistance in the United States, 1890–1994

Year	Public Social Welfare Expenditures as a Percent of GDP[a]	Social Insurance Expenditures as a Percent of GDP	Government Health Care Expenditures as a Percent of GDP
1994	21.0	8.4	5.9
1990	19.1	9.3	5.0
1987	18.4	10.8	4.2
1985	18.4	10.1	4.2
1980	18.6	8.0	3.6
1970	14.8	5.7	2.5
1955	8.6	2.6	0.9
1929	3.9	0.2	0.4
1920	—	—	—
1900	—	—	—
1890	2.4	—	0.1

[a]Social welfare expenditures include social insurance and public aid, education, veterans' programs, child nutrition, and rehabilitation programs.

Source: U.S., Department of Commerce, *Historical Statistics of the United States: Colonial Times to 1970* (Washington, D.C.: Government Printing Office, 1975), Series B236-247, H1–31, H412–432, H716–727; *Statistical Abstract of the United States* (selected years).

governmental agencies. Public elementary and secondary education has dominated the American education system for quite a while, but the government share of support for higher education has increased substantially over the last 50 years. During that time, public universities have supplanted private universities as the dominant institutions in higher education.

Two general rules have governed public assistance. The first is that, if feasible, goods should be provided on an "in-kind" basis (for example, subsidized school lunches and food stamps) rather than as income payments. This rule suggests an unwillingness to rely on freedom of choice and a feeling that the poor are not to be trusted to allocate their incomes wisely. The second general rule is that families should not have the power to shop around for education or public health, despite arguments that making such choice possible would force suppliers to be more efficient and responsive to the consumer.

In the 1996 presidential election, the issue of choice was discussed in the areas of education. The Republican candidate favored a "voucher" system, whereby parents would receive a voucher from the government, which could be used at the school of choice, be it public or private.

In the 1990s, discussion of the U.S. public assistance programs turned to their potential effects on economic efficiency and to their unanticipated consequences. It was argued that public assistance programs based on calculated "need" encouraged families on welfare to reduce their incomes. In particular, "needs-based" programs actually created incentives for fathers to desert their families in order to reduce the income of the welfare family. Government unemployment insurance programs, de-signed to mitigate the costs of unemployment, may serve to encourage longer spells of unemployment. Government health insurance programs, by increasing the demand for medical care, may cause medical costs to rise more rapidly, thereby making them less affordable to the uninsured.

U.S. Policy Toward Monopoly

In the United States, monopoly policy has been neither uniform nor consistent. In some instances, government policy restricts competition (tariffs, licensing, agricul-tural price supports); in others, it seeks to restrain monopoly power and to promote competitive behavior.

Government Ownership

Several options are open to government with regard to natural monopolies, which serve as the sole suppliers of a product. The government can nationalize them in the "public interest." It can also tax them in order to transfer monopoly profits to the state and to guarantee an output/price combination more consistent with competitive standards. A third alternative is government regulation. A fourth is for the govern-ment to auction exclusive franchises to operate natural monopolies. This option would transfer much of the monopoly return to the state.[19]

In the United States, all of these approaches have been employed, though dis-criminatory monopoly taxation and franchise auctions are rare. Public ownership of natural monopolies is common at the local and state levels but rare at the federal level. Municipal services such as local transportation, garbage collection, water, electricity, gas, public wharves, and state transit authorities are often owned and operated by state and municipal government. More than 20 percent of all electrical energy is generated by government or cooperative arrangements, and 10 percent of all utility payments go to government enterprises. In only 2 of the 10 largest cities is the municipal transit system privately owned. Approximately 3 percent of all resi-dential housing construction has been undertaken by public authorities.[20]

Government enterprise operated by the federal government is more limited: operating the postal services (now a semigovernmental operation), administering public lands (the Forest Service), lending and guaranteeing loans (the FHA and VA programs), providing insurance against various risks (social security), generating electricity (the Tennessee Valley Authority), and engaging in limited manufacturing activities (Redstone Arsenal, the U.S. Government Printing Office).

Local, state, and federal government enterprises account for less than 2 percent of national income. The government enterprise share of manufacturing is insignifi-cant.[21] The public's decision to leave natural monopolies in the hands of private owners has been in marked contrast to Europe, where the state owns and operates many natural monopolies—and even enterprises that are not natural monopolies (such as automobile manufacturing, national airlines, and railroads).

In public enterprises, the incentive to restrict output and raise prices should not be so strong as under private ownership. On the other hand, the pressures to reduce costs and to innovate are generally weaker. Moreover, red tape and civil service restrictions may impede efficiency in the public enterprise. At the empirical level, the evidence is mixed. One authority concludes (after reviewing the European experience as well) that "the evidence is presently insufficient to support a sharp choice between the alternatives on straightforward economic performance grounds."[22] Another concludes that there is a strong correlation between the share of public ownership in manufacturing and the economic efficiency of the entire economy.[23]

Regulation

The overwhelming political choice has been to regulate industries that possess monopoly power rather than to use public ownership.[24] **Regulation** has been exercised by a wide variety of local, state, and federal agencies. Other kinds of regulation—control by the courts or by the terms of franchises, charters, and city ordinances—have proved ineffective in the United States, and the public has turned instead to administrative regulation, either by an official of executive government or by semi-independent commissions operating under general legislative authority.[25]

Government regulation can be classified as *social regulation* and *economic regulation*.[26] Social regulation is regulation of health, safety, and environment. Examples include consumer product safety rules, environmental protection, and automobile safety and gasoline mileage requirements. Economic regulation is government involvement in markets, such as setting prices, restricting corporate decision making and controlling competition. Examples of economic regulation include government regulation of utility rates and market structures and the setting of local taxi rates.

Both economic regulation and social regulation impose costs and create benefits. One of the costs of regulation is the costs of compliance—the associated paper work, creating facilities for the handicapped, and so on. *The Federal Registry,* which publishes all federal regulations, reached 100,000 pages per year in the mid-1990s. Estimates of the compliance costs of regulation are provided in Table 8.5.

A rational policy of regulation requires that the benefits of regulation at least equal their costs. Obviously, it would be better for the benefits of the regulatory program far to exceed the cost. Studies of social regulation identify some programs whose benefits far exceed their costs. Regulations related to highway safety, for example, cost about $9 billion annually while yielding benefits (in terms of reduced accidents) of as much as $45 billion per year. Asbestos regulation, on the other hand, costs $66 million per year to save 1 life per year. That $66 million, if devoted to other activities, such as heart transplants, would result in 18,333 more years of life.

Economic regulation at the state and local level is principally directed at natural monopolies—specifically, the electric, gas, and telephone companies. At the national level, federal commissions have regulated both monopolistic industries (such as local telephone service) and potentially competitive industries (such as trucking and airlines). The stated rationale for federal regulation has been to ensure quality of service and to guarantee the public "reasonable" prices without discrimination. A degree of

TABLE 8.5   Compliance Costs of Regulation in the United States

	Cost ($ billions)	Percent GDP	Cost Per Capita
1976	$63	3.5	$289
1979	$103	4.0	$458
1990	$400	7.0	$1606
1992	$600	8.0	$1961

Source: Federal Reserve Bank of Dallas, *America's Economic Regulation Burden,* Fall 1996, p. 2.

monopoly power, however, is generally a necessary but insufficient condition for regulation. Buyers have to be at a disadvantage in bargaining by virtue of the fact that the service is an essential, nonpostponable one for which there are few good substitutes. Although the American automobile industry is more concentrated than the natural gas or rail industry, the latter two have been regulated, whereas the former has remained free from economic regulation. There are historical reasons for regulation as well. The railroads were placed under the supervision of the Interstate Commerce Commission at a time when they possessed considerable monopoly power. Motor and air transport lessened this power, yet the commission could not continue to regulate railroads without extending federal regulation to other forms of transport.

Generally, regulatory commissions control entry into the industry by granting franchises and licenses—for a new airline route, say, or a new interstate natural gas pipeline. Rarely are these licenses or franchises actually sold (for the purpose of diverting the ensuing profits to the public). Rather, it is assumed that regulation will prevent excessive profits.

It is the responsibility of the regulators to set "reasonable" rates for the services of regulated producers. In this, the regulatory commissions have been guided by the principle, guaranteed by the Fifth and Fourteenth Amendments protecting private property, that rates should be sufficient to cover operating costs plus a "proper" rate of return on invested capital. A second principle is that the rate structure should not discriminate among buyers, except when such discrimination is justified by cost differences.

This pricing formula raises a number of issues. How are operating costs to be defined? What is an appropriate rate of return on invested capital? How is the rate base (the value of tangible and intangible assets of the company) to be measured? The regulated price is essentially a cost-plus price, and additions to cost are, in time, passed on to the user. This may well reduce the incentive to seek out cost economies. Moreover, there is the problem of dealing with illegitimate or padded costs, such as buying materials from an unregulated affiliate at inflated prices in order to increase that company's profits.

Determining an appropriate rate of return to regulated firms has been another area of controversy. The rate of return should be high enough to attract new capital; hence the interest rate on recently floated debt has often been used as the rate of return. According to one authority, however, the rates of return that regulatory commissions and the courts have historically allowed have been "conventional or arbitrary, bearing no apparent relation to any statement of principles . . . usually based on expert testimony with little pretense of economic analysis."[26] The rates allowed have varied from state to state and from time to time, ranging between 5½% in the 1940s and 11% and higher during the 1970s and 1980s.

Auctions of Monopoly Rights

One approach to monopoly is for the government to auction monopoly rights to the highest bidder and thus capture a good portion of the future monopoly profits for the government. Historically, this approach has not been followed in the United States, which has typically allocated monopoly rights through political processes.

With the deregulation of telecommunications, however, there has been a greater willingness to use this option. Consider the case of government allocation of cellular phone frequencies and radio broadcast frequencies. If these frequencies are sold to the highest bidder, companies will be willing to pay a price that reflects the future monopoly profits of owning that broadcast frequency. In the 1980s, cellular phone franchises were allocated to established telephone companies and to new entrants, where the new entrants were awarded licenses by lottery. As the Federal Communications Commission prepared to allot new broadcast frequencies in the mid-1990s, there was considerable public discussion as to whether they would be allocated administratively or by auction. If by auction, it was estimated that broadcast-frequency sales would bring in billions of dollars of government revenues. However, established broadcasters have exerted intense political pressure in favor of administrative allocation. The outcome of this battle will be decided in the last few years of the twentieth century by the tug of war between the need for these government revenues and the power of telecommunications giants.

An Assessment of Regulation

Most authorities give regulation relatively poor marks, especially in industries that are not natural monopolies.[27] Regulation of natural monopolies has had remarkably little effect on the prices charged consumers. Opponents of regulation argue that operating costs will fall when potentially competitive industries are freed from regulation (deregulated).

Why have the regulatory commissions not had a more beneficial impact on the industries they regulate? There are several possible explanations. The first is that the balance of power between the regulators and the regulated is uneven. The regulated industries have well-paid staffs, whereas the regulatory commissions (the state commissions in particular) are understaffed and underpaid. Regulated industries appear able to circumvent regulations if necessary. Moreover, the commissioners themselves tend to keep in close contact with the industries they regulate, not with the consumers they are supposed to represent. The very *methodology* of regulation also remains a problem. A commission has no way of knowing what operating costs would be if the most efficient production techniques were used. Even if it did know, it would lack the authority to mandate use of these techniques. Instead, it must simply accept the actual operating costs of the utilities as given, except in obvious cases of corruption or gross mismanagement.

Deregulation

The **deregulation**[28] of the American economy began in the late 1970s. The Airline Deregulation Act, signed in October of 1978, allowed the airlines rather than the Civil Aeronautics Board (which went out of existence in 1984) to set fares and choose routes, according to the availability of landing slots at airports. In 1980, the Motor Carrier Act curbed the role of the Interstate Commerce Commission in interstate trucking. Also in 1980, the Staggers Rail Act led to major changes in railroad transport, and the Depository Institution Deregulation and the Monetary Control acts significantly changed the way the banking sector sets charges, enters markets, and the like. The AT&T Settlement of 1982 and the Cable Television Deregulation Act of 1984 brought major and well-known changes in the telecommunications and cable television industries, respectively.

Much of this deregulation was motivated by the message of microeconomic theory, namely that the development of competitive markets could provide benefits that would outweigh associated costs. At the same time, the opponents of deregulation warned of deteriorating service, pricing wars, and general instability in deregulated industries.

U.S. experience has shown that deregulation leads to lower prices for most—but not all—consumers. Consumers in small markets characterized by high costs are no longer protected and now have to pay prices closer to costs. Deregulation has increased the diversity of services offered and has given consumers more freedom of choice. Firms that had been protected by regulation have lowered their costs substantially, and these lower costs are being passed on to their customers. Deregulation has also had its losers. Firms that could not meet competitive pressures have gone out of business or have been acquired by more successful firms. Employees have seen their earnings fall as firms have sought ways to lower their costs.

In the airline industry, the problems of high fuel prices, terrorism, and high debt resulted in the concentration of the industry in the hands of a few giant airlines. In banking, a number of problems (such as corruption and the inflation of the 1970s and 1980s) led to massive failures both in the savings and loan industry and in commercial banking. These negative experiences have caused some to question the wisdom of deregulation. There is, however, widespread agreement that consumers have been the prime beneficiaries of deregulation. Consumers now have a broad range of choice of long-distance carriers, airline fares, and financial services, offered at competitive prices.

Support for deregulation has continued into the late 1990s. The latest area of expansion of deregulation is the electricity market. Previously, electricity was supplied by regulated electrical utilities that were granted monopolies over geographic markets subject to rate regulation by state regulatory agencies.[29] A number of experiments are currently being tried and, if successful, they will lead to a private unregulated market in electricity. With the development of transmission technology and a national grid system of high-voltage cables, electricity can now be transmitted at low cost from one geographic region to another, thereby creating the opportunity for a competitive market in electricity. Under the deregulation experiments, local utilities will serve as common carriers obligated to transmit electricity purchased from various supplies to the national power grid. They will continue to be regulated. Marketers of electricity can enter into contracts with businesses and ultimately consumers whereby they supply the end user with electricity purchased from the cheapest source. Under this system, the forces of competition, not regulatory agencies, will determine the price of electricity.

Antitrust Legislation

The major alternative to direct regulation of monopoly is legislation to control market structure and market conduct.[30] The most important piece of federal **antitrust legislation**, the Sherman Antitrust Act of 1890, confronts these issues. The Sherman Act was the government's reaction to public hostility toward the trust movement of the late 19th century in the transportation, steel, tobacco, and oil industries. The Sherman Act contains two sections. Section 1 declares "every contract, combination . . . or conspiracy" in restraint of interstate commerce illegal. Section 2 makes the attempt to monopolize interstate commerce a federal offense. Section 1 prohibits a particular type of market *conduct* (conspiring to restrain trade), whereas Section 2 enjoins a particular market *structure* (monopoly). The language of Section 2 is vague, and this imprecision has led to varying court interpretations over the years. According to the language of Section 2, **monopolization** is prohibited, not **monopolies**. The Sherman Act clearly bans the act of creating a monopoly but is ambiguous on the legality of existing monopolies.

The Sherman Antitrust Act of 1890 forms the foundation of American antitrust legislation. The Clayton and Federal Trade Commission acts of 1913 established the Federal Trade Commission to investigate "unfair" business practices and prohibited specific illegal business practices. The Wheeler–Lea Act of 1938 gave the Clayton Act more teeth by declaring unfair or deceptive business practices illegal. The Celler–Kefauver Act of 1950 tightened up the antimerger provisions of the Clayton Act. (See Table 8.6.)

American antitrust policy is made by Congress and by the courts, for it is in the courts that actual antimonopoly policy has been set. The basic issue confronting the courts was whether certain forms of market conduct were prohibited or whether the monopoly market structure was illegal per se. If so, it was then up to the courts to decide what constituted a monopoly. In the early court rulings (the American Tobacco and Standard Oil cases of 1911 and the U.S. Steel case of 1920), the courts interpreted the Sherman Act as enjoining anticompetitive market conduct (mergers, price fixing, and price cutting to eliminate competition) but not the existence of monopoly per se. This became known as the "rule of reason."[31]

TABLE 8.6   An Overview of U.S. Antitrust Legislation

Act	Date	Provisions
Sherman Act	1890	Section 1: restraint of interstate commerce illegal
		Section 2: attempt to monopolize illegal
Clayton Act	1914	Declared specific business practices illegal
Federal Trade Commission Act	1914	Established the FTC to secure compliance with Clayton Act
Wheeler–Lea Act	1938	Banned deceptive business practices
Celler–Kefauver Act	1950	Broadened ban on mergers

The rule of reason appeared to be reversed when the courts ruled in 1945 that Alcoa was in violation of the Sherman Act because it controlled more than 90% of U.S. aluminum output. Although Alcoa had not used its monopoly power to restrain trade unfairly, the courts ruled that size alone was a violation of antitrust statutes. The rule of reason had implied that companies engaging in practices that would ultimately lead to monopoly were in violation of the Sherman Act but that existing monopolies, if they behaved well, were not in violation.

The Alcoa ruling was gradually eroded by court decisions of the 1970s and 1980s. The Alcoa decision appeared to punish all monopolies, even those that became monopolies by means of superior innovation and management. The Eastman Kodak case of 1972 and the FTC ruling in favor of DuPont in 1978 established that monopolies created through superior management and innovation did not violate the Sherman Act. The Alcoa decision was also weakened when, in 1982, the Justice Department dropped its 13-year-old suit against IBM. In 1998, the Justice Department and the FTC charged the two computer industry giants Microsoft and Intel with antitrust violations.

Price Fixing and Mergers

In the United States, the courts have generally found **price-fixing** agreements among producers and **mergers** of large companies engaged in the same line of business to be in violation of the antitrust laws. Formal arrangements for fixing prices have consistently been ruled illegal restraints of trade. The United States stands virtually alone among the industrialized capitalist countries in holding that formal arrangements for price fixing are illegal per se, even if the resulting prices are "reasonable." The courts have thus avoided the difficult issue of distinguishing "reasonable" from "unreasonable" price fixing.

The more difficult enforcement issue, however, has been collusion without outright agreement on pricing policy. Prior to 1948, the courts held that informal price coordination was illegal even if a formal price conspiracy could not be shown. After

1948, in order to demonstrate an illegal conspiracy, it had to be shown that the pattern of pricing could not conceivably have occurred if each firm had acted independently in its own self-interest.

The basic legislation against mergers is found in the Clayton Act of 1914 and in the Celler–Kefauver Act of 1950. Especially since 1950, the courts have adopted a virtual prohibition of mergers between firms with substantial market shares. The merger waves of the 1990s in banking and defense industries signalled a new tolerance of mergers. Particularly in banking, mergers created a much more concentrated industry.

In its strict interpretation of antimerger statutes, the United States stands alone among the industrialized capitalist countries, most of which encourage mergers that serve to increase the scale of production. In Western Europe, for example, the burden of proof is on the government to establish that the social costs of a proposed merger exceed its benefits.

An Evaluation of Antitrust Policy

The most relevant criterion for evaluating government policy toward monopoly is its effect on U.S. economic structure and performance. Since the antitrust laws have been in effect, there has not been a significant increase in the concentration of American industry, whereas the second half of the nineteenth century witnessed a substantial increase in concentration. Many have speculated on the manner in which the antitrust laws contributed to the stability of concentration in the twentieth century. According to one authority, antitrust legislation made three important contributions to the maintenance of workable competition: It prevented European-type cartelization of American industry, it prevented consolidations that would have led to dominant industries, and it helped to preserve freedom of entry and equality of opportunity.[32]

Although it does appear that government policy has contributed to the maintenance of competition in the U.S. economy, not all such policy has been consistent. In fact, a great many government activities have been designed to *reduce* the competitiveness of the American economy: protective tariffs for selected industries, price supports for agricultural products, the patent system, licensing, and so on.

Government and Macroeconomic Stability

Planning for macroeconomic stability in the United States is limited to the use of indirect tools of monetary and fiscal policy. No national economic plan is drafted by government. In this, the United States deviates significantly from other industrialized capitalist countries, most of which have some form of national economic planning. (The case studies of capitalist variants in Chapter 10 focus on national economic planning in France and Britain.) Congressional proposals to introduce a mild form of economic planning have generated considerable controversy.[33]

Prior to the Great Depression, the prevailing notion in government circles was that monetary and fiscal policy should be neutral. "Neutral" meant interfering as little as possible with private economic activity. After the Great Depression and the acceptance of Keynesian economics, this view changed; by the 1960s both major political parties came to accept the view that discretionary monetary and fiscal policy should be used to counter cyclical unemployment and inflation. Although some American monetarists and rational-expectations theorists have spoken out in favor of a return to the traditional neutralist view, monetary and fiscal planners continue to engage in countercyclical policy.

The Federal Reserve System (the Fed) is in charge of formulating monetary policy. Established in 1913, the Federal Reserve System consists of twelve Federal Reserve district banks coordinated by the board of governors in Washington, D.C. In the United States the "central bank" is more decentralized along regional lines than is common for central banks, but it nonetheless performs the functions of a central bank—regulating the money supply through open-market operations, managing the discount rate, setting reserve requirements, and so on.

Authority over fiscal policy is diffused among the various executive and legislative bodies in charge of government spending and taxation, and the balance of authority has tended to shift over time. It is therefore difficult to describe briefly how important fiscal decisions are made. The president can propose budgets, but only Congress can approve them. The Treasury Department can propose changes in the tax structure, but it is the Congress that amends and approves such executive suggestions.

The conduct of monetary policy is more divorced from the business of day-to-day politics than is that of fiscal policy. Members of the Board of Governors of the Fed are appointed for fourteen-year terms, and although they owe their ultimate responsibility to the Congress, a tradition of independence for the Fed has evolved. Recurring proposals call for greater congressional control of the Fed, and there is evidence that the Fed does seek to pursue a monetary policy consistent with that of the current administration. The conduct of fiscal policy is very much a matter of politics, so it has proved difficult to conduct countercyclical fiscal policy. This is especially true during periods of inflation, when politically unpopular budget cuts and tax increases are shunned.

On the whole, the distinctive feature of economic planning in the United States is its virtual absence. Price and wage controls have been applied during periods of inflation, in the form of either voluntary guidelines or mandatory wage and price limitations. The most dramatic examples were the price freezes of 1971–1973, which showed the American public the disastrous consequences of wage and price controls. The negative effects of interfering in the price system were again apparent when efforts were made to control gasoline prices during the energy crises of the 1970s.

Government Activity and Externalities

In an economic system using price signals for resource allocation decisions, incorrect signals (signals that do not recognize both public and private costs and benefits) can lead to incorrect decisions in the sense of not recognizing **external costs** and

benefits. Thus externalities, like pollution, are permitted because their full cost is not always recognized. Benefits are lost because their value is not recognized. Government can play a role in lessening these imbalances. No comprehensive program for dealing with externalities exists at the federal level, and the responsibility for environmental protection is diffused among a wide variety of federal, state, and local agencies. Some of these agencies have an exceptional record of environmental protection; an example is the U.S. Soil Conservation Service. Others, such as the U.S. Environmental Protection Agency, lack sufficient authority to correct serious cases of misallocation.

Three themes should be stressed in assessing the role of the state in dealing with the externality problem. The first is that the division of authority and responsibility among local, state, and national agencies (control of air pollution, for example) has made it difficult to devise effective programs. In many cases, external effects transcend local political boundaries; dealing with them requires some form of national or regional coordination. The second theme has been the general reluctance to use market forces (such as taxes on polluters). Fines, prohibitions, and other administrative orders have been the principal means of enforcement. The third theme is the general unwillingness to consider "optimal" levels of environmental disruption— that is, the level of pollution reduction one should aim for, given the fact that it can be attained only at the expense of society's resources.[34]

As in the field of deregulation, where significant change has occurred, federal government agencies have shown a willingness to entertain new regulatory ideas in the area of environmental protection. The most significant change has been the greater use of "economic" regulation of the environment. In particular, regulatory agencies understand that different companies are able to reduce pollution at different resource costs. They have therefore allowed trading in "rights to pollute." In a particular industry, for example, the environmental regulatory agency establishes emission limits and issues the number of "licenses to pollute" that will keep emissions within the prescribed limits. The companies receiving these licenses, however, are free to sell them to the highest bidder. Companies that can reduce their emissions at low cost will be willing to sell their pollution rights to high bidders who cannot reduce their emissions efficiently. In fact, markets located in Chicago and New York now conduct active trading in pollution emission rights. Notably, the prices of emission rights have been falling steadily, spurred on by the incentive to create new pollution abatement technologies.

Government Policies and the Distribution of Income

To what extent does government in the United States redistribute income through taxation and the distribution of social services? The distribution of income is measured by the Lorenz curve (defined in Chapter 3), which compares family income by rank (say, the lowest to the highest fifth of all families) with percentage share of income either before or after taxes. Some studies "tailor" the Lorenz curve by adjusting for age differences, for differences in family size, and for the distribution of government services.[35]

As measured by the Lorenz curve before taxes and any other adjustments, the U.S. distribution of income seems to have changed little since 1950. In 1950, the lowest and the highest fifth of families accounted for 5 and 45 percent of all income, respectively. By 1982, those figures were 5 and 42 percent. The change since 1929 has been more substantial: The share of the highest fifth of U.S. families declined from 54 to 43.5 percent in all income between 1929 and 1985.[36] It has been argued that if one adjusts these figures for differences in age and family size, then the trend toward greater equality becomes even more evident.[37]

The traditional view is that government has not played a significant role in redistributing income from upper-income to lower-income groups. Although the federal tax system is progressive (upper-income families pay a higher percentage of their income in taxes than do lower-income families), state and local taxes are regressive (upper-income families pay a lower percentage of income). On balance, therefore, the total tax system is roughly proportional (each income group pays the same percentage of its income in taxes), and the after-tax distribution of income is little different from the before-tax distribution. Remember, though, that all such calculations are inexact because of the difficulty of determining what proportion of business and property taxes are passed on to the consumer in the form of higher prices. Joseph Pechman and Benjamin Okner have found that if one assumes such taxes are almost entirely passed on to the consumer, then the tax system is proportional. If one assumes they are borne by the producer, however, Pechman and Okner found that the tax system becomes progressive, but only at the very top and very bottom of the income distribution.[38]

According to some, the state plays a greater redistributive role than is commonly thought.[39] The basis for such claims is that lower-income groups receive larger shares of government in-kind benefits (food stamps, welfare, public education) than their shares of money income. If one includes the value of these benefits in income and then subtracts income and payroll taxes, the distribution of disposable income is much more nearly equal than the unadjusted figures suggest. Figure 8.4 shows calculations from a study by Edgar Browning to illustrate this position. The redistributive role of government in the United States is probably much less significant than in other industrialized capitalist countries. Thus, relatively speaking, the government plays a modest role in the redistribution of income in the United States.

Privatization

In recent years, interest has been growing in **privatization**, the shift of economic activity from the public sector to the private sector.[40] In part, this new interest stems from the vast privatization efforts taking place in the former planned socialist economies and elsewhere in Europe. In this sense, privatization represents one way to reduce the role of government in a market economy. But the contemporary American economy focuses more on efficiency, or the notion that goods and services can be more efficiently provided (that is, at lower cost) in the private sector than in the public sector.

FIGURE 8.4   Lorenz Curves: U.S. Income Distribution Before and After Income
and Transfer Payments

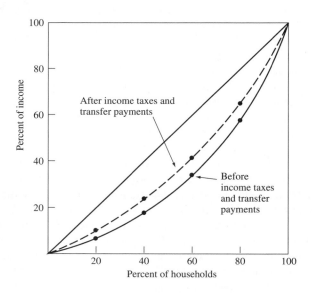

Source: Data from 1972 based on Edgar K. Browning, "The Trend Toward Equality in the Distribution of Net Income," *Southern Economic Journal* 43 (July 1976), 914.

Thus, whereas privatization in Eastern Europe consists primarily of changes in equity arrangements from public to private, privatization in the United States is more likely to consist of government contracting for the private production of traditionally public-sector goods and services, such as trash collection, homes for the elderly, local transportation services, schools, and even prisons.

Privatization is a matter of considerable controversy in the contemporary American economy. Accordingly, it is easy to find strongly held views on both sides of the subject. Those who favor privatization in the provision of municipal services, for example, argue that beyond immediate cost reduction, quality will improve as a result of competitive markets and that in the long term, the role of government in the economy will be reduced. Those who oppose privatization argue that, in fact, only limited empirical evidence indicates actual cost reductions. Moreover, because measuring its impact is difficult, the role of government might not be reduced, competitive provision of services might not prevail, and quality might, in fact, be threatened. Inevitably, privatization threatens government employees, who are likely to oppose the trend.

A case in point has been the battle over vouchers in public education. If government gave parents vouchers that could be used to pay for education in the school of the parents' choice, this would result in a de facto privatization of U.S. public education. Vouchers have therefore been strongly opposed by teacher unions.

What is the status of privatization in the United States in the late 1990s? First, although past trends have been toward contracting, there are publicly owned facilities, such as airports, roads, water systems, and sports centers, to which the privatization discussion has been applied. Second, although considerable variation exists from one city or region to another, there is a substantial amount of private initiative in the provision of local services. Finally, the message from the scholarly literature remains divided. However, as more case studies are examined, empirical evidence will doubtless help in understanding privatization, in determining whether it is a realistic alternative for cost savings, and in sorting out the preconditions that are necessary to achieve such savings.

The United States and Economic Freedom

Economies allocate resources through markets and through government allocation. This chapter has described the various ways in which governments intervene in the U.S. economy. Government influences private economic decision making through social and economic regulation, antitrust laws, income redistribution, environmental restrictions, and so on.

When compared with other countries, how much economic freedom is there in the United States economy? By *economic freedom* we mean the ability of participants in the economy to pursue their economic decision making free from government controls or intervention.

The Heritage Foundation, in cooperation with the *Wall Street Journal,* compiles an annual index of economic freedom that applies more than fifty independent criteria to assess the level of economic freedom in each country.[41] The areas examined are trade policy, taxation, government intervention, monetary policy, capital flows and foreign investment, banking policy, wage and price controls, property rights, regulation, and black market activity.

The U.S. economy ties for fifth place with Switzerland on this index of economic freedom. Only Hong Kong, Singapore, Bahrain, and New Zealand rank higher.

Comparison of the 1997 index with previous indexes reveals that wealthy countries tend to lose their ranking as time passes. The United States, however, with its deregulation process, has been able to retain its ranking, unlike other industrialized countries such as Germany and France, whose rankings have been dropping.

Another measure of economic freedom is freedom from corruption—the degree to which business transactions involve corruption or questionable practices. According to this indicator, the United States tied for first place with eight other countries (Canada, Ireland, France, The Netherlands, New Zealand, Norway, Singapore, and Switzerland).[42]

Both indicators reflect the degree to which business decision makers are free to pursue their economic decision making unencumbered either by government intervention or by government corruption. In both regards, the U.S. economy scores among the world's leaders.

Summary

Three main actors make up the American economy: firms, households, and government. The private sector consists of economic activity in which private ownership prevails, whereas the public sector comprises economic activity influenced by government. The coordination of economic activity is determined primarily by relatively decentralized product and factor markets by the forces of supply and demand. This structure conforms to the theoretical model of market capitalism, with exceptions to the existence of competitive markets both for products and for factors of production.

Government plays an important role in the American economy, although direct government ownership is more limited in the United States than in other market economies. The American government does, however, play an important role in the regulation and control of industries in which some degree of concentration of market power is said to exist. Some 25 percent of economic activity in the United States has been directly affected by such involvement as government spending and regulatory activity. The percentage of that government activity was reduced in the 1980s as a result of significant deregulation, especially in airlines, trucking, and telecommunications.

The principal mechanisms of government influence in the American economy are regulation and antitrust policy. Antitrust policy in the United States is largely spelled out in four acts: the Sherman Act, the Clayton Act, and Federal Trade Commission Act, and the Celler–Kefauver Act.

The American government, in spite of important social programs, does not play a major role in the redistribution of income. Some, however, would argue that the actual impact is greater than the visible impact because of difficulties in measuring the effect of in-kind transfers. Certainly, the redistributive role of the American government in the American economy is less than that typically found in other industrialized market economies.

In recent years, interest has increased in the privatization of government activity. Privatization is controversial largely because of the relatively limited empirical evidence of its costs and benefits. In the American economy, privatization is generally achieved not through changes in ownership but through local government attempting to reduce costs through private contracting for services. The U.S. economy is among the world's leaders in economic freedom and freedom from corruption.

Key Terms

public sector	concentration ratio	capital market
private sector	competition	future prices
sole proprietorship	price takers	financial intermediaries
partnership	perfect markets	public goods
corporation	arbitrage	military–industrial complex
product market	imperfect competition	social regulation
factor market	intermediaries	economic regulation
market power	discrimination	deregulation

antitrust legislation   price fixing   external costs and benefits
monopolization   mergers   privatization
monopolies

Notes

1. Milton Friedman, "Monopoly and Social Responsibility of Business and Labor," in Edwin Mansfield, ed., *Monopoly Power and Economic Performance*, 3rd ed. (New York: Norton, 1974), pp. 57–68.
2. Frederic Scherer, *Industrial Structure and Economic Performance*, 2nd ed. (Boston: Houghton Mifflin, 1980), p. 519.
3. Clifford Winston, "Economic Deregulation: Days of Reckoning for Microeconomists," *Journal of Economic Literature* 31, 3 (September 1993), 1263–1289.
4. Milton Friedman, "Monopoly and Social Responsibility of Business and Labor," pp. 57–68.
5. William G. Shepherd, "Causes of Increased Competition in the U.S. Economy, 1939–1980," *Review of Economics and Statistics,* November 1982, 613–626.
6. See Scherer, *Industrial Market Structure*, pp. 68–70; James V. Koch, *Industrial Organization and Prices*, 2nd ed. (Englewood Cliffs, N.J.: Prentice-Hall, 1980), p. 181; and Morris Adelman, "Changes in Industrial Concentration," in Mansfield, *Monopoly Power and Economic Performance*, pp. 83–88.
7. Joe S. Bain, *Barriers to New Competition*, pp. 192–200; H. Michael Mann, "Seller Concentration, Barriers to Entry, and Rates of Return in Thirty Industries," *Review of Economics and Statistics* 58 (August 1966), 296–307.
8. Leonard W. Weiss, "Quantitative Studies of Industrial Organization," in Michael D. Intrilligator, ed., *Frontiers of Quantitative Economics* (Amsterdam: North Holland, 1971); Leonard Weiss, "Concentration–Profits Relationship and Antitrust," in Goldschmidt *et al.,* eds., *Industrial Concentration: The New Learning* (Boston: Little, Brown, 1974), pp. 184–233.
9. The Harberger results can be found in Arnold Harberger, "Monopoly and Resource Allocation," *American Economic Review* 44 (May 1954), 77–87.
10. Anne Krueger, "The Political Economy of the Rent-Seeking Society," *American Economic Review* 64 (June 1974), 291–303; Gordon Tullock, "The Welfare Cost of Tariffs, Monopolies, and Theft," *Western Economic Journal* 5 (June 1967), 224–232; Harvey Leibenstein, "Allocative Efficiency vs. X-Inefficiency," *American Economic Review* 56 (June 1966), 392–415.
11. Harold Demsetz, "Industry Structure, Market Rivalry, and Public Policy," *Journal of Law and Economics* 16 (April 1973), 1–10.
12. Our discussion of the U.S. labor market and the figures cited are from the following sources: William Bowen and Orley Ashenfelter, eds., *Labor and the National Economy*, rev. ed. (New York: Norton, 1975); H. Gregg Lewis, *Unions and Relative Wages in the United States* (Chicago: University of Chicago Press, 1963); Stanley Masters, *Black–White Income Differentials* (New York: Academic, 1975); Cynthia Lloyd, ed., *Sex, Discrimination and the Division of Labor* (New York: Columbia University Press, 1975); Michael Boskin, "Unions and Relative Real Wages," *American Economic Review* 62 (June 1972), 466–472; George Johnson, "Economic Analysis of Trade Unionism," *American Economic Review, Papers and Proceedings* 65 (May 1975), 23–28; Albert Rees, *The Economics of Trade Unions* (Chicago: University of Chicago Press, 1963); C. J. Paisley, "Labor Union

Effects on Wage Gains: A Survey of Recent Literature," *Journal of Economic Literature* 18 (March 1980), 1–31; and Richard Freeman and James Medoff, "The Two Faces of Unionism," *The Public Interest* 57 (Fall 1979), 73–80; and Ronald G. Ehrenberg and Robert S. Smith, *Modern Labor Economics*, 3rd ed. (Glenview, Ill.: Scott, Foresman, 1988); "Rising Wage Inequality in the United States: Causes and Consequences," *American Economic Review: Papers and Proceedings* 84, 2 (May 1994), 10–33; "Lessons from Empirical Labor Economics: 1972–1992," *American Economic Review: Papers and Proceedings* 83, 2 (May 1993), 104–121.

13. The original statement of the merit goods (wants) concept is found in Richard Musgrave, *The Theory of Public Finance* (New York: McGraw-Hill, 1959).

14. For a classic debate over the proper scope of government and "nongovernment," see Paul Samuelson, "The Economic Role of Private Activity: A Dialogue on the Proper Economic Role of the State," in Paul Samuelson, ed., *Readings in Economics*, 7th ed. (New York: McGraw-Hill, 1973), pp. 78–84; and George J. Stigler, "The Government of the Economy," *A Dialogue on the Proper Economic Role of the State, ibid.,* 73–77; for a discussion of public choice, see Harvey S. Rosen, *Public Finance,* 3rd ed. (Homewood, Ill.: Irwin, 1992), Ch. 7.

15. For more on the various explanations of the U.S. weapons procurement system, see James Kurth, "The Political Economy of Weapons Procurement: The Follow-On Imperative," *American Economic Review, Papers and Proceedings* 62 (May 1972), 304–311.

16. Seymour Melman, *Pentagon Capitalism* (New York: McGraw-Hill, 1970); and Kurth, "The Political Economy of Weapons Procurement," pp. 304–311.

17. For Galbraith's view, see John Kenneth Galbraith, "Power and the Useful Economist," *American Economic Review* 63 (March 1973), 1–11.

18. For suggestions on how to improve the current procurement system, see Carl Kaysen, "Improving the Efficiency of Military Research and Development" with comments by Paul Cherington, in Mansfield, *Defense, Science, and Public Policy*, pp. 114–131.

19. For arguments in favor of the fourth approach, see Friedman, "Monopoly and Social Responsibility of Business and Labor," pp. 57–68; and George Stigler and Claire Friedland, "What Can Regulators Regulate? The Case of Electricity," in Paul MacAvoy, ed., *The Crisis of the Regulatory Commissions* (New York: Norton, 1970), pp. 39–52.

20. These statistics are from Department of Commerce, *Historical Statistics of the United States: Colonial Times to 1970* (Washington, D.C.: Government Printing Office, 1975), Series N15–29, S86–94, 6416–469, Y505–521; and Clair Wilcox, *Public Policies Toward Business*, 3rd ed. (Homewood, Ill.: Irwin, 1966).

21. James Schmitz, "The Role Played by Public Enterprises: How Much Does It Differ Across Countries?" Federal Reserve Bank of Minneapolis, *Quarterly Review,* Spring 1996, 9.

22. Scherer, *Industrial Structure and Economic Performance*, p. 421.

23. Schmitz, "The Role Played by Public Enterprises," p. 6.

24. The following discussion of regulation is based on these sources: Wilcox, *Public Policies Toward Business*, part III; Scherer, *Industrial Structure and Economic Performance*, Ch. 18; and Paul MacAvoy, "The Rationale for Regulation of Field Prices of Natural Gas," in MacAvoy, *The Crisis of the Regulatory Commissions*, pp. 152–168; Robert E. Litan and William D. Nordhaus, *Reforming Federal Regulation* (New Haven: Yale University Press, 1983); and Lawrence J. White, *Reforming Regulation* (Englewood Cliffs, N.J.: Prentice-Hall, 1981).

25. The first of these commissions was established in New England before the Civil War, with authority over the railroads, and in the Midwest in the 1870s. Commissions for the

regulation of public utilities were set up only in the early twentieth century (1907); in some instances, public utility supervision was entrusted to the already established railroad commissions. Federal regulation was initiated first in 1887 with the Interstate Commerce Commission, the first major federal regulatory commission.

State commissions in almost all states have jurisdiction over railroads, motor carriers, water, electricity, gas, and telephones, and such bodies in about half the states have the authority to regulate urban transit, taxicabs, and gas pipelines. Commissioners are either elected or appointed by the governor of the state. The staffs of the commissions are generally small and are generally poorly funded compared to the legal staffs of the industries they regulate.

There are five federal commissions. The Interstate Commerce Commission (established in 1887) regulates railroads, interstate oil pipelines, and interstate motor and water carriers. The Federal Power Commission (established in 1920) has jurisdiction over power projects and the interstate transmission of electricity and natural gas. The Federal Communications Commission (established in 1933) regulates interstate telephone and telegraph and broadcasting. The Securities and Exchange Commission (established in 1934) regulates securities markets. The Civil Aeronautics Board (established in 1938) supervised domestic and international aviation before it was closed in 1984. These federal commissions are staffed by commissioners appointed by the U.S. president for terms of five to seven years, and their staffs range from 1000 to 2000 employees. In general, the professional staffs on the federal commissions are better paid and better qualified than their state counterparts, but their salaries are not competitive with those paid by the regulated industries.

26. Federal Reserve Bank of Dallas, *America's Economic Regulation Burden,* Fall 1996, pp. 1–6.
27. See, for example, the selections by Merton Peck (on transportation), Richard Caves (on air transport), and Paul MacAvoy and E. W. Kitch (on natural gas) in MacAvoy, *The Crisis of the Regulatory Commissions,* pp. 72–93, 131–151, 152–186.
28. This discussion is based on Roy J. Ruffin and Paul R. Gregory, *Principles of Microeconomics,* 3rd ed. (Glenview, Ill.: Scott, Foresman, 1988), Ch. 14; Elizabeth E. Bailey, "Price and Productivity Change Following Deregulation: The U.S. Experience," *The Economic Journal* 96 (March 1986), 1–17. See also C. Winston, "Conceptual Developments in the Economics of Transportation," *Journal of Economic Literature* 23 (1985), 57–94; T. Keeler, *Railroads, Freight, and Public Policy* (Washington, D.C.: Brookings, 1983); A. F. Friedlander and R. H. Spady, *Freight Transport Regulation* (Cambridge, Mass.: M.I.T. Press, 1981); Clifford Winston, "Economic Deregulation: Days of Reckoning for Microeconomists," *Journal of Economic Literature* 31, 3 (September 1993), 1263–1289.
29. Robert Bradley, Jr., "The Origins of Political Electricity: Market Failure or Political Opportunism?" *Energy Law Journal* 17, 59 (1996), 59–102.
30. This discussion is based on Scherer, *Industrial Structure and Economic Performance,* Ch. 19 and pp. 469–494; A. D. Neale, *The Antitrust Laws of the United States of America* (Cambridge, England: The University Press, 1962), pp. 2–5; Eugene Singer, *Antitrust Economics* (Englewood Cliffs, N.J.: Prentice-Hall, 1968), Ch. 2; Marshall C. Howard, *Antitrust and Trade Regulation* (Englewood Cliffs, N.J.: Prentice-Hall, 1983); Oliver Williamson, *Markets and Hierarchies: Analysis and Antitrust Implications* (New York: The Free Press, 1975); and Howard, *Antitrust and Trade Regulation.*
31. The landmark cases were the Standard Oil and American Tobacco cases of 1911. In both instances, the courts ruled that these companies, both accounting for some 90 percent of industry output, should be dissolved into smaller companies. The courts' reasoning, however, was that Standard Oil and American Tobacco were in violation of the Sherman Act

not because they accounted for such a large share of industry output (that is, not because they were monopolies) but because they had engaged in "unreasonable" restraints of trade. The implication of this ruling was that if these companies had behaved better toward their competitors, they would not have been held in violation of the Sherman Act. This so-called rule of reason was the prevailing interpretation of the Sherman Act until 1945. The rule of reason was upheld in 1920 with the U.S. Steel case. The company controlled over half of industry output yet had not treated its competitors unfairly or sought to control steel prices. In this case, the courts upheld the rule of reason, stating that the law does not make mere size or the existence of unexerted power an offense.

32. These conclusions are from Simon Whitney, *Antitrust Policies*, Vol. II (New York: Twentieth Century Fund, 1958), p. 429; summarized in Wilcox, *Public Policies Toward Business*, p. 281.

33. Richard Musgrave, "National Economic Planning: The U.S. Case," *American Economic Review, Papers and Proceedings* 67 (February 1977), 50–54; see also R. D. Norton, "Industrial Policy and American Renewal," *Journal of Economic Literature* 24, 1 (March 1986), 1–40.

34. Edwin Mills, "Economic Incentives in Air-Pollution Control," in Marshall Goldman, ed., *Controlling Pollution: The Economics of a Cleaner America* (Englewood Cliffs, N.J.: Prentice-Hall, 1967), pp. 100–108.

35. See, for example, Morton Paglin, "The Measurement and Trend of Inequality: A Basic Revision," *American Economic Review* 65 (September 1975), 598–609; and Edgar Browning, "The Trend Toward Equality in the Distribution of Income," *Southern Economic Journal* 43 (July 1976), 912–923.

36. These figures are from Department of Commerce, *Historical Statistics of the United States*, series G; and *Statistical Abstract of the United States*.

37. Paglin, "The Measurement and Trend of Inequality," pp. 598–609.

38. Joseph Pechman and Benjamin Okner, *Who Bears the Tax Burden?* (Washington, D.C.: Brookings, 1974).

39. Browning, "The Trend Toward Equality," pp. 912–923. Also see Edgar Browning and William R. Johnson, *The Distribution of the Tax Burden* (Washington, D.C.: American Enterprise Institute, 1979).

40. For background, see Janet Rotherberg Pack, "Privatization of Public Sector Services in Theory and Practice," *Journal of Policy Analysis and Management* 6 (1987), 523–540; John B. Donahue, *The Privatization Decision* (New York: Basic Books, 1989); a useful summary of the American experience can be found in Richard L. Worsnop, "Privatization," *Congressional Quarterly Researcher,* November 13, 1992, 979–999.

41. Heritage Foundation and *Wall Street Journal, 1997 Index of Economic Freedom* (New York: Dow Jones, Inc., 1997).

42. Paulo Mauro, "Corruption and Growth," *Quarterly Journal of Economics* 110 (1995), 681–712.

Recommended Readings

Traditional Sources

F. M. Bator, "The Simple Analytics of Welfare Maximization," *American Economic Review* 47 (March 1957), 22–59.

———, "The Anatomy of Market Failure," *Quarterly Journal of Economics* 72 (August 1958), 351–379.

H. G. Lewis, *Unionism and Relative Wages in the United States* (Chicago: University of Chicago Press, 1963).

Paul MacAvoy, ed., *The Crisis of Regulatory Commissions* (New York: Norton, 1970).

Product Markets

William J. Baumol, John C. Panzar, and Robert D. Willig, *Contestable Markets and the Theory of Industry Structure* (New York: Harcourt Brace Jovanovich, 1982).

Oliver Williamson, *The Economic Institutions of Capitalism* (New York: The Free Press, 1985).

Factor Markets

Ronald Ehrenberg and Robert Smith, *Modern Labor Economics* 3rd ed. (Glenview, Ill.: Scott Foresman, 1988).

Richard B. Freeman, "Unionism Comes to the Public Sector," *Journal of Economic Literature* 24, 1 (March 1986), 41–86.

"Lessons from Empirical Labor Economics: 1972–1992," *The American Economic Review: Papers and Proceedings* 83, 2 (May 1993), 104–121.

James B. Rebitzer, "Radical Political Economy and the Economics of Labor Markets," *Journal of Economic Literature* 31, 3 (September 1993), 1394–1434.

Government and the Economy

Andrew B. Abel and Ben S. Bernanke, *Macroeconomics* (New York: Addison-Wesley, 1992).

Douglas H. Blair and Robert A. Pollack, "Rational Collective Choice," *Scientific American* 249, 2 (August 1983), 88–95.

John B. Donahue, *The Privatization Decision* (New York: Basic Books, 1989).

Federal Reserve Bank of Dallas, *America's Economic Regulation Burden,* Fall 1996.

Frank Levy and Richard J. Murname, "U.S. Earning Levels and Earnings Inequality: A Review of Recent Trends and Proposed Explanations" *Journal of Economic Literature* 30, 3 (September 1992), 1333–1381.

N. Gregory Mankiw, "Symposium on Keynesian Economics Today," *Journal of Economic Literature* 7, 1 (Winter 1993), 3–82.

Robert Moffitt, "Incentive Effects of the U.S. Welfare System: A Review," *Journal of Economic Literature* 30, 1 (March 1992), 1–61.

Joseph Pechman, *Who Paid the Taxes, 1966–85?* (Washington, D.C.: Brookings Institution, 1985).

Janet Rotherberg Pack, "Privatization of Public Sector Services in Theory and Practice," *Journal of Policy Analysis and Management* 6 (1987), 523–540.

Harvey S. Rosen, *Public Finance,* 3rd ed. (Homewood, Ill.: Irwin, 1992).

F. M. Scherer and David Ross, *Industrial Market Structure and Economic Performance*, 3rd ed. (Boston: Houghton Mifflin, 1990).

Eugene Singer, *Antitrust Economics* (Englewood Cliffs, N.J.: Prentice-Hall, 1968).

James Schmitz, "The Role Played by Public Enterprises: How Much Does It Differ Across Countries?" Federal Reserve Bank of Minneapolis, *Quarterly Review,* Spring 1996, 2–15.

Don E. Waldman, ed., *The Economics of Antitrust* (Boston: Little, Brown, 1986).

Leonard Weiss and Michael Klass, eds., *Regulatory Reform: What Actually Happened* (Boston: Little, Brown, 1986).

Clifford Winston, "Economic Deregulation: Days of Reckoning for Microeconomists," *Journal of Economic Literature* 31, 3 (September 1993), 1263–1289.

Richard L. Worsnop, "Privatization," *Congressional Quarterly Researcher* (November 13, 1992), 979–999.

Economic Freedom

Heritage Foundation and the *Wall Street Journal, 1997 Index of Economic Freedom* (New York: Dow Jones Inc., 1997).

Kine R. Holmes and Melanie Kirkpatrick, "Freedom and Growth," *Wall Street Journal,* December 16, 1996.

Paulo Mauro, "Corruption and Growth," *Quarterly Journal of Economics* 110, (1995), 681–712.

9

The Soviet Command Economy: Structure and Performance

Although the organization of the Soviet economy varied during the years following the 1917 **Bolshevik revolution**, state ownership, national economic planning, and the collectivization of agriculture were all introduced in the late 1920s and lasted through 1991, the last year of the Soviet Union as a country.

The **administrative command economy** was the primary mechanism for resource allocation in the former Soviet Union for more than sixty years. The Soviet experience of centrally planned socialism remains the prime example of an attempt to remake the society and to forge rapid economic development with minimal use of markets.

Although the concept of economic reform received a great deal of attention in the Soviet Union from mid-1950 on, reform did little to change the fundamentals of the system. Thus from 1928 through 1985, when Mikhail Gorbachev introduced Perestroika, there is a long period in which to examine the nature and operation of the Soviet economic system.

The demise of the former Soviet Union and other, similar systems in Eastern Europe necessarily focuses attention on issues of performance. The last section of this chapter examines their performance to understand the reasons for their demise and their legacy for transition in the 1990s.

Historical Perspectives

Our examination of American capitalism was not cast in historical perspective. The American economy is, after all, an economy undergoing change all the time. The Soviet experience was different. Just as the Gorbachev era represented a sharp break with the Soviet past, the Bolshevik revolution of 1917 represented a sharp break with the preceding **czarist era**.[1] Indeed, Soviet experimentation between 1917 and 1928 provides insights into the roots of the administrative-command system.

The era of the czars came to a close and the era of the Soviets began with the Bolshevik revolution of 1917. Although the Soviet economic system of the plan era dates from 1928, analysis of the Soviet era must begin with the *level* and *rate* of **economic development** at the end of the czarist era.

Russian economic development as of 1917 was at a relatively low level, judged by indicators such as per capita GNP. However, there had been considerable increase in rate of growth, especially industrial growth, during the last three decades of czarist rule, and the Soviets could therefore build on an existing base of transportation, industrial capacity, minerals, and so forth.

At the end of the 1920s, Joseph Stalin, the Soviet leader who had succeeded V. I. Lenin, made two momentous decisions. First, a comprehensive system of central economic planning based on compulsory state and party directives was established. An abrupt end to the prevailing system of market relations in industry ensued, and there was a sudden shift in industrial production away from consumer goods and toward producer goods. Second, agriculture was collectivized. A vast network of **collective farms (*kolkhozy*)** was created, in which more than 90 percent of Soviet peasant households were living by the mid-1930s.[2] These two major decisions, though sudden at the time, did not arise out of a vacuum.

Two economic "experiments" were conducted in the decade following the revolution of 1917: **war communism** (1917–1920) and the New Economic Policy (1921–1928).[3] Both responded to the needs to consolidate power and to marshal economic resources in a time of crisis.[4]

War communism, implemented by Lenin during the Russian Civil War, saw the introduction of substantial state ownership (nationalization), an attempt to eliminate market relationships in industry and trade, and the forced requisitioning of agricultural products from the peasants. In a sense, it seemed that Lenin was attempting to by-pass socialism and move directly from a capitalist to a communist system. Whatever the intent, the economic consequences were a disaster by the end of the civil war; the economy was in ruin.[5]

In an attempt to instill economic recovery, Lenin introduced the **New Economic Policy (NEP)** in 1921. NEP signaled a partial return to private ownership (the so-called commanding heights of industry remained nationalized), reintroduction of the market as a primary mechanism for resource allocation, and implementation of a more viable tax system on agriculture. By 1927, the Soviet economy had recovered from the losses of war communism and was at, and in some cases above, the prewar level.[6] In effect, NEP could be regarded as a primitive form of market socialism, with its combination of state ownership of industry and market allocation.

The period from 1917 to 1928 provided some lessons that permeated Soviet thinking. First, if the market were to be eliminated, some mechanism for coordination had to take its place. During war communism, Lenin nationalized industries and eliminated the market, but he did not replace the market with a plan or some other substitute mechanism. Second, partly as a result of inept state policies, the peasants came to be viewed as holding considerable power over the pace of industrialization.[7] After all, the economy was largely agricultural, so resources would have to come primarily from the rural sector. Third, the response to Lenin's attempt to introduce payment in kind and to downgrade the importance of money during war communism made it obvious that, whatever the system, **material incentives** would be crucial to motivate labor.

In addition to the experience of war communism and NEP, the 1920s witnessed open discussions: the "great industrialization debate" and the beginnings of the theory of planning.[8] The debate on industrialization focused on modes of industrialization and, in particular, on differing roles for the agricultural and industrial sectors. All participants agreed that industrialization was essential and that the peasants would play a key role. The end result, however, was not readily foreseen by the debate's participants.

The economic system that Stalin put in place in the late 1920s and early 1930s was radically different from then-existing systems. Although the economic system evolved through time, and a variety of reform attempts were made beginning in the late 1950s, the system Mikhail Gorbachev inherited in the mid-1980s looked surprisingly similar to that of earlier years.

The Setting

Before we examine the Soviet command economy, we should consider its natural setting. By almost any measure, the Soviet Union was a very large country. It occupied 8.6 million square miles, an area more than twice that of the United States. In terms of population, the Soviet Union entered the 1990s with approximately 290 million persons, some 15 percent more than the population of the United States. The majority of the Soviet population (roughly 65 percent) lived in urban areas, and approximately 80 percent of the labor force was in industry and related nonagricultural occupations. Urbanization characterized the Soviet experience, along with the traditional shift of the labor force away from rural/agricultural pursuits.

Equally significant, the Soviet Union was a very diverse nation consisting of 15 union republics. The largest of these, the Russian Republic, accounted for just over 50 percent of the Soviet population. The remainder of the population comprised the Latvians, Lithuanians, and Estonians; the Ukrainians; the peoples of Central Asia, including Uzbekistan, Kirgizstan, Tadzhikistan, and Turkmenistan; and those of the Caucasus, including Georgia, Azerbaidzhan, and Armenia. These and other peoples of the Soviet Union infused it with vast ethnic, cultural, and historical diversity. Ethnic and regional differences remained significant in the post-Soviet era, as the newly independent former Soviet republics created their own transition paths.

Sharp differences also existed in the Soviet Union's natural environment. The climate ranged from the hot, dry areas of Central Asia to the cold expanses of Siberia and the cool, wet plains of the west. Needless to say, significant regional differences in climate dictated major variations in resource usage, especially in agriculture.

Finally, the Soviet Union had an extraordinarily rich resource base. In addition to being a major producer of fish and forest products, the Soviet Union was amply endowed with minerals and was the world's largest producer of petroleum, coal, and iron ore. Indeed, there are very few minerals for which the Soviet Union had inadequate domestic reserves.

The Soviet Economy: A Framework

System differences fall into four basic categories: **decision-making** *levels*, *market* and *plan* mechanisms of information, **property rights** (*public* **versus** *private*), and incentive systems (*material* versus *moral*).

As we examine the Soviet command economy and its organizational arrangements, we must ask two questions: How did this system differ from the ideal of planned socialism? How should the actual command system be categorized according to our four criteria?

In terms of the decision-making arrangements, the Soviet economy was organized in a vertical hierarchical fashion of the sort described in Figure 2.4. The Soviet state, operating through government ministries, and the **Communist party**, operating through groups and cells in organizations, shared authority and responsibility. There were several decision-making layers, including the state and party structure at the top, the ministries and regional authorities and sometimes trust organizations in the middle, and the basic production units (enterprises and farms), at the lower level.

From the perspective of resource allocation, the Soviet system was a centralized economic system. Moreover, the dominant mechanism for generating and using information was the national economic plan and its subcomponents. The state and party organizations made key decisions on production, distribution, and accumulation that were spelled out in the long- and short-term plans. Although planning was the dominant mechanism for resource allocation, there were instances in which market forces and influences affected that process—for example, in the allocation of labor and in the second, or underground, economy.

The most striking difference between the Soviet economy and a market capitalist economy was in the area of property rights. The Soviet state as the primary property owner controlled virtually all aspects of property utilization. Although collective farms, for example, were exceptions to full state ownership, in fact such distinctions were not particularly important.

Significantly, state ownership of property meant that there were no capital or land markets and no formal system of rewards to these inputs. Rather, income generated from their use accrued directly to the state, **wage income** being the method of payment to workers. Beyond **material incentives**, however, the Communist party placed considerable emphasis on **moral incentives**, a distinguishing characteristic of socialist systems.

Organizational Features

Since the beginning of the plan era in 1928, organizational change occurred frequently in the Soviet Union. Despite the appearance of change, there was continuity in the basic arrangements, a stylized picture of which is presented in Figure 9.1. Under these arrangements, the Soviet Union was nominally governed by an elected government, the operative organ of which was the Council of Ministers at the federal (all-Union) and republic levels. A parallel structure, the Communist Party of the Soviet Union (CPSU), was the principal organ of decision making, control, and

FIGURE 9.1   The Organization of the Soviet Economy:
The Command Model

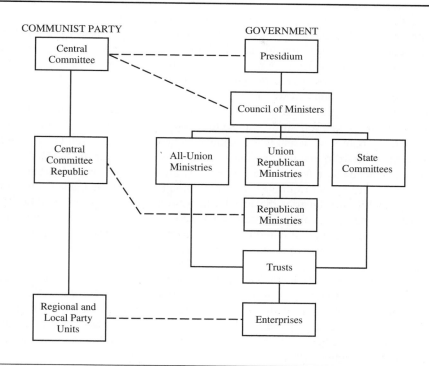

supervision. It operated through a complex centralized structure beginning at the national level and terminating with individual party cells in each industrial enterprise, farm, and organization.[9] Regional party organizations were important agents for controlling and monitoring the allocation of resources at the local level.

The means of production were, with only limited exceptions, owned by the state; firms and other organizations operated under the control of the state and party apparatus.[10] Agriculture was organized into state farms, collective farms, and a private sector, the latter governed by strict regulations. Both vertical and horizontal integration characterized the later agricultural scene, as farms and industrial processing were linked in agro-industrial combines.

The major decisions about resource allocation were made through **Gosplan**, the state planning agency. The Communist party developed the general directives on resource allocation. Gosplan then converted those directives into operative plans, with the aid of ministeries and, to a degree, the individual enterprises. Finally, it was the responsibility of the individual enterprises to carry out the plan directives. Information flowed from top to bottom and vice versa, intra-enterprise activities were plan-coordinated, and money and markets played only a limited role.

Over the years, there was remarkable stability in organizational arrangements and policy directives. The administrative-command system remained a hierarchical command system in which public ownership was combined with material incentives aimed at encouraging the carrying out of state and party directives. From an economic standpoint, two properties of the command system deserve emphasis. First, the major organization around which the industrial activity of enterprises and the agricultural activities of farms were organized was the **ministry**. Ministries were hierarchically organized by type of production: steel, agriculture, and so on. The ministerial structure was shifted to organization on a *regional* basis in 1957, under the reform leadership of Nikita Khrushchev, to break down the tendency of ministries to become self-sufficient and to ignore interactions with other ministries. The reform did not work and was abandoned when Khrushchev fell from power in 1964. Ministries differed in importance, depending on their function. The most important branches of industry were governed by all-union ministries. Investment decisions concerning, for example, steel production facilities were made at the center. Union republican ministries dispersed a measure of decision-making authority to the level of the 15 republics. The ministries were the organizational superiors of the industrial and agricultural enterprises. Organizational reforms experimented with combining enterprises into trusts to serve as an intermediary between the enterprise and the ministry.

Second, economy-wide planning was done by Gosplan, the state planning agency. Gosplan was responsible for converting general directives of the Communist party into operative plans, with the help of the ministries and individual enterprises. Although planning, in the sense of making all economic decisions, is virtually impossible, in practice the Soviet command system utilized a variety of means to simplify the planning task.

Planning in Practice

The allocation of resources in the Soviet Union was conducted primarily through the plan. There were short-term (1-year), longer-term (5- or 7-year), and even 20-year "perspective" plans. The annual plans, which directed economic activity, were of central interest.

The essence of plan formulation was the **material balance system**, the theoretical basis of which we examined in Chapter 6.[11] The plan was formulated in the following manner. General directives on the economy were provided by the CPSU and converted into control figures by Gosplan. The control figures, or tentative production targets, were transmitted through the ministries down to the level of individual enterprises, with comment and informational input being sought from each level in the hierarchy. The control figures then moved back up through the hierarchy and at the Gosplan level were "balanced"; that is, for major items in the plan, supply and demand had to balance. Once balance was achieved, the plan was disaggregated and the targets once again disseminated down through the ministries to the individual enterprises. The final result, the **techpromfinplans** (technical-industrial-financial plans), were legally binding and contained detailed directives for enterprise operations during the forthcoming year.

In practice, the formulation of this plan was time-consuming and complex, and clearly could not approach the theoretical ideals posed in Chapter 6. Intense bargaining, haggling, interplay among the various units, and delays were integral parts of planning. Frequently the new plan was late in arriving, so the enterprise would continue to operate under the old plan. The material balance system worked in large part because it had built-in flexibility. The planning process did not start from scratch each year. The plan for year t was, in effect, little more than a revision and update of the plan for year $t-1$. This practice was described as "planning from the achieved level." Although it simplified the planning process, it built in considerable inflexibility. In addition, Soviet planners did not plan all items produced by the economy and planned at the center only a relatively small number of items. Major commodities such as steel and machinery were called **funded commodities** or **limited commodities** and were planned at the center. Their number varied over time from a few hundred to a few thousand. Other commodities were planned at progressively lower and lower levels, depending on their importance. This simplified the planning process but left much to be done at the lower levels—for example, in the various republics and ministries.

In constructing balances for major materials, planners faced a dilemma. On the one hand, they wanted the **balance** to be achieved at the highest possible level; on the other hand, they knew that the more *taut* the plan—that is, the closer the targets were to maximum capacity—the more likely it was that errors and supply imbalances would occur.[12] The approach was, in practice, to attempt to find a balance at a reasonably high level through adjusting input usage, final demand, and stocks, and/or seeking foreign supplies. All these stratagems were devices for ensuring that the plan was demanding yet at the same time in balance. Soviet planners did not employ sophisticated planning techniques to "balance" supplies and demands. In fact, ad hoc tallies of sources and material requirements were compiled, and past experience was the principal guide. Accordingly, Soviet planners were usually satisfied if they were able to come up with a **consistent plan**, but they did not have the luxury of seeking out the **optimal plan** from among all possible consistent plans.

This picture of traditional Soviet planning is only an approximation of reality, for it depicts an economy that was rigidly planned and controlled by central authorities. In relative terms this view is correct. All economies combine some mix of market and plan, and the Soviet economy leaned most heavily in the direction of planning by directive. Most facets of the Soviet economy were planned, and there was almost total public ownership of the means of production. But beneath the façade of rigid centralized planning, numerous informal and some quasi-market mechanisms affected resource allocation. Little is known about the scope and workings of those informal mechanisms, although our knowledge expanded in the post-Soviet era.

We know that the formal plan was really only the initial blueprint for economic activity at both the economy-wide and the enterprise level. The manner in which the plan was revised in the course of plan fulfillment was probably as important as the initial plan itself. In fact, the changes and revisions that took place after the plan was finalized were so great that some analysts questioned whether it is appropriate to call the Soviet economy a planned economy. We also know that a variety of unofficial markets existed that were largely independent of the formal planning process.[13] Most products, in fact, were planned at regional or local levels or were not planned at all. In some instances, indirect signals such as prices, played a role in resource allocation, especially at the managerial level.

It is not possible to characterize precisely the balance between the formal and informal forces that determined resource allocation in the Soviet Union. We know that compared to market economies, the balance was strongly in favor of centralized administrative allocation, but the role of informal forces was also recognized.[14]

Our discussion of the theory of planning (Chapter 6) emphasized three stages in the planning process: plan development, implementation, and feedback. Plan development was done by the planning organizations described above with limited participation by enterprises. Plan execution and feedback were characterized by more heavy involvement of enterprises. Plan implementation was in large part the responsibility of the individual firm or agricultural enterprise. What sorts of rules were used to ensure that each enterprise was in fact motivated to follow plan directives and thus fulfill the directives of the central planners? What happened when mistakes in planning were made or when allocation decisions were omitted from plan directives?

The Soviet Enterprise

In the planned economy, all enterprises have a plan, which is usually specified in annual terms but broken down into monthly (and even shorter) periods. The plan is a comprehensive document covering many facets of the firm's operations, and it has the force of law. The plan specifies both inputs and outputs in physical and financial terms; it specifies the sources and the distribution of funds for the firm. However, it would be erroneous to think that the Soviet manager was fully regimented, mechanically followed instructions, and had little freedom of action. In fact, quite a lot of managerial freedom existed. To understand Soviet management and plan fulfillment, one must understand how managers responded in this environment and what impact they had on plan fulfillment.

Much of the traditional Soviet managerial milieu can be summed up as the **managerial success indicator problem**. Soviet managers were offered substantial rewards for achieving planned objectives, but those objectives were fuzzy and often led to dysfunctional managerial behavior,[15] a classic principal–agent problem.

Historically, **gross value of output** was the most important target from the manager's viewpoint. The manager's performance was judged on the basis of fulfillment of that target. Even if prices accurately reflected relative scarcities, it would be difficult for planners to specify output objectives unequivocally. For example, if managers were told to maximize the gross value of output, they would ignore items that made a small contribution, relative to their claim on scarce resources, to gross value and would overproduce items that made a large contribution. The *mix* or **assortment of goods** within the plan would be ignored, if ignoring it was necessary to meet the gross output target. Given Soviet managerial bonuses, such behavior, though potentially disruptive, was rewarding to the manager and the enterprise. The bonus system typically paid little or nothing until the output plan was 100 percent fulfilled. Then rewards were paid for production over this level, resulting in an average managerial bonus of 25 or 35 percent of base salary.[16] Top managers received bonuses in excess of 50 percent. Moreover, managerial perks and job tenure depended on fulfillment of the gross output target. Generally taut targets and uncertain supply (especially for "limited" goods) were combined with substantial rewards for fulfillment of planned output targets. The result was informal and dysfunctional managerial behavior— a problem not anticipated by the socialist economic theorists, who assumed that managers would obey all rules handed down by superior authorities.

How did Soviet managers protect themselves and prosper in such an environment? First, managers, during the plan formulation stage, attempted to secure "easy" targets—that is, targets that were low vis-à-vis the actual capacity of the enterprise. This is a problem of any system in which participants can manipulate the objectives by which they will be measured. And it is why the reward system was so important in a planned economy.

Second, managers could emphasize what was important in terms of their rewards and neglect other areas. Thus cost-saving targets, along with assortment targets, could be sacrificed for the sake of ensuring fulfillment of gross output targets. Neglect of assortment explained the shortage of spare parts: Their manufacture disrupted production lines and did not contribute sufficiently to rewards. Third, managers could seek "safety" in various other practices. They could stockpile materials that were in short supply; they could avoid innovation; and they could establish informal or "family" connections to ensure a supply of crucial inputs.

Many features of the informal Soviet managerial milieu were disruptive and shifted the results of production away from those envisaged by the planners. Others were necessary to correct for errors made by planning authorities and for breakdowns in the supply system. Plan execution, therefore, was subject to a substantial measure of flexibility not envisaged in the theoretical models: People simply did not do what they were told. But the state did not stand idle; it exercised control over enterprise management.

Planners monitored enterprise performance, though this was not a simple task in an economy the size of the Soviet Union. The CPSU was a key control institution. All organizations contained party cells, and enterprise managers were nearly always party members, aware of party priorities. Despite these controls, at almost all levels of the Soviet economy there was a bias in favor of reporting successful results. If local enterprises performed well, the careers of local party officials were advanced, and so on up the hierarchy. Another monitoring device was the state bank (Gosbank).[17] Most Soviet enterprises were budget-financed, which meant that funds both to and from enterprises flowed through the state bank into and out of the state budget. The state budget was the major source of enterprise investment funds or, for an enterprise that lost money, of subsidy funds. Profits, too, were channeled through the state bank, and profit taxes were the major source of Soviet budgetary revenue. Each enterprise was required to hold all accounts with the state bank where all transactions were recorded. Not only were the firm's labor requirements specified in the plan, but the fund used to pay for the labor was held and monitored by the state bank.

Second, managerial behavior was manipulated by the reward system.[18] Soviet managers earned substantial monetary bonuses for meeting targets. There were other rewards, such as housing, vacations, automobiles, and promotions. On the negative side, managers who did not perform were dismissed, a sanction that was widely used in the early days of Soviet planning.[19]

Prices and the Allocation of Land, Labor, and Capital in the Command System

So far, we have discussed the planning of inputs and outputs and managerial behavior in the Soviet economy. We now consider the role of prices and the allocation of the factors of production. Soviet plans existed in both physical and monetary variants. The financial plans were derived from the physical plans. Beginning in the reform era of the late 1950s, increasing attention was paid to financial variables and hence to the nature and rationality of the Soviet price system. In market economic systems, prices clearly influence resource allocation. Indeed, as financial variables grew more important in the command economy, the issue of price formation grew in importance.

Soviet Prices: General Features

With some exceptions, Soviet prices were set by administrative authorities.[20] In the case of the collective farm markets, and in services provided by moonlighting workers, prices were formed by supply and demand. Industrial prices were set to equal the average cost by the industrial branch plus a small profit markup. **Branch average cost** generally excluded rental and interest charges, and its use as a standard resulted in enterprises making both planned profits and planned losses within the same branch. Pricing authorities sought, through periodic price "reforms," to raise prices enough to make the average branch enterprise profitable. This meant that when the price reform was introduced, the average enterprise broke even but others made substantial profits. The administrative difficulty of instituting frequent price reforms meant that historically prices lagged behind cost increases, and the majority of enterprises in particular branches made planned losses. During the last quarter-century of the Soviet system, major price reforms were rare. Wholesale prices established in 1955 remained generally in effect until 1966. The 1966–1967 price reform remained in effect until the general price reform of 1982. Prices had limited use, because they were unrelated to relative scarcities.

As far as inter-enterprise relations were concerned, wholesale prices played primarily an accounting role, for supplies and demands were administratively planned and were not functions of prices. However, when a product left the wholesale level to be sold at the retail level, the matter was not so simple. Figure 9.2 illustrates retail price formation.

The supply of consumer goods was determined largely by the planners, although producers, if they had a choice in output mix, might choose products with higher relative prices. Thus we draw the supply curve (S) with a steep upward slope. The demand curve (D) is a function of relative prices, incomes, and tastes and could

FIGURE 9.2   Soviet Turnover Tax

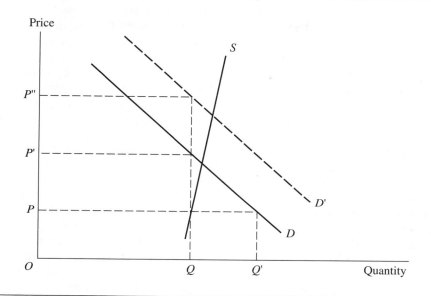

not be controlled by the planners. How could the planners achieve a balance of supply and demand? Typically, the retail price was established at or near a market-
clearing level by adding either a **turnover tax** or a subsidy (if the wholesale price
was above the clearing level). If the retail price were set at the wholesale price (P in
Figure 9.2), there would be an excess demand of $Q'Q$, for OQ would be produced
and OQ' demanded. Some form of rationing would be required in this case.

In addition to administrative rationing and rationing of goods through long lines,
Soviet authorities relied on adjusting the turnover tax to balance supply and demand.
If the authorities chose to ration via equilibrium pricing, the retail price would be set
at OP' and equilibrium would prevail. It is important to note that raising the retail
price *did not* raise the quantity supplied above OQ, because the enterprise continued
to receive the wholesale price OP for the product. The difference between the retail
and wholesale prices is the turnover tax.

The turnover tax, in this case PP', was a significant component of Soviet
budgetary revenue. Unlike Western sales taxes, its proportion differed widely from
one product to another, and it was included in the price rather than being added on
at the time of sale. Its share of retail prices declined over time, as planners increased
supplies of consumer products and raised the wholesale prices of farm products.

Although prices approached equilibrium at the retail level, the result was different from a market economy. What in the Soviet case was a tax would in the capitalist system be in effect a profit, signaling existing producers to expand supply and
new producers to enter the market. There was no such signal in the Soviet case,
because what would be profit in the capitalist context accrued as tax revenue to the

state. The producer at the wholesale level was unaware of and largely uninterested in retail prices. The link between consumer demand and the producer was broken. Say demand increases from D to D'. As the producer continues to receive the wholesale price OP, the quantity produced remains at OQ. But at the old retail price OP', there is now an excess of quantity demanded over quantity supplied. The state reacts eventually by raising the turnover tax by $P'P''$.

In the Soviet case, the mix of consumer goods was determined by **planners' preferences**, not by **consumer demand** (although planners may well have considered consumer signals when establishing plan targets). Thus prices played only a very limited allocative role and were used primarily for measurement, control, and manipulation of the distribution of income.

Soviet price policy emphasized the desirability of pricing some goods and services relatively "low" and others relatively "high." This policy reflected a very different socialist attitude toward the "equitable" distribution of income and toward necessities and luxuries. Thus the prices of books, housing, medical care, and transportation were very low, and the prices of automobiles and vodka were very high. Price policy affected the distribution of real incomes in accordance with state objectives.

In the pre-Gorbachev era, price reform was generally aimed at making prices more accurately reflect production costs to promote greater efficiency in the use of inputs. However, despite numerous reform attempts, Soviet prices remained, throughout the plan era, largely ineffective in promoting the rational allocation of resources. Given the indispensable role of prices in a market system, one can readily appreciate the difficulty of replacing plan by market under these conditions.

Input Prices: Land and Labor

In the Soviet economy, the prices of inputs—land, labor, and capital—reflected a peculiar combination of Marxian orthodoxy, pragmatism, and allocative necessity. There was, for the most part, no rental price for agricultural land. Land was allocated to collective and state farms administratively. Planners determined land utilization within the framework of the plan, taking into account technical and local conditions. The absence of land charges made farm accounting a questionable exercise, prompting an endless debate over the role of land rent under socialism. Despite some interest in land valuation, the Soviet Union never formalized a system of land valuation. However, planners attempted to extract a rent from the Soviet countryside by using regionally differentiated procurement prices and differential charges for state machine services.

The allocation of labor in the Soviet Union was a very different case, for there was a price for labor in the form of a wage rate. How were wages set and what role did relative wages have in allocating labor among that country's various occupations, uses, and regions?[21]

Historically, wage differentials were one of several mechanisms utilized to allocate labor in the Soviet Union. The demand for labor was primarily plan-determined. Once output targets were established, labor requirements were determined by applying technical coefficients that measured the amount of labor required per unit of output under existing technology. On the supply side, households were substantially free to make occupational choices and to decide between labor and leisure. The state set wage differentials—for example, by occupation and by region—in an attempt to induce appropriate supplies to meet planned demands.

The Soviet wage-setting procedure was straightforward. For an industrial branch, a base rate was established to determine the wage level for that branch relative to other branches. A schedule gave all rates above this level as a percentage of the base and established the pattern of wage differentials within the branch. Thus the level and differential could be adjusted by manipulating the base or the schedule. Trade unions and individual workers played virtually no role in setting wages; wages were set by administrative authorities. But unlike other areas in the Soviet economy, planners were willing to *use* these differentials to manipulate labor supply. There was a substantial degree of market influence on the structure of Soviet wages.[22]

In addition to wage differentials, other devices were used to manipulate labor supply. Higher- and technical-education institutions expanded in direct relation to the desired composition of the labor force, as directed by state control. In addition, nonmonetary rewards, adulation in the press, social benefits, and other moral incentives were used to affect the supply of labor. **Organized recruitment** by special organizations and the party was important in early years but declined thereafter, except for the seasonal needs of agricultural production.[23]

Soviet labor policies, including the forced-labor campaigns of the 1930s, ensured a high rate of labor force participation to promote rapid economic development. The participation rate, defined as the civilian labor force as a proportion of the able-bodied population, generally exceeded 90 percent. Structural problems grew more serious as the system matured and became a major test of the ability of central planning to allocate labor. For example, the rapid rate of urbanization left shortages in some areas, surpluses in others. Labor imbalances especially characterized the regional distribution of labor. Soviet authorities were consistently unable to meet the labor needs of Siberia and the Far North. In addition, the restrictive role of Soviet trade unions and the policy of "full employment" resulted in overemployment—artificially high levels of staffing at the enterprise level. It was quite difficult to lay off workers even if they were redundant. Although there was experimentation with programs to encourage the firing of unproductive workers, the problems of **overfull employment policies** were not solved and remained a serious problem for the transition.

Capital Allocation

Capital is not a value-creating input in the Marxian scheme.[24] Why then should capital generate a reward in the form of an interest charge? Even if capital has no value-creating capacity, less is available than is demanded. Some means must be devised for its allocation. Furthermore, even if a "price" is used in this allocation function, it will perform *only* this function. Where all capital is owned by the state, the "income" from capital accrues directly to the state, not to individuals.

In the Soviet case, investment was largely controlled by central planning authorities and the ministries. In drawing up the output plan, planners used technical coefficients to determine and authorize the investment necessary to produce the planned increases in output. Some funds were available from internal enterprise sources, but even those funds remained under control of the state banking system. The aggregate supply of investment funds was largely under the control of planners. It is not surprising, therefore, that the ratio of saving to gross national product was higher in the Soviet Union than under industrialized capitalism. The high investment rate illustrates a basic feature of planners' preferences. In a market capitalist economy, saving is influenced by government but is largely determined by individuals and businesses as they choose between consumption in the present and greater consumption in the future. In the Soviet context, the state controlled saving (primarily by the state and by enterprises). In a capitalist economy, saving arises as undistributed profits in enterprises and as income that is not consumed in households. Both *types* of saving existed in the Soviet case, but because wages and prices were set by the state, the state itself could accumulate savings at whatever rate it chose without recourse to the indirect method of taxation. The control of saving and investment was a powerful mechanism to promote more rapid capital accumulation than would be tolerated in an economy directed by consumer sovereignty.

Starting in the late 1960s, Soviet enterprises paid an interest charge for the use of capital. This charge was typically low and was designed to cover the administrative costs of making the capital funds available to the enterprise.

At the enterprise level, Soviet authorities devised rules for choosing among investment projects. Suppose there was a directive to raise the capacity to generate a certain volume of electric power. Will the capacity be hydroelectric, nuclear, coal-fueled, or what? How can one compare the capital-intensive variant that has low operating costs with the variant that requires less capital initially but has high annual operating costs? Although quasi-market techniques for making this sort of decision were rejected by Stalin in the 1930s in favor of planners' wisdom, those methods surfaced again in the late 1950s and were used widely until the end of the Soviet Union.

Soviet planners accepted the principle that the selection among competing projects should be based on cost-minimizing procedures. A general formula, called the **coefficient of relative effectiveness**, was used to compare projects:

$$C_i + E_n K_i = \text{minimum}$$

where

C_i = current expenditures of the ith investment project
K_i = the capital cost of the ith investment project
E_n = the normative coefficient

This formula was used to weigh the tradeoff between higher capital outlays (K_i) and lower operating costs (C_i). The principle was that the project variant should be selected that yields the minimal full cost, where an imputed capital charge is included in cost. The capital cost was calculated by applying a "normative coefficient" (E_n) to the projected capital outlay.

To illustrate, assume that a choice must be made between two projects, the first having an annual operating cost (C) of 10 million rubles and a capital cost (K) of 30 million rubles, the second having a C of 7 million rubles and a K of 50 million rubles. Applying a normative coefficient of 10 percent yields a full cost of 13 million rubles for the first project and 12 million rubles for the second. The second project should be chosen, because it is the minimal-cost variant. However, suppose a normative co-efficient of 20 percent is applied. In this case, the full cost of the first variant is 16 and that of the second variant is 17. In this case—and all that has changed is the normative coefficient—the first variant should be chosen.

A distinctive feature of this formula should be noted. The higher the normative coefficient, the higher the imputed capital cost, and the *less* likely that capital-intensive variants would be selected. Between 1958 and 1969, a system of differentiated normative coefficients gave priority to heavy industry by applying low E_ns to heavy-industrial branches and high E_ns to light industry. In 1969, a new **Standard Methodology** replaced the earlier differentiated system with a standard normative coefficient of 12 percent.[25] It was supposed to be applied equally to all branches of the economy.

The principle that capital should be allocated among projects on the basis of such rate-of-return calculations should not obscure the fact that the basic allocation of capital still proceeded through an administrative investment plan, which itself was a derivative of the output plan. The rate-of-return calculations were used only to select among projects that followed planners' preferences in the first place. Thus they were used to decide what type of plant should be used to generate electricity, not whether the investment should be in the generation of electricity or, for example, in steel production. In fact, the standardized coefficient introduced in 1969 was watered down thereafter by numerous exceptions for particular branches of heavy industry and for various regions.

Financial Planning

The Soviet economy was run by largely administrative rules and instructions. Although value categories (prices, costs, and profits) always existed, they played only a limited role in allocating resources. Even in a centralized economy where few decisions were made at local levels, households made decisions about working and what they would buy. How could planners ensure that there would be a **macroeconomic balance** of consumer goods? The balancing of aggregate consumer demand and supply can be illustrated in the following framework:

$$D = WL - R \tag{9.1}$$

$$S = P_1 Q_1 \tag{9.2}$$

where

D = aggregate demand
S = aggregate supply
W = the average annual wage
L = the number of worker-years of labor used in the economy
R = the amount of income not spent on consumer goods
  (equal to the sum of direct taxes and savings)
Q_1 = the real quantity of consumer goods produced
P_1 = the price level of consumer goods

The conceptual problem is quite simple. As the Soviet economy grew rapidly in the early plan years, it paid labor increasingly high wages to motivate higher participation and greater effort, but the state wanted that labor to produce producer goods, not consumer goods (Q_1). Thus the state permitted wages (W) to rise rapidly in order to encourage labor inputs (L) to rise. In so doing, planners were hoping that labor force decisions would be based on nominal and not real wages—in other words, that Soviet workers would be subject to money illusion. In the absence of sharp increases in Q_1, however, alternative steps were required to achieve a balance between S and D—notably to let P_1 rise along with R (the latter through forced bond purchases). However, prices were not allowed to rise fast enough to absorb the full increase in demand; an imbalance between aggregate supply and demand was allowed to develop. This technique, known as **repressed inflation**, was used widely in the Soviet Union.[26]

After World War II, the quantity of consumer goods increased, although simultaneous increases in purchasing power made it difficult to determine to what degree excess demand was reduced. Indeed, as noted earlier, Janos Kornai developed a general model of the socialist economy suggesting that such systems can in fact be shortage-based systems, even when expansion in the production of consumer goods is taking place.

At the end of the Soviet era, the focus of discussion was on repressed inflation.[27] In a system where excess demand is unlikely to result in price increases, **disequilibrium analysis** (see Appendix 9A) can be used as an effective tool. Soviet savings were regarded as evidence of repressed inflation, assuming that people save because there is nothing to buy at prevailing prices. Soviet authorities feared a savings overhang—forced savings that could destabilize consumer markets.

Market Forces in the Command Economy

The American economy is a market economy in which the state plays a growing and frequently controversial role. The Soviet economy, at least until the era of **Perestroika**, was a planned economy in which market forces were of only moderate and secondary importance. Markets in the Soviet economy have been viewed as an exception to the plan. The issue of markets in the planned Soviet economy deserves additional attention.

In an economic system, ownership and control are closely related. The Soviet state, as the owner of the means of production, exercised control over the direction of economic activity through the national economic plan.

Paul Craig Roberts argued that the Soviet economy was a **"polycentric" system** in which control was diversified.[28] He maintained that the interaction of enterprises at the local level, their informal interrelationships, and the control of local information flows, not the plan, were the main forces determining economic activity. Eugene Zaleski concluded from his analysis of plan fulfillment that administrative adjustments made after the plan was finalized had a stronger bearing on resource allocation than the plans themselves. Zaleski refers to the Soviet economy as an **administratively managed economy**.[29]

A number of other Western analysts questioned whether the Soviet economy was a "planned" economy. John H. Wilhelm argued that the original plan typically was not workable, was continuously changed in the course of plan fulfillment, and in the end was revised to correspond to expected fulfillment. Under these circumstances, Wilhelm argues, it is inappropriate to call the Soviet economy a planned economy.[30] We would reject the argument that the plan was not a critical determinant of economic activity. Rather, the relevant issue is whether, and how much, additional forces affected economic outcomes.

In some areas of the Soviet economy—for example, labor allocation—planners used markets to influence outcomes. Thus wage differentials were used to influence the distribution of labor by region, by season, and by profession; retail prices were used to allocate consumer goods. The fact that wages and retail prices were set by planners does not rule out market forces. In such instances, planners were actually using the market as a tool.

A third role for market forces was the **second economy**. The second economy has been analyzed extensively by Gregory Grossman, Dimitri Simes, Vladimir Treml, Michael V. Alexeev, Aron Katsenelinboigen, and others.[31] It consisted of a number of market activities of varying importance and degrees of legality, all facilitating "unplanned" exchange among consumers and producers. According to Grossman, second-economy activities must meet at least one of the following two criteria: (1) the activity is engaged in for private gain; (2) the person engaging in the activity knowingly contravenes existing law.

Examples of second-economy activities abound. Indeed, since the demise of the Soviet Union, a good deal more has been learned about the second economy. A physician would treat private patients for higher fees. A salesperson would set aside quality merchandise for customers who offered large tips. The manager of a textile firm would reserve goods for sale in unofficial supply channels. A collective farmer would divert collective farm land and supplies to his private plot. Black marketeers in port cities would deal in contraband merchandise. Owners of private cars transported second-economy merchandise. In some cases, official and second-economy transactions were intertwined. Managers would divert some production into second-economy transactions to raise cash to purchase unofficially supplies needed to meet the plan. The official activities of an enterprise would serve as a front for a prospering second-economy undertaking.

Second-economy activities were concentrated in collective farms and in transportation. Apparently, the supervision of collective farms was more lax; they therefore served as better fronts for the second economy. Transportation enterprises were critical to the second economy, for its merchandise had somehow to be moved. The increase in private ownership of automobiles apparently enhanced the operation of the second economy.

Unfortunately, it is difficult to estimate accurately the magnitude of second-economy activity. In a survey of Soviet émigrés conducted by Gur Ofer and Aron Vinokur, during the early 1970s earnings derived from activity other than that at the main place of employment were found to account for approximately 10 percent of earnings.[32] A study of Soviet alcohol production and consumption, conducted by

Vladimir Treml in the mid-1980s, found that between 20 and 25 percent of transactions were illegal. Although the second economy was important in the overall command economy, there were substantial variations from one sector to another. It was not surprising for secondary activities to arise in a setting of rising incomes and limited resources devoted to the service sector.

The second economy had its advantages and disadvantages as far as the planners were concerned. It helped to preserve incentives, because higher wages and bonus payments could be spent in the second economy. Moreover, the second economy reduced inflationary pressures on the official economy. On the negative side, the second economy diverted effort from planned tasks and loosened planners' control. Soviet authorities long tolerated the second economy. Reforms of the late 1980s moved to legalize a number of second-economy activities that did not involve the use of hired labor.

A fourth area of market influence was the private sector of Soviet agriculture. Under certain restrictions, the farm family could use a plot of land, hold animals, and raise crops. The resulting products were sold in the kolkhoz market—a practice tolerated by the authorities—at prices established by supply and demand. Such sales accounted for a substantial portion of the farm family's income. It was not by accident that the private plots produced farm products that were poorly suited to planning, such as fruits, vegetables, and dairy products—all of which required much personal care and motivation.

The existence of second-economy activity in the administrative command economy is of more than passing interest. Although it is now difficult to quantify this second economy with precision, it is nevertheless viewed as an important—if unevenly distributed—part of the overall economic system. It is of theoretical interest that such a mechanism arises in the command economy beyond the purview of the planners. Moreover, if we find that its magnitude increased over time, we may have discovered a crude indicator of the divergence between plan targets and achievements and consumer demands in the economy.

Agriculture in the Command Economy

In an advanced economy such as the United States, agriculture plays a relatively much more modest role than it did in the Soviet economy. Even at the beginning of the Gorbachev era in the mid-1980s, agriculture accounted for 20 to 25 percent of Soviet gross national product and absorbed a great deal of the Soviet labor force. However, there is a second reason for looking more closely at Soviet agriculture: It exhibited unique organizational arrangements, and the results achieved were modest in spite of continuing attention from Soviet policy makers.

During war communism and the New Economic Policy, various forms of organization existed, but private peasant agriculture dominated.[33] The rural sector was seen as crucial to any Soviet development effort, because industrialization would depend on agricultural deliveries. Whether or not the perception of agriculture in the 1920s as the key to industrialization was correct, it was the rationale for Stalin's decision to collectivize in 1929.[34]

Two major institutions dominated Soviet agriculture after 1928. The collective farms (**kolkhozy**) were operated like cooperatives; the **state farms (sovkhozy)**, in which the farmers were paid like industrial workers, in effect were "factories in the fields." The sovkhoz was a state enterprise with state-appointed management.[35] The kolkhoz was, in theory, a cooperative with elected management. Sovkhoz workers were state employees and received fixed wages like other state employees. Kolkhoz peasants initially received a dividend instead of a wage payment. Because this unique payment system was the cornerstone of Stalin's attempt to extract a surplus from the countryside, dwelling on it for a moment is worthwhile.

Before 1966, payment for peasants in the kolkhoz was established in the following fashion. For a particular task assigned to a peasant, a certain number of labor days would be recorded in the peasant's work book. The **labor day** was not necessarily a measure of time or effort, but rather an often arbitrary measure of work input. At the end of the year, the *value* of one labor day would be determined by the following formula:

$$\text{Value of one labor day} = \text{farm income after required deliveries and other expenses} \div \text{total number of labor days for entire kolkhoz}$$

Once the value of a labor day was determined, each individual was paid a "dividend" by multiplying the number of labor days accumulated by the value of one labor day.

The labor-day system of payment was highly arbitrary. The work demanded for one labor day could and did vary regionally, seasonally, and from farm to farm. Furthermore, contrary to the principles of any good incentive system, peasants had little idea in advance what they would earn per labor day. The labor-day system was finally abandoned in 1966 and replaced by a guaranteed wage.[36]

Differences Between Collective Farms and State Farms

Most input and output determinations in the kolkhoz and the sovkhoz were planned like an industrial enterprise. There were, however, some noteworthy differences. First, the method of payment for labor in the kolkhoz was, until 1966, very different from that in the sovkhoz. Second, the manner in which capital investment was provided was different: Kolkhoz investments were largely self-financed; sovkhoz investment funds came directly from the state budget.[37] Third, until the late 1950s, machinery and equipment were maintained in the Machine Tractor Stations and were provided to the collective farms for a payment.[38] Machine Tractor Stations also served as an external control over the kolkhozy. Fourth, the method of distribution of output was different. The sovkhoz, as a state enterprise, distributed its output through the normal state trade channels, as did industrial enterprises. The kolkhoz, in contrast, was required to make compulsory deliveries to the state, often at low fixed prices; but the remainder of its output was free for sale either to the state at higher prices or on the collective farm markets. This two-tier pricing arrangement allowed the state to extract output from the kolkhoz at low prices.

In both the kolkhoz and the sovkhoz, families were entitled to small plots of land (typically about half an acre) for their private use.[39] The produce from this land, important in the case of truckgarden and dairy products, could be consumed on the farm, sold to the state, or sold in collective farm markets. To give some idea of the importance of the private sector, in the 1960s, the private sector accounted for roughly 60 percent of total potato output, 70 percent of total vegetable output, and 30 percent of total milk output. Throughout the postwar period, the private sector accounted for approximately 40 percent of family income on collective farms. Peasants were also entitled to hold some animals, although the permitted number of each type varied over time. For example, roughly 40 percent of all cows were owned privately in the 1960s.

Changes in Soviet Agriculture

Organizational arrangements in agriculture changed substantially after the 1930s, although the kolkhoz, the sovkhoz, and the private sector remained at least in name through 1991. We note the main trends of change.[40]

First, after the 1940s, mergers and consolidations sharply reduced the number and importance of kolkhozy; at the same time, the number of sovkhozy increased, and their average size became greater. In 1940 there were 237,000 kolkhozy with an average sown area of 1235 acres. By the mid-1980s, the number of kolkhozy had been reduced to just over 26,000, and each kolkhoz had an average sown area of just over 8600 acres. As for sovkhozy, in 1940 there were 4200, averaging just over 6900 acres of sown area on each farm. By the mid-1980s, the number of sovkhozy had increased to almost 22,700, with an average sown area of almost 12,000 acres per farm.[41] In 1940 roughly 78 percent of all sown area was accounted for by kolkhozy; this was reduced to 44 percent by the mid-1980s.

Possibly the most important organizational change was the introduction of **agro-industrial integration** on a major scale.[42] Begun in the 1970s, agro-industrial integration brought both kolkhozy and sovkhozy together with industrial-type activity (for example, processing) into integrated production units with centralized management. These changes, along with organizational changes on the regional level introduced with the Brezhnev "Food Program" of 1982, set the scene for further changes to occur with Perestroika under Gorbachev.

Second, **Machine Tractor Stations** were abolished in 1958, and their equipment was sold to the farms, a move that gave farm managers enhanced control over farm equipment.

Third, rural incomes increased sharply after the 1950s, generally more rapidly than industrial incomes. In addition, a pension system introduced in the 1960s substantially improved the welfare of rural workers and peasants and reduced the rural–urban income differential.[43] However, expanded production costs at the farm level and unwillingness to raise retail food prices significantly resulted in a very large subsidy to the agricultural sector.[44]

Fourth, after a period of extensive campaigns by Nikita Khrushchev in the 1950s (the Virgin Land Campaign, the corn program, and so on) designed to expand inputs, the emphasis in the 1960s and 1970s shifted to improvement of productivity through increases in agricultural investment.

Fifth, there was an ongoing program to examine seriously the problems of agriculture in an urban industrial economy. For example, Soviet planners devoted (though not always successfully) considerable attention to the problems of supplying large cities with vegetables. Also, efforts were made to stem the continuing rapid flow of young males from the rural areas and hence to alleviate the problem of labor shortages and imbalances.

Soviet agriculture has been of more than passing interest to Western observers. Catastrophic crop failures, minimal supplies of meat, and the virtual absence of produce in Soviet cities in winter were puzzling in a heavily industrialized nation. Many observers laid the blame for uneven Soviet agricultural performance on unique Soviet organizational arrangements or on limited investment in agriculture.

The Brezhnev years of the 1970s and early 1980s saw important developments in Soviet agriculture. Capital investment increased from roughly 15 percent of aggregate investment to almost 27 percent—a substantial increment by any standard. Despite these efforts, agricultural productivity remained a problem, imports became necessary, and the infrastructure of Soviet agriculture remained primitive, especially food processing, storage, and distribution.

Soviet agricultural policy was a focal point of controversy from the beginning, and it remained so in those East European nations where the Soviet model was imposed after World War II. During the postwar era, there was probably no sector in the Soviet economy to which so much attention was devoted with so few results. Agriculture remains a major challenge for the leaders of the post-Soviet era.

International Trade in the Command Economy

Foreign trade played a substantive role in the Soviet development experience.[45] Moreover, the organizational arrangements used differed significantly from those in market economic systems. The policies and the systemic arrangements of foreign trade in the command model differed widely from market economies.

Throughout the Soviet period, foreign trade was planned and executed by the foreign-trade monopoly. Decision making—what will be traded, with whom, and on what terms—was centralized in three major institutions: the Ministry of Foreign Trade (MFT), the *Vneshtorgbank* or **Bank for Foreign Trade** (BFT), and the various **foreign trade organizations** (FTOs). The formal organization of Soviet foreign trade is represented in Figure 9.3. The **Ministry of Foreign Trade**, like other Soviet ministries, was a centralized body concerned with issues of foreign trade planning— the development of import/export plans, material supply plans, and balance-of-payments plans—all of which were an integral part of the Soviet material balance planning system.

Individual Soviet enterprises did not deal with the external world until the reforms of Gorbachev in 1987. Rather, for both imports and exports, enterprises dealt

FIGURE 9.3   The Organization of Soviet Foreign Trade: The Command Model

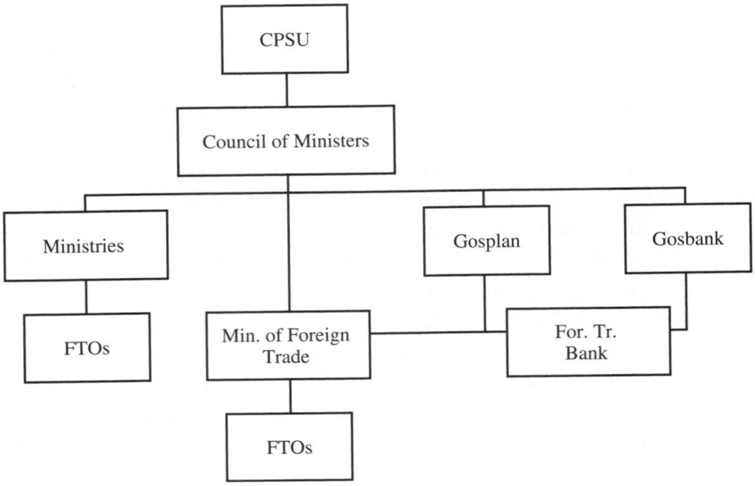

with the FTOs in domestic currency at domestic prices, and the FTOs dealt with the external world via financial arrangements handled by the Ministry of Foreign Trade and the BFT. The domestic users or producers of goods entering the foreign market were isolated from foreign markets by this foreign trade monopoly. Soviet foreign trade operated according to the rule "Export what is available to be exported to pay for necessary imports, and limit the overall volume of trade to control the influence of market forces on the Soviet economy."

Most Soviet trade, even with other socialist countries, was bilateral—that is, directly negotiated for each trade deal with each trading partner. Bilateral trade meant that Soviet exports and imports were handled largely on a barter basis. The difficulties of operating according to offsetting barter deals hampered Soviet trade volume through the years. In part, bilateral trading arrangements arose from and contributed to the nonconvertibility of the Soviet ruble, which was not used as a medium of exchange in world markets.

Soviet trading arrangements were not conducive to an expanding and competitive position in world markets, but Western economists generally argued that the Soviet Union followed a policy of deliberate **trade aversion.**[46] Dating from the late 1920s and early 1930s, Soviet trade ratios (that is, the ratio of imports and exports to GNP) generally declined. For many years they remained low by world standards. This pattern partially resulted from the Soviet Union's adverse position in world markets at that time, or it may have been in part a deliberate policy response. In any event, for the trade that was conducted, a very successful effort was made to redirect Soviet imports away from consumer goods and toward producer goods, an outcome that contributed to the development effort.

The latter years of the Soviet era witnessed some changes in Soviet foreign trade. First, Soviet trade ratios increased, signaling a growing participation in the world economy. The extent of this rise was difficult to estimate because of the peculiarities of Soviet foreign trade accounting,[47] but Soviet participation in foreign trade in the 1980s was well above the rates of the 1950s and 1960s. Second, the 1960s and 1970s saw organizational changes aimed at making enterprises more responsive to world markets and streamlining the FTOs. Third, there were changes in Soviet attitudes toward foreign trade, with renewed interest in neoclassical trade theory and in the development and application of criteria on which to base trade decisions. Fourth, the Soviet Union, though fundamentally conservative throughout the command era, displayed increasing interest in participating in world trade arrangements and organizations. Thus Soviet attitudes toward the external world changed even before the Gorbachev era.

Despite changes in attitudes toward international markets near the end of the Soviet period, the Soviet economy remained isolated from world product and capital markets. Whereas other countries became increasingly a part of globalized markets, the Soviet economy remained isolated.

Performance of the Soviet Command Economy

The Soviet administrative-command economy was installed with minimal adjustments for local conditions in Eastern Europe at the end of World War II. A different variant of the command model developed in China, as we will see in the following chapter. It makes little sense to provide separate descriptions of each of the Soviet-style economies that populated the globe from the late 1940s to 1990, because they so closely resembled the Soviet administrative-command economy.

If we wish to consider how well the Soviet command economy "worked," it is more appropriate to examine the performance of many command economies rather than that of only one, such as the Soviet Union. We have a relatively long record of economic performance for seven socialist command economies (the Soviet Union, Czechoslovakia, Hungary, East Germany, Bulgaria, Poland, and Romania) from the 1950s until their abandonment in or around 1990. Because the Soviet command economies have been abandoned, we are not faced with a moving target. The historical growth record of these economies has been written.

As was pointed out in Chapter 3, we can evaluate economic performance using a number of criteria. In this section, we provide a comparative appraisal of the economic performance of the administrative-command economies based on the most commonly used performance measures: growth of output and productivity and income distribution.

An Economic Profile: Structural Characteristics of East and West

Table 9.1 provides an economic profile of the European planned socialist countries and selected capitalist countries. This profile shows what factors should be held constant in performance comparisons, and it provides insights into the socialist model

TABLE 9.1   An Economic Profile of Socialist and Capitalist Countries in the 1980s

	(1) Per Capita GNP, 1985 (U.S. $)	(2) Population 1985 (Millions)	(3a) Share of Industry and Construction in GNP (1982)	(3b) Agriculture	(3c) Services	(4) Proportion of Labor in Agriculture (1985)	(5) Gross Investment as a Percentage of GNP (1982)
A. Planned Socialism							
East Germany	10,440	16.7	51	13	36	10	24
Czechoslovakia	8,750	15.5	49	15	36	13	25
Hungary	7,560	10.6	38	26	36	18	29
Soviet Union	7,400	278.9	42	19	39	19	30
Poland	6,470	37.2	37	27	36	29	27
Bulgaria	6,420	9.0	46	23	31	20	28
Romania	5,450	22.7	46	26	28	29	38
B. Capitalism							
Norway	16,719	4.2	41	5	54	9	26
United States	16,710	238.6	34	3	63	3	19

	(1) Per Capita GNP, 1985 (U.S. $)	(2) Population 1985 (Millions)	(3a) Share of Industry and Construction in GNP (1982)	(3b) Agriculture	(3c) Services	(4) Proportion of Labor in Agriculture (1985)	(5) Gross Investment as a Percentage of GNP (1982)
Canada	16,538	25.4	32	4	64	5	25
Denmark	14,603	5.1	22	5	73	7	16
West Germany	14,432	61.0	53	3	44	6	23
France	13,755	55.0	41	4	55	9	21
Japan	13,312	120.7	40	5	55	10	31
Belgium	13,219	9.9	42	4	54	3	18
Netherlands	12,741	14.5	33	4	63	5	18
Austria	12,343	7.6	39	4	57	9	26
United Kingdom	12,042	56.4	33	2	65	3	17
Italy	10,928	57.1	41	6	53	13	21
Spain	9,008	39.1	34	6	60	18	20
Greece	6,854	10.0	31	17	52	31	25
Turkey	2,135	45.1	31	22	47	60	25

Sources: U.S. Department of Commerce, *Statistical Abstract of the United States, 1981* (Washington, D.C.: Government Printing Office, 1981), pp. 876–879; National Foreign Assessment Center, *Handbook of Economic Statistics 1986* (Washington, D.C.: Central Intelligence Agency, 1986); World Bank, *World Tables*, 3rd ed. (Baltimore: The Johns Hopkins University Press, 1984); OECD, *Historical Statistics, 1960–1985* (Paris, OECD, 1987); Thad Alton, "East European GNPs," Joint Economic Committee, *East European Economics: Slow Growth in the 1980s*, Vol. 1 (Washington, D.C.: Government Printing Office, 1985), pp. 81–132. The East European investment rates are calculated by subtracting the rates of defense spending and the GNP from Alton's residual expenditure category (p. 95).

of industrialization.[48] We focus on the mid-1980s as a period of relative "normalcy" in Eastern Europe prior to the dramatic changes of the late 1980s.

In terms of per capita income, the Soviet Union and Eastern Europe were well behind the advanced capitalist countries in the mid-1980s. The per capita incomes in the more advanced planned socialist economies (Czechoslovakia, East Germany, and the Soviet Union) were well below those in Japan and the United Kingdom and between those in Italy and Spain. Poland, Romania, and Hungary and the less advanced Bulgaria were well below Italy and Spain but close to Greece. The planned socialist countries as a group were less advanced than the industrialized Western countries with which they were most often compared.

Despite relatively low per capita income, the share of industry and construction in GNP in the socialist countries was roughly equal to that of the capitalist countries in the mid 1980s. In fact, the socialist industry share averaged 43 percent; the average of capitalist countries (United States to Italy) was 36 percent. One would have to conclude that, if per capita income were held constant, the planned socialist industry share was high relative to capitalism. The socialist shares of agriculture and services were even more different from their Western counterparts. Agriculture's share of both GNP and labor force was quite high in the planned socialist countries if per capita income is held constant, but the share of the service sector was well below that of capitalist countries at similar levels of development. The data on investment rates do not reveal a clear trend. The socialist countries tended to have investment rates in the high ranges of 24 to 38 percent, but one can find similarly high investment rates among the capitalist countries. The East German investment rate, on the other hand, was relatively low.

Other differences, not recorded in Table 9.1, can also be noted. If one breaks down the industry sector into heavy and light industry, the planned socialist shares of heavy industry were well *above* those of a capitalist country at a similar level of development. The shares of the urban population of the socialist countries were well *below* those of a capitalist country at a similar stage of economic development.

All of these features constitute the distinguishing characteristics of the socialist industrialization model. What was the logic behind the socialist model? It aimed at "building socialism" as quickly as possible. In order to do so, it had to accord industrialization priority. Activities that did not contribute to material production, such as services, would be limited, and within industry, priority had to be granted to heavy industry, which laid the foundation for socialism. Urbanization should be retarded to limit the flow of scarce investment resources into social overhead capital, a form of capital that does not lead immediately to expanded industrial capacity. Extra resources were devoted to agriculture to promote self-sufficiency, even if this worked against comparative advantage. Resources were diverted from consumption into investment in order to achieve a high investment rate.

Economic Growth

Table 9.2 and Figure 9.4 supply data on GDP growth rates for the postwar period in socialist and capitalist countries. One should be cautious about attaching importance to small differences in growth rates, for there is measurement error in such calculations.

Moreover, the measured growth rate of economies experiencing substantial structural changes can be ambiguous—the problem of index number relativity.[49] Growth rates must be regarded as approximate and often ambiguous measures of the expansion of real goods and services. This is especially true of East–West comparisons, where substantial adjustments must be made to render the past GDP data comparable.

In Table 9.2, we have assembled growth rates of real GDP and of real GDP per capita for the entire postwar period. In panel A we supply growth rates for the Soviet Union and Eastern Europe. We also supply growth rates for a number of capitalist countries at various stages of economic development (panel B).

Are there systemic differences in growth rates? Table 9.2 examines postwar economic growth from the heady growth of the 1950s and 1960s to the generally slower growth of the mid-1970s and 1980s. It illustrates the dangers of using a pair of countries (such as the United States and the Soviet Union) to judge the growth performance of capitalism and socialism. One can find capitalist countries (such as Japan) that have grown much more rapidly than most socialist countries, and one can find socialist countries (such as Bulgaria) that grew more rapidly than most capitalist countries. Moreover, some countries grew rapidly in one period (Bulgaria in the 1950s and 1960s) and then grew slowly in another period (Bulgaria from 1975 to 1980).

If we take unweighted averages of the seven planned socialist and fifteen capitalist countries, the socialist group grew slightly more rapidly in the 1950s (5.4 percent per year versus 5.0 percent for the capitalist group). The capitalist group grew more rapidly in the 1960s (5.5 percent versus 4.5 percent in the first half and 5.5 percent versus 4.1 percent in the second half). The capitalist group experienced severe growth recessions in the mid-1970s, whereas the socialist group enjoyed a noticeable growth advantage for the first half of the 1970s (4.5 percent versus 3.9 percent). The growth of the capitalist group continued to lag during the second half of the 1970s (at 3.4 percent), but the slowdown of growth was even more severe in the socialist group (falling to 2.1 percent). For the period 1980 to 1990, the slowdown of socialist growth was marked, hovering around one percent per year, whereas the capitalist growth rates were between 2 and 3 percent. The long-term decline in socialist growth rates is very pronounced: from above 4 percent per annum, to 2 percent in the late 1970s, and to 1 percent in the 1980s. From 1985 to 1990, the collapse of socialist growth was so pronounced that Western growth outstripped socialist growth by a large factor.

Direct comparisons of planned socialist and capitalist average growth rates did not reveal significant growth differences until the last decade of the administrative-command economy. However, if one makes a rule-of-thumb adjustment for differences in per capita income by including only the capitalist countries that fall within the approximate per capita income range of the socialist sample—say $3,000 to $6,000—some striking findings emerge. The rationale for this adjustment is that growth rates in the postwar period have tended to vary inversely with the level of development. Countries with low per capita income have grown more rapidly as a group. There are four capitalist countries that fall within this income range (Spain, Greece, Italy, and Venezuela), but comparing their average growth rates with those of the former Soviet Union and Eastern Europe is nevertheless informative. For the entire postwar period, the unweighted average annual growth rate of these four capitalist economies was almost 6 percent (4.25 percent on a per capita basis).

TABLE 9.2   Average Annual Growth of GDP and GDP Per Capita in Socialist and Capitalist Countries, 1950–1990 (per capita figures in parentheses)

	1950–1960	1960–1965	1965–1970	1970–1975	1975–1980	1980–1985	1985–1990
A. Planned Socialist Countries							
Czechoslovakia	4.8 (3.9)	2.3 (1.6)	3.4 (3.2)	3.4 (2.7)	2.2 (1.5)	1.5 (1.2)	1.2 (1.2)
East Germany	5.7 (6.7)	2.7 (3.0)	3.0 (3.1)	3.4 (3.8)	2.3 (2.5)	1.8 (1.9)	1.6 (1.6)
Soviet Union	5.7 (3.9)	5.0 (3.5)	5.2 (4.2)	3.7 (2.7)	2.7 (1.8)	2.0 (1.1)	1.8 (1.1)
Poland	4.6 (2.75)	4.4 (3.2)	4.1 (3.4)	6.4 (5.4)	.7 (0)	.7 (-.1)	.2 (.2)
Hungary	4.6 (4.0)	4.2 (3.9)	3.0 (2.7)	3.4 (2.9)	2.0 (1.9)	1.7 (1.7)	.7 (.7)
Romania	5.8 (4.55)	6.0 (5.3)	4.9 (3.7)	6.7 (5.8)	3.9 (3.0)	1.0 (.8)	.6 (.6)
Bulgaria	6.7 (5.9)	6.7 (5.7)	5.1 (4.2)	4.6 (4.2)	.9 (.9)	1.2 (1.0)	.4 (.4)
Unweighted average	5.4 (4.5)	4.5 (3.7)	4.1 (3.5)	4.5 (3.9)	2.1 (1.7)	1.4 (1.1)	.9 (.8)
B. Capitalist Countries							
United States	3.3 (1.5)	4.6 (3.2)	3.1 (2.1)	2.3 (1.6)	3.7 (2.6)	2.4 (1.4)	3.1 (2.1)
Canada	4.6 (1.3)	5.7 (3.8)	4.8 (3.0)	5.0 (3.6)	2.9 (1.9)	2.2 (.9)	3.3 (2.3)
West Germany	7.9 (6.3)	5.0 (3.5)	4.4 (3.9)	2.1 (1.7)	3.6 (3.7)	1.1 (1.4)	2.8 (2.4)
Denmark	3.6 (2.9)	5.1 (4.3)	4.5 (3.7)	2.8 (2.4)	2.7 (2.4)	2.3 (2.3)	2.4 (2.4)

	1950–1960	1960–1965	1965–1970	1970–1975	1975–1980	1980–1985	1985–1990
Norway	3.6 (2.5)	4.8 (4.3)	4.8 (3.9)	4.6 (4.0)	4.6 (4.2)	3.0 (2.8)	3.3 (3.3)
Belgium	3.0 (2.5)	5.2 (4.5)	4.8 (4.4)	3.9 (3.5)	2.5 (2.3)	.4 (.4)	2.7 (2.7)
France	4.4 (3.8)	5.8 (4.5)	5.4 (4.5)	4.0 (3.2)	3.2 (2.9)	1.2 (.7)	2.7 (2.2)
Netherlands	5.0 (3.3)	4.8 (3.5)	5.5 (4.4)	3.2 (2.0)	2.6 (1.9)	.5 (.1)	2.1 (1.6)
Japan	7.9 (6.6)	10.0 (9.0)	12.2 (11.2)	5.0 (3.8)	5.1 (4.2)	3.9 (3.2)	3.8 (3.4)
Austria	5.6 (5.4)	4.3 (3.7)	5.1 (4.6)	3.9 (3.5)	4.0 (4.0)	2.8 (2.8)	2.2 (2.2)
United Kingdom	3.3 (2.3)	3.1 (2.4)	2.5 (2.2)	2.0 (1.4)	1.6 (1.6)	1.7 (1.3)	3.1 (2.9)
Italy	5.6 (4.8)	5.2 (4.3)	6.2 (5.4)	2.4 (1.5)	3.9 (3.4)	.8 (.5)	2.9 (2.7)
Spain	6.2 (5.3)	8.5 (7.5)	6.2 (5.2)	5.5 (4.6)	2.3 (1.3)	1.4 (.8)	4.1 (3.7)
Greece	6.0 (5.0)	7.7 (7.2)	7.2 (6.6)	5.0 (4.5)	4.4 (3.2)	1.0 (.4)	1.8 (1.8)
Turkey	6.4 (3.4)	4.8 (2.8)	6.6 (3.7)	7.5 (5.0)	3.1 (.6)	4.9 (2.7)	5.1 (2.7)
Unweighted average	5.0 (3.7)	5.5 (4.4)	5.5 (4.5)	3.9 (2.95)	3.4 (2.6)	2.0 (1.5)	3.2 (2.7)

Sources: Thad Alton, "Economic Structure and Growth in Eastern Europe," in U.S. Congress, Joint Economic Committee, *Economic Developments in Countries of Eastern Europe* (Washington, D.C.: Government Printing Office, 1970), p. 49; Thad Alton, "Comparative Structure and Growth of Economic Activity in Eastern Europe," in U.S. Congress, Joint Economic Committee, *East European Economies Post Helsinki* (Washington, D.C.: Government Printing Office, 1977), p. 237; Thad Alton, "Production and Resource Allocation in Eastern Europe: Performance, Problems, and Prospects," in U.S. Congress, Joint Economic Committee, *East European Economic Assessment*, Part 2 (Washington, D.C.: Government Printing Office, 1981), p. 381; U.S. Congress, Joint Economic Committee, *USSR Measures of Economic Growth and Development, 1950–1980* (Washington, D.C.: Government Printing Office, 1982), pp. 15–21; *Statistical Abstract of the United States*, 1981, pp. 878–879; Wilfred Malenbaum, "Modern Economic Growth in India and China: The Comparison Revisited, 1950–1980," *Economic Development and Cultural Change*, 31 (October 1982), 53; *Handbook of Economic Statistics 1990*; Thad Alton et al., Occasional Papers Nos. 75–79 of the Research Project on National Income in East Central Europe (New York, 1983), pp. 7–12, 25; Rush Greenslade, "The Real Gross National Product of the USSR, 1950–75," in U.S. Congress, Joint Economic Committee, *Soviet Economy in a New Perspective* (Washington, D.C.: Government Printing Office, 1975), p. 271; World Bank, *World Tables*, 3rd ed. (Baltimore: The Johns Hopkins University Press, 1983); OECD, *National Accounts, 1960–1985* (Paris: OECD, 1987); "Eastern Europe: Long Road to Economic Well-Being," Tables C-1 to C-21.

FIGURE 9.4   Average GDP Growth Rates for Planned Socialist and Capitalist
Countries, 1950–1990 (unweighted annual average growth rates)

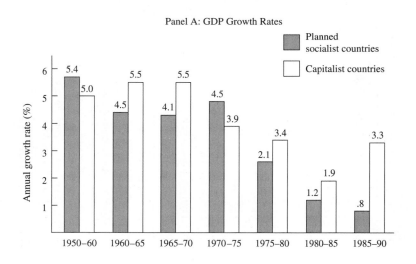

Panel A: GDP Growth Rates

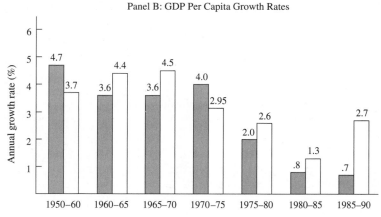

Panel B: GDP Per Capita Growth Rates

Source: Table 9.2.

Among countries at a similar stage of development, the planned socialist economies
experienced slower growth than their capitalist counterparts.[50]

Frederic Pryor examined the comparative growth rates of capitalist and socialist
economies for the period 1950 to 1979, using econometric methods to hold factors
other than the economic system constant. Pryor found that although the socialist-
system effect was negative, the system coefficient was not statistically significant
either for the growth of GNP or for the growth of GNP per capita.[51]

The pattern of decline of planned socialist growth rates goes a long way toward explaining the desire to convert from planned socialism to market resource allocation. Both East and West experienced relatively high rates of growth from 1950 through 1970. In the West, growth was well above long-term historical performance during this period. The growth rates of the planned socialist economies began their descent in the mid-1970s; lower growth rates were recorded in each successive half-decade. In the Soviet Union and Eastern Europe, economic growth had all but ceased by the latter half of the 1980s.

The Sources of Economic Growth: Efficiency

Socialist growth rates were in many ways comparable to capitalist systems through 1980. Toward the end of the planned socialist era in the Soviet Union and Eastern Europe, growth rates declined seriously. In the Soviet Union, the rate of growth of output became negative by 1990 as the collapse was imminent.

Why did rates of economic growth ultimately decline sharply in the planned socialist economic systems? Were declining rates of economic growth a symptom of more basic economic difficulties in these systems? To answer these questions, it is necessary to look closely at the sources of economic growth and especially at issues of efficiency.

Chapter 3 distinguished between extensive growth and intensive growth. Extensive growth is the growth of output from the expansion of inputs, land, labor, and capital. Intensive growth is the growth derived from increasing output per unit of factor input—that is, from the better use of available inputs.

The sources of economic growth are important for two reasons. First, historical experience shows that as economies grow and develop, the sources of growth tend to change. During the early stages of development, the task is to bring idle resources into production; output expansion is achieved largely from using more inputs. As economic development proceeds, the tendency is to generate growth from the better use of inputs (and improvements in input quality). The distinction between intensive and extensive growth is important, for input expansion comes from sacrificing leisure time and increasing work time and from reducing current consumption with the hope of greater improvements in the future. Intensive growth, however, is derived largely from increased efficiency—for example, through improved managerial systems and technological change.

It is relevant to ask which economic system has done a better job in generating economic growth, where *better* is defined in terms of the relative weights of **intensive growth** versus **extensive growth**. Two such comparisons pertain. The first, **static efficiency**, takes a snapshot of planned socialist and capitalist countries at a particular point in time to determine how much output they are generating from a given amount of factor inputs. The second, **dynamic efficiency**, probes the question of efficiency performance over time—that is, the extent to which output expands more rapidly than inputs, the difference being the growth rate of factor productivity.[52]

Table 9.3 supplies information on the dynamic efficiency of the planned socialist and the industrialized capitalist countries. Specifically, it provides the annual growth rates of aggregate employment ($\hat{L}$) and reproducible capital ($\hat{K}$), which we then compare with the growth rate of aggregate output ($\hat{Q}$). By subtracting the growth rates of employment and capital, respectively, from the growth rate of output, we obtain the growth rates of **labor productivity** ($\hat{Q} - \hat{L}$) and **capital productivity** ($\hat{Q} - \hat{K}$), respectively.

Because the productivity of labor or capital is affected by substitutions between the two factors, it is desirable to have a comprehensive measure of the growth rate of combined labor and capital productivity. One must first calculate the growth rates of labor and capital combined ($\hat{L} + \hat{K}$), or total factor input. This is typically done by taking a weighted average of the growth rates of labor and capital, where the weights represent each factor's share of national income. Thus **total factor productivity** is defined as $\hat{Q} - (\hat{L} + \hat{K})$. Here

$$\hat{K} + \hat{L} = \hat{K} W_K + \hat{L} W_L$$

where

$$W_K = \text{capital's share of income}$$
$$W_L = \text{labor's share of income}$$

We use rates of growth of labor and capital combined ($\hat{L} + \hat{K}$), calculated in this manner. Inasmuch as a return to capital was typically not included in prices in the planned socialist countries, "synthetic" factor shares must be used to calculate their $\hat{L} + \hat{K}$ growth rates.[53] Once the growth rate of combined factor inputs is calculated, it is subtracted from the growth rate of output to obtain the growth rate of factor productivity $[\hat{Q} - (\hat{L} + \hat{K})]$.

The approximative nature of these productivity calculations is worth emphasizing. Factors of production, especially labor, can expand in both quantitative and qualitative terms, yet our measure captures only its quantitative advance.[54] If comparable data were available, one could calculate a more comprehensive measure of labor's growth by adjusting for the growth in education, training, and composition of the labor force. Because we use employment rather than actual hours, we are not even capturing the quantitative growth of labor accurately. Moreover, the capitalist data do not adjust for unemployment (which rose over this period). We use the official capital stock estimates of the planned socialist economies, except for the Soviet Union. We have no way of knowing whether they are comparable to Western data or whether they are reliable.[55]

What conclusions are to be drawn from Table 9.3? The first is that through the mid-1980s, the growth rates of capital and labor inputs were similar for capitalism and socialism. The planned socialist and capitalist averages suggest roughly equivalent rates of growth of employment and, although the socialist growth rate of capital was probably slightly lower during the 1950s and higher thereafter. For the entire period, capital grew at an average rate of roughly 5 percent in each economic system. The stereotype, fostered by the rapid growth of both labor and capital in the Soviet Union, that the planned socialist system generates a more rapid rate of growth of inputs is not supported. The rates of growth of labor and capital combined round to 2 percent per annum for both capitalism and planned socialism.

Both the socialist and the capitalist countries experienced a slowdown in productivity growth after the 1960s: The planned socialist growth rate of output declined

TABLE 9.3 Annual Growth of Inputs and Output per Unit of Inputs in Socialist and Capitalist Countries

		(1) Employment ($\hat{L}$)	(2) Fixed Capital ($\hat{K}$)	(3) Labor and Capital ($\hat{L}+\hat{K}$)	(4) Output ($\hat{Q}$)	(5) Labor Productivity ($\hat{Q}-\hat{L}$)	(6) Capital Productivity ($\hat{Q}-\hat{K}$)	(7) Total Factor Productivity $\hat{Q}-(\hat{L}+\hat{K})$
				A. Planned Socialist Countries				
Czechoslovakia	1950–60	0.7	3.5	1.4	4.8	4.1	1.3	3.4
	1960–83	1.0	4.7	2.1	2.6	1.6	-2.1	0.5
East Germany	1950–60	0.0	2.0	0.5	6.1	6.1	4.1	5.6
	1960–83	0.3	4.0	1.4	2.8	2.5	-1.2	1.4
Soviet Union	1950–60	1.2	9.4	3.4	5.8	4.6	-3.6	2.4
	1960–85	1.3	7.3	2.8	3.6	2.3	-3.7	0.8
Poland	1950–60	1.0	2.6	1.4	4.6	3.6	2.0	3.2
	1960–83	1.5	4.7	2.5	3.3	1.8	-1.4	0.8
Hungary	1950–60	1.0	3.6	1.7	4.6	3.6	1.0	2.9
	1960–83	0.3	5.0	1.7	2.9	2.6	-2.1	1.2
Romania	1950–60	1.1	—[a]	—	5.9	4.8	—	—
	1960–85	0.4	—[a]	—	4.6	4.1	—	—
Bulgaria	1950–60	0.2	—[a]	—	6.7	6.5	—	—
	1960–85	0.5	—[a]	—	3.7	3.2	—	—
Unweighted average	1950–60	.8	4.2	1.7	5.5[b] (5.2)[c]	4.8	1.0	3.5
	1960–85	.8	5.1	2.1	3.3[b] (3.0)[c]	2.5	-2.1	0.9

TABLE 9.3   Annual Growth of Inputs and Output per Unit of Inputs in Socialist and Capitalist Countries (*Cont.*)

		(1) Employment ($\hat{L}$)	(2) Fixed Capital ($\hat{K}$)	(3) Labor and Capital ($\hat{L}+\hat{K}$)	(4) Output ($\hat{Q}$)	(5) Labor Productivity ($\hat{Q}-\hat{L}$)	(6) Capital Productivity ($\hat{Q}-\hat{K}$)	(7) Total Factor Productivity $\hat{Q}-(\hat{L}+\hat{K})$
		B. Capitalist Countries						
United States	1950–60	1.4	3.6	1.8	3.1	1.7	-0.5	1.3
	1960–85	2.0	3.3	2.4	3.1	1.1	-0.2	0.7
Canada	1960–85	2.7	4.7	3.3	4.2	1.5	-0.5	0.9
Belgium	1950–62	0.6	2.3	1.0	3.2	2.6	0.6	2.2
Denmark	1950–62	0.9	5.1	1.8	3.5	2.6	-1.6	1.7
	1950–60^d	0.1	4.2	1.0	4.9	4.8	0.7	3.9
	1960–85	0.7	4.8	1.8	3.9	3.1	-0.9	2.1
West Germany	1950–60^d	2.0	6.4	3.1	7.3	5.3	0.9	4.2
	1960–85	0.0	4.8	1.2	3.1	3.1	-1.7	1.9
Italy	1950–62	0.6	3.5	1.3	6.0	5.4	2.5	4.7
	1960–85	0.7	4.6	1.9	3.9	3.2	-0.5	2.0
Sweden	1962–83	0.6	3.5	1.5	2.8	2.2	-0.7	1.3
Netherlands	1950–62	1.1	4.7	1.9	4.7	3.6	0.0	2.8
Norway	1950–60^d	0.2	4.2	1.2	3.5	3.3	-0.7	2.3
	1960–85	0.5	3.6	1.4	4.2	3.7	0.6	2.8
United Kingdom	1950–60^d	0.7	3.4	1.2	2.3	1.6	-1.1	1.1
	1960–85	0.5	3.2	1.1	2.3	1.8	-0.9	1.2

	(1) Employment ($\hat{L}$)	(2) Fixed Capital ($\hat{K}$)	(3) Labor and Capital ($\hat{L} + \hat{K}$)	(4) Output ($\hat{Q}$)	(5) Labor Productivity ($\hat{Q} - \hat{L}$)	(6) Capital Productivity ($\hat{Q} - \hat{K}$)	(7) Total Factor Productivity $\hat{Q} - (\hat{L} + \hat{K})$
Japan 1953–70	1.7	9.8	3.8	10.0	8.3	0.2	6.2
1970–85	0.9	8.2	2.3	4.4	3.5	-3.8	2.1
Greece 1960–85	0.4	5.8	2.0	5.1	4.7	-0.7	3.1
Unweighted average[e] 1950–60	0.9	4.7	1.8	4.8	3.9	0.1	3.0
Unweighted average 1960–85	0.9	4.7	1.9	3.7	2.8	-1.0	1.8

Note: All figures are annual growth rates.
$\hat{L}$ = growth rate of employment
$\hat{K}$ = growth rate of reproducible capital
$\hat{Q}$ = growth rate of output
($\hat{L} + \hat{K}$) = growth rate of labor and capital combined

[a] The official Romanian and Bulgarian capital stock series are not cited because they are in current, not constant, prices.
[b] Average of all seven countries.
[c] Average of first five countries.
[d] 1950–1962.
[e] Includes Japan, 1953–1970.

Sources: Panel A: Employment: Andrew Elias, "Magnitude and Distribution of the Labor Force in Eastern Europe," in U.S. Congress, Joint Economic Committee, *Economic Developments in Countries of Eastern Europe* (Washington, D.C.: Government Printing Office, 1970), pp. 208–214; Thad Alton, "Comparative Structure and Growth of Economic Activity in Eastern Europe," in U.S. Congress, Joint Economic Committee, *East European Economies Post Helsinki* (Washington, D.C.: Government Printing Office, 1977), p. 218; *Handbook of Economic Statistics 1980,* p. 47. *Capital Stock:* Official CMEA estimates of productive funds (*osnovnye fondy*) from *Statisticheski ezhegodnik stran-chlenov Soveta Ekonomicheskoi Vzaimopomoschi 1974* (Moscow: Statistika), p. 27; Alton, "Production and Resource Allocation in Eastern Europe," p. 372; *Handbook of Economic Statistics 1980,* p. 58; and Alton, "Comparative Structure and Growth," p. 223. *Output:* Table 10.1. *Panel B: Growth Rates of Employment, Reproducible Capital, and Output:* Edward Denison, *Why Growth Rates Differ* (Washington, D.C.: Brookings, 1967), pp. 42, 190, and Ch. 21; Edward Denison, *Accounting for United States Economic Growth, 1929–1969* (Washington, D.C.: Brookings, 1974), pp. 32, 58; Edward Denison and William Chung, *How Japan's Economy Grew So Fast* (Washington, D.C.: Brookings, 1976), pp. 19, 31; OECD, Department of Economics and Statistics, *Flows and Stocks of Fixed Capital, 1960–1985* (OECD: Paris, 1987); *Handbook of Economic Statistics 1986; World Table,* 3rd ed.

after 1960 by about 40 percent; yet inputs, both labor and capital, grew more rapidly after 1960 (about one-quarter faster). Thus both labor and capital productivity and total factor productivity declined dramatically after 1960 in the planned socialist economies—labor productivity from an average of 4.8 to 2.5 percent, and total factor productivity from 3.5 to 0.9 percent. Efforts to stabilize the growth of output by raising the growth of inputs did not succeed; rather than becoming more intensive, the growth of the planned socialist economies became more extensive after 1960.

The greater extensivity of socialist growth after 1960 is apparent when we compare the growth rates of total factor productivity with the growth rates of output. Taking those five socialist countries for which capital data are available, the average GDP growth rate was 5.2 percent per annum between 1950 and 1960, whereas the growth of efficiency (factor productivity) was 3.5 percent. Thus 67 (3.5/5.2) percent of economic growth was accounted for by increasing output per unit of input. The corresponding figures for the period 1960 to 1983 are 3.0 percent and 0.9 percent. Thus from 1960 to 1983, only 30 percent of growth was accounted for by increasing factor productivity. The declining growth of productivity was felt by both labor and capital, but the decline in capital productivity from a positive rate to a negative rate of –2.1 percent per annum was especially prominent.

The capitalist group also experienced a slowdown in productivity growth after 1960. Average labor productivity growth fell from 3.9 to 2.8 percent; capital productivity growth fell from zero to –1.0 percent, and total factor productivity growth fell from 3.0 to 1.8 percent. In the 1950s, some 65 (3.0/4.8) percent of growth in the capitalist group was explained by the growth of efficiency; for the period 1960–1985, 49 (1.8/3.7) percent of growth was explained by efficiency gains.

Table 9.3 shows the planned socialist economies in a favorable light because it does not include the productivity collapse of the second half of the 1980s. During this period, all the planned socialist economies experienced negative productivity.[56]

What are the overall conclusions concerning the growth of efficiency under capitalism and planned socialism? As in the case of economic growth, there appears to be no evidence to suggest a more rapid rate of growth of productivity under planned socialism (see Figure 9.5). It appears that since 1960, at least, the productivity performance of planned socialism deteriorated seriously and that socialist growth became much more extensive in character. Indeed, recent re-examination of the Soviet growth record by William Easterly and Stanley Fischer suggests that, whereas other countries did follow an extensive growth strategy, Soviet inability to substitute capital for labor led to serious diminishing returns to capital, the major factor accounting for the dismal Soviet growth record.[57]

Income Distribution

Another measure of the performance of economic systems is the distribution of income. What constitutes a good distribution of income must be a subjective matter, but there would be agreement that a distribution in which the top 5 percent of the population receives 95 percent of all income is "unfair" and that a completely equal

FIGURE 9.5   Productivity Growth in Socialist and Capitalist Countries, 1960–1985

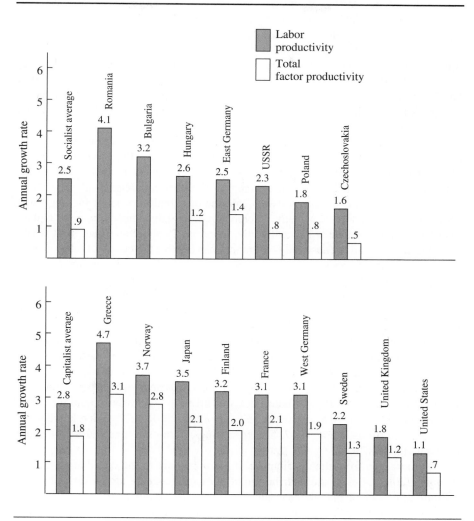

Source: Table 9.3.

distribution is "unfair." Marx himself rejected the notion of an equal distribution of income during the transition from socialism to communism, arguing instead for a distribution that reflected the individual's contribution to the well-being of society.[58]

Under both planned and market socialism, property other than consumer durables and housing is owned by the state, and the return from this state-owned property is at the state's disposal. Under capitalism, the bulk of property is owned privately, and property income accrues to private individuals.

The distribution of human capital depends on the manner in which schooling and on-the-job training are provided. Free or subsidized public schooling is available in both types of societies, although there is a greater tendency for the state to pay for higher education in socialist societies. Nevertheless, the differences between the two systems would not be expected to be great. The major distinction is the absence of private ownership of income-earning property under socialism. Unless offset by higher earnings differentials, the distribution of property plus labor income should be more nearly equal under socialism. The distribution of income after taxes depends on the extent to which the state uses redistributive taxes and transfers to equalize income distribution.

As to earnings differentials, planned socialist societies recognized that labor cannot be allocated administratively and must be allowed relative freedom of choice of occupation. Therefore, the distribution of wage and salary income under socialism should follow roughly the same principles as under capitalism.

Arguments can be made, however, that the distribution of labor income varies according to the economic system.[59] Some argue that labor income is more equally distributed under socialism because of the more nearly equal distribution of education and training and because the government can control the power of labor groups. Moreover, socialist governments have a greater doctrinal commitment to equality.

Frederic Pryor made an extensive econometric study of the distribution of labor income among workers for the late 1950s and early 1960s.[60] He found that the distribution of labor income was *more equal* under socialism, once per capita income and the size of the country were held constant. He also found that labor incomes were more unequal in the Soviet Union than in the other socialist countries; therefore, studies that generalize from the Soviet experience are likely to give a false impression.

More recent data on the distribution of earnings for full-time wage and salary earners confirm most of Pryor's findings for the 1950s and early 1960s.[61] Earnings were more nearly equally distributed in Eastern Europe, Yugoslavia, and the Soviet Union than in the United States in the 1970s. For the USSR, this was a relatively new phenomenon, for as late as 1957, Soviet earnings were more unequal than those in the United States.[62]

We now turn from the distribution of *labor income* to the distribution of *total income*. Table 9.4 gives the distribution of per capita income after income taxes in a limited number of planned socialist and capitalist countries for which data are available.[63] The socialist data generally exclude top income-earning families (party leaders, government officials, artists, and authors), including instead only families of workers and employees. Many second-economy activities considered legal in capitalist societies (the provision of private repair and medical services, for example) were not recorded. Also, a relatively larger volume of resources (even excluding free educational and medical benefits) was provided in socialist societies on an extra-market basis—shopping privileges, official cars, vacations—and was not included in reported income.

Table 9.4 shows that income was distributed more unequally in the capitalist countries in which the state played a relatively minor redistributive role either through progressive taxation or through the distribution of social services (the United States,

TABLE 9.4   Distribution of Per Capita Income Among Families After Income Taxes in Planned Socialist and Capitalist Countries

	U.K. 1969	U.S. 1968	Italy 1969	Canada 1971	Sweden 1971	Hungary 1964	Czecho-slovakia 1965	Bulgaria 1963–1965	USSR 1966
Per capita income of individual in 95th percentile ÷ that of individual in 5th percentile	5.0	12.7	11.2	12.0	5.5	4.0	4.3	3.8	5.7
Per capita income of individual in 90th percentile ÷ that of individual in 10th percentile	3.4	6.7	5.9	6.0	3.5	3.0	3.1	2.7	3.5
Per capita income of individual in 75th percentile ÷ that of individual in 25th percentile	1.9	2.6	2.5	2.4	1.9	1.8	1.8	1.7	2.0

Source: P. J. D. Wiles, *Economic Institutions Compared* (New York: Halsted Press, 1977), p. 443. Used by permission of Basil Blackwell, Oxford.

Italy, and Canada). Yet even where the state played a major redistributive role (the United Kingdom and Sweden), the distribution of income appeared to be slightly more unequal than in the planned socialist countries (Hungary, Czechoslovakia, and Bulgaria). The Soviet Union in 1966 appeared to have had a less egalitarian distribution of income than its East European counterparts. The USSR distribution was scarcely distinguishable from the British and Swedish distributions (it may even have been more unequal).

Differences in distribution of income between the planned socialist economies and the capitalist welfare states were relatively minor. This is a surprising conclusion. One would have expected the absence of private ownership of property to make more of a difference. Nevertheless, differences are apparent when one contrasts the socialist distributions with those of the capitalist nations in which the state does not play a major redistributive role. In this instance, the expected contrast emerges, although we must emphasize the difficulty of interpreting the socialist distributions because of the omitted income categories.

Summary

The administrative-command model dominated resource allocation in the Soviet Union for almost 60 years. Although Mikhail Gorbachev began a serious attempt to dismantle key features of this system, it remains as a very significant example of economic development in a largely nonmarket context. The main features of this system were as follows:

1. The administrative command system was put in place in 1928 with nationalization of the means of production, a system of national economic planning, and the collectivization of agriculture. Although there were numerous changes in this system over the years, its fundamental aspects remained remarkably stable.
2. The Soviet system was a relatively centralized economic system. The broad objectives of the Communist party were implemented through the state planning agency (Gosplan), the ministries, and individual firms and agricultural units.
3. The essence of Soviet planning was the material balance system, in which balances were developed to equate the demand and supply of key industrial commodities, labor inputs, and the like. The balance approach stressed consistency but not optimality, and there was only minimal reliance on money and prices for the allocation of resources.
4. Soviet enterprises were responsible for fulfilling plan targets, and managers were motivated within an incentive framework. In the absence of a price system reflecting relative scarcities and thus enabling managers to make rational decisions, dysfunctional behavior was a major problem.
5. Prices were cost-based, and the demand side had little or no influence. Prices served primarily an accounting and control function. Retail markets and the allocation of labor were exceptions; here the allocative role of prices was greater. Although capital was allocated in accordance with rules that resembled rates of return, capital allocation was largely accomplished by administrative decree.

6. Market-type influence existed in the allocation of labor. At the same time, market forces were prevalent in the second economy, which, though it varied in importance from one sector to another, dominated in the service sector. Market mechanisms also played an important role in the private sector of Soviet agriculture.

7. Soviet agriculture was traditionally dominated by the collective farms, the state farms, and the private sector. The latter was an important source of food products in spite of its relatively small size in terms of land area. In later years, agro-industrial integration became an important mechanism for combining farm activity with industrial processing.

8. Soviet foreign trade was a state monopoly. Soviet domestic enterprises were largely isolated from world markets through the intermediary function of the Foreign Trade Organization and the nonconvertible ruble.

9. Although cases of rapid economic growth in socialist systems do exist, and despite the importance given to economic growth in socialist systems, these systems have generally not surpassed their capitalist counterparts. Indeed, if we control for other factors, such as the level of economic development, rates of economic growth were higher in capitalist systems. Socialist growth rates slowed markedly in the final years of the Soviet and East European experiences.

10. To understand differences in economic growth, it is necessary to examine the sources of growth, especially the increased use of inputs (extensive growth) vis-à-vis the better use of inputs (intensive growth). The growth of inputs for the differing systems was broadly similar during the postwar years, though after 1980 factor inputs probably grew more rapidly under planned socialism, despite the declining rate of output growth in this era.

11. During the early postwar era, productivity growth was broadly similar in both systems. For example, during the 1950s, efficiency growth accounted for more than 60 percent of the growth in planned socialist systems, a figure close to the capitalist achievement during that same period. In the era after 1960, however, planned socialist economic growth became more extensive, a troubling sign because almost 70 percent of socialist growth was accounted for by the expansion of inputs.

12. The distributions of income are similar in the planned socialist economies and the capitalist welfare states.

Key Terms

incentives
Bolshevik revolution
administrative-command economy
czarist era
level and rate of economic development
collective farms (kolkhozy)
war communism
New Economic Policy (NEP)

decision-making levels
market
planning
public property rights
private property rights
Communist party
wage income
material incentives

moral incentives
Gosplan
ministry
techpromfinplan
material balance system
funded commodities
limited commodities
balanced plan
taut plan
consistent plan
optimal plan
gross value of output
mix or assortment of goods
branch average cost
turnover tax
planners' preferences
consumer demand
organized recruitment
overfull employment policy
coefficient of relative effectiveness
Standard Methodology
repressed inflation
Perestroika

disequilibrium analysis
polycentric system
second economy
state farms (sovkhozy)
labor day
agro-industrial integration
Machine Tractor Stations
Bank for Foreign Trade
foreign trade organizations (FTOs)
Ministry of Foreign Trade
trade aversion
nonconvertible ruble
incentives
success indicators
barter trade
intensive growth
extensive growth
static efficiency
dynamic efficiency
labor productivity
capital productivity
total factor productivity
income distribution

Notes

1. For a general treatment of the Soviet economy and references to the specialized literature, see Paul R. Gregory and Robert C. Stuart, *Soviet and Post-Soviet Economic Structure and Performance*, 6th ed. (Reading, Mass.: Addison Wesley Longman, 1997); Alec Nove, *The Soviet Economic System*, 3rd ed. (New York: Unwin Hyman, 1986); and Michael Ellman, *Socialist Planning* (New York: Cambridge University Press, 1989). For useful background papers, see U.S. Congress, Joint Economic Committee, *Soviet Economy in the 1980s: Problems and Prospects*, Parts 1 and 2 (Washington, D.C.: Government Printing Office, 1982). For a briefer treatment of the Soviet economy, see Franklyn D. Holzman, *The Soviet Economy: Past, Present, and Future* (New York: Foreign Policy Association, 1982); and James R. Millar, *The ABC's of Soviet Socialism* (Urbana: University of Illinois Press, 1981).

2. For a discussion of these years, see M. Lewin, *Russian Peasants and Soviet Power* (London: Allen and Unwin, 1968); for a brief survey, see Gregory and Stuart, *Soviet and Post-Soviet Economic Structure and Performance*, Ch. 5.

3. A considerable amount has been written about the Soviet economy during these early years. See, for example, Alec Nove, *An Economic History of the U.S.S.R.*, rev. ed. (London: Penguin Books, 1982); Eugene Zaleski, *Planning for Economic Growth in the Soviet Union, 1928–1932* (Chapel Hill: University of North Carolina Press, 1971); Maurice Dobb, *Soviet Economic Development Since 1917*, 5th ed. (London: Routledge and Kegan

Paul, 1960); E. H. Carr and R. W. Davies, *Foundations of a Planned Economy, 1926–1929*, Vol. I, Pt. 2 (New York: Macmillan, 1969); Roger Munting, *The Economic Development of the USSR* (London: Croom Helm, 1982); R. W. Davies, *The Socialist Offensive, the Collectivization of Soviet Agriculture 1929–30* (London: Macmillan, 1980); and Thomas F. Remington, "Varga and the Foundation of Soviet Planning," *Soviet Studies* 34 (October 1982), 585–600.

4. There is considerable debate about the *level* of economic development in the Soviet Union in 1917 and hence about the readiness of that country, in the Marxian schema, for the introduction of socialism. For a discussion of this issue, see Gregory and Stuart, *Soviet and Post-Soviet Economic Structure and Performance*, Ch. 2; for more detail, see Paul R. Gregory, "Economic Growth and Structural Change in Tsarist Russia: A Case of Modern Economic Growth?" *Soviet Studies* 23 (January 1972), 418–434; Paul R. Gregory, *Russian National Income 1885–1913* (New York: Cambridge University Press, 1983); and R. W. Davies, ed., *From Tsarism to the New Economic Policy* (Basingstoke, England: Macmillan, 1990).

5. By 1920 the index of industrial production (1913 = 100) had fallen to 20, the index of agricultural production to 64, and the index of transportation to 22. See Gregory and Stuart, *Soviet and Post-Soviet Economic Structure and Performance*, p. 58.

6. By 1928 the index of industrial production (1923 = 100) had risen to 102, the index of agricultural production to 118, and the index of transportation to 106. *Ibid.*, p. 56.

7. For a discussion of the policy issues of this period, see Jerzy F. Karcz, "From Stalin to Brezhnev: Soviet Agricultural Policy in Historical Perspective," in James R. Millar, ed., *The Soviet Rural Community* (Urbana: University of Illinois Press, 1971), pp. 36–70; and Davies, *The Socialist Offensive*.

8. The classic work is Alexander Erlich, *The Soviet Industrialization Debate, 1924–1928* (Cambridge, Mass.: Harvard University Press, 1960). For a translation of original contributions to the debate, see Nicolas Spulber, *Foundations of Soviet Strategy for Economic Growth* (Bloomington: Indiana University Press, 1964).

9. There was, however, only a single candidate for each position, although Gorbachev later proposed changes. For a comprehensive discussion of the Soviet government and party structure, see Jerry F. Hough and Merle Fainsod, *How the Soviet Union Is Governed* (Cambridge, Mass.: Harvard University Press, 1979). T. H. Rigby, *Political Elites in the USSR* (Brookfield, Vt.: Edward Elgar, 1990).

10. For a study of the Communist party of the Soviet Union, see Leonard Shapiro, *The Communist Party of the Soviet Union* (New York: Random House, 1971); and Hough and Fainsod, *How the Soviet Union Is Governed*. For a statistical survey of party membership, see T. H. Rigby, *Communist Party Membership in the U.S.S.R., 1917–1967* (Princeton, N.J.: Princeton University Press, 1968). For further evidence, see T. H. Rigby, "Soviet Communist Party Membership Under Brezhnev," *Soviet Studies* 28 (July 1976), 317–337; and Jan Adams, *Citizen Inspectors in the Soviet Union: The People's Control Committee* (New York: Praeger, 1977).

11. The material balance technique has been analyzed in some detail. The classic article is J. M. Montias, "Planning with Material Balances in Soviet-Type Economies," *American Economic Review* 49 (December 1959), 963–985; for a summary, see Gregory and Stuart, *Soviet and Post-Soviet Economic Structure and Performance*, p. 163 ff. For a theoretical discussion, see Raymond P. Powell, "Plan Execution and the Workability of Soviet Planning," *Journal of Comparative Economics* 1 (March 1979), 51–76.

12. This important point represents a sharp difference between the functioning of a planned economy and that of a market economy. In the market economy, the producing enterprise

normally has supply contracts for required inputs. However, the firm can, with limitations, enter the market either to secure better contractual arrangements or to find a replacement if existing arrangements are interrupted for some reason. In the planned economy, the producing enterprise relies on an inter-enterprise delivery specified in the annual plan. If this delivery is interrupted for any reason, the producing enterprise has no market to which it may turn. In such cases production is typically interrupted. Unless formal or informal stopgap measures can be taken, the imbalances tend to accumulate throughout the economy.

13. See, for example, A. Katsenelinboigen, "Coloured Markets in the Soviet Union," *Soviet Studies* 29 (January 1977), 62–85; Vladimir G. Treml, "Alcohol in the USSR: A Fiscal Dilemma," *Soviet Studies* 27 (April 1975), 161–177; and Boris Rumer, "The 'Second' Agriculture in the USSR," *Soviet Studies* 33 (October 1981), 560–572.

14. The role of the Soviet second economy was the focus of a major research effort undertaken by Gregory Grossman and Vladimir Treml. The Grossman–Treml project involved interviews with Soviet émigrés concerning their personal experiences in the second economy. Gur Ofer and Aaron Vinokur have conducted studies of second-economy earnings among Soviet émigrés to Israel, and the Soviet Interview Project has studied second-economy earnings among Soviet emigrants to the United States. For initial results from these surveys, see J. R. Millar, ed., *Politics, Work, and Daily Life in the USSR* (New York: Cambridge University Press, 1987).

15. There is a substantial body of literature on the problems of Soviet enterprise management. See Joseph Berliner, *Factory and Manager in the USSR* (Cambridge, Mass.: Harvard University Press, 1957); David Granick, *The Red Executive* (New York: Doubleday, 1960); David Granick, *Managerial Comparisons of Four Developed Countries: France, Britain, United States and Russia* (Cambridge, Mass.: M.I.T. Press, 1972); William J. Conyngham, *The Modernization of Soviet Industrial Management* (New York: Cambridge University Press, 1982); and Jan Adams, "The Present Soviet Incentive System," *Soviet Studies* 32 (July 1980), 360.

16. Gregory and Stuart, *Soviet and Post-Soviet Economic Structure and Performance*, pp. 215–216.

17. Unfortunately, relatively little research has been done on the structure and functions of the Soviet state bank. For a survey, see Paul Gekker, "The Banking System of the USSR," *Journal of the Institute of Bankers* 84 (June 1963), 189–197; and Christine Netishen Wollan, "The Financial Policy of the Soviet State Bank, 1932–1970" (Ph.D. dissertation, University of Illinois, Urbana, 1972).

18. Incentives—how to make enterprises do what the center wants—have been the subject of a considerable amount of research. See David Conn, special ed., *The Theory of Incentives*, published as vol. 3, no. 3, *Journal of Comparative Economics* (September 1979); and J. Michael Martin, "Economic Reform and Maximizing Behavior of the Soviet Firm," in Judith Thornton, ed., *Economic Analysis of the Soviet-Type System* (New York: Cambridge University Press, 1976).

19. In contemporary times, the rate of turnover of Soviet industrial managers declined.

20. For a basic survey of Soviet price policy and citation of the important literature, see Gregory and Stuart, *Soviet and Post-Soviet Economic Structure and Performance*, Ch. 8. For an update, see Morris Bornstein, "Soviet Price Policy in the 1970s," in U.S. Congress, Joint Economic Committee, *Soviet Economy in a New Perspective* (Washington, D.C.: Government Printing Office, 1976), pp. 17–66; Morris Bornstein, "The Administration of the Soviet Price System," *Soviet Studies* 30 (October 1978), 466–490; and Morris Bornstein, "Soviet Price Policies," *Soviet Economy* 3, 2 (1987), 96–134.

21. For a discussion of Soviet wage-setting procedures, see Leonard J. Kirsch, *Soviet Wages: Changes in Structure and Administration Since 1956* (Cambridge, Mass.: M.I.T. Press, 1972); B. Arnot, *Controlling Soviet Labour* (London: Macmillan, 1988); D. Granick, *Job Rights in the Soviet Union: Their Consequences* (New York: Cambridge University Press, 1987); and Silvana Malle, *Employment Planning in the Soviet Union* (Basingstoke, England: Macmillan, 1990).

22. See Abram Bergson, *The Economics of Soviet Planning* (New Haven: Yale University Press, 1964), Ch. 6.

23. The provision of appropriate manpower to the Soviet economy was a matter of both interest and complexity because it involved analysis of Soviet demographic trends. For a summary of statistical trends, see Murray Feshbach and Stephen Rapawy, "Soviet Population and Manpower Trends and Policies," in Joint Economic Committee, *Soviet Economy in a New Perspective*, 113–154. For the specific case of agriculture, see Karl-Eugen Wadekin, "Manpower in Soviet Agriculture—Some Post-Khrushchev Developments and Problems," *Soviet Studies* 20 (January 1969), 281–305. Contemporary evidence is presented in Murray Feshbach, "Population and Labor Force," in Abram Bergson and Herbert S. Levine, eds., *The Soviet Economy: Towards the Year 2000* (Winchester, Mass.: Allen and Unwin, 1983), pp. 79–111; Jan Adams, ed., *Employment Policies in the Soviet Union and Eastern Europe*, 2nd ed. (New York: St. Martin's, 1987); and P. R. Gregory and I. L. Collier, "Unemployment in the Soviet Union: Evidence from the Soviet Interview Project," *The American Economic Review* 78 (September 1988), 613–632.

24. For a brief summary of the socialist attitude toward an interest charge for capital, see A. C. Pigou, *Socialism Versus Capitalism* (London: Macmillan, 1937), Ch. 8. For a discussion of Soviet investment planning, see Gregory and Stuart, *Soviet and Post-Soviet Economic Structure and Performance*, Ch. 7. For details, see David A. Dyker, *The Process of Investment in the Soviet Union* (Cambridge, England: Cambridge University Press, 1983).

25. For a discussion of the rules, see Alan Abouchar, "The New Soviet Standard Methodology for Investment Allocation," *Soviet Studies* 24 (January 1973), 402–410; P. Gregory, B. Fielitz, and T. Curtis, "The New Soviet Investment Rules: A Guide to Rational Investment Planning?" *Southern Economic Journal* 41 (January 1974), 500–504; Frank A. Durgin, "The Soviet 1969 Standard Methodology for Investment Allocation Versus 'Universally Correct' Methods," *The ACES Bulletin* 19 (Summer 1977), 29–53; Frank A. Durgin, Jr., "The Third Soviet Standard Methodology for Determining the Effectiveness of Capital Investment (SM-80, Provisional)," *The ACES Bulletin* 24 (Fall 1982), 45–61; and Janice Giffen, "The Allocation of Investment in the Soviet Union: Criteria for the Efficiency of Investment," *Soviet Studies* 33 (October 1981), 593–609. For a useful summary, see David Dyker, *The Process of Investment in the Soviet Union* (New York: Cambridge University Press, 1981).

26. Since the mid-1970s, there has been a debate over the extent of repressed inflation in the former Soviet Union. See D. H. Howard, "The Disequilibrium Model in a Controlled Economy: An Empirical Test of the Barro-Grossman Model," *American Economic Review* 66 (December 1976), 871–879; Richard Portes, "The Control of Inflation: Lessons from East European Experience," *Economics* 44 (May 1977), 109–130; Richard Portes and David Winter, "A Planners' Supply Function for Consumption Goods in Centrally Planned Economies," *Journal of Comparative Economics* 1 (December 1977), 351–365; and Richard Portes and David Winter, "The Demand for Money and for Consumption Goods in Centrally Planned Economies," *Review of Economics and Statistics* 60 (February 1978), 8–18.

27. Joyce Pickersgill and Gur Ofer conducted early empirical studies of Soviet saving behavior and concluded that Soviet citizens appear to save for the same reasons Westerners
do. On this, see Gur Ofer and Joyce Pickersgill, "Soviet Household Saving: A Cross-
Section Study of Soviet Emigrant Families," *Quarterly Journal of Economics* 95 (August
1980), 121–144; and Joyce Pickersgill, "Soviet Household Saving Behavior," *Review of
Economics and Statistics* 58 (May 1976), 139–147. Other scholars see increases in excess
demand as the cause of increases in saving. On this, see D. W. Bronson and Barbara S.
Severin, "Recent Trends in Consumption and Disposable Money Income in the USSR,"
U.S. Congress, Joint Economic Committee, *New Directions in the Soviet Economy*,
Part II-B (Washington, D.C.: Government Printing Office, 1966); and Igor Birman, *Secret
Income and the Soviet State Budget* (Boston: Kluwer, 1981).

28. Paul Craig Roberts, "The Polycentric Soviet Economy," *Journal of Law and Economics*
12 (April 1969), 163–181.

29. Eugene Zaleski, *Stalinist Planning for Economic Growth, 1932–1952* (Chapel Hill: University of North Carolina Press, 1980).

30. John Wilhelm, "Does the Soviet Union Have a Planned Economy?" *Soviet Studies* 31
(April 1979), 268–274.

31. Gregory Grossman, "The 'Second Economy' of the USSR," *Problems of Communism*
26 (September–October 1977), 25–40; Aron Katsenelinboigen, "Coloured Markets in
the Soviet Union," *Soviet Studies* 29 (January 1977), 62–85; Dimitri Simes, "The Soviet
Parallel Market," *Survey* 21 (Summer 1975), 42–52; and *Studies on the Soviet Second
Economy* (Durham, N.C.: Berkeley–Duke Occasional Papers on the Second Economy in
the USSR, December 1987).

32. Vladimir Treml, "Alcohol in the USSR: A Fiscal Dilemma," *Soviet Studies* 41 (October
1973), 161–177; Dennis O'Hearn, "The Consumer Second Economy: Size and Effects,"
Soviet Studies 32 (April 1980), 221; and Vladimir G. Treml, *Purchase of Food from
Private Sources in Soviet Urban Areas* (Durham, N.C.: Berkeley–Duke Occasional
Papers on the Second Economy in the USSR, September 1985).

33. For a discussion of the various forms of agricultural organization, see D. J. Male, *Russian
Peasant Organization Before Collectivization* (Cambridge, England: Cambridge Uni-
versity Press, 1971); and Robert G. Wesson, *Soviet Communes* (New Brunswick, N.J.:
Rutgers University Press, 1963).

34. For a survey of thinking on this issue, see Karcz, "From Stalin to Brezhnev."

35. Because the sovkhoz was a relatively straightforward state enterprise operating under the
same general principles as the industrial enterprise, relatively little attention had been
paid to its structure and operation. It is important to note, however, that whereas the
sovkhoz was state-owned property, the kolkhoz was an ideologically inferior form of
property holding known as kolkhoz-cooperative property. Many of the changes in the
kolkhoz could be explained by the implementation of state policy designed to "improve"
the kolkhoz and raise it to the same level as the sovkhoz.

36. For a detailed discussion of the kolkhoz and the labor-day mechanism, see Robert C.
Stuart, *The Collective Farm in Soviet Agriculture* (Lexington, Mass.: Heath, 1972) and
R. W. Davies, *The Industrialization of Russia*, Vols. 1 and 2 (Cambridge, Mass.: Harvard
University Press, 1980). Research has supported the view that during the introduction of
the collectives there was no increase in the net surplus generated by agriculture. For a discussion of this question, see James R. Millar, "Soviet Rapid Development and the Agricultural Surplus Hypothesis," *Soviet Studies* 22 (July 1970), 77–93; and M. J. Ellman,
"Did the Russian Agricultural Surplus Provide the Resources for the Increase in Investment in the USSR During the First Five-Year Plan?" *Economic Journal* 85 (December

1975), 844–863. For a summary, see Gregory and Stuart, *Soviet and Post-Soviet Economic Structure and Performance*, Ch. 5. For a critical view, see David Morrison, "A Critical Examination of A. A. Barsov's Empirical Work on the Value of Balance Exchanges Between the Town and the Country," *Soviet Studies* 34 (October 1985), 570–584.

37. For a discussion of the financing of the kolkhozy, see James R. Millar, "Financing the Modernization of Kolkhozy," in Millar, *The Soviet Rural Economy*, pp. 276–303.

38. The standard work on the Machine Tractor Stations is Robert F. Miller, *One Hundred Thousand Tractors* (Cambridge, Mass.: Harvard University Press, 1970).

39. For an in-depth discussion of the private sector in Soviet agriculture, see Karl-Eugen Wadekin, *The Private Sector in Soviet Agriculture* (Berkeley: University of California Press, 1973); and A. Lane, "U.S.S.R.: Private Agriculture on Center Stage," in U.S. Congress, Joint Economic Committee, *Soviet Economy in the 1980s: Problems and Prospects*, Pt. 2 (Washington, D.C.: U.S. Government Printing Office, 1982), pp. 23–40.

40. For a survey of postwar developments in Soviet agriculture and references to the specialized literature, see Gregory and Stuart, *Soviet and Post-Soviet Economic Structure and Performance*, Ch. 6.

41. Robert C. Stuart, "The Changing Role of the Collective Farm in Soviet Agriculture," *Canadian Slavonic Papers* 26 (Summer 1974), 145–159.

42. For a survey, see K.-E. Wadekin, *Agrarian Policies in Communist Europe: An Introduction* (Totowa, N.J.: Allanheld and Osmun, 1982), Ch. 12.

43. Rural income levels are discussed in David W. Bronson and Constance B. Krueger, "The Revolution in Soviet Farm Household Income, 1953–1967," in Millar, *The Soviet Rural Economy*, pp. 214–257; and in more general terms in Gertrude E. Schroeder and Barbara S. Severin, "Soviet Consumption and Income Policies in Perspective," in Joint Economic Committee, *Soviet Economy in a New Perspective*, pp. 620–660.

44. For a discussion of subsidies, see W. G. Treml, "Subsidies in Soviet Agriculture: Record and Prospects," in U.S. Congress, Joint Economic Committee, *Soviet Economy in the 1980s: Problems and Prospects* (Washington, D.C.: U.S. Government Printing Office, 1982), pp. 171–186.

45. For a survey of Soviet foreign trade and references to the literature, see Gregory and Stuart, *Soviet and Post-Soviet Economic Structure and Performance*, Ch. 9.

46. For a different view, see Steven Rosefielde, "Comparative Advantage and the Evolving Pattern of Soviet International Commodity Specialization, 1950–1973," in Steven Rosefielde, ed., *Economic Welfare and the Economics of Soviet Socialism* (New York: Cambridge University Press, 1981), pp. 185–220.

47. See Vladimir Treml and Barry Kostinsky, *Domestic Value of Soviet Foreign Trade: Exports and Imports in the 1972 Input-Output Table*, Foreign Economic Report No. 20, U.S. Department of Commerce, October 1982.

48. Gur Ofer, "Industrial Structure, Urbanization, and the Growth Strategy of Socialist Countries," *Quarterly Journal of Economics* 90 (May 1976), 219–243; Gur Ofer, *The Service Sector in Soviet Economic Development* (Cambridge, Mass.: Harvard University Press, 1973); Paul Gregory, *Socialist and Nonsocialist Industrialization Patterns* (New York: Praeger, 1970); Frederic L. Pryor, *Public Expenditures in Communist and Capitalist Nations* (Bloomington: Indiana University Press, 1973); and Frederic L. Pryor, *Property and Industrial Organization in Communist and Capitalist Nations* (Bloomington: Indiana University Press, 1973). For a discussion of the pure methodology of econometric performance evaluation, see Edward Hewett, "Alternative Econometric Approaches for Studying the Link Between Economic Systems and Economic Outcomes," *Journal of Comparative Economics* 4 (September 1980), 274–294. For a discussion of the methodology of growth

comparisons, see Gur Ofer, "Soviet Economic Growth, 1928–1985," *Journal of Economic Literature* 25 (December 1987), 1767–1833.

49. For a discussion of index number relativity, see Bergson, *Real National Income of Soviet Russia Since 1928*, Ch. 3.
50. This result was noted first by Abram Bergson in "Development Under Two Systems: Comparative Productivity Growth Since 1950," *World Politics* 20 (July 1971), 579–617.
51. Frederic Pryor, *A Guidebook to the Comparative Study of Economic Systems* (Englewood Cliffs, N.J.: Prentice-Hall, 1985), p. 78.
52. For a discussion of the measurement of static and dynamic efficiency, see Bergson, *Planning and Productivity Under Soviet Socialism*.
53. Edward Denison and William Chung, *How Japan's Economy Grew So Fast* (Washington, D.C.: Brookings, 1976), p. 30.
54. The classic treatment of the measurement of factor productivity is Edward Denison, *Why Growth Rates Differ* (Washington, D.C.: Brookings, 1967).
55. Apparently the Romanian and Bulgarian capital stock figures are in current prices. On this, see Alton, "Comparative Structure and Growth of Economic Activity in Eastern Europe," p. 223.
56. "Eastern Europe: Long Road Ahead to Economic Well-Being," Tables C-1 to C-21.
57. William Easterly and Stanley Fischer, "The Soviet Economic Decline," *World Bank Economic Review* 9, 3 (September 1995), 341–371.
58. A considerable amount of research has gone into the subject of the relative growth of investment and consumption in Eastern Europe. Unfortunately, studies that cover the 1970s have not succeeded in calculating directly the real growth of investment. For a discussion of this point, see Alton, "Production and Resource Allocation in Eastern Europe," pp. 314–367. Also see Alton, "East European GNPs," pp. 94–98.
59. See Pryor, *Property and Industrial Organization in Communist and Capitalist Nations*, pp. 74–75.
60. *Ibid.*, pp. 74–89.
61. John R. Moroney, ed., *Income Inequality: Trends and International Compromise* (Lexington, Mass.: D. C. Heath, 1978), p. 5.
62. Janet Chapman, "Earnings Distribution in the USSR, 1968–1976," *Soviet Studies* 35 (July 1983), 410–413.
63. See also a specialized study for the Soviet Union by Alastair McAuley, "The Distribution of Earnings and Income in the Soviet Union," *Soviet Studies* 29 (April 1977), 214–237. Also see Harold Lydall, "Some Problems in Making International Comparisons of Income Inequality," in Moroney, *Income Inequality*, pp. 31–33. For recent analysis of the available evidence, see Anthony B. Atkinson and John Micklewright, *Economic Transformation in Eastern Europe and the Distribution of Income*, Cambridge: Cambridge University Press, 1992.

Recommended Readings

General Works

Robert W. Campbell, *The Soviet-Type Economies: Performance and Evolution*, 3rd ed. (Boston: Houghton Mifflin, 1981).
R. W. Davies, ed., *The Soviet Union* (Winchester, Mass.: Unwin Hyman, 1989).
David A. Dyker, *The Future of the Soviet Planning System* (Armonk, N.Y.: M. E. Sharpe, 1985).

Paul R. Gregory and Robert C. Stuart, *Soviet and Post-Soviet Economic Structure and Performance*, 5th ed. (New York: HarperCollins, 1994).

Franklyn D. Holzman, *The Soviet Economy: Past, Present, and Future* (New York: Foreign Policy Association, 1982).

Tania Konn, ed., *Soviet Studies Guide* (London: Bowker–Saur, 1992).

James R. Millar, *The ABC's of Soviet Socialism* (Urbana: University of Illinois Press, 1981).

Alec Nove, *The Soviet Economic System*, 2nd ed. (London: Unwin Hyman, 1981).

United States Congress, Joint Economic Committee, *Gorbachev's Economic Plans*, Vols. I and II (Washington, D.C.: U.S. Government Printing Office, 1987).

Soviet Economic History

E. H. Carr and R. W. Davies, *Foundations of a Planned Economy, 1926–1929*, Vol. 1, Pts. 1 and 2 (New York: Macmillan, 1969).

R. W. Davies, *The Industrialization of Soviet Russia*, Vols. I and II (Cambridge, Mass.: Harvard University Press, 1980).

R. W. Davies, Mark Harrison, and S. G. Wheatcroft, eds., *The Economic Transformation of the Soviet Union 1913–1945* (Cambridge: Cambridge University Press, 1994).

Maurice Dobb, *Soviet Economic Development Since 1917*, 5th ed. (London: Routledge and Kegan Paul, 1960).

Alexander Erlich, *The Soviet Industrialization Debate, 1924–1928* (Cambridge, Mass.: Harvard University Press, 1969).

Paul R. Gregory, *Russian National Income, 1885–1913* (New York: Cambridge University Press, 1983).

Gregory Guroff and Fred V. Carstensen, *Entrepreneurship in Imperial Russia and the Soviet Union* (Princeton, N.J.: Princeton University Press, 1983).

Moshe Lewin, *Political Undercurrents in Soviet Economic Debates: From Bukharin to the Modern Reformers* (Princeton, N.J.: Princeton University Press, 1974).

Roger Munting, *The Economic Development of the USSR* (London: Croom Helm, 1982).

Alec Nove, *An Economic History of the U.S.S.R.*, rev. ed. (London: Penguin Books, 1982).

Nicolas Spulber, *Soviet Strategy for Economic Growth* (Bloomington: Indiana University Press, 1964).

The Communist Party and the Manager

Donald D. Barry and Carol Barner-Barry, *Contemporary Soviet Politics: An Introduction*, 2nd ed. (Englewood Cliffs, N.J.: Prentice-Hall, 1982).

William J. Conyngham, *The Modernization of Soviet Industrial Management* (New York: Cambridge University Press, 1982).

Andrew Freiis, *The Soviet Industrial Enterprise* (New York: St. Martin's Press, 1974).

David Granick, *Managerial Comparisons of Four Developed Countries: France, Britain, United States, and Russia* (Cambridge, Mass.: M.I.T. Press, 1972).

Leslie Holmes, *The Policy Process in Communist States* (Beverly Hills: Sage Publications, 1981).

Jerry F. Hough and Merle Fainsod, *How the Soviet Union Is Governed* (Cambridge, Mass.: Harvard University Press, 1979).

David Lane, *Politics and Society in the USSR*, 2nd ed. (London: Martin Robertson, 1978).

Nathan Leites, *Soviet Style in Management* (New York: Crane Russak, 1985).

Leonard Shapiro, *The Government and Politics of the Soviet Union*, 6th ed. (Essex, England: Hutchinson Publishing Group, 1978).

Selected Aspects of the Soviet Economy

R. Amann and J. M. Cooper, eds., *Industrial Innovation in the Soviet Union* (New Haven: Yale University Press, 1982).

Joseph S. Berliner, *The Innovation Decision in Soviet Industry* (Cambridge, England: Cambridge University Press, 1983).

Morris Bornstein, ed., *The Soviet Economy: Continuity and Change* (Boulder, Colo.: Westview Press, 1981).

Robert W. Campbell, *Soviet Energy Technologies* (Bloomington: Indiana University Press, 1980).

David A. Dyker, *The Process of Investment in the Soviet Union* (Cambridge, England: Cambridge University Press, 1983).

Franklyn D. Holzman, *International Trade Under Communism* (New York: Basic Books, 1976).

Alastair McAuley, *Women's Work and Wages in the Soviet Union* (London: Unwin Hyman, 1981).

Mervyn Matthews, *Education in the Soviet Union* (London: Allen and Unwin, 1982).

———, *Poverty in the Soviet Union* (New York: Cambridge University Press, 1987).

James R. Millar, *Politics, Work, and Daily Life in the USSR* (New York: Cambridge University Press, 1987).

Henry W. Morton and Robert C. Stuart, eds., *The Contemporary Soviet City* (Armonk, N.Y.: M. E. Sharpe, 1984).

Robert C. Stuart, ed., *The Soviet Rural Economy* (Totowa, N.J.: Roman and Allenheld, 1983).

Murray Yanowitch, *Social and Economic Inequality in the Soviet Union* (London: Martin Robertson, 1977).

Eugene Zaleski, *Planning Reforms in the Soviet Union, 1962–1966* (Chapel Hill: University of North Carolina Press, 1967).

Planning

Alan Abouchar, ed., *The Socialist Price Mechanism* (Durham, N.C.: Duke University Press, 1977).

Edward Ames, *Soviet Economic Processes* (Homewood, Ill.: Irwin, 1965).

Abram Bergson and Herbert S. Levine, eds., *The Soviet Economy: Towards the Year 2000* (London: Allen and Unwin, 1983).

Martin Cave, Alastair McAuley, and Judith Thornton, eds., *New Trends in Soviet Economics* (Armonk, N.Y.: M. E. Sharpe, 1982).

Michael Ellman, *Soviet Planning Today: Proposals for an Optimally Functioning Economic System* (Cambridge, England: Cambridge University Press, 1971).

David Granick, *Job Rights in the Soviet Union: Their Consequences* (New York: Cambridge University Press, 1987).

Kenneth R. Gray, ed., *Soviet Agriculture* (Ames: Iowa State University Press, 1990).

Donald W. Green and Christopher I. Higgins, *SOVMOD I: A Macroeconometric Model of the Soviet Economy* (New York: Academic, 1977).

Paul R. Gregory, *The Soviet Economic Bureaucracy* (Cambridge, England: Cambridge University Press, 1990).

John Hardt *et al.*, *Mathematics and Computers in Soviet Planning* (New Haven: Yale University Press, 1977).

Peter Murrell, *The Nature of Socialist Economies: Lessons from Eastern European Foreign Trade* (Princeton, N.J.: Princeton University Press, 1990).

Steven Rosefielde, ed., *Economic Welfare and the Economics of Soviet Socialism* (New York: Cambridge University Press, 1981).

Robert C. Stuart, ed., *The Soviet Rural Economy* (Totowa, N.J.: Roman and Allenheld, 1983).

Judith Thornton, ed., *Economic Analysis of the Soviet-Type System* (New York: Cambridge University Press, 1976).

Alfred Zauberman, *Mathematical Theory in Soviet Planning* (Oxford, England: Oxford University Press, 1976).

Comparing Performance

Trevor Buck, *Comparative Industrial Systems* (New York: St. Martin's, 1982).

Irving B. Kravis, "Comparative Studies of National Incomes and Prices," *Journal of Economic Literature* 22 (March 1984).

Irving B. Kravis, Allen Heston, and Robert Summers, "Real GDP Per Capita for More Than One Hundred Countries," *Economic Journal* 88 (June 1978).

Irving B. Kravis, *World Product and Income: International Comparisons of Real Gross Product* (Baltimore: Johns Hopkins University Press for the World Bank, 1982).

Frederic L. Pryor, *Property and Industrial Organization in Communist and Capitalist Nations* (Bloomington: Indiana University Press, 1973).

———, *A Guidebook to the Comparative Study of Economic Systems* (Englewood Cliffs, N.J.: Prentice-Hall, 1985.

Economic Growth

Thad P. Alton and associates, *Economic Growth in Eastern Europe 1970 and 1975–1985*, Research Project on National Income in East Central Europe (New York: L. W. International Financial Research, Inc., (occasional paper no. 90).

Abram Bergson, *Soviet Post-War Economic Development* (Stockholm: Almquist & Wicksell, 1974).

———, "The Soviet Economic Slowdown," *Challenge* 21 (January–February 1978), 22–27.

Joseph C. Brada and Ronald L. Graves, "Slowdown in Soviet Defense Expenditures," *Southern Economic Journal* 54 (1988), 964–984.

Norman E. Cameron, "Economic Growth in the USSR, Hungary, and East and West Germany," *Journal of Comparative Economics* 5 (March 1981), 24–42.

Stanley Cohn, "The Soviet Path to Economic Growth: A Comparative Analysis," *Review of Income and Wealth*, March 1976, 49–59.

Edward Denison, *Why Growth Rates Differ: Postwar Experience in Nine Western Countries* (Washington, D.C.: The Brookings Institution, 1967).

Padma Desai, *The Soviet Economy: Efficiency, Technical Change and Growth Retardation* (Oxford, England: Basil Blackwell, 1986).

———, "Soviet Growth Retardation," *American Economic Review Papers and Proceedings* 76 (May 1986), 175–179.

William Easterly and Stanley Fischer, "The Soviet Economic Decline," *The World Bank Economic Review* 9, 3 (September 1995), 341–71.

Stanislaw Gomulka, "Soviet Growth Slowdown: Duality, Maturity and Innovation," *American Economic Review Papers and Proceedings* 76 (May 1986), 170–174.

Vladimir Kontorovich, "Soviet Growth Slowdown: Econometric vs. Direct Evidence," *American Economic Review Papers and Proceedings* 76 (May 1986), 181–185.

Sima Lieberman, *The Growth of European Mixed Economies* (New York: Halstead Press, 1977).

Angus Maddison, *Economic Growth in Japan and USSR* (New York: Norton, 1969).
———, "Growth and Slowdown in Advanced Capitalist Economies," *Journal of Economic Literature* 25 (June 1987), 649–698.
Wilfred Malenbaum, "Modern Economic Growth in India and China: The Comparison Revisited," *Economic Development and Cultural Change* 31 (October 1982), 45–84.

Productivity

Abram Bergson, "Comparative Productivity: The USSR, Eastern Europe, and the West," *American Economic Review* 77 (June 1987), 342–357.
———, *Planning and Productivity Under Soviet Socialism* (New York: Columbia University Press, 1967).
———, *Productivity and the Social System: The USSR and the West* (Cambridge, Mass.: Harvard University Press, 1978).
———, "Productivity under Two Systems: The USSR versus the West," in Jan Tinbergen *et al.*, eds., *Optimum Social Welfare and Productivity: A Comparative View* (New York: New York University Press, 1972).
———, "The U.S.S.R. Before the Fall: How Poor and Why?" *Journal of Economic Perspectivies* 5, 4 (Fall 1991), 27–44.
Padma Desai, "Total Factor Productivity in Postwar Soviet Industry and its Branches," *Journal of Comparative Economics* 9 (March 1985), 1–23.
Padma Desai and Ricardo Martin, "Efficiency Loss from Resource Misallocation in Soviet Industry," *Quarterly Journal of Economics* 98 (August 1983), 441–456.
Herbert S. Levine, "Possible Causes of the Deterioration of Soviet Productivity Growth in the Period 1976–80," in United States Congress, Joint Economic Committee, *Soviet Economy in the 1980s: Problems and Prospects*, Part 1 (Washington, D.C.: United States Government Printing Office, 1982), pp. 153–168.
Peter Murrell and Mancur Olson, "The Devolution of Centrally Planned Economies," *Journal of Comparative Economics* 15 (June 1991), 239–265.
Gertrude Schroeder, "The Slowdown in Soviet Industry, 1976–1982" *Soviet Economy* 1 (January–March 1985), 42–74.
Subramanian Swamy, "The Economic Growth in China and India, 1952–1970: A Comparative Appraisal," *Economic Development and Cultural Change* 21 (July 1973), 1–84.
United States Congress, Joint Economic Committee, *USSR: Measures of Economic Growth and Development, 1950–1980* (Washington, D.C.: U.S. Government Printing Office, 1982).
———, *East European Economies: Slow Growth in the 1980s*, Vols. 1–3 (Washington, D.C.: United States Government Printing Office, 1985).
Martin Weitzman, "Soviet Postwar Economic Growth and Capital–Labor Substitution," *American Economic Review* 60 (December 1970), 676–692.

Technology

R. Amann and J. Cooper, eds., *Industrial Innovation in the Soviet Union* (New Haven: Yale University Press, 1982).
Abram Bergson, "Technological Progress," in Abram Bergson and Herbert S. Levine, eds., *The Soviet Economy Towards the Year 2000* (London: Allen & Unwin, 1983).
Joseph S. Berliner, *The Innovation Decision in Soviet Industry* (Cambridge, Mass.: M.I.T. Press, 1976).

Income Inequality

Michael V. Alexeev and Clifford G. Gaddy, "Trends in Wage and Income Distribution under Gorbachev: Analysis of New Soviet Data," (Durham, N.C.: Berkeley–Duke Occasional Papers on the Second Economy in the USSR, No. 25, 1991).

Anthony B. Atkinson and John Micklewright, *Economic Transformation in Eastern Europe and the Distribution of Income* (Cambridge: Cambridge University Press, 1992).

Abram Bergson, "Income Inequality under Soviet Socialism," *Journal of Economic Literature* 22 (September 1984).

Janet Chapman, "Are Earnings More Equal Under Socialism? The Soviet Case, with Some United States Comparisons," in J. R. Moroney, ed., *Income Inequality: Trends and International Comparisons* (Lexington, Mass.: Heath, 1979).

———, "Earnings Distribution in the USSR, 1968–1976," *Soviet Studies* 35 (1983), 410–413.

———, "Income Distribution and Social Justice in the Soviet Union," *Comparative Economic Studies* 31 (1989), 14–45.

John Moroney, *Income Inequality: Trends and International Comparisons* (Lexington, Mass.: D. C. Heath, 1978).

Martin Schnitzer, *Income Distribution: A Comparative Study of the United States, Sweden, West Germany, East Germany, the United Kingdom, and Japan* (New York: Praeger, 1974).

P. J. D. Wiles, *The Distribution of Income, East and West* (Amsterdam: North Holland, 1974).

Appendix 9A: Measuring Outcomes in the Command Economy

Throughout, this book has emphasized both the importance and the difficulty of relating varying outcomes to different systemic arrangements. Although it is critical to understand how systems and outcomes are related, there are a variety of problems of both a general and a specific nature.

For example, to assess the Soviet economic experience, a variety of general paradigms may be used. This experience might be assessed by examining it in terms of the Marxist–Leninist vision of economic history or by using the more general concepts of economic development.

Suppose, however, that a more specific issue demands examination, such as the common conception that the Soviet Union had persistent excess demand for consumer goods—what is generally called repressed inflation. An anecdotal approach could be pursued by looking at the media and reports that attempt to gather information on consumer complaints, the existence of waiting lines, and the like. That approach might be necessary in the absence of appropriate data, even though it might not be fully satisfactory.

If the question of excess demand arose in a market economy, sophisticated techniques would be available first to develop a theory or model of the particular market and then to test the model using empirical evidence. But can such techniques, based on contemporary neoclassical economic theory and relevant econometric methods, be used in a setting as different as that which existed in the former Soviet Union? Although the immediate goal is to examine a particular issue in the Soviet context, broader methodological issues are involved.

The Market Context

If we wish to examine outcomes of the supply of and demand for, say, consumer goods in the market context, a familiar approach is to specify demand and supply equations representing the particular market. Equations 9A.1 and 9A.2 illustrate the demand and supply equations, respectively.

$$Q_d = a + bP + cY + u \tag{9A.1}$$

$$Q_s = d + eP + fC + u' \tag{9A.2}$$

This model, designed only for illustrative purposes, would allow us to give empirical content to the demand and supply relationships, where demand is viewed as a function of prices (P) and incomes (Y), and supply is a function of prices (P) and some measure of production capacity (C). Familiar techniques are available for the estimation of this sort of model.[1]

This sort of model is generally not discussed in an introductory text in economics, but an important proposition underlying the model *is* generally discussed—namely, the identification problem. As most discussions of supply and demand emphasize, when we observe prices and quantities in the real world, let us say over time, we are in fact observing a series of equilibrium positions, or intersections of supply curves and demand curves. To take a simple case in which demand is unchanged but supply is increasing through time, the price–quantity combinations that we would observe are those represented by the letters *A, B,* and *C* in Figure 9.6.

FIGURE 9.6   Supply and Demand: Equilibrium

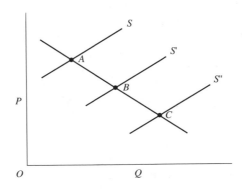

It is important to note that in this approach, the market clears; at each point in time, equilibrium prevails. Suppose, however, that the market does not clear. Let us consider the disequilibrium case.

The Disequilibrium Context

In recent theoretical and empirical work, it has been argued that the equilibrium approach may be inappropriate in the presence of persistent excess demand.[2] For example, if we consider a simple static case where the price is set by state authorities, the outcome could be represented by Figure 9.6, where the magnitude of excess demand is given by the distance Q_sQ_d, and the prevailing price is set by the state at OP'.

It is quite obvious that in this case we would not, in the real world, observe the intersection of the supply and demand curves when we examined combinations of price and quantity. Under the conditions specified in Figure 9.7, we would observe the state-set price of OP', some rationing device (about which we may or may not have information), and a resulting quantity actually sold, probably Q_s. If we move from this simple case to a more realistic case with persistent excess demand through time, it is clearly possible that the magnitude of the excess demand will change. Could we capture the increased complexity of this disequilibrium case in a formal model? One approach that has been suggested can be represented as follows:

$$Q_d = a + bP + cY + u \qquad \text{(9A.3)}$$

$$Q_s = d + eP + fC + u' \qquad \text{(9A.4)}$$

$$Q = \min(D,S) \qquad \text{(9A.5)}$$

FIGURE 9.7 Supply and Demand: Disequilibrium

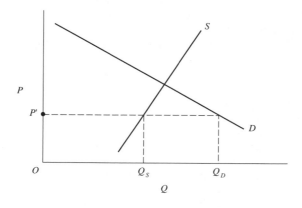

In this particular case, equation 9A.5 is introduced to provide a rule by which the suspected shortage will be handled. Once again, various methods of estimation are available, with price (P) assumed to be exogenous. In this approach, interest centers on the appropriate specification, on alternative methods of estimation, and, finally, on empirical verification of whether in fact a disequilibrium specification is appropriate.[3]

A more sophisticated variant would include the possibility that if there is excess demand in a particular market at a particular time, planners may (1) have some knowledge about this excess demand and (2) take some steps to lessen its magnitude through time. A number of attempts have been made to construct macroeconometric models of planned socialist economic systems. It is particularly appealing on a number of grounds to consider a model in which planners have available, and utilize, various policy controls for manipulation of the economic system through time. Although one can imagine a wide array of possible controls, let us, for the sake of illustration, consider a basic approach suggested by Richard Quandt.[4] Thus, to consider the response of planners over time, we specify a more complex model:

$$Q_t^d = a + bP_t + cY_t + u \tag{9A.6}$$

$$Q_t^s = d + eP_t + fC_t + u' \tag{9A.7}$$

$$Q_t = \min(D_t, S_t) \tag{9A.8}$$

$$P_t - P_{t-1} = g(D_t - S_t) + u'' \tag{9A.9}$$

In the model presented in equations 9A.6 through 9A.9, price (P) is again exogenous and is assumed to be the mechanism through which planners make adjustments. Specifically, planners vary price through time, depending on the magnitude of the excess demand. Other approaches could be considered, but this particular model captures the essence of the Lange adjustment and is thus of more than passing interest.

The disequilibrium approach is, of course, an alternative hypothesis to the equilibrium approach and is not, therefore, necessarily limited to application in the case of the command economy. The approach is, however, relatively recent in origin. There is now a substantial literature applying this approach to the Soviet case, especially in the examination of consumer markets. The approach remains controversial, and methodological difficulties complicate both specification and estimation of the model.

Notes

1. See William H. Greene, *Econometric Analysis*, 2nd ed. (New York: Macmillan, 1993). For a discussion of disequilibrium models that provides extensive references to the literature, see Richard E. Quandt, *The Econometrics of Disequilibrium* (New York: Basil Blackwell, 1988).
2. For example, Western interpretations of the Soviet consumer goods market have generally suggested that although there is excess demand, the turnover tax has been used to bring prices close to the point of equilibrium. One could argue, however, that if prices were in

fact "close" to equilibrium, planners would have sufficient knowledge and power to raise prices *to* equilibrium, thus eliminating the persistent complaints about shortages. The possibility of persistent excess demand deserves our attention, especially because it is a basic underpinning of the work of Kornai described in Chapter 7.
3. See, for example, Richard E. Quandt, "Tests of the Equilibrium vs. Disequilibrium Hypotheses," *International Economic Review* 19 (June 1978), 435–452.
4. Ibid.

Recommended Readings

R. J. Barro and H. I. Grossman, "A General Disequilibrium Model of Income and Employment," *American Economic Review* 61 (March 1971), 82–93.

W. Charemza and M. Gronicki, *Plans and Disequilibria in Centrally Planned Economies* (Amsterdam: North-Holland, 1988).

Christopher M. Davis, "The Second Economy in Disequilibrium and Shortage Models of Centrally Planned Economies," (Durham, N.C.: Berkeley–Duke Occasional Papers on the Second Economy in the USSR, July 1988).

S. M. Goldfeld and R. E. Quandt, "Estimation in a Disequilibrium Model and the Value of Information," *Journal of Econometrics* 3 (November 1975), 325–348.

———, "Single-Market Disequilibrium Models: Estimation and Testing," *The Economic Studies Quarterly* 32 (April 1981), 12–28.

———, "Some Properties of the Simple Disequilibrium Model with Covariance," *Economics Letters* 1, 4 (1978) 343–346.

David H. Howard, *The Disequilibrium Model in a Controlled Economy* (Lexington, Mass.: Lexington Books, 1979).

———, "The Disequilibrium Model in a Controlled Economy: An Empirical Test of the Barro–Grossman Model," *American Economic Review* 66 (December 1976), 871–879.

Richard Portes and David Winter, "The Demand for Money and for Consumption Goods in Centrally Planned Economies," *Review of Economics and Statistics* 60 (February 1978), 8–18.

———, "The Supply of Consumption Goods in Centrally Planned Economies," *Journal of Comparative Economics* 1 (December 1977), 351–363.

Richard E. Quandt, *The Econometrics of Disequilibrium* (New York: Basil Blackwell, 1988).

———, "Tests of the Equilibrium vs. Disequilibrium Hypotheses," *International Economic Review* 19 (June 1978), 435–452.

H. S. Rosen and R. E. Quandt, "Estimation of a Disequilibrium Aggregate Labor Market," *Review of Economics and Statistics* 60 (1978), 371–379.

10

China: Moving Toward Market Socialism?

We discussed the theory of market socialism in Chapter 7. Unlike the other theoretical models of economic systems—market capitalism and planned social-ism, both of which can be illustrated with real-world examples—market socialism lacks a clear-cut real-world manifestation. Recall that market socialism is an eco-nomic system that combines market resource allocation with state ownership. In dif-ferent market-socialist models, state ownership need not be pervasive; there may be private ownership of smaller businesses, but the state should own the most significant "means of production" of society. This ownership may be in the form of state owner-ship or ownership by workers. In the theoretical market-socialist model, the market allocates consumer goods and labor, but market simulation techniques may be used in the producer goods market. Management of state enterprises may be carried out by state managers answerable to the state, or it may be executed by managers appointed by worker-owners.

Thus there is no single form of market socialism; it is sufficiently flexible to encompass a range of institutional arrangements. Its most basic feature, however, is its combination of state ownership with market allocation.

If we search for real-world models of market socialism, we can cite the Yugo-slav economy before the disintegration of what was once Yugoslavia. The Yugoslavs abandoned the Soviet planned economy in the aftermath of World War II as Yugo-slavia, under the leadership of J. Tito, avoided being swallowed up in the Soviet bloc. Having rejected the Soviet model, the Yugoslavs settled on a system characterized by worker ownership and management, a relatively open economy, and extensive use of market allocation but tempered by strong state interventionist policies. Interest in the Yugoslav form of market socialism has declined with the collapse of Yugoslavia as a nation-state.

The transition economies of Eastern Europe and the former Soviet Union (to be discussed in later chapters) could perhaps also serve as examples of market socialism except for the fact that most of them are aiming for an end result that is not market socialism. As they go through their transitions, their economies are characterized by extensive state ownership combined with the increasing importance of market alloca-tion. However, their end goal appears to be the creation of a capitalist market econ-omy rather than a stable market-socialist economy. The market-socialist features of the transition economies, however, will be noted in our discussion of them.

China began its current economic reform in the late 1970s. Prior to the adoption of these reforms, the Chinese economy strongly resembled the Soviet administrative-command economy (almost complete state ownership, collectivized agriculture, an industry managed by directive plans, priorities set by the Communist Party) but with necessary amendments to account for China's rural nature. The reforms begun by Deng Xiaoping, however, dramatically altered the nature of the Chinese economy by permitting significant private ownership in agriculture, trade and small-scale industry, opening the economy to world product and capital markets, and allowing various financial markets and institutions to be formed, such as stock markets, commercial banks, and credit markets. Throughout these reforms, China retained two essential features of the administrative-command model: state ownership of heavy industry and other "commanding heights" activities and the continued political dictatorship of the Chinese Communist Party. The continued dominance of the Communist Party was signaled by the crackdown on dissidents in June of 1989 in Tianenmin Square in Beijing.

This chapter examines the Chinese experience as the country moved from the administrative-command model to the current model that appears to resemble market socialism. The Chinese story is not complete without accounts of the various political upheavals that, although they occurred for reasons independent of the economy, had major negative effects on economic performance. In fact, an unusual feature of Chinese development is the impact of exogenous political catastrophes, such as the Great Leap Forward and the Cultural Revolution, both of which set back economic progress, often for a decade or more.

We are attracted to China for two reasons. First, with its 1.2 billion citizens, China is the world's most populous country. It has the world's largest standing army, and it has shared borders with no fewer than 14 countries. Given its size and geographic location, China is bound to play a major role in the 21st century. Second, we are drawn to China as a part of the "East Asian economic miracle." Like several of its East Asian neighbors, China has grown at rapid rates for more than two decades. If this rapid growth continues, China could become a relatively affluent economy of immense political and economic power. There is, therefore, major interest in the contemporary Chinese economy, emerging as it has from the Soviet model, but with the introduction of markets and sustained state (party) control.

Revolution and Upheaval

The Setting

As we have said, China's 1.2 billion inhabitants make it the world's most populous country. It is sobering to compare China with Canada, another large country. Canada, with a population of approximately 30 million, has a land area of 3.8 million square miles. China, with a population of more than 1 billion, has a land area of just over 3.6 million square miles, making it one of the most densely populated countries of the globe. If the Chinese population continued to increase at the average annual rate of the past two decades, a new Canada, in terms of population, would arise in China roughly every 15 months! Both land and population are resources that can contribute to economic development, but people must eat, and considerable portions of China's land are inappropriate for agriculture without capital investment.

China is a resource-rich country, but once again, its resources must be exploited to support economic development. Although coal is a major source of energy, only recently has China undertaken to utilize its oil riches. Sharp variations in climate and fertility, along with large areas of rough terrain, mean that large amounts of capital are needed to exploit its mineral and land resources.

A nonsystemic feature is the unique Chinese historical experience. China is the oldest existing civilization in the world, a source of great pride to the Chinese people. Although there are numerous ethnic minorities in China (primarily in the western part of the country), the dominant nationality group is the *han* nationality. The Chinese language comprises many varying dialects; the Mandarin dialect is dominant. The rich heritage of the Chinese people is an important if unmeasurable influence on their attitudes toward and participation in the modernization process.

China remains today a poor country despite rapid growth. Substantial economic progress has been made since the early 1950s, but China in the mid 1990s had a per capita income of $700. China's per capita income, though above that of its immediate neighbors India and Pakistan, ranks well below that of Taiwan ($43,000).

Another feature of China is the notion of a greater China. The political definition of "Greater China" is mainland China plus Taiwan, Hong Kong, and Macao (currently the last Portuguese colony). Hong Kong is now under the rule of mainland China. The prospering Taiwan is vigorously seeking to maintain its independence in the face of mainland Chinese efforts at reunification. In addition to Greater China's geographic boundaries, the notion of a greater China also includes the diaspora of more than 50 million ethnic Chinese located mainly in Southeast Asia; their wealth is said to equal that of China's own population of 1.2 billion.

A "Greater China" would account for economic and laborpower resources that would clearly make it a fourth pillar in the world economy, along with the United States, Europe, and Japan.[1]

The Early Years and the Soviet Model

China in 1949 was probably more backward than Russia in 1917 when China adopted the Soviet economic model. Chinese leaders faced several key problems in adapting the **Soviet model**. How could the Chinese economy, in the absence of the advantages enjoyed by Russian leaders in 1917 (a basic industrial capacity, a transportation network, and so on), institute a planned socialist economic system in a large and very poor peasant economy? In developing such a planned socialist economy, modifications of the Soviet model had to be made to account for the very large Chinese population, its relative poverty, and its primarily rural character.

China at the time of the 1949 revolution was a classic poor country with low per capita income, significant population pressure on arable land and other resources, and an absence of institutions appropriate for economic development. China, with a land mass slightly larger than that of the United States and about half that of the

Soviet Union, and with a population roughly four times that of the United States and about three- and one-half times that of the Soviet Union, began in 1949 to implement the Soviet model, with substantive modifications. The result was economic growth and development interrupted when ideological and political factors gained supremacy over economic factors. Many of the policies and institutions developed in China were similar to those used in the Soviet experience. There were, however, important differences, especially the impact of ideology.

The Beginnings of Soviet-Style Industrialization and Collectivization

The Chinese People's Republic was proclaimed by Mao Zedong in 1949. Between 1949 and 1952 a period of consolidation ensued. Two main goals were sought. First, the redistribution of land to individual households was implemented in preparation for collectivization. Collectivization, however, was to be pursued without undue haste. Second, nationalization and consolidation of the holdings in industry took place in preparation for national economic planning. Other steps were taken—financial reform, educational reform, and other changes deemed necessary to stabilize the economy in preparation for the beginning of the first 5-year plan in 1953. However, the basic steps were related to changing the ownership base and the means of guiding the economy. In this respect, China's first steps were much like those of the Soviet Union in the aftermath of the revolution.[2]

China's approach to the rural sector differed from the Soviet experience of the early 1930s, especially inasmuch as Soviet collectivization brought with it some serious negative consequences that the Chinese leadership wished to avoid. On the surface, both countries utilized initial land reform and similar experimental forms of organization to eliminate class differences, distributed machinery and equipment through centralized facilities, and applied pressure to hold down rural food consumption. China's achievement was the avoidance of substantial destruction of cattle, facilities, and equipment.[3] The extremes of the Soviet model were avoided during collectivization. The Chinese countryside was better prepared in terms of ideological and organizational factors, though certainly not in terms of machinery and equipment.

The Chinese adopted the basic Soviet model of land reform and subsequent collectivization in the 1950s; the differences, however, were sufficient to avoid some of the extreme negative consequences experienced in the Soviet Union.

The second important policy of the early years was the nationalization of industry and the development of a system of national economic planning. During the early 1950s there was a gradual transition from private industry toward socialist industry—certainly more gradual than in the Soviet Union after 1928. The shift from private to socialist industry in China was targeted to be slow, though toward the latter part of the first five-year plan it became rapid. The pattern of change was from private ownership to elementary state capitalism, then to advanced state capitalism, and finally to socialist industry. By 1955, 68 percent of the gross value of output was accounted for by state industry and only 16 percent by joint state–private enterprises.

Eventually, even handicraft production was brought under state control in moves reminiscent of the excessive nationalization of Soviet war communism. Although the plans for the socialist transformation in both agriculture and industry called for a relatively gradual pace, the experience in 1955–1956 showed that ideology and political considerations could accelerate the rate of change in the case of China.

The Chinese planning structure, put in place in the early 1950s, was initially similar to the Soviet model.[4] The basic unit of production activity was the enterprise. As in the Soviet Union, a dual party–state administrative structure drew up and implemented (and often interrupted) 5-year plans for both agriculture and industry. Chinese plans are formulated by a State Planning Commission, which, like Gosplan in the Soviet Union, operated through an industrial ministry system communicating with regional and enterprise officials and ultimately assembling a plan. Once it was approved by the State Council, that plan became law for enterprises.

Chinese planning produced problems similar to those in the Soviet case: imbalance and shortages, poor quality, late plans, and deviation of results from targets. Chinese thinking on reform began to surface in the mid-1950s, but it was overshadowed by the political and ideological upheavals of the late 1950s.

The first ten years of the Chinese industrialization show the influence of the Soviet model. "In general, it can be said that during 1953–1957, the Chinese followed the broad outlines of the Stalinist strategy of selective growth under conditions of austerity with three important qualifications."[5] First, less pressure was placed on the agricultural sector, in recognition of the large, rural, poor population. Presumably Chinese leaders learned from the Soviet experience with rapid collectivization, for despite many similarities between the two cases, the extreme costs of the Soviet case were avoided in China.

Second, unlike the Soviet case, where state resources were directed through state farms and Machine Tractor Stations, agriculture in the early years of the new Chinese regime was largely self-financed. This may have reflected the much lower level of economic development in China in 1949 than in the Soviet Union in 1928.[6]

Third, the Chinese relied heavily on the state enterprise as a revenue source for state investment funds. Revenue from state enterprises accounted for roughly 35 percent of total budgetary revenue in 1953 and for 46 percent by 1957. In comparison, the most important source of budgetary revenue in the early years of Soviet industrialization was the turnover tax. The decision not to rely on taxes forced from the peasants reflected the realities of a subsistence agriculture.

During the 1950s, the Chinese generally followed the Soviet "industry first" strategy. Between 1953 and 1957, heavy industry in China absorbed an average of 85 percent of industrial investment. At the same time, only 8 percent of state investment was devoted to agriculture, whereas aggregate investment accounted for 20 to 25 percent of the national product.[7] These figures suggest a relatively high rate of accumulation for a poor country (though not nearly so high as the comparable rate for the Soviet Union in the early 1930s), with emphasis on industry in general and heavy industry in particular.

China's economic performance during the 1950s was generally strong, though uneven. There was an impressive doubling of GNP per capita, a ninefold increase in industrial production, and a modest increase in agricultural production. Overall, the early years were ones of consolidation. The first five-year plan witnessed substantial growth; the latter part of the 1950s saw a mixture of progress and retrogression (caused by China's first great upheaval) in both industry and agriculture.

The First Upheaval: The Great Leap Forward

Chinese economic development through the 1970s was characterized by intermittent political upheavals that tended to erase economic progress. Political upheavals appealed periodically to an aging group of communist revolutionaries led by Mao, who worried about the decline of revolutionary fervor and the bureaucratization of Chinese economic and political life. Chinese upheavals originated from the highest levels of the ruling elite; they were introduced to achieve goals and objectives desired by that leadership.

After the liberal **Hundred Flowers Campaign** (1956–1957), during which there was open discussion and criticism of the system, the **Great Leap Forward** was launched (1958–1960) by Mao.[8] The Great Leap was a massive resurgence of ideology, which replaced rationality. Campaigns were instigated with revolutionary fervor to emphasize a new role for the peasantry, especially through small-scale industry in the countryside and the introduction of communes. Development of water resources was also stressed. A brutal campaign against the educated elite was mounted.

The disruptions of the Great Leap were substantial. There was an economically irrational attempt to move heavy industry from the city to the countryside, contrary to all economic principles of mass production and economies of scale. Agriculture was reorganized into massive communes encompassing thousands of households. The exacting of farm products from the countryside was so stringent that massive starvation occurred in provinces that were exporting grain "surpluses."

The true toll of the great Leap Forward was initially concealed by Chinese authorities, but by all official statistics, the Great Leap caused a stagnation of Chinese economic growth.

Although the Great Leap was abandoned by 1960, the commune system, introduced in 1958, remained.[9] The **Rural Peoples Communes** were initially set up as very large units combining a number of collectives (advanced cooperatives) to produce agricultural and handicraft products and to serve as local units of government. The original communes (roughly 26,000 in number and averaging about 4,600 households each) faced difficulties. Agricultural units encompassing some 50,000 households were too difficult to coordinate, and individual incentives were overshadowed by the size of the collective. Subsequent modifications improved the commune system.

The striking feature of Chinese economic performance in the 1950s was the impact of ideological disruptions. Chinese GDP grew at an annual rate of 6 percent from 1952 to 1956.[10] The 1958 level of GDP, however, was not regained until 1963. Thus the Great Leap Forward caused an enormous setback in Chinese growth.

The Great Leap Forward was abandoned in the late 1950s at a time when relations between China and the Soviet Union were deteriorating rapidly. The ideological and economic break between the two countries was almost complete by 1960. Although the role of outside aid in the Chinese development experience was minimal, the Soviet contribution was important in the early years, especially in the area of technical assistance. The break would prove to be a sobering experience for Chinese leaders and planners.

1960–1978: Development and Disruption

Like the 1950s, the 1960s are divided into two very different periods: moderation in the early 1960s and upheaval in the late 1960s.

The early 1960s was a period of relative calm in which Chinese leaders looked toward balance in economic development, modernization in the agricultural sector, and recovery from the aftermath of the Great Leap. In industry, the 1960s was a period of rather substantial reform—a movement away from the overwhelming importance of gross output (the major success indicator of the 1950s) toward quality in production and the elimination of major deficiencies in the planning system.

Both central control and local initiative changed during this period. The center tried to put pressure on enterprises to improve quality, to be concerned with efficiency, and to enhance the role of technical expertise in the decision-making process. At the same time, many decisions, especially minor ones, were shifted to the local level. For example, local industrial establishments were set up to serve local (especially rural) needs. Although the emphasis on enterprise efficiency and profitability later came under sharp attack in the 1960s the Chinese industrial structure was modified to suit Chinese conditions, and the modifications for the most part withstood later upheavals.

During the early 1960s, new emphasis was placed on the need for mechanization and reorganization of the agriculture. The communes underwent substantial change. Because communes were found to be too large, the intermediate (brigade) and lower-level (team) units assumed new importance. Emphasis on nonmaterial rewards, a hallmark of the earlier commune system, was changed in favor of material incentives and the reintroduction of private plots. Although the number of communes was reduced during the 1960s, their role in the social, cultural, and political affairs of the countryside remained intact through the 1970s.

In addition to organizational changes and policy shifts, the 1960s witnessed a widespread educational campaign among the Chinese people. There was an effort to re-educate the population in the ways of Mao. This campaign laid the foundations for the Cultural Revolution.

If the early 1960s was a period of rationality—reform and change along a well-defined continuum—the opposite could be said of the Cultural Revolution of 1966–1969. The Cultural Revolution, which is difficult for the Western observer to fully comprehend, was an upheaval of ideas, an abandonment of much that had preceded it. Emanating from a Communist Party struggle, the Cultural Revolution was not a debate over economic ideas. In fact, its disastrous disruption of economic activity became apparent only later. However, although economic activity was substantially disturbed, the basic organizational arrangements in industry and in agriculture do not seem to have been altered in significant ways.

The Cultural Revolution had a dramatic effect on China's educated classes, including its elite. Scholars and officials were ignominiously shipped to hard labor or worse in the countryside by radical bands of youths motivated by Mao's revolutionary ideas. China's entire educational establishment ceased to function in the backlash against education and Western teaching.

Like the Great Leap, the Cultural Revolution had a devastating effect on economic performance. Disruption was so great that meaningful GDP estimates during the Cultural Revolution are not available. GDP failed to increase between 1965 and 1970, a loss of output equal to or more severe than that of the Great Leap.[11]

The early 1970s was a period of recovery from the events of the Cultural Revolution.[12] However, attempts to return to normalcy were interrupted by events of the early and mid-1970s. Zhou Enlai, an advocate of a moderate path of industrialization, died in early 1976. The following September, Mao Zedong, the father of the revolution and an advocate of continuing the revolutionary mentality, died. Shortly thereafter, in October of 1976, the **"Gang of Four,"** representing the revolutionary left and espousing a continuation of the Stalinist mode of industrialization, were arrested amid great ideological fervor.[13] These events paved the way for what would be fundamental changes in the Chinese economic system and its policies.

Reform

Reform and the Soviet Model

As we will see, events of the reform era after 1978 fundamentally changed the nature of the Chinese economic system, a system that remains in an evolutionary stage. Thus far we have emphasized the importance of the Soviet model, although this model was applied with changes in a special setting.

The impact of this Soviet-type past on the nature and outcomes of the contemporary reform era has remained a subject of interest. The starting point for reforms, however, was typical of systems influenced by the Soviet model. The growth of industry as a share of GDP was rapid. By the end of the Mao era, this industry share would be much larger than that in other countries at similar levels of economic development. A like differential could be observed in sectoral growth rates: modest rates of growth in agriculture and much more rapid rates of growth of industry.

Similar observations could be made about the uses of GDP. During the Mao era, the share of private consumption fell while the shares of both savings and investment increased. Again, compared to other countries at similar levels of economic development, China was devoting an unusually large share of its product to investment and focusing that investment on industry.

As we will see, although the reform era would take China along a very different path, the experience of the Soviet model would remain influential, for example, when the country addressed the problems of privatizing large-scale industry, an issue not discussed until late 1997.

China's Modernization Reform: The Deng Era

China has the world's largest population; the Soviet Union had the world's largest land mass. Both sought to make the administrative-command system work, the Soviet Union from 1928 to 1985 and China from 1950 to 1978. Both, disillusioned by the weaknesses of the administrative-command system, turned to great reformers to modify their systems. The Soviet Union turned to a young and vigorous general secretary of the Communist Party, Mikhail Gorbachev, who opted to alter the Soviet political, social, and economic system with the result that the Soviet Union and its centralized party dictatorship ceased to exist. China turned to an elderly veteran of the Chinese civil war and a victim of the worst of China's upheavals, Deng Xiaoping, to reform the Chinese system.[14]

The path chosen by Deng was quite different from Gorbachev's, and it yielded quite different results: Deng opted to avoid the political and social liberalization—democratization and openness—that Gorbachev introduced into the Soviet system. He chose instead to preserve the dictatorship of the Chinese Communist Party and not to tolerate dissent, but rather to unleash the productive and entrepreneurial talents of the Chinese people while retaining significant control and ownership of the "commanding heights" of the Chinese economy. This decision can be likened to V. I. Lenin's decision in 1921 to return the Soviet economy to a mixed economic system in which considerable private initiative was encouraged and openness to the outside world was promoted, but the state retained control of the "commanding heights" of the economy along with ownership of heavy industry, transportation, and finance.

Change in China and Russia differed in another important way. During the Gorbachev era in the Soviet Union and thereafter in post-Soviet Russia, agrarian reform was of limited importance. In China, on the other hand, we will see that agrarian reform was of major importance.

The Deng Strategy

Although the Deng reforms, which began to be introduced in 1978, were intended to be gradual (a process Deng described as "fording the river by feeling for the stones"), in reality the reforms moved quickly, especially in the countryside. Specifically, the Deng reforms made two major changes in the vast Chinese countryside: allowing Chinese farmers to work for themselves rather than for the collective farm and allowing townships to create "township enterprises" or "township and village enterprises" (TVEs). These reforms spread across the countryside so rapidly because the party and state chose not to stop them, and because they resulted from the unleashing of existing entrepreneurial forces.

Agricultural Reforms

Prior to 1978, the commune was the unit of organization in agriculture.[15] Basic economic activity was in the hands of the **production team**, which comprised a number of households within a village. Production teams would combine to form a brigade, brigades to form a commune. Above the commune, the county was the state unit responsible for directing agricultural activity. It played a major role in implementing the national economic plan administered by the Ministry of Agriculture and Forestry.[16]

The commune had a reward system not unlike that used in the collective farms of the former Soviet Union prior to 1966. Individuals would accumulate points for daily work done, the ultimate reward being based on residual income, which consisted of revenues less expenses.

The **contract responsibility system** was introduced in the late 1970s.[17] The release of local agricultural markets and the contracting by the state with households for the sale of major crops effectively brought collectivization to an end. The system for distributing output changed, as did the ability of households to purchase inputs. Although restrictions remained on the availability of land for household farming, by the early 1980s, the commune and production-team arrangements had virtually disappeared.[18] In effect, on both the output and the input side of Chinese agriculture, markets dominated.

The impact these changes had on agricultural performance was immediate and dramatic, though by the latter part of the 1980s there had been some retrenchment to slower rates of growth of output.

Although industry and transportation remained under state control and ownership, the Deng reforms permitted villages and townships to form their own enterprises. These enterprises, which concentrated initially on services and light industry, accounted for one-third of Chinese manufacturing by the mid-1980s. Chinese township enterprises were free to develop unencumbered by state planning and bureaucratic controls. They were also free to form joint ventures with foreign partners, who supplied capital and export-marketing expertise.

The development of services and light manufacturing outside of the state planning system promoted the growth of services. Before 1978, Stalinist priorities and restrictions against services prevailed; however, as an example of substantive change, between 1978 and 1981, the share of total investment devoted to heavy industry fell from 54.7 percent to 40.3 percent, a sharp drop in a very short time.[19] Indeed, the average annual rate of growth of services was 6.1 percent between 1970 and 1980 and 11.2 percent between 1980 and 1991.[20] Finally, the labor force in the service sector doubled from 48.7 million in 1978 to 99.5 million in 1988. What accounted for this dramatic change in the service sector?

China, like other planned socialist economies, had essentially prohibited the development of the service sector largely through outright prohibitions. Beginning in the late 1970s, however, these rules were substantially relaxed, which resulted in a sharp and sudden increase in service-sector activity. Entry was easy, markets were functioning, and large amounts of capital investment were, for the most part, unnecessary.

The Deng reform strategy did not rest on freeing up entrepreneurial forces in agriculture alone. To remedy China's lack of advanced technology and its shortages of capital, Deng decided to tap Western markets and Western capital to promote China's economic development. In focusing on the outside world, Chinese reformers knew that they had to take advantage of the presence of capital and technology in nearby Hong Kong, Taiwan, and East Asia. However, such capital would not be forthcoming unless the Chinese could offer reasonable safety for foreign investment. Given that Chinese legal protection of property rights was weak and that Chinese courts could not be counted on to enforce the property rights of foreigners, Chinese reformers set up various "free enterprise or trade zones," most located initially in close proximity to Hong Kong, that were exempted from the more restrictive Chinese taxation and regulatory arrangements. Moreover, China liberalized its joint venture laws to encourage the creation of export-oriented joint ventures in these zones.

The result of this activity was a massive influx of Western capital after 1978 (Figure 10.1). Starting initially with modest amounts, direct foreign investment in China exceeded a cumulated total of $40 billion by 1996.[21] As Figure 10.1 shows, almost 60 percent of this direct investment came from "Greater China" sources—Hong Kong, Macao, and Taiwan.

Although the increase in direct foreign investment was substantial, it remains relatively small on a per capita basis, given China's massive population. In 1994, for example, China attracted $26 of foreign investment per capita, well above India's $1 per capita but well below Mexico, Chile, Hungary, Poland, and Malaysia.[22] A major payoff from this foreign investment has been the installation of technology and the creation of marketing savvy that has permitted China to increase its exports (Figure 10.2). In 1985 Chinese companies with foreign investors exported goods worth less than one billion per annum and accounted for about one percent of Chinese exports. In 1995 they accounted for almost $50 billion of exports and for 32 percent of Chinese total exports.

China's opening of its economy to foreign investment and trade required significant change in its foreign trading arrangements.

China in the 1970s was typical of the planned socialist economic systems. Trade was centralized and fully controlled by the state. Beginning in the late 1970s, the regulations pertaining to foreign trade were relaxed and businesses were encouraged to import and export using decentralized market arrangements. Exportation has been especially important in developing arrangements to encourage the sale of manufactured goods in foreign markets and to stimulate foreign direct investment in China.

The issue of convertibility of the Yuan remains unresolved, though the sequence of steps taken in China resemble other cases. From an initial posture of total state control, dual channels were effectively implemented to combine continuing state control with "foreign exchange adjustment centers," where access to foreign currency was possible at essentially market-determined rates. Obviously, the long-term goal is full convertibility, which would allow China to advance to a higher status in international financial organizations.

China, despite its current posture of protecting its domestic industries, is also interested in membership in the World Trade Organization (WTO), a sign of acceptance by the international trading community.

The Commanding Heights

The Chinese reform strategy has been to unleash the forces of private initiative in the rural sector and in services and light industry while retaining state control and ownership of the "commanding heights" of the economy—heavy industry, banking and finance, and transportation. Although joint ventures account for a substantial

FIGURE 10.1   China: Foreign Direct Investment (FDI)[a]

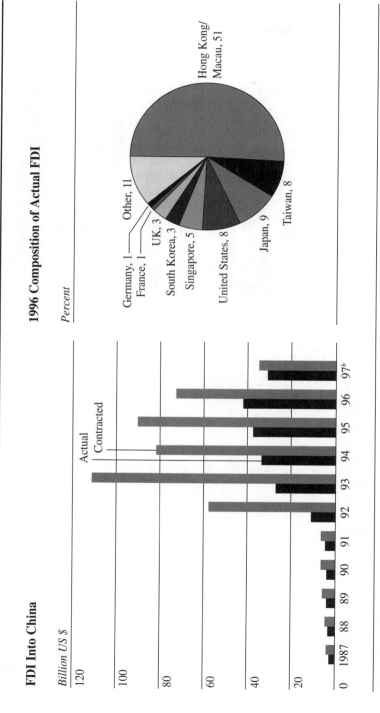

FDI Into China

1996 Composition of Actual FDI

[a]From official Chinese government statistics
[b]January–September
Source: Central Intelligence Agency, China's Economy in 1995–1997 (Washington, D.C.: C.I.A., 1997), p. 20.

FIGURE 10.2   China: Foreign Trade[a]

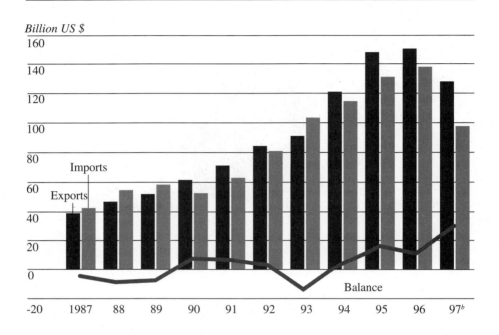

Billion US $

*[a]Based on official Chinese government statistics
[b]January–September*

Source: Central Intelligence Agency, *China's Economy in 1995–1997* (Washington, D.C.: C.I.A., 1997), p. 17.

and growing portion of exports, they still represent a small portion of China's economic output.

Heavy industrial enterprises, banks, railways, airlines, and infrastructure remain in the hands of the state. The state sector is managed along the lines of an administrative-command economy with a national economic plan. State-owned enterprises are required to fulfill the plan. If they sustain losses, they are typically bailed out by subsidies or by direct credits administered through the system of state-owned banks. The Chinese system of credit, which is based on the savings deposits of frugal Chinese citizens, is directed by a state credit and finance plan almost exclusively to state enterprises, even if the rate of return on invested funds is extremely low.

Although there is much discussion in the Chinese literature about making the system of state-owned enterprises work more efficiently, their operation is reminiscent of Soviet enterprises. They are judged on the basis of fulfillment of quantity targets; managers have an incentive to pilfer from the enterprise; any losses are covered by the state. Chinese state enterprises, like former Soviet enterprises, are operated on a patronage basis. They often have thousands of employees, whose children are taught in the enterprise-run school, whose health is taken care of by the enterprise clinic, and whose housing is owned by the state enterprise. Employees are subject to strict work rules, and their employment records are maintained in work books that move with them from job to job.

The state sector accounted for two-thirds of manufactured output in the early 1980s; by the mid-1990s, it share had fallen to 50 percent. About 70 percent of the state enterprises make losses, and bad loans to state enterprises account for about 30 percent of GDP.

Policy and Practice

China's Governance

Power in China is exercised through "the largest coercive apparatus in the world."[23] At the top of this apparatus are 25 to 35 people who make the major policy decisions for the country—the politburo of the Chinese Communist Party. Its standing committee consists of seven individuals who oversee the main functional areas of power, such as public security, the education system, propaganda, and the economy.

The branch of the party that influences Chinese daily life the most is concerned with personnel and organization. Every employee of a state enterprise is assigned to a work unit, which controls the employee's housing and oversee the employee's work record. Job moves are approved by personnel committees.

The Chinese legal system lacks a legal framework to protect property rights and provide due process. Businesspeople seeking guarantees for their investments cannot turn to legal processes. Instead, they must seek out patrons in the political elite who will act as their backstage protectors against arbitrary and predatory actions.

The Chinese financial system remains under state ownership and control. To date, only one private commercial bank has been registered. Lacking alternatives, Chinese savers must deposit their savings in state banks, and these state banks then allocate available credit according to government plans. These government plans dictate that all credit go to state enterprises, even though higher rates of return can be obtained from private companies.

Economic Performance

China's economic performance is summarized in Figure 10.3. Although there is doubt as to the reliability of China's statistics on real GDP, there is little doubt that China has grown rapidly since 1978. Prior to 1978, China experienced periods of negative growth associated with the upheavals of the Great Leap and the Cultural Revolution (which would then be followed by rapid growth as the country recovered). Since 1978, however, Chinese growth has been on a par with the extraordinarily rapid growth of Hong Kong and Taiwan.

FIGURE 10.3   Growth of Real GDP[a]

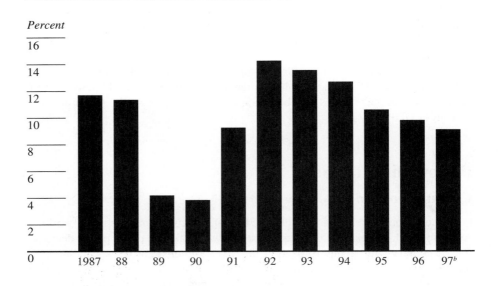

[a] Official Chinese government statistics
[b] January–September, compared to same period in 1996

Source: Central Intelligence Agency, *China's Economy in 1995–1997* (Washington, D.C.: C.I.A., 1997), p. viii.

China's rapid growth is the result of more than 30 percent of China's GDP being invested in capital formation. It is also the consequence of rapid growth in exports. In this regard, China's economic growth is similar to Soviet growth and to the growth of the East Asian economies (discussed in a later chapter), both of which were based on rapid growth of capital.

China's growth has been highly uneven among regions (see Figure 10.4). Those regions that have served as free enterprise zones have grown most rapidly (they are located in close proximity to Hong Kong). There has also been rapid growth in some major urban centers, such as Shanghai. Whereas China's per capita income in 1995 was $687, GDP per capita in Shenzhen was $3,360, Shanghai's was $2,084, and Beijing's was $1,335.

China's Future

Clearly, if China's growth were to continue for two more decades to be as rapid as it has been over the past 20 years, China would be a relatively affluent country by the year 2015. With its vast population, China would have the world's largest economy and the world's largest army. We must therefore consider whether China can continue to grow at such a rapid pace.

FIGURE 10.4   China's Regional Growth Patterns

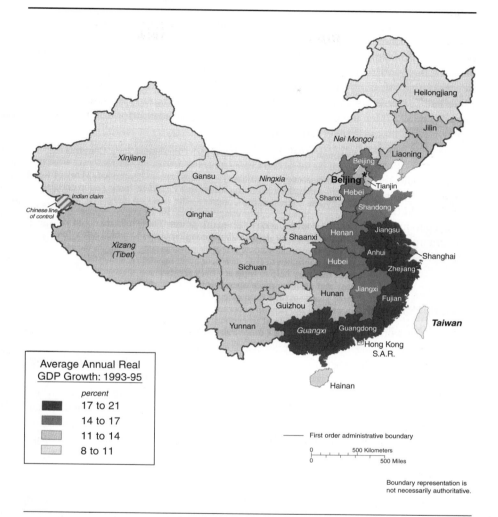

Source: Central Intelligence Agency, *China's Economy in 1995–1997* (Washington, D.C.: C.I.A., 1997), p. vi.

On the positive side, China still has considerable underutilized potential. Rapid growth has touched only a minority of China's regions. The bulk of China remains decisively a part of the underdeveloped world. As private enterprise spreads to the hinterlands, we would expect them to begin to grow more rapidly. The growth of specific Chinese regions, however, has been stimulated by foreign investment as investment has moved into protected enterprise zones. Chinese authorities are not able to declare all parts of China special enterprise zones, so the movement of foreign capital into China's hinterlands will depend more on improvement in China's general legal and social institutions.

The major unknown concerning China's future is the fate of its commanding heights. According to material presented in this chapter, the Chinese state economy operates inefficiently, in a manner scarcely indistinguishable from Soviet enterprises. China's financial system allocates scarce capital to activities yielding a low rate of return. A country can have a high rate of capital formation but can use this capital so inefficiently as to negate the benefits of high capital formation. Like the Soviet Union, China appears to be involved in a futile search for solutions to the problems of Chinese state enterprises.

At some point, China's reform process will have fully exploited the opportunities that exist outside the state sector. At this time, the Chinese leadership will have to decide whether it is prepared to privatize the state sector and subject it to hard budget constraints. If it continues to coddle the state sector, Chinese economic growth could falter. Change in the state sector is likely to be slow. In the fall of 1997, it was announced at the Communist Party Congress that 10,000 of the 13,000 large state enterprises would be sold, though it was also clear that this process would be both difficult and slow.

Summary

China is the world's most populous country. As we approach a new century, China commands our attention for many reasons. The economic growth of China has been exceptionally rapid for more than two decades as it moves toward a model of market socialism that combines market forces with strong state and party control.

During the early years of communist rule in China, the Soviet model was applied in a large and very poor country with substantial regional diversity but abundant natural resources. Between 1949 and the contemporary reform era, the beginnings of Chinese socialism unfolded under Mao Zedong, including the importance of ideology in explaining both policy and systemic change—events that would form the preconditions for the contemporary reform era.

During the first decade of socialism in China, the basic Soviet model was implemented, characterized by the socialization of agriculture, by nationalization, and by the development of a system of national economic planning. Although there were important deviations from the Soviet model, a major feature of the early years was the dominance of ideology, exhibited, for example, in the Great Leap Forward campaign of the mid- and late 1950s.

Whereas the first half of the 1960s was a period of relative tranquility, the latter half gave way to major disruption and the dominance of ideology in the Cultural Revolution. Although the ideological upheaval of this era had a major impact on the overall performance of the Chinese economy, the basic organizational arrangements of the economic system seemed to undergo relatively little change.

The 1970s began with a period of recovery after the Cultural Revolution, followed by a number of important events that would shape the contemporary reform era. The death of both Zhou Enlai and Mao Zedong provided the opportunity for reassessment in a period when economic performance dictated a need for change. Specifically, many of the problems that had become evident in the Soviet Union also plagued China after a long and persistent application of the Stalinist model of industrialization. Heavy industry was overemphasized, there was regional imbalance, investment ratios were unusually high and incentives minimal, the latter being a special problem in the agricultural sector.

Beginning in the late 1970s, the reforms of Deng Xiaoping fundamentally altered the Chinese economic system while at the same time maintaining state and party control, a path markedly different from that being pursued in the transition economies, where in most cases both political and system changes were crucial. Beginning with an effective end to collectivization in agriculture, market forces were introduced in a meaningful way, leading to a sharp increase in agricultural output as the rural population responded to new incentive arrangements.

Major changes were also introduced in industry, services, and especially international trade. Although discussion of the privatization of large Chinese industrial enterprises was delayed until the summer of 1997, privatization of small-scale industry proceeded earlier. The service sector expanded and the rigidities of the foreign trade arrangements were fundamentally altered, along with the introduction of foreign trade zones. These changes sharply increased the importance of foreign trade and at the same time attracted foreign investment.

The post-1978 reform era has again fundamentally changed the nature of the Chinese economy as it has moved toward a variant of market socialism. Although the economic performance has been positive, the presence of market forces combined with traditional controls in some spheres has spawned problems—for example, fluctuations in economic activity. However, the introduction of market forces has paved the way for the long-term development of a basic infrastructure radically different from that of the prereform era.

Key Terms

Soviet model
Hundred Flowers Campaign
Great Leap Forward
Rural Peoples Communes
Cultural Revolution
Gang of Four

Four Modernizations
eight-point program
production team
contract responsibility system
market socialism

Notes

1. Survey China, *The Economist,* March 8, 1997, p. 5.
2. For a useful long-term comparison of basic economic and developmental indicators, see Arthur G. Ashbrook, Jr., "China: Economic Modernization and Long-Term Performance," in U.S. Congress, Joint Economic Committee, *China Under the Four Modernizations,* Part 2, Section V (Washington, D.C.: U.S. Government Printing Office, 1982), pp. 151–368.

3. There was some unrest and disruption in China, but markedly less than that which occurred in the Soviet Union. For a comparison, see Jan S. Prybyla, *The Political Economy of Communist China* (Scranton, Pa.: International Textbook, 1970), Ch. 5.

4. For a useful outline of the basic features of the Chinese administrative structure and changes through time, see Thomas G. Rawski, "China's Industrial System," in U.S. Congress, Joint Economic Committee, *China: A Reassessment of the Economy* (Washington, D.C.: U.S. Government Printing Office, 1975), pp. 175–198. For a recent comparison of the Chinese experience and the Soviet experience, see Robert F. Dernberger, "The Chinese Search for the Path of Self-Sustained Growth in the 1980s: An Assessment," in Joint Economic Committee, *China Under the Four Modernizations*, Part 1, pp. 19–76.

5. Prybyla, *The Political Economy of Communist China*, pp. 144–145.

6. For example, in terms of agricultural performance, we might make the following crude comparison. In China in 1949, grain production was 0.20 metric ton per capita; in the Soviet Union in 1928–1929, grain production was 0.47 metric ton per capita. Chinese data are from Ashbrook, "China: Economic Modernization and Long-Term Performance," p. 104; Paul R. Gregory and Robert C. Stuart, *Soviet Economic Structure and Performance*, 3rd ed. (New York: Harper & Row, 1986), p. 244; and TsSU (Central Statistical Administration), *Naselenie SSSR 1973* (Moscow: Statistika, 1975), p. 7.

7. These data are from Prybyla, *The Political Economy of Communist China*, pp. 135 ff.

8. For a discussion of this period, see Roderick MacFarquhar, *The Hundred Flowers Campaign and the Chinese Intellectuals* (New York: Praeger, 1960).

9. For a discussion of the early commune, see Kenneth R. Walker, "Organization of Agricultural Production," in Alexander Eckstein, Walter Galenson, and Ta-Chung Liu, eds., *Economic Trends in Communist China* (Chicago: Aldine, 1968), pp. 440–452. For a study of the private sector, see Kenneth R. Walker, *Planning in Chinese Agriculture: Socialization and the Private Sector, 1956–1962* (Chicago: Aldine, 1965). For an update of organizational changes into the 1970s, see Frederick W. Crook, "The Commune System in the People's Republic of China, 1963–74," in Joint Economic Committee, *China: A Reassessment of the Economy*, pp. 366–410; a useful recent source is Frederic M. Surls and Francis C. Tuan, "China's Agriculture in the Eighties," in Joint Economic Committee, *China Under the Four Modernizations*, Part 1, pp. 419–448.

10. Subramanian Swamy, "Economic Growth in China and India 1952–1970: A Comparative Appraisal," *Economic Development and Cultural Change*, 21 (July 1973), 62.

11. *Ibid.*

12. An excellent survey of these years can be found in Dernberger, "The Chinese Search for the Path of Self-Sustained Growth," pp. 19–76.

13. For a discussion of the revolutionary left in the economic context, see Robert F. Dernberger and David Fasenfest, "China's Post-Mao Economic Future," in U.S. Congress, Joint Economic Committee, *Chinese Economy Post-Mao* (Washington, D.C.: U.S. Government Printing Office, 1978), pp. 3–47.

14. There is a great deal of literature pertaining to the Chinese economy. For a useful survey of contemporary events, see Dwight Perkins, "Completing China's Move to the Market," *Journal of Economic Perspectives* 8 (Spring 1994), 23–46; Gary H. Jefferson and Thomas G. Rawski, "Enterprise Reform in Chinese Industry," *Journal of Economic Perspectives* 8 (Spring 1994), 47–70; Shahid Yusuf, "China's Macroeconomic Performance and Management During Transition," *Journal of Economic Perspectives* 8 (Spring 1994), 71–92; "China's Economic Reforms: Structural and Welfare Aspects," *American Economic Review Papers and Proceedings* 84 (May 1994), 266–284; *China: Statistical Yearbook 1993* (Bejing: State Statistical Bureau of the Peoples Republic of China, 1993).

15. Frederick W. Crook, "The Commune System in the People's Republic of China, 1963–1974," in U.S. Congress, Joint Economic Committee, China: A Reassessment of the Economy (Washington, D.C.: U.S. Government Printing Office, 1975), 411–437.

16. For a discussion of pre-reform arrangements, see Henry J. Groen and James A. Kilpatrick, "China's Agricultural Production," in U.S. Congress Joint Economic Committee, Chinese Economy Under Post-Mao, Vol. 1 (Washington, D.C.: U.S. Government Printing Office, 1978), pp. 607–652.

17. For a discussion of changes in the rural economy, see Kuan-I Chen, "China's Changing Agricultural System," *Current History* 82 (September 1983), 259–263, 277–278; Kuan-I Chen, "China's Food Policy and Population," *Ibid.*, 257–260, 274–276; Yak-Yeow Kueh, "China's New Agricultural-Policy Program: Major Economic Consequences, 1979–1983," *Journal of Comparative Economics* 8 (December 1984), 353–375; Nicholas R. Lardy, *Agriculture in China's Modern Economic Development* (Cambridge, England: Cambridge University Press, 1983); Dwight Perkins and Shahid Yusuf, *Rural Development in China* (Baltimore: The Johns Hopkins University Press, 1984); Kenneth R. Walker, "Chinese Agriculture During the Period of Readjustment, 1978–83," *China Quarterly* 100 (December 1984), 783–812; Kenneth R. Walker, *Food Grain Procurement and Consumption in China* (Cambridge, England: Cambridge University Press, 1984); Peter Nolan and Dong Fureng, eds., *Market Forces in China* (London: Zed Books Ltd., 1990); Anthony Y. C. Koo, "The Contract Responsibility System: Transition from a Planned to a Market Economy," *Economic Development and Cultural Change* 38 (July 1990), 797–820.

18. Dwight Perkins, "Completing China's Move to the Market," 26.

19. Chu-yuan Cheng, "China's Industrialization and Economic Development," *Current History* 82 (September 1983), 266.

20. World Bank, *World Development Report 1993* (New York: Oxford University Press, 1993), Table 2.

21. *The Economist,* 1997, p. 10.

22. *The Economist,* 1997, p. 10.

23. *The Economist,* p. 18; Kenneth Lieberthal, *Governing China* (New York: Norton, 1995).

Recommended Readings

General Works

Richard Baum, ed., *China's Four Modernizations: The New Technological Revolution* (Boulder, Colo.: Westview Press, 1980).

Chu-yuan Cheng, *China's Economic Development: Growth and Structural Change* (Boulder, Colo.: Westview Press, 1982).

Gregory Chow, *The Chinese Economy* (New York: Harper & Row, 1984).

Robert F. Dernberger, ed., *China's Development Experience in Comparative Perspective* (Cambridge, Mass.: Harvard University Press, 1980).

Audrey Donnithorne, *China's Economic System* (New York: Praeger, 1967).

Alexander Eckstein, *China's Economic Development: The Interplay of Scarcity and Ideology* (Ann Arbor: University of Michigan Press, 1975).

———, *China's Economic Revolution* (New York: Cambridge University Press, 1977).

———, *Communist China's Economic Growth and Foreign Trade* (New York: McGraw-Hill, 1969).

Alexander Eckstein, Walter Galenson, and Ta-Chung Liu, eds., *Economic Trends in Communist China* (Chicago: Aldine, 1968).

Christopher Howe, *China's Economy: A Basic Guide* (New York: Basic Books, 1978).

Gary H. Jefferson and Wenyi Yu, "The Impact of Reform on Socialist Enterprises in Transition: Structure, Conduct, and Performance in Chinese Industry," *Journal of Comparative Economics* 15 (January 1991), 45–54.

Zhiling Lin and Thomas Robinson, eds., *The Chinese and Their Future: Beijing, Taipei, and Hong Kong* (Washington, D.C.: AEI Press, 1994).

Thomas P. Lyons, *Economic Integration and Planning in Maoist China* (New York: Columbia University Press, 1987).

Nicholas Lardy, *Economic Growth and Distribution in China* (New York: Cambridge University Press, 1979).

Jun Ma, *Intergovernmental Relations and Economic Management in China* (New York: St. Martin's Press, 1997).

Jan S. Prybyla, *The Chinese Economy: Problems and Policies*, 2nd ed. (Columbia: University of South Carolina Press, 1981).

———, *The Political Economy of Communist China* (Scranton, Pa.: International Textbook, 1970).

Carl Riskin, *China's Political Economy* (New York: Oxford University Press, 1987).

Kai Yuen Tsui, "China's Regional Inequality, 1952–1985," *Journal of Comparative Economics* 15 (March 1991), 1–21.

U.S. Congress, Joint Economic Committee, *China: A Reassessment of the Economy* (Washington, D.C.: U.S. Government Printing Office, 1975).

———, *China Under the Four Modernizations* (Washington, D.C.: U.S. Government Printing Office, 1982).

———, *Chinese Economy Post-Mao* (Washington, D.C.: U.S. Government Printing Office, 1978).

———, *An Economic Profile of Mainland China*, Vols. I and II (Washington, D.C.: U.S. Government Printing Office, 1967).

———, *China's Economic Dilemmas in the 1990s: The Problems of Reforms, Modernization, and Interdependence*, Vols. 1 and 2 (Washington, D.C.: U.S. Government Printing Office, 1991).

The Rural Economy

William A. Byrd and Lin Qingsong, eds., *China's Rural Industry* (New York: Oxford University Press, 1991).

Kang Chao, *Man and Land in Chinese History: An Economic Analysis* (Stanford: Stanford University Press, 1987).

Kuan-I Chen, "China's Food Policy and Population," *Current History* 86 (September 1987), 257–260, 274–276.

Christopher Findlay, Andrew Watson, and Harry X. Wu, eds., *Rural Enterprises in China* (New York: St. Martin's, 1994).

Yak-Yeow Kueh, "China's New Agricultural-Policy Program: Major Economic Consequences, 1979–1983," *Journal of Comparative Economics* 8 (December 1984), 353–375.

Justin Yitu Lin, "Rural Reforms and Agricultural Growth in China," *American Economic Review* 82 (March 1992), 34–51.

Nicholas R. Lardy, *Agriculture in China's Modern Economic Development* (Cambridge, England: Cambridge University Press, 1983).

Victor Nee and Frank W. Young, "Peasant Entrepreneurs in China's `Second Economy': An Institutional Analysis," *Economic Development and Cultural Change* 37 (January 1991), 293–310.

Dwight H. Perkins, *Agricultural Development in China, 1368–1968* (Chicago: University of Chicago Press, 1969).

————, ed., *Rural Small-Scale Industry in the People's Republic of China* (Berkeley: University of California Press, 1977).

Shugiei Wao, *Agricultural Reform and Grain Production in China* (New York: St. Martin's, 1994).

Economic Reform

Willam A. Byrd, ed., *Chinese Industrial Firms Under Reform* (Oxford: Oxford University Press, 1992).

Richard Conroy, *Technological Change in China* (Paris: OECD, 1992).

Kang Chen, Gary H. Jefferson, and Inderjit Singh, "Lessons from China's Economic Reform," *Journal of Comparative Economics* 16 (1992), 201–225.

Directorate of Intelligence, *The Chinese Economy in 1991 and 1992: Pressure to Revisit Reform Mounts* (Washington, D.C.: Central Intelligence Agency, 1992).

————, *China's Economy in 1992 and 1993: Grappling with the Risks of Rapid Economic Growth* (Washington, D.C.: Central Intelligence Agency, 1993).

————, *China's Economy in 1994 and 1995: Overheating Pressures Recede, Tough Choices Remain* (Washington, D.C.: Central Intelligence Agency, 1995).

————, *China's Economy in 1995–97* (Washington, D.C.: Central Intelligence Agency, 1997).

Qimiao Fan and Peter Nolan, *China's Economic Reforms* (New York: St. Martin's Press, 1994).

Joseph Fewsmith, *Dilemmas of Reform in China* (Armonk, N.Y.: M.E. Sharpe, 1994).

David Granick, *Chinese State Enterprises: A Regional Property Rights Analysis* (Chicago: University of Chicago Press, 1990).

Keith Griffin and Zhao Renwei, eds., *The Distribution of Income in China* (New York: St. Martin's Press, 1993).

————, *China's Economy in 1983 and 1984: The Search for a Soft Landing* (Washington D.C., Central Intelligence Agency, 1994).

Gary H. Jefferson and Thomas G. Rawski, "Enterprise Reform in Chinese Industry," *Journal of Economic Perspectives* 8 (Spring 1994), 47–70.

Gary H. Jefferson, Thomas G. Rawski, and Yuxin Zheng, "Growth, Efficiency, and Convergence in China's State and Collective Industry," *Economic Development and Cultural Change* 40 (1992a), 239–266.

Hsueh Jien-tsung, Sung Yun-wing, and Yu Jingyuan, *Studies on Economic Reform and Development in the People's Republic of China* (New York: St. Martin's Press, 1993).

Deborah A. Kaple, *Dream of a Red Factory* (New York: Oxford University Press, 1994).

Anthony Y. C. Koo, "The Contract Responsibility System: Transition from a Planned to a Market Economy," *Economic Development and Cultural Change* 38 (July 1990), 797–820.

Deepak Lal, "The Failure of the Three Envelopes: The Analytics and Political Economy of the Reform of Chinese State-Owned Enterprises" *European Economic Review* 34 (September 1990), 1213–1231.

Nicholas R. Lardy, *China in the World Economy* (Washington, D.C.: Institute for International Economics, 1984).

Justin Yitu Lin, Fang Cai, and Zhou Li, *The China Miracle* (Hong Kong: The Chinese University Press, 1996).

Ike Mathur and Chen Jui-Sheng, *Strategies for Joint Ventures in the People's Republic of China* (New York: Praeger, 1987).

Barry Naughton, *Growing Out of the Plan: Chinese Economic Reform, 1978–1993* (New York: Cambridge University Press, 1993).

Ole Odgaard, *Private Enterprises in Rural China* (Brookfield, Vermont: Ashgate Publishing Company, 1992).

Dwight H. Perkins, "Completing China's Move to a Market Economy," *Journal of Economic Perspectives* 8 (Spring 1994), 23–46.

Elizabeth J. Perry and Christine Wong, *The Political Economy of Reform in Post-Mao China* (Cambridge, Mass.: Harvard University Press, 1987).

Jan S. Prybyla, "Mainland China's Economic System: A Study in Contradictions," *Issues & Studies* 30, 8 (August, 1994), 1–30.

Susan L. Shirk, *The Political Logic of Economic Reform in China* (Berkeley: University of California Press, 1993).

Clement Tisdell, *Economic Development in The Context of China* (New York: St. Martin's Press, 1993).

George Totten and Zhou Shulian, eds., *China's Economic Reform* (Boulder: Westview Press, 1992).

Lim Wei and Arnold Chao, eds., *China's Economic Reforms* (Philadelphia: University of Pennsylvania Press, 1983).

Gordon White, "The Politics of Economic Reform in Chinese Industry: The Introduction of The Labour Contract System," *The China Quarterly* 11 (September 1987), 365–389.

Christine P. Wong, "The Economics of Shortages and Problems of Reform in Chinese Industry," *Journal of Comparative Economics* 10 (December 1986), 363–387.

Susumi Yabuki, *China's New Political Economy: The Giant Awakes* (Boulder: Colo.: Westview Press, 1995).

Shahid Yusuf, "China's Macroeconomic Performance and Management During Transition," *Journal of Economic Perspectives* 8 (Spring 1994), 71–92.

11

The European Model: Variants of Industrialized Capitalism

Europe versus Asia

Economic historians have claimed that there exist distinct "European" and "Asian" models of development. Such distinctions have been put forward by diverse writers ranging from the noted economic historian Alexander Gerschenkron to the communist leader V. I. Lenin and other, more recent writers such as Angus Maddison.[1]

The "European model" explains the economic development of those countries on the European continent that began their modern economic growth in the 19th century, following the United Kingdom's Industrial Revolution of some 50 to 100 years earlier. The Industrial Revolution began in England in the mid-18th century and was characterized by sustained growth of population and per capita GDP and by structural transformations. The European continent and the offshoots of European development in North America and Australia/New Zealand followed England's lead as "follower countries" to create the core of industrial economies that dominated the 20th century.

According to Gerschenkron's analysis, each of the follower countries of Europe took a slightly different path to industrialization to make up for missing preconditions. Germany and France, for example, lacked a developed private capital market and a strong middle class of entrepreneurs. They therefore substituted universal banks to economize on acquiring entrepreneurial skills and to compensate for a weak capital market. Russia was even more relatively backward than Germany and France. Accordingly, Russia had to make more substitutions for missing preconditions. In the Russian case, state administrators substituted for missing entrepreneurs, and foreign capital substituted for missing domestic capital formation.

Because the European countries began their development from a higher level of per capita income, they were able to create sustained economic growth without the substantial sacrifices made by the poorer countries of Asia. They were not faced with the need for massive and rapid shifts of resources. Although agriculture was less productive than industry, population pressures had not driven marginal productivity of agricultural workers to zero. European households were accumulating savings. They weren't just being put to effective use.

After the European countries began modern economic growth, the innovation of their economic institutions continued.[2] Germany developed the first state-run social welfare system under Bismarck in the mid-nineteenth century. France, with its long experience with mercantilism in the eighteenth century, experimented with government ownership and direction of the economy—later called *dirigisme* and indicative planning. Sweden, the most rapidly growing economy of Europe in the nineteenth and early twentieth centuries, built on the German idea of state social welfare systems to create the most advanced social welfare state of the twentieth century. In addition, Sweden experimented with the limits of income redistribution through progressive taxes.

England, initiator of the Industrial Revolution, conducted its own experiments with respect to the economic system. Ever subject to a changing balance between conservative and labor parties, England experimented with rising and falling tides of state ownership and put in place a social welfare system that borrowed many of the elements of German and Swedish welfare systems. England entered the twentieth century as the world's most prosperous nation. In entered the last quarter-century as an economy that was losing ground to the rest of Europe, afflicted by the "English disease." England's recovery to economic health during the last two decades of the twentieth century has rewarded the measures it took to recover its lost relative position.

The story of Europe is also one of changes in attitude toward economic integration. Europe began the nineteenth century with a mercantilist attitude toward international trade. Each country should protect its domestic industry and should try to sell as much as possible to other countries while buying as little as possible. As the European continent began its modern economic growth, attitudes toward trade changed. The major European economies joined the international gold standard in the late nineteenth century, international trade expanded, as did the trade in capital, with England supplying the capital needs of other countries. The trend toward economic integration ended with World War I, which was followed by the Great Depression.[3] The last half of the twentieth century, however, has witnessed a remarkable movement toward European economic integration, and a single European market was created in 1992. As Europe moves to a single currency in 1999 (The Euro) and to the complete integration of markets, it remains to be seen to what extent national boundaries will remain important in the Europe of the twenty-first century.

European Profiles

Table 11.1 provides an economic and demographic profile of the European countries studied in this chapter as compared to the United States. Although only four European countries are included, they give an indication of the size and level of affluence of the European market as a whole.

Europe does contain some large countries, the largest of which is now Germany (with a population of 81 million after the reunification of East and West Germany in 1989). France, Germany, and the United Kingdom's populations alone add up to more than half of the U.S. population. The affluent European countries have been growing slowly, compared to the United States, and most of this growth has occurred through immigration rather than through rates of natural increase. They therefore exhibit the demographic dynamics of very mature countries whose populations are aging.

With the exception of the U.K. (whose growth performance we will discuss in detail), the most affluent European nations have per capita GDPs within 80 percent

TABLE 11.1   The European Model: A Profile of the Mid-1990s

	Population (millions)	Growth (1980 = 100)	GDP per Capita	Growth (1985 = 100)	Taxes as % of GDP	Social Security Tax Rate (%)	CPI (1980 = 100)	Unemployment Rate (%)
U.S.	263	116	$25,780	116	29	12.50	187	5.30
France	58	108	$21,962	114	44	48	207	12.70
Germany	81	104	$21,442	100	42	31	151	11.30
U.K.	58	106	$17,165	120	35	12	224	13.40
Sweden	9	104	$20,963	102	50	25	226	8.80

Sources: Statistical Abstract of the United States, 1995, "International Statistics"; *IMF Survey* 26, 7 (April 7, 1997); *The Economist,* March 29/April 4, 1997, "Economic Indicators"; and *Economic Report of the President,* February 1996, "International Statistics."

of the U.S., the world's most affluent country, as measured on a purchasing power parity basis. Since 1985, France and the U.K. have grown at about the same rate as the United States, but Germany and Sweden have grown scarcely at all.

All of the affluent European countries except the U.K. have exceptionally high tax burdens; France, Germany, and Sweden collect between 40 and 50 percent of their GDP in taxes. Again with the exception of the U.K., their taxes on employment (social security taxes paid by employers and employees on wages) are between double and quadruple those of the United States.

Figure 11.1 provides further structural information about state ownership in the three largest European nations in 1980 as compared to public ownership in the United States. State ownership of the major industries was much more widespread in Europe than in the United States. This prompted a move toward privatization in the late 1980s and early 1990s, the United Kingdom leading the way in the 1980s.

European Performance

It is difficult to evaluate the performance of the European economy. The European economies were the first to experience modern economic growth, with sustained rates of GDP growth well in excess of the growth of population. As Figure 11.2 shows, Europe has gone through various growth phases in which the region as a whole has grown either rapidly or slowly. The prewar industrialization period was

FIGURE 11.1   Extent of State Ownership of Industry, 1980

	Telecommunications	Electricity	Gas	Oil Production	Coal	Railways	Airlines	Automobile Production	Steel	Shipbuilding
United States	○	◔	○	○	○	◔	○	○	○	○
Germany	●	◕	◐	◔	◐	●	●	◔	○	◔
France	●	●	●	na	●	●	◕	◐	◕	○
United Kingdom	●	●	●	◔	●	●	◕	◐	◕	●

Private Sector: ○ More than 75 percent

Public Sector: ● More than 75 percent; ◕ 75 percent; ◐ 50 percent; ◔ 25 percent;
na = not available

Source: J. Vickers and V. Wright, *The Politics of Privatisation in Western Europe* (London: Frank Cass, 1989), p. 11, based on *The Economist*.

FIGURE 11.2   Long-term Growth Rates in Europe Compared to the United States

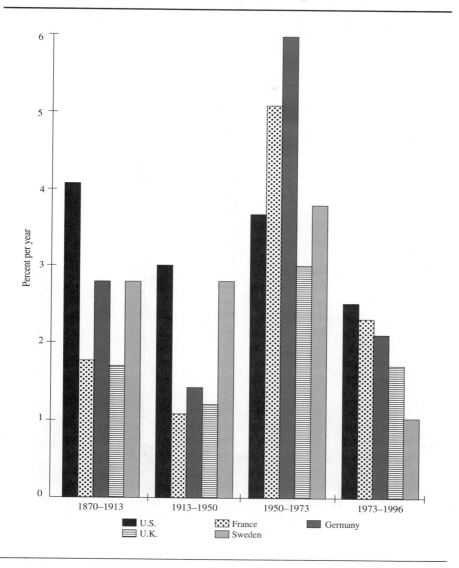

one of generally rapid growth, with Germany and Sweden growing quite rapidly and the U.S. and France lagging behind. The period 1913–1950 was one of relatively slow growth that witnessed two world wars and the Great Depression. Only Sweden continued to grow rapidly during this period. The period 1950–1973 has been iden-tified as the "Golden Age" of growth for Europe; all the European countries recorded exceptional growth. Since 1973, growth has fallen, with Sweden moving from its position as a growth leader to stagnant growth.

FIGURE 11.3   Inflation and Unemployment in the United States and Europe,
1960–1970 and 1995–1997

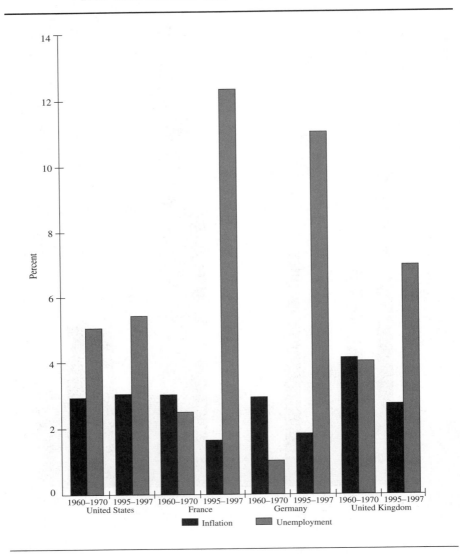

With the exception of Germany, the affluent European countries have experienced higher inflation than the United States since 1985, and in the mid-1990s, they had much higher unemployment rates than the United States. In fact, Figure 11.3 shows the rising unemployment problems of Europe in the 1980 and 1990s. Whereas United States inflation and unemployment in the mid-1990s had basically returned to their levels of the period 1960 through 1970, European unemployment rates in the mid-1990s were large multiples of their 1960s rates.

France: Indicative Planning

The post-World War II French economic system provided a significant test of whether national economic planning and a democratic capitalist society can be effectively and harmoniously combined.[4] For those who believe that some or all of the ills of capitalism require some form of state intervention, the French example has been cited on both practical and theoretical grounds.[5] French planning used noncoercive intervention while preserving the market economy. Moreover, the French planning mechanism remained modest in size, contrary to the warnings raised by Hayek and others in the socialist controversy. Moreover, the postwar French economy provides an example of extensive state ownership combined with an exceptionally high rate of taxation and state expenditures.

Interest in the French system was aroused by France's generally good economic performance in the immediate postwar period. As Figures 11.2 and 11.3 indicate, since 1973 French economic performance has deteriorated (a phenomenon not limited to France). Deteriorating performance has caused France to examine alternative approaches. France has moved away from the planning model described in this chapter to a milder form of industrial policy.

France: The Setting

Countries possess features, such as location, size, and cultural and historical characteristics, that influence the economic system. Although such features frequently cannot be isolated and measured, they may be of great importance in molding the course of events. France, a country whose history and traditions bore heavily on its acceptance of national economic planning, is certainly a case in point.

France is a major world power with a long, rich, and varied history. It has a population of roughly 57 million people residing predominantly in urban areas and has a total land area slightly larger than twice the size of the state of Colorado. Although France enjoys excellent agricultural conditions, agriculture represents a relatively small proportion of GDP (as is the case in most developed countries). By international standards, France is a developed country with a high standard of living and a record of sustained economic growth.

To understand the French economic system, one must understand the postwar French political system. France is a republic whose president is elected to serve for a term of seven years. The president in turn appoints the prime minister. The National Assembly or Parliament is elected.

Although one might look to earlier times to discover the roots of French thought on the appropriate economic role of the state, it is worth emphasizing that during the Fifth Republic, under the leadership of Charles De Gaulle (1958–1969), the power of the French presidency was substantially enhanced. This power has been retained during the post–De Gaulle era.

During the 1970s, with growing concern for inflation, unemployment, and balance-of-payments problems, austerity was imposed under the conservative leadership of Georges Pompidou and Valéry Giscard d'Estaing. This was a period of declining interest in planning as a mechanism to guide recovery. France became less and less interesting as a case of indicative planning.[6]

In the spring of 1981 François Mitterrand, a socialist, was elected to the French presidency, and a socialist majority was sent to the French National Assembly. Mitterrand was reelected in 1988. Although one might have expected a socialist government to be more sympathetic to planning, this was not necessarily the case. Nevertheless, planning continued in France, where the tenth plan terminated in 1992, the year unification of the European market began.

Since 1995, France has had a conservative President, Jacques Cirac. Under Cirac, France has turned its attention from planning to privatization of the French economy. In the case of France, the change from conservative to socialist and back to conservative presidents has probably had less effect than such change in the U.K.

French Indicative Planning: The Background

France has a long history of a strong state and of acceptance of a strong role for the state in management of the nation's economic affairs.[7] This historical experience contrasts sharply with that of the United States, Canada, and Great Britain, where it is an article of faith, at least in most business circles, that the least government is the best government.[8] French history was an important element in the widespread post-war acceptance of planning. Indeed, the early development of the plan by M. Jean Monnet (the founder of the European Common Market) was predicated on acceptance of planning by influential business leaders.

The French have tended to view their economy in a rather long-term perspective, emphasizing the primary importance of balanced economic growth and development.[9] Faith in the ability of the unfettered market mechanism to produce economic harmony has not been strong. Even within the framework of national economic planning, the French were willing to utilize mechanisms that are often viewed with skepticism in other countries. For example, the mixed enterprise in which the state and the private sector combine their entrepreneurship and managerial skills has a long history in France. The pattern of interchanging executives between the public and the private sector has created a tight-knit network of officials.[10] The recruitment of top executives for the public sector from the upper echelons of management creates a managerial style very different from that found elsewhere.[11]

Although these characteristics of the French economy facilitated the introduction of a planning mechanism, such a step presented both practical and theoretical problems. The path to national economic planning in capitalist economic systems has generally been slow and unsure. In France, planning played its most important roles in the first two postwar decades.

The basic case for indicative planning—the theoretical underpinning of the French planning system—rested on using information to guide the economic system in the face of uncertainty.[12] Specifically, it was argued that decision making can be improved if some planning agency collects, processes, and disseminates information to any and all decision makers. Indicative planning of this variety is nonauthoritarian in the sense that no directive targets are issued and that economic agents are encouraged to pursue plan objectives via indirect incentives. The nonauthoritarian nature of indicative planning was viewed as a major positive feature.

French planning began immediately after World War II, when countries such as England and Germany were dismantling the controls and planning mechanisms of the war years. As in other countries that began to experiment with planning at that time, planning in France subsequently underwent significant change, especially as the economy moved away from the immediate postwar problems toward more "normal" operations. The first plan, begun in 1946 and subsequently extended to 1952, was a transitional plan closely associated with the name of Jean Monnet.[13] Monnet headed the General Planning Commissariat, working closely with the Marshall Plan, and utilized direct controls to manipulate economic activity.

French planning changed significantly over the years in response to the changing needs of the French economy. The changes, however, were mostly in terms of *goals* and the *means* to achieve these goals rather than in the administrative machinery of the plan. Each plan on a five-year horizon had a theme. The first plan focused on the development of key sectors: transportation, agricultural machinery, steel, electricity, coal, and cement. The second five-year plan emphasized the improvement of productivity. The third was devoted to economic growth and the foreign sector. The plans thereafter departed from the traditional sectoral emphasis and focused instead on improved economic performance in general. They also placed strong emphasis on social goals: lessening income differentials, and redressing regional economic imbalances.

As time passed, French indicative planning moved away from direct controls to reliance on more indirect mechanisms. These indirect controls became the hallmark of French planning.[14]

Plan Administration

The organizational arrangements of French planning remained relatively unchanged from after World War II until the early 1980s, at which time substantial modifications were made.

French planning relied on an unpretentious institutional structure to forge a social consensus among various interest groups, such as business, trade unions, and regions. The main planning organ was the General Planning Commissariat, a small and relatively modest operation. Under the General Planning Commissariat, some thirty "vertical" and "horizontal" **modernization commissions** were responsible for sectoral projections. The "vertical" commissions dealt with various sectors of the economy, whereas the "horizontal" commissions dealt with economy-wide matters such as finance. Consultation, a major feature of the French system, was achieved through the work of the Economic and Social Council.

The plan itself was based on a series of alternative projected growth paths for the French economy, including major state priorities, which were formulated by the Planning Commissariat. Subsequent elaboration was developed by the modernization commissions with help from various state agencies. In essence, the French plan consisted of broad sectoral growth targets related to input, output, investment, and productivity. These targets were derived from macroeconomic projections for the aggregate economy and included state objectives, but they also recognized important constraints, such as the foreign sector.

Characteristics of Indicative Planning

The traditional French plan, unlike its Soviet counterpart, did not order firms to do things. The plan was indicative; it offered suggested targets at a fairly high level of aggregation. The plan projections were a source of information that firms could use, along with traditional market signals, to make decisions. Why would a firm be guided by the plan if it is not compulsory? The mechanisms for plan implementation, both direct and indirect, were another distinctive feature of French planning.[15]

The state had two major instruments for influencing economic outcomes: the *budget* and *public ownership*. Not all forms of investment that flowed through the state were governed by the national economic plan. Furthermore, the degree of control the plan agencies exerted over state investment was not uniform.[16] Plan control over investment in large public enterprises was considerable, but such control was limited in the case of local government investments. However, in the French case, almost one-third of investments in structures were undertaken by government—more than double the proportion of public investment in the U.K.[17] Statistics do not differentiate between private investments and those made by French public enterprises. Given the significant public ownership of French industry, the share of investment undertaken by state-owned industry must be substantial. French public investment, moreover, has been concentrated in key sectors such as housing.

Like state investments, public ownership in France is concentrated in key sectors such as banking, coal, gas and electricity, transportation, and auto and aircraft production. As a producer, consumer, and financier, the state sector has influenced economic activity in both the public sector and the private sector through its control over the availability of credit and of crucial inputs such as electricity, the regional distribution of resources, and tax incentives.

Plan fulfillment depends on whether firms follow the plan. The logic of the plan suggests that the plan is designed to achieve the best possible economic performance that is consistent with intersectoral balance. Thus a firm, especially a large firm, operating in accordance with plan directives should be able to do *its* best and to avoid unpredictable constraints. This, if true, would be an attractive feature of French planning: the creation of a predictable and harmonious business environment.[18] Evidence suggests that French firms in fact paid attention to the plans, especially firms important enough to know that the plan might influence their operation.

Monnet argued that a plan is likely to be carried out if those who will be implementing it have a voice in its creation.[19] This aspect of the French system is exemplified by the administrative structure of planning, especially the modernization commissions where the diverse interests of labor, the state, and business were supposed to come together to forge a consensus. The relationship between business and the state in France has fostered an interchange of ideas and understanding where there would otherwise be antagonism.

Events of the 1970s (especially external shocks to the economy) resulted in a loss of interest in planning. France was ruled by a conservative government from 1974 to 1981. The election of a socialist president in 1981 presented an opportunity for renewed planning activity. Although domestic economic problems and external events continued to keep planning on a back burner throughout the 1980s, interest in planning reappeared.[20]

In the early 1980s, a special commission was set up to assess the French planning system. While this assessment was in progress, external economic conditions resulted in termination of the eighth five-year plan (1981–1985) and its replacement with an interim plan (1982–1983). Ultimately there was a new, ninth, five-year plan for the years 1984 to 1988. Although the interim plan reflected the socialist government's policy of expanding the role of the public sector, conditions created by the worldwide recession took priority. French economic policies, therefore, were designed primarily to address the realities of weak foreign markets, inflation, and unemployment. These issues, along with the matter of European integration, remained important in the tenth plan (1988–1992).

The socialist government of François Mitterrand created a Ministry for Economic Planning and Regional Policy in 1981. Next, a National Planning Commission was established to bring together, in addition to the Minister of Planning, interest groups such as trade unions, regions, and employers for the purpose of spelling out plan priorities and methods of plan fulfillment. Along with these organizational changes, procedural changes were introduced. The new planning process introduced after 1981 distinguished between identification of plan objectives and designation of the methods by which plan objectives were to be achieved. The first phase placed new emphasis on realistic macroeconomic projections; the second was concerned with regional development, technological advancement, and so forth.

Another change of the 1980s was that regional plans were developed and incorporated into the national plan. In addition, contracts became an important mechanism for achieving plan fulfillment. One might argue that the changes introduced in the 1980s were more an attempt to revitalize planning than to change its basic nature. However, the organizational framework of French planning clearly had undergone change. The notion of achieving objectives spelled out in a national consensus was given new force through the use of contractual arrangements. Moreover, in addition to emphasizing better planning in a number of dimensions, the arrangements of the 1980s were supposed to harmonize regional and national objectives.

Did French Planning Work?

The features that made French planning attractive to many, especially its apparent consistency with the values of a Western pluralistic society, would be of little value if the plan did not work. As Figure 11.2 indicated, French economic performance (especially between 1950 and 1973) was relatively good. Did indicative planning contribute to that performance?

There are three reasons why it is difficult to assess the impact of the French planning system on economic performance.

First, the planning system changed in many ways. In the 1950s, planners were concerned with sectoral goals in what was almost a developmental context. During the 1960s, the plan grew more sophisticated and plan objectives broadened. By the 1970s, especially under conservative leadership, interest in planning waned. During that period, traditional economic difficulties such as inflation, unemployment, and trade deficits were countered largely via traditional monetary and fiscal policy.[21] Market allocation was strengthened through the reduction of controls, less emphasis on the public sector, and more attention to the development of efficient capital markets. The 1970s was an era of reduced state intervention and of movement toward an industrial policy. Although considerable attention was paid to changing the planning arrangements in the 1980s, the need to resolve macroeconomic problems overshadowed improvement of the planning system.

A second and closely related issue was the effectiveness of planning. Some observers argue that French planning was of limited importance, especially in recent years, because planning was poorly done.[22] Only limited amounts of information were used to generate the plan, and plan objectives (consisting of single projections) were much too simplistic. Furthermore, this sort of information was of little value to industrial firms, even state-owned firms, operating independent of state control. The 1970s witnessed declining coordination in the business sector, further reducing the potential usefulness of the plan to decision makers. The 1980s saw renewed emphasis on plan execution. Procedures were established to monitor plan performance. In addition, both public and private sectors became more involved in monitoring plan performance and received more information. Even so, available evidence suggests that these changes did little to enhance the importance of planning.

Third, in a mixed economy like that of France, what indicators can we use to judge the effectiveness of the plan? When specific results are examined—for example, sectoral growth targets in the 1950s—there tended to be considerable difference between plan and actual achievement. On this basis, plan performance was rather poor. Other observers, however, focus on more general outcomes, such as growth in GDP, arguing that the plan must have had something to do with improved growth.

One way to look at the impact of the plan is to ask business firms, both public and private, to what extent their decision making was influenced by plan directives. Hans Schollhammer found that, on balance, French firms did consider the plan important, especially in providing useful information and creating a dynamic business environment.[23] The firms that paid attention to the plan were for the most part large, capital-intensive, and domestically owned. One could argue that this evidence, in combination with good economic performance in the early postwar years, presents a circumstantial case in favor of the French planning system.

Another test is to examine the record of plan fulfillment. Were the mechanisms of plan implementation so strong and the targets so realistic that plan fulfillment was generally achieved?

In a study of plan fulfillment, Vera Lutz, a critic of French planning, argues that, on balance, the achievement record of French planning was dismal.[24] In fact, Lutz argues, the French system of planning was not central planning at all. It was little more than "collective forecasting." Lutz's examination of the plan target and achievement data suggests that the degree to which targets were achieved varied widely from one target to another and, overall, probably did not improve over time.

In another study, John J. McArthur and Bruce R. Scott argue that "the national planning process did have some influence on the *general* measures and macroeconomic programs used by the state to shape the economic environment in which companies and industries worked."[25] They contend that the plan mechanism influenced economic outcomes through its *indirect* use of state influence. The plan had very little direct influence on corporate decision making, nor, they claim, did it have indirect influence through the state's manipulation of selective means of control. This lack of influence can be explained at least in part by the inability of planners to adapt to the changing needs and circumstances of the French economy.

A survey by J. R. Hough suggests that the planning system may have contributed to a favorable climate for the relatively good economic growth that France achieved, at least prior to the energy crisis of the 1970s.[26]

A consensus on the French experience is provided in a study by Stephen S. Cohen.[27] Cohen points out that when economic progress is rapid, it is easy to be generous in interpreting the economic impact of planning. Although we have stressed improved French economic performance in the early postwar era, that record changed for the worse after the 1970s. It may be that the plan mechanism did not adapt from its original objective of postwar recovery to the needs of what Cohen describes as "general resource allocation planning." With adverse macroeconomic conditions, the French government turned to traditional techniques for manipulating economic activity. Failure of those economic policies, combined with growing lack of interest in planning, resulted in a virtual halt in plan adaptation.[28]

Saul Estrin and Peter Holmes argue that in spite of its theoretical basis, planning in France "lost practically all practical relevance after 1965."[29] Thus Estrin and Holmes emphasize the growing lack of interest in planning, poor planning, and inadequate mechanisms to implement plans.

Martin Cave concerns that indicative planning ceased to play an important role, even after Mitterrand's socialist governments tried to revive it in the early 1980s.[30] Cave notes that many of the reforms of the 1980s (for example, the National Planning Commission) have simply not worked. Moreover, the Mitterrand government, preferring traditional macroeconomic tools, did not place confidence in the plan.

Structural Change

Like the United Kingdom, the French economy has been affected by changes in electoral politics. France has had a lengthy tradition of strong leftist parties, ranging from the French Communism Party to the French Socialist Party. Although France has been ruled throughout much of the postwar period by conservative Gaulist presidents and legislatures, it did have a lengthy period of socialist rule under President Francois Mitterrand (from 1981 to 1995).

As in the U.K., French policies toward structural reforms of the French economy have been dictated by swings in electoral outcomes. During the regime of Mitterrand,

France moved in the direction of nationalization of industry. Under later conservative rule, France has moved in the direction of denationalization and privatization. Under socialist rule, France has expanded the role of the welfare state; under conservative rule, there has been some effort to place limits on the French welfare state. One constant has been the strong role of French labor, France being among the most widely unionized of European nations.

The initial years of the Mitterrand government witnessed a substantial increase in the role of government in the French economy. Beginning in late 1981 and early 1982, a policy of nationalization was announced, especially in relation to the large industrial trusts where state involvement was already substantial. Substantial nationalization took place in the banking sector as well.

In a study of the early years of the Mitterrand government, Bela Balassa notes that the public sector share "[rose] from zero to 71 percent in iron ore, from 1 to 79 percent in iron and steel, from 16 and 66 percent in other metals, from 16 to 52 percent in basic chemicals, and from zero to 75 percent in synthetic fibers."[31] This certainly constituted a trend toward greater government involvement in the French economy, evident even in the 1970s.

After the return of the Gaulists to legislative power in the mid-1980s, there was a reversal in the trend toward nationalization and growth of the public sector.

In France during the first period of privatization, from 1986 to 1988, the transfers to the private sector yielded 70 billion French francs. From 1988 to 1990, official policy aimed at maintaining the status quo ("neither privatization nor nationalization"). Partial privatizations began in 1991. Then a new law (of July 19, 1993) earmarked 21 crucial companies in banking and industry for privatization. By 1995, total privatization sales (including those of 1986–1988) had yielded 185 billion French francs (roughly $37 billion). The sales of this period included the great companies Rhône-Poulenc, Banque Nationale de Paris, Elf-Acquitaine, and Union des Assurances de Paris, but the effort encountered market resistance when it proved difficult to find major investors for Usinor-Sacilor. The total yield 185 billion French francs was also rather modest when compared to the total budget expenditures for 1995 of 1,592 billion French francs, and to a deficit for that same year of 322 billion French francs (some 4.5 percent of GDP).[32]

Even under conservative government, France's commitment to privatization and market resource allocation remain questionable. Nicolas Spulber summarizes the situation as follows:

> The role of the government after privatization is also not as simple and transparent as one might assume. Of course, *in principle* privatization aims to free enterprises from government's ownership and control in order to increase their efficiency. Indeed, in some cases, the government does remove itself up to a point from the operation of the privatization firms. But more often than not, the government decides to *continue to play* a role—for instance, that of a critical shareholder—while in other cases, it vests new and extensive controlling powers over the privatized enterprises in the hands of regulatory authorities. Furthermore, shares are not always placed competitively through the financial markets.

As part of underlying arrangements, a substantial number of shares are kept by the state or are placed in the hands of certain groups of investors. As we already know, the government may reserve "golden shares" for itself or may select a "hard core" (*noyaux durs*) of investors to whom it allocates a proportion of the capital, with restrictions placed on its disposal over a number of years. Again, privatization, just like its opposite, nationalization, allows the state bureaucracies and the party in power to transfer wealth and award patronage to their supporters. In all the Western countries considered, and in particular under both Thatcher's and Chirac's privatizations, reliable political friends were placed at the head of privatized public enterprises. On the other hand, change-resistant employees of public enterprises may also be encouraged to acquire stock in these companies as they are privatized. Methods including offering free shares to the employees or giving the latter priority in the allocation of shares sold to the public. This much-advertised way of promoting "popular capitalism" does not, however, necessarily lead to "shareholder democracy," since people are attracted to this kind of transaction mostly in order to make a quick profit. In any case, ill-informed and largely uninterested small shareholders have few effective powers. In sum, privatization does not necessarily herald a more market oriented economy, but only a *differently structured* economy.[33]

The future of the French economy remains unclear. Much depends on the course of French politics and on whether there will be political support for basic structural change in the direction of privatization and competition. Although privatization appears as a plank in the Gaullist economic platform, real privatization has proceeded more slowly in France than in other European countries. The privatizations that have occurred have been a form of "insider" privatization involving an interlocking directorate of government officials and industrialists. Most privatized French companies remain closely held with outside shareholders owning minority interests. Thus outside shareholders find it difficult to motivate management to maximize shareholder value.

The future of the French economy also hinges on the government's ability to deal with the massive worker and union unrest that accompanies any effort to reduce the scope of the French welfare state. To date, no French government has waged a winning struggle against such protests. French politicians also have had difficulty exposing large French enterprises, such as Air France, Credit Lyonnais, and Airbus Industrie, to market forces. Instead, the French government has stood by with credits and subsidies.

Great Britain: Sclerosis and Recovery?

In contrast to France and Germany, Britain projected during the first three decades of the postwar era an image of poor economic performance, called the "British disease." Britain was classified as a capitalist welfare state because of the public provision of services such as medical care, highly progressive taxes, and the nationalization of important sectors of the British economy. Postwar British economic performance was poor until the 1980s.[34]

The election of a Conservative government under the leadership of Margaret Thatcher in 1979 was a pivotal point in contemporary British economic history. British economic performance improved in the 1980s under a package of Conservative economic reforms focusing on deregulation, privatization, incentives, and a redefined role for trade unions. In effect, these reforms were designed to undo the welfare state. It is difficult to separate the effects of these policies from those of other events, such as the discovery and exploitation of North Sea oil and gas. Thatcher was replaced in 1990 by John Major, who continued Conservative rule. However, the British general election in late 1997 saw a Labour Party victory end almost 20 years of Conservative government.

Britain is a mature economy; it was the first to experience industrialization in the eighteenth century. It remains at a high level of development in terms of the structure of production, urbanization ratios, and demographic characteristics. *Maturity* refers to Britain's longer experience with economic development.

Comparative analysts who look at the British economy often do so for the wrong reasons—to study nationalization, public services, and sharply progressive taxes. These features are important components of the British economy, but they are not unique. Other economies resemble Britain in terms of nationalization, public services, and progressive taxes. We consider broader questions: In the long run, are maturity and stagnation inevitable bedfellows? What combination of economic and political forces are required to deal with maturity?

In the year 1913, British per capita GDP was the highest in Europe and was second only to that of the United Sates on a worldwide basis. But by 1980, Britain had fallen behind a number of European countries and was tied for 13th place with Italy. This relative decline is the most abrupt on record; the U.K. is the first highly industrialized country to have fallen dramatically relative to its immediate neighbors.

Why did Britain decline? A number of explanations have been offered. They are all related to Britain's loss of international competitiveness, to a deterioration in its economic and social institutions, to a welfare state run aground. One of the most convincing explanations has been offered by Mancur Olson, who coined the term *Eurosclerosis,* which he first applied to the U.K.[35]

Olson's argument is that mature and stable societies are prone to suffer sclerosis because their very stability breeds the seeds of economic inefficiency. In dynamic societies, it is difficult for distributional coalitions—vested-interest groups that engage in monopoly rent seeking—to establish themselves. There are too many temptations to cheat on the coalition by acting as a free rider or by breaking its rules. However, when a society is stable for a long period of time, powerful distributional coalitions form—unions, monopolies, trade associations, etc.—which pass special-interest legislation, which gain monopolies, which divide the spoils of the economy among themselves. As these distributional coalitions become more and more powerful, economic performance lags.

According to Olson, Britain was the first mature economy to succumb to Eurosclerosis. The U.K. emerged from World War II with the same society and the same interest groups as before the war. Germany, France, and Japan, on the other hand, emerged from the war with entirely new social and economic structures. These dynamic changes meant that France, Germany, and Japan had to start from scratch. Distributional coalitions had to be formed anew.

As the end of this section, we shall address Olson's indictment of Britain's stability and the partial attack on vested interests, in particular on labor and on the English welfare state launched during the Thatcher years. We shall also consider the effects of the Thatcher policies on British economic performance. And we must speculate about whether the lagging performance of the European industrialized economies is a general result of the forces that earlier caused Britain's relative decline.

Great Britain: The Setting

Great Britain is an island economy; its land area is slightly greater than that of Minnesota. Britain's history of achievement and its rise to world power have not been matched by good economic performance in contemporary times. Much of the literature on the British economy focuses on the reasons for its decline, relative to its West European neighbors, in the postwar era.

Great Britain has a population of more than 57 million people, roughly 89 percent of whom live in urban areas. Although Great Britain was the home of the Industrial Revolution and the source of much innovative industrial activity, the resource base of the economy is quite limited. Thus it is not surprising that in modern times, the fate of the British economy is very closely tied to performance in the foreign sector. The British economy is dominated by the service and industrial sectors. The agricultural sector contributes only a very small fraction of GDP.

Great Britain has limited amounts of good agricultural land, and given its relatively large population, intensive land use is essential. Although Great Britain has substantial deposits of coal and iron ore, these deposits have been heavily exploited and are not of high quality. From the 1960s through the 1990s, attention has focused on the discovery of substantial reserves of oil and natural gas in the North Sea and on the extent to which these reserves can be utilized to sustain and improve British economic performance.

Background of the British Economy

Great Britain is an open economy, particularly vulnerable to external shifts over which it has no control. Developments in the foreign sector have been a key theme of the postwar period. As an indicator of the importance of the foreign sector to the British economy, the sum of merchandise imports and exports accounts for half of British GDP, whereas the comparable figure for the United States is 15 percent.

The British concept of the state's role in economic affairs is very different from that prevailing in France.[36] France had experienced slow growth in the interwar years and was acutely aware of the need for economic recovery. Whatever the motivating force, the state would play an important role in the direction of the French economy, and planning was viewed as the appropriate mechanism. In Britain, however, in spite of substantial war damage, the immediate postwar emphasis was on preserving the independence of small business and on intervening in the economy only through fiscal and monetary policy. The Keynesian revolution convinced the British of the superiority of "demand management" over central economic planning. Though impossible to quantify, this attitude toward the role of the state has been a factor in the divergent economic paths taken by France and Britain.

Britain has suffered from rather significant regional inequalities.[37] Regional inequalities always existed. Modernization has fostered urbanization, and the increased mobility of labor brought the problems of regional differences to the attention of policy makers and the public.

The British political structure is based on strong conservative and labor parties, both of which have a role in the parliamentary structure, thus providing a testing ground for the capitalist and socialist ideologies. Labor policy has been basically socialist, particularly on questions of nationalization and income distribution. But there is an erroneous tendency to associate socialism with planning, which is contrary to the British socialist tradition. As Andrew Schonfield points out, "By 1948, the basic elements of modern planning were present in Britain as in no other major Western country."[38] But there it ended until the limited introduction of planning in the 1960s. The basic elements of planning to which Schonfield refers were the Development Councils set up in the late 1940s to exert state control over the private sector, the nationalized sectors, state ownership of the Bank of England, and the wartime experience with planning.[39] All could have been important elements in a planning system, but with the advent of a Conservative government in 1951, national economic planning was not seriously discussed for more than a decade.

Probably the most important reason for the lack of interest in planning was the British Labour Party's view of socialism, which was based on old-style ideological convictions that had no connection to modern economic planning. Furthermore, wartime planning was short-term crisis planning that had little to do with long-term planning of the entire economy. After the war, wartime controls were phased out, though the nationalized industries remained. However, nationalization did not mean planning. In postwar Britain, the mechanism employed to coordinate economic activity was predominantly the market.

War damage in Britain (as in Germany and Japan) was extensive. The war years called for special means to direct British economic activity toward the single purpose of military victory. During the transition to peace, wartime controls were largely replaced by market allocation, but there was growing concern for the health of the economy. In the middle and late 1950s, this concern became an obsession with poor economic performance.[40]

The British experience, like that of France, is a special case. It is a case for which the theoretical underpinning—the economics of maturity—is limited.[41] It is therefore interesting, because it may ultimately be relevant for other mature economic systems.

The British Economy: The Early Postwar Era

When a market economy has been operating for some time under controls, release from those controls can create adjustment difficulties. Such was the case in the immediate postwar British economy. Although British economic performance was relatively good in the late 1940s and early 1950s, the roots of subsequent poor economic performance were evident even then. Policy measures taken to offset the subsequent malaise were at best useless and at worst harmful.[42] What were the roots and the dimensions of the impending economic problems?

British economic problems of the 1950s and 1960s are now familiar. The most visible was a growing balance-of-payments deficit produced in large part by Britain's declining ability to compete in export markets and by its overextended aid program. This problem was combined with growing home demand for imports, a slackening rate of economic growth, and increasing regional inequalities surfacing through inadequate mobility of labor and growing unemployment. Rather than treat underlying causes, the British government chose to stimulate and stabilize economic growth through the macroeconomic policy of **demand management**. Subsequent evidence suggests that the experience was destabilizing—and sufficiently so for it to be described as a period of **"stop-go" policies**.[43] In a sense, however, it was a continuation of the immediate postwar concern for the short run and a neglect of long-run policy remedies.

The main explanations for the poor performance of the British economy in the first decade and a half after the war were inflexible supplies of labor, inadequate investment, poor distribution of investment in non–growth-producing areas, inability to move ahead technologically, the burden of progressive taxation, and a heavy defense burden. In addition, demand management was inept and contributed to poor performance. Attention has focused on the foreign sector, notably the growing pressure of imports, worsened by the declining role of sterling as a key world currency and by the inability of Britain to maintain a strong competitive position in world export markets.

Many would consider these features symptoms rather than causes. True, the inability of exports to keep up with the growth of imports was obviously a factor in the balance-of-payments problems, but why this backsliding in the growth of exports? Above all, why was the British economy in the early postwar years unable to adapt to change? The British managerial structure in industry and the civil service power structure were both molded by tradition, which for years served in place of expertise. Trade unions, on balance, opposed technological change, seeing it as leading to unemployment. In short, the British economy proved incapable of adapting to its new role in the world economic community and to the new role of the British consumer, whose expectations were high in the 1950s.

The British Economy: Planning

Although the main elements of national economic planning were present in the immediate postwar British economy, the subject received no attention after the election of a Conservative government in 1951 and languished until 1961, when the Conservative government itself introduced a measure of planning into the British economy. Alarm over economic difficulties caused this policy shift, though the instigation of planning meant very little under Conservative guidance and continued to mean little under subsequent Labour leadership.

In a period of poor economic performance, a balance-of-payments crisis in 1961, and concern for the shape of future relations with the emerging European Economic Community, the Conservative government in 1962 established the National Economic Development Council.[44] Both labor and industry supported the idea of planning, though each had a different concept of what planning was. Both also shared a rather peculiar view that there must be an "arm's-length" relationship between the state and the plan. In addition to creation of the main plan organization, a professional staff was organized in the newly created National Economic Development Office. Economic development committees (initially about 30) were created to serve as a forum for planning discussions by leaders of labor, business, and government.

There were really two economic plans prepared for the 1960s. One, begun in 1962, was to govern the growth of the economy through 1966. The second plan, introduced in 1965 and abandoned in 1966, was to govern the growth of the economy through 1970. Both plans were sectoral elaborations on a projected aggregate growth rate. Both were based on inadequate information and had no means of implementation. Both failed.

As Werner Z. Hirsch observes, the years that followed were not really years of economic planning. They were, at least until the mid-1970s, merely a continuation of the British government's effort to develop macroeconomic forecasting and use it to manipulate economic outcomes.[45] The culmination of this exercise was the passage, under a Labour government, of the Industry Act of 1975, which created the National Enterprise Board and Planning Agreements. The National Enterprise Board was provided with funds to assist private industry and also to extend the scope of the public sector. The Planning Agreements were designed to increase collaboration between the private sector and government and to coordinate government assistance.

The British experience with national economic planning did not alter economic outcomes in desired ways. However, as Hirsch points out, it might be more appropriate to consider the experience as one designed to improve communication, information flows, and decision making, not as an exercise in planning per se. What were some of the more general problems of this experience?

First, any planning system must have accurate and up-to-date information. During the early years of planning, there was no close relationship between the planning body and those who made the important decisions in government, especially the treasury. Planners were not even informed of government financial and budgetary decisions.

Second, there was a continuous struggle over how various interest groups—unions, corporations, and the state—would be represented. Even if one is skeptical about French claims of harmony, the contrast between the British and the French experiences is striking. In Britain, instead of a state plan formulated with the inputs of interest groups and with built-in incentives for fulfillment, the planning structure proved to be a bargaining arrangement with an arm's-length relationship between the state and the planners. Schonfield notes that "the crucial issue in modern capitalist planning, which is the relationship between public power and private enterprise, remains open and undecided in the British case."[46]

Third, powerful tools used for plan implementation in France—bank control over investment, tax incentives, and others—were not brought to bear in Britain. In the British case, the state did have a substantial degree of control over state spending and over investment, but both were directed within a traditional framework of monetary and fiscal policy, and neither had much to do with the plan.

Fourth, organizational change was a frequent and destabilizing element, especially with the shifts between Labour and Conservative governments. Throughout the 1960s, traditional policy measures continued to be used. Discussion focused more on the necessity for formulating an incomes policy to combat inflation.[47] Fiscal and monetary policy were used, along with efforts to reach agreements with labor and management concerning wage and price increases. Such policies were described as stop-go policies in the 1950s, as income policies in the 1960s, and as demand management thereafter.

The "British Disease"

We can identify a number of specific problem areas—investment levels and patterns, a noncompetitive position in export markets, a high burden of taxation, problems in the allocation of labor, and the defense burden—as manifestations or causes of Britain's economic difficulties of the first 30 years of the postwar era.

Britain's investment was well below that of France and Germany. Furthermore, although government and public enterprises accounted for over 40 percent of domestic capital formation, there is little evidence that the government played any useful role in directing investment activity toward growth-producing sectors or regions. Moreover, the British capital stock per worker was below that of other countries.[48]

The British tax system has also been singled out as a cause of economic problems. Britain's tax on personal income was more progressive than in the United States, but its tax on corporations was significantly lower. The disparity between the British personal and corporate tax widened between the 1950s and the 1960s, a change that depressed personal incentives. The loss of skilled professionals (physicians, engineers, and so forth) to other countries during this period is certainly consistent with this interpretation. The outcome of steeply progressive taxation—namely, a lessening of income differentials—can be seen. In the mid-1960s, the income distribution in Britain was narrower than that in Germany, France, or even Yugoslavia.[49]

Compared with countries such as France, Germany, and Italy, the British economy did not do well in obtaining economic growth from increases in the quality and quantity of the labor force. At the same time, the process of collective bargaining in Britain contributed to low industrial productivity. Contrary to the popular concept that Britain was plagued by strikes, for the period 1955–1964 far fewer days (as a proportion of employment in key sectors) were lost to strikes in Britain than in France, Germany, Italy, or the United States.[50] However, this statistic may simply indicate a greater willingness on the part of private and public management to accede to wage and work-rule demands.

The share of GDP devoted to defense in Great Britain was smaller than that in the United States but considerably larger than that in Germany, France, or Italy. Although defense spending shifts resources away from other potential uses, it is not clear that this process depressed Britain's economic growth.

Nationalization

Britain, at least prior to the long Conservative rule beginning in 1979, was frequently described as a socialist economic system.[51] This identification is based on the state's playing a substantial role through the budgetary process, nationalized firms in key sectors, and (to a much lesser degree) the existence of national economic planning. Although there is no single indicator of the state's role in an economic system, most available evidence supports the view that the role of the state in the British economy was smaller than generally perceived and did not justify classification of the system as socialist.

A study by Frank Gould of public expenditure patterns in a number of Western industrialized countries sheds light on the growth of government spending.[52] General government spending as a proportion of GDP in the early 1960s was 37 percent for France, 33 percent for the United Kingdom, and 28.5 percent for the United States. By the late 1970s, these shares had risen to 46 percent, 45 percent, and 34 percent, respectively. During that period, real general government expenditures grew at an average annual rate of 6 percent in France, 4 percent in the United Kingdom, and almost 5 percent in the United States. Gould concludes that although state and local government spending assumed greater importance, the major explanation for the rise in general government spending can be found in the growth of government transfers. As a proportion of general government spending, government transfers during the late 1970s represented 60 percent in France, 47 percent in the United Kingdom, and 41 percent in the United States. Patterns of public expenditure in the United Kingdom did not appear different from those in other industrialized European countries at the aggregate level.

The public sector in Britain also played a substantial role in both savings and investment. Public saving as a proportion of aggregate saving in the economy fluctuated from a low of 21 percent (1960) to a high of 46 percent (1950) over the period 1950–1966. For the same years, public investment as a proportion of total investment fluctuated from a low of 31 percent (1950) to a high of 56 percent (1952) and in recent years has been just over 40 percent. Over those years, public savings averaged 31 percent of total savings, while public investment averaged 42 percent of total investment. Judged by the experience of other industrialized countries, these ratios were average or, at best, slightly above average.[53] Thus, although the public sector was important in the British economy, it was no larger than in other industrialized European economies.

Public enterprise is highly visible in some sectors of the British economy, but its overall contribution was really not large.[54] Although the share of public corporations in the capital formation of the public sector grew (largely at the expense of capital formation by the central government), the contribution of public enterprises to output remained small. In 1950, for example, the net output of the public-enterprise sector in Britain accounted for just over 8 percent of British GDP; the equivalent figure for 1967 was just over 7 percent.[55]

It is difficult to quantify the effects of British public enterprise on overall economic performance. What counts is not only the relative size of the public sector but also how well or poorly it was operated in the British economic environment. Many public enterprises (such as coal and steel) were nationalized not because of ideology but to prevent their bankruptcy. Others were large, visible companies, such as British Airways, that were run by coalitions of unions and management. Others, like British Gas, were operated according to political rather than economic rules.

The British Economy Under Thatcher

Some have argued that the problems plaguing the British economy are unique to that system: the "British disease."[56] Others have argued that the British economy is in a phase of deindustrialization brought on by a decline in the importance of manufacturing.[57]

Prior to the 1980s, Britain's economic performance was inferior to that of other industrialized European economies. This performance gap arguably stemmed from a poor labor–management system, poor work attitudes, the welfare state, and a management system incapable of growth and change. Those deeply ingrained forces resulted in low growth of productivity, an inability to compete in export markets, and a growing domestic demand for imports.

British performance was inferior relative to its European neighbors for the period 1950 to 1979. Real GDP per person grew by 2.4 percent per annum in Britain in the 1960s and by 1.9 percent in the 1970s. Comparable figures for the United States were 2.9 percent and 1.8 percent; for Japan they were 15.9 and 4.8 percent, respectively.[58] In the 1970s Britain lost further ground. In 1967, the per capita GDP of Great Britain was 86 percent of the OECD (Organization for Economic Cooperation and Development) average; by 1978, the comparable figure was 72 percent.[59] Most countries experienced rapid inflation in the 1970s. However, the British rate of inflation generally exceeded in all OECD countries.

Turning to the question of labor–market performance, unemployment increased substantially in the 1970s, though not always to levels experienced in other countries. At the same time, wages increased without concomitant rises in labor productivity. The increasing unit labor costs made British exports less competitive abroad. This latter trend was partially offset by the declining value of the pound sterling. Between 1966 and 1977, the average annual increase in unit labor costs in Britain was 11.5 percent while the comparable figures for Japan, France, and the United States were 8.1 percent, 7.7 percent, and 4.4 percent, respectively.[60] Britain's share in the world export of manufactures declined between 1951–1955 and 1973–1977 by 11.4 percent. The United States experienced a comparable decline of 7 percent, but Germany's share grew by 8 percent, Japan's by 9.8 percent, and France's by 0.3 percent.[61]

How bad the "British disease" was depends on one's perspective. Recall that the period 1950–1973 was the "Golden Age" of growth in Europe. In a study of British economic performance in the 1970s, W. B. Reddaway concluded that the "disease" view is one-sided, saying that although other economies had done better, "Even in the less-satisfactory 1970s the economy made faster progress, in real terms, than in any pre-war decade, and the two previous decades might be regarded as a golden age."[62] At the same time, a Brookings study argued that in the decade between 1967 and 1978, Britain lost ground among OECD countries, markedly so after 1973. The authors conclude, "Britain's economic malaise stems largely from its productivity problem, whose origins lie deep in the social system."[63]

The discovery of North Sea oil in the late 1970s and early 1980s was an important factor limiting the bad economic news for Britain. This positive input has a finite life span, however, and continuing improvement must rest on more fundamental changes in the British economy.[64]

Thatcher's economic policies starting in 1979 clearly represented a significant departure from earlier years. Such a departure is difficult to evaluate in the short run, although the volume of literature on the subject is already large.[65]

It is not surprising that the conservative Thatcher government placed the blame for past failures squarely on past economic policies, especially the ambitious role of the government in the British economy. Accordingly, economic polices in the 1980s were designed to reduce the role of government in four important areas.[66]

First, to improve market stability, a monetary policy designed to reduce the rate of inflation was instituted. A reduction in the rate of growth of the money supply was combined with less public-sector borrowing and less use of fiscal policy. This aspect of the Thatcher economic policy became known as a *monetarist* macroeconomic policy and has been compared with policies of the Reagan administration in the United States. It became known officially as the Medium Term Financial Strategy.

Second, to reinstitute a competitive market economy, government controls and regulations were reduced. This policy, designed to stimulate private market initiative, applied to both the domestic and the international economy.

A third area of emphasis, related to the issue of a competitive market economy, involved "privatization," or the return of the public sector (especially nationalized industries) to private ownership and operation.

British Telecom was Britain's first privatization in a series of large utility companies—such as British Airport Authority, British Gas, British Airways, Rolls-Royce, and various electricity and water authorities. They were subsequently joined by British Steel, British Coal, and Northern Ireland Electricity. To be added eventually were British Rail, the U.K. nuclear power industry, and even the London Underground. Privatization proceeds from sales of public enterprises were between 8 and 15 percent of the deficit in the period 1994–1997. The British government has also been seeking, through a so-called "Private Finance Initiative" (PFI) program, to increase private-sector participation in the provision of both capital assets and services in areas that had previously been restricted to the public sector.[67]

Finally, steps were taken to reduce the powers of trade unions and make them more responsive to their members. Like Ronald Reagan in the United States, Thatcher faced down a strike of miners to show her resolve against British trade union power.

Have **deregulation** and the **privatization** of the British economy succeeded? To the extent that the British effort to deregulate can be described as an industrial policy, it has been selective and difficult to evaluate. As one author has noted, British policy is based in large part on the notion that private ownership is in itself sufficient to generate efficient markets; at the same time, however, selective government support has increased.[68] For example, the British government has attempted to invigorate regional policy, stimulate industries where advanced technology is important, and boost the quality of investment. There has also been substantial privatization of firms, ranging from British Petroleum in the early 1980s to British Airports, British Airways, and automobile producers in the mid- and late 1980s.

Traditionally, little empirical evidence has been available for assessing the impact of privatization. However, a recent study of a large number of newly privatized firms (including the British case) has revealed significant benefits. Specifically, those that were documented include important performance improvements (sales, profitability, and the like) and sustained employment.[69] For example, British Airways, one of the more poorly performing international air carriers, has become an innovative and highly profitable carrier since its privatization.

Cure of the British Disease?

When Margaret Thatcher took office in 1980, she promised to cure the British disease. Have her programs of privatization, reduction of the welfare state, and monetary stability[70] had the desired effect?[71]

Table 11.2 summarizes the economic performance of Great Britain before and after Thatcher. From the 1950s throughout the 1970s, Great Britain did indeed have the sickest economy of Europe. The English malady, as the figures show, resulted from a lack of participation in Europe's phenomenal economic performance between 1950 and 1970. The British economy during this period was much like that of the United States.[72]

The 1970s and 1980s witnessed a decline in the European economy, which experienced a rise in unemployment and a slowdown in economic growth. In fact, the 1980s narrowed the differences among the economies such that Great Britain's rates of growth and unemployment matched those of Europe and the United States.

TABLE 11.2   Great Britain: Before and After Thatcher (1980s)

	1950–1960	1960–1970	1970–1980	1980–1990	1990–1996
Growth of real GDP					
Great Britain	2.8	2.9	1.9	2.6	1.3
European Community	5.3	4.8	3.0	2.3	1.7
U.S.	3.3	4.2	2.8	2.6	2.2
Unemployment rate (end of decade)					
Great Britain	2.3	9.2	13.3	6.9	8.8
European Community	2.6	2.3	5.2	7.0	10.0
U.S.	5.5	8.2	8.1	5.2	6.0

Source: World Tables 1976, Handbook of Economic Statistics, various years.

A wide-ranging study by Nicholas Crafts suggests that according to a number of growth and productivity measures, the U.K. has indeed reversed its relative decline compared to the rest of Europe and is, in fact, improving its relative position in per capita GDP.[73]

Germany: The Social Market Economy[74]

The economy of Germany, the Federal Republic of Germany, belongs in a discussion of the variants of capitalism for three reasons. First, the economic performance of the German economy is generally perceived to be the strongest of the major European countries throughout the postwar era. Germany has emerged as the economic leader of Europe. The second reason is Germany's combination of free market forces with significant state intervention to achieve desired social goals. The Germans label this combination the **social market economy** *(soziale Marktwirtschaft)*.[75] The combination of good economic performance with some of the ideals of a welfare state makes Germany a valuable case study. Third, unification of East and West Germany provides a unique historical example of the integration of a planned socialist economy into a market economy.

Background

The Federal Republic of Germany *(Bundesrepublik Deutschland)* came into existence as a federal republic in the late 1940s as the three allied occupation forces (the United States, England, and France) converted their occupation zones into a unified economic area *(Vereinigtes Wirtschaftsgebiet)* in 1947. The 1948 currency reform established the three occupation zones as a single currency area; Soviet authorities kept the Soviet occupation zone out of this currency union. This event signaled the splitting of Germany into two Germanys. The Basic Law for the Federal Republic of Germany was passed on June 23, 1949. It established West Germany as a federal republic consisting of a federal government (with two legislative houses and a federal bureaucracy of ministries), the states *(Länder)*, and the local governments *(Gemeinden)*. The Federal Republic is a democracy with two major parties, the Christian Democratic Union (CDU) and the Socialist party (SPD), that have dominated the political scene throughout the postwar era. Along with governmental bodies and agencies, a number of quasi-state organizations such as labor unions, employer organizations, and chambers of commerce are active in economic affairs.

The collapse of the communist governments of Eastern Europe took place in 1989 and 1990, as it became clear that the Soviet Union under Gorbachev would not use military force to prop up unpopular communist regimes in the region. On May 18, 1990, the West German chancellor and the East German prime minister signed the State Treaty on the establishment of a monetary, economic, and social union between East and West Germany. East Germany became part of the Federal Republic, accepting the constitution and laws of the Federal Republic. The monetary union between East and West Germany included the East in the German mark currency area, and East German citizens were allowed to exchange their East German marks for German marks at generous exchange rates. East German citizens were given all voting rights, and the former East German states were represented in the German parliament, according to the same rules and requirements as the West German states.

The integration of the former German Democratic Republic into the Federal Republic of Germany created the largest European nation. These two formerly distinct nations now occupy a land area of approximately 350,000 square kilometers, and in 1997 they had a total population of 81 million. Germany now has a land area roughly two-thirds that of France and a population some 22 million greater.

Origins of the Social Market Economy

The social market economy originated in the immediate postwar years. Its intellectual heritage can be traced to the so-called Freiburg school of neoliberalism, headed by Walter Eucken and Alfred Muller-Armack.[76] The Freiburg school believed that the state should play an active role in ensuring the workability of the competitive market system and that the market system should serve as the major instrument for allocating resources. The state should be prepared to intervene, however, to achieve necessary social goals. Intervention should be compatible with the underlying market order; thus policies that disrupt the working of the market, such as direct orders and price freezes, should be avoided.

The political background of the social market economy can be traced to the immediate postwar years of Allied occupation. The initial Allied policy was to continue the wartime controls. Until 1947 its objective was to enforce payment of reparations and to destroy the German military industry potential. When the emphasis turned to rehabilitation and recovery, direct controls were dismantled and the running of the country's economy was gradually returned to German hands. Ludwig Erhard, the minister of economics during the Adenauer years, was a proponent of the teachings of the Freiburg school. He strongly favored decontrol, deregulation, and the turning of economic decisions over to the impersonal hands of the market.[77] The choice of market versus plan was heatedly debated, the social democrats favoring strong state planning. Memories of the chaos of the inflationary 1920s and the depression of the 1930s convinced many German politicians of the dangers of a market economy. Two major political events signaled the return to market resource allocation: the Currency Reform and Price Reform of June 1948 and the passage of the Basic Law (Grundgesetz) of the Federal Republic in May 1949, the latter serving as the German constitution. Those events established the principle of the sanctity of private property, which was to serve as the foundation of economic policy in the postwar era.

In contrast to the United States, where national economic goals (with the exception of full employment) are unwritten, the economic goals of the Federal Republic have been written into law. These goals are price stability, a stable currency, full employment, balance-of-payments equilibrium, and stable economic growth. Three social goals, closely associated with the notion of the social market economy, are also identified: social equity, social security, and social progress. The social goals provided much of the basis for state intervention in economic affairs in the Federal Republic.[78]

Characteristics of the Social Market Economy

The principal features of the social market economy have evolved over the years. The first principle is the sanctity of private property. The second is that resource allocation should follow the dictates of the market unless there is a serious conflict with national social objectives. There is no significant planning apparatus in Germany, and the macroplanning that does exist works through traditional monetary and fiscal policy, with principal emphasis on monetary policy as carried out by the central bank (the *Bundesbank*).[79] German fiscal policy coordinates the budgets of the different levels of government. Unlike the United States, where fiscal policy is the responsibility of the federal government, the German "stability law" sets up a Business Cycle Commission *(Konjunkturrat)* and Finance Planning Commission *(Finanzplanungsrat)* to coordinate the federal, state, and local budgets for fiscal policy goals. In the area of monetary policy, German policymakers were never strongly caught up in the Keynesian revolution. The Bundesbank is more politically independent than the American Federal Reserve, and a country that has experienced hyperinflation is more likely to see inflation as a monetary phenomenon. Monetarism has been a long-run feature of German macropolicy. The economic forecasting of macroeconomic variables is a relatively recent phenomenon and is done by semi-independent research institutes, which serve as consultants for the federal government. In fact, a striking characteristic of Germany is the virtual absence of planning machinery at the federal level.

In view of the emphasis the Freiburg school placed on the state's responsibility to ensure the workability of competition, it is informative to see what procompetition arrangements emerged. Government policies in favor of competition are based on the anticartel law of 1957.

The Law Against Limitations on Competition *(Gesetz gegen Wettbewerbsbeschränkungen)* differs from American antitrust legislation. First, the German law is quite specific, and the courts have played a relatively minor role in interpreting the law. Second, the German law singles out labor unions as a clear exception to the anticartel rule. Labor is recognized as being unlike other commodities, and labor's right to form unions is clearly affirmed. Third, the German law uses both the *Verbotsprinzip* (outright prohibition) and the option to correct market abuses. Horizontal cartel contracts and agreements are illegal outright, whereas firms that occupy market-dominating positions are merely subject to the control and scrutiny of the cartel authorities. The law provides detailed definitions of "market-dominating" firms based on market shares (33 percent single-firm concentration ratio), financial power, and barriers to entry. Cartel authorities are supposed to disallow mergers if the merger produces a market-dominating firm.

The Law Against Limitations on Competition allows exceptions and exemptions that appear to contradict the basic principles of the social market economy. Agricultural, credit, insurance, transportation, rebate, "structural crisis," and "rationalization" cartels are exempt from the cartel laws. A "structural crisis" cartel is permitted when there has been a long-term decline in demand that requires the creation of a cartel to salvage an industry. A "rationalization" cartel can be formed when a cartel is deemed necessary to introduce new technologies into the industry. Critics point out that cartel authorities are in the position of having to judge whether a structural crisis exists or whether a new technology will be introduced only if a cartel is formed. This practice tends to lessen competition during economic downturns.[80]

The state actively limits competition in a number of areas on the basis of its social responsibilities to the public. Examples of such interventions are strict state regulation of business hours, state support of minimum-price legislation for brand-name articles, rent controls, laws that give renters virtual property rights, and government rules on the firing of employees, none of which is very unusual by European standards.

One type of state activity should be singled out—the extensive role played by state *(Länder)* governments in managing the occupational training of young workers. The chambers of commerce allocate young people into apprenticeships in industry and establish rules whereby local industries are responsible for the training of young workers, at the expense of these industries.

Social Correctives of the Market Economy

In the Federal Republic, social correctives of market resource allocations are actively pursued in cases of conflict between private economic decision making and national social objectives. Such social correctives occur in five major areas: (1) the security of employment, (2) the protection of employees, (3) insurance against the risks that workers run, (4) improvement of the distribution of income, and (5) other measures that have a significant impact on social policy.

The first three instances are typical of most industrialized capitalist countries and involve programs of employment services; protection against dangerous employment conditions and protection of teen-age workers; unemployment, hospitalization, and accident insurance; and so on. The unusual aspects of the German case are that such programs were instituted so early (under Bismarck in 1881) and that they are so comprehensive in contemporary terms.

The German welfare state is highly developed and rapidly expanding. State expenditures as a share of GDP rose from 32.5 percent in 1960 to about 50 percent in the 1990s. The share of GDP that social expenditures represent rose in the same time period from 21 percent to about one-third. Between 1960 and the 1990s, expenditures for the state health insurance system rose by a factor of 10. Critics of the rising share of government expenditures point to the inefficiencies that such government programs eventually produce.

Correctives aimed at improving the distribution of income are more unusual. In Germany, progressive income taxes are not the principal vehicle for making the market-determined distribution of income more equitable. Rather, the objective has been to use other instruments—the promotion of asset formation among lower-income groups, direct transfer payments (examples include child allowances and subsidization of rental payments), and direct state intervention (government funding of public housing and obligatory health insurance). Finally, the state has supported programs to allow workers to share in the profits of their enterprises as well as to have a say in the conduct of enterprise affairs (codetermination), all of which may affect the real distribution of income.

Let us first consider state policies to promote capital formation in general and savings of lower-income groups in particular. In some instances, the state supplements the savings of low-income families through a schedule of premiums, especially for savings, that cannot be withdrawn for seven or more years. Savings for home purchases receive similar treatment, and employer contributions to employee life insurance or other savings programs receive favorable tax treatment. These two features, in addition to government programs to ensure workers' access to the distribution of enterprise profits, seek to render even the lower-paid workers less dependent on their wage income. Earnings from assets should serve as income supplements. A side benefit of such pro–capital-accumulation (and anticonsumption) policies is to encourage a high domestic savings rate and a higher domestic growth rate.

In addition to these policies to promote capital formation even among working families, the income distribution is made more nearly equal by direct government interventions. A prime example is the fact that most apartment construction in contemporary Germany is funded (or sponsored) by state organizations for the purpose of making low-cost housing available to lower-income groups.

Codetermination and Labor Unions

A key aspect of government social policy is codetermination *(Mitbestimmung)*. **Codetermination** means having worker representatives on the boards of directors of corporations. The objective of this policy is "industrial democracy," or forcing management to take workers' interests into consideration when making policy. Initially applied only to selected industries, codetermination has applied to nearly all industry since German law was revised in 1976.[81] Firms with 2,000 or more employees fall under the codetermination legislation. A separate codetermination law applies to the coal, iron, and steel industries.

According to the law, stockholders and workers should have an equal number of representatives on the board of directors. For example, if the board consists of twelve members, six should represent the stockholders and six, the employees. Of the latter, two must be representatives of the labor union, and at least one must be a "leading employee" (such as a foreman). The codetermination law requires the election of a chairman *(Vorsitzender)* of the board of directors. In the absence of a majority, the chairman is elected by the representatives of the stockholders. In this way, the codetermination law seeks to avoid a stalemate by giving the chairman the deciding vote in the case of an evenly split board. Although labor and stockholders appear to have parity on the board of directors, the stockholders actually have the advantage because of the way the chairman is selected and because "leading employees" often side with the stockholders.

The 1976 regulations are still being tested in the German courts. Because codetermination rules call for a nearly equal labor voice, they call into question the protection of private property guaranteed in the German constitution. Another objection raised to the codetermination legislation is that it puts labor representatives on both sides of the collective bargaining table and thus gives labor an unfair advantage. In steel industry negotiations, however, labor representatives on the management boards have sided with management against the steel workers' demand for a 35-hour work-week. It is not obvious, therefore, how labor representatives will behave when they in effect join management.

The codetermination law gives labor a voice in major policy decisions, but the board of directors rarely deals with shop-level issues. The Enterprise Constitution Law *(Betriebsverfassungsgesetz*, or BVG) of 1972 gives labor a voice in shop-floor decisions. The BVG requires the election of an enterprise council in enterprises that employ five or more workers; "leading employees" are not eligible for election to that council. The enterprise council has codetermination responsibilities in the following areas: wages, length of the working day, firings, and layoffs. The influence of the enterprise council is strongest in personnel areas; every termination requires the approval of the enterprise council.

The BVG law of 1972, on paper at least, substantially constrains management in the area of personnel decisions. How the law works in practice remains to be fully researched. It is not yet known whether most enterprises actually follow the letter of the BVG law. Also, its effect on productivity remains to be measured. On the positive side, worker participation may boost worker loyalty and enthusiasm and reduce turnover; on the negative side, worker participation may prevent management from making necessary personnel changes.

Labor and Collective Bargaining

The right of workers to join together to form trade unions is recognized in the German constitution and the cartel laws. Workers have the freedom to contract with management or management organizations through collective bargaining. The "closed shop" (wherein all workers must belong to the union) is not allowed in Germany. The percentage of the labor force belonging to unions in Germany is more than 40 percent, much higher than the current American ratio of less than one in five. German unions are organized on an industry basis to prevent competition among individual unions for members. German unions are grouped into federations, the most important being the German Federation of Unions *(Deutscher Gewerkschaftsbund)*, which accounts for 84 percent of all union membership.

Collective bargaining between unions and management generally proceeds at a relatively high level. Unions have the right to strike, and management has the right to lock workers out *(Aussperrungen)* or close down firms in which workers are striking. The volume of strikes is relatively low in Germany (58 days per 1,000 workers per year for the period 1970–1979), but management has been willing to respond to strikes with lockouts. For example, 1971 and 1978 were years of relatively high strike activity in Germany. In both years, the number of workdays lost through lockouts was about two-thirds of the number of workdays lost through strikes. German labor laws do not require compulsory arbitration, but it is commonly used to settle stalemates. Once unions and management agree to arbitration, they must hold their peace. Arbitration proposals are not binding, but they impose strong psychological pressure on the parties to agree.

The low frequency of strikes in Germany and the relatively low nominal wage increases agreed to by unions in the postwar period point to comparatively successful labor–management relations in postwar Germany. Many factors could contribute to this success: the codetermination laws, the role of the enterprise council, and the traditional German fear of inflation.

An interesting feature of German social policy is the notion that problems of income distribution should not be solved by collective bargaining on wages by unions and management. Although German workers are organized into powerful unions and the German social democratic party is strongly influenced by organized labor, collective bargaining in Germany has been more quiescent than in other European countries. Whether the government's social policies can be credited for this or whether fear of inflation is at the root we cannot determine, but the failure of German unions to be more demanding has probably been an important factor in the lower rates of inflation in Germany.

Public Enterprise

The role of public enterprise is greater in Germany than in the United States. Not only do state enterprises dominate transportation, communication, and the construction of apartment dwellings, but there is also significant state participation in mining and metallurgy.[82] In some cases, government participation is indirect (as in the recent case of the Krupp industries); in others it is carried out through holding companies. Nevertheless, one cannot cite government enterprises as a unique feature of the German social and market economy, for it is quite typical of Europe in general.

In fact, at least prior to the 1980s, the German experience with nationalization was the reverse of the British experience. In Germany, the emphasis was on denationalization *(Privatisierung)*. The Federal Treasury Ministry *(Bundesschatzministerium)* was established in 1957 to deal with public enterprises. It was set up not as an instrument of central management but rather to lay the foundations for denationalization. The management of public enterprises has typically been decentralized to the enterprise itself. Two methods of denationalization have been used: (1) the sale of formerly public enterprises to private persons or private groups and (2) social **denationalization**, which is achieved by establishing a new type of equity, the so-called popular share, to be sold to low-income citizens on a preferential basis. The main denationalizations were those carried out at Volkswagen and Veba.

Union-owned and -organized enterprises represent a mix of public and private enterprise. For example, the union-owned *Gruppe Neue Heimat* was once the largest European apartment construction firm, the *Bank für Gemeinwirtschaft* is the fourth-largest German interregional bank, and the *Coop-Unternehmen* forms the second-largest retail trade organization in Germany. Officially, these firms were founded to serve the common good, not to maximize profits.

Germany: Unification

The **unification** of the German Democratic Republic (GDR) with the Federal Republic of Germany (FRG), an event of major political and economic significance, took place in May of 1990. Prior to unification, the GDR was a centrally planned socialist economic system patterned after the Soviet economy. The new German economy is therefore an economy formed through the unification of what were two very different economic systems.[83]

This section offers a brief analysis of the systemic arrangements of the former GDR. It also discusses the two economies on the eve of unification and examines the process of unification and the problems of integrating the former GDR into the market economic system of the FRG.

The GDR as a Planned Socialist Economic System   The FRG and the GDR prior to unification provided a case study of the differences between capitalism and socialism. This comparison was especially fruitful because the two countries were similar in most dimensions *except* the economic system and economic policies.

1. The two economies had, at the end of the war, a very similar stock of human capital and an essentially homogeneous population.
2. They had shared traditions, culture, and tastes.
3. At the outbreak of World War II, the FRG and the GDR were roughly equivalent in per capita income, per capita industrial output, and foreign trade patterns.

If there were similarities, however, there were also differences, some of which affected economic outcomes in the postwar period.

1. The GDR was a much smaller economy (the population of the GDR was roughly 25 percent of that of the FRG) at the end of the war. This proportion declined further, in part because of the "republic flight" (the ongoing loss of population from the GDR to the FRG, between 1945 and 1961, which varied annually from 144,000 to 365,000).
2. The resource base of the GDR was inferior. Nevertheless, lignite coal was relatively abundant for fuel and for generation of electricity. And with a smaller population, the GDR had a more favorable ratio of population to land.
3. Approximately 50 percent of the GDR's industrial capacity was destroyed by the end of the war, compared with 25 percent of the FRG's. And whereas the GDR was making reparation payments in the early postwar period, the FRG benefited from assistance under the Marshall Plan. (At the same time, the FRG eventually paid out to the FRG some 33 billion marks in *Wiedergutmaching* payments, a sum double the amount of Marshall Plan aid.)

The Soviet model was introduced into the GDR after the war, and by the end of the 1940s, virtually all industry, banking, and transportation had been nationalized and were functioning under a system of central planning. Collectivization in agriculture began seriously in the early 1950s and was completed by the end of the decade. The only private ownership that survived was in some retail trade and in handicrafts.

The model of planning and management introduced into the GDR after the war was basically the same as the Soviet administrative-command model. The Communist party dictated priorities to a state planning commission, which, in conjunction with ministries, established binding plans to govern enterprise operations. As in the Soviet Union, the system of balances was used for planning.

Beginning in the early 1960s, the GDR introduced the New Economic System to decentralize some decision making to groups of state enterprises. The objective was to improve lagging economic performance through limited devolution of planning authority. The New Economic System was abandoned in the early 1970s.

As in the Soviet administrative command model, emphasis was on economic growth through high investment in industry. Moreover, policies in agriculture were similar to those in the Soviet Union, and the GDR was integrated into the Eastern COMECON system.

The FRG and the GDR on the Eve of Unification   During the 1960s and 1970s, the East German economy was regarded as the most successful of the centrally planned economies. According to many statistical sources, its growth was close to that of the West German economy—one of the world's leading economic performers—and its GDP and living standard gaps *vis-à-vis* West Germany did not appear to be great. Moreover, neither the East German population nor its labor force was growing, so its economic growth was of the rare "intensive" variety.

Table 11.3 provides summary information about the East German and West German economies on the eve of reunification. These figures show that in the last nearly 20 years of separation, the GDR grew at a slightly slower pace, that West German living standards were much higher, and that West German families had more financial wealth.

The enthusiasm with which the general East German population accepted reunification suggests that official statistics understated the economic differences between the "old" and the "new" federal states. Moreover, reunification exposed the weaknesses of GDR enterprises in a market setting: They were geared to supply the Soviet market, their labor staffing was inefficient, and their attention to the environment was wanting.

Unification and Transition   West German laws were transferred east by treaty, and in 1990, the Deutschmark replaced the East German Ostmark, prices were freed, and trading arrangements were relaxed. The *Treuhandanstalt* (**Federal Privatizing Trust**) held all the shares of East German firms (which were converted into joint-stock companies) and assumed responsibility for privatization. Much of the transition process in the former GDR focused on the issue of privatization.

The Treuhand was more than a mechanism to hold the shares of formerly state-owned firms. The Treuhand was set up to be responsible for assembling the talent necessary to value and restructure, or to liquidate these firms. Valuation proved very difficult. The most attractive firms found immediate buyers, but less attractive firms were faced with either liquidation or the need for interim support—another function of the Treuhand. In many cases, financial discipline could not be imposed. The loss

TABLE 11.3   The Federal Republic of Germany and the German Democratic
Republic: Selected Social and Economic Indicators, 1988

	Federal Republic of Germany	German Democratic Republic
Area and population		
Area (*in 1,000 square kilometers*)	249	108
Population (*millions*)	61.4	16.7
(*in percent of population*)		
Of working age	67.0[a]	65.0
Pensioners	18.5[a]	16.0
Employment		
Total employed (*in millions*)	27.4	9.0
(*in percent of population*)	44.5	53.9
Female employment (*in percent of total employment*)	38.1[a]	48.6
Employment by sector		
(*in percent of total*)		
Agriculture and forestry	4.0	10.8
Mining, manufacturing, and construction	39.8	47.1
Other sectors	56.2	42.1
Household income, consumption, and saving		
Average monthly gross earnings (*DM/M*)	3,850	1,270
Household saving (*in percent of disposable income*)	12.8	7.1
Households with:		
(*in percent of total*)		
Automobile	97	52
Color television	94	52
Telephone	98	7[b]
GDP and prices		
(*Annual real growth rate, 1970–1989*)		
GDP	3.1	2.3
Consumer prices (*annual percent rate of change, 1980–1988*)	2.9	—
External trade in goods		
(*in percent of total exports*)		
Exports to state-trading countries	4.4	69.5
Imports from state-trading countries	4.7	68.7
Trade balance		
(*in percent of GNP/NMP*)	6.0	1.0
Of which: State-trading countries	0.2	1.0
Monetary accounts of households		
Household financial assets[c] (*billions DM/M*)	1,196.6	167.2
Velocity of money[d]	1.11	0.97

[a] 1987.
[b] 1985.
[c] Currency and bank deposits. Year-end for the FRG and year average for the GDR.
[d] Private disposable income divided by household financial assets.

Sources: Statistisches Bundesamt, *Statistisches Jahrbuch der Bundesrepublik Deutschland,* 1989; Staatliche Zentralverwaltung für Statistik der DDR, *Statistisches Jahrbuch der DDR, 1989;* and Deutsche Bundesbank; *Handbook of Economic Statistics, 1991,* p. 37.

of markets combined with the fact that wages in the former GDR had been sustained at inappropriately high levels, led to a surge in unemployment. Unemployment grew from roughly 1.6 percent in June of 1990 to almost 15 percent by 1996, a major cost to be borne by the new unified German economy.[84]

Germany in the 1990s: The End of the Economic Miracle?

The reunification of Germany created the largest European state in terms of both population and GDP. Other European countries feared that a powerhouse had been created that would overwhelm and dominate the rest of Europe. This fear of the German behemoth, perhaps, caused the other countries of Europe to welcome the creation of a single European economy, the European Union and the European Monetary Union.

The German economy, since reunification, has had more than its share of economic problems. First, German unemployment, which in the 1950s and 1960s had been less than one percent of the labor force, exceeded 10 percent in the mid-1990s. Second, German economic growth faltered after reunification. Its average growth rate from 1990 to 1996 was a meager 1.6 percent per annum. Third, Germany's inflation rate averaged 3 percent during this same period—a rate high by German postwar standards and no better than that of the United States during the same period. Fourth, the German government deficit, as a percentage of GDP, rose to 4 percent and above, the consequences of rising state deficits during the 1990s.

What were the causes of this faltering economic performance? Are the causes temporary and associated with the world business cycle, or are Germany's problems more deep-rooted? To what extent are they the consequence of the German reunification?

The Costs and Mistakes of Reunification

On a theoretical level, it would appear that the integration of the former command economy of the East into the market economy of the West would be a fairly simple matter. One of the major difficulties of transition from command economy to market economy is the need to create the institutions of a market economy. In the case of German reunification, West German institutions were transferred *en masse* to the new German federal states in the east. Businesspeople and investors did not have to worry about the legislative and legal structures under which they were to operate. Other signs for optimism were the relatively high levels of education of the East German population and the rather small gap in living standard suggested by the official statistics.

Even so, for a number of reasons, the transition of the new East German federal states proved to be more difficult than anticipated.

First, as we have noted, because of political pressure from German labor unions and from the new German states themselves, wage rates in the east were set roughly equivalent to those in the west, despite growing evidence of large productivity differentials. This action meant that the less efficient eastern labor force was priced out of the market and high rates of unemployment in the east were created.

Second, German financial authorities agreed to allow the exchange of East German marks for Deutschmarks at a rate of one to one for most savings. It was hoped that the reunification of the East German economy with the West German economy would add production of consumer goods roughly equal to the increased supply of Deutschmarks that had to be created to convert eastern savings. In fact, the German money supply increased substantially without much of an increase in real goods and services. This accounts for the increase in the German inflation rate that accompanied reunification.

Third, the provisions of the extensive German welfare state were applied *in toto* to the new eastern federal states. Eastern citizens received the same welfare, pension, and unemployment benefits as those in the west. The additional benefits exerted pressure on the German state budget and raised German deficits as a percent of GDP. The higher deficits were accompanied by higher German interest rates, which represent German economic growth.

Fourth, the process of privatizing East German enterprises proved more difficult than had been anticipated.

1. The privatization process had to deal first with the issue of *claims* from past confiscation of property. Accordingly, the privatization process was slower and substantially more complex.
2. The technological state of industry in the former GDR proved to be far lower than anticipated.
3. There was substantial concentration in the existing industrial structure on activities designed to supply an administrative-command economy, not a market economy. A good portion of East German enterprises would never be viable in a market economy.
4. The social costs of privatization were higher than anticipated. In addition to the need for direct financial support of the transition, the issues of unemployment, retraining, inflation, and the like have made defining a new social contract difficult.

The Limits of Consensus

The German social market economy was designed to operate on the basis of consensus among employers, employees, and government. The difficulties the German economy has encountered in the 1990s have raised questions about the limits of consensus. Is it possible for an advanced industrialized economy to operate efficiently on the basis of consensus?

The German consensus model created a massive welfare state with generous provisions for unemployment, retirement, and medical care. Workers work fewer days per year in Germany than in any other advanced industrialized economy, given their liberal holiday and vacation system. Wage negotiations are carried out at the national level, rather than at the local level, thereby depriving the wage-setting process of the flexibility to consider local conditions (such as the lower productivity in the new eastern federal states). The consensus model has also created a system of protection of declining industries, such as coal mining and agriculture, to reduce the social costs of economic change.

The German consensus also is very expensive. It is paid for by high marginal rates of income taxation (which exceed 50 percent) and by social security payroll taxes that approach 50 percent. In addition, Germany has a national value-added tax that increases the overall tax burden.

All these factors have combined to make the German worker among the most expensive in the world economy. Despite the German worker's relatively high productivity, the cost of German labor has become excessive, and legal restrictions on labor staffing and firings and layoffs have deprived German employers of the means to raise German labor productivity further.

Although Germany has been ruled by a conservative coalition since 1984 (German Chancellor Helmut Kohl is now the longest-serving government leader in Europe), the German political structure makes it exceedingly difficult to attack vested interests. Kohl's attempts in 1997 to reduce coal subsidies were repulsed by an angry attack by miners. The effort of one of Germany's largest steel makers to merge with another in 1997 was again repulsed by angry workers who felt their jobs would be threatened by such a move.

Although we cannot determine whether Germany's economic problems of the 1990s are cyclical, structural, or temporary (associated with the absorption of the new eastern federal states), we can say that Germany will continue to test the limits of its consensus model.

Sweden: The Capitalist Welfare State

The Swedish economic system and its performance are of interest to many for a single but vitally important reason. Sweden was able, over an extended period of time, to sustain economic progress through the efficiency of the market while implementing an egalitarian distribution of income typical of a welfare state. Although the past three decades were a challenge to Sweden, nevertheless the Swedish system continued to be admired by many as a "middle way" to economic reform and change. This focus remains important, though in recent years, many have questioned the long-term viability of Swedish arrangements. Indeed, changes have altered substantially the Swedish economic system in the 1990s.

As with other system variants, it is useful to examine the nature of economic outcomes in the Swedish case and the forces that influence these outcomes, specifically the environmental setting, the systemic or organizational arrangements of the Swedish economy, and Swedish economic policies.[85]

Sweden: The Setting

Sweden is a relatively small but highly industrialized country. It has a total area of roughly 450,000 square kilometers (somewhat larger than the state of California), and it had a population of just over 8.5 million in 1995. As of 1995, Sweden had a per capita GDP of almost $24,000 measured in U.S. dollars among the highest in

Europe. The bulk of this income is derived from industry and services; agriculture plays a very small role.

Since World War II, Sweden has experienced a long period of economic progress based on the development of its resources (timber, hydroelectric energy, and iron ore) with major reliance on a market economy and participation in foreign trade. During the 1960s, the growth of real GDP in Sweden was 5.3 percent per annum, among the highest growth rates in Europe. Historically, long-term growth has generally been higher in Sweden than in other European countries. It was Sweden's rapid growth over a long period of time that created Sweden's postwar affluence. Foreign trade is of vital importance to Sweden. In recent years, foreign trade turnover (exports plus imports) has accounted for more than 70 percent of GDP, a very high proportion by international standards.

Sweden is the prototype of a developed industrial society that has a significant involvement in foreign trade and a high standard of living based on an educated labor force functioning largely in an urban, industrial setting. It is a system, however, that has combined market efficiency with an egalitarian distribution of income in a democratic political setting.

The Swedish Welfare State

We have emphasized that the Swedish economy achieved a high level of output based on a good growth record. Although productivity growth was substantial in the 1960s, the decades after the 1960s brought this rapid growth in productivity to an end and presented a challenge to be faced in the 1990s. This challenge was serious: A system with declining economic performance simply could not support the pace at which private and public standards of living had been growing. Moreover, many began to question whether Sweden had really achieved compatibility between efficiency and equity.

Although the role of the state in influencing distribution can be measured in a variety of ways, a few basic numbers illustrate the Swedish case. The Swedish economy is predominantly a private-enterprise economy in production, but a very different picture emerges when we examine the distribution of the product. For example, in the late 1980s, fully 26 percent of aggregate demand was that of government, compared to 20 percent in the United States and 9 percent in Japan. For the same year, total government expenditure in Sweden accounted for 40.8 percent of GDP; the comparable figure for the United States was 22.9 percent.[86]

Who receives the benefits of Swedish government spending? Not surprisingly, housing, public amenities, social security, and welfare accounted for fully 54.2 percent of government spending in 1988—more than 20 percentage points greater than the equivalent sort of spending in the United States. Education also commands a much greater share of government spending in Sweden than in the United States, though the Swedish share of defense spending is much lower. Surprisingly, health accounted for a modest 1.1 percent of central government spending in 1988, compared to 12.5 percent in the United States.

Major government programs in Sweden are financed by major taxes. In 1988, total central government revenue in Sweden accounted for 42.9 percent of GDP; the

comparable figure for the United States was 19.7 percent, and for the United Kingdom 36.4 percent. In addition to this much larger role for the state in Sweden, the
sources of government revenue also differ significantly. In 1988, taxes on income,
profits, and capital gains accounted for only 17.8 percent of Swedish central government revenue; the comparable figure for the United States was a whopping 51.5
percent. Social security contributions claim a high and similar share in both countries,
but Sweden relies heavily on taxes on goods and services. This category accounts for
29.0 percent of central government revenue in Sweden, compared to a paltry 3.6 percent in the United States.

Possibly the ultimate test of state policies designed to redistribute income is
the actual distribution outcomes. In this area, the impact of the welfare state does
show up in the Swedish case. On the basis of household income for the mid-1980s,
the lowest-earning 20 percent of households in Sweden received 8 percent of all
household income, whereas the top-earning 20 percent of households received
26.9 percent of income. Comparable figures for the United States are 4.7 and 41.9
percent, respectively.[87]

Sweden: The Economic System

The Swedish economy is a market economy based largely on private ownership but
wherein the state plays a major role as an agent of income redistribution. Although
there have been important changes, the nature of the Swedish economic system is
more complex and deserves additional attention.

1. Sweden's resource base dictates to a large measure economic outcomes. Sweden,
    as a small country that needs to import fossil fuels, must be a major player in world
    markets. Moreover, with a highly educated labor force, one would expect a pro-
    duction structure and economic policies appropriate to the available factor mix.
2. The essence of the Swedish model is the setting of social democracy, a system
    where, as one observer put it, a complementary rather than a competitive rela-
    tionship exists between the competitive and the cooperative aspects of social
    existence.[88] Thus, in terms of goals and the means through which goals will be
    achieved, the views of the population are articulated through participation in a
    variety of groups such as unions, clubs, and the like.
3. Within the framework of social democracy, market information is shared in such
    a way that the process is viewed as contributing to social gain for most if not all
    of the population. Thus, in the sphere of labor allocation, the Swedish economy
    is viewed as having a very active labor market in which labor mobility is critical
    to the effective allocation of labor. At the same time, the existence of industry-
    wide collective agreements preserves a measure of control over wage increases
    that is designed to promote both economic growth and stability.
4. Employees can participate in enterprise management, at least on an advisory
    basis, through worker councils. In addition, workers can participate in ownership
    through employee investment funds—a mechanism to, in effect, convert profits

into employee ownership. Employee ownership is controversial, but its basic thrust is to create harmony between the interests of worker and enterprise.

5. The Swedish state is an active participant in the economy through the use of traditional tools of monetary and fiscal policy, which is especially important in an open economy.

6. Sweden maintains an egalitarian distribution of income largely through transfers of various types, providing generous benefits for retirement, medical care, education, and the like. These programs, and Sweden's continuing commitment to full employment, create an environment of substantial economic security.

Performance: An End to the Swedish Model?

A key theme in this book has been how various systems responded to the economic challenges of the 1970s, 1980s, and 1990s. We have emphasized that most economies of Europe experienced difficulty during these times.

The Swedish economy was no exception. Indeed, the problems of the 1970s and 1980s led many to question whether the Swedish model had outlived its usefulness. Simply put, the energy shocks of the 1970s increased domestic costs, which, along with poor productivity performance, led to an erosion of the Swedish position in external markets. But the government followed a policy of expanding deficits, which in turn stimulated inflation. Although it was more complex than this simple description suggests, the situation appeared to many to illustrate a case where planners failed to find the appropriate policy mix, rather than betraying any fundamental problems in the Swedish system. Some, however, argued that more basic changes were at work.

In a survey of the Swedish model published in 1985, Erik Lundberg noted that in addition to failures of stabilization policies, support for the social democrats became more fragmented, and policy objectives were contradictory.[89] A theme noted by Lundberg and other observers was the conflict between existing wage-setting arrangements and the continued drive for an egalitarian distribution of income— a conflict that squeezed profits and limited the attractiveness of investment, while at the same time generating low levels of unemployment in largely artificial and noncompetitive ways. Finally, Lundberg emphasized the changing nature of the international economy, a setting where Sweden faced increasingly limited policy options and a greater need to conform to policies of other major countries. In essence, the problems were more than simply policy mistakes incorporating basic elements of the Swedish system.

From the vantage point of the late 1990s, it is evident that the early and mid-1980s marked a major turning point for the Swedish economy. During that time, the Swedish economy fundamentally changed course, partly in response to a severe recession but also because of the basic changes in Swedish society and its long pursuit of the welfare state.[90]

The evidence presented in Table 11.4, illustrates the direction of change in the economy. In the past, the Swedish economy experienced modest growth, low levels

TABLE 11.4   Sweden: Contemporary Performance

	1980–1991	1991	1992	1993	1994	1995	1996
GDP (% change)	2.0[a]	−1.7	−1.7	−2.8	1.2	2.5	1.8
Unemployment (%)	—	2.9	5.3	8.0	8.7	8.6	8.8
Consumer Price Index (% change)	7.4[b]	9.4[c]	2.3	4.6	1.9	2.7	−0.4
Current Account Deficit	—	20.3	29.9	—	36.7	59.5	—

[a] Average annual
[b] Average annual rate of inflation
[c] Year to year

Sources: Data for 1980–1991 from World Bank, *World Development Report 1993* (New York: Oxford University Press, 1993), various tables; remaining data from *The Swedish Economy Autumn 1993* (Stockholm: National Institute of Economic Research, 1993), 6; *The Economist*, "Financial Indicators."

of unemployment, high rates of inflation, and a sustained negative current-account balance. The system relied on fiscal and monetary controls and an income policy that provided a close relationship between wage increases and productivity growth.

Since the late 1980s, the economy shifted away from a high-inflation–low-unemployment posture to a more traditional monetarist perspective that relied increasingly on market mechanisms to allocate resources. In 1991, a new coalition of four conservative parties ousted the long-ruling social democrats from power. The new coalition was elected on pledges to cut taxes and reduce the welfare state. A weakened social-democratic party returned to power in 1994, ruling as a minority coalition. Controls were reduced, real interest rates were allowed to rise significantly, which has resulted in a growing government budget deficit, a redistribution of income in favor of wealthier families, and a shrinking of domestic demand. In addition, changes were introduced to shift the economy away from public consumption, especially at the local government level, through changes in the social insurance system.

During the latter years of increasingly serious economic reform in the planned socialist economic systems, the Swedish model was often cited as a potentially attractive model that seemed to combine efficiency with a socialist view of equity. Contemporary changes now imply that this model has become as vulnerable as the planned socialist model and that markets have become the future path for both in the next century.

Growth or Eurosclerosis?

We have completed our examination of four European countries: France, Germany, the United Kingdom, and Sweden. Do they, in varying fashion and in varying degrees, represent a "European" model?

Despite their differences, the four mature European economies do have similar features that appear to qualify them to be called a "model."

1. They all have extensive safety nets that provide income and employment security as a part of a comprehensive welfare state.
2. The role and size of the state, as measured by the state's share of resources and the state's intrusion into economic life, are great.
3. Although these economies have tried to reduce its role, state enterprise is still an important fact of life.
4. There is a tendency to protect vested interests from economic change, through subsidization and protective legislation.
5. These societies have been stable for more than a half-century, so strong vested-interest groups have formed.

Mancur Olson, beginning with his study of the decline of Great Britain, raised the question of whether the mature industrialized European economies would succumb to what he called Eurosclerosis. If Eurosclerosis were allowed to proceed, Olson predicted that European growth would stagnate over the long term as a consequence of paralysis imposed by special vested interests. Olson warned that in stable mature economies there is a tendency for distributional coalitions to form that engage in monopoly rent seeking. Stable mature economies can therefore be dominated by monopolies, cartels, powerful labor unions, and the like, which are interested in maximizing their share of economic output at the expense of others.

Europe in the mid-1990s bears a resemblance to Olson's Eurosclerotic states: Vested interests support the status quo of a heavy tax burden, the continuation of subsidies, the imposition of rigid work rules, and the perquisites of the welfare state. Vested interests continue to dominate industrial life, the old guard being awarded management of newly privatized enterprises. One of the most powerful interest groups—the employed—continue to demand rules that prevent them from becoming unemployed, thereby reducing the flexibility of managers to restructure their businesses.

Can Europe's declining growth of the 1990s be attributed to Eurosclerosis and can Eurosclerosis be reversed? The example of Great Britain under Thatcher can perhaps be characterized as an attack on Eurosclerosis—at least an attack on Britain's powerful trade unions. Britain's recovery after 1979, therefore, might be at least partially the result of Thatcher's assault on excessively high marginal tax rates, on irresponsible monetary policy, and on the power of trade unions.

The most powerful force against Eurosclerosis may be Europe's decision in 1991 to reduce and even eliminate differences among national markets by making the entirety of Europe one common market with one common currency. By 1999, Europe is supposed to have a single currency, the Euro, and to eliminate national currencies. In order to make Europe one single market, as the United States constitutes one single market, trade barriers must be eliminated, common monetary and fiscal policies must be enacted, and uniform policies of competition must be observed. Steps have already been taken to allow open access to national markets of enterprises from all member nations in air transport, telecommunications, and utilities.

If Europe does indeed create a single market, powerful forces will be set in motion to combat special interests within any particular nation. France will no longer be able to subsidize its state enterprises; inefficient companies from one country will not be able to survive competition with efficient enterprises from other countries. Germany's restrictive work rules will simply cause jobs to go to other European countries.

European experts believe that the creation of a single European market will indeed boost Europe's economic growth and enable it to achieve again the high growth rates of the 1950s and 1960s.

Summary

In this chapter we examined the European model—specifically, the contemporary experience of the advanced industrialized nations of Western Europe. The countries we discussed in this chapter are important to the systems analyst for several reasons. First, the industrialization of Europe differs in important ways from that of Asia. Second, the economic systems of Western Europe differ considerably one from another. Third, contemporary European economic performance has varied considerably from what we often expect in the United States. Finally, the move toward the creation of a single European market has dominated discussion of the 1990s and will continue to do so as we enter a new century.

We chose to examine four major West European economic systems: Great Britain, France, Germany, and Sweden. Significant systemic and policy differences among these cases shed light both on the European experience as a whole and on the extent to which system-specific characteristics can be varied to achieve differing national objectives.

For most of the systems we examined, the 1950s and 1960s were relatively tranquil decades without substantial "shocks." The 1970s and early 1980s were anything but tranquil, giving us an opportunity to examine these systems under shock—for example the energy crisis of the 1970s.

If it is reasonable to generalize, the focus of the 1980s and 1990s has been concern for the basic indicators of performance: economic growth, productivity, unemployment and—of great importance—the emergence of new trade patterns in the global economy of the 1990s. In addition to these concerns, the demise of the major planned socialist economic systems placed a new emphasis on the subtle yet possibly important differences among the systems we have examined—for example, the relevance of differing degrees of government intervention in the economy. Each of the cases we examined shed light on important system differences.

The economy of France is of interest for the use of indicative planning in a mature market-capitalist economy. Although the French attitude toward planning arrangements has changed over time, the planning system has survived. However, there is relatively little agreement on whether the French plan has been important in explaining the performance of the French economy. This disagreement reflects both methodological issues and the basic difficulties of associating performance differences with system differences.

The British economy is of interest as a mature economy in which the role of the state has always been important, not through a process of economic planning, but rather through public ownership and the budgetary process. Although past British economic performance has been modest, the conservative government of Margaret Thatcher significantly changed British economic policy and improved the performance of the economy. The Thatcher approach was based on the use of monetary policy, incentives and competitive markets, and privatization. Although critics question the costs associated with improved economic performance (for example, the persistent problem of unemployment), enterprise-level analysis of privatization is generally positive. But in the 1990s, the political power of Margaret Thatcher's successor (John Major) waned, and concern lingered about the eventual decline of the importance of North Sea oil in the British economic equation. In the era of a new Prime Minister (Tony Blair), domestic performance issues remain at the forefront but are definitively cast within the debate over a single European market.

Germany is usually described as a social market economy, because it has been characterized by a strong combination of government intervention and worker participation in a market economy. Traditionally, the German economy was viewed as an "economic miracle," though recent inflation and unemployment have tarnished this image. In the 1990s, the German economy has attempted to respond to the new European economic arrangements, but most important, it has also had to cope with the large costs of unification after the collapse of the German Democratic Republic (GDR).

For many observers, Sweden is the classic example of a welfare state in which an egalitarian distribution of benefits is achieved, the state playing a major role but the economy benefiting from the efficiency of market arrangements. In the 1990s there has been growing disillusionment with this model as performance has weakened, leading to increased questioning of the dominant role of government in the economy. At the same time, former socialist systems undergoing transition have looked to the Swedish model as a possible system variant.

Key Terms

the European model

indicative planning

mature capitalism

social market economy

welfare state

modernization commissions

European community

industrial policy

income policy

demand management

"stop-go" policies

nationalization

deregulation

privatization

codetermination

denationalization

unification

New Economic System

Federal Privatizing Trust

dual economy

share economy

Notes

1. Alexander Gerschenkron, *Economic Backwardness in Historical Perspective* (Cambridge, Mass: Harvard University Press, 1962); V. I. Lenin, *The Development of Capitalism in Russia* (Moscow: Foreign Languages Publishing House, 1956); Angus Maddison, *Phases of Capitalist Development* (Oxford, England: Oxford University Press, 1982); Angus Maddison, *Explaining the Economic Performance of Nations* (Cambridge, England: Cambridge University Press, 1995).

2. Nicolas Spulber, *Redefining the State: Privatization and Welfare Reform in Industrial and Transitional Economies* (Cambridge, England: Cambridge University Press, 1997).

3. Jeffrey Williamson, "Globalization, Convergence, and History," *Journal of Economic History* 56, 2 (June 1996), 227–305. Also see Stephen Broadberry, "Manufacturing and the Convergence Hypothesis: What the Long-Run Data Show," *Journal of Economic History* 53, 4 (December 1993), 772–795.

France

4. There is a large body of literature on the French economy. For an overview, see J. R. Hough, *The French Economy* (New York: Holmes & Meier, 1982); Stephen S. Cohen, *Modern Capitalist Planning: The French Model* (Berkeley: University of California Press, 1977); and Stephen S. Cohen and Peter A. Gourevitch, eds., *France in a Troubled World Economy* (Boston: Butterworth, 1982). For a discussion of the French economy and a survey of the literature on indicative planning, see Saul Estrin and Peter Holmes, *French Planning in Theory and Practice* (Boston: Allen and Unwin, 1983); for a survey of this period, see Bela Balassa, *The First Year of Socialist Government in France* (Washington, D.C.: American Enterprise Institute, 1982). For a discussion of planning institutions, see John and Anne Marie Hackett, *Economic Planning in France* (Cambridge, Mass.: Harvard University Press, 1963). For an examination of the effectiveness of French planning, see John H. McArthur and Bruce R. Scott, *Industrial Planning in France* (Boston: Graduate School of Business Administration, Harvard University, 1969). For a critical view, see Vera Lutz, *Central Planning for the Market Economy: An Analysis of the French Theory and Experience* (London: Longmans Green, 1969). For an in-depth treatment of French economic performance, see J.-J. Carre, P. Dubois, and E. Malinvaud, *French Economic Growth* (Stanford, Calif.: Stanford University Press, 1975); for an historical survey, see Richard F. Kuisel, *Capitalism and the State of Modern France* (New York: Cambridge University Press, 1981); for a recent discussion, see Bernard Cazes, "Indicative Planning in France," *Journal of Comparative Economics* 14, 4 (December 1990), 607–620; Klaus-Walter Riechel, "Indicative Planning in France: Discussion," *Journal of Comparative Economics* 14, 4 (December 1990), 621–624. For background, see Richard F. Kuisel, *Capitalism and the State in Modern France*; and Andrew Schonfield, *Modern Capitalism: The Changing Balance of Public and Private Power* (New York: Oxford University Press, 1965).

5. In market economic systems where planning has been introduced, and in planned economies where economic reform has meant the introduction of market forces, there have tended to be difficulties bringing the two different sorts of instruments together. This case has been argued in David Granick, "An Organizational Model of Soviet Industrial Planning," *Journal of Political Economy* 67 (1959), 123–124; for an analysis, see Benjamin N. Ward, *The Socialist Economy: A Study of Organizational Alternatives* (New York: Random House, 1967), pp. 178–181.

6. See, for example, the discussion in Saul Estrin and Peter Holmes, *French Planning in Theory and Practice*, Ch. 8.

7. This case is argued in Andrew Schonfield, *Modern Capitalism: The Changing Balance of Public and Private Power*, Ch. 5.

8. For a detailed examination of the growth of the public sector in different countries, see Frederic L. Pryor, *Public Expenditures in Communist and Capitalist Nations* (London: Allen and Unwin, 1968); D. Cameron, "The Expansion of the Public Economy: A Comparative Analysis," *American Political Science Review* 92 (1978), 1243–1261; and Frank Gould, "The Development of Public Expenditures in Western Industrialized Countries: A Comparative Analysis," *Public Finance* 38, 1 (1983), 38–69.

9. Schonfield, *Modern Capitalism*, pp. 156–157.

10. The importance of technical planning experts in different planning efforts has been emphasized: a major role in the French case, a minimal role in the British case. For a comparison, see ibid., pp. 155–156.

11. The differing national styles of executive development have been examined in David Granick, *The European Executive* (New York: Doubleday, 1962). For a recent comparative analysis, see David Granick, *Managerial Comparisons of Four Developed Countries: France, Britain, United States and Russia* (Cambridge, Mass.: M.I.T. Press, 1972).

12. For a survey of views on planning in the United States, see Zoltan Kenessey, *The Process of Economic Planning* (New York: Columbia University Press, 1977). For a comparative viewpoint, see Morris Bornstein, ed., *Economic Planning, East and West* (Cambridge, Mass.: Ballinger, 1975). On the relevance of the French planning experience, see Stephen S. Cohen, *Recent Developments in French Planning: Some Lessons for the United States* (Washington, D.C.: U.S. Government Printing Office, 1977). For an excellent survey of views, see Estrin and Holmes, *French Planning in Theory and Practice*, Chs. 1–2.

13. See Schonfield, *Modern Capitalism*, Ch. 7.

14. Lutz, *Central Planning for the Market Economy*, Ch. 6.

15. Any discussion of the French planning system invariably devotes a great deal of attention to the mystique of the planning system, the ability of the state and the planners to get things done in the absence of coercive power, flexibility and strength, democracy, and direction. For a generally balanced treatment of these features of French planning, see Schonfield, *Modern Capitalism*, Ch. 7; for a critical view, see Lutz, *Central Planning for the Market Economy*; for a brief but useful discussion of pro and con views and references to the literature, see Hough, *The French Economy*, Ch. 5; for a recent view, see Bernard Cazes, "Indicative Planning in France," *Journal of Comparative Economics* 14, 4 (December 1990), 607–620.

16. See Hans Schollhammer, "National Economic Planning and Business Decision Making: The French Experience," in Morris Bornstein, ed., *Comparative Economic Systems: Models and Cases*, 3rd ed. (Homewood, Ill.: Irwin, 1974), pp. 52–76.

17. For a useful discussion of the relationship among the state, the sources of investment funds, and the plan, see Carre, Dubois, and Malinvaud, *French Economic Growth*, Ch. 10.

18. Changing the nature of the business environment and the extent to which planning (as opposed to simple forecasting) is useful have been controversial. For a discussion of information flows and the French planning system, see *Ibid.*, Ch. 14; for a discussion of the theoretical question of reducing uncertainty through planning, see J. E. Meade, *The Theory of Indicative Planning* (Manchester, England: Manchester University Press, 1970); see also Estrin and Holmes, *French Planning in Theory and Practice*, Chs. 1–2; see also Joseph Brada and Saul Estrin, eds., "Advances in Indicative Planning," *Journal of Comparative Economics* 14, 4 (December 1990), 523–812.

19. Lutz, *Central Planning for the Market Economy*.
20. For a discussion of changes in the French planning system, see Martin Cave, "Decentralized Planning in Britain: Comment," *Economics of Planning* 19, 3 (1985), 141–144; Martin Cave, "French Planning Reforms, 1981–1984," *The ACES Bulletin* 26, 2–3 (1984), 29–38; Saul Estrin, "Decentralized Economic Planning: Some Issues," *Economics of Planning* 19, 3 (1985), 150–156.
21. Robert Eisner argues that obsession with trade deficits has been a major focus of policy in the early 1980s. See his article "Which Way for France?" *Challenge* 20 (July/August 1983), 34–41.
22. Such a case is made in Estrin and Holmes, *French Planning in Theory and Practice*.
23. See Schollhammer, "National Economic Planning and Business Decision Making," pp. 52–76.
24. Lutz, *Central Planning for the Market Economy*.
25. McArthur and Scott, *Industrial Planning in France*, pp. 26–27.
26. Hough, *The French Economy*.
27. Cohen, *Modern Capitalist Planning*.
28. *Ibid.*, pp. 238–279.
29. Estrin and Holmes, "Preface," *French Planning in Theory and Practice*, p. vii.
30. Martin Cave, "French Planning Reforms."
31. Balassa, *The First Year of Socialist Government in France*, pp. 2–5.
32. Measures of government involvement are from Gould, "The Development of Government Expenditures in Western Industrialized Countries: A Comparative Analysis," pp. 42–43.
33. Nicholas Spulber, *Redefining the State: Privatization and Welfare Reform in Industrial and Transitional Economies* (Cambridge, England: Cambridge University Press, 1997) p. 59.

Great Britain

34. For a discussion of the British economy in the socialist mold, see Allan G. Gruchy, *Comparative Economic Systems*, 2nd ed. (Boston: Houghton Mifflin, 1977), Ch. 11. For a more recent statement, see Michael Meacher, *Socialism with a Human Face* (London: Allen and Unwin, 1982). The following are useful sources: John and Anne Marie Hackett, *The British Economy: Problems and Prospects* (London: Allen and Unwin, 1967); Richard E. Caves and Associates, *Britain's Economic Prospects* (Washington, D.C.: Brookings, 1968); Sir Alec Cairncross, ed., *Britain's Economic Prospects Reconsidered* (Albany: State University of New York Press, 1970); Richard E. Caves and Lawrence B. Krause, eds., *Britain's Economic Performance* (Washington, D.C.: Brookings, 1980); and W. P. J. Maunder, ed., *The British Economy in the 1970s* (London: Heinemann Educational Books, 1980); Sidney Pollard, *The Wasting of the British Economy* (New York: St. Martin's, 1982). A useful introductory survey is National Institute of Economic and Social Research, *The United Kingdom Economy* (London: Heinemann Educational Books, 1976); for a helpful update, see W. B. Reddaway, "Problems and Prospects for the U.K. Economy," *The Economic Record* 59 (September 1983), 220–231.
35. Mancur Olson, *Rise and Decline of Nations* (New Haven: Yale University Press, 1982).
36. Andrew Schonfield, *Modern Capitalism: The Changing Balance of Public and Private Power* (New York: Oxford University Press, 1965), Ch. 6.
37. On the regional question, see B. E. Coates and E. M. Rawstron, *Regional Variations in Britain* (London: Batsford, 1971).
38. Schonfield, *Modern Capitalism*, p. 88.

39. For an interesting discussion of a particular case of British wartime planning, see Ely Devons, *Planning in Practice* (Cambridge, England: Cambridge University Press, 1950).
40. In the period when British concern for poor economic performance, especially unemployment, was growing rapidly, actual performance was quite good, though possibly not on a par with that of the fast-growing nations of the period. For example, between 1959 and 1966, the average annual rate of unemployment was 2.6 percent in Britain, 5.4 percent in the United States, and 5.5 percent in Canada. For the period 1955–1964, per capita national income grew in Britain at an average annual rate of 2.1 percent, compared to 1.4 percent in the United States, 4.7 percent in Italy, and 4.3 percent in West Germany.
41. For a discussion, see Carlo M. Cipolla, ed., *The Economic Decline of Empires* (London: Methuen, 1970); see also Frank Blackaby, ed., *De-industrialisation* (London: Heinemann Educational Books, 1979).
42. We shall not discuss the details of British stabilization policy in this short survey. The interested reader should refer to the discussion in Hackett, *The British Economy*, Ch. 1; for a more recent brief survey, see G. D. N. Worswick, "Fiscal Policy and Stabilization in Britain," in Cairncross, *Britain's Economic Prospects Reconsidered*, pp. 36–60; for useful background, see Charles Feinstein, ed., *The Managed Economy* (Oxford, England: Oxford University Press, 1983). See also G. D. N. Worswick, "The End of Demand Management?" *Lloyd's Bank Review* 123 (January 1977), 1–18.
43. Worswick, "Fiscal Policy and Stabilization in Britain."
44. For a brief but excellent survey of the British experience with national economic planning, see Werner Z. Hirsch, *Recent Experience with National Economic Planning in the United Kingdom* (Washington, D.C.: U.S. Government Printing Office, 1977).
45. *Ibid.*, pp. 13–15.
46. Schonfield, *Modern Capitalism*, p. 173.
47. Hackett, *The British Economy*, p. 162.
48. Caves and Associates, *Britain's Economic Prospects*, pp. 271–274.
49. Chenery and Syrquin, *Patterns of Development*, Table 5–4.
50. Caves and Associates, *Britain's Economic Prospects*, Ch. 8.
51. Meacher, *Socialism with a Human Face*.
52. The data presented here are from Frank Gould, "The Development of Public Expenditures in Western Industrialized Countries: A Comparative Analysis," *Public Finances* 38, 1 (1983), 38–69.
53. See World Bank, *World Tables*, 2nd ed. (Baltimore: The Johns Hopkins University Press, 1980).
54. A great deal has been written about the nationalized industries in Great Britain. For a brief survey, see Richard Pryke, "Public Enterprise in Great Britain," in Morris Bornstein, ed., *Comparative Economic Systems: Models and Cases*, 3rd ed. (Homewood, Ill.: Irwin, 1974), pp. 77–92. For in-depth treatment, see R. Kelf-Cohen, *Twenty Years of Nationalisation* (London: Macmillan, 1969); R. Kelf-Cohen, *British Nationalisation, 1945–1973* (New York: St. Martin's, 1973); and Leonard Tivey, ed., *The Nationalized Industries Since 1960: A Book of Readings* (Toronto: University of Toronto Press, 1973). For a discussion of issues in the 1970s, see T. G. Weyman-Jones, "The Nationalised Industries: Changing Attitudes and Changing Roles," in W. P. J. Maunder, ed., *The British Economy in the 1970s*, Ch. 8.
55. Steel (denationalized in 1954 and nationalized again in 1965) is not included. See Pryke, "Public Enterprise in Great Britain," p. 82.
56. See, for example, the discussion in Reddaway, "Problems and Prospects for the U.K. Economy."
57. For a useful discussion, see Blackaby, *De-industrialisation*.

58. Reddaway, "Problems and Prospects for the U.K. Economy," Table 1.
59. Computed from Caves and Krause, *Britain's Economic Performance*, Table 2, p. 3.
60. Pollard, *The Wasting of the British Economy*, Table 3.3, p. 53.
61. *Ibid.*, Table 1.2, p. 12.
62. Reddaway, "Problems and Prospects for the U.K. Economy," p. 225.
63. Caves and Krause, *Britain's Economic Performance*, p. 19.
64. For interesting background, see Bernard N. Nossiter, *Britain—A Future That Works* (Boston: Houghton Mifflin, 1978).
65. Useful sources include David S. Bell, ed., *The Conservative Government, 1979–84: An Interim Report* (London: Croom Helm, 1985); Paul Hare, *Planning the British Economy* (London: Macmillan, 1985); Grahame Thompson, *The Conservatives' Economic Policy* (London: Croom Helm, 1986); Alan Walters, *Britain's Economic Renaissance* (New York: Oxford University Press, 1986); and "Planning in Britain," *Journal of Comparative Economics* 19, 3 (1985).
66. Alan Walters, *Britain's Economic Renaissance*, pp. 4–5.
67. Nicolas Spulber, *Redefining the State: Privatization and Welfare Reform in the East and West* (Cambridge, England: Cambridge University Press, 1997).
68. Grahame Thompson, *The Conservatives' Economic Policy*, Ch. 7.
69. William L. Megginson, Robert C. Nash, and Mathias van Randenburgh, "The Financial and Operating Performance of Newly Privatized Firms: An International Empirical Analysis," *The Journal of Finance* 44 (June 1994), 403–452.
70. See also John Vickers and George Yarrow, "Regulation of Privatized Firms in Britain," *European Economic Review* 32 (1988), 465–472.
71. To the extent that systemic change is involved, assessment of the Thatcher years will require a much longer time horizon.
72. World Bank, *World Development Report 1987*, p. 223.
73. Nicolas Crafts's study is summarized in "Government Reforms May Have Halted Decline," *Financial Times,* March 17, 1997. According to Crafts's study, between 1979 and 1994, GDP per capita grew 1.5 percent faster in the U.K. than in France and the United States and kept pace with Germany. The only European country to grow faster was Italy.

Germany

74. Our discussion of the early years is based on the following sources: Heinz Lampert, *Volkswirtschaftliche Institutionen* (Munich: Verlag Franz Vahlen, 1980); G. Gutman, W. Klein, S. Paraskewopolous, and H. Winter, *Die Wirtschafts-Verfassung der Bundesrepublik Deutschland*, 2nd ed. (Stuttgart: Fischer, 1979); Hannelore Hamel, ed., *Bundesrepublik Deutschland-DDR, Die Wirtschaftssysteme*, 4th ed. (Munich: C. H. Beck, 1983); and Gerhard Brinkman, *Okonomik der Arbeit*, Vol. I (Stuttgart: Ernst Klett Verlag, 1981).
75. This label is credited to A. Muller-Armack, "Soziale Marktwirtschaft," in *Handwörterbuch der Sozialwissenschaften*, Band IX (Stuttgart: Fischer, 1956), p. 390.
76. H. Jorg Thieme, *Soziale Marktwirtschaft: Konzeption und wirtschaftspolitische Gestaltung in der BRD* (Hanover: Berenberg, 1973), pp. 12–28; and Wolfram Engels, *Soziale Martwirtschaft: Verschmähte Zukunft* (Stuttgart: Seewald, 1973), pp. 40–45.
77. L. Erhard and A. Muller-Armack, *Soziale Marktwirtschaft* (Frankfurt am Main: Ullstein, 1972).
78. See Gutman *et al.*, *Wirtschaftsverfassung*, Ch. 8.
79. Thieme, *Soziale Marktwirtschaft*, pp. 83–87.
80. Lampert, *Institutionen*, pp. 31–49.

81. Martin Schnitzer and James Nordyke, *Comparative Economic Systems*, 2nd ed. (Cincinnati, Ohio: Southwestern, 1977), p. 328.
82. J. H. Kaiser, "Public Enterprise in Germany," in W. G. Friedman and J. F. Garner, *Government Enterprise: A Comparative Study* (New York: Columbia University Press, 1970).
83. For a discussion of the GDR and comparisons to the FRG, see Paul R. Gregory and Gert Leptin, "Similar Societies Under Differing Economic Systems: The Case of the Two Germanys," *Soviet Studies* 29 (October 1977), 519–541.
84. For recent comparative data, see George A. Akerlof, Andrew K. Rose, and Janet L. Yellen, "East Germany in from the Cold: The Economic Aftermath of Currency Union," paper presented at the Conference of the Brookings Panel on Economic Activity, Washington, D.C., April 4, 1991, p. 92. For recent analyses of the East German transition, see Helmut Wagner, "Reconstruction of the Financial System in East Germany," *Journal of Banking and Finance* 17 (1993), 1001–1029; Roy Vogt, "Transforming the Former GDR Into a Market Economy," *Comparative Economic Studies* 34 (Fall–Winter 1992), 68–80.

Sweden

85. For a discussion of the Swedish model, see Henry Milner, *Sweden: Social Democracy in Action* (New York: Oxford University Press, 1989); for background and a critique of the contemporary system, see Erik Lundberg, "The Rise and Fall of the Swedish Model," *Journal of Economic Literature* 23 (March 1985), 1–36; for an American assessment, see Barry P. Bosworth and Alice M. Rivlin, eds., *The Swedish Economy* (Washington, D.C.: Brookings, 1987); Timothy A. Canova, "The Swedish Model Betrayed," *Challenge* 37 (May–June 1994), 36–40; *The Swedish Economy Autumn 1993* (Stockholm: National Institute of Economic Research, 1993).
86. World Bank, *World Development Report 1990* (New York: Oxford University Press, 1990).
87. *World Development Report 1990.*
88. See Henry Milner, *Sweden: Social Democracy in Action.*
89. Erik Lundberg, "The Rise and Fall of the Swedish Model."
90. For a discussion of this point, see Assar Lindbeck, "Is the Welfare State in Trouble?" *Eastern Economic Journal* 13 (October–December 1987), 345–351; Timothy A. Canova, "The Swedish Model Betrayed"; and Assar Lindbeck, "The Swedish Experiment," *Journal of Economic Literature* XXXV, 3 (September 1997), 1273–1319.
91. Mancur Olson, "The Varieties of Eurosclerosis: The Rise and Decline of Nations Since 1982," in Nicholas Crafts and Gianni Toniolo, *Economic Growth in Europe Since 1945* (Cambridge, England: Cambridge University Press, 1996), pp. 73–94.

Recommended Readings

General Sources

Clive Archer and Fiona Butler, *The European Union: Structure and Process,* 2nd ed. (New York: St. Martin's, 1996).
Bart van Art and Nicholas Crafts, eds., *Quantitative Aspects of Post-War European Economic Growth* (New York: Cambridge University Press, 1996).
Robert Leonardi, *Convergence, Cohesion and Integration in the European Union* (New York: St. Martin's, 1994).

Stelios Stavridis, Elias Mossialos, Roger Morgan, and Howard Machin, *New Challenges to European Union* (Brookfield, Vt.: Ashgate, 1997).

William Wallace, Regional Integration: The West European Experience (Washington, D.C.: Brookings, 1994).

France

Bela Balassa, *The First Year of Socialist Government in France* (Washington, D.C.: American Enterprise Institute, 1982).

Joseph Brada and Saul Estrin, eds., "Advances in Indicative Planning," *Journal of Comparative Economics* 14 (December 1990), 523–812.

Bernard Cazes, "Indicative Planning in France," *Journal of Comparative Economics* 14 (December 1990), 607–619.

J.-J. Carre, P. Dubois, and E. Malinvaud, *French Economic Growth* (Stanford, Calif.: Stanford University Press, 1975).

Juny Chater and Brian Jenkins, *France: From the Cold War to the New World Order* (New York: St. Martin's Press, 1996).

Stephen S. Cohen, *Modern Capitalist Planning: The French Model* (Berkeley: University of California Press, 1977).

————, *Recent Developments in French Planning: Some Lessons for the United States* (Washington, D.C.: Government Printing Office, 1977).

Stephen S. Cohen and Peter A. Gourevitch, eds., *France in a Troubled World Economy* (Boston: Butterworth, 1982).

Saul Estrin and Peter Holmes, *French Planning in Theory and Practice* (Boston: Allen and Unwin, 1983).

John and Anne Marie Hackett, *Economic Planning in France* (Cambridge, Mass.: Harvard University Press, 1963).

Stanley Hottman and William Andrews, eds., *The Fifth Republic at Twenty* (New York: State University of New York Press, 1980).

J. R. Hough, *The French Economy* (New York: Holmes & Meier, 1982).

Richard F. Kuisel, *Capitalism and the State in Modern France* (New York: Cambridge University Press, 1981).

Vera Lutz, *Central Planning for the Market Economy: An Analysis of the French Theory and Experience* (London: Longmans Green, 1969).

John H. McArthur and Bruce R. Scott, *Industrial Planning in France* (Boston: Graduate School of Business Administration, Harvard University, 1969).

John Sheahan, *An Introduction to the French Economy* (Columbus, Ohio: Merrill, 1969).

W. Allen Spivey, *Economic Policies in France 1976–1981* (Ann Arbor: University of Michigan Graduate School of Business Administration, 1983).

Great Britain

David S. Bell, ed., *The Conservative Government, 1979–84: An Interim Report* (London: Croom Helm, 1985).

Frank Blackaby, ed., *De-industrialisation* (London: Heinemann Educational Books, 1979).

M. J. Buckle and J. L. Thompson, *The United Kingdom Financial System* 2nd ed. (New York: St. Martin's, 1995).

Richard E. Caves and Associates, *Britain's Economic Prospects* (Washington, D.C.: Brookings, 1968).

Richard E. Caves and Lawrence B. Krause, eds., *Britain's Economic Performance* (Washington, D.C.: Brookings, 1980).

Carlo M. Cipolla, ed., *The Economic Decline of Empires* (London: Methuen, 1970).

B. E. Coates and E. M. Rawstron, *Regional Variations in Britain* (London: Batsford, 1971).

T. A. J. Cockerill and R. Brown, eds. *Prospects for the British Economy* (Brookfield, Vt., Ashgate, 1997).

Charles Feinstein, ed., *The Managed Economy* (Oxford, England: Oxford University Press, 1983).

Andrew Gamble, *Britain in Decline* (New York: St. Martin's, 1995).

John and Anne Marie Hackett, *The British Economy: Problems and Prospects* (London: Allen and Unwin, 1967).

Paul Hare, *Planning the British Economy* (London: Macmillan, 1985).

Werner Z. Hirsch, *Recent Experience with National Economic Planning in Great Britain* (Washington, D.C.: U.S. Government Printing Office, 1977).

Ken Holden, Kent Matthews, and John Thompson, *The U.K. Economy Today* (New York: St. Martin's, 1995).

R. Kelf-Cohen, *British Nationalization, 1945–1973* (New York: St. Martin's, 1973).

W. P. J. Maunder, ed., *The British Economy in the 1970's* (London: Heinemann Educational Books, 1980).

F. V. Meyer, D. C. Corner, and J. E. S. Parker, *Problems of a Mature Economy* (London: Macmillan, 1970).

National Institute of Economic and Social Research, *The United Kingdom Economy* (London: Heinemann Educational Books, 1976).

Sidney Pollard, *The Wasting of the British Economy* (New York: St. Martin's, 1982).

Grahame Thompson, *The Conservatives' Economic Policy* (London: Croom Helm, 1986).

Alan Walters, *Britain's Economic Renaissance* (New York: Oxford University Press, 1986).

Germany

George A. Akerlof, Andrew K. Rose, and Janet L. Yellen, "East Germany in from the Cold: The Economic Aftermath of Currency Union," paper presented at the Conference of the Brookings Panel on Economic Activity, Washington, D.C., April 4, 1991.

Gary R. Beling, "Selling Off the Family Silver? The Privatization of State Enterprises: The East German Case," unpublished paper, Princeton University, May 17, 1991.

Eduardo Borensztein and Manmohan S. Kumar, "Proposals for Privatization in Eastern Europe," Washington, D.C.: IMF Working Paper, April 1991.

Doris Cornelsen, "GDR: Current Issues," in NATO, *The Central and East European Economies in the 1990s: Perspectives and Constraints* (Brussels: NATO, 1990).

Irwin Collier, "The Estimation of Gross Domestic Product and Its Growth Rate for the German Democratic Republic" (Washington, D.C.: World Bank Staff Working Papers, #773, 1985).

Paul Gregory and Gert Leptin, "Similar Societies Under Differing Economic Systems: The Case of the Two Germanys," *Soviet Studies* 29, 4 (October 1977), 519–544.

Lutz Hoffmann, "Integrating the East German States Into the German Economy: Opportunities, Burdens, and Options," paper presented at the American Institute for Contemporary German Studies, The Johns Hopkins University, Washington, D.C., November 13, 1990.

Barry W. Ickes, "What to Do Before the Capital Markets Arrive: The Transition Problem in Reforming Socialist Economies," paper presented at the Conference on the East European Transformation, Princeton University, May 3, 1991.

Henning Klodt, "Government Support for Restructuring the East German Economy," paper presented at the American Institute for Contemporary German Studies, The Johns Hopkins University, Washington, D.C., November 14, 1990.

Jack K. Knott, *Managing the German Economy* (Lexington, Mass.: Heath, 1981).

Oliver Letwin, *Privatizing the World* (London: Cassell, 1988).

Leslie Lipschitz and Donough McDonald, *German Unification: Economic Issues*, Washington, D.C., IMF, Occasional Paper #75, December 1990.

Philip L. Paarlberg, "Sectoral Adjustments in Eastern Germany Due to Market Forces," *Review of International Economics* 2 (June 1994), 112–122.

Martin Myant, Frank Fleischer, Kurt Hornschild, Křůžena Vintrová, Karel Zeman, and Zdeněk Sovček, *Successful Transformations?* (Broofield, VT., Edward Elgar, 1997).

Claus Schnabel, "Structural Adjustment and Privatization of the East German Economy," paper presented at the American Institute of Contemporary German Studies, The Johns Hopkins University, Washington, D.C., December 1990.

Martin Schnitzer, *East and West Germany: A Comparative Economic Analysis* (New York: Praeger, 1990).

———, *Income Distribution: A Comparative Study of the United States, Sweden, West Germany, East Germany, the United Kingdom, and Japan* (New York: Praeger, 1974).

Wolfgang Stolper, *The Structure of the East German Economy* (Cambridge, Mass.: Harvard University Press, 1960).

Helmut Wagner, "Reconstruction of the Financial System in East Germany," *Journal of Banking and Finance* 17 (1993), 1001–1029.

Norbert Walter, "Beyond German Unification," *The International Economy*, (October/November 1990).

Sweden

Barry P. Bosworth and Alice M. Rivlin, eds., *The Swedish Economy* (Washington, D.C.: Brookings, 1987).

Timothy A. Canova, "The Swedish Model Betrayed," *Challenge* 37 (May–June, 1994), 36–40.

Richard Freeman, Birgitta Swedenborg and Robert Topel (eds.), *Reforming the Welfare State: The Swedish Model in Transition* (Chicago: University of Chicago Press, 1997).

Peter Lawrence and Tony Spybey, *Management and Society in Sweden* (London: Routledge and Kegan Paul, 1986).

Assar Lindbeck, "The Swedish Experiment," *Journal of Economic Literature* XXXV, 3 (September 1997), 1273–1319.

Assar Lindbeck *et al.*, *Turning Sweden Around* (Cambridge, Mass.: M.I.T. Press, 1994).

Erik Lundberg, "The Rise and Fall of the Swedish Model," *Journal of Economic Literature* 23 (March 1985), 1–36.

Michael Maccoby, ed., *Sweden at the Edge* (Philadelphia: University of Pennsylvania Press, 1991).

Per-Martin Meyerson, *The Welfare State in Crisis—The Case of Sweden* (Stockholm: The Federation of Swedish Industries, 1982).

Henry Milner, *Sweden: Social Democracy in Action* (New York: Oxford University Press, 1989).

Bengt Ryden and Villy Bergstrom, eds., *Sweden: Choices for Economic and Social Policy in the 1980s* (London: Allen and Unwin, 1982).

The Swedish Economy Autumn 1993 (Stockholm: National Institute of Economic Research, 1993).

12

The Asian Model

The "Asian" model has been applied to those countries located east of the industrialized core countries of Europe and North America. The Eurasian country with the most "Eastern" pattern of economic development was tsarist Russia and thereafter the Soviet Union—the pioneer of *the socialist planned-economy model of development.* Other countries to the east of the European core that followed an Asian pattern are Japan—as the notable pioneer of the *Asian capitalist model of development*—and then, in the second half of the 20th century, the Four Tigers of Southeast Asia: Taiwan, South Korea, Singapore, and Hong Kong. Another country known for its Asian development features is China, a country that has experienced rapid growth only in the last three decades. China began its development as a planned socialist economy and now appears to be developing as a *market socialist economy.*

The Asian model applies to countries that began their development from a low initial level of per capita income in a largely rural economy. Their main task was not the more efficient utilization of resources, as in Europe, but the creation of capital resources and the drawing of labor out of agriculture, where workers were underemployed or completely redundant, into industry. In order for this transfer to take place, capital formation in industry must take place, which requires the mobilization of savings, be it savings from the predominant rural sector or saving from other sources, such as foreign capital.

One of the most controversial features of the Asian model is the mechanism it uses to raise capital formation proportions, to allocate that capital, and to draw labor from agriculture to industry. Given the greater gap in per capita incomes, the Asian model argues that greater sacrifices are called for and that a strong state hand may be required to enforce these sacrifices.

Just as Gerschenkron provided the general model for European industrialization (discussed in Chapter 11), the two-sector model enunciated by W. Arthur Lewis, John Fei and Gustav Ranis, and Soviet economists such as Preobrazhenksy provides the intellectual basis for the Asian model.

The Asian model covers a wide gamut of choices. At one extreme is the *Stalinist model,* which uses considerable state power to force high rates of capital formation and rapid transfer of resources from agriculture to industry. At the other extreme, we have the predominantly free-market models of Southeast Asia, influenced by state industrial policy to direct investment resources to defined targets. In the middle, we have the pioneering model of Japan, with its heavy emphasis on land taxes and other devices to shift savings from industry to agriculture and its heavy-handed reliance on industrial policy supported by a close alliance between the state and big business.

The Lewis Two-Sector Model

The Nobel laureate economist W. Arthur Lewis pioneered the **two-sector model** that was later refined by J. Fei and G. Ranis.[1] Lewis's two-sector model assumed a traditional agricultural sector in which, because of population pressures, labor is redundant; the marginal worker produces no additional output; and agricultural output is allocated among the farm population by tradition rather than by commercial decision making. Alongside the traditional agricultural sector, there exists a relatively small modern industrial sector in which decisions are made commercially. The task of development, therefore, is to transfer labor from agriculture, where it is redundant, to industry, where its marginal product is positive.

The Theory

Figure 12.1 contrasts the traditional agricultural sector with the modern industrial sector. Figure 12.1A shows agriculture with an employment level of N_a, and a production level of Q_a. From the shape of agriculture's production function, it is clear that agricultural output would not decline if employment in agriculture could be reduced. The average wage in agriculture is Q_a/N_a. Agricultural workers simply decide to divide the available output evenly among themselves according to tradition and custom.

Panel B shows labor supply and demand in industry. The demand for labor depends on the marginal product of labor MP_L (remember that in industry, decisions are made on the basis of standard marginal analysis). Initial industry employment is N_i; the marginal product of labor in industry is positive. If additional employment could be created in industry, more industrial output could be produced.

The development task of this poor, agricultural economy is therefore to transfer labor from agriculture to industry—which will occur only if the demand for industrial labor can be increased. In order for industrial labor demand to increase, there has to be an increase in industrial investment. Additional industrial investment raises the marginal product of labor and increases the demand for labor. The supply of labor to industry will be horizontal at Q_a/N_a (the traditional agricultural wage), because there will be a ready supply of labor to industry as long as the traditional agricultural wage is not bid up. This bidding up will not occur until agricultural surplus labor is transferred out of agriculture.

Consider what would happen if, by some mechanism, the supply of labor to agriculture could be reduced to N'_a. Because agricultural labor is redundant, the same amount of agricultural output (Q_a) continues to be produced. Workers who remain in agriculture will continue to receive the same wage as before, so a "surplus" is created that equals agricultural output (Q_a) minus the wages (in the form of agricultural

FIGURE 12.1   The Two-Sector Model

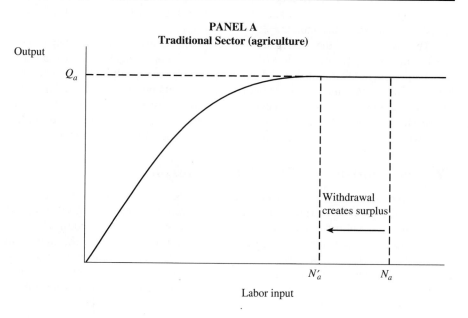

PANEL A
Traditional Sector (agriculture)

Output

Q_a

Withdrawal
creates surplus

N'_a N_a

Labor input

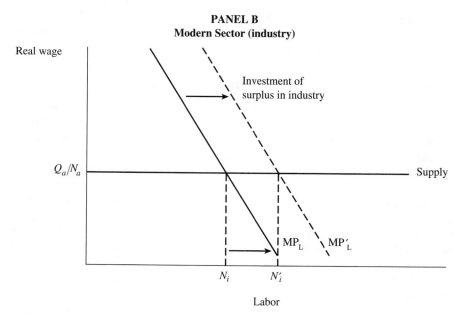

PANEL B
Modern Sector (industry)

Real wage

Investment of
surplus in industry

Q_a/N_a Supply

MP_L MP'_L

N_i N'_i

Labor

goods) received by those workers who remain in agriculture. As long as the agricultural population continues to receive the same wage as before, the transfer of labor out of agriculture generates a surplus, which is free to flow from agriculture to industry as industrial investment.

The investment of the agricultural surplus in industry raises the marginal product of labor in industry (from MP_L to MP'_L), which raises the demand for industrial labor, which increase industrial output and employment. The net result is that the economy has not lost any agricultural output but has increased its production of industrial output. Thus, as long as a mechanism can be found to harness the agricultural surplus for industrial investment, labor can continue to be transferred out of agriculture, industrial investment can continue to grow, and economic development can proceed.

The Mechanism for Transferring Surplus

The theoretical model is clear. What is unclear is the mechanism that will cause the agricultural surplus to be transferred from agriculture to industry and will keep the agricultural wage at its initial level even though labor is leaving agriculture?

A number of mechanisms have been suggested. One is to use the market to transfer the surplus. The farm population could be offered the opportunity to deposit savings into financial intermediaries, which would then lend these funds to industry. Agricultural entrepreneurs could supply capital to industrial firms in return for ownership shares. Another mechanism would be for the state to impose taxes on the agricultural population to force them to save. The state would then accumulate budget surpluses that could be used as a fund to invest in industry. Finally, the state could "nationalize" agriculture, through collectivization or some other means, to force the transfer of savings from agriculture to industry.[2]

The Asian Model and the Surplus

At the start of the industrialization process, the dominant sector in the economy is agriculture. Hence the major source of capital accumulation must be the agricultural population, unless significant foreign savings can be attracted. This is true whether the agricultural labor force is initially redundant or not.

The Asian countries studied in this chapter are, for the most part, examples of successful industrialization. Japan industrialized later than Europe but was the first case of modern economic growth in Asia. The Four Tigers (Hong Kong, Taiwan, Singapore, and South Korea) industrialized after World War II. Other Asian countries, such as Malaysia, Indonesia, and Thailand, may be in the process of initiating modern economic growth in the 1990s. Other poor Asian countries, such as India, still have not initiated modern economic growth in the 1990s.

This chapter examines how the successful Asian economies marshaled savings both domestic and foreign, made the necessary changes in agriculture, and created institutions suitable for economic growth. They used varying approaches, some relying more on state intervention, others more on market forces. The two-sector model is a convenient way to organize thinking about these economies.

Japan: Growth Through Capital Formation

Japan's postwar rate of economic growth is the highest among the major industrialized countries. For the admirer of high rates of economic growth, thought to be a hallmark of the early years of planned socialist systems, Japan was earlier cited as a capitalist alternative to the Soviet model for the developing nations. However, in Japan as in other countries, growth rates have slowed. In the 1980s attention focused on how, and how well, the Japanese economy could adjust to external shocks from the world economy. Indeed, by the mid-1990s, there was considerable pessimism about the performance of the Japanese economy.

This discussion of Japan stresses three areas: the historical traditions and special circumstances of Japan, its economic performance, and various observers' explanations of Japan's impressive growth record. It concludes with observations on contemporary performance issues.

Background of the Japanese Economy

Japan is a country with a large population but limited supplies of natural resources and land. Before the Meiji restoration, which began in 1868, Japan was "a fossilized and closed society."[3] Therefore, interest in Japanese economic performance centers on the period since 1868, though the roots of modern development may be found in the Tokugawa period prior to the Meiji restoration.[4]

Japan, like Great Britain, is an island economy. With a population of approximately 123 million, 77 percent of whom live in urban areas, and a land area slightly smaller than that of California, Japan is densely populated. Japan is a developed economy dominated by the service sector, the industrial sector, and a small agricultural sector.

Japan has a long, varied, and controversial history. Since its defeat in World War II, Japan has been governed under a democratic political system established by the Allied occupation forces. The Japanese parliament *(Diet)* is elected by the people; it chooses the prime minister, who is the leader of the country.

The Japanese have achieved rapid growth in a country whose natural resource base is minimal. Japan is not well endowed with minerals or fertile agricultural land. Thus Japanese performance must be explained by its economic system, its organizational arrangements, and its people.[5] Between the late 1860s and the early 1900s, Japan developed policy measures for economic growth based on special features of the Japanese system.

First of all, there was (and still is) among the Japanese population a unity of purpose fostered by the state and facilitated by Japanese cultural traditions and history. There are a discipline and devotion to work on the part of the laborers and a degree of paternalism on the part of employers seldom seen in other countries. Although it is difficult to pinpoint the sources of this unity, one observer has suggested that a long period of development of the labor market, based on the discipline of the home production process, and the generation of information for an efficient market combined to create an efficient and disciplined worker.

Second, the state has performed important functions, although Table 12.1 suggests a modest role for the state in the Japanese economy. However, such statistics may understate the role of the state in postwar Japan. For example, in the crucial area of capital formation, the government played a key role, not only in promoting savings and investment, but also in attracting foreign capital, which was important in the early years of Japanese development.

Although the rate of capital formation in postwar Japan has been much higher than in other mature economies, the *direct* role of the state has been smaller than in other nations. Government purchases have also been smaller proportionally than in any of these countries. The state's role, then, has been to stimulate *private* investment through strong incentives such as low tax rates, proinvestment state financial policy, and the limited provision of social services.

The role of the Japanese state as a purchaser was significant in earlier times, especially in its capacity as an entrepreneur—a role that carries over to present-day Japan. This state function has been important not only in getting industry started but also in focusing investment in growth sectors, at the best scale of operation, and utilizing the best available technology.

Third, historical experience is crucial to understanding modern economic growth in Japan. During the Meiji restoration, the Japanese economy was opened up to Western technology. Enrollment in formal educational programs increased rapidly, as did participation in the labor force, and a "dual economy" developed. The dual economy consisted of a large, increasingly modern industrial sector requiring skilled labor, existing alongside relatively primitive industrial operations where labor with minimal skills was utilized.

Agricultural development accelerated during this period, and technological progress and the expansion of conventional inputs (labor and fertilizer) created the agricultural surplus emphasized by the Lewis model. Agriculture's role in Japanese

TABLE 12.1   Asian versus European Models

	Europe	Japan	Hong Kong	Singapore	Korea	Taiwan
Per capita GDP, 93 $	17,089	20,523	16,601	13,021	6,548	7,249
GDI/GDP	20%	33%	27%	35%	35%	18%
Gross saving	20%	34%	35%	43%	37%	31%
Literacy	100	100	88	91	96	92
People/doctor	611	609	933	753	1078	9811
Taxes/GDP	40%	29%	14%	21%	19%	n.a.*

*not available

Sources: Roy Ruffin, "The Role of Foreign Investment in the Economic Growth of the Asian and Pacific Region," *Asian Development Review* 11, 1 (1993), 3–5; Cormac O'Grada and Kevin O'Rourke, "Irish Economic Growth, 1945–88," in Nicholas Crafts and Gianni Toniolo, eds. *Economic Growth in Europe Since 1945* (Cambridge, England: Cambridge University Press), 1996, p. 405; and *The World Factbook 1988,* country statistics.

development—in particular, the use of high taxation to extract the surplus—remains a matter of controversy.[6]

Fourth, military activity has been an important factor. The rapid pace of development after the 1860s through World War I was fostered in part by military spending. Thereafter, at least until 1946, war was a dominant theme. World War II warped the structure of production and led to an economy governed by controls and, later, manipulated by the American occupation forces. American occupation policies were primary land reform (large holdings were broken up), deconcentration of industrial ownership, the introduction of trade unionism, and an end to the military commitment.[7] All had lasting implications for Japan's development in the postwar period. No one set of features can explain Japanese growth.

Sources of Japanese Economic Growth

Although the Japanese economy grew rapidly for a long time, the interesting facet of this record, as Kazushi Ohkawa and Henry Rosovsky emphasize, was the accelerating trend of economic growth at a particularly high level. The rate of growth of output of the Japanese economy in the postwar years was exceptionally high by international standards until the past two decades, averaging close to 10 percent annually. This rate meets or exceeds even those of such rapidly growing countries as Germany and (earlier) the Soviet Union. Growth rates through the 1990s have been much slower, though they remain respectable by international standards. In the 1990s, Japanese growth was anemic.

The Japanese economy is a market economy in which national economic planning has played only a marginal role. One cannot look to extra market mechanisms, such as planning, to explain Japanese growth. What, then, has led to this impressive economic performance? It is very difficult to isolate the key features that have influenced any economic system's performance. However, the path-breaking work of Ohkawa and Rosovsky identifies two general influences: those that are narrowly economic and those of a broader nature.[8] Let us examine each in turn.

The economic explanations for postwar (and earlier) Japanese economic development, according to Ohkawa and Rosovsky, were a technology gap, a high rate of capital formation, and the availability of labor. After being a closed economy, Japan had a technology gap and thus could benefit in a major way from the absorption of Western technology. Technology assimilation was facilitated by sharp increases in the size of the capital stock (through imports of capital, a high propensity to save, and the state's promotion of capital formation) and by elastic supplies of labor. Furthermore, the dual labor market permitted the shift of labor from the primitive to the modern sector at a rate dictated by the needs of the advanced sector, and wage increases lagged behind advances in productivity.[9]

At the same time, the Japanese economy was able to achieve a growing role in foreign markets. During the early stages of development, while modern industry was growing, exports were derived primarily from traditional industries such as textiles.

As modern technology was assimilated, Japanese exports shifted away from the traditional products toward the high-technology products that Japan, owing to its productive but relatively inexpensive labor, could produce with comparative advantage. In part, industrial development at home was enhanced by the state's policy of starting import-competing industries. These factors, combined with reparations from China and an aggressive external posture, made the foreign sector an important contributor to Japan's growth.

The factors emphasized by Ohkawa and Rosovsky are familiar—technology, capital creation, development of the labor force. The difference may be Japan's ability to assemble these features in a harmonious way. Ohkawa and Rosovsky place great emphasis on the noneconomic, or special, features of the Japanese nation. What are the important noneconomic features of the Japanese development experience?

First, we must again emphasize the multidimensional role of the state. The state gave impetus and direction to the drive for economic growth. The state intervened selectively and was a catalyst for ensuring not only a high rate of investment but also its distribution. For example, beyond the approval of general economic policies by the Diet, government is also more directly involved in business. Government offices *(genkyoku)* supervise individual industries, and ministries supervise sectors of the economy. Also, there are ministries (such as the Ministry of Finance) the interests of which cross specific industrial borders. Finally, the government is directly involved in a wide range of economic matters: the encouragement of designated industrial projects through low-interest loans from the Japan Development Bank, regulation of antitrust matters by the Fair Trade Commission, and so on.[10] Prior to the deregulation of Japanese financial markets in April of 1998, Japanese savers had few choices for saving. Restrictions on financial intermediation meant that over half of personal savings was held in checking and savings accounts.

The role of the state in the Japanese economy remains one of the intriguing aspects of the Japanese economic system. In terms of readily quantifiable indicators of state economic activity such as revenue and expenditure, the role of the state is relatively small. At the same time, the state has been a facilitator of the market process, the creator of a harmonious business environment, and an entrepreneur and overseer of the development process.

Second, what Ohkawa and Rosovsky describe as the "human element" has been a factor in the Japanese story. In Japan, labor has a peculiar and growth-conducive attitude toward industry: the "permanent employment" system and the submissive attitude of labor toward the industrial establishment.[11] In addition, rising family incomes produced unusually high levels of savings—most appropriate for rapid growth but hard to explain on other than traditional and cultural grounds.

Prior to World War II, the government suppressed the growth of trade unions. Having gained recognition in the postwar period, trade unions have since had a voice in wages, supplemental benefits, and working conditions. They are constrained, however, in that they are enterprise unions, enrolling long-term employees. Their primary strength is in the largest industrial enterprises.[12]

Third, one could cite a number of other factors—some narrowly economic, others less so—that have affected growth: favorable population growth and hence labor supplies, the end to military expenditure, and the limiting of low-growth sectors (such as housing).

Industrial Organization

An economy's industrial organization can affect its performance, and most theories associate competition with "good" economic performance. The Japanese economy presents a test case, for it appears to have combined an industrial structure dominated by giant vertical and horizontal trusts with rapid economic growth.

Before World War II, Japanese industry was dominated by giant holding companies called *zaibatsu*, which represented a complex maze of interlocking directorships, banking relationships, and family ties.[13] By the end of the war, this concentration of ownership had proceeded to the point where fewer than 4,000 zaibatsu-connected families owned almost 50 percent of all the outstanding shares. The American occupation forces sought to eliminate zaibatsu dominance by outlawing holding companies, breaking up monopolies, and making mutual shareholdings among zaibatsu firms illegal.

In the postwar era, shareholding in industry and banking has become more evenly distributed among the population. New industrial groupings called *kieretsu* replaced the old zaibatsu organizations. Kieretsu can be either vertical or horizontal: either a large firm in charge of smaller ("children") firms or a horizontal association of interest groups. These new groups are less powerful than the old zaibatsu, and it is possible for a firm within a grouping to place its own interests above those of the group, an action inconceivable before the war.

One enduring feature of the large Japanese company is its emphasis on industrial paternalism. Established employees of large companies are, in effect, guaranteed lifetime employment. They are taught to think of the company as their family, and they believe that if they work hard for the company, the company will take care of them. John M. Montias singled out this characteristic of the Japanese enterprise for study and found that this "permanent employment" constraint on Japanese management is likely to alter resource allocation patterns.[14]

Indeed, the Japanese economy has been characterized as a **share economy**, based on a framework suggested by Martin Weitzman.[15] The evidence for this characterization—the bonus system in Japan—is not strong, though differences in the allocation system make Japanese labor markets of great interest to the comparative analyst.[16]

The concepts of industrial paternalism and lifetime employment have received a great deal of attention, in large part because the system seems so different from other capitalist countries. How can labor be allocated in a rapidly changing environment if it is not mobile?

The answer to this question lies largely in the difference between appearance and substance. In fact, a number of forces at work in the Japanese economy limit the impact of guaranteed employment.[17] First, not all members of the Japanese labor force are covered by guaranteed employment. Roughly 30 percent of the industrial labor force is covered by some form of guaranteed employment.[18] Second, Japanese firms have ways to create flexibility in employment. For example, a temporary labor force can be utilized, and the bonus payment system serves as an inducement for employees to work hard. Third, Japanese firms rely on subcontracting for industrial parts, thus lessening the need to hire the labor force necessary to produce these parts on a sustained basis. Finally, guaranteed employment does not mean that inefficient firms are in some way maintained. On the contrary, both the pressures of the market and the role played by government agencies encourage the productive sectors and discourage the unproductive sectors. All these factors substantially mitigate what would otherwise appear to be a starkly different system of labor–management relations.

Japanese Planning

Economic planning has not been an important element in the Japanese economy. Japan has had a planning agency since the late 1940s and has assembled numerous plans. Japanese plans have been very pragmatic, with frequently shifting goals. They have been highly aggregative and are based on a simple extension of the national accounts. The plan targets (in addition to being highly aggregative) have been projected only to terminal years of the 5-year planning period, which makes them of minimal value to private firms even when those firms want to be integrated into the plan projections.

One measure of the value of a plan is how closely it is fulfilled. Japanese economic performance has typically been better than that called for by the plan. Plan targets have typically been exceeded, sometimes by very large amounts. This sort of inaccuracy renders the plan targets of little use for purposes of coordination and leads to skepticism about the plan and about the necessity for continued corrections by individual firms.

Although the discipline of Japanese firms and their management would make them look at and consider the plan, the real force of intervention in the life of the economy has been the state, not the planning agency.[19] Although we have emphasized this fact, it is worth noting again that discussion of intervention in the Japanese economy focuses not on the Economic Planning Agency but on the Ministry of International Trade and Industry, where the real power lies. In this sense, the state, its agencies, and its budget are the focus of attention.

In a study of Japanese economic planning, Kazuo Sato describes the Japanese system as indicative planning but emphasizes the sectoral impact of planning and the role of the government through the Ministry of International Trade and Industry, rather than through traditional macroeconomic channels.

Japan: Industrial Policy?

Few would identify the Japanese economy as a planned economy, though many would argue that it is an economy in which the state plays a major role. This role is played in part through the Japanese industrial structure, which we have discussed. However, it also arises through both organizational arrangements (the economic system) and policy measures, especially industrial policy. These issues deserve additional attention.

First, Japanese social structure differs markedly from other countries. Above all, Japan is a country dominated by both vertical and horizontal organization, where group allegiance, formal and informal, is very important. Japanese society might be likened to a family, where the role of each member contrasts markedly with the sort of individualism familiar to us in the United States.

Second, government does play an important role in the Japanese economy, yet its role is difficult to measure.[20] The Japanese ministerial structure has a substantial impact on the economy, not only through direct participation in key aspects of economic life, but also through its indirect influence. For example, the Ministry of Finance, along with the Bank of Japan, is responsible for the traditional functions of monetary control. In the outside world, however, it is the **Ministry of International Trade and Industry (MITI)** that receives the most attention.[21]

Third, the close relationships among manufacturing, banks, and government has meant that banks have allocated capital on the basis of an implicit industrial policy, unlike elsewhere where banks are more independent of industrial borrowers. Prior to 1998, this meant that Japanese enterprises were virtually guaranteed cheap capital through the banking system.

MITI has an impressive formal role, being responsible for international trade, domestic production, and domestic industrial structure. Whether formal or informal, though, MITI is frequently viewed as the purveyor of an "industrial policy" geared to promoting rapid economic growth.[22] MITI is responsible for guiding and influencing economic decisions by promoting key sectors of the economy and carefully phasing out other, low-productivity sectors. MITI uses public funds for research and development and provides assistance for organizational change, such as mergers. Although MITI is an important vehicle for transmitting information in the Japanese economy, few describe this function as planning.

Beyond the ministerial system, there is considerable government involvement in the economy. This activity ranges from the traditional provision of "public goods" to activities in less traditional areas. For example, special financial institutions provide supplementary services to the private industrial sector.

Traditional measures of government involvement in an economic system probably don't capture the essence of the Japanese system. In the absence of a major formal role for government and planning, the government is nevertheless able to influence both short- and long-term decision making. Rather than formal and powerful involvement in a few traditional and noticeable areas, the government exerts its influence through a myriad of arrangements that guide economic growth. Enthusiasts of an industrial policy cite the Japanese experience.

During the 1970s, outside admiration for the Japanese economic system grew. In a time of general economic turmoil, the Japanese were perceived to have found the keys to sustained economic growth. Many writers attempted to discover what forces were responsible for this growth—whether industrial policy, a special role for the government, the managerial system, the labor–management arrangements, or the nature of Japanese society and the Japanese work force. This admiration was limited only by our apparent inability to transplant these growth forces and by continuing friction in Japanese–American trade relations.

The 1970s, however, were not a tranquil decade for the Japanese economy. In the early 1970s, Japan sustained two major shocks. The first was the Nixon administration's action to end the long-fixed exchange rate between the American dollar and the Japanese yen and move toward a flexible exchange rate.[23] The second event was the initial impact of the energy crisis in 1973. The average annual rate of growth of real GDP declined from above 10 percent in the late 1960s to generally lower rates in the mid-1970s. The average annual rate of inflation reached almost 25 percent in 1974. Other performance indicators showed similar trends. Output per labor-hour in manufacturing declined, and manufacturing unit costs increased dramatically.

The late 1970s brought on a second, less severe energy crisis and (possibly more important) a sharply increasing positive balance on the current account. Once again, the problem of balancing Japanese–American trade became a major issue.

Nevertheless, the condition of the Japanese economy was generally positive: Although the rate of economic growth declined in the 1980s, performance was still impressive. Between 1965 and 1980, GDP grew at an average annual rate of 6.3 percent, and from 1980 to 1987, 3.7 percent. For the same periods, the average annual rate of inflation declined from 7.5 to 1.5 percent.[24] Policies of restraint, intended to bring inflation under control and to restore economic growth and balance-of-payments equilibrium, were largely successful.

From the late 1980s through the mid-1990s, two themes dominated discussions about Japan.[25] First, after a period of strong economic performance, negative changes increased pessimism and concern among the people of Japan. This led many in the West to question the economic strength and seeming invincibility of the Japanese economic system. Second, the Japanese trade surplus, especially its large imbalance with the United States, remained a point of contention for many and was a dominant theme of U.S.–Japanese relations during the Clinton administration.[26] These situations are interrelated and will undoubtedly be important issues throughout the decade.

A slower rate of economic growth for Japan in the 1990s, along with the end of a lengthy tenure for the Liberal Democratic Party, changed the Japanese domestic economic scene. Increasing unemployment fueled discussion about the future of the Japanese economy, especially regarding its position in research and development.

Although the United States has taken steps to reduce the large trade deficit with Japan, free trade implies a Japanese economy capable of sustaining growth of imports, and fewer "structural mechanisms" that inhibit the growth of imports, such as domestic regulations and business practices. These tend to limit the potential of foreign competitors in Japanese domestic markets.[27]

Change in the Japanese Model?

In the 1960s and 1970s, the Western world studied the Japanese economic system to determine whether its best features could be transferred to Western economies. The Japanese model of industrial policy, tight-knit relationships between the state bureaucracy and big business, close linkages among large banks, government, and bank industrial clients, and lifetime employment appeared to generate high rates of growth. Books were written and business seminars held on the Japanese way of doing business.

Japan's dramatic decline in economic performance in the 1990s has dimmed the luster of the Japanese model. The reliance on large industrial conglomerates has been seen to inhibit competition and to retard the growth of smaller and more innovative businesses. The intimate relationship between banks and large industrial concerns has caused banks (often prompted by government) to make large, unprofitable loans. The cozy relationship between government and business has created a vast system of corruption, where more than half of Japan's business enterprises have admitted to breaking the law in order to conduct their routine business operations. The close link between government and business has created campaign funding abuses that are more severe than those encountered in the United States. The system of lifetime employment offered by Japan's large industrial concerns has prevented them from downsizing to become more efficient in the world market place.

Japan's famous industrial policy—the attempt on the part of the state bureaucracy to pick upcoming industrial winners—has also been questioned—for example, the Japanese government's ill-fated decision to promote high-definition television. Japan still lags well behind the United States in technological innovation, a gap that many attribute to the Japanese economic system.

It remains to be seen whether Japan's decline in the 1990s is cyclical or more deep-rooted. We do not know whether Japan can recover its status as one of the world's fastest-growing economies. At the end of the 1990s, prospects did not appear bright. Japan's political system was in paralysis, unable to implement meaningful reforms. Growth remained anemic. Japan's banks were left with large portfolios of questionable loans, and respected financial enterprises were forced to close their doors.

Asian Tigers: South Korea, Singapore, Taiwan, and Hong Kong

The **Four Tigers**—South Korea, Singapore, Taiwan, and Hong Kong—are characterized as the newly industrialized countries of Asia.[28] These countries are the object of considerable interest in a region of the world where contemporary economic progress has been great but uneven. Moreover, they have achieved significant rates of economic growth, judged by world historical standards, and have made progress through the market mechanism and a strategy of export-led industrialization. Although there are substantive differences among these countries, it is their similarities and their economic progress that stand out. These Asian success stories deserve our attention.

Background

The Four Tigers vary considerably in size and natural endowment. In terms of population, the smallest country is Singapore (6 million) and the largest is South Korea (43 million). None is particularly well endowed with natural resources. For example,

Singapore is a wholly urban society with a strong manufacturing base, an active service sector, and virtually no agriculture. At the other end of the spectrum, South Korea is an industrialized country with a substantial agricultural sector, an urbanization level of roughly 70 percent at the end of the 1990s, and limited amounts of such resources as coal. Taiwan has an important agricultural sector, but its natural and climatic conditions are less than ideal, and minerals are in short supply. Agriculture is relatively unimportant in Hong Kong.

Performance: System and Policy

Table 12.2 summarizes, in a few simple numbers, an economic success story. All these countries have attained within three decades significant levels of per capita product. At the end of World War II, the Asian Tigers were all poor countries. Now two of them, Hong Kong and Singapore, have per capita incomes that place them in the affluent, developed world. The other two, South Korea and Taiwan, will join the ranks of the world's most affluent nations within a decade if their rapid growth continues. And though this dimension is difficult to measure accurately, the Four Tigers seem to have achieved these gains with little if any increases in inequality. They are, therefore, systems generating both efficiency and equity. Table 12.2 indicates that these countries have been able to generate exceptionally high rates of saving, most of which is invested at home, but significant amounts are also invested abroad in nearby developing Asian economies. They have also invested in people's health and education. The burden of taxes is generally light.

Economic growth has been driven by export-led industrialization. Exports have been largely manufactures, but in recent years a somewhat more diversified export

TABLE 12.2   Growth of GDP and Total Factor Productivity for the Four Tigers and Other Economies

	Annual Growth of GDP	Total Factor Productivity
Four Tigers		
Hong Kong, 1966–1991	7.3	2.3
South Korea, 1961–1990	10.3	1.7
Taiwan, 1966–1990	9.4	2.6
Singapore, 1970–1990	8.5	0.2
Other Countries		
Canada, 1960–1989	4.2	0.5
France, 1960–1989	2.7	1.5
Germany, 1960–1989	3.1	1.6
Japan, 1960–1989	5.0	2.0
Italy, 1960–1989	3.9	2.0

Source: Alwyn Young, "The Tyranny of Numbers: Confronting the Statistical Realities of the East-Asian Growth Experience," *Quarterly Journal of Economics* 110, 3 (August 1995), 657–673.

pattern has emerged (for example, financial services in the case of Singapore).[29] Growth has been achieved with a traditional mix of inputs. Although external capital played a role in earlier years, rates of domestic saving have increased rapidly, as have rates of investment, the latter largely supported by domestic sources.

For example, in the case of South Korea, gross domestic savings accounted for 8 percent of GDP in 1965 and for 38 percent in 1988. Between the same years, gross domestic investment as a share of GDP increased from 15 to 30 percent.[30] Similar changes occurred in Singapore; in Hong Kong, the ratios were high for both years but fell somewhat in the latter period.

Most of these countries have had modest and declining rates of population growth, though the transformation of agriculture has resulted in substantial growth of the labor force to support the industrialization process, most notably in South Korea and Taiwan. Structural change has been quite rapid.

The Role of the State

Each of the Four Tigers has a different political system. The governments of South Korea and Singapore have been more repressive than that of Hong Kong, which has not suppressed labor unions. Singapore, however, is strongly opposed to trade unionism and has invoked economic arguments against unionism. In South Korea, an active and noisy form of trade unionism has developed.

The common feature of state policy in this region has been the consistent support of the policy of *export promotion* over *import substitution*. Export promotion refers to state policies to promote exports. Such policies can range from subsidies of export industries to free-trade practices for the economy as a whole. Import-substitution policies are those that protect domestic industries from foreign competition by tariffs or other barriers against foreign products. Industrial policies in some developing nations may be directed toward planning and protectionism. Industrial policy in the Four Tigers aims to promote the export of industries in the context of generally free trade.

The World Bank provides evidence of the success of the free-trade orientation of the Four Tigers. The World Bank has classified Hong Kong, Singapore, and South Korea as the world's most strongly outward-oriented economies among the developing countries during the periods 1963–1973 and 1973–1985. Notable, the same study classified India as among the most strongly inward-oriented of the developing economies.[31] More general statistical studies, though plagued by conceptual and empirical difficulties, generally conclude that the relationship between export orientation and economic growth is positive.[32]

Rightly or wrongly, the Four Tigers have the reputation of having achieved their success through reliance on free markets. This view is disputed by some, who claim that the Tiger's success has depended on government action in many instances. According to a 1997 study by Britain's Overseas Development institute, Asia's Four Tigers' economies owe their success to the entrepreneurial successes of their governments rather than to classic free-market principles.[33] The study disputes the contention that deregulation and free markets created high growth in Hong

Kong, Singapore, South Korea, and Taiwan. The notion that government's alliance with business played a key role in the success of the region is also being fostered by the Asian Development Bank located in Japan.

The contention is that governments, in different ways, played the role of result-oriented entrepreneurs in a dynamic framework for government intervention. There is no disguising the role of government in South Korea, Taiwan and Singapore, and the hidden role of government in Hong Kong was great as well. In Hong Kong, the government subsidized housing to maintain social stability and reduce the cost of labor. The Hong Kong government used revenue from land sales to sustain a welfare system, while maintaining low corporate and personal taxation. The Hong Kong government did not seek to pick winners, but it did find it necessary to intervene in the housing market and the planning of infrastructure.

In the other three tigers, government's approach was more direct. The other three routinely targeted specific industries and specific companies for assistance, but the emphasis on export performance pushed industry toward international standards.

Asian Growth and Income Distribution

As we have seen, East Asia recorded a remarkable record of economic growth from 1965 to the present. One of the often-overlooked aspects of this growth is that the East Asian economies have combined high growth with relatively low and declining inequality of income.

Figure 12.2 is a scatter diagram for 40 economies, showing the relationship between economic growth and income inequality as measured by the ratio of the income share of the richest 20 percent to that of the poorest 20 percent of the population. As the figure shows, there are seven high-growth–low-income-equality countries, and all seven are in East Asia. The East Asian economies began their era of rapid growth with relatively equal distributions of income, and most of them have ended with a more nearly equal distribution than when they started.[34] As the author of a substantial survey of the East Asian growth experience comments, "East Asian economies have relatively equal income distributions, and growth in the region is especially noteworthy in that it has not been at the expense of equity."[35]

How was it that East Asia was able to combine growth and equity? One factor has been that the governments of the region adopted policies to ensure that all groups benefited from economic growth. These programs included universal education and public housing programs, land reform, and control of fertilizer and agricultural prices to raise rural incomes. History also explains the more nearly equal distribution of income: Japan's defeat in World war II, the destruction of the Korean War, and the defeat of the Chinese nationalist forces made possible rural land reform and eliminated the property assets of the elite.[36]

East Asia's relatively equitable distributions of income may contribute to their more rapid growth. Less inequality usually means greater political stability. It also means a more equitable distribution of education. A high degree of income inequality may promote labor unrest and political conflict, both of which inflict greater risks on the economy and raise the cost of capital.[37]

FIGURE 12.2   Income Inequality and Growth of GDP, 1965–1989

GDP growth per capita (percent)

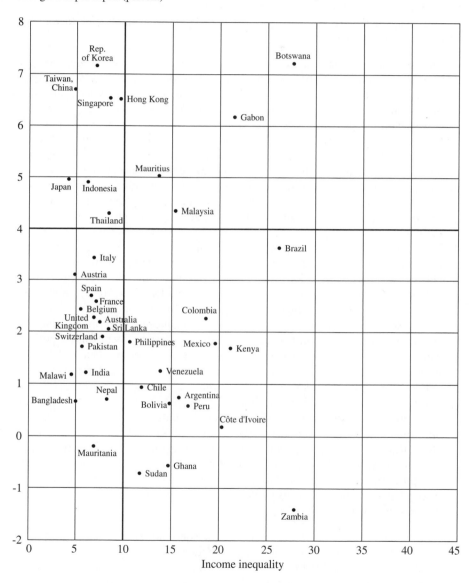

Note: Income inequality is measured by the ratio of the income shares of the richest 20% and the poorest 20% of the population.

Source: World Bank data.

Explanations of the Asian Miracle

The rapid economic growth of the East Asian region is clearly not explained by any single factor. It must be attributed to the history of the region, the policies of the governments, and by the economic institutions established.

Scholars of the East Asian miracle have identified a number of factors that explain the rapid growth:

1. The fact that the East Asian economies went rapidly through their demographic transitions from high fertility and high mortality to low fertility and low mortality caused substantial increases in savings rates. With declining fertility, the ratio of dependents to adult workers fell, freeing discretionary income for savings.[38]
2. Governments in the region promoted a stable investment climate by adopting stable macroeconomic policies and providing stability, secure property rights, and tranquil industrial relations. Some governments created development banks that took a longer-run view of investment and monitored industrial borrowers carefully.
3. The government of East Asia promoted universal education and investment in human capital, such as in public health. The high levels of human capital at the starting point of rapid growth is thought to have contributed substantially to the rapid economic growth.[39]
4. Many experts believe that openness to international trade was one of the most important factors in the region's rapid growth. Developing countries can choose between outward orientation (attempting to grow on the basis of exports) and import substitution (attempting to boost the domestic economy by substituting domestic production for imports). The outward-oriented policies that the East Asian countries employed varied from the use of incentives to undervalued exchange rates, the avoidance of import restrictions, trade liberalization policies, and so on.[40] Competing in world markets forced domestic producers to become more efficient and to learn new technologies. Exports generated foreign exchange that could be used to import raw materials and capital goods.
5. Some but not all East Asian governments promoted foreign direct investment to supplement domestic saving and attract new technologies. Policies toward foreign direct investment varied widely; Japan and Korea were hostile, whereas Hong Kong and Singapore promoted foreign investment. Foreign direct investment has been significant in parts of East Asia, but only in Singapore was direct foreign investment more than 10 percent of capital formation. In all cases, steps were taken to introduce new technologies, in some cases through the use of multinational corporations.

The most controversial issue related to the source of East Asian growth is the extent to which it was made possible by market-oriented policies versus state-interventionist policies. Experts are divided between the conventional view that East Asian growth has been driven primarily by free-market policies and the "revisionist" view that growth was promoted by strong government intervention.[41]

The World Bank supports the conventional view that East Asian growth was promoted by the largely noninterventionist policies of area governments. Evidence of the free-market orientation includes the limited price distortions (the use of world market and market-determined prices), the relatively limited size of government, the limited protection of the export orientation of economic policies. Moreover, there is evidence that export policies promoting domestic markets, and were pursued generally, rather than selectively to give an advantage to particular government-favored industries and companies.

The conventional views and revisionist views differ most markedly in the area of the effect of industrial policy—the use of financial incentives, subsidies, and credit allocation to specific government-favored sectors of the economy to achieve growth.

In this regard, industrial policy appears to have been used in Japan, Korea, and Taiwan where governments singled out specific industries and companies for favorable credits, protection of domestic markets, direct foreign investment controls, export promotion, and government allocation of foreign exchange. In other East Asian economies, most notably in Hong Kong, there was a clear absence of industrial policy.

Whereas there is agreement that industrial policy was actively pursued in certain East Asian economies, there is less agreement about its effectiveness. Empirical studies of Korean and Taiwanese industrial policy conclude, for example, that there were negative correlations between the amount of government support to an industry and that industry's total factor productivity growth.[42] Other supporters of the conventional view suggest that, if anything, industrial policies simply conformed to the results that the market would have achieved if it had been left alone.

Revisionists, on the other hand, claim that industrial policy played a major positive role because of the initial weakness of the East Asian capital markets. Without strong interventionist policies the growth industries would not have been financed. In addition, the revisionists argue that state industrial policy did not pick winners; it made winners. Without state intervention, the industrial success stories of East Asia would not have happened. To argue that state industrial policy can pick winners means that the state must have greater insights into the economic future than private entrepreneurs.

The Future Growth of East Asia

East Asian growth has been very rapid over the past three decades.[43] Can it continue to be as rapid in the future? In this respect, East Asia bears a strong resemblance to the Soviet economy of the 1930s, 1950s, and 1960s. In both cases, much of the rapid growth was explained by the rapid growth of inputs—in particular by the rapid growth of capital—but also by the rapid growth of the labor force. Further, as in the case of the Soviet Union, it is not possible for an economy to continue indefinitely to expand its inputs at extremely rapid rates. In East Asia, the demographic transition has been completed, so the growth of the adult population will be less rapid than in the past. High rates of capital formation require continued sacrifice by a population that refrains from consuming and prefers instead to save. Even if high rates of saving continue, there is the question of whether high rates of return can persist, given the growing imbalance between capital and labor inputs.

The End of the Asian Miracle?

The GDP growth of the Four Tigers from 1970 to 1996 is shown in Table 12.3. All four recorded rates of growth more than double those of the industrialized world. It is this rapid growth over two decades that made the Four Tigers either "rich" countries or "future rich" countries.

Notably, the success of the Four Tigers spread to other parts of Southeast Asia (the ASEAN region—Association for Southeast Asian Nations)—to Malaysia, Thailand, and Indonesia and, to some extent, to the Philippines. These countries also began to achieve rapid growth by adopting some of the policies of the Four Tigers. Perhaps more important, the Four Tigers themselves began to invest in the region. This investment was funded by the growing difference between domestic saving and domestic investment.

Never before has a region sustained economic growth in the neighborhood of 8 percent per annum for more than three decades, as have the economies of East Asia. The original Four Tigers—Hong Kong, South Korea, Singapore, and Taiwan—have joined the ranks of the developed countries in terms of per capita income. Hong Kong and Singapore are now richer than Great Britain. In the last two decades, the poorer countries of East Asia—Indonesia, Malaysia, and Thailand (we discussed China in Chapter 10)—have grown rapidly and have started to chase the leaders of East Asia, even though they started from a much lower level of income.

In 1996 and 1997, the growth of the ASEAN countries slowed; they logged export growth of only 5 percent per year. There were other signs of trouble: Malaysia, South Korea, and Thailand ran current account deficits; South Korea was beset by labor unrest and political crisis. The Korean and Thai stock markets fell, and GDP growth for the region slowed from 9 percent in 1995 to 7 percent in 1996. Growth slowed even more for the richest three tigers—to 5 percent for the year.[44]

It is clearly too early to determine whether the Four Tigers' economies are slowing. Analysts fall into two groups, the optimists and the pessimists, who debate the original sources of rapid growth in East Asia and hence its sustainability.[45]

The pessimist case was advanced by Paul Krugman, who has argued that East Asia's growth was achieved primarily through the rapid growth of the capital stock and through shifts in resources from agriculture to industry. Thus East Asian growth was similar to that of the Soviet Union: It was primarily extensive in nature. Although a rapid expansion in resources can lead to higher growth as it did in the Soviet Union, such growth cannot be sustained, because a country cannot indefinitely expand its resources without exhausting the resource-generating ability of the population.

According to Krugman, growth based on the expansion of inputs is self-limiting. His statistics suggest that very little of East Asia's growth has been based on the growth of the residual—the growth of total factor productivity.

Krugman based his conclusions on the empirical work of Alwyn Young, who analyzed the growth experiences of 118 countries from 1970 to 1985, splitting GDP growth into growth due to the expansion of inputs and growth due to the more productive use of these inputs.[46] Young found that the growth of total factor productivity was no higher in the East Asian countries than in the industrialized countries.

TABLE 12.3   The ASEAN Economies

		GDP Growth		
	GDP Per Capita	1970–1980	1980–1989	1990–1996
Hong Kong	23,900	9.2	7.5	5.0
Singapore	22,600	9.4	7.2	8.3
Taiwan	13,200	10.2	8.1	6.3
South Korea	11,900	9.3	8.0	7.7
Malaysia	10,400	8.0	5.7	8.8
Thailand	8,000	7.3	7.2	8.6
Indonesia	3,800	7.8	5.7	7.2
Philippines	2,800	6.1	1.8	2.8
Industrialized countries	19,400	3.4	2.6	2.0

Sources: IMF, ING Barings, national statistics.

Thus, if deprived of the rapid expansion of inputs, the Tigers would have had no higher growth than the rich industrialized economies. (See Table 12.3)

The optimists argue that the East Asian economies can continue to expand at more rapid rates than the industrialized West. They argue that the East Asian economies have created a solid basis for growth with enlightened free-market policies and openness to world capital and product markets. The Union Bank of Switzerland, for example, studied the productivity growth of 104 countries for the period 1970 to 1990 and concluded that five of the ASEAN economies ranked among the top 12 economies in terms of total factor productivity growth. This conclusion was supported by a study of the International Monetary Fund, which concluded that Three of the east Asian economies had total factor productivity growth between 2 percent and 2.25 percent per annum between 1978 and 1996, compared with the U.S. annual rate of 0.3 percent.

Moreover, the optimists argue that their high investment rates gave the East Asian economies the opportunity to introduce advanced leading-edge technology. With investment rates averaging 35 percent of GDP, the East Asian economies had the opportunity to import technology from the rest of the world at a high rate.

High savings rates alone do not guarantee rapid growth. Investments must be put to good use. In this respect, the optimists point to structural features of the East Asian economies that allowed them to invest their savings wisely: their openness, low taxation, strict monetary and fiscal policies, commitment to education, and flexible labor markets. The relative openness of markets ensured that resources would be allocated according to price signals.

The dispute over the future of East Asia is related to the growth opportunities that remain. Can East Asia continue to narrow the income gap between itself and the rich industrialized economies? Workers in East Asia still work with much less capital per worker than in the rich industrialized economies; there is still an education gap. On the negative side, the future growth of East Asia could be retarded by the rapid growth of wages, which make East Asia less of an attraction for investment. The Tigers must compete with China, Eastern Europe, and the former Soviet Union, all of which offer labor at lower rates.

The Asian Crisis

During the second half of 1997, the Asian miracle appeared to collapse, beginning with Thailand and spreading to Indonesia, Malaysia, South Korea, and even Japan. Although the reasons for collapse vary, a common thread appeared to be a loss of confidence in the currency followed by drastic devaluations of the currency. In many cases, Asian countries had tied their own currency to the U.S. dollar. As they experienced higher inflation than the United States, their currencies became overvalued, prompting attacks on their currencies by speculators. As their currencies fell in value, they were unable to service their large external debts, and they had to petition their foreign creditors for debt relief. Given the magnitude of the debt problem, they had to negotiate with the International Monetary fund for stand-by credits.

The currency collapse also exposed the weakness of the banking system, which had made too many real estate loans which were backed by office buildings and other real estates whose values had also collapsed. The collapse also revealed the extent of corruption, whereby low-interest loans had been granted to well-connected families and business groups.

Countries particularly hard-hit by the Asian crisis were Thailand, Indonesia, and South Korea. It is too early to determine the long-term outcome. We do not know whether these countries can restore long-term rapid growth.

India: The Failed Quest for Economic Growth

This chapter examines two models of economic development—one unsuccessful, the other successful. India, the unsuccessful model, is one of the world's largest countries that has used heavy state intervention to promote economic development. Taiwan, South Korea, Hong Kong, and Singapore—the Four Tigers that we have just discussed—make up the successful model. These four East Asian countries have experienced extremely rapid economic development over the past three decades. They have relied more on market forces and on free trade than on the state to promote their economic development.

Earlier, this book posed a question: Does any one economic system appear better suited than others to solving the development problems of low-income countries? It is therefore incumbent on us to study a low-income country. There are more poor countries than affluent ones. In fact, affluence is limited to a very small proportion of the world's population. The difficulty is that there is more diversity among the **less-developed countries** (the **LDCs**) than among the industrialized economies. Some LDCs are only a step removed from the economic arrangements they have exhibited for centuries; others appear to be on their way to transforming themselves into developed countries. Moreover, the LDCs have diverse political and social in-stitutions. In some LDCs, tribal or traditional authority still prevails; others have adopted Western democratic political institutions; and still others are controlled by dictatorships of one kind or another.

What common features can be extracted from this diversity? LDCs possess the characteristics generally associated with low levels of income: the dominant role of agriculture, high fertility and mortality rates, limited use of advanced technology, and lower saving rates. In addition to these features, LDCs share other characteris-tics: concentration of the ownership of wealth, reliance on indirect taxes, extensive government control of international transactions, poorly developed capital markets, and monopoly power in the limited industrial sector.[47]

Poor countries used to admire what was then viewed as the rapid economic progress of planned socialist systems. This admiration was reflected in such features as cooperative arrangements in agriculture and a major role for the state in economic development, not to mention the appeal of policies to influence the distribution of income. Will recent developments in the Soviet Union and Eastern Europe alter these views, and if so, what will be the results?

Rather than attempt to deal with the LDCs as a group, we have selected one from the heart of Asia—India. The Indian economy is reasonably representative of the operation of the capitalist economic system at low levels of economic development.

India is an important example of capitalism in a large and poor country. Unlike China, India has chosen an economic system that is basically capitalist in character, but it combines this system with a significant degree of state influence, the latter im-plemented through various types of controls and a state planning system. Economic growth and economic development are key goals of Indian economic policy. Thus it makes more sense to compare India and China than, for example, India and the United States. Moreover, India is a country with economic policies that have been redirected, in the 1990s, away from the socialist path toward greater reliance on markets.

Characteristics[48]

Table 12.4 shows summary statistics for India, with comparisons to China and the United States. India is the world's second most populous country (almost 850 million in 1990), with approximately 15 percent of the world's population. On the other hand, India accounts for under 2 percent of world GDP. These two facts highlight India's very low per capita income (roughly $300–$400 in U.S. dollars). Approximately 31 percent of India's GDP originates in agriculture, and only 1 in 4 persons lives in urban areas. Some 70 percent of the labor force works in agriculture. Population has tended to grow at a rate of over 2 percent per annum (compared with about 0.5 per-cent in the industrialized countries), and life expectancy is under 50 years. Only 1 in every 3 adults is literate.

Although India is a large country, natural conditions are less than ideal both from a climatic perspective and in terms of environmental decay resulting, for example, from industrial pollution and land use arrangements. India has substantial mineral deposits and large reserves of coal.

TABLE 12.4   Selected Structural Features of India

Feature	India	China	United States
Per capita GNP, 1991, in U.S. $	330.0	370.0	22,240.0
Percent of population urban, 1991	27	60	75
Percent of GDP derived from industry, 1991	27	42	33[a]
Government expenditure as a percent of GNP, 1991	17.5	n.a.[b]	25.3
Gross domestic investment as a percent of GDP, 1991	20	36	15
Average annual rate of inflation, 1980–91	8.2	5.8	4.2
Defense expenditures as a percent of total central government expenditure, 1991	17.0	n.a.	21.6

[a] 1988
[b] not available

Source: All data are from World Bank, *World Development Report 1993* (New York: Oxford University Press, 1993), Tables 1–32.

India has been called the world's largest democracy. Its government is patterned on the English parliamentary system, and Indian politics was dominated until the 1990s by the Congress Party. India comprises a multiplicity of ethnic groups who speak different languages, and it has suffered over the years from ethnic and regional strife. Indeed, this strife remains important in the late 1990s.

The Indian Economy: Historical Background[49]

The Indian economy prior to India's achieving independence from Britain in 1947 makes an ideal case study of a traditional society with a long history of colonial domination. Prior to British rule (first under the British East India Company and then under the Crown), the Indian moghul economy (so called because a Moslem minority was the ruling elite) operated according to long-standing traditional rules. Society was divided into castes: the religious leaders, warlords, and their retainers were at the top, and the small peasant and "untouchable" castes were at the bottom. In this hierarchical system, one's place in society, as well as one's occupation, was determined at birth. Occupations were not distributed according to the skills, qualifications, and wishes of individuals or according to the needs of society. Moreover, work was considered beneath the dignity of the upper castes; physical labor could be engaged in only by the lower castes.

In contrast to other feudal societies, the ruling class itself generally did not own the means of agricultural production and was not involved in its management. Instead, the actual land cultivators paid taxes (tribute, often 50 percent of the harvest) to the ruling classes according to custom and in return for protection, which was necessary in an area torn by regional factionalism, warlordism, and civil strife. Agricultural taxes were levied not only to meet the needs of general government but also to support the high living standards of the upper castes. In the village community, the ruling class controlled the land, but because property rights were poorly defined, the farm family (and the landlords) had little incentive to undertake land improvements. In the farm family, an extended family system prevailed whereby income was shared among brothers, cousins, uncles, and so on.

The wealthy classes were not motivated to make productive investments; instead, their savings were devoted to acquiring precious metals, and little social overhead investment (such as irrigation) was undertaken. Foreign trade was conducted primarily by foreigners, who traded Indian spices and handicrafts for gold and silver. The limited education that did exist was purely religious in character, and the education of women was proscribed.

Economic progress under the moghul economy was limited. Population did not increase for two thousand years. It is likely that in the sixteenth century, per capita income in India was on a par with that of Western Europe, and contemporary European visitors even felt that average living standards were higher in India than at home. By the time of British rule, however, per capita income in India was very low compared with that of Western Europe. Thus during the era when Europe was preparing for its initial industrialization and population expansion, the Indian moghul economy was becoming relatively backward. The reasons for this declining economic position are not hard to identify: the rigid caste system, religious restrictions, uncertain property rights, barriers against productive investment, and civil strife. It was this last, particularly the enmity between the majority Hindu population and their Moslem rulers (as well as regional factionalism)—that allowed the British to turn India easily into a colonial dominion.

The Indian economy under British rule was not dramatically different, but the British did remove the old moghul warlord aristocracy, replacing it with a new indigenous ruling elite (supportive of the British) and a professional British bureaucracy, both designed to preserve law and order. Britain's objective was not to promote the economic development of India but to use India as a guaranteed market for British products. Tariff barriers were erected against the sale of Indian textiles abroad, and the removal of the moghul princes reduced the demand in India for the traditional luxury products of Indian handicraft. The British accepted and even intensified the caste system by establishing themselves as a separate ruling class. After 1930, native Indians gradually infiltrated the bureaucracy. This native bureaucracy became a wellspring of nationalism and was instrumental in achieving independence for India in 1947.

During British rule, the population of India began to grow for the first time over an extended period, and the economy grew along with it. Nevertheless, per capita income failed to increase perceptibly. Although British colonial rule did establish conditions for the growth of output and population, it did not allow output growth to exceed population growth. The positive economic features of the colonial period included the creation of a professional bureaucracy, the introduction of a secular education system to replace the system of religious education, a reduction of the tax burden on agriculture, and the creation of some property rights in agriculture (for the new ruling class). Under British rule, the proportion of national income going to the nonvillage economy declined somewhat with elimination of the moghul elite, and a lower proportion of national income went to the new ruling elite (British officials, native princes, and their retainers). However, the share of income received by those at the bottom of the ladder did not increase.

The Modern "Socialist" Indian Economy

The modern Indian economy is the creation of the Congress party and its leaders, Mahatma Gandhi and Jawaharlal Nehru, who referred to India as a "socialist" economy, though they differed on the appropriate course of **Indian socialism**. Gandhi extolled the traditional village community as the ideal economic organization and downgraded industrialization and the profit motive. Nehru favored industrialization and emphasized heavy industry as the appropriate path for Indian socialism. According to our definition, *socialism* is largely a misnomer in the case of India, except for government ownership in industry and commerce. Indian leadership has not pursued a socialist distribution of income. India is still primarily an agricultural country, and the distribution of income depends mainly on the distribution of agricultural property. Since independence, only limited progress has been made in land reform. Although there have been some efforts to distribute land to the poor peasants, land remains unequally distributed, and there is no evidence that the range of income inequality has been reduced.[50] It is true that the pensioning off of the native princes and limitations on landholdings have reduced the number of enormous estates, but the land-limiting legislation has been circumvented, and many Indian states have not been able (or willing) to push land reform because of the strength of vested landed interests. The tax system continues to be regressive, direct taxes are rarely levied on land, and the nominally high urban income taxes are ameliorated by evasion and through numerous exemptions.

The pretax income distribution figures sum up the failure to establish a more equitable distribution of income. In 1960, the bottom 10 percent of families accounted for less than 1 percent of all income, whereas the top 10 percent accounted for more than one-third. This income distribution is less equitable than in the industrialized capitalist countries (a less equitable distribution is characteristic of less-developed countries).[51] The after-tax distribution is not significantly different from this pretax distribution because of the predominance of regressive indirect taxes. A native Indian elite of civil servants, the military, and capitalists has replaced the British and the native princes at the top of the income distribution. Landless agricultural laborers, small landholders, and the urban poor remain at the bottom.

Rather than seeking to achieve "socialist" objectives through income redistribution, the architects of the modern Indian economy emphasized state ownership in industry. The feeling was that socialism could be achieved through state control of industry, which would serve as a surrogate for social change. State promotion of heavy industry (through ownership and government controls) was to lead to economic development and limit the concentration of wealth in private hands, and it was assumed that economic development would inevitably bring about necessary social change. In the early postwar period, the Indians adopted one basic feature of the Soviet development model: the priority of heavy industry over light industry and agriculture. It was argued that the creation of a domestic heavy-industry base would lead to more rapid development, would promote domestic savings, and would make India less dependent on the outside world (freeing India to pursue an independent political course).[52]

India's heavy-industry strategy was reflected in the public ownership of heavy industries and banking. Steel, heavy machinery, chemicals, power, fuel, communication, transportation, and life insurance were nationalized in the early 1950s. In the 1970s the state moved to enlarge the public sector by nationalizing the large banks, the copper industry, the wholesale grain and jute trade, and a number of coal mines and textile mills. In some instances, the Indians followed the British pattern of nationalization to rescue failing private companies. In others (such as the wholesale grain trade), nationalization was undertaken to expand state control over the private economy. Nationalization was usually accomplished by compensation of previous owners (rather than expropriation), and an increasing "Indianization" of industrial ownership has evolved as foreign owners have been displaced.

Despite substantial nationalization, the scope of the public sector remains limited. Private enterprise still accounts for some 90 percent of industrial output.[53] The public sector (general government and public enterprises) accounts for approximately 15 percent of national output.[54] The government's share of savings is 13 percent.[55] These figures indicate that the role of the public sector in India is below average or small compared to that in the industrialized countries.[56] Thus the strategy of pursuing socialism through public ownership has had only a limited effect on the aggregate economy. However, one must bear in mind that the Indian economy is still highly underdeveloped and that most of the labor force remains concentrated in agriculture and personal services. This means that the share of the heavy-industry sector (the focal point of nationalization) must necessarily be limited. Moreover, the impact of public policy on economic affairs may be greater than the figures indicate because of a pervasive system of indirect controls and planning.

The organization of the private industrial sector is quite concentrated in India, and the objective of limiting industrial wealth holdings has not been achieved. At the end of the 1950s, the twenty largest industrial groups owned one-third of the share capital of the private corporate sector.[57] Although measures have been introduced since then to reduce this concentration of private wealth and power (the most significant being the nationalization of large banking interests), large private interests are probably promoted by the existing system of economic control. In addition, major industrialists are key figures in the Congress party.

Economic Planning in India[58]

Economic planning in India has attracted considerable attention because India is one of the few LDCs to have well-organized and sophisticated planning machinery. The planning apparatus in a typical LDC is as underdeveloped as the economy, so the Indian example serves as a useful test case of the potential contribution of planning in an LDC.

Indian planning would be classified as indicative, even though its heritage is the Soviet experience. It is a noncompulsory form of planning, in keeping with the Indian philosophy that the use of force is contrary to Indian democracy. This is not to suggest that Indian plan directives have not been implemented. In the industrial sector a wide range of enforcement mechanisms have been available. Much heavy industry is directly owned by the state and can be expected to follow plan guidelines; industrial credit is largely state-controlled; import licenses are also granted by the state. The fact that the Indian economy has developed a relatively large heavy-industry sector for an LDC demonstrates better than anything else that planning has mattered. Nevertheless, India continues to be an agricultural country, and agriculture, which cannot be planned in any effective way, remains largely out of the control of planners.

India has concentrated on long-term plans, typically of five years in duration. Attempts to devise annual operational plans have not been successful. Planning goals and planning methods have changed over the years, although the general objectives (raising the rate of economic growth and the investment ratio, reducing inequalities, and stimulating employment) are familiar to observers of national economic planning. The first plan was based on simple Keynesian growth models. The second plan (1956–1961) emphasized the priority of heavy industry. Later plans have concentrated on multisectoral balances and have to some extent moved away from the emphasis on heavy industry.

Balances for the major industrial sectors have been constructed (via either rudimentary methods or input–output tables) to determine the consistency of the plan. A crucial component of the plan is the investment subplan, which indicates the growth rates of investment in the public and private sectors. The investment plan, which determines the basic direction of the economy, is most amenable to enforcement because of the state's control of public enterprises, raw-material allocations, investment credit, and imports.

Economic planning in India is carried out on an aggregated level; specific output directives are not normally issued to the private industrial sector. In the public sector, an industry often consists of a small number of publicly owned enterprises, so the aggregate directives can be converted into actual production and investment targets. On the surface, it would appear that Indian planners are in a better position to influence the behavior of industry with the arsenal of controls at their disposal, but it is difficult to establish what degree of control they actually exercise over the private sector.

Recent studies of Indian planning reveal a system that has had both successes and failures. On balance, however, the Indian planning system did not always achieve its objectives, and it failed to adapt to change in an economy in which private ownership and markets have been important.

Economic Controls[59]

Governmental controls over resource allocation are more extensive in India than in the industrialized capitalist countries. In addition to the planning apparatus, a whole range of extramarket controls are utilized. The rationale for these controls is the widespread belief that the free market cannot be trusted to allocate resources in a low-income country.

The basic instrument for control of private industry was the Industries Act of 1951, which covered almost all manufacturing, mining, and power. It gave the government authority to grant licenses for expanding capacity and to control the allocation and prices of raw materials and, in some instances, the prices of finished products. The prices of basic agricultural products are controlled by the state, and a complex zonal pricing system exists to regulate the flow of agricultural products from regions of surplus to regions of deficit. Moreover, the state disburses food products received under foreign aid programs and in this way exerts further influence over agricultural prices.

A most important instrument of state control is state regulation of foreign exchange and imports. Since the mid-1950s, India has been on a strict import and exchange control system. Imported capital equipment, crucial to industrial expansion, has been regulated by industrial licensing, and input and raw-material licenses have regulated the disbursement of imported materials to industrial users. The import control system has operated on the principles of essentiality and indigenous nonavailability. In order to justify an import, the domestic user has to demonstrate that the commodity is essential and that it cannot be purchased at home. Import restrictions, when strictly applied, have given automatic protection to domestic industry and, according to many economists,[60] have reduced the efficiency of the Indian economy.

In the late 1960s, the Indian system of **economic controls** was reexamined, and an attempt was made to limit controls (except for agricultural pricing) to large firms. The retention of controls, despite the growing recognition of their inefficiency, can be attributed to three factors.[61] The first is that many large firms actually like controls because they reduce risk and guarantee profits. Second, controls enhance the power and positions of bureaucrats. Third, distrust of the market is ingrained in the Indian bureaucracy.

It is difficult to quantify the effect of government controls on Indian resource allocation because one cannot know to what extent they are circumvented. What one can say is that the system of state controls is more comprehensive than that in the advanced capitalist countries.

Growth Performance

The growth of the Indian economy after 1947 represents a marked improvement over its historical performance. As we have already noted, the moghul economy was stagnant for centuries, and per capita income failed to grow during British colonial rule; therefore, any growth of per capita income is an improvement over historical standards. The difficulty in evaluating Indian growth performance is that the world economy experienced accelerated growth after World War II, and India would be expected to participate in this acceleration.

India's per capita GDP averaged a 1.7 percent annual growth for the period 1965–1985. According to Angus Maddison, the reasons for this per capita growth rate are the expansion of government services (education and credit assistance), a high investment rate, the increase in both public and private investment, foreign aid, and the importation of advanced technology. Although inflation averaged about 7 percent annually in the 1980s, growth in real output has been sustained largely as a result of growth in the industrial sector.

On the positive side of the ledger is the steady but unspectacular rise in per capita income despite substantial population pressures. In the crucial agricultural area, output has expanded slightly more rapidly than population (at a per capita rate of about one-half of 1 percent per year). India's dependence on imported grains has declined over the years, and now India is largely self-sufficient in basic food grains. On the negative side, India's growth in per capita income has been slow relative to the performance of other developing countries (whose per capita income growth tended to be around 2 to 3 percent per year). India's growth performance has been well below that of China, although China and India began their postcolonial development from an equivalent point. Because of lower growth, India's per capita income today is less than three-quarters that of China.[62] Additional negative features include persistent high unemployment (and underemployment), rapid inflation, and susceptibility to external shocks (such as the oil price explosion of the 1970s).

Maddison and Malenbaum argue that Indian growth has been substandard for the LDCs in the postwar era, and Maddison calculates that the Indian growth rate has been 25 percent below its potential.[63] The reasons for this underutilization of growth potential are India's extremely low per capita income, its relatively small per capita receipts of foreign capital, its poor natural resources, the drain of a large military, the retention of institutional constraints (caste restrictions, maldistribution of agricultural land, taboo on the slaughter of livestock), and the inefficiency of public enterprise, which has been operated at a loss throughout most of the postwar era.

Capitalism in India

Notwithstanding the large share of government ownership of heavy industry and finance, India is a capitalist economy. The public-enterprise sector is a small part of the total economy, and private ownership prevails throughout the rest of the economy. The dominant sector, agriculture, is characterized by private ownership of land. There has been no significant change in the distribution of income, and the inequality of income distribution is greater in India than in the advanced capitalist countries, whether calculated on a pretax or a posttax basis. Economic planning is primarily indicative, although planning of the public enterprise sector may carry with it some compulsory elements. Nevertheless, noncoercion remains the foundation of Indian planning.

Government intervention in private economic decision making is probably more extensive in India than in the advanced capitalist countries, although the actual degree of compliance is difficult to establish. Government controls have been placed on prices, imports, foreign exchange, raw materials, and capacity expansion. One reason for these controls is a rather deep-seated distrust of market resource allocation. On the other hand, controls seem to be a characteristic feature of capitalism under conditions of underdevelopment, so in this sense, India conforms to the general pattern of underdevelopment.

Problems and Prospects

The basic challenge facing India over the coming decades is to improve the utilization of its abundant resource, labor. Endemically high rates of unemployment and underemployment attest to labor's underutilization, but the best means of correcting the situation remains a hotly debated issue. Should there be more or less planning? Should government intervention and controls be increased or reduced? Can ways be found to remove the remaining vestiges of feudalism and the caste system? Can centuries-old regional and ethnic factionalism be removed? Can there be any narrowing in income inequality? In a sense, the biggest decision facing India appears to be whether to choose more market or more plan. Should resource allocation be more fully entrusted to the market, with government acting on the sidelines to protect property rights and promote competition? Or is it dangerous to trust market guidance in a developing country?

The Indian Economy in the Twenty-First Century

The past Soviet experience with national economic planning, especially, had a significant impact on the policies and on the systemic arrangements of the Indian economy. At the same time, performance problems with sectoral difficulties, in particular, led to an ongoing reassessment of the planning system in the 1980s. The result reduced the extent to which government controls intervened in the private sector, though the actual magnitude of change at this time has been the subject of debate.[64]

By the summer of 1991, however, India began moving toward the implementation of market strategies using traditional macroeconomic tools to handle budgetary deficits, inflation, and balance of payments. There has also been a move toward deregulation in the private sector and decentralization of decision making in the public sector. It has been argued that these changes represent an important shift in the arrangements of the Indian economic system.[65]

In the mid-1990s, a coalition government replaced the ruling Congress party for the first time since Indian independence. The coalition government began pursuing reforms to convert India into a modern market economy, starting with privatization and the attraction of foreign capital. India's sleepy stock market began to rise as risk capital flowed into India. In 1997 the coalition government failed, and political instability frightened away a considerable amount of foreign investment.

The success stories of China and the Four Tigers will make it difficult for India to forego significant reform in the future. It cannot afford to be left behind when its most immediate neighbors are growing rapidly.

Summary

In this chapter, we have examined the experience of several developing nations that are using variants of market capitalism to promote economic growth and economic development. Although less-developed nations share a number of characteristics, the examples we have chosen to examine also exhibit unique features that make them of compelling interest to the study of different economic systems.

India has always been of interest to economists as a large and poor country that has, in the past, pursued economic growth through the market, but with a significant socialist overlay. In the Indian case, the socialist overlay was derived from the Soviet experience. India has promoted economic growth through a policy of investment expansion guided in part by state controls and a system of economic planning.

The comparison of India to China has always been interesting because of both the similarities and the differences between these two countries. This comparison has remained of interest in the 1990s because China has pursued major economic reforms tending toward greater emphasis on markets, and India has also reduced its reliance on controls, focusing more on market mechanisms for both macroeconomic and microeconomic decision making.

The original Four Tigers (South Korea, Singapore, Taiwan, and Hong Kong) are important examples of economic growth through export-led industrialization. It is often argued that the model of export-led industrialization can be transplanted to other settings. Whether the Tigers' experience can be replicated in other parts of Southeast Asia (the ASEAN region) is of great interest, and attention at the end of the century focuses on the fundamental issue of whether rapid economic growth can be generally sustained.

The countries we examine in this chapter began the process of economic development under very different existing conditions and represent various approaches to industrialization. The critical issue in these cases is isolating the forces that have (and those that have not) led to economic growth and economic development and then assessing their durability and transferability. It is too early to determine whether these countries can restore high rates of economic growth following the consequences of the Asian Crisis, which began in 1997.

Key Terms

agricultural surplus

less-developed country (LDC)

Indian socialism

Indian planning

Industrial policy

economic controls

Four Tigers

economic growth

export-led industrialization

share economy

Ministry of International
   Trade and Industry (MITI)

the Asian model

the ASEAN region

the Lewis two-sector model

Notes

1. W. Arthur Lewis, "Economic Development with Unlimited Supplies Labor." Manchester School, Vol. 22 (May, 1954), 139–191; John Fei and Gustav Ranis, Development of the Labor Surplus Economy (Homewood, Ill.: Irwin, 1964).
2. As is well known, collectivization was the transfer mechanism used in the Soviet Union in the 1930s and in China in the 1950s.

Japan

3. Angus Maddison, *Economic Growth in Japan and the USSR* (London: Allen and Unwin, 1969), Ch. 1.
4. For an excellent survey of the early years of Japanese economic development, see Kazushi Ohkawa and Henry Rosovsky, *Japanese Economic Growth* (Stanford, Calif.: Stanford University Press, 1973).
5. For an examination of the Japanese growth experience, see Lawrence Klein and Kazushi Ohkawa, eds., *Economic Growth: The Japanese Experience Since the Meiji Era* (Homewood, Ill.: Irwin, 1968); Japan Economic Research Center, *Economic Growth: The Japanese Experience Since the Meiji Era*, Vols. I and II (Tokyo: Japan Economic Research Center, 1973); and Hugh Patrick and Henry Rosovsky, eds., *Asia's New Giant: How the Japanese Economy Works* (Washington, D.C.: Brookings, 1976). For a discussion of Japanese economic planning, see Shuntaro Shishido, "Japanese Experience with Long-Term Economic Planning," and Tsunshiko Watanabe, "National Planning and Economic Growth in Japan," both in Bert G. Hickman, ed., *Quantitative Planning of Economic Policy* (Washington, D.C.: Brookings, 1965); and William Lockwood, ed., *The State and Economic Enterprise in Japan* (Princeton, N.J.: Princeton University Press, 1965). For an analysis of Japanese labor markets, see Koji Taira, *Economic Development and the Labor Market in Japan* (New York: Columbia University Press, 1970). For a discussion of Japanese multinationals, see Ozawa Terutomo, *Multinationalism Japanese Style* (Princeton, N.J.: Princeton University Press, 1979); Yoshi Tsurumi, *The Japanese Are Coming: A Multinational Interaction of Firms and Politics* (Cambridge, Mass.: Ballinger, 1976); and M. Y. Yoshino, *Japan's Multinational Enterprises* (Cambridge, Mass.: Harvard University Press, 1976). For a general discussion of the Japanese economic system, especially its organizational features, see G. C. Allen, *The Japanese Economy* (London: Weidenfeld and Nicolson, 1981).
6. For a brief discussion, see Allen, *The Japanese Economy*, Ch. 5; for background, see I. J. Nakamura, *Agricultural Production and the Economic Development of Japan, 1873–1922* (Princeton, N.J.: Princeton University Press, 1966).
7. Maddison, *Economic Growth in Japan and the USSR*, Ch. 4.
8. For a survey of Japanese economic growth, see Ohkawa and Rosovsky, *Japanese Economic Growth*, Ch. 2.
9. Various aspects of the Japanese labor market are discussed in Allen, *The Japanese Economy*, Ch. 9; and Taira, *Economic Development*.
10. For a useful survey of organizational features of the Japanese economic system, see Kanji Haitani, *The Japanese Economic System* (Lexington, Mass.: Heath, 1976).
11. Ohkawa and Rosovsky, *Japanese Economic Growth*, Ch. 5.
12. In addition to Taira, *Economic Development*, see Robert E. Cole, *Japanese Blue-Collar: The Changing Tradition* (Berkeley: University of California Press, 1971); for a summary, see Robert E. Cole, "Industrial Relations in Japan" in Morris Bornstein, ed., *Comparative Economic Systems, Models and Cases*, 3rd ed. (Homewood, Ill.: Irwin, 1974), pp. 93–116.

13. Kozo Yamamura, "Entrepreneurship, Ownership and Management in Japan," in M. M. Postan et al., *Cambridge Economic History of Europe*, Vol. VII, pt. 2 (Cambridge, England: Cambridge University Press, 1978), pp. 215–264. See also Eleanor M. Hadley, *Antitrust in Japan* (Princeton, N.J.: Princeton University Press, 1970); Richard E. Caves and Masu Uekusa, *Industrial Organizations in Japan* (Washington, D.C.: Brookings, 1976); and Haitani, *The Japanese Economic System.*

14. John M. Montias, *The Structure of Economic Systems* (New Haven: Yale University Press, 1976), Pt. 5.

15. Martin Weitzman, *The Share Economy* (Cambridge, Mass.: Harvard University Press, 1984).

16. Merton J. Peck, "Is Japan Really a Share Economy?" *Journal of Comparative Economics* 10 (1986), 427–432.

17. For a recent discussion, see Gregory B. Christainsen and Jan S. Hagendorn, "Japanese Productivity: Adapting to Changing Comparative Advantage in the Face of Lifetime Employment Commitments," *Quarterly Review of Business and Economics* 23 (Summer 1983), 23–39. For a discussion of the labor–management issue in a growth context, see Harry Oshima, "Reinterpreting Japan's Postwar Growth," *Economic Development and Cultural Change* 31 (October 1982), 1–43.

18. Christainsen and Hagendorn, "Japanese Productivity," p. 30.

19. The classic work on the Japanese factory is J. G. Abegglen, *The Japanese Factory* (Glencoe, Ill.: Free Press, 1958).

20. Assessing the role of government in the importance of the "public" sector in the Japanese economy is difficult for definitional reasons. For a discussion, see Chalmers Johnson, *Japan's Public Policy Companies* (Washington, D.C.: American Enterprise Institute, 1978).

21. Much has been written about MITI. For basics, see Haitani, *The Japanese Economic System*; for more detail, see Chalmers Johnson, *MITI and the Japanese Miracle* (Stanford, Calif.: Stanford University Press, 1982); and Christainsen and Hagendorn, "Japanese Productivity."

22. For a more restrained view of the role of MITI in the 1970s, see Kozo Yamamura, "Success That Soured: Administrative Guidance and Cartels in Japan," in Kozo Yamamura, ed., *Policy and Trade Issues of the Japanese Economy* (Seattle: University of Washington Press, 1982), pp. 77–112. On the role of the state in supporting key sectors, see also Gary R. Saxonhouse, "What Is All This About 'Industrial Targeting' in Japan?" *The World Economy* 6 (September 1983), 253–273.

23. The movement from fixed to flexible exchange rates was, of course, much more an issue than U.S.–Japanese trade. See Patrick and Rosovsky, *Asia's New Giant*, Ch. 6. See also Takafusa Nakamura, *The Postwar Japanese Economy* (Tokyo: University of Tokyo Press, 1981), Pt. 3; for specific references to the impact of oil shortages, see Yoichi Shinkai, "Oil Crises and Stagflation in Japan," in Yamamura, *Policy and Trade Issues of the Japanese Economy*, pp. 173–193.

24. Data are from World Bank, *World Development Report 1987* (New York: Oxford University Press, 1987), pp. 202–205.

25. Useful sources for analyzing contemporary adjustment policies include Ronald Dore, *Flexible Rigidities* (London: The Athlone Press, 1986); Chikara Higashi and G. Peter Lauter, *The Internationalization of the Japanese Economy* (Boston: Kluwer Academic Publishers, 1987); Edward J. Lincoln, *Japan: Facing Economic Maturity* (Washington, D.C.: Brookings, 1988); and Yoshio Suzuki, *Money, Finance, and Macroeconomic Performance in Japan* (New Haven: Yale University Press, 1986); Ryuzo Sato, "U.S.–Japan Relations Under the Clinton and Hosokawa Administrations," *Japan and the World*

Economy 6, 1 (1994), 89–103; Gregory W. Noble, "Japan in 1993," *Asian Survey* 34 (January 1994), 19–29.

26. See Ryuzo Sato, "U.S.–Japan Relations" and Gregory W. Noble, "Japan in 1993."
27. Ryuzo Sato, "U.S.–Japan Relations," 95.

South Korea, Singapore, Taiwan, Hong Kong

28. There is a large literature on these economies. See, for example, Edward K. Y. Chen, *Hyper-Growth in Asian Economies* (London and Basingstoke, England: The Macmillan Press Ltd., 1979); Eddy Lee, ed., *Export-Led Industrialization and Development* (Geneva: ILO, 1981); Roy A. Matthews, *Canada and the Little Dragons* (Montreal: The Institute for Research on Public Policy, 1983); Miron Mushkat, *The Economic Future of Hong Kong* (Boulder, Colo., and London, England: Hong Kong University Press, 1990); Miyohei Shinohara and Fu-chen Lo, *Global Adjustment and the Future of Asian-Pacific Economy* (Tokyo and Kuala Lumpur: Institute of Developing Economies and Asian and Pacific Development Centre, 1989); Julian Weiss, *The Asian Century* (New York: Facts on File, 1989); and Jon Woronoff, *Asia's "Miracle" Economies* (Armonk, N.Y.: M. E. Sharpe, 1986).
29. Eddy Lee, ed., *Export-Led Industrialization and Development* (Geneva: ILO, 1981); Robert A. Scalapino, Seizaburo Sato, and Jusuf Wanandi, eds., *Asian Economic Development—Present and Future* (Berkeley: University of California Press, 1985).
30. World Bank, *World Development Bank 1990* (New York: Oxford University Press, 1990).
31. World Bank, *World Development Report 1987* (Oxford: Oxford University Press, 1987).
32. Sebastian Edwards, "Openness, Trade Liberalization and Growth in Developing Countries," *Journal of Economic Literature* 31 (September 1993), 1387.
33. Overseas Development Institute, *Development Policy Review,* March 1997, London, England.
34. World Bank. The East Asian Miracle: Economic Growth and Public Policy (Oxford: Oxford University Press, 1993). Fig. 1.3, p. 31; Fig. 3, p. 4.
35. John Bauer, "Economic Growth and Policy in East Asia," Conference on Population and the Asian Economic Miracle. Program on Population. East-West Center, Honolulu, Hawaii, January 7–10, 1997.
36. D. H. Perkins, "There Are at Least Three Models of East Asian Development," *World Development*, 4 (April 1994), pp. 655–662.
37. For a discussion of income distribution and growth, see Vito Tanzi and Ke-young Chu (eds.), Income Distribution and High-Quality Growth (Cambridge Mass.: MIT Press, 1998).
38. Geoffrey Carliner, "Comment on Anne Krueger, "East Asian Experience and Endogenous Growth Theory," in Taakatoshi Ito and Anne Krueger, eds., *Growth Theories in Light of the East Asian Experience* (Chicago: University of Chicago Press, 1995), pp. 30–33; Joseph Stiglitz and Marilow Uy, "Financial Markets, Public Policy, and the East Asian Miracle," *The World Bank Research Observe* 1, 2 (August 1996), 249–276.
39. Ronald Lee, Andrew Mason, and Timothy Miller, "Saving, Wealth, and the Demographic Transition in East Asia," Conference on Population and the East Asian Miracle, Program on Population, East-West Center, Honolulu, Hawaii, January 7–10, 1997; Jeffrey Williamson and Mathew Higgins. "The Accumulation and Demography Connection in East Asia," Andrew Mason, ed., *Population and the East Asian Miracle* (forthcoming).
40. Robert Barro and Xavier Sala-l-Martin, "Economic Growth (New York: McGraw-Hill, 1995).

41. Anne Krueger, "East Asian Experience and Endogenous Growth Theory," in Takatoshi Ito and Anne Krueger, eds., *Growth Theories in Light of the East Asian Experience* (Chicago: University of Chicago Press, 1995), pp. 9–30; Bela Balassa, *Economic Policies in the Pacific Area Developing Economies* (New York: New York University Press, 1991).

42. World Bank, The East Asian Miracle, pp. 123–147.

43. This summary is based on Bauer, pp. 46–52.

44. Krueger, *Growth Theories in Light of the East Asian Experience,* p. 24.

45. The Asian Miracle: Is It Over?" *The Economist,* March 1, 1997, 23–25; Paul Krugman, "The Myth of the Asian Miracle," *Foreign Affairs* 73, 6; "The Asian Miracle," *UBS International Finance* 29 (1996); IMF Conference, "Growth and Productivity in the ASEAN Economies," Jakarta, Indonesia, November 1996.

46. Alwyn Young, "The Tyranny of Numbers: Confronting the Statistical Realities of the East Asian Growth Experience," *Quarterly Journal of Economics* 110, 3 (August 1995), 64–680.

India

47. The literature on the economic characteristics of LDCs is summarized in Marvin Miracle, "Comparative Market Structures in Developing Countries" (Association for Comparative Economics, Proceedings in Conjunction with the Midwest Economic Association, Detroit, April 1970). Also see John Due, *Indirect Taxes in Developing Countries* (Baltimore: The Johns Hopkins University Press, 1970). Indian and Chinese economic growth are compared in Subramanian Swamy, "Economic Growth in China and India, 1952–1970: A Comparative Appraisal," *Economic Development and Cultural Change* 21 (July 1973), 1–84; and Wilfred Malenbaum, "Modern Economic Growth in India and China: The Comparisons Revisited," *Economic Development and Cultural Change* 3 (October 1982), 45–84.

48. Data here are compiled from World Bank, *World Development Report 1990* (New York: Oxford University Press, 1990), Tables 1–32.

49. This discussion is based principally on Angus Maddison, *Class Structure and Economic Growth: India and Pakistan Since the Moghuls* (New York: Norton, 1971), Chs. 2–4.

50. Raj Krishna and G. S. Raychaudhuri, "Trends in Rural Savings and Capital Formation in India, 1950–1951 to 1973–1974," *Economic Development and Cultural Change* 30 (January 1982), 289–294.

51. Maddison, *Class Structure and Economic Growth*, Ch. 6.

52. For a discussion of the Indian controversy over planning priorities, see Jagdish Bhagwati and Sukhamoy Chakravaty, "Contributions to Indian Economic Analysis: A Survey," *American Economic Growth,* 59 (September 1969), 4–29; and V. V. Bhatt, "Development Problem, Strategy, and Technology of Choice: Sarvadaya and Socialist Approaches in India," *Economic Development and Cultural Change* 21 (October 1982), 85–100.

53. Maddison, *Class Structure and Economic Growth*, p. 119.

54. Allan G. Gruchy, *Comparative Economic Systems*, 2nd ed. (Boston: Houghton Mifflin, 1977), p. 638.

55. World Bank, *World Tables, 1976*, p. 428.

56. *Ibid.,* summary tables.

57. Maddison, *Class Structure and Economic Growth*, p. 127.

58. Our discussion of Indian planning is based on Gruchy, *Comparative Economic Systems*, pp. 639–653; and Bhagwati and Chakravaty, "Contributions to Indian Economic Analysis," pp. 2–73; for a contemporary discussion, see Rakesh Mohan and Vandana Aggarwal, "Commands and Controls: Planning for Indian Industrial Development, 1951–1990,"

Journal of Comparative Economics 14 (December 1990), 681–712; William A. Byrd, "Planning in India: Lessons from Four Decades of Development Experience," *Journal of Comparative Economics* 14 (December 1990), 713–735.; Arvind Panagariya, "Indicative Planning in India: Discussion," *Journal of Comparative Economics* 14 (December 1990), 736–742; E. Wayne Nafziger, *The Economics of Developing Countries,* 2nd ed. (Englewood Cliffs, N.J.: Prentice-Hall, 1990), Ch. 19.

59. This discussion is based on Maddison, *Class Structure and Economic Growth* pp. 120–125.
60. Bhagwati and Chakravaty, "Contributions to Indian Economic Analysis," pp. 60–66.
61. Maddison, *Class Structure and Economic Growth*, pp. 122–124.
62. Malenbaum, "Modern Economic Growth in India and China," pp. 45–84; World Bank, *World Tables, 1980*, pp. 372–375.
63. Maddison, *Class Structure and Economic Growth*, p. 81.
64. See, for example, Rakesh Mohan and Vandana Aggarwal, "Commands and Controls."
65. J. S. Uppal, "India's New Economic Policy," *Journal of Economic Development* 18 (December 1993), 33–61.

Recommended Readings

Japan

J. G. Abegglen, *The Japanese Factory* (Glencoe, Ill.: Free Press, 1958).
G. C. Allen, *The Japanese Economy* (London: Weidenfeld and Nicolson, 1981).
W. G. Beasley, *The Rise of Modern Japan* 2nd ed. (New York: St. Martin's, 1995).
Thomas F. Cargill, Michael M. Hurchison, and Takatoshi Ito, *the Political Economy of Japanese Monetary Policy* (Cambridge, Mass.: The M.I.T. Press, 1997).
Edward F. Denison and William K. Chung, *How Japan's Economy Grew So Fast: The Sources of Postwar Expansion* (Washington, D.C.: Brookings, 1976).
Ronald Dore, *Flexible Rigidities* (London: The Athlone Press, 1986).
Kanji Haitani, *The Japanese Economic System* (Lexington, Mass.: Heath, 1976).
Christopher Hause, *The Origins of Japanese Trade Supremacy: Development and Technology in Asia from 1540 to the Pacific War* (Chicago: University of Chicago Press, 1996).
Ronald I. McKinnon and Kenichi Ohno, *Dollar and Yen: Resolving Economic Conflict Between the United States and Japan* (Cambridge, Mass.: The M.I.T. Press, 1997).
Toru Iwami, *Japan in the International Financial System* (New York: St. Martin's, 1996).
Japanese Economic Research Center, *Economic Growth: The Japanese Experience Since the Meiji Era*, Vols. I and II (Tokyo: Japanese Economic Research Center, 1973).
Chalmers Johnson, *Japan's Public Policy Companies* (Washington, D.C.: American Enterprise Institute, 1978).
———, *MITI and the Japanese Miracle* (Stanford, Calif.: Stanford University Press, 1982).
Lawrence Klein and Kazushi Ohkawa, eds., *Economic Growth: The Japanese Experience Since the Meiji Era* (Homewood, Ill.: Irwin, 1968).
Edward J. Lincoln, *Japan: Facing Economic Maturity* (Washington, D.C.: Brookings, 1988).
William Lockwood, ed., *The State and Economic Enterprise in Japan* (Princeton, N.J.: Princeton University Press, 1965).
Angus Maddison, *Economic Growth in Japan and the USSR* (London: Allen and Unwin, 1969).
Ryoshim Minami, Kwan S. Kim, Fumio Makino and Joung-Hae Seo, *Acquisition, Adaptation and the Development of Technologies* (New York: St. Martin's, 1994).

Ryoshin Minami, *The Economic Development of Japan* (London: Macmillan, 1986).

Carl Mosk, *Competition and Cooperation in Japanese Labor Markets* (New York: St. Martin's, 1994).

Takafusa Nakamura, *The Postwar Japanese Economy* (Tokyo: University of Tokyo Press, 1981).

Meiko Nishimizu and Charles R. Hulten, "The Sources of Japanese Economic Growth, 1955–71," *Review of Economics and Statistics* 60 (August 1978), 351–361.

Kazushi Ohkawa and Henry Rosovsky, *Japanese Economic Growth* (Stanford, Calif.: Stanford University Press, 1973).

Kazushi Ohkawa and Hirohisa Kohama, *Lectures on Developing Economies: Japan's Experience and Its Relevance* (Tokyo: University of Tokyo Press, 1989).

Hugh Patrick and Henry Rosovsky, eds., *Asia's New Giant: How the Japanese Economy Works* (Washington, D.C.: Brookings, 1976).

M. M. Postan et al., eds., *Cambridge Economic History of Europe*, Vol. VII, Pt. 2 (Cambridge, England: Cambridge University Press, 1978), Chs. 3–5 on Japan.

Ozawa Terutomo, *Multinationalism Japanese Style* (Princeton, N.J.: Princeton University Press, 1979).

Kazuo Sato, *The Transformation of the Japanese Economy* (Armonk, N.Y.: M.E. Sharpe, 1996).

———, *The Japanese Economy and Business* (Armonk, N.Y.: M.E. Sharpe, 1996).

Ryuzo Sato, "U.S.–Japan Relations Under the Clinton and Hosokawa Administrations," *Japan and the World Economy* 6, 1 (1994), 89–103.

Yoshio Suzuki, *Money, Finance, and Macroeconomic Performance in Japan* (New Haven: Yale University Press, 1986).

Yosho Tsurumi, *The Japanese Are Coming: A Multinational Interaction of Firms and Politics* (Cambridge, Mass.: Ballinger, 1976).

Kozo Yamamura, ed., *Policy and Trade Issues of the Japanese Economy* (Seattle: University of Washington Press, 1982).

M. Y. Yoshino, *Japan's Multinational Enterprises* (Cambridge, Mass.: Harvard University Press, 1976).

South Korea, Singapore, Taiwan, Hong Kong

Edward K. Y. Chen, *Hyper-Growth in Asian Economies* (London and Basingstoke, England: The Macmillan Press Ltd., 1979).

Shirley W. Y. Kao, Gustav Ranis, and John C. H. Fei, *The Taiwan Success Story: Rapid Growth with Improved Distribution in the Republic of China, 1952–1979* (Boulder, Colo.: Westview, 1981).

Paul Krugman, "The Myth of Asia's Miracle," *Foreign Affairs* 73 (November–December 1994), 62–78.

Paul Kuzner, "Indicative Planning in Korea," *Journal of Comparative Economics* 14 (December 1990), 657–676.

Eddy Lee, ed., *Export-Led Industrialization and Development* (Geneva: ILO, 1981).

Roy A. Matthews, *Canada and the Little Dragons* (Montreal: The Institute for Research on Public Policy, 1983).

Miron Mushkat, *The Economic Future of Hong Kong* (Boulder, Colo., and London, England: Hong Kong University Press, 1990).

George Rosen, *Economic Development in Asia* (Brookfield, Vt.: Ashgate, 1996).

J. L. Saking, "Indicative Planning in Korea: Discussion," *Journal of Comparative Economics*, 14, 1 (December, 1990), 677–680.

Robert A. Scalapino, Seizaburo Sato, and Jusuf Wanandi, eds., *Asian Economic Development—Present and Future* (Berkeley: University of California Press, 1985).

Miyohei Shinohara and Fu-chen Lo, *Global Adjustment and the Future of the Asian-Pacific Economy* (Tokyo and Kuala Lumpur: Institute of Developing Economies and Asian and Pacific Development Centre, 1989).

A. H. Somjee and Geeta Somjee, *Development Success in Asia Pacific* (New York: St. Martin's, 1995).

Julian Weiss, *The Asian Century* (New York: Facts on File, 1989).

Jon Woronoff, *Asia's "Miracle" Economies* (Armonk, N.Y.: M. E. Sharpe, 1986).

World Bank, *The East Asian Miracle: Economic Growth and Public Policy* (Washington, D.C.: The World Bank, 1993).

India

A. N. Agrawal, *Indian Economy*, 2nd ed. (New Delhi: Vikas Publishing House, 1976).

Jagdish Bhagwati and Sukhamoy Chakravaty, "Contributions to Indian Economic Analysis: A Survey," *American Economic Review* 59 (September 1969), 4–29.

Kaushik Basu, *Agrarian Questions* (Delhi: Oxford University Press, 1998).

William A. Byrd, "Planning in India: Lessons from Four Decades of Development Experience," *Journal of Comparative Economics* 14 (December 1990), 713–736.

Pramit Chaudhuri, ed., *Aspects of Indian Economic Development* (London: Allen and Unwin, 1971).

Francine R. Frankel, *India's Green Revolution* (Princeton, N.J.: Princeton University Press, 1971).

———, *India's Political Economy, 1947–1977* (Princeton, N.J.: Princeton University Press, 1978).

Ira N. Gang, "Small Firm 'Presence' in Indian Manufacturing" *World Development* 20 (1992), 1377–89.

Raj Krishna and G. S. Raychaudhuri, "Trends in Rural Savings and Capital Formation in India, 1950–1951 to 1973–1974," *Economic Development and Cultural Change* 30 (January 1982), 271–298.

William A. Long and K. K. Seo, *Management in Japan and India* (New York: Praeger, 1977).

Angus Maddison, *Class Structure and Economic Growth: India and Pakistan Since the Moghuls* (New York: Norton, 1971).

Wilfred Malenbaum, "Modern Economic Growth in India and China: The Comparison Revisited, 1950–1980," *Economic Development and Cultural Change* 31 (October 1982), 45–84.

Dilip Mookhergee, *Indian Industry: Policies and Performance* (Delhi: Oxford University Press, 1997).

Rakesh Mohan and Vandana Aggarwal, "Commands and Controls: Planning for Indian Industrial Development, 1951–1990," *Journal of Comparative Economics* 14 (December 1990), 681–712.

Arvind Panagariya, "Indicative Planning in India: Discussion," *Journal of Comparative Economics* 14 (December 1990), 736–742.

Prabhat Patnaik, *Macroeconomics* (Delhi: Oxford University Press, 1997), pp. 12–36.

C. H. Shah and C. N. Vakil, eds., *Agricultural Development of India: Policy and Problems* (New Delhi: Orient Longman, 1979).

Subramanian Swamy, "Economic Growth in China and India, 1952–1970: A Comparative Appraisal," *Economic Development and Cultural Change*, 21 (July 1973), 1–84.

13

The Command Economies: Performance and Decline

There is probably no issue in the field of comparative economic systems of greater relevance than the issue of comparative performance. After all, in the early chapters of this book, we emphasized that systems and policies differ and that performance differences can be related to these differences. If we are to assess the relative merits of different arrangements, then we need to be able to associate these arrangements with performance.

In this chapter, we focus on two important performance issues. First, returning to the classification of economic systems that we developed in the early chapters of this book, can we compare performance across real-world variants of these systems such that some basic judgments can be made about comparative performance as it relates to the economic system? Second, in light of the demise of a number of the planned socialist economic systems, can we relate economic performance problems to systemic arrangements in these cases? To put it differently, what factors led to the demise of the administrative command systems?

The reader might well ask why are we interested in the performance of systems that have collapsed. There are several reasons. From both a theoretical and a practical standpoint, the reasons for the decline of the planned economies are important. These were major system variants, some of which still exist, that experienced major economic problems. Moreover, as these systems collapsed, many of the economic problems that they experienced remained (and in some cases still remain) in the transition era. Moreover, many contemporary systems are in fact mixed systems, in which components from a wide variety of systems are employed. Their experience is therefore fundamental to our knowledge about contemporary economic systems— and especially about the nature of change in modern economic systems.

Problems of Evaluation

In Part I of this book, we emphasized that system objectives differ from one case to another. Socialist systems have typically pursued different objectives than capitalist systems. The pursuit and achievement of each objective represent a cost in terms of resources used, so difficult choices must be made in any system. Unfortunately, unless different systems pursue the same goals and in fact assign the same weight to each, it is difficult to evaluate the overall performance of the differing economic systems. There is no way in which we can identify single or dominant goals, so in the end, we find ourselves making subjective judgments about which goals are "best" as we make performance comparisons.

Evaluating economic performance is not easy even if we isolate a single dominant objective—for example, economic growth. Suppose we wish to compare the growth experience of socialist and capitalist economic systems. Assuming that we can agree on basic system definitions, how will we select the systems to be evaluated, and over what time frame will the evaluation be performed? How will we control non-system characteristics such as the level of economic development? Some criterion for selection must be used. For example, should we choose "representative" economic systems, and if we do so, how will the approach be defined? If we consider a sampling approach, the relatively small number of planned socialist systems in that particular population poses serious problems.

For performance comparisons to be valid, the *ceteris paribus* assumption must hold. The economies compared should be alike *in all respects* except their economic systems. In Chapter 3, the *ceteris paribus* problem was described as follows: Outcomes (O) are a function of a variety of environmental factors (ENV; for example, natural and human resource endowments and level of development), economic policy (POL), and the economic system (ES).

$$O = f(ENV, POL, ES) \qquad (13.1)$$

Because ENV and POL differ by country, one cannot make a statement about the impact of ES on outcomes without clearly understanding the role of the ENV and POL factors.

Labor productivity in the Soviet Union was always low relative to that in the United States and industrialized Western Europe.[1] The question, however, is whether this was a consequence of the *system* or a product of the other factors (ENV, POL). The level of economic development of the Soviet Union always lagged behind that of the United States and Western Europe, and productivity is positively associated with economic development. Can the Soviet productivity gap be accounted for entirely by these other factors, or was the economic system itself to blame? *Long-term* economic growth in the Soviet Union outpaced that in the United States and Western Europe through the 1970s.[2] Was this a consequence of the economic system or of other factors?

Two related approaches can be used to deal with this problem. The first is to compare economies that are alike in all respects other than economic system. In terms of equation 13.1, this means making performance comparisons only in instances where ENV and POL are equal so that any differences in performance can be attributed to the system. The nearest (though imperfect) example would be the comparison of previously unified countries that belonged to different economic blocs (East and West Germany or North and South Korea, for example), but such examples are rare.[3] The basic drawback is that real-world cases where all factors other than the economic system are constant do not exist.

The econometric approach to the *ceteris paribus* problem requires estimation of the impact of the ENV and POL factors on O. Once their impact is known, these factors can be held constant, revealing the impact of the economic system on performance. This approach requires the investigation of *groups* of capitalist and socialist economies that differ in ENV and POL characteristics, so that their impact can be isolated and held constant.[4]

Because economic systems are multidimensional, their attributes are difficult to measure, and we cannot formulate an *objective* and *quantitative* measure of ES that differentiates among economies in terms of the degree of capitalism or of planned or market socialism. We cannot determine whether the Soviet economy was more "planned socialist" than the East German economy was or whether the U.S. economy is more "capitalist" than the British economy. Therefore, we must bunch real-world economies into political–economic groupings without being able to hold constant the effect of variations in ES *within* a particular group.

Real-world economies are grouped into two categories: capitalism and planned socialism. This requires combining economies that differ in important respects. In the comparisons that follow, intermediate- and low-income countries such as Greece, Spain, Turkey, and India are included in the "capitalist" group, despite their substantial differences from industrialized capitalist countries. There was much greater homogeneity within the planned socialist group prior to the reforms of the late 1980s. Yet even they had differences (ownership and control arrangements in agriculture), so the planned socialist economies were by no means uniform.[5]

How well the representatives of economic systems have actually performed is the appropriate standard for evaluating the performance of economic systems. What counts is not how an economic system might conceivably perform under ideal circumstances, but how well it performs in the real world.

The Performance of Systems

Recognizing the difficulties inherent in evaluating economic systems, we use the most important performance indicators—economic growth, economic efficiency, the "fairness" of the distribution of income, and economic stability—to determine how well selected representatives of capitalism and socialism have performed. The available empirical evidence is updated with new evidence, where it exists.

The Choice of Countries

The selection of representatives of capitalism and socialism is constrained by the availability of data. Data limitations dictate that we emphasize comparisons of the former Soviet Union and East European nations with the industrialized and near-industrialized capitalist nations.[6] The data for the smaller Asian communist countries (North Korea, Vietnam, Cambodia, and Mongolia) are too meager to support meaningful comparisons.[7]

How about the performance of China vis-à-vis its noncommunist Asian counterparts? China may be representative of planned socialism in a large and backward economy. Chinese economic performance has been significantly affected by political upheavals. There is the further difficulty of finding appropriate counterparts against which to gauge China's economic performance. Should China be measured against Japan (an immediate Asian neighbor), against India[8] (another Asian neighbor, almost equally populous), or against the large and small noncommunist Asian nations combined? If the yardstick is Japan, then Chinese performance will not be impressive; if Bangladesh, it will be. Moreover, in the era since the late 1970s, major reforms in China (examined in Chapter 10) have significantly altered the nature of the Chinese economic system.

Data: Concepts and Reliability

Economic aggregates, such as GDP, industrial production, and per capita consumption, were not compiled uniformly by the statistical agencies in Eastern and Western countries.[9] The planned socialist nations excluded from final output "nonproductive" services—those that did not directly support material production. The aggregate figures used in this chapter are recalculations that make the planned socialist figures conform as closely as possible to Western national accounting practices.[10] Western recalculations of Soviet and East European national accounts made adjustments for omitted costs and for omitted product categories (such as services). They all used the **adjusted factor cost concept** pioneered by Abram Bergson.[11] Western economists were not in a position to recalculate the output of planned socialist economies on the basis of utility values. If planners dictated the production of goods and services that did not raise welfare (such as excessively heavy reinforced concrete, inferior shoes, and the collected works of Leonid Brezhnev), we have no choice but to value those goods and services at the cost of supplying them. A market economy might reject these goods and services (by setting zero prices), but a planned socialist economy dictated by planners' preferences would continue to order their production.

The *Glasnost* movement that swept through the Soviet Union and Eastern Europe in the second half of the 1980s raised serious questions about statistical reliability.[12] For example, Romanian statistical authorities subsequently revealed that their statistics contained wild exaggerations of economic performance. Independent estimates by Soviet economists and journalists claim that official Soviet statistics overstated growth by a factor of more than 2.[13]

The demise of the Soviet Union and the other planned socialist economies of Eastern Europe has made the matter of accessing accurate and meaningful statistical information complex. Although the situation may appear dramatically better, that is not necessarily the case. First, because the former planned socialist systems generally began the conversion to Western accounting practices at or just prior to the end of the plan era, new series for earlier years (for example, relating to the components of national income) were not necessarily generated. Second, new empirical evidence that has become available is highly variable. Finally, the availability of new data does not necessarily mean that new analysis has been done in the 1990s.

An Economic Profile: Structural Characteristics of East and West

Table 13.1 provides an economic profile of the planned socialist countries and selected capitalist countries. This profile shows what factors should be held constant in performance comparisons, and it offers insights into the socialist model of

TABLE 13.1   An Economic Profile of Socialist and Capitalist Countries in the 1980s

	(1) Per Capita GNP, 1985 (U.S. $)	(2) Population 1985 (millions)	(3a) Share of Industry and Construction in GDP (1982)	(3b) Agriculture	(3c) Services	(4) Proportion of Labor in Agriculture (1985)	(5) Gross Investment as a Percentage of GDP (1982)
A. Planned Socialism							
East Germany	10,440	16.7	51	13	36	10	24
Czechoslovakia	8,750	15.5	49	15	36	13	25
Hungary	7,560	10.6	38	26	36	18	29
Soviet Union	7,400	278.9	42	19	39	19	30
Poland	6,470	37.2	37	27	36	29	27
Bulgaria	6,420	9.0	46	23	31	20	28
Romania	5,450	22.7	46	26	28	29	38
China	340	1,042.4	45	35	20	68	28
B. Capitalism							
Norway	16,719	4.2	41	5	54	9	26
United States	16,710	238.6	34	3	63	3	19

	(1) Per Capita GNP, 1985 (U.S. $)	(2) Population 1985 (millions)	(3a) Share of Industry and Construction in GDP (1982)	(3b) Agriculture	(3c) Services	(4) Proportion of Labor in Agriculture (1985)	(5) Gross Investment as a Percentage of GDP (1982)
Canada	16,538	25.4	32	4	64	5	25
Denmark	14,603	5.1	22	5	73	7	16
West Germany	14,432	61.0	53	3	44	6	23
France	13,755	55.0	41	4	55	9	21
Japan	13,312	120.7	40	5	55	10	31
Belgium	13,219	9.9	42	4	54	3	18
Netherlands	12,741	14.5	33	4	63	5	18
Austria	12,343	7.6	39	4	57	9	26
United Kingdom	12,042	56.4	33	2	65	3	17
Italy	10,928	57.1	41	6	53	13	21
Spain	9,008	39.1	34	6	60	18	20
Greece	6,854	10.0	31	17	52	31	25
Turkey	2,135	45.1	31	22	47	60	25
India	250	767.7	26	36	38	70	25

Sources: U.S. Department of Commerce, Statistical Abstract of the United States, 1981 (Washington, D.C.: U.S. Government Printing Office, 1981), pp. 876–879; National Foreign Assessment Center, Handbook of Economic Statistics 1986 (Washington, D.C.: Central Intelligence Agency, 1986); World Bank, World Tables, 3rd ed. (Baltimore: The Johns Hopkins University Press, 1984); OECD, Historical Statistics, 1960–1985 (Paris, OECD, 1987); Thad Alton, "East European GNPs," Joint Economic Committee, East European Economics: Slow Growth in the 1980s, Vol. 1 (Washington, D.C.: U.S. Government Printing Office, 1985), pp. 81–132. The East European investment rates are calculated by subtracting the rates of defense spending and the GDP from Alton's residual expenditure category (p. 95).

industrialization.[14] We focus on the mid-1980s as a period of relative "normalcy" in Eastern Europe prior to the dramatic changes of the late 1980s.

In terms of per capita income, the Soviet Union and Eastern Europe were well behind the advanced capitalist countries in the mid-1980s. The per capita incomes in the more advanced planned socialist economies (Czechoslovakia, East Germany, and the Soviet Union) were well below those in Japan and the United Kingdom and between those in Italy and Spain. Poland, Romania, and Hungary and the less advanced Bulgaria were well below Italy and Spain but close to Greece. The planned socialist countries as a group were less advanced than the industrialized Western countries with which they were most often compared.

Despite relatively low per capita income, the share of industry and construction in GDP in the socialist countries was roughly equal to that of the capitalist countries in the mid-1980s. In fact, the socialist industry share averaged 43 percent; the average of capitalist countries (United States to Italy) was 36 percent. One would have to conclude that if per capita income were held constant, the planned socialist industry share would be high relative to capitalism. The socialist shares of agriculture and services were even more different from their Western counterparts. Agriculture's share of both GDP and labor force emerged as quite high in the planned socialist countries once per capita income was held constant, but the share of the service sector was well below that of capitalist countries at similar levels of development. The data on investment rates do not yield a clear trend. The socialist countries tended to have investment rates in the high ranges of 24 to 38 percent, but one can find similarly high investment rates among the capitalist countries. The East German investment rate, on the other hand, was relatively low.

Other differences, not recorded in Table 13.1, can also be noted. If one breaks down the industry sector into heavy and light industry, the planned socialist shares of heavy industry were well *above* those of a capitalist country at a similar level of development. The shares of the urban population of the socialist countries were well *below* those of a capitalist country at a similar stage of economic development.

All of these features constitute the distinguishing characteristics of the socialist industrialization model. What was the logic behind the socialist model? It aimed at "building socialism" as quickly as possible. In order to do so, industrialization had to be accorded priority. Activities that did not contribute to material production, such as services, would be limited, and within industry, priority had to be granted to heavy industry, which laid the foundation for socialism. Urbanization should be retarded to limit the flow of scarce investment resources into social overhead capital, a form of capital that does not lead immediately to expanded industrial capacity. Extra resources were devoted to agriculture to promote self-sufficiency, even if this worked against comparative advantage. Resources were channeled away from consumption into investment in order to achieve a high investment rate.

The socialist industrialization model is of interest for several reasons. First, it has been of great interest in Third World countries, such as India, where socialist economic policies and economic planning were borrowed from the past Soviet experience. Second, examining the socialist growth record will reveal that these countries were not indifferent to what was being produced. Thus, although growth has been emphasized in these systems, that emphasis has been directed toward particular sectors, such as heavy industry, whereas others, such as services, have been neglected. It is important to note that when we examine efficiency measures, inputs are related to all output, not just the output of priority sectors.

Economic Growth

Table 13.2 and Figure 13.1 supply data on GDP growth rates for the postwar period in socialist and capitalist countries. One should be cautious about attaching importance to small differences in growth rates, for there is measurement error in such calculations. Moreover, the measured growth rate of economies experiencing substantial structural changes can be ambiguous—the problem of index number relativity.[15] Growth rates must be regarded as approximate and often ambiguous measures of the expansion of real goods and services. This is especially true of East–West comparisons, where substantial adjustments must be made to render the past GDP data comparable.

In Table 13.2, we have assembled growth rates of real GDP and of real GDP per capita for the entire postwar period. In panel A we supply growth rates for the Soviet Union, Eastern Europe, and China. We also supply growth rates for a number of capitalist countries at various stages of economic development (panel B). We include comparative growth data for China and India, two poor and populous Asian giants, one a planned socialist economy, the other a basically capitalist economy.

Are there systemic differences in growth rates? Was economic growth more rapid in the planned socialist economies? Table 13.2 examines postwar economic growth from the heady growth of the 1950s and 1960s to the generally slower growth of the mid-1970s and 1980s. It illustrates the dangers of using a pair of countries (such as the United States and the Soviet Union) to judge the growth performance of capitalism and socialism. One can find capitalist countries (such as Japan) that have grown much more rapidly than most socialist countries, and one can find socialist countries (such as Bulgaria and China) that have grown more rapidly than most capitalist countries. Moreover, some countries grew rapidly in one period (Bulgaria in the 1950s and 1960s) and then grew slowly in another period (Bulgaria in the period 1975 to 1980).

It is difficult to reach firm conclusions about the growth performance of capitalism and socialism on the basis of these data. If one simply takes unweighted averages of the eight planned socialist and the sixteen capitalist countries, the socialist group grew slightly more rapidly in the 1950s (5.7 percent per year versus 5.0 percent for the capitalist group). The capitalist group grew more rapidly in the 1960s (5.5 percent versus 4.4 percent in the first half and 5.5 percent versus 4.3 percent in the second half). The capitalist group experienced severe growth recessions in the mid-1970s, whereas the socialist group enjoyed a noticeable growth advantage for the first half of the 1970s (4.8 percent versus 3.9 percent). The growth of the capitalist group continued to lag during the second half of the 1970s (at 3.4 percent), but the slowdown of growth was even more severe in the socialist group (growth fell to below 3 percent). For the period 1980 to 1985, the average socialist growth rate

TABLE 13.2   Average Annual Growth of GDP and GDP Per Capita in Socialist and Capitalist Countries, 1950–1990, percentage (per capita figures in parentheses)

	1950–1960	1960–1965	1965–1970	1970–1975	1975–1980	1980–1985	1985–1990
A. Planned Socialist Countries							
Czechoslovakia	4.8 (3.9)	2.3 (1.6)	3.4 (3.2)	3.4 (2.7)	2.2 (1.5)	1.5 (1.2)	1.2 (1.2)
East Germany	5.7 (6.7)	2.7 (3.0)	3.0 (3.1)	3.4 (3.8)	2.3 (2.5)	1.8 (1.9)	1.6 (1.6)
Soviet Union	5.7 (3.9)	5.0 (3.5)	5.2 (4.2)	3.7 (2.7)	2.7 (1.8)	2.0 (1.1)	1.8 (1.1)
Poland	4.6 (2.75)	4.4 (3.2)	4.1 (3.4)	6.4 (5.4)	.7 (0)	.7 (−.1)	.2 (.2)
Hungary	4.6 (4.0)	4.2 (3.9)	3.0 (2.7)	3.4 (2.9)	2.0 (1.9)	1.7 (1.7)	.7 (.7)
Romania	5.8 (4.55)	6.0 (5.3)	4.9 (3.7)	6.7 (5.8)	3.9 (3.0)	1.0 (.8)	.6 (.6)
Bulgaria	6.7 (5.9)	6.7 (5.7)	5.1 (4.2)	4.6 (4.2)	.9 (.9)	1.2 (1.0)	.4 (.4)
China	7.9 (5.6)	4.0 (2.5)	7.1 (4.0)	7.0 (4.5)	6.2 (4.6)	9.3 (8.0)	8.6 (7.2)
Unweighted average	5.7 (4.7)	4.4 (3.6)	4.3 (3.6)	4.8 (4.0)	2.6 (2.0)	2.4 (2.0)	1.9 (1.5)
Without China	5.4 (4.5)	4.5 (3.7)	4.1 (3.5)	4.5 (3.9)	2.1 (1.7)	1.4 (1.1)	.9 (.8)
B. Capitalist Countries							
United States	3.3 (1.5)	4.6 (3.2)	3.1 (2.1)	2.3 (1.6)	3.7 (2.6)	2.4 (1.4)	3.1 (2.1)
Canada	4.6 (1.3)	5.7 (3.8)	4.8 (3.0)	5.0 (3.6)	2.9 (1.9)	2.2 (.9)	3.3 (2.3)

	1950–1960	1960–1965	1965–1970	1970–1975	1975–1980	1980–1985	1985–1990
West Germany	7.9 (6.3)	5.0 (3.5)	4.4 (3.9)	2.1 (1.7)	3.6 (3.7)	1.1 (1.4)	2.8 (2.4)
Denmark	3.6 (2.9)	5.1 (4.3)	4.5 (3.7)	2.8 (2.4)	2.7 (2.4)	2.3 (2.3)	2.4 (2.4)
Norway	3.6 (2.5)	4.8 (4.3)	4.8 (3.9)	4.6 (4.0)	4.6 (4.2)	3.0 (2.8)	3.3 (3.3)
Belgium	3.0 (2.5)	5.2 (4.5)	4.8 (4.4)	3.9 (3.5)	2.5 (2.3)	.4 (.4)	2.7 (2.7)
France	4.4 (3.8)	5.8 (4.5)	5.4 (4.5)	4.0 (3.2)	3.2 (2.9)	1.2 (.7)	2.7 (2.2)
Netherlands	5.0 (3.3)	4.8 (3.5)	5.5 (4.4)	3.2 (2.0)	2.6 (1.9)	.5 (.1)	2.1 (1.6)
Japan	7.9 (6.6)	10.0 (9.0)	12.2 (11.2)	5.0 (3.8)	5.1 (4.2)	3.9 (3.2)	3.8 (3.4)
Austria	5.6 (5.4)	4.3 (3.7)	5.1 (4.6)	3.9 (3.5)	4.0 (4.0)	2.8 (2.8)	2.2 (2.2)
United Kingdom	3.3 (2.3)	3.1 (2.4)	2.5 (2.2)	2.0 (1.4)	1.6 (1.6)	1.7 (1.3)	3.1 (2.9)
Italy	5.6 (4.8)	5.2 (4.3)	6.2 (5.4)	2.4 (1.5)	3.9 (3.4)	.8 (.5)	2.9 (2.7)
Spain	6.2 (5.3)	8.5 (7.5)	6.2 (5.2)	5.5 (4.6)	2.3 (1.3)	1.4 (.8)	4.1 (3.7)
Greece	6.0 (5.0)	7.7 (7.2)	7.2 (6.6)	5.0 (4.5)	4.4 (3.2)	1.0 (.4)	1.8 (1.8)
Turkey	6.4 (3.4)	4.8 (2.8)	6.6 (3.7)	7.5 (5.0)	3.1 (.6)	4.9 (2.7)	5.1 (2.7)
India	3.8 (1.9)	4.0 (1.7)	5.0 (2.6)	3.0 (1.0)	3.4 (1.6)	4.1 (1.9)	6.0 (3.9)
Unweighted average	5.0 (3.7)	5.5 (4.4)	5.5 (4.5)	3.9 (2.95)	3.4 (2.6)	2.0 (1.5)	3.2 (2.7)

Sources: Thad Alton, "Economic Structure and Growth in Eastern Europe," in U.S. Congress, Joint Economic Committee, *Economic Developments in Countries of Eastern Europe* (Washington, D.C.: U.S. Government Printing Office, 1970), p. 49; Thad Alton, "Comparative Structure and Growth of Economic Activity in Eastern Europe," in U.S. Congress, Joint Economic Committee, *East European Economies Post Helsinki* (Washington, D.C.: U.S. Government Printing Office, 1977), p. 237; Thad Alton, "Production and Resource Allocation in Eastern Europe: Performance, Problems, and Prospects," in U.S. Congress, Joint Economic Committee, *East European Economic Assessment*, Part 2 (Washington, D.C.: U.S. Government Printing Office, 1981), p. 381; U.S. Congress, Joint Economic Committee, *USSR Measures of Economic Growth and Development, 1950–1980* (Washington, D.C.: U.S. Government Printing Office, 1982), pp. 15–21; *Statistical Abstract of the United States, 1981*, pp. 878–879; Wilfred Malenbaum, "Modern Economic Growth in India and China: The Comparison Revisited, 1950–1980," *Economic Development and Cultural Change* 31 (October 1982), 53; *Handbook of Economic Statistics 1990*; Thad Alton et al., Occasional Papers Nos. 75–79 of the Research Project on National Income in East Central Europe (New York, 1983), pp. 7–12, 25; Rush Greenslade, "The Real Gross National Product of the USSR, 1950–75," in U.S. Congress, Joint Economic Committee, *Soviet Economy in a New Perspective* (Washington, D.C.: U.S. Government Printing Office, 1975), p. 271; World Bank, *World Tables*, 3rd ed. (Baltimore: The Johns Hopkins University Press, 1983); OECD, *National Accounts, 1960–1985* (Paris: OECD, 1987); "Eastern Europe: Long Road to Economic Well-Being," Tables C-1 to C-21.

FIGURE 13.1   Average GDP Growth Rate, Planned Socialist and Capitalist
Countries, 1950–1990 (unweighted annual average growth rates)

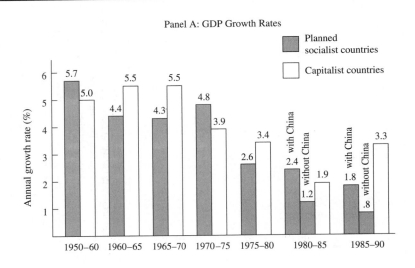

Panel A: GDP Growth Rates

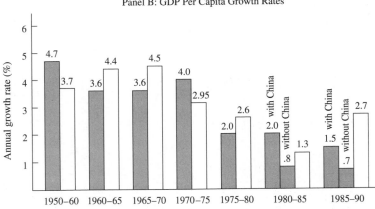

Panel B: GDP Per Capita Growth Rates

Source: Table 13.2.

exceeded the average capitalist rate. The marked slowdown of socialist growth in the
second half of the 1980s (coupled with the recovery of capitalist growth rates) gives
the clear advantage to the capitalist group. Trends in per capita GDP, given in parentheses in Table 13.2, mirror these GDP growth trends.

Because only eight planned socialist countries are covered, growth of any one
has a strong effect on the averages of the group. As Table 13.2 shows, China's growth
up to the mid-1970s was not so different from that of the other socialist countries.

From 1975 onward, however, China's rapid growth stood in marked contrast to the slowing growth rates of the other socialist countries. If China is excluded from the socialist group, their average growth rate sinks well below that of the capitalist group from 1975 on. For example, for the period 1980 to 1985, the average socialist growth rate without China was a meager 1.2 percent per annum, compared to the capitalist rate of 1.9 percent per annum. In fact, if one omits the soaring Chinese growth rates of the mid-1970s and 1980s, the decline in socialist growth rates is very pronounced: from above 4 percent per annum, to 2 percent in the late 1970s, to 1 percent in the 1980s. From 1985 to 1990, the collapse of socialist growth is so pronounced that Western growth outstrips socialist growth by a large factor, whether China is included or not. We will return to this point later in the chapter.

One contrast between capitalism and planned socialism that holds over the entire postwar period is the lesser variability of socialist country growth rates. From 1950 to 1960, for example, the gap between the lowest and highest socialist growth rates was the difference between 4.6 percent and 7.9 percent; for the capitalist group, the difference was that between 3.0 percent and 7.9 percent The capitalist averages conceal more variation than the socialist averages. This pattern was altered somewhat by the marked contrast in growth rates between China and the other socialist countries after 1975, but it persisted within the Soviet and East European group. The planned socialist economies avoided the extreme differences among capitalist countries.

Direct comparisons of planned socialist and capitalist average growth rates did not reveal significant growth differences. However, if one makes a rule-of-thumb adjustment for differences in per capita income by including only the capitalist countries that fall within the approximate per capita income range of the socialist sample—say $3,000 to $6,000—some striking findings emerge. The rationale for this adjustment is that growth rates in the postwar period have tended to vary inversely with the level of development. Countries with low per capita income have grown more rapidly as a group. Only four capitalist countries fall within this income range (Spain, Greece, Italy, and Venezuela), but comparing their average growth rates with those of the former Soviet Union and Eastern Europe is nevertheless informative. For the entire postwar period, the unweighted average annual growth rate of these four capitalist economies was almost 6 percent (4.25 percent on a per capita basis). Even when China is included, the planned socialist average was around 4.5 percent per annum (3.8 percent on a per capita basis). Among countries at a similar stage of development, the planned socialist economies experienced slower growth than their capitalist counterparts.[16]

Frederic Pryor examined the comparative growth rates of capitalist and socialist economies for the period 1950 to 1979, using econometric methods to hold factors other than the economic system constant. Pryor found that although the socialist-system effect was negative, the system coefficient was not statistically significant either for the growth of GDP or for the growth of GDP per capita.[17]

The pattern of decline of planned socialist growth rates goes a long way toward explaining the desire to convert from planned socialism to market resource allocation. Both East and West experienced relatively high rates of growth from 1950 through 1970. In the West, growth was well above long-term historical performance during this period. The growth rates of the planned socialist economies began their descent in the mid-1970s; lower growth rates were recorded in each successive half-decade. In the Soviet Union and Eastern Europe, economic growth had all but ceased by the latter half of the 1980s.

On the other hand, the West (after slow growth in the early 1980s) continued to grow at approximately its long-term historical rates. For the West, the first two decades after the war were periods of peak economic performance, after which it returned to its long-run historical pattern. The West, with two hundred years of recorded growth history, had demonstrated its ability to grow over the long run. The East, on the other hand, with a limited history of economic growth, feared that the planned socialist system had lost its ability to generate economic growth.

The Chinese and Indian comparisons shed light on the growth performance of capitalism and planned socialism in large and very poor countries. Although the Chinese data are fairly rough, most authorities agree that China has outperformed India in GDP growth and per capita GDP growth. It is likely that India and China entered the postwar era with similar levels of per capita income. China's current advantage in per capita income is the consequence of its more rapid growth.

The importance of China as a development model for poor, populous countries requires a further look at Chinese economic growth in an Asian context. Table 13.3 gives the annual growth rates of seven Asian countries for the period 1960–1985. It shows that Chinese economic growth has indeed been rapid even compared with that of other rapidly growing Asian economies, such as Japan, South Korea, and Taiwan. Chinese economic performance looks even better when compared with that of poor, populous Asian countries. Chinese growth has been more than double that of India and Pakistan.[18]

There is no evidence that the planned socialist countries as a group outgrew their capitalist counterparts. One would have to conclude that the growth rates of capitalism and planned socialism were quite similar until the collapse of growth in the East after 1985.

The conclusion that economic growth was not more rapid in the planned socialist economies is a strong one in view of the priority of growth in these countries and the low weight attached to economic growth by many of the capitalist countries. If

TABLE 13.3   Annual GDP Growth Rates of Selected Asian Economies, 1960–1991

China	6.9
Taiwan	7.6
South Korea	7.9
Japan	5.7
Philippines	4.2
India	4.1
Pakistan	4.0

Source: National Foreign Assessment Center, *Handbook of International Economic Statistics 1992* (Washington, D.C.: Central Intelligence Agency, 1992), Table 8 and Table 13.2.

one makes a crude *ceteris paribus* adjustment for differences in per capita income, capitalist growth even emerges as more rapid.

The Sources of Economic Growth

Socialist growth rates were in many ways comparable to those in capitalist systems, though differences in priorities, levels of economic development, and other such influences affect this conclusion. Toward the end of the planned socialist era in the Soviet Union and Eastern Europe, growth rates declined seriously. In the Soviet Union, the rate of growth of output became negative by 1990 as the collapse drew near.

Why did rates of economic growth ultimately decline sharply in the planned socialist economic systems? Were declining rates of economic growth a symptom of more basic economic difficulties in these systems? To answer these questions, it is necessary to look closely at the sources of economic growth and especially at issues of efficiency.

Chapter 3 distinguished between extensive growth and intensive growth. Extensive growth is the growth of output from the expansion of inputs, land, labor, and capital. Intensive growth is the growth derived from increasing output per unit of factor input—that is, from the better use of available inputs.

The sources of economic growth are important for two reasons. First, historical experience shows that as economies grow and develop, the sources of growth tend to change. During the early stages of development, the task is to bring idle resources into production, a model where output expansion is achieved largely from using more inputs. As economic development proceeds, the tendency is to generate growth from the better use of inputs (and improvements in input quality). The distinction between intensive and extensive growth is important, for input expansion comes from sacrificing leisure time, increasing work time, and reducing current consumption with the hope of greater improvements in the future. Intensive growth, however, is derived largely from increased efficiency—for example, through improved managerial systems and technological change.

It is relevant to ask which economic system has done a better job in generating economic growth, where *better* is defined in terms of the relative weights of **intensive growth** and **extensive growth**. Two such comparisons are relevant here. The first, **static efficiency**, takes a snapshot of planned socialist and capitalist countries at a particular point in time to determine how much output they are generating from a given amount of factor inputs. The second, **dynamic efficiency**, probes the question of efficiency performance over time—that is, the extent to which output expands more rapidly than inputs, the difference being the growth rate of factor productivity.[19]

Dynamic Efficiency

Table 13.4 supplies information on the dynamic efficiency of the planned socialist and the industrialized capitalist countries. Specifically, it provides the annual growth rates of aggregate employment ($\hat{L}$) and reproducible capital ($\hat{K}$), which we then compare with the growth rate of aggregate output ($\hat{Q}$) By subtracting the growth rates of employment and capital, respectively, from the growth rate of output, we obtain the growth rates of **labor productivity** ($\hat{Q} - \hat{L}$) and **capital productivity** ($\hat{Q} - \hat{K}$), respectively.

Because the productivity of labor or capital is affected by substitutions between the two factors, it is desirable to have a comprehensive measure of the growth rate of combined labor and capital productivity. One must first calculate the growth rates of labor and capital combined ($\hat{L} + \hat{K}$), or total factor input. This is typically done by taking a weighted average of the growth rates of labor and capital, where the weights represent each factor's share of national income. Thus **total factor productivity** is defined as $\hat{Q} - (\hat{L} + \hat{K})$. Here

$$\hat{K} + \hat{L} = \hat{K}W_K + \hat{L}W_L$$

where

$$W_K = \text{capital's share of income}$$
$$W_L = \text{labor's share of income}$$

We use rates of growth of labor and capital combined ($\hat{L} + \hat{K}$), calculated in this manner. Inasmuch as a return to capital was typically not included in prices in the planned socialist countries, "synthetic" factor shares must be used to calculate their $\hat{L} + \hat{K}$ growth rates.[20] Once the growth rate of combined factor inputs is calculated, it is subtracted from the growth rate of output to obtain the growth rate of factor productivity [$\hat{Q} - (\hat{L} + \hat{K})$]. All of these figures are given in Table 13.4.

The approximate nature of these productivity calculations is worth emphasizing. Factors of production, especially labor, can expand in both quantitative and qualitative terms, yet our measure captures only its quantitative advance.[21] If comparable data were available, we could calculate a more comprehensive measure of labor's growth by adjusting for the growth in education, training, and composition of the labor force. Because we use employment rather than actual hours, we are not even capturing the quantitative growth of labor accurately. Moreover, the capitalist data do not adjust for unemployment (which rose over this period). We use the official capital-stock estimates of the planned socialist economies, except for the Soviet Union. We have no way of knowing whether they are comparable to Western data or of assessing their reliability.[22]

What conclusions are to be drawn from Table 13.4? The first is that through the mid-1980s, the growth rates of capital and labor inputs were similar for capitalism and socialism. The planned socialist and capitalist averages suggest roughly equivalent rates of growth of employment, and although the socialist growth rate of capital was probably slightly lower during the 1950s and higher thereafter, for the entire period capital grew at an average rate of roughly 5 percent in each economic system. The stereotype, fostered by the rapid growth of both labor and capital in the Soviet Union, that the planned socialist system generates a more rapid rate of growth of inputs is not supported. The rates of growth of labor and capital combined round to 2 percent per annum for both capitalism and planned socialism.

Unlike GDP growth, the variability of factor-input growth by country appears to have been as great under planned socialism as under capitalism. Some planned

TABLE 13.4 Annual Growth of Inputs and Output per Unit of Inputs in Socialist and Capitalist Countries

		(1) Employment ($\hat{L}$)	(2) Fixed Capital ($\hat{K}$)	(3) Labor and Capital ($\hat{L}+\hat{K}$)	(4) Output ($\hat{Q}$)	(5) Labor Productivity ($\hat{Q}-\hat{L}$)	(6) Capital Productivity ($\hat{Q}-\hat{K}$)	(7) Total Factor Productivity $\hat{Q}-(\hat{L}+\hat{K})$
			A. Planned Socialist Countries					
Czechoslovakia	1950–60	0.7	3.5	1.4	4.8	4.1	1.3	3.4
	1960–83	1.0	4.7	2.1	2.6	1.6	-2.1	0.5
East Germany	1950–60	0.0	2.0	0.5	6.1	6.1	4.1	5.6
	1960–83	0.3	4.0	1.4	2.8	2.5	-1.2	1.4
Soviet Union	1950–60	1.2	9.4	3.4	5.8	4.6	-3.6	2.4
	1960–85	1.3	7.3	2.8	3.6	2.3	-3.7	0.8
Poland	1950–60	1.0	2.6	1.4	4.6	3.6	2.0	3.2
	1960–83	1.5	4.7	2.5	3.3	1.8	-1.4	0.8
Hungary	1950–60	1.0	3.6	1.7	4.6	3.6	1.0	2.9
	1960–83	0.3	5.0	1.7	2.9	2.6	-2.1	1.2
Romania	1950–60	1.1	—[a]	—	5.9	4.8	—	—
	1960–85	0.4	—[a]	—	4.6	4.1	—	—
Bulgaria	1950–60	0.2	—[a]	—	6.7	6.5	—	—
	1960–85	0.5	—[a]	—	3.7	3.2	—	1.0
Unweighted average	1950–60	0.8	4.2	1.7	5.5[b] (5.2)[c]	4.8	1.0	3.5
	1960–83(85)	0.8	5.1	2.1	3.3[b] (3.0)[c]	2.5	-2.1	0.9

TABLE 13.4 Annual Growth of Inputs and Output per Unit of Inputs in Socialist and Capitalist Countries *(Cont.)*

		(1) Employment ($\hat{L}$)	(2) Fixed Capital ($\hat{K}$)	(3) Labor and Capital ($\hat{L}+\hat{K}$)	(4) Output ($\hat{Q}$)	(5) Labor Productivity ($\hat{Q}-\hat{L}$)	(6) Capital Productivity ($\hat{Q}-\hat{K}$)	(7) Total Factor Productivity $\hat{Q}-(\hat{L}+\hat{K})$
				B. Capitalist Countries				
United States	1950–60	1.4	3.6	1.8	3.1	1.7	−0.5	1.3
	1960–85	2.0	3.3	2.4	3.1	1.1	−0.2	0.7
Canada	1960–85	2.7	4.7	3.3	4.2	1.5	−0.5	0.9
Belgium	1950–62	0.6	2.3	1.0	3.2	2.6	0.6	2.2
Denmark	1950–62	0.9	5.1	1.8	3.5	2.6	−1.6	1.7
	1950–60^d	0.1	4.2	1.0	4.9	4.8	0.7	3.9
	1960–85	0.7	4.8	1.8	3.9	3.1	−0.9	2.1
West Germany	1950–60^d	2.0	6.4	3.1	7.3	5.3	0.9	4.2
	1960–85	0.0	4.8	1.2	3.1	3.1	−1.7	1.9
Italy	1950–62	0.6	3.5	1.3	6.0	5.4	2.5	4.7
Finland	1960–85	0.7	4.6	1.9	3.9	3.2	−0.5	2.0
Sweden	1962–83	0.6	3.5	1.5	2.8	2.2	−0.7	1.3
Netherlands	1950–62	1.1	4.7	1.9	4.7	3.6	0.0	2.8
Norway	1950–60^d	0.2	4.2	1.2	3.5	3.3	−0.7	2.3
	1960–85	0.5	3.6	1.4	4.2	3.7	0.6	2.8
United Kingdom	1950–60^d	0.7	3.4	1.2	2.3	1.6	−1.1	1.1
	1960–85	0.5	3.2	1.1	2.3	1.8	0.9	1.2

	(1) Employment ($\hat{L}$)	(2) Fixed Capital ($\hat{K}$)	(3) Labor and Capital ($\hat{L}+\hat{K}$)	(4) Output ($\hat{Q}$)	(5) Labor Productivity ($\hat{Q}-\hat{L}$)	(6) Capital Productivity ($\hat{Q}-\hat{K}$)	(7) Total Factor Productivity $\hat{Q}-(\hat{L}+\hat{K})$
Japan	1953–70						
	1.7	9.8	3.8	10.0	8.3	0.2	6.2
1970–85	0.9	8.2	2.3	4.4	3.5	-3.8	2.1
Greece	1960–85						
	0.4	5.8	2.0	5.1	4.7	-0.7	3.1
Unweighted average[e] 1950–60	0.9	4.7	1.8	4.8	3.9	0.1	3.0
Unweighted average 1960–85	0.9	4.7	1.9	3.7	2.8	-1.0	1.8

Note: All figures are annual growth rates.
$\hat{L}$ = growth rate of employment
$\hat{K}$ = growth rate of reproducible capital
$\hat{Q}$ = growth rate of output
$(\hat{L}+\hat{K})$ = growth rate of labor and capital combined

[a] The official Romanian and Bulgarian capital-stock series are not cited because they are in current, not constant, prices.
[b] Average of all seven countries.
[c] Average of first five countries.
[d] 1950–1962.
[e] Includes Japan, 1953–1970.

Sources: **Panel A:** *Employment:* Andrew Elias, "Magnitude and Distribution of the Labor Force in Eastern Europe," in U.S. Congress, Joint Economic Committee, *Economic Developments in Countries of Eastern Europe* (Washington, D.C.: U.S. Government Printing Office, 1970), pp. 208–214; Thad Alton, "Comparative Structure and Growth of Economic Activity in Eastern Europe," in U.S. Congress, Joint Economic Committee, *East European Economies Post Helsinki* (Washington, D.C.: U.S. Government Printing Office, 1977), p. 218; *Handbook of Economic Statistics 1980*, p. 47. *Capital Stock:* Official CMEA estimates of productive funds (*osnovnye fondy*) from *Statisticheski ezhegodnik stran-chlenov Soveta Ekonomicheskoi Vzaimopomoschi 1974* (Moscow: Statistika), p. 27; Alton, "Production and Resource Allocation in Eastern Europe," p. 372; *Handbook of Economic Statistics 1980*, p. 58; and Alton, "Comparative Structure and Growth," p. 223. *Output:* Table 10.1. **Panel B:** *Growth Rates of Employment, Reproducible Capital, and Output:* Edward Denison, *Why Growth Rates Differ* (Washington, D.C.: Brookings, 1967), pp. 42, 190, and Ch. 21; Edward Denison, *Accounting for United States Economic Growth, 1929–1969* (Washington, D.C.: Brookings, 1974), pp. 32, 58; Edward Denison and William Chung, *How Japan's Economy Grew So Fast* (Washington, D.C.: Brookings, 1976), pp. 19, 31; OECD, Department of Economics and Statistics, *Flows and Stocks of Fixed Capital, 1960–1985* (OECD: Paris, 1987); *Handbook of Economic Statistics 1986*; *World Table*, 3rd ed.

socialist countries (East Germany, for example) experienced low growth of both labor and capital, whereas others (the Soviet Union and Poland, for example) experienced rapid input growth. One finds similar variability among the capitalist countries, with some (notably Japan) experiencing quite rapid growth of both labor and capital inputs.

Both the socialist and the capitalist countries experienced a slowdown in productivity growth after the 1960s: The planned socialist growth rate of output declined after 1960 by about 40 percent; yet inputs, both labor and capital, grew more rapidly after 1960 (about one-quarter faster). Thus both labor and capital productivity and total factor productivity declined dramatically after 1960 in the planned socialist economies—labor productivity from an average of 4.8 percent to 2.5 percent, total factor productivity from 3.5 percent to 0.9 percent. Efforts to stabilize the growth of output by raising the growth of inputs did not succeed; rather than becoming more intensive, the growth of the planned socialist economies became more extensive after 1960.

The greater extensivity of socialist growth after 1960 is apparent when we compare the growth rates of total factor productivity with the growth rates of output. Taking those five socialist countries for which capital data are available, the average GDP growth rate was 5.2 percent per annum between 1950 and 1960, whereas the growth of efficiency (factor productivity) was 3.5 percent. Thus 67 percent (3.5/5.2) of economic growth was accounted for by increasing output per unit of input. The corresponding figures for the 1960 to 1983 period are 0.9 percent and 3.0 percent. Thus from 1960 to 1983, only 30 percent of growth was accounted for by increasing inputs. The declining growth of productivity was felt by both labor and capital, but the decline in capital productivity from a positive rate to a negative rate of 2.1 percent per annum was especially prominent.

The capitalist group also experienced a slowdown in productivity growth after 1960. Average labor productivity growth fell from 3.9 percent to 2.8 percent; capital productivity growth fell from zero to 1.0 percent; and total factor productivity growth fell from 3.0 percent to 1.8 percent. In the 1950s, some 65 percent (3.0/4.8) of growth in the capitalist group was explained by the growth of efficiency; for the period 1960–1985, 49 percent (1.8/3.7) of growth was explained by efficiency gains.

Table 13.4 shows the planned socialist economies in a favorable light because it does not include the productivity collapse of the second half of the 1980s. During this period, all the planned socialist economies experienced negative productivity growth except the USSR, which experienced zero productivity growth. The special features of the Soviet case, notably extensive growth and a low elasticity-substitution of capital for labor, are discussed in a recent contribution by Easterly and Fischer.[23]

What are the overall conclusions concerning the growth of efficiency under capitalism and planned socialism? As in the case of economic growth, there appears to be no evidence to suggest a more rapid rate of growth of productivity under planned socialism (see Figure 13.2). It appears that the productivity performance of planned socialism deteriorated seriously since 1960, at least, and that socialist growth became much more extensive in character. We must emphasize that these conclusions are based on approximate data and do not reflect the qualitative growth of inputs. We believe, however, that they would hold up even if more exhaustive data were available.

Consumption Costs of Growth

One cost of economic growth is the sacrifice in current consumption required to add to the nation's stock of capital. Although growth rates in the East and West have been similar, it is not true that this growth was achieved with a similar allocation of resources between consumption and investment. Information on resource-allocation policies is summarized in Table 13.5.[24] Although the capitalist and socialist data cover

FIGURE 13.2   Productivity Growth in Socialist and Capitalist Countries, 1960–1985

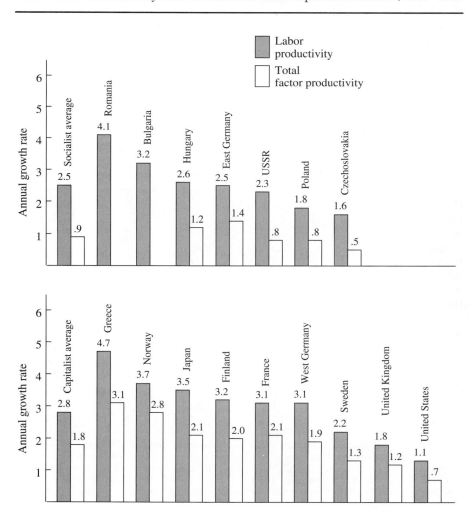

Source: Table 13.4

TABLE 13.5   Annual Rates of Growth of Personal Consumption, Investment, and GDP in Planned Socialist and Capitalist Countries

Country	(1) Personal Consumption	(2) Gross Investment	(3) GDP	(4) Consumption Growth as a Percentage of Investment Growth, (1) ÷ (2)
A. Planned Socialist Countries				
Czechoslovakia (1950–1967)	2.2	5.2	3.2	0.42
East Germany (1960–1975)	3.7	6.1	4.9	0.61
Hungary (1950–1967)	3.4	5.2	4.0	0.65
Poland (1950–1967)	4.2	7.9	5.1	0.53
Soviet Union (1950–1980)	4.3	7.7	4.7	0.56
Unweighted average	3.6	6.4	4.4	0.56
B. Capitalist Countries, 1950–1977				
United States	3.4	3.1	3.6	1.10
Canada	4.7	4.6	4.8	1.02
West Germany	4.7	5.0	4.8	0.94
Denmark	3.5	4.9	3.8	0.71
Norway	3.9	4.6	4.2	0.85
Belgium	3.7	4.6	4.0	0.81
France	5.0	6.1	5.0	0.82
Netherlands	4.6	4.2	4.5	1.09
Japan	7.8	11.0	8.4	0.71
Austria	5.4	5.1	4.9	1.06
United Kingdom	2.2	4.4	2.5	0.50
Italy	4.6	5.0	4.8	0.92
Greece	6.0	7.1	6.4	0.85
Spain	5.2	6.7	5.6	0.77
Turkey	6.1	8.2	6.3	0.74
Unweighted average	4.7	5.6	4.9	0.84

Sources: Thad Alton, "Economic Structure and Growth in Eastern Europe," in U.S. Congress, Joint Economic Committee, *Economic Developments in Countries of Eastern Europe* (Washington, D.C.: U.S. Government Printing Office, 1970), pp. 52–53; *Deutsches Institut fur Wirtschaftsforschung Wochenbericht*, 44 (June 1977), p. 199; Rush Greenslade, "The Real Gross National Product of the USSR, 1950–75," in U.S. Congress, Joint Economic Committee, *Soviet Economy in a New Perspective* (Washington, D.C.: U.S. Government Printing Office, 1975), p. 275; World Bank, *World Tables 1980* (Baltimore: The Johns Hopkins University Press, 1980), country tables; U.S. Congress, Joint Economic Committee, *USSR: Measures of Economic Growth and Development, 1950–80* (Washington, D.C.: U.S. Government Printing Office, 1982), pp. 65–67.

slightly different time periods, they tell an interesting story. Again the GDP growth rates are quite similar, but personal consumption fared relatively better than invest-ment under capitalism. In fact, where as personal consumption grew on the average at a more rapid rate in the capitalist sample (4.7 percent versus 3.6 percent), gross investment grew faster under planned socialism (6.4 percent versus 5.6 percent).

Of even greater interest, when one takes the ratio of the growth rates of con-sumption and investment as a measure of resource allocation, a distinct pattern emerges. Although there seems to be a positive relationship between this ratio and per capita income, the socialist consumption–investment ratios appear to be well below those of capitalist countries at a similar stage of development. The achieve-ment of similar rates of growth in East and West has required a greater sacrifice of current consumption under planned socialism. In fact, the resource-allocation pat-tern of the socialist countries was remarkably uniform and was closest to the pattern of the less-industrialized capitalist countries (such as Turkey and Spain).

Given the higher investment rates under planned socialism in the 1950s and 1960s, it follows that socialist per capita consumption was lower for a given level of per capita national income *ceteris paribus*. This is the other side of the coin— namely, the cost of maintaining economic growth through expansion of capital in-puts.[25] The absolute level of per capita consumption depends on the economic poten-tial of the country, and to argue that one country has outperformed the other simply because its standard of living is higher begs the question. The major issue is what standard of living is being supplied, given the economic resources at the nation's disposal. Such a comparison shows that the socialist living standards are low relative to per capita income. This reflects the decision of growth-oriented socialist planners to devote a relatively larger share of GDP to investment than under capitalism. How-ever, the telling point is that this decision did not lead to a notably higher rate of growth for the planned socialist nations. The planners' consumption policies did not pay off in terms of more rapid growth.

These findings have negative implications concerning the viability of the planned socialist systems. We have not yet considered the reasons for the productivity prob-lem, but the incentive impact on the socialist consumer must have been harmful to these economies. First, the systems, especially that of the former Soviet Union, em-phasized a basic socialist postulate—sacrifice now through expanded savings and reduced consumption (such as that which took place in the 1930s) to enjoy significant gains in consumption in the future. But in general those gains did not materialize. When they did, the pace of improvement was slow, a fact that Soviet consumers could recognize as they watched other countries outperform their own system. Although these patterns are not easily quantifiable, the effort contributed by the Soviet worker must have suffered, especially in the 1970s and 1980s.

Static Efficiency

Static efficiency is a difficult concept to measure. To do so correctly requires first a notion of an economy's productive potential, as defined by its total resources, and then a determination of how closely the economy comes to meeting that potential.

This problem is explained in Figure 13.3. To show that the Soviet Union, for example, obtained half as much output as the United States from a given amount of conventional labor and capital inputs would not unambiguously prove the greater static efficiency of the American economy. The measurement of conventional inputs may fail to capture the full range of resources (in both qualitative and quantitative terms) at the disposal of each economy.

One way to illustrate the problem of measuring static efficiency is to note the strong positive relationship between the level of economic development and output per unit of input. Any evaluation of the static efficiency of capitalism and planned socialism must distinguish between "normal" differences caused by unequal economic development and differences due to the economic system. What is missing is information on what the economy should be able to produce at maximum efficiency from its resources.

FIGURE 13.3   Why It Is Difficult to Evaluate Static Efficiency: Different Country Production Possibilities

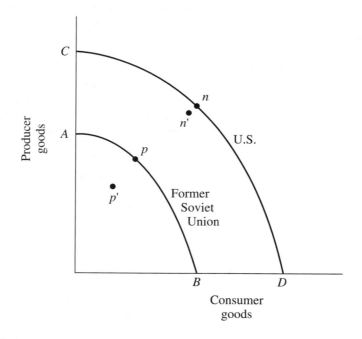

Explanation: CD represents the production possibilities frontier (PPF) of, say, the United States. AB is the PPF of, say, the former Soviet Union. The U.S. PPF is to the northeast of the Soviet PPF because of greater resources and better technology. The relevant measure of static efficiency is how closely each economy comes to operating on its PPF. If, for example, the United States operates very close to n at n' and the Soviet Union operates at p', which is very far from p, then the United States is more efficient. In real-world measurement, all we observe is p' and n'. We have no way of knowing what p and n are.

Abram Bergson has made a careful study of comparative productivity under capitalism and socialism that sheds light on the issue of relative productivity performance.[26] Bergson's data for 1975 are reproduced in Table 13.6. They give per capita outputs and labor (adjusted for quality differences), capital, and land inputs of various capitalist and socialist countries (where the socialist group includes Yugoslavia) as a percentage of the U.S. per capita figures. Table 13.6 shows, for example, that Italy had a per capita output 61 percent of that of the United States, a per capita employment 75 percent of that of the United States, and a per capita capital stock 62 percent of that of the United States. The Soviet Union had a per capita output 60 percent of that of the United States, a per capita employment 104 percent of that of the United States, and a per capita capital stock 73 percent of that of the United States.

The issue is whether the socialist countries systematically obtained less output from their available inputs than the capitalist countries. The data for Italy and the Soviet Union show that Italy obtained more output from its available inputs. Italy and the Soviet Union had the same per capita output when compared with the United States, yet the Soviet Union used more labor and capital per capita to produce that output.

Bergson demonstrates that there was a systematic tendency for the output per worker (labor productivity) in socialist economies to fall short of output per worker in capitalist countries, when inputs are held constant. According to Bergson's calculations, output per worker in the socialist group fell 25 percent to 34 percent short of output per worker in the capitalist group *ceteris paribus*.

TABLE 13.6   Per Capita Output, Employment, Capital, and Land, 1975
(United States = 100)

Country	Output per Capita	Employment per capita Adjusted for Labor Quality	Reproducible Capital per Capita	Farm Land per Capita
United States	100.0	100.0	100.0	100.0
West Germany	90.0	84.0	107.3	14.8
France	92.2	88.3	83.0	40.1
Italy	61.3	75.2	61.6	24.9
United Kingdom	67.2	89.6	77.2	14.5
Japan	82.8	129.0	95.2	5.4
Spain	64.6	95.4	47.7	67.0
Soviet Union	60.0	104.1	73.2	103.5
Hungary	61.1	115.6	70.9	59.8
Poland	54.8	122.7	51.6	50.4
Yugoslavia	41.5	98.8	35.9	45.6

Source: Abram Bergson, "Comparative Productivity: The USSR, Eastern Europe, and the West," *American Economic Review* 77 (June 1987), 347. Used by permission.

Bergson's findings are important, though this sample is small. It will be a long time before a similar experiment on a larger number of countries can be performed. Meanwhile, we believe it is appropriate to conclude that socialist economies have relatively lower productivity, *ceteris paribus*, than industrialized capitalist countries.[27]

As previously shown, it is difficult to assess the comparative static efficiency of socialist and capitalist economic systems because determining how closely real-world economies operate to their production possibilities frontier is not possible. However, beginning with the work of Judith Thornton in 1971, a number of predictive studies inclusive of the early 1990s have attempted to examine **allocative efficiency** by estimating various production functions and by focusing on the allocation of inputs among industries in socialist economies.[28] These studies generally found that there was allocative inefficiency in that reallocation could raise the value added; that was increasingly so through the 1970s. Similar studies conducted in the 1980s resulted in similar conclusions, though the estimated magnitudes of inefficiency were generally not very large. These types of studies generally supported the existence of allocative inefficiency, but their results have sparked controversy, especially because of a variety of basic measurement problems that remain unresolved.

A number of studies of **enterprise (technical) efficiency** have looked at enterprises in socialist and capitalist systems and, in some cases, have made comparisons. Although generalizing across a wide variety of studies that differ in scope and approach is difficult, most studies have not shown unusually low levels of efficiency in enterprises of planned socialist economic systems. But, like measures of allocative efficiency, these measures of technical efficiency are difficult to interpret because of basic underlying measurement problems.

In sum, these studies have led to a general presumption that efficiency was lower in the planned socialist systems than in market capitalist systems. The issue, remains controversial, however, and undoubtedly will spur further analyses in the future.

Income Distribution

Another measure of the performance of economic systems is the distribution of income among the members of society. What constitutes a good distribution of income must be a subjective matter, but there would be agreement that a distribution in which the top 5 percent of the population receives 95 percent of all income is "unfair" and that a completely equal distribution is "unfair." Marx himself rejected the notion of an equal distribution of income during the transition from socialism to communism, arguing instead for a distribution that reflected the individual's contribution to the well-being of society.[29]

Another reason why most people reject a perfectly equal distribution of income is that rewards must be offered for differential effort and for scarce resources; otherwise, incentives will diminish and the economy will not produce its potential output. The issue therefore is now to construct a distribution of income that both is "fair" and provides necessary incentives. Both socialism and capitalism must address this issue.

What differences would one expect in the distribution of incomes under capitalism and socialism? In capitalist societies, the two major sources of income inequality are the unequal distribution of property ownership (land and capital resources) and that of human capital. Both forms of capital yield income—the first in the form of property income from rent, interest, dividends, and capital gains, the second from wages and salaries.

Under both planned and market socialism, property other than consumer durables and housing is owned by the state, and the return from this state-owned property is at the state's disposal. Under capitalism, the bulk of property is owned privately, and property income accrues to private individuals.

The distribution of human capital depends on the manner in which schooling and on-the-job training are provided. Free or subsidized public schooling is available in both types of societies, although there is a greater tendency for the state to pay for higher education in socialist societies. Nevertheless, the differences between the two systems would not be expected to be great.

The major distinction is the absence of private ownership of income-earning property under socialism. Unless offset by higher earnings differentials, the distribution of property plus labor income should be more nearly equal under socialism. The distribution of income after taxes depends on the extent to which the state uses redistributive taxes and transfers to equalize income distribution.

As to earnings differentials, planned socialist societies recognized that labor cannot be allocated administratively and must be allowed relative freedom of choice of occupation. Therefore, the distribution of wage and salary income under socialism should follow roughly the same principles as under capitalism.

Arguments can be made, however, that the distribution of labor incomes varies according to the economic system.[30] Some maintain that labor income is nearly more equally distributed under socialism because of the more nearly equal distribution of education and training and because the government can control the power of labor groups. Moreover, socialist governments have a greater doctrinal commitment to equality.

Frederic Pryor made an extensive econometric study of the distribution of labor income among workers for the late 1950s and early 1960s.[31] He found that the distribution of labor income was *more nearly equal* under socialism, once per capita income and the size of the country were held constant. He also found that labor incomes were less nearly equal in the Soviet Union than in the other socialist countries; therefore, studies that generalize from the Soviet experience are likely to give a false impression.

More recent data on the distribution of earnings for full-time wage and salary earners confirm most of Pryor's findings for the 1950s and early 1960s.[32] Earnings were more nearly equally distributed in Eastern Europe, Yugoslavia, and the Soviet Union than in the United States in the 1970s. For the USSR, this was a relatively new phenomenon, for as late as 1957, Soviet earnings were less nearly equal than those in the United States.[33]

We now turn from the distribution of *labor income* to the distribution of *total income*. Table 13.7 gives data on the distribution of per capita income, after income taxes, in a limited number of planned socialist and capitalist countries for which data are available.[34] The socialist data generally excluded top income-earning families

TABLE 13.7   Distribution of Per Capita Income Among Families After Income Taxes in Planned Socialist and Capitalist Countries

	U.K. 1969	U.S. 1968	Italy 1969	Canada 1971	Sweden 1971	Hungary 1964	Czecho-slovakia 1965	Bulgaria 1963–1965	USSR 1966
Per capita income of individual in 95th percentile ÷ that of individual in 5th percentile	5.0	12.7	11.2	12.0	5.5	4.0	4.3	3.8	5.7
Per capita income of individual in 90th percentile ÷ that of individual in 10th percentile	3.4	6.7	5.9	6.0	3.5	3.0	3.1	2.7	3.5
Per capita income of individual in 75th percentile ÷ that of individual in 25th percentile	1.9	2.6	2.5	2.4	1.9	1.8	1.8	1.7	2.0

Source: P. J. D. Wiles, *Economic Institutions Compared* (New York: Halsted Press, 1977), p. 443. By permission of Basil Blackwell, Oxford.

(party leaders, government officials, artists, and authors), including instead only families of workers and employees. Many second-economy activities considered legal in capitalist societies (the provision of private repair and medical services, for example) were not recorded. Also, a relatively larger volume of resources (even excluding free educational and medical benefits) was provided in socialist societies on an extramarket basis—shopping privileges, official cars, vacations—and such resources were not included in reported income.

Table 13.7 shows that income is distributed more unequally in the capitalist countries in which the state plays a relatively minor redistributive role either through progressive taxation or through the distribution of social services (the United States, Italy, and Canada). Yet even where the state played a major redistributive role (the United Kingdom and Sweden), the distribution of income appeared to be slightly more unequal than in the planned socialist countries (Hungary, Czechoslovakia, and Bulgaria). The Soviet Union in 1966 appeared to have had a less egalitarian distribution of income than its East European counterparts. The USSR distribution was scarcely distinguishable from the British and Swedish distributions (it may even have been more unequal). Table 13.8 reveals that Soviet income distribution was more nearly equal than that in Australia, Canada, and the United States but not much different from that in Norway and the United Kingdom.

TABLE 13.8   An International Comparison of Income Shares of Selected Percentile Groups, Distributions of Households by Per Capita Household Income, and GDP Per Capita

Distribution, Country and Year	Percentage Income Share of			
	Lowest 10%	Lowest 20%	Highest 20%	Highest 10%
Nonfarm households (pretax)				
USSR, 1967	4.4	10.4	33.8	19.9
Urban households (post-tax)				
USSR, 1972–1974	3.4	8.7	38.5	24.1
All households (pretax)				
Australia, 1966–1967	3.5	8.3	41.0	25.6
Norway, 1970	3.5	8.2	39.0	23.5
U.K., 1973	3.5	8.3	39.9	23.9
France, 1970	2.0	5.8	47.2	31.8
Canada, 1969	2.2	6.2	43.6	27.8
U.S., 1972	1.8	5.5	44.4	28.6
All households (post-tax)				
Sweden, 1972	3.5	9.3	35.2	20.5

Source: Abram Bergson, "Income Inequality Under Soviet Socialism," *Journal of Economic Literature* 22 (September 1984). Used by permission.

The **Gini coefficient** is a convenient summary measure of income inequality. The higher the Gini coefficient, the more unequal the distribution of income. A Gini coefficient of zero denotes perfect equality; a Gini coefficient of 1 denotes perfect inequality. Gini coefficients for Great Britain and Sweden for the early 1970s are both around 0.25. The Czech, Hungarian, and Polish Gini coefficients for the same period are 0.21, 0.24, and 0.24, respectively—that is, very close to the British and Swedish coefficients. The Canadian and U.S. Gini coefficients, on the other hand, are 0.34 and 0.35, respectively, well above the socialist coefficients.[35]

Figure 13.4 provides Lorenz curves for Hungary, Sweden, West Germany, Spain, Mexico, and Yugoslavia. The reader will recall from Chapter 3 that the further the Lorenz curve departs from the line of perfect equality, the more unequal the distribution. These curves, which refer to the early 1970s, confirm the basic pattern shown in Table 13.7: Hungary was about the same as Sweden but was much more egalitarian than West Germany and Spain (two capitalist countries without considerable state income redistribution); Yugoslavia did not differ significantly from West Germany and Spain. However, there apparently was a narrowing of differentials in Yugoslavia between the early 1960s and the early 1970s.

The Mexican Lorenz curve is included to make a general point about the Yugoslav (and Hungarian, Polish, Soviet, and Czech) distributions. As the Mexican curve shows, inequality tends to be negatively related to the level of development.[36] If one could adjust for lower per capita income, the socialist distributions would appear even more nearly equal than they do in direct comparisons.

In general, we conclude that the differences in distribution of income between the planned socialist economies and the capitalist welfare states have been relatively minor. This is a surprising conclusion. One would have expected the absence of private ownership of property to make more of a difference. Nevertheless, differences are apparent when one contrasts the socialist distributions with those of the capitalist nations in which the state does not play a major redistributive role. In this instance, the expected contrast emerges, although we must re-emphasize the difficulty of interpreting the socialist distributions because of the omitted income categories.

Economic Stability

A final indicator of economic performance is economic stability. By economic stability we mean the absence of excessive movements in prices, unemployment, and output. Stability also refers to the absence of persistent (as opposed to cyclical) high unemployment rates or inflation rates.

The postwar era witnessed several recessions in the major capitalist countries, the most severe occurring in the mid-1970s and at the start of the 1980s. Socialist countries experienced "growth recessions"—that is, periods when the growth rate declined but remained positive, but they largely avoided recessions before 1980. In the 1980s, however, the majority of the planned socialist countries experienced periods of negative growth.

The literature recognizes that cyclical fluctuations are present in planned socialist economies, but it was believed that socialist fluctuations were less pronounced. However, Frederic Pryor found that socialist fluctuations in GDP, industrial output,

FIGURE 13.4   Lorenz Curves of the Distribution of Per Capita Income in Hungary, Sweden, West Germany, Spain, Yugoslavia, and Mexico[a,b]

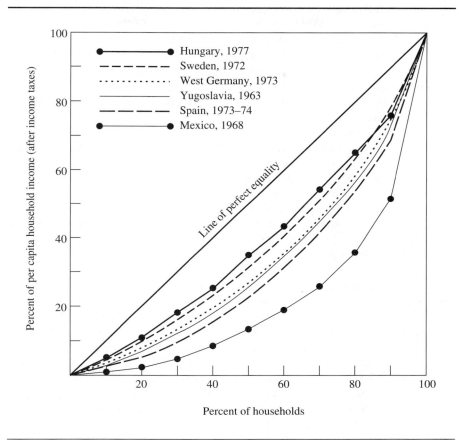

[a] For an explanation of the Lorenz curve, see Chapter 3.
[b] Mexican data are prior to income taxes, but we doubt that their inclusion would move the Mexican Lorenz curve dramatically.

Sources: Malcolm Sawyer, *Income Distribution in OECD Countries* (Paris: OECD, 1976), p. 17; Jan Adams and Miloslav Nosal, "Earnings Differentials and Household-Income Differentials in Hungary—Policies and Practice," *Journal of Comparative Economics* 6 (June 1982), 197; and Wouter van Ginneken, "Generating Internationally Comparable Income Distribution Data," *Review of Income and Wealth* 28 (December 1982), 374.

and investment are not statistically distinguishable from capitalist fluctuations. Moreover, socialist fluctuations in agricultural output were more pronounced than those in capitalist agriculture.[37]

The planned socialist economies claimed that socialist planning "liquidated" unemployment. No society can eliminate unemployment entirely, for at any given time some people are in the process of changing jobs. It does appear that the planned socialist economies reduced the rate of unemployment to small proportions relative to capitalist economies.[38] This was a consequence of deliberate full-employment planning. Enterprises were either unwilling or unable to release underemployed workers, which created such a problem that experiments were attempted to encourage the laying off of redundant workers. Generally, however, enterprises were given hiring quotas for new graduates, and the planning system served to provide employment for able-bodied individuals, whether in a necessary or an underemployed position.[39]

Moreover, the planned system avoided unemployment problems by not allowing enterprises to fail. Enterprises have typically been rewarded on the basis of output rather than sales, and the existence of the enterprise has been guaranteed regardless of its performance.

If one examines price inflation under capitalism and planned socialism, a striking contrast emerges from the official statistics (see Table 13.9). Between 1960 and 1980, for example, the capitalist countries experienced considerable inflation, which accelerated after 1970. According to official socialist indexes, on the other hand, consumer prices rose at a very modest pace over this period. The planned socialist economies' claims of virtual price stability for the 1960s and 1970s evoke skepticism about the official consumer price series.[40] First, the official price series ignored substantial price increases for "new" or "higher-quality" products. Often an enterprise could obtain a higher price by claiming superficial or nonexistent quality improvements in its products. Second, the official series failed to capture the price increases of goods sold in legal and illegal free markets. Third, the official indexes did not include the costs of standing in line or of the bribes required to obtain goods. When these circumstances prevail, demand exceeds supply at the established official price, and **repressed inflation** results. Supplies offered at established state prices were rationed out by standing in line, special shopping privileges, or ration coupons.

There is evidence that the official price series understated actual inflation in the socialist countries. Recalculated price indexes (shown in parentheses in Table 13.9) suggest that prices rose more rapidly than official sources claim for the period 1960 to 1980. The relatively stable state retail prices concealed an unknown degree of repressed inflation, which has had a serious destabilizing effect in some planned socialist economies, such as Poland. For political and other reasons, authorities were unwilling to raise official consumer prices to market-clearing levels. Price stability was achieved only at the cost of serious shortages, redirection of purchasing power into collective farm markets and black markets, and growing discontent.

The second column of Table 13.9 gives inflation rates for 1980 to 1989, a period that saw the partial liberalization of state price controls in the East. In the two countries that have converted most to market prices (Poland and Hungary), inflation well outpaced the West. Even in the Soviet Union, Bulgaria, and Romania, where prices remained state-controlled during this period (and where the official statistics probably understated inflation), inflation was about the same as in such low-inflation Western countries as Japan, Germany, and the Netherlands.

The rapid increase of prices in Poland and Hungary show the extent of repressed inflation on the eve of liberalization. The freeing of prices led to very high rates of inflation. In Poland, the result was a 65-fold increase in prices in 1989 as price controls were removed, after which prices stabilized. The apparent price stability of

TABLE **13.9**   Indexes of Consumer Prices in 1980 and 1989
(recalculated socialist indexes in parentheses)

	1980 (1960 = 100)		1989 (1980 = 100)	
	A. Socialist Countries			
	Official	Recalculated	Official	Recalculated
Soviet Union	100	(140)	109	(—)
Bulgaria	130	(207)	113	(126)
Czechoslovakia	126	(173)	116	(115)
East Germany	98	(127)	110	(114)
Hungary	169	(210)	215	(220)
Poland	185	(254)	6515	(—)
Romania	120	(—)	130	(141)
Yugoslavia	1449		246560	

	B. Capitalist Countries	
United States	280	150
Canada	287	170
Belgium	261	150
France	382	178
Italy	546	236
Japan	420	119
Netherlands	295	124
United Kingdom	547	172
West Germany	213	126

Sources: Statistical Abstract of the United States, 1981, p. 881; *Economic Report of the President, 1981*, p. 355; Martin Kohn, "Consumer Price Developments in Eastern Europe," in U.S. Congress, Joint Economic Committee, *Eastern European Economic Assessment*, Part 2 (Washington, D.C.: U.S. Government Printing Office, 1981), p. 3330; Thad Alton *et al., Official Alternative Consumer Price Indexes in Eastern Europe, 1960–1980*, OP-68, Research Project on National Income in East Central Europe (New York, 1981); Directorate of Intelligence, CIA, *Soviet Gross National Product in Current Prices, 1960–80*, SOV 83-10037 (March 1983), pp. 6, 22; *Handbook of Economic Statistics 1990*, p. 45; "Eastern Europe: Long Road Ahead to Economic Well-Being," 1990, Tables C-2 to C-21; and *Narodnoe Khoziaistvo SSSR 1988*, p. 125.

earlier periods (as reflected in the official statistics) has concealed churning inflationary forces. In fact, the pent-up inflationary forces present a serious obstacle to economic reform. The conversion to a market economy requires releasing inflationary pressures. In Eastern Europe, both the governments and the public have a strong fear of inflation—of its effect on output and on the distribution of income. This fear of inflation reduces public support for market reform.

Yugoslavia has experienced a more rapid rate of inflation than any capitalist country in our sample. After 1980, Yugoslavia experienced hyperinflation. Moreover, the Yugoslav unemployment rate was higher than that in the planned socialist countries.[41] Thus Yugoslavia does not appear to match the planned socialist record of stability but is more like a capitalist LDC in this regard. In fact, Yugoslavia's rates approximated those of Portugal and Turkey.

Performance Comparisons and Decline

At the beginning of this chapter we posed two questions: First, to what extent and in what ways did the performance of the former planned socialist economic systems differ from the performance of market capitalist systems? Second, to what extent and in what ways can the demise of many of these systems be attributed to economic factors?

Economic Decline in the Planned Socialist Systems

Although empirical evidence suggests that some aspects of socialist performance were good in earlier years, noticeable declines in the growth rate of output and productivity were observed in the 1970s and 1980s. That declining performance attracted considerable attention as well as many explanations.

A popular approach to understanding the growth slowdown in the planned socialist economies focused on analysis of input and output growth (production function analysis).[42] Such analyses seemed to suggest that the growth of total factor productivity, while generally (though not always) positive, declined rather steadily during the 1970s and 1980s. Moreover, studies examining labor and capital productivity usually demonstrated a positive and declining labor productivity and an increasingly negative capital productivity. The simple conclusion was that overall diminishing returns and/or declining marginal product of capital occurred in a setting where capital was substituted for labor. This evidence was used to conclude that planned socialist systems, rather than becoming more intensive, were in fact, achieving increasingly less growth from a given input expansion.

Examination of these concepts required the use of production function analysis to relate inputs to outputs in a formal econometric model. Lack of technological progress has been a problem, but for some periods, diminishing returns to capital has also been an explanatory factor.

Beyond the statistical analysis of economic growth in the planned socialist economic systems, a variety of other theories have attempted to provide reasons for the observed slowdown. Many of these theories focus on problems with information and/or incentives.

The microeconomics of the planned socialist systems revealed various sources of inefficiency. In the absence of the pressures of competition and for cost minimization, socialist industrial and agricultural production units demonstrated little interest in efficiency, functioning in an environment of persistent, excess demand along with shortages and bottlenecks in the material supply system. Moreover, lack of innovative activity became understandable in a system where few if any rewards were reaped for either product or process innovation.[43]

Besides the microeconomic problems, a number of observations have been made about more general macroeconomic issues. For example, the evolutionary approach to change may have been a growth advantage for the early years of such systems, but in fact, it became a disadvantage in later years.[44] Thus it has been argued that the devolution of the planned economies occurred because micro-units, responding to central directives, could be directed and controlled in the early years. But as time passed, those units learned how to collude, restricting and manipulating information flows, which limited the effectiveness and control the central planners had over the economy.

In addition, the growing complexity of the planned socialist systems could have contributed to the lagging performance.[45] There is, in fact, empirical evidence to suggest that as an economy grows, more units produce more products with increasingly varied inputs. As a result, the basic coordination function becomes increasingly difficult, especially when efforts have been made to avoid the decentralizing of decision making to local levels where the necessary information is available.

A major problem in the planned socialist systems was the nature of incentives. Incentive arrangements may possibly provide the broadest indictment of the planned socialist systems. Although it is difficult to demonstrate empirically, some have argued that the lack of perceived improvements in standards of living, and especially shortages of quality consumer goods, caused the labor force to become increasingly unwilling to make the effort required to stimulate growth and efficiency.

Finally, a variety of issues are related to the general development patterns of socialist economic systems. In a variety of dimensions, especially structural ones, socialist development patterns were different from those observed in market capitalist systems. Sectoral expansion paths differed; for instance, the socialist system emphasized heavy industry at the expense of consumer and service sectors. Although attempts were made to offset the slow growth in private consumption, such as the expansion of social consumption, the bias against market patterns undoubtedly influenced the forces affecting economic growth. Although structural issues were discussed in a growth context during the era of the planned socialist economic systems, as will be seen in this book's discussion of transition issues, those issues remain important as forces influencing the rate and pattern of adjustment in the 1990s.

Although there is no general and decisive explanation for the decline of the planned socialist economic systems, the so-called strengths at lower levels of economic development might have become weaknesses in subsequent years. These systems were largely incapable of institutional adaptation. To put it another way, traditional economic reform failed, and even last-minute efforts, such as the Soviet Union's attempts at perestroika, were too little and too late. Moreover, in places like Hungary, where change may have been more successful, it served mainly to make the ultimate transition to markets easier as political support for the socialist regime collapsed.

Summary

This chapter focuses on two issues: comparisons of the performance of planned socialist systems with market capitalist systems, and the economic reasons for the decline and ultimate demise of many of the socialist systems.

Although performance comparisons are important for understanding different economic systems, meaningful comparisons and overall conclusions are difficult to make without using some subjective criteria—for example, whether economic growth is more or less important than, say, full employment. It is possible, however, to consider comparative economic performance by using a series of separate indicators to see how well different systems measure up.

Cases of rapid economic growth in socialist systems do exist, but these systems have generally not surpassed their capitalist counterparts despite the importance given to economic growth in socialist systems. Indeed, if one were to control for other factors, such as the level of economic development, rates of economic growth were highest in capitalist systems, even though there has been a capitalist slowdown in contemporary times. Socialist growth rates slowed markedly in the final years of the Soviet and East European experiences.

Structural differences between socialist and capitalist economic systems are also important. If one attempts to control for per capita income, a comparison of the two systems reveals that industry shares were high under socialism, service sector shares low, and urbanization underemphasized, all of which are characteristic of the socialist industrialization model.

To understand differences in economic growth, it is necessary to examine the sources of growth, especially the increased use of inputs (extensive growth) vis-à-vis the better use of inputs (intensive growth). The growth of inputs for the differing systems was broadly similar during the postwar years, though after 1980 factor inputs probably grew more rapidly under planned socialism, despite the declining rate of output growth in this era.

During the early postwar era, productivity growth was broadly similar in both systems. For example, during the 1950s, efficiency growth accounted for more than 60 percent of the growth in planned socialist systems, a figure close to the capitalist achievement during that same period. In the era after 1960, however, planned socialist economic growth became more extensive, a troubling sign because almost 80 percent of socialist growth was accounted for by the expansion of inputs.

The phenomenon of a more extensive growth pattern in the socialist systems was evident in both the levels and the differential growth rates of consumption and investment; this indicates greater consumer sacrifices in the socialist systems, precisely the opposite of what socialist theory would suggest for advanced levels of economic development. Other inputs remaining constant, the planned socialist countries generally achieved less output per unit of labor input than their capitalist counterparts.

Income distribution was always difficult to measure in the socialist systems because of the lack of meaningful data. However, past studies have generally argued that income is distributed more nearly equally in those systems in which the state plays a major redistributive role. Thus the differences between the planned socialist systems and the capitalist welfare states are surprisingly small.

Conventional measures of stability suggest, for the most part, that the socialist systems were more stable than the capitalist systems. But common measures, such as inflation and unemployment, are difficult to interpret across systems because of the serious underemployment and repressed inflation in the socialist setting.

The apparent decline of rates of economic growth in the planned socialist systems has been analyzed largely by using production function analysis. Although the evidence is mixed, the focus is on diminishing returns and/or declining productivity of capital due to substitution of capital for labor with lack of technological change.

In addition to an analysis of slowdowns in growth, a number of more general explanations have been given for the slowing economy, including the growing complexity and the devolution of the system and its general inability to adjust to changes over time.

Key Terms

system objectives
representative economic system
net material product
nonproductive services
adjusted factor cost concept
economic growth
intensive growth
extensive growth
static efficiency
dynamic efficiency
labor productivity

capital productivity
total factor productivity
income distribution
Gini coefficient
allocative efficiency
enterprise (technical) efficiency
total income
labor income
repressed inflation
underemployment

Notes

1. Abram Bergson, *Planning and Productivity Under Soviet Socialism* (New York: Columbia University Press, 1968).
2. Paul R. Gregory and Robert C. Stuart, *Soviet Economic Structure and Performance*, 6th ed. (Reading, Mass.: Addison Wesley Longman, 1998), Chs. 11–12.
3. See Joseph Chung, "The Economies of North and South Korea" (Annual Meeting of the American Economic Association, Atlantic City, N.J., September 1976) and Paul Gregory and Gert Leptin, "Similar Societies Under Differing Economic Systems: The Case of the Two Germanys," *Soviet Studies* 24 (October 1977), 519–542. Also see the papers on the panel: "Different Strategies, Similar Countries: The Consequences of Growth and Equity" (Annual Meeting of the American Economic Association, New York, December 1982).
4. Gur Ofer, "Industrial Structure, Urbanization, and the Growth Strategy of Socialist Countries," *Quarterly Journal of Economics* 90 (May 1976), 219–243; Gur Ofer, *The Service*

Sector in Soviet Economic Development (Cambridge, Mass.: Harvard University Press, 1973); Paul Gregory, *Socialist and Nonsocialist Industrialization Patterns* (New York: Praeger, 1970); Frederic L. Pryor, *Public Expenditures in Communist and Capitalist Nations* (Bloomington: Indiana University Press, 1973); and Frederic L. Pryor, *Property and Industrial Organization in Communist and Capitalist Nations* (Bloomington: Indiana University Press, 1973). For a discussion of the pure methodology of econometric performance evaluation, see Edward Hewett, "Alternative Econometric Approaches for Studying the Link Between Economic Systems and Economic Outcomes," *Journal of Comparative Economics* 4 (September 1980), 274–294. For a discussion of the methodology of growth comparisons, see Gur Ofer, "Soviet Economic Growth, 1928–1985," *Journal of Economic Literature* 25 (December 1987), 1767–1833.

5. For example, Gregor Lazarcik found that the centrally planned economies with more decentralized agriculture (such as Hungary and Poland) have performed better in terms of output and efficiency than those with centralized agriculture. On this, see Gregor Lazarcik, "Comparative Growth, Structure, and Levels of Agricultural Output, Inputs, and Productivity in Eastern Europe, 1965–79," in U.S. Congress, Joint Economic Committee, *East European Economic Assessment*, Pt. 2 (Washington, D.C.: U.S. Government Printing Office, 1981), pp. 587–634.

6. The major sources of data on the Soviet Union, Eastern Europe, and China are reports to the U.S. Congress prepared by the Joint Economic Committee. See, for example, *East European Economies: Slow Growth in the 1980s*, Vols. 1–3 (Washington, D.C.: U.S. Government Printing Office, 1986) and *Gorbachev's Economic Plans*, Vols. 1–2 (Washington, D.C.: U.S. Government Printing Office, 1987). Another useful statistical compendium is the Central Intelligence Agency, Directorate of Intelligence, *Handbook of Economic Statistics*. The most useful official East European source is the CMEA handbook: *Statisticheski ezhegodnik stran chlenov Sovet Ekonomicheskikh Vzaimopomoshichi*, various annual editions. For data on the Chinese economy, see U.S. Congress, Joint Economic Committee, *China: A Reassessment of the Economy* (Washington, D.C.: U.S. Government Printing Office, 1975); and Alexander Eckstein, ed., *Quantitative Measures of China's Economic Output* (Ann Arbor: University of Michigan Press, 1980).

7. Statistical comparisons of industrialized capitalism and planned socialism include Maurice Ernst, "Postwar Economic Growth in Eastern Europe," in U.S. Congress, Joint Economic Committee, *Economic Developments in Countries of Eastern Europe* (Washington, D.C.: U.S. Government Printing Office, 1970), pp. 41–67; and Thad Alton, "East European GNPs," Joint Economic Committee, *East European Economies: Slow Growth in the 1980s*, Vol. 1, pp. 81–132. Also see Andrew Stollar and G. R. Thompson, "Sectoral Employment Shares: A Comparative Systems Context," *Journal of Comparative Economics* 11 (March 1987), 62–80; and Thad Alton, "Production and Resource Allocation in Eastern Europe: Performance, Problems, and Prospects," in Joint Economic Committee, *East European Economic Assessment*, Pt. 2, pp. 348–408.

8. See, for example, Subramanian Swamy, "Economic Growth in China and India, 1952–1970: A Comparative Appraisal," *Economic Development and Cultural Change* 21 (July 1973), 1–84; and Wilfred Malenbaum, "Modern Economic Growth in India and China: The Comparison Revisited," *Economic Development and Cultural Change* 31 (October 1982), 45–84.

9. For a discussion of CMEA statistical practices, see Thad Alton, "Economic Structure and Growth in Eastern Europe," in Joint Economic Committee, *Economic Developments in Countries of Eastern Europe*, pp. 43–45; and Alton, "Production and Resource Allocation in Eastern Europe," pp. 384–408.

10. The pioneering work on reconstructing planned socialist national income accounts was for the Soviet Union and was carried out by Abram Bergson and his associates. For an account of these efforts, see Abram Bergson, "Introduction," *Real National Income of Soviet Russia Since 1928* (Cambridge, Mass.: Harvard University Press, 1961).

11. *The Real National Income of Soviet Russia Since 1928*, Chs. 2 and 3.

12. On this, see Directorate of Intelligence, *Measuring Soviet GNP: Problems and Solutions: A Conference Report*, SOV 90–10038, September 1990; "Eastern Europe: Long Road Ahead to Economic Well-Being," A Paper by the Central Intelligence Agency Presented to the Subcommittee on Technology and National Security of the Joint Economic Committee, May 1990; and Directorate of Intelligence, *Revisiting Soviet Economic Performance Under Glasnost: Implications for CIA Estimates*, SOV 88–10068, September 1988.

13. *Measuring Soviet GNP: Problems and Solutions*, p. 187.

14. For discussions of the socialist industrialization model, see Gregory, *Socialist and Nonsocialist Industrialization Patterns*; Ofer, "Industrial Structure, Urbanization, and the Growth of Socialist Countries" and *The Service Sector in Soviet Economic Development*; and Gregory and Stuart, *Soviet Economic Structure and Performance*, Ch. 12.

15. For a discussion of index number relativity, see Bergson, *Real National Income of Soviet Russia Since 1928*, Ch. 3.

16. This result was noted first by Abram Bergson in "Development Under Two Systems: Comparative Productivity Growth Since 1950," *World Politics* 20 (July 1971), 579–617.

17. Frederic Pryor, *A Guidebook to the Comparative Study of Economic Systems* (Englewood Cliffs, N.J.: Prentice-Hall, 1985), p. 78.

18. See, for example, Swamy, "Economic Growth in China and India," pp. 81–83; and Malenbaum, "Modern Economic Growth in India and China," pp. 45–84.

19. For a discussion of the measurement of static and dynamic efficiency, see Bergson, *Planning and Productivity Under Soviet Socialism*.

20. Edward Denison and William Chung, *How Japan's Economy Grew So Fast* (Washington, D.C.: Brookings, 1976), p. 30.

21. The classic treatment of the measurement of factor productivity is Edward Denison, *Why Growth Rates Differ* (Washington, D.C.: Brookings, 1967).

22. Apparently the Romanian and Bulgarian capital-stock figures are in current prices. On this, see Alton, "Comparative Structure and Growth of Economic Activity in Eastern Europe," p. 223.

23. Wililam Easterly and Stanley Fischer, "The Soviet Economic Decline," *The World Bank Economic Review* 9, 3 (September 1995), 341–371.

24. A considerable amount of research has gone into the subject of the relative growth of investment and consumption in Eastern Europe. Unfortunately, studies that cover the 1970s have not succeeded in calculating directly the real growth of investment. For a discussion of this point, see Alton, "Production and Resource Allocation in Eastern Europe," pp. 314–367. Also see Alton, "East European GNPs," pp. 94–98.

25. See the following studies of per capita consumption in the USSR and Eastern and Western Europe: Terence Byrne, "Levels of Consumption in Eastern Europe," in Joint Economic Committee, *Economic Developments in Countries of Eastern Europe*, pp. 297–315; and U.S. Congress, Joint Economic Committee, *Consumption in the USSR: An International Comparison* (Washington, D.C.: U.S. Government Printing Office, 1981).

26. Abram Bergson, "Comparative Productivity: The USSR, Eastern Europe, and the West," *American Economic Review* 77 (June 1987), 342–357. For Bergson's earlier work on this subject, see his discussion of relative Soviet output per unit in Abram Bergson, *The Economics of Soviet Planning* (New Haven: Yale University Press, 1964), Ch. 14. Also see

Bergson, *Production and the Social System: The USSR and the West* (Cambridge, Mass.: Harvard University Press, 1978).

27. This view is shared by Pryor, *Property and Industrial Organization in Communist and Capitalist Nations*, p. 80.
28. Padma Desai and Ricardo Martin, "Efficiency Loss from Resource Misallocation in Soviet Industry," *Quarterly Journal of Economics* 98 (August 1983), 441–456. Also see Judith Thornton, "Differential Capital Charges and Resource Allocation in Soviet Industry," *Journal of Political Economy* 79 (May/June 1971), 545–561. A useful summary of major studies can be found in Peter Murrell, "Can Neoclassical Economics Underpin the Reform of Centrally Planned Economies?" *Journal of Economic Perspectives* 5 (Fall 1991), 59–76.
29. For comprehensive discussions of income distribution under capitalism and socialism, see P. J. D. Wiles, *Economic Institutions Compared* (New York: Halsted Press, 1977), Ch. 16; Martin Schnitzer, *Income Distribution: A Comparative Study of the United States, Sweden, West Germany, East Germany, the United Kingdom, and Japan* (New York: Praeger, 1974); and Abram Bergson, "Income Inequality Under Soviet Socialism," *Journal of Economic Literature* 22 (September 1984); C. Morrison, "Income Distribution in East European and Western Countries," *Journal of Comparative Economics* 8 (1984), 121–138. Anthony B. Atkinson and John Micklewright, *Economic Transformation in Eastern Europe and the Distribution of Income.* (Cambridge, England: Cambridge University Press, 1992).
30. See Pryor, *Property and Industrial Organization in Communist and Capitalist Nations*, pp. 74–75.
31. *Ibid.,* pp. 74–89.
32. John R. Moroney, ed., *Income Inequality: Trends and International Compromise* (Lexington, Mass.: Heath, 1978), p. 5.
33. Janet Chapman, "Earnings Distribution in the USSR, 1968–1976," *Soviet Studies* 35 (July 1983), 410–413.
34. See also a specialized study for the Soviet Union by Alastair McAuley, "The Distribution of Earnings and Income in the Soviet Union," *Soviet Studies*, 29 (April 1977), 214–237.
35. Harold Lydall, "Some Problems in Making International Comparisons of Income Inequality," in Moroney, *Income Inequality*, pp. 31–33. For recent analysis of the available evidence, see Anthony B. Atkinson and John Micklewright, *Economic Transformation in Eastern Europe and the Distribution of Income.*
36. Simon Kuznets, *Modern Economic Growth* (New Haven: Yale University Press, 1966).
37. For studies of socialist business and trade cycles, see C. W. Lawson, "An Empirical Analysis of the Structure and Stability of Communist Foreign Trade, 1960–68," *Soviet Studies* 26 (April 1974), 224–238; G. J. Staller, "Patterns and Stability in Foreign Trade, OECD and COMECON," *American Economic Review* (September 1967); Josef Goldman, "Fluctuations and Trends in the Rate of Economic Growth in Some Socialist Countries," *Economics of Planning* 4, 2 (1964), 89–98; Oldrich Kyn, Wolfram Schrette, and Jiri Slama, "Growth Cycles in Centrally Planned Economies: An Empirical Test," Osteuropa Institute, Munich, *Working Papers*, No. 7 (August 1975); Gerard Roland, "Investment Growth Fluctuations in the Soviet Union: An Econometric Analysis," *Journal of Comparative Economics* 11 (June 1987), 192–206. Pryor's results are in Pryor, *A Guidebook*, pp. 114–118.
38. P. J. D. Wiles, "A Note on Soviet Unemployment in U.S. Definitions," *Soviet Studies* 23 (April 1972), 619–628. David Granick, *Job Rights in the Soviet Union: Their Consequences* (Cambridge, England: Cambridge University Press, 1987).
39. Morris Bornstein, "Unemployment in Capitalist Regulated Market Economies and Socialist Centrally Planned Economies," *American Economic Review, Papers and Proceedings*

68 (May 1978), pp. 38–43; and Paul Gregory and Irwin Collier, Jr., "Unemployment in the Soviet Union: Evidence from the Soviet Interview Project," *American Economic Review* 78 (September 1988), 613–632.

40. Authoritative discussion of official socialist price indexes and repressed inflation are found in Richard Portes, "The Control of Inflation: Lessons from East European Experience," *Economica* 44 (May 1977), 109–129. For some empirical estimates, see Richard Portes and David Winter, "The Demand for Money and Consumption Goods in Centrally Planned Economies," *Review of Economics and Statistics* 60 (February 1978), 8–18; and Martin J. Kohn, "Consumer Price Developments in Eastern Europe," in Joint Economic Committee, *East European Economic Assessment*, Pt. 2, pp. 328–347.

41. World Bank, *World Tables 1976* (Baltimore: The Johns Hopkins University Press, 1976).

42. For a summary of views, see "The Soviet Growth Slowdown: Three Views," *American Economic Review: Papers and Proceedings* 76 (May 1986), 170–185.

43. See, for example, Joseph S. Berliner, *The Innovation Decision in Soviet Industry* (Cambridge, Mass.: M.I.T. Press, 1976).

44. Peter Murrell and Mancur Olson, "The Devolution of Centrally Planned Economies," *Journal of Comparative Economics* 15 (June 1991), 239–265.

45. Abhijii V. Banerjee and Michael Spagat, "Productivity Paralysis and the Complexity Problem: Why Do Centrally Planned Economies Become Prematurely Gray?" *Journal of Comparative Economics* 15 (December 1991), 646–660.

Recommended Readings

General References

Trevor Buck, *Comparative Industrial Systems* (New York: St. Martin's, 1982).

William Easterly and Stanley Fischer, "The Soviet Economic Decline," *The World Bank Economic Review* 9, 3 (September 1995), 341–71.

Irving B. Kravis, "Comparative Studies of National Incomes and Prices," *Journal of Economic Literature* 22 (March 1984).

Irving B. Kravis, Allen Heston, and Robert Summers, "Real GDP Per Capita for More Than One Hundred Countries," *Economic Journal* 88 (June 1978).

Irving B. Kravis, *World Product and Income: International Comparisons of Real Gross Product* (Baltimore: Johns Hopkins University Press for the World Bank, 1982).

Frederic L. Pryor, *Property and Industrial Organization in Communist and Capitalist Nations* (Bloomington: Indiana University Press, 1973).

——, *A Guidebook to the Comparative Study of Economic Systems* (Englewood Cliffs, N.J.: Prentice-Hall, 1985).

Economic Growth

Thad P. Alton and associates, *Economic Growth in Eastern Europe 1970 and 1975–1985*, Research Project on National Income in East Central Europe (New York: L. W. International Financial Research, Inc., (occasional paper no. 90).

Abram Bergson, *Soviet Post-War Economic Development* (Stockholm: Almquist & Wicksell, 1974).

——, "The Soviet Economic Slowdown," *Challenge* 21 (January–February 1978), 22–27.

Norman E. Cameron, "Economic Growth in the USSR, Hungary, and East and West Germany," *Journal of Comparative Economics* 5 (March 1981), 24–42.

Stanley Cohn, "The Soviet Path to Economic Growth: A Comparative Analysis," *Review of Income and Wealth*, March 1976, 49–59.

Edward Denison, *Why Growth Rates Differ: Postwar Experience in Nine Western Countries* (Washington, D.C.: Brookings, 1967).

Padma Desai, *The Soviet Economy: Efficiency, Technical Change and Growth Retardation* (Oxford: Basil Blackwell, 1986).

———, "Soviet Growth Retardation," *American Economic Review Papers and Proceedings* 76 (May 1986), 175–179.

Stanislaw Gomulka, "Soviet Growth Slowdown: Duality, Maturity and Innovation," *American Economic Review Papers and Proceedings* 76 (May 1986), 170–174.

Vladimir Kontorovich, "Soviet Growth Slowdown: Econometric vs. Direct Evidence," *American Economic Review Papers and Proceedings* 76 (May 1986), 181–185.

Sima Lieberman, *The Growth of European Mixed Economies* (New York: Halstead Press, 1977).

Angus Maddison, *Economic Growth in Japan and USSR* (New York: Norton, 1969).

———, "Growth and Slowdown in Advanced Capitalist Economies," *Journal of Economic Literature* 25 (June 1987), 649–698.

Wilfred Malenbaum, "Modern Economic Growth in India and China: The Comparison Revisited," *Economic Development and Cultural Change* 31 (October 1982), 45–84.

Productivity

Abram Bergson, "Comparative Productivity: The USSR, Eastern Europe, and the West," *American Economic Review* 77 (June 1987), 342–357.

———, *Planning and Productivity Under Soviet Socialism* (New York: Columbia University Press, 1967).

———, *Productivity and the Social System: The USSR and the West* (Cambridge, Mass.: Harvard University Press, 1978).

———, "Productivity Under Two Systems: The USSR versus the West," in Jan Tinbergen *et al.,* eds., *Optimum Social Welfare and Productivity: A Comparative View* (New York: New York University Press, 1972).

Padma Desai, "Total Factor Productivity in Postwar Soviet Industry and Its Branches," *Journal of Comparative Economics* 9 (March 1985), 1–23.

Padma Desai and Ricardo Martin, "Efficiency Loss from Resource Misallocation in Soviet Industry," *Quarterly Journal of Economics* 98 (August 1983), 441–456.

Herbert S. Levine, "Possible Causes of the Deterioration of Soviet Productivity Growth in the Period 1976–80," in United States Congress, Joint Economic Committee, *Soviet Economy in the 1980s: Problems and Prospects*, Pt. 1 (Washington, D.C.: U.S Government Printing Office, 1982), 153–168.

Peter Murrell and Mancur Olson, "The Devolution of Centrally Planned Economies," *Journal of Comparative Economics* 15 (June 1991), 239–265.

Gertrude Schroeder, "The Slowdown in Soviet Industry, 1976–1982" *Soviet Economy* 1 (January–March 1985), 42–74.

Subramanian Swamy, "The Economic Growth in China and India, 1952–1970: A Comparative Appraisal," *Economic Development and Cultural Change* 21 (July 1973), 1–84.

United States Congress, Joint Economic Committee, *USSR: Measures of Economic Growth and Development, 1950–1980* (Washington, D.C.: U.S. Government Printing Office, 1982).

———, *East European Economies: Slow Growth in the 1980s*, Vols. 1–3 (Washington, D.C.: U.S. Government Printing Office, 1985).

Martin Weitzman, "Soviet Postwar Economic Growth and Capital–Labor Substitution," *American Economic Review* 60 (December 1970), 676–692.

Technology

R. Amann and J. Cooper, eds., *Industrial Innovation in the Soviet Union* (New Haven: Yale University Press, 1982).
Abram Bergson, "Technological Progress," in Abram Bergson and Herbert S. Levine, eds., *The Soviet Economy Towards the Year 2000* (London: Allen & Unwin, 1983).
Joseph S. Berliner, *The Innovation Decision in Soviet Industry* (Cambridge, Mass.: M.I.T. Press, 1976).

Income Inequality

Michael V. Alexeev and Clifford G. Gaddy, "Trends in Wage and Income Distribution under Gorbachev: Analysis of New Soviet Data," (Durham, N.C.: Berkeley–Duke Occasional Papers on the Second Economy in the USSR, # 25, 1991).
Anthony B. Atkinson and John Micklewright, *Economic Transformation in Eastern Europe and the Distribution of Income* (Cambridge, England: Cambridge University Press, 1992).
Abram Bergson, "Income Inequality under Soviet Socialism," *Journal of Economic Literature* 22 (September 1984).
Janet Chapman, "Are Earnings More Equal Under Socialism? The Soviet Case, with Some United States Comparisons," in J. R. Moroney, ed., *Income Inequality: Trends and International Comparisons* (Lexington, Mass.: D. C. Heath, 1979).
———, Earnings Distribution in the USSR, 1968–1976," *Soviet Studies*, 35 (1983), 410–413.
———, "Income Distribution and Social Justice in the Soviet Union," *Comparative Economic Studies*, 31 (1989), 14–45.
John Moroney, *Income Inequality: Trends and International Comparisons* (Lexington, Mass.: D. C. Heath, 1978).
Martin Schnitzer, *Income Distribution: A Comparative Study of the United States, Sweden, West Germany, East Germany, the United Kingdom, and Japan* (New York: Praeger, 1974).
P. J. D. Wiles, *The Distribution of Income, East and West* (Amsterdam: North Holland, 1974).

Welfare Issues

Anthony B. Atkinson and John Micklewright, *Economic Transformation in Eastern Europe and the Distribution of Income* (Cambridge, England: Cambridge University Press, 1993).
Abram Bergson, "The USSR Before the Fall: How Poor and Why?" *Journal of Economic Perspectives* 5 (Fall 1991), 29–44.
M. Matthews, *Privilege in the Soviet Union* (London: Allen & Unwin, 1978).
Alastair McAuley, *Economic Welfare in the Soviet Union* (Madison: University of Wisconsin Press, 1979).
———, "The Welfare State in the USSR," in T. Wilson and D. Wilson, eds., *The State and Social Welfare* (London: Longmans, 1991).
G. Ofer and A. Vinokur, *The Soviet Household Under the Old Regime* (Cambridge, England: Cambridge University Press, 1992).
A. Vinokur and G. Ofer, "Inequality of Earnings, Household Income, and Wealth in the Soviet Union in the 1970s" in James R. Millar, ed., *Politics, Work, and Daily Life in the USSR* (Cambridge, England: Cambridge University Press, 1987).
Murray Yanowitch, *Social and Economic Inequality in the Soviet Union* (White Plains, N.Y.: M. E. Sharpe, 1977).

Appendix 13A:
The Index Number Problem in
International Comparisons

In this chapter we cited a large number of statistics comparing the level of GDP, output per worker, and so on among capitalist and socialist countries.[1] For purposes of simplicity, we glossed over the fact that the price system that underlies these valuations can have a substantial impact on the outcome. For example, for us to compare levels of GDP meaningfully, the GDPs of all countries being compared must be valued in some common currency (dollars, rubles, marks, pounds, whatever). These issues bear scrutiny because they are basic to international comparisons, even in the 1990s as systems change.

Let us take the case of comparing the levels of GDP of the Soviet Union and the United States in 1980. To simplify the illustration, let us say that both countries produce only two goods, wheat and lathes. In the USSR, wheat is expensive relative to lathes; in the United States, wheat is cheap relative to lathes (as judged by Soviet prices). Production and domestic prices of these two commodities in each country are given in Table 13A.1.

From this information, we can make two types of calculations: We can calculate the GDPs of both countries using U.S. prices, or we can calculate the GDPs of both countries using Soviet prices.

In U.S. prices, we get

$$\text{Soviet GDP} = (\$2 \times 10) + (\$2 \times 20) \quad \text{or} \quad \$60$$
$$\text{U.S. GDP} = (\$2 \times 30) + (\$2 \times 40) \quad \text{or} \quad \$140$$

Result: In U.S. prices, Soviet GDP is 60/140 = 43 percent of U.S. GDP.

In Soviet prices, we get

$$\text{Soviet GDP} = (5R \times 10) + (1R \times 20) \quad \text{or} \quad 70R$$
$$\text{U.S. GDP} = (5R \times 30) + (1R \times 40) \quad \text{or} \quad 190R$$

Result: In Soviet prices, Soviet GDP is only 70/190 = 37 percent of U.S. GDP.

The comparison is more favorable when the prices of the other country are used than when the country's own prices are used. Why is this typically the case? It is an

TABLE 13A.1

	Output		Price	
	Wheat	Lathes	Wheat	Lathes
Soviet Union, 1980	10	20	5R	1R
United States, 1980	30	40	$2	$2

empirical fact that the relative prices of any country tend to be inversely related to the relative quantities produced by that country. Products that can be produced relatively cheaply (because of abundant domestic resources) tend to be produced in abundance, and products that can be produced relatively expensively tend to be limited in production. Insofar as relative prices differ among countries (as a result of differences in human capital and natural resources), we find that each country emphasizes the production of relatively cheap commodities. Therefore, when the GDP of one country is valued using the different relative prices of another country, its total output appears relatively large.

To take a real-world example of this index number phenomenon, we can cite studies of Soviet per capita consumption as a percentage of U.S. consumption. In 1976, Soviet and U.S. consumption per capita were 1,116R and 4,039R, respectively, when valued in rubles. In other words, the Soviet Union stood at 28 percent of the U.S. level. Valued in dollars, Soviet and U.S. per capita consumption were $2,395 and $5,598, respectively; that is, Soviet consumption per capita was 43 percent of the U.S. level. Which figure (28 percent or 43 percent) is the correct one? There is no "true" value in such comparisons. One comparison is as real as the other, for each system of relative prices yields a different answer.

It should be noted that for the comparisons in this chapter, we consistently use dollar valuations. Dollar valuations make Soviet and East European values look more favorable than they would have if, say, ruble prices had been used.

Note

1. U.S. Congress, Joint Economic Committee, *Consumption in the USSR: An International Comparison* (Washington, D.C.: Government Printing Office, 1981), p. 6.

References

Trevor Buck, *Comparative Industrial Systems* (New York: St. Martin's, 1981), Ch. 5.

Irving B. Kravis et al., *A System of International Comparisons of Gross National Product and Purchasing Power* (Baltimore: The Johns Hopkins University Press, 1975).

Richard Moorsteen, "On Measuring Productive Potential and Relative Efficiency," *Quarterly Journal of Economics* 75 (August 1981), 451–467.

Moving Toward a Market Economy

14

Transition

In Chapter 13, we examined the economic performance of planned socialist economic systems and identified a variety of rather obvious reasons for their economic difficulties and, ultimately, their political and economic collapse. Whatever the combination of forces present in each case, the collapse of the Soviet and East European command economies at the end of the 1980s ushered in an era of transition that dominates any discussion of economic systems in the decade of the 1990s.

Transition is the replacement of one economic system by another. In the cases discussed in this book, we are generally dealing with replacement of the administrative-command economy by markets. In a very real sense, the economies of the 1990s are mixed systems, and although we now know that they differ considerably one from another, in this chapter we address the basic issues that have surfaced in most if not all transition economies.

Before we turn to some specifics, it is important to note that even though the performance problems of the command economies were widely recognized, few observers expected sudden and total collapse. Moreover, as the command economies collapsed, there was no textbook model of transition to follow. Indeed, the basics of transition did not exist in the textbooks of the 1980s but rather emerged through practical experience in the 1990s. For this reason, the story of transition has been a developing story and one that has exhibited great variation from country to country. It is within this context that we attempt to present a survey of basic issues that surround transition.

Transition: The Basics

Although there is some lack of precision in the terminology that is used, economists tend to refer to transition as the replacement of one economic system by another—in the 1990s, generally the replacement of the plan by the market. At the same time, major changes such as those experienced by China are generally referred to as **reform.** In the case of China, the Communist party has retained political power, and along with sanctioning the introduction of market forces, has maintained a degree of centralized command planning.

In those cases where the collapse of the old order was fairly rapid, immediate discussions of transition placed considerable emphasis on issues of the appropriate speed and sequencing of transition. How should markets be introduced? Specifically, should an attempt be made to put market arrangements in place as quickly as possible, or would the gradual development of market forces be more appropriate? In either case, how should the problems of sequencing be handled? In what sequence should the components of the market be introduced? In the absence of a blueprint for transition, the dichotomy appeared to be between "big bang," or rapid, approach and the slower "gradualist" approach. We are now a decade beyond the initial experience, and though few would argue that there is a coherent "theory of transition," the earlier dichotomy between the big-bang and gradualist approaches is recognized as simplistic. The problems of sequencing, however, remain important.[1]

If there is to be a replacement of plan by market, what are the elements of the market that are to be established and in what sequence will these components be introduced? The literature on transition broadly classifies the major components of the market system along four major dimensions.

First, the **microeconomics of transition** emphasizes the creation of markets and associated market price signals. Recall from our earlier discussion of command system that this aspect of transition would imply the creation of product markets (both consumer and producer goods) and factor markets (labor markets, capital markets, and land markets). The essence of the market economy is the existence of private property rights, to be introduced into the former command economies through the process of privatization. As we will soon see, the process of privatization is the centerpiece of transition, and yet the creation of private property rights has proved to be a difficult and continuing task.

Second, the **macroeconomics of transition** focuses on the creation of a money–financial system. The components of such a system include a financial infrastructure, (financial markets), the introduction of a new role for the state through major changes in the budgetary process (revenues and expenditures), and monetary and fiscal policy mechanisms designed to guide macroeconomic performance in the emerging market setting. If the creation of private property rights has been a daunting task, it is important to recall that the command economies functioned largely without money–financial mechanisms of the sort with which we in market economies are familiar. In both a microeconomic and a macroeconomic sense, the mechanisms designed to guide economic activity must undergo fundamental changes.

Third, a major element of the market economy is reliance on **international trade** and **international finance**, which have become increasingly important as the global economy has burgeoned in the latter half of the twentieth century. For the transition economies, these changes have involved the creation of new arrangements for the conduct of foreign trade (elimination of the state trade monopoly) and related new trade policies. Another essential element of change has been the creation of new financial arrangements for the conduct of foreign trade in both goods and services and greater participation in international financial markets and mechanisms, the cornerstone of which is the introduction of a convertible currency. Once again, these changes fundamentally altered the nature of the arrangements typical of the command economies, which tended to be characterized by state-directed (barter) trade and nonconvertible currencies and by state-set (meaningless) exchange rates.

Fourth, state-provided social services are a hallmark of socialist economies, and such arrangements have undergone change as markets have emerged. Thus a major component of the transition process has been the development and introduction of an appropriate **safety net**. From the vantage point of ten years of transition experience, we now know that the development of appropriate safety nets has been difficult; in many cases, it has been neglected. The most important components of the safety net are medical services, unemployment benefits, retirement benefits (pensions), and the like. As we have emphasized in previous chapters, the provision of these benefits has been fundamentally different in the command economies. The privatization of such services, along with the difficulties of sustaining state funding in transition settings, has changed the degree of availability of services, the means of delivery and payment, and the distribution of services.

Although this fourfold classification of transition elements is simplistic, it provides us with a convenient starting point from which to examine the important real-world cases. It also enables us to depart from the narrow confines of classification to consider the interface among system components during transition and, most important, the nature of nonsystem characteristics, such as differential resource endowments and the varying political and economic preconditions from which the transition process emerged.

Transition: The Importance of Preconditions

Throughout this book, we have emphasized the fact that however we judge the arrangements of the command economy that preceded transition, they differed fundamentally from the arrangements of the market economy and left a lasting imprint on those economies. Moreover, these different system arrangements, in combination with different (socialist) policy objectives, resulted in allocation arrangements and results very different from what might be anticipated under market arrangements in similar natural settings. To put it differently, the mechanisms for resource allocation in the command systems were fundamentally different, and—most important—these mechanisms and (socialist) policies implemented over a period of many years put in place an economic structure fundamentally different from what would have evolved under market arrangements. The failure of economic reform in the planned socialist systems left those economic systems, at the time of collapse, fundamentally unchanged from their beginnings. Thus both the policies and the mechanisms used to implement those policies generally had a long period of time in which to leave their imprint.

We argue that on the eve of transition, one could envision the success or failure of the transition process to be broadly influenced by two sets of forces: the condition of economy as the transition began—what we term **initial conditions**—and the nature and effectiveness of the **transition policies** implemented during the transition process itself.[2] We turn first to a discussion of initial conditions and how they may affect the transition process in different cases.

Initial Conditions

The impact of the initial conditions is an important element for our understanding of the transition era. Moreover, there are important differences in the impact of initial conditions from one transition case and component to another. Recall that our general understanding of initial conditions is the structural and related differences (from those occurring in market economies) brought about by the long-term impact of the command arrangements and related (socialist) economic policies. For example, the emphasis on heavy industry left behind an industrial structure different from that which would have emerged under market arrangements. There are few areas in which the command era did not leave such unusual legacies.

Consider, for example, the case of foreign trade. We know that the command economies used a set of trade mechanisms and implemented policies that led to outcomes different from what might have been expected under market arrangements. These outcomes—specifically the reduction of the magnitude of trade, the alteration of the commodity and regional composition of trade, and differential terms on which trade took place–all differed from the outcomes that might have been expected under market arrangements. Quite apart from the costs and benefits of such arrangements, they resulted in different trade patterns and may have had different effects from one transition case to another. Perhaps converting to market arrangements (and thus immediately changing outcomes) might be easier for a pretransition economy freer of the distortions of the command era—specifically, for our trade example, a small and relatively open economy. On the other hand, consider a larger, resource-rich economy subject to the trade mechanisms typical of the command economies. The absolute magnitude of trade might be greater, but its magnitude relative to the size of the economy would be less, and its potential allocative distortions would be greater in the sense of providing a means through which to pursue trade avoidance. Moreover, the nature of trade arrangements in the command economies (specifically the centralization of trade decisions) must have resulted in a lack of experience in dealing with foreign markets, and issue critical during the transition era.

Let's look at a very different example, on the microeconomic side. Where there has been little if any private activity, and ownership claims from earlier generations must be arbitrated, privatization may be slow as the old order collapses and new arrangements struggle to emerge, the result being a sharp decline in real output. Moreover, one might expect a direct relationship between ease of privatization (and especially restructuring) and the nature of the pretransition industrial structure. Consider two extreme theoretical cases. On the one hand, where the industrial structure is less biased against the light-industrial and service sectors, privatization may be accomplished quickly with limited impact on the level of output. On the other hand, where the industrial structure is biased in favor of heavy industry using outdated technology and capital stock, creating a corporate structure may not be particularly difficult, but changing the decision-making arrangements in that new formal corporate structure may be quite difficult. Thus one could argue that the nature of privatization in transition settings would be influenced by the nature of the industrial structure that prevailed at the onset of transition.

Consider one further example: the initial requirements for macroeconomic stabilization. One could certainly argue that the greater the degree of macroeconomic disequilibrium, broadly defined, the more difficult the initial stages of the transition process, when stabilization measures are needed but requisite tools are not in place. There are a variety of specific outcomes for which the degree of pretransition distortion is important but very difficult to measure. For example, if there is a quick and rather general lifting of state-controlled prices in a setting of at best primitive market mechanisms, how much inflationary pressure will be released? Clearly, the extent of pretransition distortions will matter in a variety of ways.

Transition Policies

A rather different but closely connected set of issues pertains to the strategy of implementing transition policies and programs. Apart from (but related to) differences in initial conditions, how should the various components of the transition program be sequenced, and with what speed should they be implemented? Both are important issues in the transition experience. Consider the case of privatization as an example.

A major goal of privatization, as we will see, is the creation of new property rights and thus markets in which prices will be determined by the force of supply and demand, prices to reflect relative scarcities useful for the process of resource allocation. To the extent that one of the initial conditions is the distortion of prices left over from the plan era, the speed with which prices are released becomes an important policy issue. From the point of view of expectations, it makes sense to release prices quickly. However, in the absence of market institutions, and especially in the absence of appropriate macroeconomic mechanisms and policies for stabilization purposes, the potential for inflation may be a serious issue. Prices are formed in markets, but markets don't exist in the early stages of transition. Should price setting be a state function until markets are established?

The issue raised here pertain not only to the components of transition but also to the **sequencing** of the transition process. For example, if the price-setting function of the state is to be eliminated, is it reasonable to release prices to be determined by market forces before those market forces exist? In real-world cases, the issue of sequencing is much more complex than our discussion here suggests, because it is seldom a simple choice between the existence or nonexistence of one institution or another. For example, in most transition economies, the state may well sustain control over the prices in certain sectors (such as energy), while releasing prices to market forces in other sectors. Indeed, the broader issue of state and nonstate sectors remains unresolved in many transition economies. Moreover, in transition economies, especially during the early stages of the process, it is very unlikely that newly emerging markets will be competitive.[3] Clearly, these sorts of difficulties pertain to most if not all of the transition components that we have outlined. How can we be guided in these cases?

We have already emphasized that even during the relatively short experience with transition in the 1990s, our thinking on these issues of speed and sequencing has changed. A great deal of the early literature on transition treated the process in a somewhat mechanical manner, arguing for the "big bang"—the rapid and simultaneous (to the greatest extent possible) implementation of new system components. Markets are to be the guiding force, and markets require new property rights, so it was thought best to introduce these new rights as quickly as possible. Moreover, there was considerable fear that market (and political) reforms might be reversed, so it was argued that acting rapidly would help sustain the new era even when socioeconomic changes might make reforms unpopular.

The paradigm of **evolutionary economics** offers a different perspective.[4] Although it is clearly inappropriate to suggest that there are exactly two incompatible approaches and that only one will be chosen, nevertheless, the contrast is instructive. The advocates of the evolutionary paradigm have argued that contemporary neoclassical microeconomic theory does not provide an adequate underpinning for understanding change. Specifically, whereas **neoclassical economic theory** sees change as emerging from the behavior of rational agents maximizing known objectives with available information, resulting in the achievement of observable equilibria through time, the evolutionary approach presents a different picture. Proponents of the evolutionary view argue that institutions emerge only slowly and sequentially in a path-dependent world and that they do so through the behavior of agents whose knowledge and foresight are limited. In this world, which differs fundamentally from the neoclassical world, the emergence of new institutions is a slow and a sequential process. Must we choose a paradigm?

The transition experiences of the 1990s have taught us a lot, though the difficulty of understanding change within the framework of neoclassical economic theory remains. Moreover, although we now have the ability to look at the various (very different) transition cases, so many factors influenced the outcomes we observe that gaining insight into appropriate strategies of speed and sequencing is difficult. We do know, however, that it is not a simple matter of choosing a paradigm but rather entails relating a complex set of transition arrangements to a particular setting. This is typically a very difficult task. Moreover, there are other issues that complicate the process.

One could argue that with known initial conditions and a clear-cut vision of an end point, it would be easier to develop and implement transition policies. The case of the public sector is, however, instructive as an example. In the real world, few transition economies have a clear-cut vision of an appropriate role of the public sector, whether it be for energy production or for the provision of social services (both of which are amenable to privatization). It is difficult to design instruments to achieve objectives when the latter are unclear or unknown.

Transition and the Policy Setting

The focus of this book is economics, not politics. At the same time, it is evident in much of what we have said that the two are inextricably bound together in the transition era. As we discuss real-world transition cases in subsequent chapters, it will be appropriate to devote some attention to political arrangements and to how these arrangements influence the policy process. For example, in the Russian case, the continuing struggle between the president and the legislature has unquestionably been of major importance in the shaping of economic policies and in their implementation. At the same time, the quicker demise of communism in countries such as Poland, the Czech Republic, and Hungary has facilitated the policy process. In these cases, though, the emergence of interest groups (such as that of labor through the solidarity movement in Poland) will be important for understanding the policy process.

Another key issue in the policy process is the extent to which there exists popular support for transition policies. As we will see when we discuss performance in the transition era, the end of the command era brought with it a sharp reduction of real output in most cases. The severity of this decline differed considerably from case to case (severe in Russia, limited in Poland), but popular support for transition has varied and has had important political repercussions. Apart from the initial collapse, the transition era has inevitably brought significant changes in living levels for major segments of the population.

Finally, the policy agenda must extend far beyond the focus on transition issues outlined above. In Russia for example, important regional issues must be addressed through the evolution of a new federalism. To cite another example, sectors such as energy have tended to function under a set of rules rather different from those applied to the typical industrial enterprise.

Thus, in addition to the basic political stability so important for economic progress, the political governance of the transition era is a major challenge.

Transition and Convergence: When Does Transition End?

Much of our discussion here pertains to the early and difficult stages of transition when, as we have emphasized, there has been no blueprint. As transition proceeds, those systems lucky enough to survive the initial shocks will be in the fortunate position of fine-tuning system arrangements and policies. However, if the systems of an earlier era produced distorted outcomes, one would expect new arrangements to change these outcomes. In a sense, one might expect a convergence of economic outcomes (for instance, structures)—but for reasons very different from those proposed in the discussions of the convergence hypothesis earlier in this book. In a very real sense, this implies major restructuring, though this term has typically been applied to changes in the decision making of privatized enterprises, not to economy-wide changes. What is fundamental, however, is a set of arrangements and (most important) outcomes that differ fundamentally from those of the socialist era.[5] Such an outcome is far more difficult to characterize than, for example, simply changing the decision-making arrangements of an industrial enterprise.

The Microeconomics of Transition: Privatization

Our discussion of differing economic systems has emphasized the general absence of private property as a key feature of socialist economic systems. The absence of private property in socialist systems fundamentally altered the nature of the allocation process, and especially the outcomes of that process, with important effects on efficiency and equity. Essential to the market (capitalist) economy is a different set of property-holding arrangements: private property. It is not surprising, therefore, that the microeconomics of the transition process consists in large part of **privatization**, a crucial issue in transition economies.[6] What is the basic for privatization, and how will it be achieved in transition economies?

As we will see throughout our discussion, the concept of privatization is not unique to the transition economies, though one could argue the process itself differs from the sale of a state-owned enterprise (SOE) in a market economy. Although the process of privatization in transition economies has differed from case to case, the sequence of events typically observed is illustrated in Figure 14.1

As we noted earlier, privatization has been a focal point of economic policy since the 1980s. Moreover, it is a critical theme both in market capitalist economies and in the former command economies. There are fundamental differences, however, and these are critical to understanding the transition era.

In market economies, privatization has typically been pursued for perceived gains in efficiency. The process of privatization in these cases is facilitated because it is taking place in a market economy where the nature of property rights can be changed with reasonable speed. Thus if a state-owned production facility is to be privatized, there exists a market for valuation and sale. If a state-run service is to be privatized, contracts can be arranged and a post-privatization assessment of gains can be made. Privatization in the transition setting is much more complex and has varied considerably from one case to another.

The process of privatization in transition economies often begins with **small-scale privatization** (for example, the introduction of cooperatives in the Soviet Union in the 1980s) or with what is sometimes termed **spontaneous privatization** (the immediate introduction of small-scale retail trade or service establishments). In fact, most privatization in such transition cases is termed **mass privatization**. In principle, all of the state-owned assets are to be privatized, and the process is to take place in what has been a nonmarket setting. This is a setting very different from selective privatization of some state assets in market economies.

As Figure 14.1 illustrates, the process of privatization can be characterized by a rather typical sequence of steps. In most cases, a state agency (the Truehandstaldt in Germany, Gosimushchestvo in Russia) is created to oversee the process of privatization. These agencies are to be guided by a legislative program, although such programs differ considerably. Broadly speaking, though, the legislation provides the rules under which privatization will take place: what assets will be privatized and what process will be used to implement changes in ownership.

Although there is a need for broad policy agreement on issues of privatization (Will the energy sector be privatized? What will be done about common land?), the process itself typically begins with the specific identification of state properties— for example, a state-owned factory—that are to be privatized. Then it is necessary to prepare the properties for sale, a procedure often termed corporatization. **Corporatization** is the development of a corporate share structure that will facilitate the transfer of ownership from the state to new (potential) buyers. The sale of the assets (shares) is another complex element in the privatization process and deserves additional comment.

FIGURE 14.1   The Sequence of Privatization

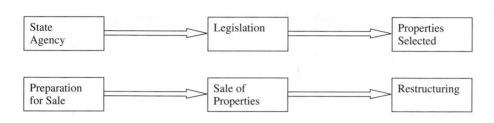

Source: Adapted from Paul R. Gregory and Robert C. Stuart, *Russian and Soviet Economic Structure and Performance,* Sixth Edition, p. 279. © 1998 Addison Wesley Educational Publishers, Inc. Reprinted by permission of Addison Wesley Longman.

Conceptually, the selling of shares in a market setting presents no special problems, but in the transition economies, there are serious difficulties. First, in the absence of meaningful markets, a process of valuation must be discovered. Traditional methods such as present-value calculations, accounting valuations, and market valuations are typically of limited use, especially during the early stages of privatization. Moreover, there may be claimants from past arrangements such that some form of **restitution** must be considered.[7] Again, cases differ, though in most of the former command economies, restitution (fundamentally an equity issue) was not an insurmountable problem. However, even with some sense of valuation in hand, the actual sale of shares is a daunting task that has been approached in a variety of ways.

First, it is possible simply to sell the shares directly to buyers—through an auction, for example. Direct sale has a distinct advantage over alternative approaches in that it helps raise funds that the firm needs for modernization and development. However, the lack of transparency, or openness, in such arrangements in transition settings makes it difficult to find buyers (let alone foreign buyers), to say nothing of the fact that in most transition economies, potential buyers lack the funds necessary to become actual buyers, and financial markets are virtually nonexistent, a condition that breaks any possible link between savers and investors. As we will see, with the possible exception of Hungary, the use of foreign direct investment to stimulate privatization has been very limited. Thus, for a variety of reasons, direct sale is a necessary though limited approach.

Second, the most common form of privatization is probably through the voucher process, a mechanism used in a variety of transition settings with quite different arrangements and different outcomes. Although voucher privatization does not provide a source of working capital, it is relatively simple and fast, and it has potential equity advantages. Specifically, the voucher approach has been viewed as a means of dispersing ownership widely. In some transition cases, the voucher mechanisms has been important; in other cases, less so.

Voucher privatization works in the following way. First, the state issues to the population vouchers with a specified face value. In the Russian case, each member of the population was issued (in 1993) a voucher with a face value of 10,000 rubles, roughly one month's pay at that time.[8] Obviously, a secondary market emerged, and some sold their vouchers, especially the elderly who needed funds for daily expenditures. The intention, of course, was that vouchers would be exchanged for shares (probably at the place of work) such that the workers would become the owners.

The distribution of shares to managers, workers, and others was specified in state legislation discussed above. However, through a variety of mechanisms (including the secondary market) managers would generally have an upper hand in gaining control of the enterprise—an outcome usually termed **insider privatization**. Thus, even though the voucher approach to privatization is designed to provide the population with widespread access to ownership, the outcome may be different. The nature of the rules governing the distribution of shares, in combination with insider skill in accumulating vouchers, may lead to insider privatization essentially as a form of **employee buyout** (EBO). In these cases, the outcome is probably less attractive from an equity viewpoint, though the efficiency issues remain to be examined fully. Finally, although vouchers could be used for financial investment through mutual funds and similar arrangements, the generally primitive state of financial markets and the general distrust of such mechanisms meant that, in practice, very few vouchers were utilized in this manner.

It is instructive to look back at the early discussions of privatization. Indeed, from the beginning, much of the emphasis was (appropriately at the time) placed on issues of mechanics: How will privatization proceed? What will be the equity outcomes and who will be able to purchase equities? The emergence of markets in transition settings is now viewed as a substantially more complex issue than was thought ten years ago.[9] Moreover attention is now focused on the critical—and as yet substantially unresolved—set of issues known as **restructuring**. Most would agree that the creation of new property rights through privatization is an initial step in the transition process, but the obvious next step is that of fundamentally changing decision-making arrangements such that there are desperately needed gains in efficiency. The concept of restructuring involves changing the nature of the enterprise decision-making process to achieve the objective of improved enterprise performance.

Although the gathering of evidence on enterprise restructuring in transition is still in its early stages, some initial observations can be made. First, empirical evidence seems to suggest that the outcomes of privatization in Western market economies (both developed and underdeveloped) have been positive as reflected by improved performance indicators such as profits, productivity, and the like.[10] Second, as we will emphasize when we examine selected transition cases, restructuring, though difficult to define and measure, has apparently been limited. There is evidence that enterprises have found it difficult to impose hard budget constraints and thus, in the absence of functioning capital markets, face a shortage of working capital. Pricing signals are of limited usefulness, so a barter economy thrives, along with the continued use of inter-enterprise credits out of reach of the money economy. In other words, it has been difficult to impose a hard budget constraint on enterprises in the transition economies.[11] Grasping the subtleties of restructuring will be critical to understanding the effectiveness of privatization, and ultimately the success of transition, as we move into the next century.

Transition and the Macroeconomy: Monetary and Fiscal Arrangements

One of the most difficult aspects of transitions is the establishment of new monetary and fiscal arrangements and policies.[12] Again, we have emphasized that the money and fiscal arrangements of the administrative-command economy were fundamentally different from those of the market economy. Indeed, traditional macroeconomics tools played only a limited role in the command economy.

As we know, the state was a dominant player in the command economy, though its operations were financed in large part directly from the returns of enterprise activity rather than through a tax system, as is typical of market economies. As the command systems collapsed, the demands on the state, whether for sustaining employment, education, or the provision of services for the elderly, did not shrink to the same degree that revenues fell. In this setting, even with the development of a broad-based "Western style" tax system, state spending typically exceeded state revenues. At the same time, in the absence of developed financial markets, the resulting deficit was monetized through the printing of money. The result, though it varied from one case to another, was unusually large deficits that created strong inflationary pressures. These pressures, along with the release of administered prices, resulted in severe price increases. Developing a "normal" state structure on both revenue and the expenditure side has proved to be a difficult task.

A critical element of the macroeconomy is the development of financial markets and a banking structure. Although financial markets have generally begun to develop, they are shallow and typically lack transparency. At the same time, with exceptions, there has been a rapid expansion of small, unprofitable, poorly capitalized banks. The development of a central bank and appropriate banking legislation is a typical path to avoiding financial difficulties, especially in the many cases where external aid has been of limited importance.

The strategy of macroeconomic policy making and implementation during the transition era is a related and complex set of issues. Again, as we examine different countries, it will become apparent that the potential for macroeconomic instability during the early years of transition differed considerably from one case to another. However, an examination of macroeconomic indicators would suggest that many of the countries in transition have had a degree of success in stabilizing their economies, arresting the decline of output, and moving toward a path of reasonable if not steady economic growth. Indeed, the issue is more complex. The policies appropriate for the early and medium term may be different from those appropriate to sustaining long-term economic growth. We examine the issue of performance in a later chapter.

Opening a Closed Economy: Transition and Trade

The transition economies of the 1990s are a fundamentally very diverse group of countries in which we would expect to find very different international trade and financial arrangements. At the same time, the transition economies that emerged from the command era entered the transition process with a similar legacy—specifically a major degree of isolation from the world trade and financial arrangements, from which they were sheltered by peculiar foreign trade decision-making arrangements and by an isolated or nonconvertible currency. The two major tasks of the early transition era were to effect changes in both critical areas.

First, it is necessary to abolish the old arrangements and to create the policies and infrastructure necessary for the conduct of foreign trade on a decentralized basis. This task has been different for the various transition cases for generally obvious reasons. In some cases (such as Romania and Albania), the economies were isolated, whereas in other cases (Poland and the Czech republic), there was considerably less isolation. The Soviet Union is of special interest from the trade perspective in that a single political entity with fifteen internal political divisions (republics) became fifteen distinct countries.

Second, it is necessary to create the financial underpinnings required for the conduct of foreign trade, most notably the conditions needed for establishing and sustaining a convertible currency. Although the initial emphasis in transition economies seemed to be on the need for external assistance, events demonstrated that domestic reform was also necessary to establish a competitive position in the global economy.

As we examine the performance outcomes of the various transition economies, it will be evident that the trade experience has varied considerably from case to case.

The Safety Net During Transition

Throughout this book, we have emphasized the fundamental differences between the administrative-command economy and the market economy. One of the most important differences is in the nature of the social contract—that is, the implicit agreement between a government and its citizens that defines the responsibilities of each. Thus the transition from planned socialism to market capitalism entails a fundamental change in the social contract.[13] Although the impact of socialist thought varied considerably from one case to another, the pattern was for the state to provide social services without charging users significant fees. Although it was generally argued that unemployment did not exist (a posture that largely eliminated the need for unemployment insurance), the "social wage" in command economies was a significant contribution to family income, providing subsidized or "free" medical care, pensions, education, and the like. Whether this package was attractive to recipients is not the issue here. It quickly became clear from the earliest days of transition that the social contract would be changed. Moreover, as might be expected, the impact of these changes would be quite different for different segments of the population. Again as might be expected, the shift to market arrangements typically increased the unevenness of the income distribution. In addition, segments of the populations (the elderly, for example) have fared much less well under transition than the young.

Although the safety net issues have received much less attention than other micro-economic and macroeconomic issues, the changes have been in understandable directions. There has been a movement away from state-provided toward private, fee-based services. In addition, there has been a substantial shift in the distribution of benefits.

Summary

In this chapter we have surveyed the basic issues of transition, leaving the details of different cases for subsequent discussion. It is important for the reader to appreciate the fact that after roughly ten years of transition experience, the issues that are the focus of discussion have changed. A case in point is that of the strategy of transition.

From the beginning, there has been interest in the admittedly artificial contrast between the "big bang," or rapid, approach and the slower, "gradualist" approach. This discussion originally occupied center stage, but we now treat the distinction as much more subtle, though it nevertheless incorporates interesting issues, especially those pertaining to institution building in a new socioeconomic setting.

Our discussion in this chapter has focused on four major components of transition: microeconomic (privatization) issues, macroeconomic issues (the role of the state and financial issues), trade (integration into the world economy) and safety net issues (pensions, medical care, assistance for the elderly, and so on).

Although these issues overlap in interesting ways, they are discrete and identifiable components of the transition experience in which the organizational arrangements and policies of the command economy, in some cases in place for many years, are replaced by the fundamentally different arrangements and policies of the market economy.

Transition from a command to a market-driven economy involves privatization, which usually entails preparing properties for sale and changing equity arrangements through methods such as direct sale and/or a voucher arrangement. Beyond the formal change of ownership arrangements, contemporary interest is also focused on restructuring—that is, on changing the decision-making arrangements to improve enterprise performance. This phase (which is now in progress) will be crucial to the long-term viability of the transition economies.

A second major component of transition involves macroeconomic issues, specifically the introduction of a money economy and financial markets, along with a state structure capable of sustaining a desired level of government spending based on a radically new and different "Western style" tax system. In a sense, there is a parallel between the microeconomic and the macroeconomic reforms. Thus enterprises can be privatized while undergoing only limited change (restructuring). At the same time, financial markets and infrastructure can exist, but they play only a very limited role in the operation of the economy. Both are areas to watch as transition proceeds into a new century.

Third, we have emphasized that the trade and financial arrangements of the command economies were fundamentally different from those of market economies. Thus transition involves the instituting of new trade arrangements and the creation of new financial mechanisms and arrangements, most notably a convertible currency. Though these changes are initially difficult, given an economic system substantially isolated from world market forces, they can be expected to affect international trade in fundamental ways.

Finally, safety net issues are important if constituent populations are to continue to support the efforts to change of the regime in transition. The social contract has undergone fundamental change as the old order collapsed and new private, fee-based services have gradually been introduced. This process has been slow and irregular, and it has understandably resulted in a very uneven distribution of services both by region and (most notably) by income class.

Key Terms

transition	neoclassical economic theory
reform	restructuring
microeconomics of transition	restitution
macroeconomics of transition	small-scale privatization
international trade	spontaneous privatization
international finance	mass privatization
safety net	corporatization
initial conditions	insider privatization
transition policies	employee buyout (EBO)
sequencing	valuation
evolutionary economics	voucher privatization

Notes

1. A number of authors have discussed the issues of the speed and sequencing of transition. See Peter Murrell, "Evolutionary and Radical Approaches to Economic Reform," *Economics of Planning* 25, 1 (1992); Joseph Brada, "The Transformation from Communism to Capitalism: How Far? How Fast? *Post-Soviet Affairs* 9, 2 (1993); Paul Hare and Tamas Revesz, "Hungary's Transition to the Market: The Case Against a Big-Bang," *Economic Policy* 14 (1992); Herman W. Hoen, "Theoretically Underpinning Transition to the Market: An Austrian View," *Economic Systems* 19, 1 (1995); Jozef van Brabant, "Lessons from the Wholesale Transformations in the East," *Comparative Economic Studies* 35, 4 (1993); Peter Murrell, "Evolution in Economics and in the Economy Reform of the Centrally Planned Economies," in Christopher Clague and Gordon C. Rausser, eds., *The Emergence of Market Economies in Eastern Europe* (Cambridge, Mass.: Blackwell, 1992), pp. 35–53; Hans Van Ees and Harry Garretsen, "The Theoretical Foundations of the Reforms in Eastern

Europe: Big Bang versus Gradualism and the Limitations of Neo-Classical Theory," *Economic Systems* 18, 1 (1994); Herman W. Hoen, "Shock versus Gradualism in Central Europe Reconsidered," *Comparative Economic Studies* 38, 1 (Spring 1996).

2. For a discussion of transition policies, see Stanley Fischer and Alan Gelb, "The Process of Socialist Economic Transformation," *Journal of Economic Perspectives* 5, 4 (Fall 1991); Maurice Ernst, Michael Alexeev, and Paul Marer, *Transforming the Core* (Boulder: Westview Press, 1996), Chs. 1–2; World Bank, *World Development Report 1996* (Washington, D.C. World Bank, 1996); Norbert Funke, "Timing and Sequencing of Reforms: Competing Views and the Role of Credibility," *Kyklos* 3 (1993).

3. This issue is discussed in Peter Murrell and Yijiang Wang, "When Privatization Should Be Delayed: The Effects of Communist Legacies on Organizational and Institutional Reforms," *Journal of Comparative Economics* 17 (1993).

4. See, for example, Peter Murrell, "Evolution in Economics and in the Economic Reform of the Centrally Planned Economies," in Christopher Clague and Gordon C. Rausser, eds., *The Emergence of Market Economies in Eastern Europe* (Cambridge, Mass.: Blackwell, 1992), pp. 35–53; Peter Murrell and Mancur Olson, "The Devolution of Centrally Planned Economies." *Journal of Comparative Economics* 15 (1991).

5. It was argued that the command economies were "distorted" vis-à-vis allocation patterns that would be typical of market economies. These distortions pertained to a variety of outcomes, such as industry emphasis and especially heavy-industry emphasis, low ratios of consumption to output and high ratios of savings and investment to output. Under the market arrangements of the transition era, one would expect the former command economies to converge to more "normal" patterns of resource allocation.

6. The literature on privatization is extensive. The literature of the 1980s focuses primarily on the economics of privatization and the nature of privatization in Western market economies. The literature of the early 1990s focuses on strategies of privatization in transition economies. The literature of the mid- and late 1990s focuses on the strategies of privatization and especially on the outcomes of privatization and the nature of restructuring in transition economies.

7. Although there was much discussion of restitution (equity) issues during the early days of the transition era, in fact restitution (beyond examples such as the Czech Republic and the Baltic states) has been statistically unimportant as a mechanism for privatization. For a discussion, see World Bank, *From Plan to Market: World Development Report 1996* (Washington, D.C.: World Bank, 1996), Ch. 3.

8. For a discussion of the Russian voucher program, see L. D. Nelson, and I. Y. Kuzes, "Evaluating the Russian Voucher Privatization Program," *Comparative Economic Studies* 36 (Spring 1994); for a general survey, see Maxim Boycko, Andrei Shleifer, and Robert Vishny, *Privatizing Russia* (Cambridge, Mass.: M.I.T. Press, 1997); Joseph R. Blasi, Maya Kroumova, and Douglas Kruse, *Kremlin Capitalism: Privatizating the Russian Economy* (Ithaca, N.Y.: Cornell University Press, 1997).

9. There is a large literature on these issues. See, for example, Horst Brezinski and Michael Fritsch, eds., *The Emergence and Evolution of Markets* (Lyme, Conn.: Edward Elgar, 1997).

10. See, for example, W. C. Megginson, R. C. Nash, and M. van Randenborgh, "The Financial and Operating Performance of Newly Privatized Firms: An International Empirical Analysis," *Journal of Finance* 49 (June 1994), 403–452.

11. There is large and growing literature on restructuring in transition economies. For a discussion of the Russian case and references, see Susan J. Linz, "Russian Firms in Transition: Champions, Challengers, and Chaff," *Comparative Economic Studies* 2, 39 (Summer 1997), 1–36.

12. There is now a substantial literature on macroeconomic issues during transition. For a discussion of the early stages of transition, see R. McKinnon, "Financial Control in the Transition from Classical Socialism to a Market Economy," *Journal of Economic Perspectives* 5, 4 (Fall 1991); O. J. Blanchard, K. A. Froot, and J. D. Sachs, eds., *The Transition in Eastern Europe,* Vol. 1 and 2 (Chicago: University of Chicago Press, 1994). More recent works on selected aspects of the macroeconomy are listed at the end of this chapter.
13. For a discussion of these issues, see Lucjan T. Orlowski, "Social Safety Nets in Central Europe: Preparation for Accession to the European Union?" *Comparative Economic Studies* 37, 2 (Summer 1995); Victor A. Pestoff, ed., *Reforming Social Services in Eastern Europe—An Eleven Nation Overview* (Cracow: Cracow Academy of Economics and Friedrich Ebert Stiftung, 1995); World Bank, *From Plan to Market: The World Development Report 1996* (Washington, D.C.: World Bank, 1996), Chapter 4; OECD, *The Changing Social Benefits in Russian Enterprises* (Paris: OECD, 1996); James R. Millar and Sharon J. Wolchik, eds., *The Social Legacy of Communism* (New York: Cambridge University Press, 1994).

Recommended Readings

Transition: General Sources

Oliver Jean Blanchard, Kenneth A. Froot, and Jeffrey D. Sachs, eds., *The Transition in Eastern Europe,* Vols. 1 and 2 (Chicago: University of Chicago Press, 1994).
Horst Brezinski and Michael Fritsch, eds., *The Emergence and Evolution of Markets* (Lyme, Conn.: Edward Elgar, 1997).
Christopher Clague and Gordon C. Rausser, eds., *The Emergence of Market Economies in Eastern Europe* (Cambridge, Mass.: Blackwell, 1992).
Bruno, Dallago and Luigi Mittone, *Economic Institutions: Markets and Competition* (Cheltenham, England: Edward Elgar, 1996).
M. Dewatripont and G. Roland, "Transition as a Process of Large-Scale Institutional Change," *Economics of Transition* 4, 1 (1996), 1–30.
Jerzy Hausner, Bob Jessop, and Klaus Nielsen, *Strategic Choice and Path-Dependency in Post-Socialism* (Cheltenham, England: Edward Elgar, 1995).
Shafiqul Islam and Michael Mandelbaum, eds., *Making Markets: Economic Transformation in Eastern Europe and the Post-Soviet States* (New York: Council on Foreign Relations, 1993).
Edward P. Lazear, ed., *Economic Transition in Eastern Europe and Russia* (Stamford, Conn.: Hoover Institution Press, 1995).
Martin Myant, Frank Fleischer, Kurt Hornschild, Ruzena Vintrova, Karel Zeman, and Zdenek Soucek, *Successful Transformations? The Creation of Market Economies in Eastern Germany and the Czech Republic* (Cheltenham, England: Edward Elgar, 1996).
Nicolas Spulber, *Redefining the State: Privatization and Welfare Reform in Industrial and Transitional Economies* (New York: Cambridge University Press, 1998).
"Symposium on Economic Transition in the Soviet Union and Eastern Europe," *Journal of Economic Perspectives* 5, 4 (Fall 1991).
Wing Thye Woo, Stephen Parker, and Jeffrey D. Sachs, eds., *Economies in Transition: Comparing Asia and Europe* (Cambridge, Mass.: M.I.T. Press, 1997).

Privatization: General Sources

Joan W. Allen *et. al., The Private Sector in State Service Delivery: Examples of Innovative Practices* (Washington, D.C.: Urban Institute, 1989).

Masahiko Aoki and Hyung-Ki Kim, *Corporate Governance in Transitional Economies* (Washington, D.C.: The World Bank, 1995).

William J. Baumol, "On the Perils of Privatization," *Eastern Economic Journal* 19 (Fall 1993), 419–440.

P. Bolton and G. Roland, "Privatization Policies in Central and Eastern Europe," *Economic Policy* 15 (1992), 276–309.

Deiter Bos, *Privatization: A Theoretical Treatment* (Cambridge, Mass.: Blackwell, 1992).

Maxim Boycko, Andrei Shleifer, and Robert W. Vishny, "A Theory of Privatisation," *The Economic Journal* 106 (March 1996), 309–319.

Ralph, Bradford, "Privatization of Natural Monopoly Public Enterprises: The Regulation Issue," *Review of Industrial Organization* 10, 3 (June 1995), 249–267.

F. Cornelli and D. D. Li, "Large Shareholders, Private Benefits of Control and Optimal Schemes of Privatization," *The Rand Journal of Economics* 28, 4 (Winter 1997), 585–604.

John D. Donahue, *The Privatization Decision* (New York: Basic Books, 1989).

Saul Estrin and Robert Stone, "A Taxonomy of Mass Privatization," *Transition* 7, 11–12 (November–December 1996).

John B. Goodman and Gary W. Loveman, "Does Privatization Serve the Public Interest?" *Harvard Business Review* (November/December 1992), 26–38.

Pierre Guislain, *The Privatization Challenge: A Strategic, Legal and Institutional Analysis of International Experience* (Washington, D.C.: The World Bank, 1997).

Leroy P. Jones, Tankaj Tandon, and Ingo Vogelsgang, *Selling Public Enterprises: A Cost-Benefit Methodology* (Cambridge: M.I.T. Press, 1990).

J. A. Kay and D. J. Thompson, "Privatization: A Policy in Search of a Rationale," *Economic Journal* 96 (March 1986), 18–32.

Michael McLinden, *Privatization and Capital Market Development: Strategies to Promote Economic Growth* (Westport, Conn.: Praeger, 1996).

V. V. Ramanad Lam, ed., *Privatization and Equity* (New York: Routledge, 1995).

Philip Morgan, ed., *Privatization and the Welfare State: Implications for Consensus and the Welfare* (Brookfield, Vt.: Dartmouth, 1995).

John Nellis, "So Far So Good? A Privatization Update," *Transition* 7, 11–12 (November–December, 1996).

OECD, *Methods of Privatising Large Enterprises* (Paris: OECD, 1993).

———, *Valuation and Privatisation* (Paris: OECD, 1993).

Janet Rothenberg Pack, "Privatization of Public-Sector Services in Theory and Practice," *Journal of Policy Analysis and Management* 6 (1987), 523–540.

Dominique Pannier, ed., *Corporate Governance of Public Enterprises in Transitional Economies* (Washington, D.C.: The World Bank, 1996).

Andrew Pendleton and Jonathan Winterton, eds., *Public Enterprise in Transition* (London and New York: Routledge, 1993).

E. S. Savas, *Privatization: The Key to Better Government* (Chatham, N.J.: Chatham House, 1987).

Elliot Sclar, *The Privatization of Public Service: Lessons from Case Studies* (Washington, D.C.: The Economic Policy Institute, 1997).

Horst Seibert, ed., *Privatization: A Symposium in Honor of Herbert Giersch* (Tubingen, Germany: Institut fur weltwirtschaft an der Universitat Kiel, 1992).

Mary Shirley and John Nellis, *Public Enterprise Reform: The Lessons of Experience* (Washington, D.C.: The World Bank, 1991).

E. E. Suleiman and J. Waterbury, *The Political Economy of Public Sector Reform and Privatization* (Boulder, Colo.: Westview Press, 1990).

John Vickers and George Yarrow, *Privatization: An Economic Analysis* (Cambridge, Mass.: M.I.T. Press, 1988).

Charles Wolf Jr., *Markets or Governments: Choosing Between Imperfect Alternatives* (Cambridge Mass.: M.I.T. Press, 1988).

Privatization Cases

Dieter Bos, "Privatization in Europe: A Comparison of Approaches," *Oxford Review of Economic Policy* 9, 1 (1993), 95–110.

Maxim Boycko, Andrei Schleifer, and Robert Vishny, *Privatizing Russia* (Cambridge, Mass.: M.I.T. Press, 1995).

Trevor Buck, Igor Filatotchev, and Mike Wright, "Employee Buyouts and the Transformation of Russian Industry," *Comparative Economic Studies* 36 (Summer 1994), 1–16.

Wendy Carlin and Colin Mayer, "The Truhandanstalt: Privatization by State and Market," in Oliver Jean Blanchard, Kenneth A. Froot, and Jeffrey D. Sachs, *The Transition in Eastern Europe,* Vol. 2 (Chicago: University of Chicago Press, 1994), pp. 184–207.

Gunnar Eliasson, "The Micro Frustrations of Privatizing Eastern Europe," working paper, Stockholm: The Industrial Institute for Economic and Social Research, 1992.

Maurice Ernst, Michael Alexeev, and Paul Marer, *Transforming the Core* (Boulder, Colo.: Westview Press, 1996).

Saul Estrin, "Privatization in Central and Eastern Europe: What Lessons Can Be Learnt for Western Experience," *Annals of Public and Cooperative Economy* 62, 2 (April–June, 1991), 159–182.

Saul Estrin and Xavier Richet, "Industrial Restructuring and Microeconomic Adjustment in Poland: A Cross Sectoral Approach," *Comparative Economic Studies* 35, 4 (Winter 1993), 1–19.

Roman Frydman and Andrzej Rapaczynski, eds., *Privatization in Eastern Europe: Is the State Withering Away?* (New York: Oxford University Press, 1994).

Dominique Hachette and Rolf Luders, *Privatization in Chile* (San Francisco: ICS Press, 1993).

Ira W. Liberman *et al.,* eds., *Mass Privatization in Central and Eastern Europe and the Former Soviet Union: A Comparative Analysis* (Washington, D.C.: The World Bank, 1995).

Eva Marikova Leeds, "Voucher Privatization in Czechoslovakia," *Comparative Economic Studies* 35, 3 (Fall 1993), 19–38.

Lynn D. Nelson and Irina Y. Kuzes, "Evaluating the Russian Voucher Privatization Program," *Comparative Economic Studies* 36 (Spring 1994), 55–68.

Jeremy Richardson, ed., *Privatisation and Deregulation in Canada and Britain* (Brookfield, Vt.: Aldershot, 1990).

Darrell Slider, "Privatization in Russia's Regions," *Post Soviet Affairs* 10, 4 (October–December, 1994), 367–396.

Robert H. Wissel, "Privatization in the United States," *Business Economics* 30, 4 (October 1995), 45–50.

Privatization in LDCs

Paul Cook and Colin Kirkpatrick, eds., *Privatisation in Less Developed Countries* (New York: St. Martin's Press, 1988).

Steve H. Hanke, ed., *Privatization and Development* (San Francisco: ICS Press, 1987).

Attiat F. Ott and Keith Hartley, eds., *Privatization and Economic Efficiency: A Comparative Analysis of Developed and Developing Countries* (Cheltenham, England: Edward Elgar, 1991).

Jonas Prager, "Is Privatization a Panacea for LDC's? Market Failure versus Public Sector Failure," *The Journal of Developing Areas* 26 (April 1992), 301–322.

Gabriel Roth, *The Private Provision of Public Services in Developing Countries* (Oxford, England: Oxford University Press, 1987).

Results of Privatization

Matthew Bishop, John Kay, and Colin Mayer, eds., *Privatization and Economic Performance* (New York: Oxford University Press, 1994).

Simon Commander, Qimiao Fan, and Mark E. Schaffer, *Enterprise Restructuring and Economic Policy in Russia* (Washington, D.C.: The World Bank, 1996).

Saul Estrin, Josef C. Brada, Alan Geld, and Inderjit Singh, eds., *Restructuring and Privatization in Central Eastern Europe,* (Armonk, N.Y.: Sharpe, 1995).

Ahmed Galal, Leroy Jones, Pankaj Tandon, and Ingo Vogelsgang, *Welfare Consequences of Selling Public Enterprises: An Empirical Analysis* (New York: Oxford University Press, 1994).

Susan J. Linz, "Russian Firms in Transition: Champions, Challengers, and Chaff," Department of Economics, Michigan State University, 1996.

Sunita Kikeri, John Nellis, and Mary Shirley, *Privatization: The Lessons of Experience* (Washington, D.C.: The World Bank, 1992).

William C. Megginson, Robert C. Nash, and Matthias van Randenborgh, "The Financial and Operating Performance of Newly Privatized Firms: An International Empirical Analysis," *Journal of Finance* 49 (June 1994), 403–452.

OECD, *Mass Privatisation: An Initial Assessment* (Paris: OECD, 1995).

Milica Uvalic and Daniel Vaughan-Whitehead, eds., *Privatization Surprises in Transition Economies: Employee Ownership in Central and Eastern Europe* (Cheltenham, England: Edward Elgar, 1997).

Macroeconomics of Transition

Richard Bird, *et al., Decentralization of the Socialist State: Intergovernment Finance in Transition Economies* (Brookfield, VT: Ashgate, 1996).

Steve H. Hanke, Lars Jonung, and Kurt Shuler, *Russian Currency and Finance: A Currency Board Approach to Reform* (New York: Routledge, 1993).

Hansjorg Herr, ed., *Macroeconomic Problems of Transformation: Stabilization Policies and Economic Restructuring* (Cheltenham, England: Edward Elgar, 1994).

Ronald I. McKinnon, "Financial Control in the Transition from Classical Socialism to a Market Economy," *Journal of Economic Perspectives* 5 (Fall 1991), 107–122.

———, *The Order of Economic Liberalization: Financial Control in the Transition to a Market Economy* (Baltimore: The Johns Hopkins University Press, 1991).

Janet Mitchell, "Managerial Discipline, Productivity and Bankruptcy in Capitalist and Socialist Economies," *Comparative Economic Studies* 32 (Fall 1990), 93–137.

OECD, *Transformation of the Banking System: Portfolio Restructuring, Privatisation, and the Payment System* (Paris: OCED, 1993).

The World Bank, *Russia: The Banking System During Transition* (Washington, D.C.: The World Bank, 1993).

Transition and International Trade

Patrick Artisien-Maksimento and Yuri Adjubei, eds., *Foreign Investment in Russia and Other Successor States* (New York: St. Martin's Press, 1996).

Richard N. Cooper and Janos Gacs, eds., *Trade Growth in Transition Economies* (Cheltenham, England: Edward Elgar, 1997).

OECD, *Barriers to Trade with the Economies in Transition* (Paris: OCED, 1994).

———, *Trade Policy and the Transition Process* (Paris: OCED, 1996).

Zhen Kun Wang, "Integrating Transition Economies Into the Global Economy," *Finance and Development* 33, 3 (September 1996), 21–23.

The Safety Net

Nicholas Barr, "People in Transition: Reforming Education and Health Care," *Finance and Development* 33, 3 (September 1996), 24–27.

Nicholas Barr, ed., *Labor Markets and Social Policy in Central and Eastern Europe: The Transition and Beyond* (New York: Oxford University Press, 1996).

Ke-Young Chu and Sanjeev Gupta, "Protecting the Poor: Social Safety Nets During Transition," *Finance and Development* 30 (June 1993), 24–27.

Christopher Mark Davis, "The Health Sector in the Soviet Union and Russian Economies: From Reform to Fragmentation to Transition," in United States Congress, Joint Economic Committee, *The Former Soviet Union in Transition,* Vol. 2 (Washington, D.C.: U.S. Government Printing Office, 1993), 852–872.

Ellen Goldstein, Alexander S. Preker, Olusoji Adeyi, and Gnanaraj Chellaraj, *Trends in Health Status, Services, and Finance: The Transition in Central and Eastern Europe,* Vols. I and II (Washington, D.C.: The World Bank, 1997).

Jeni G. Klugman and George Schieber, *A Survey of Health Reform in Central Asia* (Washington, D.C.: The World Bank, 1997).

George Kopits, "Reforming Social Security Systems," *Finance and Development* 30, 2 (June 1993), 21–23.

James R. Millar and Sharon L. Wolchik, eds., *The Social Legacy of Communism* (New York: Cambridge University Press, 1994).

OECD, *The Changing Social Benefits in Russian Enterprises* (Paris: OECD, 1996).

———, *Unemployment in Transition Economies: Transient or Persistent?* (Paris: OECD, 1994).

George Schieber, "International Report: Health Care Financing Reform in Russia and Ukraine," *Health Affairs,* supplement (1993), 294–299.

The World Bank, *Social Indicators of Development* (Washington, D.C.: The World Bank, 1996).

15

The Russian Economy in Transition

With the breakup of the former Soviet Union at the end of 1991, the fifteen Soviet republics became fifteen independent countries of which Russia is by far the largest. In terms of land area, Russia represents roughly 76 percent of the Soviet land mass, 70 percent of the Soviet population, and the bulk of Soviet oil production.

Our examination of the contemporary Russian economic system is complicated by the fact that it is in a state of flux. However, because of its size, past development experience and contemporary political and economic significance, Russia is a very important case of transition from plan to market.

We have already examined the nature of the administrative-command economy and noted the performance problems of that system. However, insofar as we place importance on prior conditions for understanding the transition era, we provide a brief overview of the final days of the Soviet era. Thereafter, we turn to a discussion of transition in the 1990s.

The Natural Setting

Russia is by far the largest of the former Soviet republics and, as a new and separate nation, remains a country with great economic potential. At the beginning of this decade, Russia accounted for roughly 60 percent of the total output of the Soviet Union and had a population of just under 150 million, 75 percent of whom lived in an urban setting. Because of the significant educational and career achievements of a substantial part of the populace under very different political and economic arrangements, the breakup of the Soviet Union has been an event of great importance.

Although the breakup of the Soviet Union changed the resource balance among the former republics, Russia remains the wealthiest with substantial supplies of most basic natural resources from oil to timber and minerals. The issue is not reserves, then, but rather the effective use of these reserves in a manner that contributes to economic growth and to improvement in the standard of living of the Russian people.

From a geographic perspective, it is important to appreciate the diversity of the vast Russian landscape and to recognize that Russia is a northerly country with wide variations in climate and substantial land areas that are relatively inhospitable. These characteristics have dictated the nature and location of economic activity, especially agricultural production, and they will continue to do so. Indeed, the Soviet response to these factors has a major influence on contemporary transition.

The immense size of Russia is important in another way. As Russia moves toward a decentralized market economy, both economic and political power will shift from upper to lower levels. Under these new arrangements, we can expect a very different sectoral and regional pattern of economic activity from that which prevailed in the past, though such changes will emerge over a relatively long span of years.

The End of the Command Era

Our discussion of the administrative-command in Chapter 9 emphasized the fact that this system was in place for a long time, significantly longer than was the case in Eastern Europe, beginning in 1928.[1] Thus, to the extent that resource-allocation patterns of Russia in, say, 1991 did not reflect those of market forces, major changes could be anticipated. Moreover, one might expect such changes to be more difficult to develop and implement in Russia (and especially the other former republics) than in Eastern Europe, where the planned socialist economic system had prevailed for a relatively short time. The impact of the past on the transition process and the differences from one case to another remain to be assessed in the future.

For the Russian economy, change began before the events of the late 1980s and early 1990s. There were important changes even during the Stalin era. However, we have emphasized that economic reform in the post-World War II era was focused on regime-directed programs designed to improve the working arrangements of the planned economy. Beginning in the late 1950s and early 1960s, there were a variety of modest reform attempts that had relatively little impact either on Soviet working arrangements or on Soviet economic performance.

The final attempt at reform was **perestroika**, or restructuring, which began with the ascendancy of Mikhail Gorbachev in 1985.[2] This economic reform program, along with its political counterpart **democratization** and its social counterpart **glasnost**, or openness, brought forth wide-ranging changes in the old Soviet order—charges that failed to improve economic performance and contributed to the end of the Soviet economic and political systems. In some respects, the attempted reforms of perestroika suffered from the same problems associated with earlier Soviet reform efforts. But in other ways, many viewed them as exciting and as capable of making the Soviet economic and political systems effective in a new era.

The motivation for perestroika was declining performance of the Soviet economy. By the mid-1980s the Soviet economy, like other planned economies, had experienced years of declining rates of economic growth and major productivity problems. Declining economic performance was attributed to serious information and incentive deficits of the command system. Indeed, when Gorbachev announced the beginnings of perestroika, he suggested that his new policies would be a cure for the "period of stagnation" (period **zastoia**) that characterized the Brezhnev era and especially the 1970s and early 1980s. In addition to emphasizing technological change, opening the economy to the external world, and improving internal enterprise decision-making rules, Gorbachev placed great reliance on what he termed the **human factor**—an attempt to revive the enthusiasm that characterized the efforts of

Soviet citizens in the early 1930s. However, the many years of unkept economic promises made stimulating the population to greater effort impossible.

Unlike earlier cosmetic reforms, perestroika was of great significance because it was **radical economic reform**, combined with a significant opening of Soviet society and increased citizen participation. The sense that this was real economic reform created some enthusiasm for change at first.

Indeed, through the late 1980s, a great deal of new reform legislation passed. For example, foreign trade was markedly liberalized on critical issues such as foreign ownership, repatriation of profits, and joint management arrangements. In other areas, such as the development of cooperatives and new land laws, the legislation of the period was very conservative. Initially, the cooperatives were limited to small operations in the service sector, and severe limitations were imposed on their ability to hire labor and on their access to capital. Gorbachev showed little interest in the concept of private property and price reform, both critical issues of making real changes in the allocation procedures. Changes to be made in the system of enterprise guidance seemed to be important, yet they proved complex, often contradictory, and difficult to implement.[3]

One can criticize perestroika as less than a complete reform program and as poorly sequenced and coordinated, but if the legislative decrees had been fully implemented, they would have changed the nature of the Soviet economy. However, traditional problems of resistance to reform emerged. Indeed, there was so much legislation in this period that it became hard to tell which rules and laws applied in which cases. The result was an attempt to implement changes that could not be successful in isolation. The traditional system began to disintegrate, and toward the end of the decade there was an attempt at retrenchment. The net result of perestroika was the worst of all worlds. It destroyed the old system without creating a cohesive new one. By the end of the 1980s, confusion reigned.

In Table 15.1, we present some basic performance indicators for the Soviet economy during the perestroika era. Although the performance of the economy showed some improvement during the first 2 years of perestroika, the reform began to crumble during and after 1989. At the time, observers attributed declining performance to the partial nature of the reform, to its overemphasis on the human factor, to sequencing problems, and to delays in implementation. The Soviet command system was markedly weakened during these years even though there was an attempted recentralization—a response to lagging performance—in the latter part of the decade.

The beginning of the new decade was pivotal from both an economic and a political standpoint.[4] Through 1990, attention focused increasingly on **transition** rather than reform, as major transition programs, the "500 day plans," were developed and discussed. Although these plans were limited in many ways, they were very different from earlier reform programs. First, they were, for the time, reasonably comprehensive. Second, they prescribed a specific timetable, including the sequencing of key changes. Third, they called for fundamental change in areas such as prices and privatization. To put it another way, though they varied in style and to some degree in substance, all the plans included a discussion of a shift to a market economy

TABLE 15.1   The Soviet Economy Under Perestroika

	Average Annual Rate of Growth				
	1986	1987	1988	1989	1990
Gross domestic product[a]	4.1	0.3	2.2	1.4	−2.0
Per capita consumption[b]	−2.1	0.4	3.0	3.2	n.a.[e]
Consumer price index (1980 = 100)	111.0	116.0	119.0	122.0	139.0
Soviet exports[c]	97.0	107.7	110.7	109.3	104.1
Soviet imports[c]	88.9	96.0	107.3	114.7	120.9
Net hard-current debt[d]	20.9	26.4	26.8	36.1	45.4

[a] GDP is measured by sector of origin at factor cost in 1928 prices.
[b] 1982 established prices.
[c] Includes all trade, in billions of current U.S. dollars.
[d] Gross debt minus assets in western banks, in millions of current U.S. dollars.
[e] not available

Source: Central Intelligence Agency, *Handbook of Economic Statistics 1990* (Washington, D.C.: CIA, 1990); and *Beyond Perestroika: The Soviet Economy in Crisis* (Washington, D.C.: CIA, 1991).

(transition) rather than simply the reform of existing institutions. It was in this era that the concept of transition from plan to market was born.

The performance problems of the Soviet economy became markedly more serious in 1990 and 1991. Following the coup of August 19, 1991, Mikhail Gorbachev resigned as head of the Communist party on August 25, effectively bringing the power of that body to an end. Thereafter, the republics of the Soviet Union began to declare their independence from Moscow, and by December of 1991, the Soviet Union as a political and economic entity came to an end. Boris Yeltsin, the leader of a new Russia, had been active on both the political and the economic front and was prepared to move quickly in the new era.

The Transition Era

As the Soviet Union entered its final days in 1991, the stamp of Boris Yeltsin, then head of the Russian republic, became increasingly apparent. By October of 1991, Yeltsin was promoting a transition plan that focused on macroeconomic stabilization, the freeing of prices, the expansion of foreign trade, and privatization of the means of production. These steps were fundamentally more aggressive than those developed by Gorbachev under perestroika, though during the early months of transition, political turmoil and a generally recalcitrant population limited the transition process and its initial achievements. It is important to reemphasize that political stability is critical if transition programs are to be carefully developed and fully implemented. Political stability in the Russia case has been precarious at the central level, not to mention at the regional and local levels.

The Political Setting

Our discussion of the basics of transition in Chapter 14 focused on the economic rather than the political aspects of transition. However, the policy process is based in the political sphere, which changed radically after the demise of the Soviet Union.[5] Boris Yeltsin having been elected president of Russia in June of 1991, the end of the Soviet era (which occurred formally in December of 1991) resulted in a new country to be run by a president, a cabinet, and a legislature. The basis of this political structure became the Russian constitution, which was approved in 1993 to replace the last Soviet constitution. Under the new arrangements, the president is elected for up to two four year terms (Yeltsin was elected for his second term in June of 1996).

The president appoints the prime minister and the cabinet and a number of other top officials, with legislative ratification. The cabinet structure is responsible for the management and operation of the various components of the economy.

Under the 1993 Russian constitution, Russia is governed by a bicameral **Federal Assembly** that consists of an upper house (the **Federation Council**) and a lower house (the **State Duma**). The Federation Council consists of two representatives each from 89 regions of Russia, whereas the State Duma comprises 450 representatives.[6]

The early history of transition in Russia is a history of struggle between the president and the legislature. Although the attempted coup in August of 1993 has been the most open demonstration of this friction, the persistent difficulties of developing and implementing transition policies, and ongoing personnel shifts, confirm the pattern. As in any emerging democracy, the problems of defining the boundaries of central and local power remain, along with unresolved issues of policy formulation and implementation. Although the Russian constitution and associated laws provide the framework of a market economy, it will be apparent as we discuss the economics of transition that the setting is fragile, which greatly complicates the actual process of transition.

Since the beginning of the transition era, the focus of concern about the viability of transition in Russia has shifted to some degree. At the outset, there was discussion about whether the transition process might be reversed, and if so, what would be the implications for transition policies, specifically the speed and sequencing of changes. As we come to the end of the 1990s, the focus is much more on sustaining systemic change and implementing polices such that the Russian economy can reverse its significant economic downslide and achieve positive economic growth. As we will see, the output of the Russian economy fell by some 50 percent through 1996, though in 1997, positive economic growth was achieved for the first time since the beginning of the transition era.

Microeconomic Issues

In Chapter 14 we emphasized the fact that the creation of private property is fundamental to instituting a market economy. Privatization has moved forward quickly in Russia, and yet the underlying story is complex.[7]

In January of 1992, there was a general freeing of prices (with important exceptions, such as in the energy sector). At the same time, foreign exchange was liberalized, trade restrictions removed, and an effort made to achieve budget balance through new taxes and restrictions on government expenditures. These programs bore the stamp of Deputy Prime Minister Egor Gaidar, who had been named Yeltsin's major economic advisor. Although there was an attempt to index wages, the general result was inevitable: Significant though varied price increases, at first roughly double the increase in money wages, led to a notable decline in real wages. Early changes in the state budget and an initially very restrictive monetary policy caused an immediate but short-term shortage of roubles. At the end of 1992, the prices of consumer goods had increased by approximately 2,300 percent over the previous year, whereas for the same period, money wages had increased by roughly 994 percent.[8]

Through decrees beginning in late 1991, the privatization of industry and services began; changes in agriculture were handled separately in a decree of April of 1992.[9] The pace of privatization was slow and uneven at first. However, in October of 1992, the Russian government (through the **State Property Committee**) began to issue **vouchers**, and the pace of privatization increased significantly through 1993 and 1994.[10] This early stage of Russian privatization meant that those holding vouchers (managers, workers, or the general population) could exchange them for shares in the enterprises that had been converted into joint stock companies (what we have described as corporatization). Vouchers could also be used in auctions, or they could be utilized through private investment funds. The rules governing the distribution of enterprise shares were specified, although the ultimate distribution of shares turned out to be different from that envisioned when the rules were drawn up, leading to concern about some individuals exploiting their position to seize control through what would be termed insider privatization.

In 1994 a second phase of privatization began when the process of selling enterprise shares was opened up through auctions and other mechanisms, with the objective of substantially completing the privatization process. Between 1992 and 1996, roughly 120,000 Russian enterprises, accounting for approximately 65 percent of the industrial capital stock, became private, though there was significant variation by region and by sector.[11] By the end of 1995, roughly 34 percent of Russian medium- and large-scale enterprises were still in state hands, the remainder having been privatized through equal-access vouchers (11 percent) and management–employee buyouts (55 percent).[12] At first the valuation process was carried out in 1992 prices; then, beginning in mid-1994, the prices for January of 1994 were used. Privatization in this phase was intended to include large state firms, but in 1995 additional measures were taken to privatize these firms through the granting of equity to banks in return for their providing long-term loans.

Privatization moved in yet another direction in 1998. Whereas the emphasis was first on smaller and thereafter on medium-sized and large state enterprises, contemporary policy is focusing on the privatization of the largest and most successful Russian enterprise, such as utilities and energy enterprises to be privatized through stock offerings. By any standard, privatization in Russia has been aggressively pursued. The next major step, as we will see later in this chapter, is **restructuring**, or the modification of decision-making arrangements within enterprises to introduce a hard budget constraint, increase efficiency, and contribute to positive economic growth through the end of the decade.

Macroeconomic Perspectives

From a macroeconomic perspective, the initial stages of transition were difficult. The end of the administrative-command economy put enterprises in an awkward position. With the gradual elimination of state orders and the collapse of inter-republic trade, enterprise activity plummeted and inventories increased. Traditional sources of state revenue declined sharply in the absence of a Western-style system of taxation to replace dwindling enterprise contributions. At the same time, subsidies continued, and enterprises, unable to pay their bills, accumulated a large volume of inter-enterprise debt.[13]

In a very real sense, the early stages of transition were difficult because market-type guidance mechanisms were being introduced (market price for both inputs and outputs). Enterprises were increasingly being required to respond to these signals, yet they had to do so with little or no market infrastructure. We turn now to an examination of developments in both the monetary and the fiscal sector of the Russian transition economy.

The most fundamental macroeconomic element in the transition economies has been the development of capital markets for the purpose of **financial intermediation**, or the channeling of savings into investment. In the emerging market economy, savings may come from individuals or businesses, from abroad, or through the government when taxes exceed government spending.[14]

The development of capital markets in Russia has been of special importance because of the absence of these arrangements and the use of very different mechanisms during the Soviet era. Although the Soviet economy was characterized by high investment ratios, investment had fallen to negligible amounts in 1990 and had declined every year thereafter. In this setting, the creating of new financial mechanisms—and especially the emergence of a modern banking system—became critical.

Although financial intermediation takes place through a variety of mechanisms, the banking system is fundamental in the Russian case. The transition era has been characterized by the emergence of many small, private banks and by the reorganization of Soviet-era banks. The period from 1991 to 1995 heralded significant legislation on banking, but it was not until the passage of the Federal Law of the CBR in 1995 that the **Central Bank of Russia (CBR)** emerged as the central bank, with responsibility for the value of the Russian ruble and a new role vis-à-vis the state budget.[15]

During the early 1990s, the Russian banks had limited ability to make loans. Moreover, the persistence of directed credits to enterprises, along with the ability of the CBR to grant credits to finance the budget deficit directly, created the potential for serious inflation. Although the legislation passed in 1995 significantly improved the operation of the CBR, the Russian banking system still suffers from an industry-specific focus and a lack of financial depth. Both deposits and loans are limited in a setting where there is limited faith in the banking system.

Banks should be a major source of credit, but in the early years of the Russian transition, cash was provided to enterprises by government grants through the banks, a system subsequently but slowly replaced by the emergence of treasury bills (GKOs).[16] In addition, as we have emphasized, there has been a great deal of inter-enterprise credit in Russia. These arrears, which are large in magnitude, reflect a number of factors present in Russia: a continuation of Soviet-era behavior, the lack of healthy and transparent financial markets, and high inflation.

An important aspect of the macroeconomics of transition has been the creation of **equity markets**. Various types of investment funds emerged quickly in Russia, and the onset of privatization in 1992 led to the creation of stock markets characterized largely by over-the-counter trading of a limited number of stocks with limited value. The combination of a burdensome tax system, poor registration practices, and a general lack of transparency in these markets has limited the significance of their activities.

An important aspect of the emerging financial arrangements is the ability to conduct both monetary and fiscal policy. Indeed, at the time of the Soviet collapse and the beginning of the transition era, a number of issues complicated the policy setting. No such policies existed in the Soviet era, and until the institution of the CBR, there was no central bank capable of conducting monetary policy in an emerging market setting. Moreover, the collapse of the USSR created fifteen new countries, a setting where once-domestic issues quickly became foreign issues—a case rather different from that in many of the other transition economies. However, as we have noted, the banking legislation developed in 1995 effectively brought to an end the era in which government deficits were, in effect, directly financed by the bank. In this setting, monetary and fiscal policy have been closely intertwined through the financing of the government sector.

During transition, the Russian government has faced significant and continuing demands on the expenditure side, with a collapsing set of arrangements on the revenue side. Privatization brought to an end to direct state access to enterprise revenues, although the emergence of a new "Western-style" tax system placed modest burdens on individuals and major burdens on the enterprise sector. However, the complexity of the tax system and the problems of avoidance and evasion have seriously hamstrung the revenue side—a major issue for the development of a new tax code. The net result has been a significant (though difficult to measure) budget deficit.[17] However, although there is dispute over the magnitude of the deficit, alternative measures indicate a decline in the deficit as a share of GDP after 1994 (see Table 15.2)

Thus the combination of a reduction in the rate of growth of the money supply and more realistic financing of the government sector has reduced the inflationary pressures in the Russian economy. In 1997 the volume of domestic financing (GKOs) increased, along with Russian access to the Eurobond market. It is too early to make meaningful predictions about the contemporary macroeconomy of Russia, but the emergence of basic capital markets has replaced the mechanisms of the administrative-command era. At the same time, these debt and equity markets are shallow and lack the transparency necessary to play a greater role in the Russian economy. Their importance must grow over time if they are to contribute to the improving performance of the Russian economy.

TABLE 15.2   The Russian Budget Deficit (Deficit/GDP)

	International Monetary Fund Definition	Ministry of Finance Definition
1993	6.5	9.8
1994	11.4	10.7
1995	5.4	3.0
1996 (estimate)	7.7	3.3

Source: Russian European Center for Economic Policy, *Russian Economic Trends,* April 29, 1997, p. 2.

The Russian Economy: Performance and Sectoral Issues

Throughout our discussion of transition economies, we have emphasized the distinction between performance indicators, such as economic growth, and longer-term restructuring indicators, such as privatization and structural (sectoral) shifts in resource allocation. Although Russia is in the early stages of transition, it is important that we learn from the available preliminary evidence. We turn first to a discussion of basic performance indicators, after which we examine general patterns of restructuring.

Performance[18]

In Table 15.3 we have assembled basic performance indicators for the contemporary Russian economy. Despite the real difficulties of generating and interpreting accurate data in a transition era, these data nevertheless provide some guidance to trends in the Russian economy.[19]

First, although estimates have differed, the expected significant drop in output materialized, with a possible trough in 1992. The largest single-year decline in real GDP, a drop of 14.5 percent, occurred in 1992.[20] The decline in investment is understandable and was especially sharp in 1992. These patterns represent a significant decrease in the activity of large state enterprises, only partially offset by the smaller, emerging private sector. Significant annual reductions in output continued through 1996.[21]

When prices were released in January of 1992, there was a general expectation of significant increases driven in part by the perception of existing excess demand and also by the pre-existing distortion of prices. As we have noted, these expectations were realized, as prices increased sharply in 1992 and again during 1993. Although the prices of both producer and consumer goods continued to increase through 1994, the magnitude of these increases was less than in earlier years. By 1997 the rate of inflation had been significantly reduced.[22]

There has been considerable discussion and debate over the issue of levels of living in the post-Soviet era. A variety of indicators are used to judge changes in levels of living and to make comparisons with other countries, but such indicators of

TABLE 15.3   Russia: Basic Performance Trends

	1990	1991	1992	1993	1994	1995	1996	1997
Real GDP (% change)	0.1	−13.1	−14.5	−8.7	−12.6	−4.0	−6.0	0.4
Investment: (% change, constant prices)		−15.0	−40.0	−12.0	−26.0	−13.0	−18.0	n.a.[a]
Retail prices (end of period)		144	2318	841	203	131	22	17
Money supply (end of period)	17.6	126	643	409	200	126	34	n.a.
Unemployment	n.a.	n.a.	n.a.	5.5	7.1	8.2	9.3	n.a.

[a] not available

Source: Economics of Transition 5, 1 (1997), Tables 1, 9.

standard of living are not generally very reliable, so it is difficult to draw firm conclusions. The unemployment rate, based on International Labor Organization definitions, was just over 9 percent in 1996 and 1997.[23] The available data on unemployment have indicated low levels during the Russian transition, though the reported modest levels of unemployment are often viewed with skepticism. For example, it is not uncommon for a person working in a failing enterprise to be on "extended leave." In addition, part-time employment and the holding of several jobs by individuals are widespread. The generally unattractive nature of official unemployment benefits offers little incentive for the genuinely unemployed to apply for them. Thus actual levels of unemployment may be significantly higher than those officially reported.

Though money wages have risen, we have already noted that prices increased considerably faster, causing a significant decline in real wages until the mid-1990s.[24] The average monthly money wage in medium-sized and large enterprises in 1996 was 805,924 rubles, an increase of 12 percent in real terms over 1995.[25] However, wage arrears remained substantial, at 25.7 percent of GDP, in the middle of 1997.[26] We would expect changes in the distribution of income and, especially, increases in the proportion of the labor force at the lower end of the distribution. Although the evidence is difficult to gather, it is likely that there has been a significant widening in the gap between rich and poor. According to World Bank estimates, the Gini co-efficient for Russia in 1993 was 48, an increase of some 14–24 points from 1987 to 1988, whereas in 1993, judged on the basis of income levels, some 38 million Russians were below the poverty level.[27] The minimum (monthly) money wage in 1997 was 83,490 rubles, whereas the monthly subsistence minimum was roughly 407,000 rubles, and some 21 percent of the population lived below this level.[28]

It is difficult to summarize these trends. Most were expected, and the pattern of changes over time offers some encouragement. However, comparing these data to similar data for Hungary and Poland suggests that the latter have made it past the economic trough much more quickly, though with more open evidence of costs—for example, high levels of unemployment.

Restructuring

Ultimately, the success of transition will depend on restructuring, or the shift from the command economy to market arrangements. There are problems in assessing restructuring. First, the time frame is unclear. How long should fundamental changes in resource allocation take? Societies cannot be expected to resolve such a basic issue quickly. Second, the generation of accurate data and hence the measurement of change are difficult in a time of transition.

This is a comment we have made frequently in this book, yet it cannot be overemphasized. Some would argue with good cause that many of the numbers we are examining during transition represent broad trends at best. At worst, they represent inaccurate pictures and are becoming less meaningful over time. For example, when firms are privatized, basic definitions are complex issues, and when new tax arrangements are put in place, there are strong incentives to avoid accurate reporting. Reporting problems are especially serious for small cooperative firms and for retail and service-sector operations. For example, data on the share of total output from the subsidiary economy (however defined) must be suspect, and yet we would expect this sector to be an important and potentially growing component of total output. In this sense, we may be misled even by basic output series and especially by short-term shifts in those series.

Ideally, it would be useful to know about the role of the state in the new Russian economy, the expansion of the private sector, and the impact of both on the structure of the Russian economy. The impact of privatization will take time to discover, but the *pace* of privatization, though initially quite slow, accelerated significantly through 1997. As we have already emphasized, however, privatization is an initial step. Even when the privatization of large firms has proceeded successfully, restructuring (and the conversion of those firms involved in military production) has been much more difficult.[29]

The concept of restructuring involves fundamental changes in the organizational arrangements of the enterprise and in the nature of the decision-making process within the enterprise. Through privatization, one expects both structure and rules to change such that new coalitions of influence emerge within the enterprise, in a sense doing things differently than in the past. Thus in newly privatized enterprises, where in the past there were soft budget constraints, direct access to state capital funding, and production of inappropriate or nonmarketable products using outdated technology, major changes could be expected. Have such changes in fact taken place?

Restructuring in medium-sized and large enterprises has been hindered by the absence of depth in capital markets and by the fact that the methods of privatization, although they speed up the process, have nevertheless not provided capital for modernization. In these types of enterprises, there has been a tendency for viable subunits to thrive while larger and more questionable components of the enterprise remain troubled. Whereas official state statistics tell us something about the overall pace of privatization, sample surveys of enterprises are beginning to reveal a picture of how enterprise behavior is changing. The evidence suggests that even though managerial control in Russian firms remains strong, there is a considerable degree of managerial consultation in a setting of reasonably dispersed ownership arrangements. From a performance perspective, there is evidence that as firms were privatized, their output declined, as did their levels of employment—both results understandable in light of the overall trends in the Russian economy after 1990. However, there is also evidence that restructuring differs considerably by region and especially by industrial sector.[30]

Sectoral Issues

The process of transition will have a significant impact on every sector of the Russian economy, whether the urban sector, the defense sector, energy, or the agricultural sector. Of special interest, however, are developments in both agriculture and foreign trade.

Although many Western observers had viewed the rural economy as likely to be the basis for the beginnings of a shift from plan to market, the transitions of the former Soviet Union and Eastern Europe have generally not followed this pattern. In this (and in other respects), they differ markedly from the changes that have occurred in China.

Whereas Gorbachev was reluctant to move ahead with privatization in Russia, Yeltsin moved aggressively, but not in agriculture. By the latter part of 1991, legislation had provided a number of options for collective and state farms, with change being implemented mainly through local channels. Individual peasant farms could emerge, joint stock companies could be formed, producer cooperatives could be formed, or farms could remain essentially in the then-existing form.[31]

Judged by the amount of land that has, by some definition, been privatized, change has been very slow. At the same time, much of the conversion of state and collective farms to joint stock companies has been primarily an action on paper, though decision-making arrangements on farms have changed.

Although agricultural output has declined, the amount of decline has generally been less than the decline in total output because of a much sharper decline in industrial output. Moreover, the liberalization of prices in 1992 and the gradual emergence of markets seem to have eliminated what was at that time perceived to be a serious excess demand for food products. The general patterns of contemporary Russian agricultural performance are presented in Table 15.4. It is also important to note that there have been significant structural changes in the agricultural sector. Market forces are playing a substantially increased role, leading both to changes in domestic production and consumption patterns and to changes in agricultural trade patterns. With prices largely set in markets, the state's role in agriculture (both state purchases and state subsidies) has declined. The importance of the livestock sector has decreased, meat imports have risen, and imports of grains have fallen sharply.

Fundamental change in the Russian rural economy has been very limited. As we have emphasized, formal changes in ownership arrangements of state and collective farms have not included much restructuring. The absence of significant land markets, the large amounts of debt, and the lack of profitability of farms are issues to be faced in the future. In this setting, improvements in agricultural performance can be expected to be modest.

TABLE 15.4   Agricultural Performance in Russia During Transition

	Meat (thousand tons)	Milk (thousand tons)	Eggs (millions)	Grain[a] (thousand tons)
1991	9,315	51,886	46,875	116,676
1993	7,513	46,524	40,297	99,000
1995	5,930	39,306	33,714	63,400
1996	5,350	36,000	31,500	69,285

[a] Total grains (cleanweight), calendar year.

Source: U.S. Department of Agriculture, *International Agriculture and Trade Reports: Former USSR* (Washington, D.C.: USDA, May 1996 and 1997); U.S. Department of Agriculture, *Former USSR Update* (Washington, D.C.: USDA, October 1996).

One of the important developments of the Russian transition has been the change in the foreign trade sector.[32] We emphasized in Chapter 13 the peculiar nature and impact of foreign trade arrangements and policies during the administrative-command era. Moreover, even during the Gorbachev era, changes in the Soviet trade regime did not resolve the complaints Gorbachev voiced about the lack of access to world technology and the inadequate diversification of Soviet exports. In short, Russia entered the era of transition with serious distortions and imbalances in the foreign trade sector.

Not only was Russia saddled by an outmoded and totally inappropriate set of foreign trade arrangements and policies, but any movement of the Russian economy toward an open posture in foreign trade necessitated a convertible ruble. However, in the face of price liberalization, financial markets in their infancy, and a general lack of legal infrastructure, a changing regime of multiple exchange rates gradually emerged over time and offered increasing degrees of access to foreign currencies, in part supported by a stabilization fund provided through the International Monetary Fund. Beginning in April of 1991, there was a "market" rate of exchange for the ruble, along with other rates set for special purposes. These latter rates were employed because those who were involved in exporting were required to remit a portion of their export earnings to the state to be used for servicing Russian foreign debt. During the early years of Russian transition, there was ongoing change in the nature of the currency rules, but by 1996 the ruble was fully convertible.

Although the money exchange rate of the ruble has declined throughout the transition era and has varied over time, the real exchange rate increased after 1992. Moreover, the Russian government has been able to keep the ruble within a set corridor. Critical to Russian transition is the emergence of new trade arrangements and patterns.

During the transition era, several developments have seriously hampered the smooth adjustment of the foreign trade sector from the command to the market era. First, trade among the former Soviet republics collapsed as the republics became independent, gradually pursuing the introduction of their own independent national currencies.[33] Although there would be continuing discussion of a "ruble zone," close integration between Russia and other former republics was actually sustained only in limited cases such as Belarus. Moreover, the fact that these new countries had been a single country for so long presented important trading complications. Second, the CMEA system of foreign trade disintegrated.

The net result of changes in the transition era has been a sharp drop in Russian foreign trade during transition and a significant redirection of that trade. Between 1990 and 1992, the volume of Russian exports fell by roughly 50 percent while the volume of Russian imports fell by more than 50 percent. There was understandably a sharp reduction in trade with former CMEA countries, a reduction greater than that with other non-CMEA countries. Moreover, the initial commodity composition of Russian foreign trade has been exports of raw materials and imports of consumer goods and technology. We summarize aggregate trends in Table 15.5.

With the transition to markets, the Russian payments position has taken on new importance. Through the mid-1990s, Russia had a positive balance on current account,

TABLE 15.5   Aspects of Russian Foreign Trade

	Exports[a]	Imports[a]	Real Exchange Rate
1993	59.7	44.3	225.1
1994	67.5	50.5	107.3
1995	81.1	60.8	79.2
1996	89.2	62.3	59.7

[a] Including trade with the CIS, in millions of U.S. dollars.

Source: Russian European Center for Economic Policy, *Russian Economic Trends,* April 29, 1997, pp. 4, 6.

resulting from a strong export position in spite of net import of services. However, it increased its net indebtedness to foreigners from roughly 10 percent of GDP in 1990 to about 33 percent of GDP by 1995.[34] This debt burden is not especially high, but Russian access to capital markets will be determined in part by the future ability of the Russian government to service external debt obligations.

Unfortunately, the role of foreign investment in Russia has been minimal. For example, according to World Bank estimates of the sum of direct investment inflows for the period 1989–1995, Russia received 3.9 billion dollars (roughly 2 percent of 1994 GDP), whereas Hungary for the same period received 10.6 billion dollars (roughly 30 percent of 1994 GDP).[35] These are extreme cases, but they indicate the limited importance of direct foreign investment in Russia. In addition, in recent years, whereas foreigners have purchased Russian securities, Russians themselves have purchased foreign securities in greater magnitude. Both of these trends are examples of **capital flight**, and the actual volumes are undoubtedly larger as a result of unregistered transactions.

Summary

Russia is a contemporary political power whose transition from plan to market necessarily captures our attention. Although Russia enjoys great natural wealth, the breakup of the Soviet Union created both political and economic realities quite different from those in most other transition economies.

The empirical evidence suggests that the path of Russian transition has been difficult. The policy framework for transition has emerged in a volatile political setting, and the early stages of transition were especially difficult. Even so, privatization has proceeded, prices for the most part have been freed from state control, and macroeconomic balance has been achieved and sustained. The output of the economy has been reduced by roughly 50 percent with declines in both industry and agriculture, the former more severe than the latter. The decline of output was finally arrested in 1997 with the achievement of a modest but positive rate of economic growth of output.

The next stage of transition in Russia has begun; it involves subtle, difficult, but critical issues. On the microeconomic side, enterprise restructuring is of major importance as decision-making arrangements change and efficiency objectives are pursued. Market forces in both product and factor markets must be enhanced.

On the macroeconomic side, financial markets (debt markets and equity markets) must grow in importance, yet to do so they must increase in sophistication and transparency, and an appropriate legal infrastructure must evolve. The financial infrastructure of the Russian economy will emerge as the state budget on both the revenue and expenditure sides grows in importance as a component of the Russian economy.

The initial stages of change in the Russian foreign trade sector have been completed in the sense that the old trading arrangements have been dismantled and new trading arrangements have emerged. Currently convertibility has been achieved, although the stability of the currency remains a matter of concern. The real value of the ruble increased after a period of significant decline, but changes in the geographic and commodity composition of Russian foreign trade have been slow to take place.

Agriculture has not been a success story of the Russian transition process. Although the decline in agricultural output has been less than that in industrial output, organizational change in agriculture—especially privatization—has been formal and modest.

The Russian transition has been difficult and is currently entering a new stage. Initial changes have been implemented. The next task is achieving a significant rate of economic growth.

Key Terms

perestroika	vouchers
democratization	joint stock companies
glasnost	corporatization
zastoia	insider privatization
human factor	restructuring
radical economic reform	financial intermediation
transition	Central Bank of Russia
Federation Council	equity markets
State Duma	debt markets
State Property Committee	GKOs
wages arrears	

Notes

1. For a discussion of the Soviet era, see Paul R. Gregory and Robert C. Stuart, *Russian and Soviet Economic Structure and Performance*, 6th ed. (Reading, Mass.: Addison Wesley Longman, 1998).

2. A great deal has been written about perestroika. For a summary, see Paul R. Gregory and Robert C. Stuart, *Russian and Soviet Economic Structure and Performance*, Ch. 12; Anders Aslund, *Gorbachev's Struggle for Economic Reform*, rev. ed. (London: Pinter Publishers, 1991); Padma Desai, *Perestroika in Perspective* (Princeton, N.J.: Princeton University Press, 1991); E. A. Hewett, *Reforming the Soviet Economy* (Washington, D.C.: The Brookings Institution, 1988); Joseph L. Wieczynski, ed., *The Gorbachev Encyclopedia* (Salt Lake City, Utah: Charles Schlacks, Jr., Publisher, 1993).

3. For a discussion of the enterprise law, potentially central to changes in planning and management, see R. E. Ericson, "The New Enterprise Law," *Harriman Forum* 1 (1988).

4. For a discussion of these early years of transition, see J. H. Noren, "The Russian Economic Reform: Progress and Prospects," *Soviet Economy* 8, 1 (1992), 3–41.

5. For a discussion of political issues, see J. W. Hahn, ed., *Democratization in Russia* (Armonk, N.Y.: Sharpe, 1996).

6. For a discussion of legal issues, see G. B. Smith, *Reforming the Russian Legal System* (New York: Cambridge University Press, 1996).

7. There is a large and growing literature on privatization in general and on privatization in Russia in particular. For a survey of the Russian case, see Joseph R. Blasi, Maya Kroumova, and Douglas Kruse, *Kremlin Capitalism* (Ithaca, N.Y.: Cornell University Press, 1997); Maxim Boycko, Andrei Shleifer, and Robert Vishny, *Privatizing Russia* (Cambridge, Mass.: M.I.T. Press, 1997).

8. *Economics of Transition* 5, 1 (1997), 263.

9. Although agriculture has been subjected to considerable legislative activity, the concept of a land market in Russia is limited and shallow largely because of unresolved controversies about land use. A land code is scheduled to be completed in 1998.

10. These aspects of Russian privatization are discussed in depth in Paul R. Gregory and Robert C. Stuart, *Russian and Soviet Economic Structure and Performance*, Ch. 14.

11. *Ibid.*, p. 301.

12. The World Bank, *World Development Report 1996* (Washington, D.C.: The World Bank, 1009), 53.

13. Inter-enterprise debt is a problem in that it is large in magnitude and substantially beyond the control of monetary authorities. For a discussion, see B. W. Ickes and Randi Ryterman, "The Enterprise Arrears Crisis in Russia," *Post-Soviet Affairs* 8, 4 (1992), 331–361.

14. For a discussion of capital markets in Russia, see Paul R. Gregory and Robert C. Stuart, *Russian and Soviet Economic Structure and Performance*, Ch. 16.

15. For detail on the Russian banking system, see J. Rautava, ed., *Russia's Financial Markets and the Banking System in Transition* (Helsinki: Bank of Finland, 1995); A. Robinson, *Russia and Its Banking System* (London: 1995).

16. The GKO, or *gosudarstvennye kratkosrochnye obligatsii,* is a short-term debt instrument similar to a treasury bill in the United States.

17. The size of the budget deficit has been a matter of controversy largely because of measurement problems. Although the magnitude of the deficit grew through 1994 (in absolute terms and as a share of GDP), the latter measure peaked at about 10 percent in 1994.

18. Note that in January of 1998 the ruble was redenominated, dividing by 1,000. Unless otherwise noted, pre-1988 numbers are reported in pre-redenomination values.

19. The transition era is characterized by major increases in the amounts and types of data available, often using generally accepted definitions. However, for a variety of reasons, the available data are fragile. For example, accurate measurement of change is difficult when the magnitude of change is large and reporting systems are not necessarily in place.

Moreover, many of our traditional performance indicators do not capture the impact of the subsidiary economy, which arguably is important in transition settings.

20. *The Economics of Transition* 5, 1 (1997), 263.
21. There are differing estimates of Russian GDP. According to *The Economics of Transition* 5, 1 (1997), 263, real GDP was projected to grow by 1.5 percent in 1997. According to the *Wall Street Journal,* January 28, 1998, 1, the Russian GDP increased in 1997 by 0.4 percent. Whatever the actual number, if it is positive, then a lengthy and significant economic decline has finally come to an end.
22. One source estimates the increase in prices in 1997 to have been 11 percent. See. U.S. Department of Commerce, *Bisnis*, January 30, 1998, 1.
23. The official data can be found in Goskomstat Rossii, *Rossiia v. Tsifrakh* (Moscow: Goskomstat, 1997), section 3.
24. For example, the annual average increases in wages outstripped those in consumer prices through 1995. See *The Economic of Transition* 5, 1 (1997), 263.
25. *Rossiia v. Tsifrakh* 1997, 59; U.S. Department of Commerce, Business Information Service, *Bisnis,* January 30, 1998, 1.
26. *Russian Economic Trends* 9.
27. For a discussion of these issues and the data, see The World Bank, *World Development Report 1996* (Washington, D.C.: The World Bank, 1996), Ch. 4.
28. *Bisnis*, 1.
29. The literature on restructuring is emerging in the mid-1990s. See, for example, Milica Uvalic and Daniel Vaughan-Whitehead, eds., *Privatization Surprises in Transition Economies* (Lyme, Conn.: Edward Elgar, 1997); Trevor Buck, Igor Filatotchev, Mike Wright, and Yves van Frausum, "The Process and Impact of Privatization in Russia and Ukraine," *Comparative Economic Studies* 38, 2/3 (Summer/Fall, 1996), 45–69; Trevor Buck, Igor Filatotchev, and Mike Wright, "Employee Buyouts and the Transformation of Russian Industry," *Comparative Economic Studies* 36, 2 (Summer, 1994), 1–15; Susan J. Linz, "Production and Employment in Privatized Firms in Russia," *Comparative Economic Studies* 36, 3 (Fall 1994), 104–113; Susan J. Linz, "Russian Firms in Transition: Champions, Challengers and Chaff," *Comparative Economic Studies* 39, 2 (Summer 1997), 1–36; Saul Estrin *et al.,* "Shocks and Adjustment by Firms in Transition: A Comparative Study," *Journal of Comparative Economics* 21, 2 (October 1995), 131–153.
30. See Susan J. Linz, "Red Executives in Russia's Transition Economy," *Post-Soviet Geography and Economics* 37, 10 (1996), 633–651.
31. For a discussion of initial changes in agriculture, see Stephen K. Wegren, "Private Farming and Agrarian Reform in Russia," *Problems of Communism* 41, 3 (1992), 107–121; R. J. Mcintyre, "The Phantom of Transition: Privatization of Agriculture in the Former Soviet Union and Eastern Europe," *Comparative Economic Studies* 34 (Fall–Winter, 1992), 81–95.
32. For a discussion of Russian foreign trade and references to the literature, see Paul R. Gregory and Robert C. Stuart, *Russian and Soviet Economic Structure and Performance*, Ch. 17.
33. This early collapse was of particular importance in the Russian case. For a discussion, see David Tarr, "Terms of Trade Effect of Moving to World Prices on Countries in the Former Soviet Union," *Journal of Comparative Economics* 18, 1 (February 1994).
34. Paul R. Gregory and Robert C. Stuart, *Russian and Soviet Economic Structure and Performance*, 401–402.
35. The World Bank, *World Development Report 1996* (Washington, D.C.: The World Bank, 1996), 64.

References

The Soviet Era

Paul R. Gregory and Robert C. Stuart, *Russian and Soviet Economic Structure and Perform-ance* 6th ed. (Reading, Mass.: Addison Wesley Longman, 1998).
Tania Konn ed., *Soviet Studies Guide* (London and New Jersey: Bowker-Saur, 1992).

Perestroika

Anders Aslund, *Gorbachev's Struggle for Economic Reform,* rev. ed. (London: Pinter Pub-lishers, 1991).
Padma Desai, *Perestroika in Perspective* (Princeton, N.J.: Princeton University Press.)
E. A. Hewett, *Reforming the Soviet Economy* (Washington, D.C.: The Brookings Institution, 1988).
William Moskoff, *Hard Times: Impoverishment and Protest in the Perestroika Years* (Armonk, N.Y.: Sharpe, 1993).
Joseph L. Wieczynski, ed., *The Gorbachev Encyclopedia* (Salt Lake City, Utah: Charles Schlacks, Jr., Publisher, 1993).

Transition: General Sources

Anders Aslund, ed., *Economic Transformation in Russia* (London: Pinter Publishers, 1994).
Oliver Jean Blanchard, Kenneth A. Froot, and Jeffrey D. Sachs, *The Transition in Eastern Europe*, Vols. 1 and 2 (Chicago and London: University of Chicago Press, 1994).
J. Hahn, "Attitudes Towards Reform Among Provincial Russian Politicians," *Post-Soviet Affairs* 9, 1 (1993), 66–85.
———. ed., *Democratization in Russia* (Armonk, N.Y.: Sharpe, 1996).
Peter Murrell, *et al.,* "Symposium on Economic Transition in the Soviet Union and Eastern Europe," *Journal of Economics Perspectives* 5, 4 (Fall 1991), 3–16.
James H. Noren, "The Russian Economic Reform: Progress and Prospects," *Soviet Economy* 8, 1 (1992), 3–41.
M. Keren and G. Ofer, eds., *Trails of Transition: Economic Reform in the Former Communist Bloc* (Boulder, Colo.: Westview Press, 1994).
Kenneth K. Koford *et al.,* "Symposium: Economic Reform in Eastern Europe and the Former Soviet Union," *Eastern Economic Journal* 19, 3 (Summer 1993), 329–393.
G. B. Smith, *Reforming the Russian Legal System* (New York: Cambridge University Press, 1996).
P. Sutela, ed., *The Russian Economy in Crisis and Transition* (Helsinki: Bank of Finland, 1993).
United States Congress, Joint Economic Committee, *The Former Soviet Union in Transition*, Vols. 1 and 2 (Washington, D.C.: U.S. Government Printing Office, 1993).
The World Bank, *Russian Economic Reform: Crossing the Threshold of Structural Change* (Washington, D.C.: The World Bank, 1992).

Privatization and Restructuring

A. S. Bim, D. C. Jones, and T. Weisskopf, "Hybrid Forms of Enterprise Organization in the Former USSR and the Russian Federation," *Comparative Economic Studies* 35, 1 (Spring 1993), 1–38.

Joseph R. Blasi, Maya Kroumova, and Douglas Kruse, *Kremlin Capitalism* (Ithaca, N.Y.: Cornell University Press, 1997).

Morris Bornstein, "Russia's Mass Privatization Programme," *Communist Economies and Economic Transformation* 6, 4 (1994), 419–457.

Maxim Boycko, Andrei Shleifer, and Robert Vishny, *Privatizing Russia* (Cambridge, Mass.: The M.I.T. Press, 1996).

T. Buck, I. Filatotchev, and M. Wright, "Employee Buyouts and the Transformation of Russian Industry," *Comparative Economic Studies* 39, 2/3 (Summer–Fall 1996), 1–16.

Central Intelligence Agency, *Measuring Russia's Emerging Private Sector* (Washington, D.C.: CIA, 1992).

B. W. Ickes and Randi Ryterman, "The Enterprise Arrears Crisis in Russia," *Post-Soviet Affairs* 8, 4 (1992), 331–361.

G. Krueger, "Transition Strategies of Former State-Owned Enterprises in Russia," *Comparative Economic Studies* 37, 4 (Winter 1995), 89–110.

S. J. Linz, "Russian Firms in Transition: Champions, Challengers, and Chaff," *Comparative Economic Studies* (Summer, 1997), 1–36.

Lynn D. Nelson and Irina Y. Kuzes, "Evaluating the Russian Voucher Privatization Program," *Comparative Economic Studies* 36, 1, (Spring 1994), 55–68.

Andrei Schleifer and Robert W. Vishny, "Privatization in Russia: First Steps" in Oliver Jean Blanchard, Kenneth A. Froot and Jeffrey D. Sachs, *The Transition in Eastern Europe*, Vol. 2 (Chicago: University of Chicago Press, 1994), 137–160.

The Macroeconomy

Richard M. Bird *et al., Decentralization of the Socialist State* (Brookfield, Vt.: Ashgate, 1996).

———, *Russia: The Banking System During Transition* (Washington, D.C.: The World Bank, 1993).

J. Rautava, ed., *Russia's Financial Markets and the Banking Sector in Transition* (Helsinki: Bank of Finland, 1995).

A. Robinson, *Russia and Its Banking System* (London: 1995).

C. I. Wallich, *Russia and the Challenge of Fiscal Federalism* (Brookfield, Vt.: Ashgate, 1996).

The World Bank, *Fiscal Management in Russia* (Washington, D.C.: The World Bank, 1996).

International Trade

G. Michalopoulos and D. Tarr, eds., *Trade Performance and Policy in the Newly Independent States* (Washington, D.C.: The World Bank, 1996).

N. Pautola, "Trends in EU-Russia Trade, Aid, and Cooperation," *Review of Economies in Transition* 4 (1996).

Alan Smith, *Russia and the World Economy: Problems of Integration* (London and New York: Routledge, 1993).

D. Tarr, "The Terms of Trade Effect of Moving to World Prices on Countries of the Former Soviet Union," *Journal of Comparative Economics* 18, 1 (February, 1994).

Agriculture

Frank A. Durgin, "Russia's Private Farm Movement: Background and Perspectives," *The Soviet and Post-Soviet Review* 21, 2–3 (1994).

Zvi Lerman and Karen Brooks, "Russia's Legal Framework for Land Reform and Restructuring," *Problems of Post-Communism* 43, 6 (November–December 1996).

R. J. Mcintyre, "The Phantom of Transition: Privatization of Agriculture in the Former Soviet Union and Eastern Europe," *Comparative Economic Studies* 34, 3–4 (Fall–Winter 1992), 81–95.

Don Van Atta, ed., *The Farmer Threat: The Political Economy of Agrarian Reform in Post-Soviet Russia* (Boulder, Colo.: Westview, 1993).

Stephen K. Wegren, "Private Farming and Agrarian Reform in Russia," *Problems of Communism* 41, 3 (1992), 107–121.

———, ed., *Land Reform in the Former Soviet Union and Eastern Europe* (New York: Routledge, 1998).

———, "Land Reform and the Land Market in Russia: Operation, Constraints, and Prospects," *Europe-Asia Studies* 49, 6 (September 1997).

Stephen K. Wegren and Frank A. Durgin, "The Political Economy of Private Farming in Russia," *Comparative Economic Studies* 39, 3–4 (Fall–Winter 1997), 1–24.

Data and Commentary

Central Intelligence Agency, *Handbook of International Statistics* (Washington, D.C.: CIA, annual).

———, *World Fact Book* (Washington, D.C.: CIA, annual).

The Economist, Intelligence Unit, *Quarterly Reports* (London: *The Economist*).

The Economics of Transition: Reports and Statistical Data (Oxford: England: Oxford University Press).

Goskomstat, *Rossia v. Tsifrakh 1997* (Russia in Figures 1997) (Moscow: Goskomstat, 1997).

International Monetary Fund, *International Financial Statistics: Supplement on Countries of the Former Soviet Union* (Washington, D.C.: International Monetary Fund, 1993).

Russian Economic Trends (Lawrence, Kansas: Whurr Publishers, quarterly).

OECD, *Short-Term Economic Indicators: Transition Economies* (Paris: OECD, quarterly).

———, *National Accounts for the Former Soviet Union* (Paris: OECD, 1993).

———, *Transformation of the Banking System: Portfolio Restructuring, Privatisation, and the Payment System* (Paris: OECD, 1993).

———, *Trends and Policies in Privatisation* (Paris: OECD, biannual).

Jan Vanous, ed., *PlanEcon Reports* (Washington, D.C.: PlanEcon, various.)

Jaclyn Y. Shend, *Agricultural Statistics of the Former USSR Republics and the Baltic States* (Washington, D.C.: U.S. Department of Agriculture, 1993).

The World Bank, *Historically Planned Economies 1993: A Guide to the Data* (Washington, D.C.: The World Bank, 1993).

16

Eastern Europe: Poland, Hungary, and the Czech Republic

Transition patterns deviate considerably one from another in differing real-world settings. Such is certainly the case in the countries of Eastern Europe to which we turn our attention in this chapter.

Although it is difficult to talk about the basic transition issues in isolation from real-world cases, our discussion in Chapter 14 was designed to present contemporary economic thinking on transition somewhat in the abstract, with only limited attention to real-world cases. As we begin our discussion of Eastern Europe, it is important that we understand how these countries differ from others we have studied and how these differences have affected the transition process and will continue to do so.

The East European Setting

Prior to the era of glasnost and perestroika in the mid- and late 1980s, the Soviet Union had not been a leader in the sphere of economic reform and change in the planned socialist economic systems. At the same time, within political constraints, a number of countries in Eastern Europe, such as Hungary, pursued economic reform to such an extent that these countries were in a different position as transition began seriously in the early 1990s. Thus, although the Soviet Union was the political and economic model for Eastern Europe after World War II, important differences had developed between the Soviet Union and the systems of Eastern Europe by the mid-1980s.

First, the economic history of Eastern Europe was very different from that of the Soviet Union. The political and economic systems of Eastern Europe was very different from that of the Soviet Union. The political and economic systems of Eastern Europe were imposed externally by the Soviet Union after World War II, and with the possible exception of Yugoslavia, the arrangements followed the Soviet pattern very closely. The means of production were nationalized, agriculture was collectivized, and balance planning was the primary mechanism for allocating resources. Within a few years after World War II, the economic systems of Eastern Europe closely resembled that of the Soviet Union.

Second, as the breakdown of the older order led to transition in the early 1990s, the nations of Eastern Europe had functioned under the Soviet model for roughly 35 years, a relatively short time compared to the Soviet experience. In contrast, the political and economic arrangements of the administrative-command economy in the Soviet Union had been in place since the late 1920s, a relatively long time. Thus the characteristics of the command economy had a much shorter period of time to take hold in Eastern Europe, making both the memory and the impact of market forces much stronger than in the Soviet Union.

Third, although there was a great deal of discussion in the Soviet Union in the 1920s about the nature of economic growth and development and the appropriateness of alternative strategies, there was no such discussion in Eastern Europe. Indeed, the countries of Eastern Europe were at a very different starting point in the early 1950 than the Soviet Union was in 1928. These differences were important then, and they became important again in the 1990s as these countries reverted to market arrangements.

Fourth, the countries of Eastern Europe differed from one another, but most important, they differed fundamentally from the Soviet Union. Most were relatively small, were resource-poor, and had to rely on foreign trade in any development strategy. If planned socialist systems were **trade-averse,** the impact of such a policy must have been significantly less in these relatively small, trade-oriented nations.

Fifth, there was significant differences in the rigor with which the Soviet model was applied in Eastern Europe and thus in the extent of reform and change during the plan era. For example, one might contrast the extreme variant of Albania, always considered a rigid Stalinist model, with Yugoslavia, a country that broke with the planned socialist model relatively soon after making an attempt to implement it. In the middle ground between these extremes, the cases of Hungary and the Czech Republic were themselves different. Hungary began to experiment with economic reform in the late 1960s, whereas political repression in Czechoslovakia limited the extent and meaning of economic reform. As we will see later, Czechoslovakia became two distinct nations, the Czech Republic and the Slovak Republic, in 1993. In our discussion and presentation of data, when we refer to the period through 1992, we speak of Czechoslovakia, whereas for events from 1993 forward, we refer to the Czech Republic.

Sixth, the countries of Eastern Europe differed significantly from the Soviet Union (and from the now-independent countries) in yet another important dimension: their cultural, religious, and ethnic composition and their experiences based on these differences. Although there are critical exceptions (such as Yugoslavia), in many countries of Eastern Europe there is a measure of ethnic and religious harmony that can provide a basis for political consensus and the stability so necessary for economic change.

As we examine the cases selected for analysis in this chapter, it will be important to appreciate the impact of these forces on the successes and failures of the transition process.

Eastern Europe: Selecting the Cases

In this chapter we pay special attention to Poland, Hungary, and the Czech Republic. These countries were better able to pursue transition and thus have had greater success than other countries. Foreign trade was much more important for these countries than for other East European countries. Economic reform had been pursued in Hungary for decades, and there was, prior to the end of the planned socialist era, a strong political opposition in Poland through the Solidarity movement.

In spite of the differences among them, we will approach Poland, Hungary, and the Czech Republic similarly. We will begin each discussion with a brief account of background and then trace how the transition process unfolded and assess the results achieved.

Poland: From Plan to Market via a Shock Therapy

Until Solidarity won the parliamentary elections in Poland in the summer of 1989, the Polish economy had been, in the post-World War II era, a typical planned socialist economic system following the Soviet model.[1] State ownership predominated, industry was emphasized, and although reform was attempted at various stages, it was largely unsuccessful. Rates of growth of output declined over the years, and the country experienced recurring shortages, inflation, and a declining work ethic.

The critical initial years of transition were 1990 and 1991. The approach was sudden, dubbed **shock therapy** in contrast to the more gradualist approach used elsewhere.[2] In a nutshell, prices were generally freed, the growth of the money supply was controlled, the zloty was made convertible into hard currencies, and steps were taken to control wage increases. Initially, the Polish approach was viewed as unique and laudable, though as we have seen in our discussion of transition issues, the shock therapy approach is not without critics. Before we examine the Polish transition experience in greater detail, some background is necessary.

The Setting

By European standards, Poland is a relatively large country. With a land area just over 300,000 square kilometers, it is slightly more than half the size of France. Moreover, at approximately 38 million, Poland's population is 68 percent the size of France.

Poland can be characterized as a relatively homogeneous society, a factor that greatly facilitates transition. Although there are urban-rural differentials in standard of living, 95 percent of the population of Poland is Catholic, 98.7 is Polish, and only a few very small minority groups exist.

Urbanization and industrialization have clearly changed the nature of Polish life and customs, and yet the church has remained strong, and family and folk ties have been sustained. Clear identity has made social and economic change much easier to implement than would otherwise have been the case.

In terms of natural resources, Poland is a country with considerable regional diversity, though major portions of the land area are not especially fertile, and environmental decay remains a serious problem. Poland's main source of energy is coal, and there are also some deposits of oil and natural gas.

The Command Economy

The Polish command system was established immediately after World War II and closely resembled that of the Soviet Union. There was widespread nationalization, the implementation of central planning as a mechanism for resource allocation, and the socialization of agriculture. In addition to these systemic arrangements, Polish economic policies of the era largely echoed those of the Soviet model.

Like other planned socialist systems, Poland attempted economic reform on several occasions.[3] The first major attempt was in 1956, when a program was developed to make changes in the management guidance system through the decentralization of decision making. Although collectivization of agriculture was abandoned, little actually changed as the state neglected private agriculture. By the latter part of the decade of the 1950s, reform attempts were of little consequence.

The second reform attempt occurred in the early 1970s under the new prime minister, Edward Gierek. The 1970s were a difficult decade for Poland. Polish economic performance was deteriorating, and imbalances in the economy were becoming more serious. The Polish strategy was to increase real wages and stimulate the economy through the importation of foreign technology to be paid for in part by the expansion of exports to hard-currency markets. The strategy was reasonable, but the effort to stimulate exports failed, in part because of downturns in Western economies. The projected impact of Western technology was minimal, the main outcome being the accumulation of a large hard-currency debt. It was increasingly apparent that retrenchment would be necessary—a difficult path given the state of unrest among Polish workers.

The 1980s began with roughly three years of martial law and new reform attempts under the military General Wojciech Jaruzelski. These attempts were in some respects similar to those proposed in the 1950s. However, analysis of Polish economic reforms in the 1980s suggests that they had limited impact and that the Polish economy had not been converted to market socialist arrangements in this decade. Serious changes would begin at the end of the decade.

The economic difficulties of the period are evident in Table 16.1. There were serious fluctuations in the growth of output after secular declines in earlier years. The volume of industrial employment fell by roughly 20 percent in the 1980s, and inflation became a serious problem that blossomed into hyperinflation in 1989. The Polish external hard-currency debt roughly doubled during this period. These economic difficulties formed the setting for the beginning of transition in 1990.

Polish Transition: The "Big Bang" in Practice

The Polish reform program officially began on January 1, 1990, several months after the collapse of the former communist government.[4] At this time, the economy was in a state of disequilibrium. Although the exact magnitude of the monetary overhang has been the subject of debate, money wage increases were out of control, there was a significant budget deficit, and hyperinflation was in progress. The initial transition program consisted of four basic components: fiscal control and elimination of the budget deficit, control of domestic credit expansion, limits to the growth of wages, and convertibility of the zloty.[5]

TABLE 16.1   The Polish Economy in the 1980s

	1971–1980	1981–1985	1987	1988	1989	1990	1991	1992
			Average Annual Rate of Growth					
Real GDP	3.6	0.6	-1.5	2.3	-1.6	-9.6	-7.6	-1.5
Real GDP per Capita	2.6	-0.3	-2.0	2.0	-2.0	-9.8	-8.1	-1.7
CPI 1980 = 100	—	—	575	938	3325	—	—	—

Source: Central Intelligence Agency, *Handbook of International Statistics, 1992* (Washington, D.C.: CIA, 1992), Table 13; *Handbook of International Statistics 1993,* Tables 8 and 9.

In the fall of 1989, most price controls on both producer and consumer goods were lifted, rationing was ended, public spending was reduced, and the zloty was devalued. In early 1990, further reductions in the state budget were implemented through the reduction of subsidies to state enterprises. A positive real rate of interest was to be implemented, and the market was to be used to signal real changes in the value of the zloty. Foreign trade was a key component of the transition program. In January of 1990, the government set the exchange rate of the zloty at 9,500 to the dollar (roughly the rate in black market exchanges) and established convertibility. Many trade restrictions were eliminated, and internal exchanges were established to handle the buying and selling of hard currencies. Although these changes resulted in domestic inflation, the initial price increases proved to be short-term, and the exchange rate of the zloty proved to be reasonable. Wage increases were controlled through wage indexation and a new tax on wage increases that exceeded established guidelines.

In the middle of 1990, a privatization law was passed and a Ministry of Ownership Change was established to oversee the privatization process.[6] Although the process of privatization would turn out to be complicated, the initial steps proceeded in a familiar manner, focusing on the gradual privatization of state enterprises through initial corporatization, the sale of smaller enterprises through auctions, and finally the development of small new enterprises through reduced entry restrictions—a process already in progress in the late 1980s. Unlike other cases in Eastern Europe, restitution was controversial and was the subject of continuing debate and discussion in the early 1990s.

In practice, privatization was uneven largely because it proceeded primarily for services and small-scale industry, not for the large state enterprises. Mass privatization was delayed through the mid-1990s but has now proceeded, with citizen participation in the privatization process, in part through the sale of stock to national investment funds. Delays in the privatization of the largest firms persist. Moreover, the role of local authorities and the issue of worker participation in new arrangements were controversial. Although private employment was reported to be 45 percent of total employment (including agriculture) at the end of 1991, privatization in the state sector lagged behind. This lack of progress motivated the creation of an Industrial Restructuring Agency and the beginning of privatization in the state sector through the instituting of stock funds and a voucher system. These policies were designed to offset problems typical of large-scale privatization in Eastern Europe, specifically the initial absence of capital markets and the limited savings of potential individual investors. Investment funds were important in Polish privatization, though the problem of debt in the formerly state-owned enterprises has been a major hurdle. There has been significant growth in Polish financial markets.

Although privatization has been slow in the major state sector, it would be wrong to conclude that changes have not been made. Apparently there have been considerable changes in the management system, largely through the active operation of workers' councils established in the 1980s. According to one study, by the end of 1990, half of the managers of these enterprises had been reconfirmed by the councils and forty percent were new managers. Measurement of the private sector in Poland is complicated by the existence of a significant second economy that is largely outside regular statistical reporting procedures. However, the private sector in Poland probably accounts for roughly two-thirds of output and employment.

Prior to the beginning of the transition in Poland, the agricultural sector was already predominantly private. By the end of the 1980s, 75 percent of arable land was in private hands, and 85 percent of net agricultural output was generated in the private sector. However, during the command era, private Polish agriculture did not have adequate access to inputs in a policy setting that favored the socialized sector. Thus modernization of an already private but technologically backward agriculture will be the focus of agricultural development in Poland during transition. The output performance of Polish agriculture in the 1990s has been uneven: significant declines in output from 1990 through 1992, a recovery in 1993, and further decline in 1994. Grain production has fluctuated in the 1990s, with an overall decline from roughly 28 million metric tons in 1990 to 26 million metric tons in 1995.

Not surprisingly, as the country weathered the onset of transition and the collapse of the old order, the Polish economy suffered a significant decline in output in 1990. That having been said, however, there is little agreement on just how serious the decline was or on the nature of the underlying causes. Obviously, one would expect the performance in the state sector and the private sector to be different, though isolation of these sectors has been difficult. Much of the decline was in the state sector, and this because of a decline in demand, changing enterprise rules, and other factors that made the conduct of economic activity problematic, such as disruption of the supply system and the difficulty of obtaining credit.

Beyond the difficulties of 1990, the collapse of the CMEA trading arrangements at the beginning of 1991 created a serious set of problems for East European nations. Trade essentially collapsed, and the move to change Polish/Soviet trade from zloty/ruble exchanges to hard-currency exchanges began. In Poland, there was considerable debate over the causes of this decline, and especially over the potential role of domestic macroeconomic policies. In any event, the collapse of CMEA trade was a serious problem for all of the countries concerned.

As Table 16-2 indicates, after an initial but modest decline in output (compared to most other transition economies), Polish output began to grow at a relatively rapid

TABLE 16.2   The Polish Economy in Transition

	1990	1991	1992	1993	1994	1995	1996	1997
GDP (constant prices) (percentage change)	−11.6	−7.6	2.6	3.8	5.2	7.0	6.0	5.5
Consumer prices (annual average percent)	585.5	70.3	43.0	35.3	32.2	27.8	19.9	16.0
Unemployment (year-end rate percent)	6.3	11.8	13.6	16.4	16.0	14.9	13.6	n.a.

Source: The Economics of Transition 5, 2 (1997), 544.

rate in the 1990s. Inflation dropped to an annual rate of 25 percent, though unemployment remained stubbornly high at around 15 percent of the labor force.

What generalizations can we make about the Polish experience with shock therapy? Although a longer span of years will provide us with a better perspective on the economic events in Poland, the early outcomes show that after an initial collapse of output and high inflation during the period of rapid transformation, Poland was able to return to positive growth in output and to limit inflation more quickly than other transforming economies. However, there were costs associated with these policies. The rate of unemployment increased significantly during the transformation, though the level of Polish unemployment was not unusually high relative to that in other transforming economies. However, as in other transition cases, the Polish outcome is a result of a variety of conditioning forces—a setting more complex than simply shock therapy. Of special importance has been the impact of changes in the foreign trade sector.

We have emphasized the importance of foreign trade in the transition setting, especially for small, relatively open economies such as Poland. As we have noted, Polish authorities moved quickly, after the collapse of communism, to establish a fully convertible currency. In January of 1990, the zloty was pegged at 9,500 to the U.S. dollar. Subsequent inflation led to the introduction of a "**crawling peg**" regime and to the maintenance of a real effective exchange rate largely unchanged through the mid-1990s.[7]

Along with the introduction of this new currency regime, trade restrictions were for the most part eliminated. The result was a significant expansion of both imports and exports, though imports exceeded exports by 1993, and the difference grew through the mid-1990s (see Table 16.3). During the early years of transition in Poland, the importance of trade with the former CMEA block declined significantly, trade being reoriented toward the European Economic Community, with which trade agreements were signed.

TABLE 16.3   The Polish Foreign Trade Sector

	1990	1991	1992	1993	1994	1995	1996
Exports*	10.9	12.8	14.0	13.6	17.0	22.9	24.4
Imports*	8.6	12.7	13.5	15.9	17.8	24.7	32.6
Foreign direct investment**	0.0	0.1	0.3	0.6	0.5	1.1	2.7
Debt service***	53.7	68.9	19.3	20.1	14.3	6.7	7.6

  * Billions of U.S. dollars.

 ** Foreign direct investment is probably considerably larger than the estimates presented here. Voluntary reporting to the State Foreign Investment Agency places the sum of inflows (1989–1996 inclusive) to be 12 billion (U.S. dollars). See *Economics of Transition* 5, 2 (1997), 551. The World Bank estimates the sum of inflows (1989–1995 inclusive) to be 6.45 billion (U.S. dollars). See The World Bank, *World Development Report 1996* (Washington, D.C.: World Bank, 1996), 64.

*** As a percent of current-account revenues, excluding transfers.

Source: Economics of Transition 5, 2 (1997), 544.

Another notable development in the globalization of the Polish economy has been the role of direct foreign investment. Though initially modest, the volume of direct foreign investment (especially from the United States, Germany, and Italy) has grown significantly. Moreover, because of the importance of this investment in relatively small firms, there may be considerable underreporting such that FDI is in fact much more important than statistical indicators suggest.

In sum, the changes in the foreign sector of the Polish economy were quick and significant. Although these policies fundamentally changed the nature of the Polish foreign trade sector, implementing them entailed adjustment costs in industry and (especially) in agriculture.

Hungary: The New Economic Mechanism and Transition

Unlike most East European economic systems functioning in terms of the Soviet model, Hungary has been of interest for its early attempts to implement economic reform. Prior to 1968, Hungary was a typical centrally planned socialist economic system.[8] Beginning in 1968, however, Hungary tried to introduce the most radical economic reform that had been attempted up to that time (with the exception of Yugoslavia). Although the program, known as the New Economic Mechanism (NEM), was only partially successful, some of the changes implemented may in fact have facilitated the subsequent transition to markets as the communist government collapsed. But in other dimensions, such as size and the importance of foreign trade, Hungary has been typical of the East European experience.

The Setting

Hungary is located in central Europe and, with a land area just over 92,000 square kilometers, is slightly larger than the state of Indiana. Hungary has a population of roughly 11 million, about the same as the state of Illinois. Although Hungary is not self-sufficient in energy, it does have supplies of coal, oil, and a number of minerals, including substantial bauxite deposits.

From a geographic perspective, Hungary is a flat country with good agricultural land and a favorable climate. As elsewhere in Eastern Europe, the period since World War II has witnessed considerable shifts of the Hungarian population from rural to urban areas and from agricultural to industrial and service activities. Today, roughly half of the Hungarian population lives in urban areas.

Hungary is not a particularly prosperous nation. Most estimates of the Hungarian GDP or GDP per capita place it in the middle of the East European countries—wealthier than Bulgaria, Yugoslavia, and certainly Albania, but behind the former GDR and Czechoslovakia. The per capita income of Hungary is close to that of Greece.

The Hungarian Command Economy: Implementation and Reform

The postwar construction of the Hungarian economy began modestly in 1945. Before the implementation of a three-year plan in 1947 (to cover the years 1947–1949), the main policies were currency stabilization, changes in the nature of rural landholding and the beginnings of nationalization. A system of economic planning was established, and investment shares increased sharply; at this time balanced development was envisioned, though this policy perspective came to an end in the early 1950s when the Soviet model was implemented.

A number of basic problems plagued the Hungarian economy during these early years, partly as a result of the command system. There were problems with labor supply—specifically, low productivity and limited ability to offset this problem with new labor from rural areas. There was considerable waste and imbalance, especially in the material supply system. Excess demand for investment often led to unfinished construction and a neglect of traditional facilities.

In the mid-1960s, Hungarian leaders began a discussion of economic reform that culminated in the NEM program announce in 1969.[9] This program sought to combine traditional state control of the major sectors of economic activity with increasing reliance on market-type forces to assist in routine decision making. To put it another way, the NEM was widely interpreted as an attempt to decentralize decision making in the Hungarian command economy. This sort of change would come from a reduction in the number of targets promulgated by central planners. Compulsory output targets were ended in many cases, with enterprise managers relying on local market forces, especially for the coordination of interenterprise activities.

In addition to changes in the plan and the rules governing its application, changes were made in the use of financial indicators. Profits were elevated in importance and were to be a source of enterprise financing and decentralized incentives for managers and workers. Local flexibility was to be limited by state guidelines, but within these guidelines, there would be flexibility in areas such as wages and profits.

Foreign trade reform was a major component of the NEM. Firms were to be able to engage directly in foreign trade, and changes were made to facilitate such a process. It was even suggested that price flexibility would allow changes in foreign prices to influence domestic Hungarian prices.

The NEM was of great interest to observers of planned socialist economies for several reasons. It was announced shortly after the largely unsuccessful and more conservative Kosygin reform program of 1965 in the former Soviet Union. It was clearly an alternative to the sorts of changes envisioned in the former GDR, and it seemed to represent a major attempt to implement what had been suggested many years earlier by Oskar Lange: central control of major economic issues combined with local control of the day-to-day functioning of the economy.

Although most observers would probably argue that the NEM program was not successfully implemented, it nevertheless had an impact on the Hungarian economy. There were, however, a variety of familiar problems.

First, these types of reforms (and NEM was no exception) were subject to political constraints. There were real limits on what central power would in fact be delegated to lower levels. This fact, combined with traditional political rigidities, limited the extent to which change was possible.

Second, there were always difficulties for any reform of planned socialist systems. Combining plan and market proved difficult. Moreover, any reform would be implemented from the "starting point" of the given economic structure, which was often not suited to a market environment.

Third, the implementation of reform in these systems implied acceptance of goals and outcomes that were typically unacceptable to the political leaders. If the labor market were to function, there had to be mobility and unemployment. If prices were to be freed, inflation was likely to ensue. These results were generally unacceptable to the leaders of the planned systems.

As time passed, it became evident that the NEM would not be implemented as originally designed. Although it was argued that the Hungarian economy had been decentralized to some degree, it was considerably less decentralized than had originally been envisioned. In fact, state control of the economy increased. For example, taxes and subsidies were introduced to protect the Hungarian economy from the influence of world market forces—the opposite of what was envisioned in the original NEM blueprint. The net result for Hungary was an economy facing rather typical economic problems in the 1980s: worsening economic performance and a growing external hard-currency debt.

Although Hungary was able to translate past improvements in economic performance into improvements in standard of living, performance slipped in the 1970s and 1980s (see Table 16.4). Inflationary pressures (though not so serious as those in Poland) plagued the Hungarian economy, as did internal microeconomic imbalances and a growing hard-currency debt. Although the volume of Hungarian commercial hard-currency debt was roughly half that of Poland, it doubled in the 1980s.

Hungarian leaders responded to these economic difficulties by implementing policies designed to sustain the standard of living while at the same time bringing the trade balance under control. A stabilization program was introduced, and Hungary joined the IMF in the early 1980s. Controls were implemented to limit import growth and expand export growth. The growth of investment was to be constrained through the state budget, the growth of consumption through limitations in the growth of wages. Although some changes took place (for example, adjustments in prices), the persistence of Soviet-type controls limited the nature and extent of change, leaving the Hungarian economy with a wide range of unresolved economic problems as the communist era came to an end.

Gradual Transition to Markets

Transition in Hungary has been different from other cases.[10] Not only has it been gradual but also it is not based on a "grand design," and it began earlier and under different circumstances from those that prevailed in Poland. Inflation was not a major problem that necessitated immediate stabilization measures, though issues

TABLE 16.4   The Hungarian Economy in the 1980s

						Average Annual Rate of Growth			
	1971–1980	1981–1985	1987	1988	1989	1990	1991	1992
Real GDP (annual rate of growth)	2.7	0.3	1.5	1.5	-2.3	-6.8	-6.8	-7.8
Real GDP per capita (annual rate of growth)	2.1	0.9	1.8	3.5	-2.1	-6.8	-5.9	-7.8
Consumer Price Index (1980 = 100)	—	—	164	184	240	—	—	—

Source: Central Intelligence Agency, *Handbook of International Statistics 1992* (Washington, D.C.: CIA, 1992), Table 13; *Handbook of International Statistics, 1993*, Tables 8 and 9.

related to foreign trade assumed great importance, partly because of the size of Hungary's hard-currency debt and because of the collapse of the CMEA in 1990.

In the absence of a specific reform program, the beginning of transition is generally dated to 1985. Since that time, a series of ongoing policy and systemic changes have shifted the Hungarian economy toward a market economy, but they have done so on a sequential and continually changing basis. The changes have been in the areas that we would expect: privatization, macroeconomic policies, microeconomic policies, and foreign trade.

Beginning in the 1980s, the means for selecting enterprise managers changed as enterprises themselves gained a voice. This managerial revolution not only changed personnel; it also changed the decision-making environment and began to change the way enterprise managers functioned. Therefore, the Company Act was passed in 1988, and in 1990 the State Property Agency was created. Privatization began largely on a small scale in services and related areas and proceeded slowly. Whereas less than 10 percent of GDP originated in the private sector in 1985, the private-sector share reached 20 to 30 percent by 1991. In the early 1990s, a serious effort began to formalize the legal structure and especially to isolate the state enterprises in corporate form.

Privatization in Hungary has differed from that carried out elsewhere. Both the pace and the magnitude of privatization have been modest. Restitution has been an issue, but the restitution program and its implementation have both been small in scope. Buyouts by managers and employees (formally an employee buyout program but with management control) have been used with significant foreign involvement and much less involvement by Hungarian financial markets. Although restitution has existed, mass privatization has been of limited importance, and debt problems have constrained restructuring.

Throughout the late 1980s and into the 1990s, efforts were begun to change the role of government in the Hungarian economy. The share of subsidies decreased by half (from 15 to 7 percent of GDP) between 1985 and 1991. Efforts began to redefine income maintenance programs, and prices were freed on a gradual basis. Unemployment increased and real wages declined. Hungarian economic performance during transition is summarized in Table 16.5. Since the end of a decline through 1993, modest real economic growth has been achieved, with continuing inflation.

TABLE 16.5 The Hungarian Economy in Transition

	1990	1991	1992	1993	1994	1995	1996	1997
GDP (constant prices) (percentage change)	−3.5	−11.9	−3.1	−0.6	2.9	1.5	1.0	3.0
Consumer prices (annual average: percent)	28.9	35.0	23.0	22.5	18.8	28.2	23.6	18.0
Unemployment (year-end rate)	−3.1	−9.6	−9.3	−5.0	−2.2	−1.4	−5.6	n.a.

Source: Economics of Transition 5, 2 (1997), 541.

As with Poland and the Czech Republic, changes in the Hungarian foreign sector have been important (see Table 16.6). During the early 1990s, the forint was devalued on an irregular basis, a policy that changed in 1995.[11] However, during the transition era, Hungarian trade patterns have changed significantly. Although there were variations from year to year, through 1994 exports declined and imports increased, resulting in a negative trade balance that persisted through 1997. Faced with a substantial external debt, Hungarian policy makers encouraged direct foreign investment. Between 1989 and 1995, the sum of inflows to Hungary amounted to over 10.6 billion dollars, or roughly 30 percent of GDP—by far the largest such inflow among the European transition economies.[12] This investment was an important component in Hungarian privatization and Hungarian foreign trade.

Although Hungary began the transition era with a large and growing external debt, assistance was provided, and in spite of the virtual collapse of CMEA trade in the early 1990s, a reduction of imports and significant increases in exports (especially in Western markets) reduced the current-account deficit significantly between 1989 and 1991. On the capital account, the increase in private transfers and the sizable inflow of foreign capital were both of major benefit.

The Czech Republic: Planning, Politics, and Transition

In 1993 the former Czechoslovakia was divided into the Czech Republic and the Slovak Republic. Throughout the period after World War II until the end of the 1980s, the economy of Czechoslovakia was like other East European economies: a planned socialist system on the Stalinist model. However, in addition to political and economic differences, Czechoslovakia was much more developed in the late 1940s than other East European economies. Even so, there were significant regional differences within Czechoslovakia, with industrialization being largely confined to the Czech lands.

TABLE 16.6   The Hungarian Foreign Trade Sector

	1990	1991	1992	1993	1994	1995	1996
Exports*	n.a.	9.3	10.0	8.1	7.6	12.8	14.2
Imports*	n.a.	9.1	10.1	11.3	11.2	15.3	16.8
Foreign direct investment**	0.3	1.5	1.5	2.3	1.1	4.5	2.0
Debt service***	48.2	33.9	34.4	43.2	54.8	47.3	50.4

* Billions of U.S. dollars.
** The cumulative FDI (1989–1995 inclusive) is reported by the World Bank as 10.63 billion U.S. dollars.
   See The World Bank, *World Development Report 1996* (Washington, D.C.: World Bank, 1996), 64.
*** Percent of current-account revenues, excluding transfers.
Source: Economics of Transition 5, 2 (1997), 541.

Although the case of Czechoslovakia was different in some respects, the long period of central planning culminated in a economy with distortions similar to those found elsewhere, in combination with declining economic performance. For convenience, we deal with the history as it was, examining issues related to Czechoslovakia at large. Later, as we discuss transition, we will look at the separate Czech Republic.

Natural Setting

Czechoslovakia had a land area of approximately 125,000 square kilometers, slightly larger than that of New York state. After 1993 the land area stood at 79,000 and 49,000 square kilometers for the Czech Republic and the Slovak Republic, respectively. The population of the Czech Republic in 1994 was 10.3 million, that of the Slovak Republic 5.3 million.

Although Czechoslovakia is strategically located and has a moderate climate and good agricultural lands, the industry that it developed during the plan era is outmoded, and in spite of a high-quality labor force, close linking of the economy to the former Soviet Union limited the ability of Czechoslovakia to compete in world markets.

Czechoslovakia is deficient in energy and raw materials, and as in many other contemporary East European nations, environmental disruption is a serious problem. In order to understand the contemporary transition to markets that began in late 1989 and early 1990, we will first review the basic elements of the former command system.

The Command Experience

The Communist party of Czechoslovakia took control of the country in 1948.[13] Immediately afterwards, the Soviet model was introduced, including nationalization of property and collectivization of agriculture. The familiar priorities of high investment in industry and reorientation of foreign trade toward the Soviet Union and other East European countries were instituted.

Although there was good economic growth in the initial plan years, early attempts in the mid-1950s to decentralize the economy were abandoned until the late 1960s. After a period of sharply slower growth rates in the early and mid-1960s, there were serious discussions of reform. These discussions focused on the concept of market socialism, with a plan for significant decentralization of decision making along with important market influences.

The potential for reform in the late 1960s arose under a new leader, Alexander Dubček. Moreover, there was substantial popular support for both economic and political reform, factors important to Dubček's position. This receptivity to economic and political reform culminated in what was called the Prague Spring of 1968. The outcome of the Prague Spring is well known. Alarmed by potential democratization, Moscow ordered Warsaw Pact troops to invade, bringing an immediate end to reform and a recentralization of the economy.

Although there were some piecemeal reform efforts in the 1970s, this decade and the 1980s were difficult times for Czechoslovakia for reasons similar to those that affected Poland and Hungary. Czechoslovakia had to import energy and faced serious problems in the era of OPEC after 1973. In addition to having a serious impact on domestic industry, rising costs significantly reduced the Czech ability to compete in foreign markets.

The data in Table 16.7 tell a familiar story, but with some exceptions. Czech economic performance fluctuated, exhibiting a significant slowdown through the 1970s and 1980s. But unlike Poland, Czechoslovakia began the subsequent transition era with a very small external hard-currency debt, in large part because of conservative financial management. Finally, there was very limited inflation. This history put the economy of Czechoslovakia in an interesting position at the starting block of transition. Some of the adverse indicators common in other cases (inflation and external debt) were lacking, yet the economy of Czechoslovakia had been significantly repressed after the Prague Spring of 1968.

Transition and Political Change

At the beginning of 1987, a major program of economic reform was announced.[14] This program bore a resemblance to earlier reform attempts, yet it was modest in character. Implementation was also modest—until the events of late 1989 and the free elections of 1990 that brought communist power to an end. The transition government announced its intention to move toward the creation of a market economy, but it was not until late 1990, after considerable discussion, that a transition plan was announced. Transition steps began in earnest in early 1991.

In January of 1991, the liberalization of producer and consumer prices began, along with devaluation of the koruna and its pegging to a basket of five Western currencies. A surcharge was also levied on imports, and steps were taken to control the growth of wages. These changes were made within the context of a set of stabilization policies and the pursuit of privatization. As in other transition cases, a great deal of attention has been focused on privatization in the Czech and Slovak republics.

Privatization began in Czechoslovakia in three broad forms: restitution, small-scale privatization through auctions (1990), and finally, in 1991, voucher privatization as part of a large-scale privatization initiative through the Ministry of Finance.[15] In addition to direct sales and sales of enterprises converted to joint stock operations, individual access to property has been achieved through the voucher system. Citizens could purchase vouchers with investment points that could be used for bidding on enterprises listed for privatization. The bidding could be direct, with public announcement of the results, or it could be made through investment diversification funds, a mechanism to encourage diversification. In the initial stages of privatization, a majority of citizens chose to invest through the investment diversification funds.

Although the Czech voucher approach has been praised for facilitating rapid privatization with citizen participation in the absence of developed financial markets, there have been problems with restructuring, management issues, and the sale of remaining stock in privatizing firms. Thus, although most points have been exchanged for shares with a great deal of participation by the population, the bulk of privatized firms were not able to sell all of their shares. Preparations began earlier, but the Prague stock exchange did not begin operations until the spring of 1993.

TABLE 16.7 The Economy of Czechoslovakia in the 1980s

	1971–1980	1981–1985	1987	1988	1989	1990	1991	1992
Real GDP (annual average)	2.8	1.2	0.5	2.2	0.7	–2.8	–14.8	–5.3
Real GDP per Capita (annual average)	2.0	1.0	–1.0	2.2	0.7	–3.4	–14.6	–5.3
Consumer price Index (1980 = 100)	—	—	110	112	114	—	—	—

Source: Central Intelligence Agency, *Handbook of International Statistics 1992* (Washington, D.C.: CIA, 1992), Table 13; *Handbook of International Statistics, 1993,* Tables 8 and 9.

The separation of the Czech and Slovak republics inevitably complicated the process of privatization. In particular, the two countries began to pursue different approaches to privatization, the Czech Republic remaining committed to the voucher approach and the Slovak Republic preferring more traditional means. However, by the mid-1990s, roughly two-thirds of the output of the Czech Republic originated from the private sector. At the same time, the process of privatization was facilitated by the growth of the financial sector, especially financial intermediaries.

Beyond the pursuit of the basic objectives of transition, substantial efforts were made in 1991 and 1992 to change the pattern of government spending (for example, reduction of subsidies to enterprises), to develop domestic financial markets, and to install a new social safety net. The latter is important in light of early reductions in the standard of living, even though unemployment in the Czech Republic has not been high and there has always been substantial support for serious transition measures. Probably the most important item on the agenda in the mid-1990s is restructuring, to take place in a setting of generally restrictive economic policies.

The performance of the Czech economy in the transition era is summarized in Table 16.8. The pattern of initial downturn and a recovery in 1993 is familiar, though healthy real economic growth after 1993 was not sustained in 1997. However, both the rate of inflation and the level of unemployment have been modest compared to similar performance indicators in other transition economies.

The significant slackening in the output performance of the Czech economy in 1996 and 1997 can be explained in part by developments in the foreign trade sector. In Table 16.9 we summarize relevant changes in that sector.[16]

Although there has been export growth during the transition era, the growth of imports has been much more rapid, resulting in a current-account deficit of about 8 percent of GDP by the end of 1996. These developments have resulted from both weaknesses in export markets and shrinkage in the growth of domestic output, partly because of restrictive monetary policies implemented to control inflation.

There has been a decisive shift of trade toward the EU countries and away from the former CMEA countries. The share of exports to the CMEA from the Czech Republic (Czechoslovakia) in 1989 was 47 percent, a figure that declined to 31 percent in 1994.[17]

TABLE 16.8   The Czech Economy in Transition

	1994	1991	1992	1993	1994	1995	1996	1997
Real GDP (annual percentage change)	−1.2	−11.5	−3.3	0.6	2.7	4.8	4.1	1.0
Consumer prices (annual average: percent)	10.8	56.6	11.1	20.8	10.0	9.1	8.8	9.5
Unemployment (year-end rate)	0.8	4.1	2.6	3.5	3.2	2.9	3.5	5.2

Source: Economics of Transition 5, 2 (1997), 538; PlanEcon, *Czech Economic Monitor,* January 30, 1998, pages 5–6.

TABLE **16.9**   The Czech Foreign Trade Sector

	1993	1994	1995	1996	1997
Exports*	13.0	14.0	21.5	21.7	n.a.
Imports*	13.3	14.9	21.4	27.7	n.a.
Foreign direct investment**	0.5	0.7	2.5	1.4	n.a.
Debt service***	8.4	13.1	10.3	12.8	n.a.

   *Billions of U.S. dollars.
  **Net basis.
***Percent of exports of goods and services.
Source: Economics of Transition 5, 2 (1997), 538.

The currency (the Czechoslovak koruna) was made convertible in 1991, ultimately tied to a combination of the dollar and deutsche mark. After 1993, trade between Czech and Slovak republics declined, and separate financial systems were developed, with the Czech Republic managing the Czech koruna. Although the underlying causal factors are a matter of debate, there was a real appreciation of the Czech koruna through the mid-1990s. Although there are difficulties in the measurement of foreign direct investment, the evidence in Table 16.9 suggests that the volume of FDI has been growing. According to World Bank estimates, the cumulative sum of FDI to the Czech Republic between 1989 and 1995 was just under 4 billion U.S. dollars.[18]

Eastern Europe: Transition, Performance, and Restructuring

Thus far we have examined Poland, Hungary, and the Czech Republic in light of the special circumstances of each country and the more general transition issues. Although there are broad similarities among these cases, there are also differences. We have examined the basic performance indicators for these three important transition cases. Estimates suggest that at the end of 1996, the per capita GDP, measured in U.S. dollars, was $4,357 for Hungary, $3,459 for Poland, and $5,340 for the Czech Republic.[19] These levels represent important increases from the low point of transition around 1993. At the same time, the ability to sustain positive economic growth will depend in large part on restructuring. In Table 16.10 we present some data related to restructuring in Poland, Hungary, and the Czech Republic.

The available evidence on basic restructuring is limited, but the data presented in Table 16.10 deserve comment. First, although the private sector seems to have expanded significantly, there are notable differences among these three cases, differences that we emphasized earlier in this chapter. Most important, as we come to the end of the century, major components of all these economies remain to be privatized.

TABLE 16.10   Transition and Restructuring in Poland, Hungary, and the Czech Republic

	1990	1991	1992	1993	1994	1995	1996
GDP: Private Sector							
Poland	30.9	30.0	40.0	45.0		57.0	
Hungary	10–20	20–30				60	
Czech Republic	13.2	17.7	27.7	45.1	56.3	63.8	
GDP: Industry Share							
Poland	44.9	40.2	34.0	32.9	28.9		
Hungary	28.8	26.8	24.4	23.2	22.8	23.9	
Czech Republic			40.2	34.9	33.6	34.1	33.8
GDP: State Budget (%)							
Poland	36.7	33.0	33.4	32.5			
Hungary	53.5	54.3	61.6	62.2	62.1	56.1	50.0
Czech Republic	60.1	54.2	29.8	35.6	33.2	32.8	32.5

Source: Economics of Transition 2 (March 1994), Tables 3, 4, 5. Private-sector data for Hungary are from Kermal Dervis and Timothy Condon, "Hungary—Partial Success and Remaining Challenges: The Emergence of a 'Gradualist' Success?" in Oliver Jean Blanchard, Kenneth A. Froot, and Jeffrey D. Sachs, *The Transition in Eastern Europe,* vol. 1 (Chicago: University of Chicago Press, 1994), p. 125. Private-sector data for the Czech Republic are Ministry of Finance estimates and refer to the nonstate portion of GDP. Private-sector data for Poland and Hungary for 1995 are from The World Bank, *World Development Report 1996* (Washington, D.C.: World Bank, 1996,) p. 15.

Second, structural (sectoral) changes have been quite striking. For example, in both Hungary and the Czech Republic, the importance of industry in total output has declined markedly, reversing a long-standing pattern of resource allocation that dates from the command era. Although the change has been different in the Hungarian case, it can be accounted for by Hungary's very different starting point.

Third, although the time frames for our evidence differ considerably, the reduction of the state sector, measured in terms of the state budget as a share of GDP, has been quite modest, especially if we date the Czech case to 1993. Although these data are crude and difficult to interpret, they suggest a continuing state role in these transition settings, especially in Hungary.

Summary

In this chapter we have examined three important transition economies: Poland, Hungary, and the Czech Republic. There are similarities among these cases, but there are also important differences.

All three countries are relatively small and have limited resources. All had been market economies at differing levels of economic development before World War II and the subsequent imposition of the Soviet administrative-command model. This model included new political arrangements, nationalization, collectivization of agriculture, and the implementation of central planning as the dominant mechanism for resource allocation.

In all cases, a number of attempts were made to reform the command economic system. These reform attempts generally failed—although their origins differed, and in the end so did their impact. However, as in other cases, the performance of these economies lagged, and the structural distortions generated by the Soviet model were thoroughly embedded.

After the Prague Spring of 1968, Czechoslovakia experienced little change. Change was also limited in Poland, though the rise of a political alternative to the Communist party—namely Solidarity—would turn out to be pivotal. In Hungary, the NEM (New Economic Mechanism) introduced in 1968 was a partial and limited reform program, though it has been credited with leaving a meaningful legacy for the development of markets in the transition era.

The general pattern of transition in these economies focused on familiar components (macroeconomic issues, microeconomic issues, and foreign trade), but Poland rapidly instituted change in system and policy (the "Big Bang"), whereas Hungary and the Czech Republic (the Czech and Slovak republics became separate countries in 1993) pursued a more gradual approach. There were important differences in macroeconomic policies and in privatization policies.

Performance outcomes of the transition era have been similar: declines followed by a bottoming out and a recovery to positive real rates of economic growth. There have been significant changes in foreign trade patterns. As the century comes to an end, the emphasis continues to be on stable economic growth, a challenge as restructuring takes place.

Key Terms

trade-averse
shock therapy
big bang
CMEA
crawling peg

Notes

1. A great deal has been written about the command experience in Poland. The publications of the Joint Economic Committee provide a useful set of papers. See, in particular, United States Congress, joint Economic Committee, *East European Economies Post-Helsinki* (Washington, D.C.: U.S. Government Printing Office, 1977); United States Congress, Joint Economic Committee, *East European Economic Assessment* (Washington, D.C.: U.S. Government Printing Office, 1981); United States Congress, Joint Economic Committee, *East European Economies: Slow Growth in the 1980s* (Washington, D.C.: U.S. Government Printing Office, 1985).

2. For an interesting survey perspective, see Jozef M. van Brabant, "Lessons from the Whole-sale Transformations in the East," *Journal of Comparative Economics* 35, 4 (Winter 1993), 73–102; see also Norbert Funke, "Timing and Sequencing of Reforms: Competing Views and the Role of Credibility," *Kyklos* 3 (1993), 337–362.

3. In addition to the sources cited in note 1, a summary discussion of Polish economic re-forms can be found in Raphael Shen, *Economic Reform in Poland and Czechoslovakia* (Westport, Conn.: Praeger, 1993).

4. For a discussion of Poland on the eve of transition, see David Lipton and Jeffrey Sachs, "Creating a Market Economy in Eastern Europe," *Brookings Papers on Economic Activity* 1 (1990), 75–147; Stanislaw Wellisz, "Poland Under 'Solidarity' Rule," *Journal of Economic Perspectives* 5, 4 (Fall 1991), 211–217.

5. This discussion is based on Andrew Berg and Oliver Jean Blanchard, "Stabilization and Transition: Poland, 1990–91," in Oliver Jean Blanchard, Kenneth A. Froot, and Jeffrey D. Sachs, eds., *The Transition in Eastern Europe.* vol. 1 (Chicago: University of Chicago Press, 1994), 51–91; John P. Bonin, "On the Way to Privatizing Commercial Banks: Poland and Hungary Take Different Roads," *Comparative Economic Studies* 35, 4 (Winter 1993), 103–20; Jeffrey Sachs and David Lipton, "Poland's Economic Reform," *Foreign Affairs* 69 (Summer 1990), 47–66; Saul Estrin and Xavier Richet, "Industrial Restructur-ing and Microeconomic Adjustment in Poland: A Cross-Sectoral Approach," *Comparative Economic Studies* 35, 4 (Winter 1993), 1–19; John P. Farrell, ed., "The Economic Trans-formation in Eastern Europe," *Comparative Economic Studies* 33, 2 (Summer 1991), 1–177; S. Gomilka, "Polish Economic Reform, 1990–91: Principles, Policies and Out-comes," *Cambridge Journal of Economics* 16 (September 1992), 355–372; Alain de Crom-brugghe and David Lipton, "The Government Budget and the Economic Transformation of Poland," In Oliver Jean Blanchard, Kenneth A. Froot, and Jeffrey Sachs, *The Transition in Eastern Europe,* vol. 2 (Chicago: University of Chicago Press, 1994), 111–133; Morris Bornstein, "Non-Standard Methods of Privatization Strategies of the Czech Republic, Hungary and Poland," *Economics of Transition* 5, 2 (1997), 323–338.

6. Andrew Berg and Oliver Jean Blanchard, "Stabilization and Transition: Poland, 1990–91," 69–70; see also Zbigniew M. Fallenbuchl, "Polish Privatization Policy," *Comparative Eco-nomic Studies* 33, 2 (Summer 1991), 53–69; M. Shaffer, "The Polish State-Owned Enter-prise Sector and The Recession of 1990," *Comparative Economic Studies* 34, 1 (Spring 1992), 58–85; Andrew Berg, "The Logistics of Privatization in Poland," in Oliver Jean Blanchard, Kenneth A. Froot, and Jeffrey D. Sachs, *The Transition in Eastern Europe,* vol. 2 (Chicago: University of Chicago Press, 1994), 165–186.

7. For a discussion of Polish foreign trade, see Stanislaw Wellisz, "Poland," in Padma Desai, ed., *Going Global: Transition from Plan to Market in the World Economy* (Cambridge, Mass.: M.I.T. Press, 1997), 209–239; Iliana Zloch-Christy, ed., *Eastern Europe and the World Economy* (Cheltenham, England: Edward Elgar, 1998); for background on similar economies, see Richard N. Cooper and Janos Gacs, eds., *Trade Growth in Transition Economies* (Northampton, Mass.: Edward Elgar, 1997).

8. For a discussion of the Hungarian economy after World War II, see the publications of the United States Congress, Joint Economic Committee, cited in note 1.

9. P.G. Hare, H.K. Radice, and N. Swain, eds., *Hungary: A Decade of Economic Reform* (London: Allen and Unwin, 1981); Bela Csikos-Nagy, "The Hungarian Economic Reform After Ten Years," *Soviet Studies,* 30 (October 1978), 540–546; Bela Balassa, "The Hungarian Economic Reform, 1968–82," *Banca Nazionale Del Lavoro Quarterly Review* 145 (June 1983), 163–184; Bela Balassa, "Reforming The New Economic Mech-anism in Hungary, "Journal of Comparative Economics 7, 3 (1983), 253–276; J. Kornai,

"The Hungarian Reform Process: Visions, Hopes, and Reality," *Journal of Economic Literature* 24 (1986), 1687–1737; J. Kornai, *Contradictions and Dilemmas* (Cambridge, Mass.: The M.I.T. Press, 1986).

10. This discussion is based on Kemal Dervis and Timothy Condon, "Hungary—Partial Successes and Remaining Challenges: The Emergence of a 'Gradualist' Success Story?" in Oliver Jean Blanchard, Kenneth A. Froot, and Jeffrey D. Sachs, eds., *The Transition in Eastern Europe,* vol. 1 (Chicago: University of Chicago Press, 1994), 123–153; D.M. Newberry, "Tax Reform, Trade Liberalization and Industrial Restructuring in Hungary," *European Economy* 43 (March 1990), 67–96; Erzsebet Szalai, "Integration of Special Interests in the Hungarian Economy: The Struggle Between Large Companies and the Party and State Bureaucracy," *Journal of Comparative Economics* 15, 2 (June 1991), 107–124; P. G. Hare, "Hungary: In Transition to a Market Economy," *Journal of Economic Perspectives* 5, 4 (1991), 195–202; Janos Kornai, *The Road to a Free Economy* (New York: Norton, 1990); Morris Bornstein, "Non-Standard Methods in the Privatization Strategies of the Czech Republic, Hungary and Poland," *Economics of Transition* 5, 2 (1997), 323–338.

11. For a discussion of Hungarian foreign trade, see Richard N. Cooper and Janos Gacs, eds., *Trade Growth in Transition Economies* (Northhampton, Mass.: Edward Elgar, 1997); Andras Blaho and Peter Gal, "Hungary," in Padma Desai, ed., *Going Global: Transition from Plan to Market in the World Economy* (Cambridge, Mass.: M.I.T. Press, 1997), 135–172.

12. The World Bank, *World Development Report 1996* (Washington, D.C.: World Bank, 1996), 64.

13. For a discussion of the post-World War II era in Czechoslovakia, see the publications of the United States Congress, Joint Economic Committee, cited in note 1.

14. This discussion is based on Karel Dyba and Jan Svejnar, "Stabilization and Transition in Czechoslovakia," in Oliver Jean Blanchard, Kenneth A. Froot, and Jeffrey D. Sachs, eds., *The Transition in Eastern Europe,* vol. 1 (Chicago: University of Chicago Press, 1994), 93–122; Jan Svejnar and Miroslav Singer, "Using Vouchers to Privatize an Economy: The Czech and Slovak Case, "*Economics of Transition* 2, 1 (March 1994), 43–70; Raphael Shen, *Economic Reform in Poland and Czechoslovakia* (Westport, Conn.: Praeger, 1993); Josef C. Brada, "The Economic Transition of Czechoslovakia from Plan to Market," *Journal of Economic Perspectives* 5, 4 (Fall 1991), 171–177; Karel Dyba and Jan Svejnar, "Czechoslovakia: Recent Economic Developments and Prospects," *American Economic Review Papers and Proceedings* 81 (May 1991), 185–190; Eva Marikova Leeds, "Voucher Privatization in Czechoslovakia," *Comparative Economic Studies* 35, 3 (Fall 1993), 19–38; The World Bank, *World Development Report 1996* (Washington, D.C.: World Bank, 1996).

15. For an excellent discussion of privatization, see Jan Svejnar and Miroslav Singer, "Using Vouchers to Privatize an Economy: The Czech and Slovak Case" and Eva Markiova Leeds, "Voucher Privatization in Czechoslovakia," and Karel Dyba and Jan Svejnar, "Stabilization and Transition in Czechoslovakia," 113–116; Morris Bornstein, "Non-Standard Methods of the Privatization Strategies of the Czech Republic, Hungary and Poland," *Economics of Transition,* 5, 2 (1997), 323–338; Milica Uvalic and Daniel Vaughan-Whitehead, eds., *Privatization Surprises in Transition Economies* (Cheltenham, England: Edward Elgar, 1997).

16. For a discussion of foreign trade in the Czech Republic, see Josef C. Brada and Ali M. Kutan, "The Czech Republic," in Padma Desai, ed, *Going Global: Transition from Plan to Market in the World Economy* (Cambridge, Mass.: M.I.T. Press, 1997), 97–134; Richard N. Cooper and Janos Gacs, eds., *Trade Growth in Transition Economies* (Cheltenham, England: Edward Elgar, 1997).

17. Richard N. Cooper and Janos Gacs, eds., *Trade Growth in Transition Economies* (Cheltenham, England: Edward Elgar, 1997), p. 6.
18. The World Bank, *World Development Report 1996* (Washington, D.C.: World Bank, 1996), 64.
19. *Economics of Transition* 5, 2 (1997), 538, 541, 544.

Recommended Readings

General Sources: Eastern Europe

Anthony B. Atkinson and John Micklewright, *Economic Transformation in Eastern Europe and the Distribution of Income* (Cambridge, England: Cambridge University Press, 1992).

Mario Baldassarri, Luigi Paganetto, and Edmund S. Phelps, eds., *Privatization Processes in Eastern Europe* (New York: St. Martin's Press, 1993).

Oliver Jean Blanchard, Kenneth A. Froot, and Jeffrey D. Sachs, eds., *The Transition in Eastern Europe: Country Studies,* vol. 1 (Chicago: University of Chicago Press, 1994).

———, *The Transition in Eastern Europe: Restructuring,* vol. 2 (Chicago: University of Chicago Press, 1994).

Tito Boeri, "Learning from Transition Economies: Assessing Labor Market Policies Across Central and Eastern Europe," *Journal of Comparative Economics* 25, 3 (December 1997), 366–384.

Morris Bornstein, "Non-Standard Methods in the Privatization Strategies of the Czech Republic, Hungary and Poland," *Economics of Transition* 5, 2 (1997), 323–338.

Michael L. Boyd, *Organization, Performance and System Choice: East European Agricultural Development* (Boulder, Colo.: Westview Press, 1991).

Jozef M. van Brabant, *Economic Integration in Eastern Europe* (New York: Routledge, 1989).

———, ed., *The New Eastern Europe and The World Economy* (Boulder, Colo.: Westview, 1993).

Christopher Clague and Gordon C. Rausser, eds., *The Emergence of Market Economies in Eastern Europe* (Cambridge, Mass.: Blackwell, 1992).

Padma Desai, ed., *Going Global: Transition from Plan to Market in the World Economy* (Cambridge, Mass.: The M.I.T. Press, 1997).

Maurice Ernst, Michael Alexeev, and Paul Marer, *Transforming the Core: Restructuring Industrial Enterprises in Russia and Central Europe* (Boulder, Colo: Westview, 1996).

S. Estrin, ed., *Privatization on Central and Eastern Europe* (London: Longmans, 1994).

Hans van Ees and Harry Garretsen, "The Theoretical Foundation of the Reform in Eastern Europe: Big Bang Versus Gradualism and the Limitations of Neo-Classical Economic Theory," *Economic Systems* 18, 1 (March 1994), 1–13.

John P. Farrell, ed., "The Economic Transition in Eastern Europe," *Comparative Economic Studies* 33, 2 (Summer 1991), 1–177.

Daniel S. Fogel, ed., *Managing in Emerging Market Economies: Cases from Czech and Slovak Republics* (Boulder, Colo.: Westview, 1994).

Petr Hanel, "Trade Liberalization in Czechoslovakia, Hungary, and Poland Through 1991: A Survey," *Comparative Economic Studies* 34, 3–4 (Fall–Winter, 1992), 34–53.

C. Clague and G. Rausser, eds., *The Emergence of Market Economies in Eastern Europe* (Cambridge, Mass.: Blackwell, 1992).

Michael Kaser, ed., *The Economic History of Eastern Europe 1919–1975,* vols. I–III (Oxford: Clarendon Press, 1986).

Michael Keren and Gur Ofer, eds., *Trials of Transition: Economic Reform in the Former Communist Bloc* (Boulder, Colo.: Westview Press, 1992).

A. Schipke and A. M. Taylor, eds., *The Economics of Transformation* (New York: Springer-Verlag, 1994).

Raphael Shen, *Economic Reform in Poland and Czechoslovakia* (Westport, Conn.: Praeger, 1993).

Milica Uvalic and Daniel Vaughan-Whitehead, eds., *Privatization Surprises in Transition Economies* (Cheltenham, England: Edward Elgar, 1997).

Jozef M. van Brabant, "Lessons from the Wholesale Transformations in the East," *Comparative Economic Studies* 35, 4 (Winter 1993), 73–102.

Kenneth J. Koford *et al.* "Symposium: Economic Reform in Eastern Europe and the Former Soviet Union," *Eastern Economic Journal* 19, 3 (Summer 1993), 329–393.

The World Bank, *The World Development Report 1996* (Washington, D.C.: World Bank, 1996).

Poland

James Angresano, "Poland After the Shock," *Comparative Economic Studies* 38, 2/3 (Summer–Fall 1996), 87–111.

Andrew Berg and Oliver Jean Blanchard, "Stabilization and Transition: Poland, 1990–91," in Oliver Jean Blanchard, Kenneth A. Froot, and Jeffrey D. Sachs, eds., *The Transition in Eastern Europe,* vol. 1 (Chicago: University of Chicago Press, 1994), 51–91.

John P. Bonin, "On the Way to Privatizing Commercial Banks: Poland and Hungary Take Different Roads," *Comparative Economic Studies* 35, 4 (Winter 1993), 103–20.

Maurice Ernst, "Dimensions of the Polish Economic Transition: The Ingredients of Success," *Post-Soviet Geography and Economics* 38, 1 (1977), 1–46.

Saul Estrin and Xavia Richet, "Industrial Adjustment and Restructuring in Poland: A Cross-Sectoral Approach," *Comparative Economic Studies* 35, 4 (Winter 1993), 1–20.

Zbigniew M. Fallenbuchl, "Polish Privatization Policy," *Comparative Economic Studies* 33, 2 (Summer 1991), 53–69.

Irena Grosfeld, "Prospects for Privatization in Poland," *European Economy* 43 (March 1990), 139–158.

David Lipton and Jeffrey Sachs, "Creating a Market Economy in Poland," *Brookings Papers on Economic Activity,* 1 (1990).

Jan Mujzel, "Polish Economic Reforms and the Dilemma of Privatization," *Comparative Economic Studies* 33, 2 (Summer 1991), 29–52.

Leon Podkaminer, "Estimates of Disequilibria in Poland's Consumer Markets 1965–1978," *Review of Economics and Statistics* 62 (August 1982), 423–432.

D. M. Nuti, "Internal and International Aspects of Monetary Disequilibrium in Poland," *European Economy* 43 (March 1990), 169–182.

R. Rapacki, "Privatization in Poland: Performance, Problems and Prospects," *Comparative Economic Studies* 37, 3 (Fall 1995), 57–75.

Jeffrey Sachs and David Lipton, "Poland's Economic Reform," *Foreign Affairs* 69 (Summer 1990), 47–66.

Jeffrey Sachs, "Poland's Big Bang: A First Report Card," *The International Economy,* January/February 1991, 40–43.

Mark Schaeffer, "State Owned Enterprises in Poland: Taxation, Subsidization and Competition Policies," *European Economy* 43 (March 1990).

Ben Slay, "Polish Banks on the Road to Recovery," *Post-Soviet Geography and Economics* 37, 8 (1996), 511–522.

Richard Portes, "Introduction to Economic Transformation in Hungary and Poland," *European Economy,* 43 (March 1990).

Hungary

Jan Adam, "Work Teams: A New Phenomenon in Income Distribution in Hungary," *Comparative Economic Studies* 31 (Spring 1989), 46–65.

James Angresano, "A Mixed Economy in Hungary? Lessons from the Swedish Experience," *Comparative Economic Studies* 34, 1 (Spring 1992), 41–57.

Cees van Beers and Guido Biessen, "Trade Possibilities and Structure of Foreign Trade: The Case of Hungary and Poland," *Comparative Economic Studies* 38, 2/3 (Summer–Fall 1996), 1–20.

Josef C. Brada, Inderjit Singh, and Adam Torok, *Firms Afloat and Firms Adrift: Hungarian Industry and Economic Transition* (Armonk: M.E. Sharpe, 1993).

Kemal Dervis and Timothy Condon, "Hungary—Partial Successes and Remaining Challenges: The Emergence of a 'Gradualist' Success Story?" in Oliver Jean Blanchard, Kenneth A. Froot, and Jeffrey D. Sachs, eds., *The Transition in Eastern Europe,* vol. 1 (Chicago: University of Chicago Press, 1994), 123–153.

A. L. Hillman, "Macroeconomic Policy in Hungary and Its Microeconomic Implications," *European Economy* 43 (March 1990), 55–60.

Janos Kornai, *The Road to a Free Economy* (New York: Norton, 1990).

———, *Struggle and Hope: Essays on Stabilization and Reform in the Post-Socialist Economy* (Cheltenham, England: Edward Elgar, 1997).

Peter Mihalyi, "On the Quantitative Aspects of Hungarian Privatization," *Comparative Economic Studies* 39, 2 (Summer 1997), 72–95.

D. M. Newberry, "Tax Reform, Trade Liberalization and Industrial Restructuring in Hungary," *European Economy* 43 (March 1990), 67–96.

Gabor Oblath and David Tarr, "The Terms-of-Trade Effects from the Elimination of State Trading in Soviet–Hungarian Trade," *Journal of Comparative Economics* 16, 1 (March 1992), 75–93.

Erzsebet Szalai, "Integration of Special Interests in the Hungarian Economy: The Struggle Between Large Companies and the Party and State Bureaucracy," *Journal of Comparative Economics* 15, 2 (June 1991), 284–303.

I. Szekely, "The Reform of the Hungarian Financial System" *European Economy* 43 (March 1990), 107–124.

The Czech Republic

David L. Bartlett, "Commercial Banks and Corporate Governance in the Czech Republic and Hungary," *Post-Soviet Geography and Economics* 37, 8 (1996), 503–510.

Tito Boevi, "'Transitional' Unemployment," *Economics of Transition* 2, 1 (March 1994), 1–26.

Josef C. Brada, "The Economic Transition of Czechoslovakia from Plan to Market," *Journal of Economic Perspectives* 5, 4 (Fall 1991), 171–177.

Raj M. Desai, "Reformed Banks and Corporate Governance in the Czech Republic, 1991–1996," *Post-Soviet Geography and Economics* 37, 8 (1996), 463–494.

Karel Dyba and Jan Svejnar, "Czechoslovakia: Recent Economic Developments and Prospects," *American Economic Review Papers and Proceedings* 81 (May 1991), 185–190.

———, "Stabilization and Transition in Czechoslovakia," in Oliver Jean Blanchard, Kenneth A. Froot, and Jeffrey D. Sachs, eds. *The Transition in Eastern Europe,* vol. 1 (Chicago: University of Chicago Press, 1994), 93–122.

John Ham, Jan Svejnar, and Katherine Terrell, "The Emergence of Unemployment in the Czech and Slovak Republics" *Comparative Economic Studies* 35, 4 (Winter 1993), 121–134.

J. Kotrba and J. Svejnar, "Rapid and Multifaceted Privatization: Experience of the Czech and Slovak Republics," *Most* 4, 2 (1994), 147–185.

Eva Marikova Leeds, "Voucher Privatization in Czechoslovakia," *Comparative Economic Studies* 35, 3 (Fall 1993), 19–38.

J. Svejnar, ed., *The Czech Republic and Economic Transition in Eastern Europe* (San Diego: Academic Press, 1995).

Jan Svejnar and Miroslav Singer, "Using Vouchers to Privatize an Economy: The Czech and Slovak Case," *Economics of Transition* 2, 1 (March 1994), 43–70.

Martin Myant *et al.,* eds. *Success Transformations? The Creation of Market Economies in Eastern Germany and the Czech Republic* (Cheltenham, England: Edward Elgar, 1996).

17

Conclusions and Prospects

The field of comparative economic systems investigates the impact of the economic system on economic performance. Economists have even begun to correlate various measures of the economic system, such as "economic freedom," the independence of the central bank, and the level of "corruption," with economic growth, and they have found that "good" economic institutions create "good" economic performance.[1] Economic performance is measured in various ways—growth of GDP or of GDP per capita or of productivity, economic stability, or employment. A more general term for economic performance is *economic development,* which entails the transformation of economies from lower levels of economic achievement to higher levels. Economic development consists of a broader range of economic outcomes, not just economic growth. Economic development refers to the rising education of the population, to its demographic transition, to the urban–rural mix, and to the economy's industrial structure.

Earlier chapters have demonstrated that the economic system does matter. The Soviet planned socialist economic system was abandoned in the former Soviet Union and in Eastern Europe because it failed to produce acceptable economic performance. The economic system adopted by the Four Tigers of Southeast Asia throughout the postwar period—low taxation, promotion of exports, and human capital enhancement—clearly led to a remarkable economic result. The Four Tiger economies, which began the postwar era as poor economies, either have joined or are on their way to joining the ranks of the affluent countries. Other countries, such as India, which had as much promise as the Four Tigers, have thus far failed to generate enough economic growth to raise their level of economic development.

The Chinese economy has, after decades of political turmoil, adopted market-oriented reforms that have generated rates of growth among the highest in the world. Whereas in the 1960s there was talk that the Soviet Union would become a dominant power in the world economy, this is now said of China.

After being held up as examples of high performers in the 1950s and 1960s, the economies of Europe have failed since then to generate economic growth on a par with other mature and industrializing economies. Although there are differences among them, the mature European economies have settled into consensus models based on heavy social protection, employee rights, worker representation, and high taxation. These economies in the 1970s, 1980s, and 1990s have tested the limits of the welfare state to determine whether consensus and worker protection are consistent with economic growth. Whether they can change their system in the face of powerful vested interests remains an open question. The distributional coalitions, which Mancur Olson blames for Eurosclerosis, mount great political resistance to change.[2]

One exception to Eurosclerosis appears to be Great Britain, the traditional economic laggard of Europe during the early postwar period. Under policies initiated by Margaret Thatcher, the economic growth of the UK revived, and the UK's per capita GDP has begun to rise again relative to the other European nations.

The most fascinating question that this book raises is the eventual outcome of the transition from planned socialism to market capitalism that is currently underway in the former Soviet Union and in Eastern Europe. The answer is far from clear from the vantage point of the last few years of the twentieth century. What is clear is that some countries have indeed been able to navigate the treacherous waters of transition; they include Poland, the Czech Republic, and Hungary. Others, such as the Baltic States and Solvenia, show clear signs of success. However, even in the case of these apparent successes, the costs of transition have been high and the political consequences brutal.

Another case of "successful" transition occurred in the eastern part of the now-reunified Germany, which began its transition from a planned to a market economy in 1990. Again the economic costs have been substantial, although they have been borne largely by German taxpayers.

The outcome of the transition process in the rest of Eastern Europe and the former Soviet Union is far from clear. The most important economy of the region, Russia, has made significant changes in its fiscal and monetary systems, has begun structural reforms, and has completed much of the formal first phase of privatization. However, the privatization process put in charge of Russian industry nomenklatura (or insider) capitalists—managers whose interests appear to be different from those of the economy at large and the real owners of industry. It remains to be seen whether Russia can overcome the challenges of this period of "wild" or "frontier" capitalism, effect major restructuring, and settle down to a more productive form of capitalism.

The other countries of the former Soviet Union, with the exception of the Baltic states, suffer many of the same problems and woes as Russia. They lack the enormous natural wealth of Russia, and given their dependence on Russia for markets and materials, their revival depends very much on the success of the Russian transition. Moreover, for many of these countries at low levels of economic development, the focus will be on the fundamentals of economic growth and economic development, not on transition.

Changing Economic Thought

John Maynard Keynes remarked in his *General Theory,* published in 1936, that we are all captives of the economic ideas and philosophies of the past. Just in the postwar period, we have seen a number of economic ideas and philosophies come and go. In the 1950s, economists naively believed that state planning was the way. The Soviet Union appeared to be growing rapidly; the Soviets, not the Americans, were the first in space, and the Soviet premier, Nikita Khrushchev, threatened to "bury" capitalism beneath the wheels of the communist economic machine. A different form of planning, indicative planning, was being carried out in France with apparent success.

The fact that the Soviet Union appeared to overcome the consequences of backwardness in less than a decade in the 1930s had enormous appeal for the countries of the less-developed world. India wholeheartedly adopted the Soviet planning philosophy, although political and other constraints prevented India from adopting the Soviet economic system.

The 1960s was the period of the European economic miracle, the "Golden Age" of growth not only in Europe but also in other parts of the globe. The world's wealthiest country, the United States, appeared to be losing out during this period and even sent emissaries to Europe to study the European model. Germany grew at such rapid rates in the 1950s and 1960s that the term *Wirtschaftswunder* was coined to describe this process. Europe appeared able in the 1960s to combine rapid economic growth with a burgeoning welfare state in which workers were protected from all risks.

Events of the late 1960s and 1970s diverted attention from Europe to Japan. The Japanese economy appeared to be experiencing accelerating growth despite the costs of a world energy crisis that should have affected the resource-poor Japanese economy more adversely than other economies. Japan's success focused attention on its system of lifetime worker tenure and industrial policy. Japan's powerful Ministry for Industry and Trade appeared to be able to pick the industrial winners of the future. The close alliance between business and the state seemed to be the key to Japan's economic success.

The 1980s and 1990s have been decades of deregulation and free enterprise. Two of the world's major economies, the United States and Great Britain, elected conservative governments that deregulated industry, communications, finance, and transportation and lowered marginal tax rates. Although U.S. economic performance was not exceptional during this period, it was nevertheless superior to that of the other mature market economies of Europe. Great Britain's long affliction with the "British Disease" ended, and England began slowly to catch up with the other countries of Europe.

The other impetus to free enterprise emanated from the Four Tigers of Southeast Asia, whose rates of growth over two decades were sufficient to transform them from poor to relatively wealthy economies. In the face of this exceptional performance, China embarked on ambitious marketization reforms, and the Soviet Union and its former empire collapsed.

The 1990s has been a period of proposing new ideas and questioning old ones. The transition of the former planned socialist economies to market economies required economists to address an entirely new issue: How do these economies make the transition from central planning to market resource allocation? This question had not been addressed by economists before, but reality demanded the rapid generation of ideas. Questions also arose in relation to the welfare states of Europe. Can an economy that guarantees its citizens participation *and* security continue to grow? Or must it change itself—and its citizens' expectations—in order to keep up with the rest of the world?

We do not know what ideas and philosophies will govern the first decade of the twenty-first century. We will probably be in for a number of surprises. For instance, we may hear arguments that the socialist planned economy is sound in principle and that if the leaders of these economies had done a better job, the experiment with planned socialism would have been a success.

If transition from plan to market is a temporary state of affairs, then the process of transition, which has occupied so much of our attention in the 1990s, will eventually come to an end. Economies currently in transition will be judged not by criteria now applied to the transition era, but rather by criteria applied to all economies. The classification of differing economic systems will clearly be more subtle than in the era of the polar opposites of plan and market.

One of the major intellectual changes of the last two decades of the twentieth century has been a rethinking of the function of the state in economic life. We began the postwar period with a view of the state as a benign instrument for good that could overcome problems of underdevelopment and inequity. We have ended the twentieth century with a less benign view that recognizes the state as a potential problem, not as a panacea.

Rising and Falling Economic Fortunes

In earlier chapters, we have cited the work of Angus Maddison, whose empirical studies identify countries and periods in which economic growth has been rapid or slow.[3] Economic growth has been uneven among the different regions of the world. Africa and Latin America have grown very slowly or not at all; the industrialized core countries of Europe and North America have experienced sustained growth over a long period of time. The past century has witnessed two major changes of economic fortunes. One was the rapid growth of Asian countries (starting with Japan and then spreading to Southeast Asia) from the 1930s on; the second was the rise and decline of the European periphery, consisting primarily of the former Soviet Union and Eastern Europe. For a brief period of time, the European periphery of planned socialist economies appeared to outgrow the industrialized core, but their growth faltered after 1970. Their failure to make further progress vis-à-vis the industrialized core explains why the system of planned socialism was abandoned.

What are the prospects for further reversals—that is, the prospects for a region that has typically grown slowly to move to a posture of fast economic growth sufficient to overcome part or all of the income gap?

First, it should be emphasized that as of the end of the twentieth century, underdevelopment and low incomes are more typical than development and high incomes. In 1995 the population of the world stood at 5.7 billion persons, with a world GDP of 33.5 trillion U.S. 1995 dollars.[4] As Table 17.1 shows, the distribution of product is uneven. More than two-thirds of the world's people still live in developing economies, where they receive barely two-fifths of the world's total product and subsist at low levels of income and wealth, with minimal education, and in poor health. Less than 20 percent of the world's population lives in high-income countries. Underdevelopment remains a fact of life.

Second, these figures can be changed by one or two significant events. One of these events would be the continued rapid economic growth of China, a country that accounts for more than a billion of the world's five billion inhabitants. The second

TABLE 17.1   World Gross Domestic Product and Population in 1995

	Gross Domestic Product (percent)	Population (percent)
Less-developed countries	38	76.3
Eastern Europe and the former USSR	6	7.3
United States	22	4.6
European Union	20	6.2
Japan	8	2.2
Total: World	100	100

Source: Central Intelligence Agency, *Handbook of International Economic Statistics, 1996* (Washington, D.C.: CIA, 1996), Figure 4.

factor would be the continued growth of Central and Latin American countries, countries that for the first time appear to be growing rapidly.

Starting with Chile under Augusto Pinochet in 1981, and then spreading to six other countries in Latin America (Argentina, Bolivia, Colombia, Mexico, Peru, and Uruguay), a Latin American model of reform has been created. This Latin model uses privatization, strengthening of private-property rights, pension reform, and deregulation—combined with monetary and fiscal austerity—to create a favorable climate for growth and foreign investment.[5] As a consequence of these actions, Latin American government deficits fell from 5.5 percent of GDP in 1988 to 1.8 percent in 1995. Average tariff rates have fallen to the level of those of the United States. Since 1991 the Latin American economies have achieved an average annual rate of growth of 3.1 percent, a rate not deemed a sufficient reward for the difficult reforms that have been undertaken. However, if the reforms have been sufficient to create a climate for growth, their payoff should be felt during the last five years of the twentieth century. Credible forecasts of growth rate are predicting average annual growth for Latin America in the neighborhood of 5 percent—a rate that, if sustained, would be sufficient to improve Latin America's relative economic position.[6]

A Golden Age?

World economic growth appears to go through cyclical or longer swings, which have been studied in the past by such eminent students of the business cycle as N. D. Kondratiev,[7] Simon Kuznets, and W. C. Mitchell. Table 17.2 shows that the 1990s have been a period of rising world economic growth—a development that economist Jeffrey Sachs has described as "an important historical event. The positive side is spectacular."[8] Several factors have been offered to explain the upsurge in economic growth in the 1990s: the vast expansion of economic freedom and property rights, the reduction in the scope of government, and an explosion in trade and private investment. Whole new industries have sprung up in computer networking and biotechnology. Even the Secretary General of the United Nations sees the world

TABLE 17.2   World Economic Growth

Year	Rate of Growth
1991	1.4
1992	2.25
1993	2.3
1994	2.7
1995	3.5
1996	3.8

Source: "Global Growth Attains a New, Higher Level That Could Be Lasting," *Wall Street Journal,* March 13, 1997. Reprinted by permission of the *Wall Street Journal,* © 1997 Dow Jones & Company, Inc. All rights reserved worldwide.

as "entering a new golden age" fostered by soaring private investment and technical advances that will enable poorer nations to avoid some of the growing pains that others had to go through to develop.

The world has experienced a number of "golden ages" of growth. The first was the 40-year period before World War I. During this period, world economic growth averaged 2.1 percent per annum—relatively slow growth by today's standards but more than double the rate of the previous half-century. The second golden age ran from 1950 to the oil shock of 1973. During this second golden age, world economic growth averaged 4.9 percent per year. The first golden age was the consequence of the spread of the Industrial Revolution. The second golden age resulted from the release of bottled up technology that had been restrained by the Great Depression and World War II and by the wartime devastation in Europe and Japan that wiped out entrenched interests and outmoded infrastructure.

From 1973 to 1993, world economic growth averaged 2 percent per year. Now Wharton Econometric Forecasting Associates expects worldwide growth in the coming 20 years to average 4 percent per annum.

A major factor in this worldwide growth has been the ongoing process of economic integration and the elimination of controls on international capital flows. Most of the world's governments are now convinced that economic liberalization is the surest path to economic growth. To quote a Mexican specialist, "Governments all over the world are moving in the same direction—deregulating, cutting their deficits and vying for foreign investment."[9] Economist Steve Hancke has studied the relationship between economic freedom and economic growth, where economic freedom is defined in terms of strong property rights, absence of currency controls, and lack of official corruption and bribes. He finds that for every 10% increase in economic freedom, GDP per capita rises between 7 and 14 percent.[10]

Poorer countries are in a position to play rapid catch-up in today's world, because relatively backward countries are not saddled with old equipment. They can use the latest equipment, which operates at lower cost and more efficiently. In prior eras, the relatively backward countries had to make do with older technology, but now new Pentium chips are manufactured in China using the latest Intel technology.

Direct investment between the developed and the less-developed countries tripled between 1990 and 1996 to 122 billion. Private capital flows, which include both direct and passive investments, rose 30 percent on an annual basis in the 1990s, to reach $231 billion in 1996.

The spectacular rise in investment flows can be explained by a number of factors. First, the savings rates in the developing countries are typically higher than in the rich countries. China's savings rate, for example, is about one-third of its GDP. Second, demographic trends favor the flow of capital from the rich to the poor nations. The rich countries are beset by demographic stagnation in their populations and work forces. The poorer countries therefore offer young and growing labor forces and growing consumer markets.

Convergence of Incomes

When comparative economics was primarily about the differences between capitalism and socialism, there was much discussion of the notion of "convergence." Convergence is the process of socialist and capitalist economies becoming more alike, whether a socialist economy becoming more like a capitalist economy or vice versa. With the transition of the socialist planned economies to capitalist market economies, it is clear that convergence is taking place. However, the nature of the convergence process has turned out to be very different from what was once expected.

There is another way to look at convergence; it can be seen as the lessening of income or earnings differentials among economies. In other words, instead of looking for a lessening of institutional differences among economies, we look instead for a lessening of differentials in outcomes.

The world economy has experienced periods of convergence and divergence. If we restrict our field of vision to the industrialized core of countries, we find that there was considerable convergence between the 1870s and the outbreak of World War I.[11] The interwar period was one of deconvergence. Income and wage differentials among countries increased as reversion to protectionism restricted the flow of labor and capital among countries. The postwar period has been one of convergence, as income differentials have diminished not only among the industrialized core of countries but between the industrialized core and Southeast Asia.

The sources of convergence have been identified by economic historians. Convergence occurs when labor and capital are free to move from country to country and when there is free trade in goods and services. The sources of convergence before World War I and then after World War II are therefore apparent. Both were periods of rapid expansion of trade and of the relatively free flow of labor and capital.

The postwar period has seen the creation of institutions that promote convergence. First GATT and then the World Trade Organization have worked through international negotiations to lower trade barriers among countries. There also has been a tendency to create regional free-trade zones, such as the European Union and the North American Free Trade Agreement. The ultimate stimulus for convergence among the European nations will be the complete integration of the European Union countries into one economic zone with a common currency, an event scheduled to take place in 1999.

Economic Systems in the Twenty-First Century

There has certainly been convergence, and the polar extremes of plan and market have largely disappeared, but in a fundamental sense, the economic system's influence on economic outcomes has increased. In the past, we found it difficult to relate institutions to outcomes, and organizations were only indirectly viewed as mechanisms for resource allocation. Contemporary economic theory focuses directly on the nature of organizations as mechanisms for allocation, whether they be identified as corporate entities within a nation or as a more general set of system arrangements that differ from one country to another.

Clearly the agenda of interest has changed, and yet the nature of the economic system—especially the importance of subtle differences from one system to another—remains important as we try to untangle systemic mechanisms from other factors that influence resource allocation. These sorts of issues will remain important as we attempt to understand why so many nations remain poor as we enter the twenty-first century.

Notes

1. Heritage Foundation and Dow Jones Corporation, *1997 Index of Economic Freedom;* Robert Barro, "Economic Growth in a Cross Section of Countries," *Quarterly Journal of Economics* 106 (1991), 407–443; Mauro Paulo, "Corruption and Growth," *Quarterly Journal of Economics* 110 (1965), 681–712.
2. Mancur Olson, "The Varieties of Eurosclerosis: The Rise and Decline of Nations Since 1982," in Nicholas Crafts and Gianni Toniolo, eds., *Economic Growth in Europe Since 1945* (Cambridge, England: Cambridge University Press, 1996), pp. 73–94.
3. Angus Maddison, *Explaining the Economic Performance of Nations* (Cambridge, England: Cambridge University Press, 1995); *Economic Growth in the West* (London: George Allen & Unwin, 1964).
4. Central Intelligence Agency, *Handbook of International Economic Statistics,* 1996 (Washington, D.C.: CIA, 1996), Figure 4.
5. "Lure of the Latin Model," *Financial Times,* April 9, 1997; *Financial Times Survey, Latin America,* March 14, 1997.
6. Union Bank of Switzerland, *Global Economic Outlook,* First Quarter 1997, p. 41.
7. L. A. Nefiodow, *Der Sechste Kondratieff* (Frankfurt: Rhein-Sieg Verlag, 1996).
8. "Global Growth Attains a New, Higher Level That Could Be Lasting," *Wall Street Journal,* March 13, 1997.
9. *Ibid.*
10. *Ibid.*
11. Jeffrey Williamson, "Globalization, Convergence, and History," *Journal of Economic History* 56, 2 (June 1996), 277–305.

Index

Index